GENDER, RACE AND CLASS IN MEDIA

GENDER, RACE AND CLASS IN MEDIA

A TEXT-READER

EDITED BY
GAIL DINES & JEAN M. HUMEZ

SAGE Publications
International Educational and Professional Publisher
Thousand Oaks   London   New Delhi

For information address:

SAGE Publications, Inc.
2455 Teller Road
Thousand Oaks, California 91320
E-mail: order@sagepub.com

SAGE Publications Ltd.
6 Bonhill Street
London EC2A 4PU
United Kingdom

SAGE Publications India Pvt. Ltd.
M-32 Market
Greater Kailash I
New Delhi 110 048 India

Printed in the United States of America

Library of Congress Cataloging-in-Publication Data

Main entry under title:

Gender, race, and class in media: A text-reader / edited by Gail
    Dines, Jean M. Humez.
        p. cm.
    Includes bibliographical references and index.
    Partial Contents: pt. 1. A cultural studies approach to gender,
race, and class in media — pt. 2. Advertising — pt. 3. Modes of
sexual representation I : romance novels and slasher films — pt.
4. Modes of sexual representation II : pornography — pt. 5. TV by
day — pt. 6. TV by night — pt. 7. Music videos and rap music :
cultural conflict and control.
    ISBN 0-8039-5163-9. — ISBN 0-8039-5164-7 (pbk.)
    1. Sex in mass media—United States. 2. Mass media and sex—
United States. 3. Mass media and race relations—United States.
4. Afro-Americans in mass media—United States. 5. Social classes
in mass media—United States. 6. Mass media—Social aspects—United
States. 7. Popular culture—United States. 8. United States—
Social conditions — 1980–   I. Dines, Gail. II. Humez, Jean
McMahon, 1944–
P96.S452U64 1994
306.7—dc20   94-22960

96 97 98 99 00 13 12 11 10 9 8 7 6 5

Sage Production Editor: Astrid Virding

Contents

ACKNOWLEDGMENTS   xv

PREFACE: Goals and Assumptions of This Reader   xvii

| PART I: | A Cultural Studies Approach to Gender, Race and Class in the Media | 1 |

Introduction

1. Cultural Studies, Multiculturalism and Media Culture   5
    DOUGLAS KELLNER

Ideology and Race

2. The Whites of Their Eyes: Racist Ideologies and the Media   18
    STUART HALL

Representation and the Social Construction of Race

3. White Negroes   23
    JAN NEDERVEEN PIETERSE

Race, Gender and Textual Analysis

4. Madonna: Plantation Mistress or Soul Sister?   28
    BELL HOOKS

History of Racism in Media Representation and Ownership

5. The Visibility of Race and Media History   33
    JANE RHODES

Defining the Working Class

6. The Silenced Majority: Why the Average Working Person
    Has Disappeared From American Media and Culture   40
    BARBARA EHRENREICH

Social Class, Television and the Consumer

7. The Meaning of Memory: Family, Class and Ethnicity
    in Early Network Television   43
    GEORGE LIPSITZ

Encoding/Decoding Model and Race

8. *The Color Purple*: Black Women as Cultural Readers   52
    JACQUELINE BOBO

Symbolic Annihilation and Gays and Lesbians as Audiences

9. Out of the Mainstream: Sexual Minorities and
    the Mass Media   61
    LARRY GROSS

PART II: Advertising   71

Consumer Culture and the Image

10. Image-Based Culture: Advertising and Popular Culture   77
     SUT JHALLY

Selling the Female Audience to Advertisers

11. Constructing and Addressing the Audience
     as Commodity   88
     ROBERT GOLDMAN

African American Ownership in the Advertising Industry

12. The Black Experience in Advertising: An Interview
    With Thomas J. Burrell   93
    MARSHA CASSIDY
    RICHARD KATULA

Racist "Stereotyping" in Television Advertisements

13. Different Children, Different Dreams:
    Racial Representation in Advertising   99
    ELLEN SEITER

Targeting African Americans

14. Separate, But Not Equal: Racial Segmentation in
    Cigarette Advertising   109
    RICHARD W. POLLAY
    JUNG S. LEE
    DAVID CARTER-WHITNEY

Advertising and the Corporate Control of Women's Magazines

15. Sex, Lies and Advertising   112
    GLORIA STEINEM

Images of Femininity in Advertising

16. Beauty and the Beast of Advertising   121
    JEAN KILBOURNE

Textual Analysis of Advertisements

17. Reading Images Critically:
    Toward a Postmodern Pedagogy   126
    DOUGLAS KELLNER

Representations of Masculinity in Advertising

18. Advertising and the Construction of Violent
    White Masculinity   133
    JACKSON KATZ

Targeting the Gay and Lesbian Reader and Consumer

19. Commodity Lesbianism   142
    DANAE CLARK

Selling to the Working-Class Home TV Viewer

20. Watching the Girls Go Buy: Shop-at-Home Television   152

    MIMI WHITE

PART III: **Modes of Sexual Representation 1— Romance Novels and Slasher Films**   **161**

Textual Analysis of Slasher Movies

21. Her Body, Himself: Gender in the Slasher Film   169

    CAROL J. CLOVER

Public Concern Over Slasher Movies

22. Do Slasher Films Breed Real-Life Violence?   185

    ALISON BASS

Textual Analysis of Romance Novels

23. Mass Market Romance: Pornography for Women Is Different   190

    ANN BARR SNITOW

Reader Reception of Romance Novels

24. Women Read the Romance: The Interaction of Text and Context   202

    JANICE A. RADWAY

The Romance Novel Formula Explained to Would-Be Writers

25. The Traditional Romance Formula   215

    MARILYN M. LOWERY

The Working Conditions of Harlequin Romance Writers

26. What's in a Pseudonym: Romance Slaves of Harlequin   223

    RICHARD POLLAK

| PART IV: | Modes of Sexual Representation 2— Pornography | 229 |

Radical Feminist Analysis of Pornography

27. Pornography and Male Supremacy 237
    ANDREA DWORKIN

The Anti-Anti-Pornography Position

28. Misguided, Dangerous and Wrong: An Analysis
    of Anti-Pornography Politics 244
    GAYLE RUBIN

Cultural Production and Pornography

29. "I Buy It for the Articles": *Playboy* Magazine and the
    Sexualization of Consumerism 254
    GAIL DINES

*Reading Images of Women's Bodies in Advertising
and Pornography*

30. Towards a Feminist Erotica 263
    KATHY MYERS

Deconstructing the Pornographic Text (Still Photos)

31. Lawless Seeing 271
    ANNETTE KUHN

Pornography and the Construction of African-American Femininity

32. Pornography and Black Women's Bodies 279
    PATRICIA HILL COLLINS

A Content Analysis of Pornographic Books and Videos

33. Racism in Pornography 287
    ALICE MAYALL and DIANA E. H. RUSSELL

A New Look at Effects Research

34. Pornography and the Limits of Experimental Research 298
    ROBERT JENSEN

Pornography: A Consumer's Testimony

35. Confessions of a Feminist Porn Watcher   307
    SCOTT MACDONALD

Pornography: An Anti-Pornography Activist's Testimony

36. Surviving Commercial Sexual Exploitation   314
    EVELINA GIOBBE

PART V: TV by Day   **319**

Feminist Critique of Soap Operas

37. Daze of Our Lives: The Soap Opera as
    Feminine Text   325
    DEBORAH D. ROGERS

Reading Race, Sexuality, and Class in Soap Operas

38. Race, Sexuality and Class in Soapland   332
    KAREN LINDSEY

Gender and Television Genres: Soap Opera as Feminine TV

39. Gendered Television: Femininity   340
    JOHN FISKE

Textual Analysis of Soaps

40. The Search for Tomorrow in Today's Soap Operas   348
    TANIA MODLESKI

Audience-Based Research on Soaps

41. Women Watching Together: An Ethnographic Study
    of Korean Soap Opera Fans in the United States   355
    MINU LEE
    CHONG HEUP CHO

Family Viewing TV Research

42. Home, Home on the Remote: Does Fascination
    With TV Technology Create Male-Dominated
    Family Entertainment?   362

Reading Geraldo

43. Constellation of Voices: How Talkshows Work   367
    WAYNE MUNSON

Textual Analysis of the Afternoon Talk Show

44. Daytime Inquiries   377
    ELAYNE RAPPING

Reading an African American Secondary Text of Soap Operas

45. His Name Was Not on the List: The Soap Opera Updates
    of Ti-Rone as Resistance to Symbolic Annihilation   383
    GLORIA ABERNATHY-LEAR

PART VI: TV by Night   395

Television Production and Social Class

46. Ralph, Fred, Archie and Homer: Why Television Keeps
    Recreating the White Male Working-Class Buffoon   403
    RICHARD BUTSCH

Race and Audience Reception

47. Is This What You Mean by Color TV? Race, Gender,
    and Contested Meanings in NBC's *Julia*   413
    ANIKO BODROGHKOZY

Representation of African American Women on Television

48. Television's Realist Portrayal of African-American
    Women and the Case of *L.A. Law*   424
    JANE RHODES

Representation of African American Men on Television

49. Television, Black Americans and the American Dream   430
    HERMAN GRAY

Race and the Potential Polysemic Text

50. Laughing Across the Color Barrier: *In Living Color*   438
    NORMA MIRIAM SCHULMAN

Women as a Target Audience for Social Issue Drama

51. The Movie of the Week   445
    ELAYNE RAPPING

The Politics of Production and Gender as an Unstable Category

52. Defining Women: The Case of *Cagney and Lacey*   454
    JULIE D'ACCI

Reading a TV Sitcom as Feminist Text

53. Subversive Sitcoms: *Roseanne* as Inspiration for
    Feminist Resistance   469
    JANET LEE

A Lesbian Reads a Family Sitcom

54. Confessions of a Sitcom Junkie   476
    SARAH SCHUYLER

PART VII: Music Videos And Rap Music: Cultural Conflict and Control in the Age of the Image   479

MTV and the Dominance of the Image

55. A Post-Modernist Moment: 1980s Commercial
    Culture and the Founding of MTV   488
    JOHN PETTEGREW

Textual Analysis of Music Videos

56. Form and Female Authorship in Music Video   499
    LISA A. LEWIS

Audiences Reading Madonna Videos

57. The Effects of Race, Gender, and Fandom on Audience
    Interpretations of Madonna's Music Videos   508
    JANE D. BROWN
    LAURIE SCHULZE

Locating Rap Music in African American Culture

58. Reconstructions of Nationalist Thought in Black Music
    and Culture 518
    KRISTAL BRENT ZOOK

Feminist Voices in Hip-Hop

59. It's My Thang and I'll Swing It the Way That I Feel!
    Sexuality and Black Women Rappers 524
    IMANI PERRY

"Policing" Rap Music and Its Audiences

60. "Fear of a Black Planet": Rap Music and
    Black Cultural Politics in the 1990s 531
    TRICIA ROSE

White Appropriation of African American Hip-Hop

61. Imitation of Life 540
    JAMES LEDBETTER

AFTERWORD: Media Activism 545

Television Violence: The Power and the Peril 547
    GEORGE GERBNER

RESOURCES FOR MEDIA ACTIVISM 558

GLOSSARY 567

BIBLIOGRAPHY 576

AUTHOR INDEX 621

SUBJECT INDEX 627

NOTES ON THE CONTRIBUTORS 641

Acknowledgments

In shaping this selection of chapters, we received useful suggestions, contacts, bibliographical information, and critical judgments from many colleagues, friends, and students. We gratefully acknowledge in particular the helpful contributions of: Stanley Aronowitz, Bernice Buresch, Richard Butsch, Hazel Carby, Linda Dittmar, John Downing, Stewart Ewen, Fred Feijes, John Fiske, George Gerbner, Richard Goldman, Herman Gray, Sut Jhally, Jackson Katz, Peter Kiang, Doug Kellner, Sarah Kurko, Cheryl Lees, Justin Lewis, Karen Lindsey, Theresa Perry, Jane Rhodes, Ann Russo, Erin Senack, Valerie Smith, Pat Turner, Ellen Wartella, and Mary Helen Washington.

Preface

Goals and Assumptions of This Reader

This reader is intended to introduce undergraduate students to some of the richness, sophistication and diversity that characterizes contemporary media scholarship in a way that is accessible and builds on students' own media experiences and interests. We aim to help demystify the nature of media culture by examining its production, construction and the meaning-making processes by which media imagery or messages help shape our personal, social and political worlds. Our ultimate goal is a more media-literate and activist public.

The editors are both teachers of undergraduate courses in media studies, sociology, literature, and interdisciplinary women's studies. We both have a strong interest in antiracist feminism and progressive social activism. In our own teaching, we have had difficulty finding in one volume the kinds of current articles by media critics and activists that (a) would introduce the most powerful theoretical concepts in contemporary media studies, (b) survey some of the most influential and interesting genres of contemporary media, and (c) focus on issues of gender, class and race from a critical perspective. We designed this volume to do these three things.

Most of the readings in this book take an explicitly critical political perspective. They assume, as we do, that Western industrialized societies such as our own are stratified along lines of **race, class** and **gender;**[1] that everyone living in such a society "has" race, class and gender as well as other aspects of social identity that help structure our experience; and that economic and other resources, advantages and privileges are distributed inequitably in part because of power dynamics involving these categories of experience (as well as others). We believe that one goal of a critical education is to enable people to conceptualize social justice more clearly and work toward it more effectively. For us, greater social justice would mean fairer distribution of our society's cultural and economic resources.

Contemporary (multicultural) cultural studies argues that many dimensions of social stratification influence the unequal distribution of power and resources in our society. **Racism, sexism, classism, heterosexism,** ageism, ableism and others—each system of social domination has its own separate history, dynamic, conditions of existence and material and ideological components. Moreover, each has produced its own social movement in the 20th-century United States—including the labor movement, the civil rights movement, the farmworkers' and Native American rights movements, the women's and gay/lesbian liberation movements and the disability rights movement. Each of these social movements has generated changed consciousness, the desire to change institutions and some real institutional change—although never as much as activists in these movements have sought. To a large extent, moreover, participants in one movement have developed ideology and learned strategy in part from those who have gone before.

Since the 1960s, each of these social movements has criticized media imagery for **stereotyping** and **"symbolic annihilation"** (the latter term, coined by George Gerbner, is used by Larry Gross in "Out of the Mainstream: Sexual Minorities and the Mass Media," Chapter 9) and has worked to change media imagery directly. Through demonstrations, testimony at congressional hearings, press conferences, published critiques and the creation of alternative cultural products, social groups conscious of their cultural marginalization have repeatedly attempted to raise consciousness and influence public opinion and public media policy.

These social movements have also produced educational reform movements within the educational institutions where knowledge is generated and transmitted. In the 1960s and 1970s, faculty and students with changed consciousness influenced college and university curricula in significant ways, through pointing out and resisting former social denigration, stereotyping, exclusion and institutional power imbalances—witness the development of such fields as Black or African American studies, Chicano, Latino, Native American, Asian American, and Third World or ethnic studies, as well as women's studies or feminist studies and labor studies.

In bringing the critical insights of activists into the academy, however, scholars have inevitably transformed the language of activism into academic discourse, for better or for worse. Thus powerful political ideas such as "media stereotyping" have been reconceptualized in ways that incorporate a more complex analysis of how media culture operates within a society characterized by social and economic inequality, as the articles in this reader will demonstrate.

In the 1990s, the insights of those critical groups who are still marginalized in academia are effecting research and teaching beyond the self-contained academic units in which they have been institutionalized (such as

Black studies or women's studies). Although the movement toward a more "multicultural" curriculum has detractors and critics, it is the most recent manifestation in colleges and universities of the impulse to change the paradigms of knowledge in ways that will help promote a more egalitarian society.

Media studies today is a complex, **multidisciplinary** and international field that has both resisted and embraced socially critical perspectives. The social movement to have influenced media studies the most dramatically so far has undoubtedly been the women's movement. Although feminists outside of the field of communications had been publishing important critiques of media imagery of women since Betty Friedan's (1963) analysis of women's magazines, in the *Feminine Mystique*, it was not until the late 1970s that feminists within the field had articles and anthologies that could be used in media education—notably, Gaye Tuchman's (1978) *Hearth and Home* and Butler and Paisley's (1980) *Women and the Mass Media*. But by the mid 1980s, **feminist media theory and criticism** had become a major research and publication area, and it continues to be a central approach today (Kaplan, 1987).

The major tasks of feminist work in media studies so far have been (a) making visible the *patriarchal* domination of media industries, in terms of both ownership and *representation*; (b) critiquing the male biases in the field of study itself; (c) bringing formerly neglected and undervalued **"women's genres"** (cultural entertainment forms targeting women audiences) to the foreground as legitimate areas of study; (d) beginning an examination of women's experiences as consumers of media imagery; and (e) encouraging women media producers to experiment with new approaches and themes.

This feminist work in media studies has not been without its critics— most notably women of color. **Black feminist theorists** in particular have argued that (White) feminist theory has been largely blind to the way that women experience the world, not just as gendered but also as racialized and class-located beings (e.g., Bobo & Seiter, 1991; Hill Collins, 1990; hooks, 1990; see also Gaines, 1988). This is part of a wider critique of media studies by scholars of color, who rightly point out that the field has not adequately grappled with the ways in which the politics of race in the United States have informed the development, production, distribution and consumption of media culture, from the 19th century to the present. In the last several years, however, there has been much exciting work in these issues, covering a range of media forms, both historically and in the present—some of which are represented in this reader.

Many scholars who are particularly interested in race and gender have been attracted in recent years to what is called the British "cultural studies" approach or paradigm, because of its progressive politics; because it offers a broader and more democratic definition of **culture** than was used in humanistic areas such as literary criticism in the past; and because of its research methodology, which is more flexible than that of the largely empirical social-scientific research of traditional U.S. communications studies. This book largely reflects this new cultural studies orientation, which the editors find congenial with their own critical perspective. (For a more extended history and definition of cultural studies, see Chapter 1, by Douglas Kellner, a leading proponent of this approach.)

Although there are now dozens of books and hundreds of journal articles available that take a cultural studies approach to media, the great majority of these are written with graduate students or other scholars in mind. We believe in developing broad-based media literacy at all levels in our society. Therefore, we have taken it as our task to attempt to convey the most powerful insights of this complex new work in as brief and clear a way as possible, in an effort to make it accessible to undergraduate students, including those in introductory media courses.

For the purposes of this book, our subject is a selection of modern U.S. popular cultural forms as conveyed by a variety of mass media technologies, including print (e.g., advertising images in magazines, pornographic pictures or romance novels) and broadcasting/cablecasting technology (e.g., talk shows, soap operas, sitcoms, MTV videos and rap music). We selected forms of **media culture** that we know to be heavily consumed and highly influential among our student populations—although, of course, because of space limitations we could not include everything that falls into this category. Although at the outset we had hoped to be as comprehensive as possible, we ultimately decided to sacrifice some breadth for greater depth in selected areas. Thus, regretfully, we have dropped chapters once planned on film and news—topics that we think are comparatively well covered in other media anthologies and in many excellent individual books—to do more with less well covered forms that we know produce animated discussions among our own students.

This collection of essays includes published journal articles, selections from recent books and several new essays commissioned for this book. Most of the published pieces have been edited by us for length. When editing, we tried to emphasize the essential arguments made in each piece. Readers should be aware, however, that in some cases we have taken just a portion, or highly edited excerpts, of the original, long essay or book chapter, as appropriate for our purposes.

Despite our best efforts, we realize that gender and race are still better represented in our book than is class. Although the British cultural studies orientation reflects the strong emphasis on class of **Marxism**—not surprisingly, given its historical debt to the thinking of Karl Marx—in U.S. academic analysis, in contrast, the concept of class has tended to be "invisible" since the 1950s for complex historical reasons. These include the eclipse of the labor movement, the anti-Communist climate created by House Un-American Activities Committee work of the early 1950s, the Cold War of the last several decades and the primacy of race as the category of social analysis acknowledged by U.S. social science.

We also acknowledge that writings from and about the perspectives of African Americans and White Americans constitute the dominant treatment of "race," with only a few contributions from other non-White perspectives. So far as we could determine from our bibliographic research, it is primarily in contemporary film studies that sophisticated analyses of racialized media imagery are reaching beyond the White-Black dichotomy, which still largely characterizes much of U.S. critical writing on race and TV. Similarly, with regard to gender, film studies has seen a wonderful efflorescence of work on gay and lesbian imagery and artists in the last few years (see bibliographies), but the attention to other media forms from this perspective has lagged somewhat behind. Thus the collection is also less comprehensive on heterosexism than on sexism.

Inevitably, any selection of readings reflects the perspectives, values, knowledge and limitations of knowledge of its editors. We welcome comments by users of this book about our selections, about what worked well in the classroom and what did not. And we especially invite suggested articles for future editions.

NOTE

1. For all boldfaced terms encountered in our introductory essays, please see the glossary for more extended definitions.

REFERENCES

Bobo, J., & Seiter, E. (1991, Fall). Black feminism and media criticism: *The Women of Brewster Place. Screen*, 32, 286-302.

Butler, M., & Paisley, W. (1980). *Women and the mass media: Sourcebook for research and action*. New York: Human Sciences Press.

Friedan, B. (1963). *The feminist mystique*. New York: Dell.

Gaines, J. (1988, Winter). White privilege and looking relations: Race and gender in feminist film theory. *Screen*, 29.

Hill Collins, P. (1990). *Black feminist thought: Knowledge, consciousness, and the politics of empowerment*. London: Harper Collins.

hooks, b. (1990). *Yearning: Race, gender and cultural politics*. Boston: South End Press.

Kaplan, E. A. (1987). Feminist criticism and television. In R. C. Allen (Ed.), *Channels of discourse: Television and contemporary criticism*. Chapel Hill: University of North Carolina Press.

Tuchman, G., et al. (Eds.). (1978). *Hearth and home: Images of women in the mass media*. New York: Oxford University Press

PART I

A CULTURAL STUDIES APPROACH TO GENDER, RACE AND CLASS IN THE MEDIA

All of the chapters in this part were selected and edited to bring issues of **gender, race** and/or **class** to the foreground, as well as to introduce major concepts of a **cultural studies** approach to media literacy. These articles are in dialogue with one another in many ways—what follows is only one reading of their main themes in relation to our reader.

We open our book with "Cultural Studies, Multiculturalism and Media Culture," by Douglas Kellner (Chapter 1). This sets out the three-part approach to cultural studies of media (**political economy**/production, **textual analysis**, and **audience reception**) that informs this book. With Professor Kellner, we believe that to understand fully a media cultural product such as a TV show or advertising image or romance novel, ideally, one needs to be able to (a) understand the socioeconomic context in which it is created (political economy/production), (b) analyze its constructed meaning(s) through careful attention to its particular visual/verbal/auditory languages or **codes** (textual analysis), and (c) determine through **ethnographic research** what its real-world audiences contribute to the meaning-making process (audience reception). In addition, Kellner points to the importance of better integrating considerations of race and gender as categories of social analysis in cultural studies work in the future.

Central to the project of cultural studies is the concept of **ideology** defined in Stuart Hall's essay (Chapter 2) as "those images, concepts and premises through which we represent, interpret, understand and 'make sense' of some aspect of social existence." For critical media theorists, the study of ideology is intimately connected to the study of media texts, because these play a major role in producing and reproducing ideologies. In

1

this article, Hall brings Western racist ideologies to the foreground. By examining the construction of "Blackness" in media texts, Hall highlights the degree to which "race is a complex, dynamic and changing construct."

In "White Negroes" (Chapter 3), Jan Pieterse demonstrates the historically unstable nature of "race" as a social construct—as a matter of power relations rather than skin color or genes. For example, he reminds us that in the 19th century the Irish were conceptualized as "black" by the Anglo-American elite and that the first Chinese immigrants to America were stereotyped according to a conceptual template similar to that which had already been worked out for African Americans. By examining the symbolic process whereby groups that are coded as "the other" change according to political, social and economic circumstances, Pieterse emphasizes the constructedness of both "Blackness" and "Whiteness." Although not denying the different histories and conditions of oppression of different non-White peoples, he emphasizes similarities with respect to symbolic communication in dominant (White) racial ideology.

Reading a more contemporary cultural text, bell hooks analyzes the White cultural icon Madonna from a **Black feminist perspective** (Chapter 4), thus rendering the Whiteness of Madonna's "blonde ambition" visible to those for whom Whiteness is usually taken as the norm. Showing how gender ideology is racialized, hooks critiques Madonna, as the producer of the Madonna media image, for failing to reject "the conventional racist defined beauty ideal," which she both thoroughly understands and "mocks." The hooks essay also introduces the complex issue of the cultural **appropriation** of Blackness by contemporary media industries and artists—"Black wannabes" as they are sometimes derisively called—which is picked up again in the section on rap/MTV (Part VII).

Implicit in these last three essays is the recognition that the symbolic construction of Blackness in our media culture has mostly taken place in **cultural artifacts** produced by a media industry that is owned and largely controlled by Whites. The authors all show in various ways that dominant media texts have encoded ideologies that help to create, sustain and legitimize White supremacy.

Thus because of the influential role that media owners and producers play in the construction of ideology in media texts, it is vital that we always contextualize an analysis of media **images** or **representations** themselves within an analysis of the politics and economics of media ownership. Jane Rhodes's article, "The Visibility of Race and Media History" (Chapter 5), reminds us of the need for culturally/economically marginal people to own their own media outlets and produce their own media imagery. By tracing the history of African American newspapers and independent filmmaking in the 19th and early 20th centuries, she also shows how a dominant White perspective has distorted the history of media production by rendering African American "alternative media" of the past largely invisible.

People of color are not the only group to be rendered invisible in dominant media imagery. As Barbara Ehrenreich points out in her article, "The Silenced Majority" (Chapter 6), the White working class has virtually disappeared from view in the media imagery of recent decades. Social class is much "mystified" in the contemporary United States, and its impact on people's access to resources is denied because of our society's "American dream" of untrammeled individualism and universal equal opportunity, which insists that if people are economically marginal, it must be because they are just not trying hard enough. Ehrenreich contributes to a demystification of class by presenting pragmatic definitions of class identity and highlighting the degree to which the professional-class background of media producers contributes to the perpetuation of negative stereotypes of the working class.

Attitudes toward inequality and cultural differences that cannot be discussed in class terms (because of the lack of a conceptual framework) are frequently displaced onto both gender and race. For example, Richard Butsch (1992) has argued that "class is symbolically coded in gender terms" when working-class males are devalued in television situation comedy through being characterized with stereotypically "feminine" attributes.

Although the working class is comparatively absent in dominant media imagery today, George Lipsitz, in "The Meaning of Memory" (Chapter 7) points to a time when blue-collar and ethnic immigrant people were highly visible in a group of situation comedies in the immediate post-World War II period and through the 1950s. He argues that these sitcoms were one of the key agents used to transform a traditional, ethnic immigrant ideology, which stressed values of community, thrift and commitment to labor unions, into an American dream ideology, which stressed individualism, consumerism and suburban domesticity—values consistent with the needs of the expanding postwar capitalist economy. The Lipsitz article helps us see connections between the ideology embodied in the texts and the wider political economy system (including media ownership). However, this approach cannot tell us how specific audience groups actually **decode** (or make meaning from) a given text. For that piece of the equation, we must turn to audience reception studies, such as Jacqueline Bobo's and Larry Gross's.

Even when material ownership of the media is unavailable to culturally marginalized groups, audiences have some power to resist demeaning imagery—as consumers of the media, we need not be conceptualized as mere passive pawns of media imagery controlled by the dominant culture. In her piece on African American women's responses to the film *The Color Purple* (Chapter 8), Bobo introduces the influential concept of **oppositional readings,** first proposed by Stuart Hall (also discussed by Kellner in Chapter 1). The meaning of media texts cannot simply be established by one critic's decoding of the text—no matter how subtle and full—because all texts are to some degree open, **polysemic** or capable of multiple meanings. Therefore, we must also seek to know how different audiences (often subcultural communities), bringing different experiences and identities to the process of reading/viewing, actually understand these texts. Specific audiences can either accept those meanings that are **preferred** by the text or produce **negotiated** or even oppositional readings of their own. Bobo's research emphasizes the complex "process by which black women were able to form a positive engagement with *The Color Purple*," despite its production by the mostly White Hollywood film industry and its textual "similarities to past films that have portrayed Black people negatively."

In a similar argument, in "Out of the Mainstream: Sexual Minorities and the Mass Media" (Chapter 9) Larry Gross shows that culturally marginal groups can relate to mainstream imagery in a wide variety of ways. Arguing that the heterosexual gender role system traditionally has depended on the **symbolic annihilation** of gays and lesbians, Gross presents from an activist's perspective a useful schema for analyzing the responses of "colonized" people to invisibility and stereotyping in media culture: internalization, subversion, secession and **resistance.**

Some media theorists have begun to warn (as Kellner does) of the dangers of overemphasizing the power of media audiences to resist the ideologies encoded in dominant media texts. We would agree that audience resistance alone cannot serve as a counterbalance or substitute for political efforts, either to get mainstream producers to change imagery or, ultimately, to achieve a more democratic system of media ownership and access. But as long-term battles are being waged on the political fronts, we would also advocate taking a view of ourselves as media audiences that is grounded in respect for our own agency, values and intelligence.

The issues of race, class and gender in media culture that have been highlighted in Part I will be important to bear in mind throughout the subsequent chapters as well, where a wide array of media cultural forms are examined in more depth.

REFERENCE

Butsch, R. (1992). Class and gender in four decades of television situation comedy: Plus ça change . . . *Critical Studies in Mass Communication, 9,* 387-399.

Cultural Studies, Multiculturalism and Media Culture

DOUGLAS KELLNER

Radio, television, film and the other products of media culture provide materials out of which we forge our very identities, our sense of selfhood; our notion of what it means to be male or female; our sense of class, of ethnicity and race, of nationality, of sexuality, of "us" and "them." Media images help shape our view of the world and our deepest values: what we consider good or bad, positive or negative, moral or evil. Media stories provide the symbols, myths and resources through which we constitute a common culture and through the appropriation of which we insert ourselves into this culture. Media spectacles demonstrate who has power and who is powerless, who is allowed to exercise force and violence and who is not. They dramatize and legitimate the power of the forces that be and show the powerless that they must stay in their places or be destroyed.

We are immersed from cradle to grave in a media and consumer society, and thus it is important to learn how to understand, interpret and criticize its meanings and messages. The media are a profound and often misperceived source of cultural pedagogy: They contribute to educating us about how to behave and what to think, feel, believe, fear and desire—and what not to. The media are forms of pedagogy that teach us how to be men and women; how to dress, look and consume; how to react to members of different social groups; how to be popular and successful and avoid failure; and how to conform to the dominant system of norms, values, practices and institutions. Consequently, the gaining of critical media literacy is an important resource for individuals and citizens in learning how to cope with a seductive cultural environment. Learning how to read, criticize and resist media manipulation can help empower oneself in relation to dominant media and culture. It can enhance individual sovereignty vis-à-vis media culture and give individuals more power over their cultural environment.

In this essay, I will discuss the potential contributions of a cultural studies approach to media literacy. In recent years, **cultural studies**[1] has emerged as a new set of approaches to the study of culture and society. The project was inaugurated by the University of Birmingham Centre for Contemporary Cultural Studies, which developed a variety of critical approaches for the analysis, interpretation and criticism of **cultural artifacts**.[2] Through a set of internal debates, and responding to social struggles and movements of the 1960s and the 1970s, the Birmingham group came to focus on the interplay of representations and ideologies of class, gender, race, ethnicity and nationality in cultural texts, including media culture. They were among the first to study the effects of newspapers, radio, television, film and other popular cultural forms on audiences. They also focused on how various audiences interpreted and used media culture differently, analyzing the factors that made different audiences respond in contrasting ways to various media texts.

Through studies of youth subcultures, British cultural studies demonstrated how culture came to constitute distinct forms of identity and group membership. For cultural studies, media culture provides the materials for constructing identities, behavior and views of the world. Those who uncritically follow the dictates of media culture tend to "mainstream" themselves, following the dominant fashion, values and behavior. Yet cultural studies is also interested in how subcultural groups resist dominant forms of culture and identity, creating their own style and identities. Individuals who conform to dominant dress and fashion codes, behavior and political ideologies thus produce their identities within the mainstream group, as members of specific social groupings (such as White, middle-class conservative Americans). Individuals who identify with subcultures, such as punk culture or Black nationalist subcultures, look and act differently from those in the mainstream and thus create oppositional identities, defining themselves against standard models.

Cultural studies insists that culture must be studied within the social relations and system through which culture is produced and consumed and that the study of culture is therefore intimately bound up with the study of society, politics and economics. Cultural studies shows how media culture articulates the dominant values, political ideologies and social developments and novelties of the day. American culture and society is a contested terrain with various groups and ideologies struggling for dominance. Television, film, music and other popular cultural forms are thus often liberal or conservative or occasionally express more radical or oppositional views.

Cultural studies is valuable because it provides some tools that enable one to read and interpret one's culture critically. It also subverts distinctions between "high" and "low" culture by considering a wide continuum of cultural artifacts, ranging from novels to television, and by refusing to erect any specific cultural hierarchies or canons. Previous approaches to culture tended to be primarily literary and elitist, dismissing media culture as banal, trashy and not worthy of serious attention. The project of cultural studies, by contrast, avoids cutting the field of culture into high and low or popular against elite. Such distinctions are difficult to maintain and generally serve as a front for normative aesthetic valuations and, often, a political program (i.e., either dismissing mass culture for high culture or celebrating what is deemed "popular" while scorning "elitist" high culture).

Cultural studies, however, allows us to examine and critically scrutinize the whole range of culture without prior prejudices toward one or another sort of cultural text, institution or practice. It also opens the way toward more differentiated political, rather than aesthetic, valuations of cultural artifacts in which one attempts to distinguish critical and oppositional from conformist and conservative moments in a cultural artifact. For instance, studies of Hollywood film show how key 1960s films promoted the views of radicals and the counterculture and how film in the 1970s was a battleground between liberal and conservative positions; late 1970s films, however, tended toward conservative positions that helped elect Ronald Reagan as president (see Kellner & Ryan, 1988).

There is an intrinsically critical and political dimension to the project of cultural studies that distinguishes it from empirical and apolitical academic approaches to the study of culture and society. British cultural studies, for example, analyzed culture historically in the context of its societal origins and effects. It situated culture within a theory of social production and reproduction, specifying the ways that cultural forms served either to further social domination or to enable people to resist and struggle against domination. It analyzed society as a hierarchical and antagonistic set of social relations characterized by the oppression of subordinate class, gender, race, ethnic and national strata. Employing Gramsci's (1971) model of **hegemony** and **counterhegemony,** it sought to analyze **"hegemonic,"** or ruling, social and cultural forces of domination and to seek "counter-hegemonic" forces of resistance and struggle. The project was aimed at social transformation and attempted to specify forces of domination and resistance to aid the process of political struggle and emancipation from oppression and domination.

For cultural studies, the concept of **ideology** is of central importance, for dominant ideologies serve to reproduce social relations of domination and subordination.[3] Ideologies of **class,** for instance, celebrate upper-class life and denigrate the working class. Ideologies of **gender** promote sexist representations of women, and ideologies of **race** use racist representations of people of color and various minority groups. Ideologies make inequalities and subordination appear natural and just and thus induce consent to relations of domination. Different groups, of course, have different ideologies (liberal, conservative, radical, etc.), and cultural studies specifies what, if any, ideologies are operative in a given cultural artifact. In the course of this study, I will provide some examples of how different ideologies are operative in media cultural texts and will accordingly provide examples of ideological analysis and critique.

Because of its focus on representations of race, gender and class and its critique of ideologies that promote various forms of oppression, cultural studies lends itself to a multiculturalist program that demonstrates how culture reproduces certain forms of racism, sexism and biases against members of subordinate classes, social groups or alternative lifestyles. **Multiculturalism** affirms the worth of different types of culture and cultural groups, claiming, for instance, that Black, Latino, Asian, Native American, gay and lesbian and other oppressed and marginal voices have their own validity and importance. A critical multiculturalism attempts to show how various people's voices and experiences are silenced and omitted from mainstream culture and struggles to aid in the articulation of diverse views, experiences and cultural forms, from groups excluded from the mainstream. This makes it a target of conservative groups who wish to preserve the existing canons of White male, Eurocentric privilege and thus attack multiculturalism in fierce cultural wars now raging over education, the arts and the limits of free expression.

Cultural studies thus promotes a multiculturalist politics and media pedagogy that aims to make people sensitive to how relations of power and domination are **encoded,** or embodied, in cultural texts, such as those of television or film. But it also specifies how people can resist the dominant encoded meanings and produce their own critical and alternative readings. Cultural studies can show how media culture manipulates and indoctrinates us and therefore can empower individuals to resist the dominant meanings in media cultural products and to produce their own meanings. It can also point to moments of **resistance** and criticism within media culture and thus help promote development of more critical consciousness.

A critical cultural studies—embodied in many of the articles collected in this reader—develops concepts and analyses that will enable readers to critically dissect the artifacts of contemporary media culture and to gain power over their cultural environment. By exposing the entire field of culture to critical scrutiny, cultural studies provides a broad, comprehensive framework to undertake studies of culture, politics and society for the purposes of individual empowerment and social and political struggle and transformation. In the following pages, I will therefore indicate some of the chief components of the type of cultural studies that I find most useful.

COMPONENTS OF
CRITICAL CULTURAL STUDIES

At its strongest, cultural studies contains a threefold project of analyzing the production and **political economy** of culture, cultural **texts** and the **audience reception** of those texts and their effects. This comprehensive approach avoids too narrowly focusing on one dimension of the project to the exclusion of others. To avoid such limitations, I propose a multiperspective approach that (a) discusses production and political economy, (b) engages in textual analysis, and (c) studies the reception and use of cultural texts.[4]

Production and Political Economy

Because it has been neglected in many trends of recent cultural studies, it is important to stress the importance of analyzing cultural texts within their system of production and distribution, often referred to as the *political economy* of culture.[5] Inserting texts into the system of culture within which they are produced and distributed can help elucidate features and effects of the texts that textual analysis alone might miss or downplay. Rather than being antithetical approaches to culture, knowledge of political economy can actually contribute to textual analysis and critique. The system of production often determines what sort of artifacts will be produced, what structural limits there will be as to what can and cannot be said and shown and what sort of audience effects the text may generate.

Study of the codes of television, film or popular music, for instance, is enhanced by studying the formulas and conventions of production. These cultural forms are structured by well-defined rules and conventions, and the study of the production of culture can help elucidate the codes actually in play. Because of the demands of the format of radio or music television, for instance, most popular songs are 3 to 5 minutes long, fitting into the format of the distribution system. Because of their control by giant corporations oriented primarily toward profit, film and television production in the United States is dominated by specific genres, such as talk and game shows, soap operas, situation comedies, action/adventure shows and so on. This economic factor explains why there are cycles of certain genres and subgenres, sequelmania in the film industry, crossovers of popular films into television series and a certain homogeneity in products constituted within systems of production with rigid generic codes, formulaic conventions and well-defined ideological boundaries.

Likewise, study of political economy can help determine the limits and range of political and ideological discourses and effects. My study of television in the United States, for instance, disclosed that takeover of the television networks by major transnational corporations and communications conglomerates was part of a "right turn" within U.S. society in the 1980s whereby powerful corporate groups won control of the state and the mainstream media (Kellner, 1990). For example, during the 1980s, all three networks were taken over by major corporate conglomerates: ABC was taken over in 1985 by Capital Cities, NBC was taken over by GE, and CBS was taken over by the Tisch Financial Group. Both ABC and NBC sought corporate mergers, and this motivation, along with other benefits derived from Reaganism, might well have influenced them to downplay criticisms of Reagan and to generally support his conservative programs, military adventures and simulated presidency.

Furthermore, one cannot really analyze the role of the media in the Persian Gulf war without analyzing the production and political economy of news and information, as well as the actual text of the Persian Gulf war and its reception by its audience (see Kellner, 1992). Or one cannot fully grasp the Madonna phenomenon without analyzing her marketing strategies, her political environment and her cultural artifacts and their effects

(Kellner, 1994). Likewise, in appraising the full social impact of pornography, one needs to be aware of the sex industry and the production process of, say, pornographic films, not just of the texts themselves and their effects on audiences.

Yet political economy alone does not hold the key to cultural studies, and important as it is, it has limitations as a single approach. Some political economy analyses reduce the meanings and effects of texts to rather circumscribed and reductive ideological functions, arguing that media culture merely reflects the ideology of the ruling economic elite that controls the culture industries and is nothing more than a vehicle for capitalist ideology. It is true that media culture overwhelmingly supports capitalist values, but it is also a site of intense struggle between races, classes, genders, and social groups. Thus, to fully grasp the nature and effects of media culture, one needs to develop methods to analyze the full range of its meanings and effects.

Textual Analysis

The products of media culture require multidimensional close textual readings to analyze their various forms of discourses, ideological positions, narrative strategies, image construction and effects. There have been a wide spectrum of types of textual analysis of media culture, ranging from quantitative **content analysis** that analyzes the number of, say, episodes of violence in a text, to qualitative analysis that applies various critical theories to explain how texts function to produce meaning. Traditionally, the qualitative analysis of texts has been the task of **formalist** literary criticism, which explicates the central meanings, values and ideologies in cultural artifacts by attending to the formal properties of imaginative literature texts—such as style, verbal imagery, characterization, narrative structure and point of view, symbolism, and so on. In more recent years, literary-critical textual analysis has been enhanced by methods derived from **semiotics,** a system for analyzing the creation of meaning not only in written languages but also in other, nonverbal languagelike codes, such as the visual and auditory languages of film and TV.

Semiotics analyzes how linguistic and nonlinguistic cultural "signs" form widely understood systems of meanings, as when giving someone a rose is a sign of love or getting an A on a college paper is a sign of mastery of the rules of the specific assignment. Semiotic analysis can be connected with **genre analysis** (the study of conventions governing established cultural forms, such as soap operas) to reveal how the codes and forms of particular genres help to produce meaning. A semiotic and generic analysis of *Rambo,* for instance, would show how this film follows the conventions of the Hollywood genre of the "war film," which dramatizes conflicts between the United States and its "enemies," and provides a happy ending that portrays the victory of good over evil. It would study the strictly cinematic and formal elements of the film, dissecting the ways that camera angles present Rambo as a god or how slow-motion images of him gliding through the jungle "code" him as a force of nature. One would also notice that images of Rambo being tortured adopt familiar crucifixion iconography, valorizing him as a Christlike martyr, and images of his headband and clothing code him as an individualist, thus appropriating 1960s countercultural iconography for the political right.[6]

If it is not to be purely formalistic, however, textual analysis needs to be concerned with showing how the cultural meanings encoded into a text's various "languages" convey ideological effects. A textual critic can combine a variety of different analytical methods with a Marxist, feminist, Third World anti-imperialist, antiracist, or other political perspective—or indeed with some combination of more than one of these—to produce **ideological textual analysis.**

Each critical perspective and analytical method has its own strengths and limitations, its optics and blind spots. Traditionally, Marxian ideology critiques have been strong on class and historical contextualization and weak on formal analysis, and some approaches include analyses of gender and race, whereas some versions are highly "reductionist"—reducing textual analysis to denunciation of ruling class ideology. Feminism excels in gender analysis, and in some versions it is formally sophisticated, drawing on such methods as semiotics and psychoanalysis, although some versions are reductive, and early feminism often limited itself to analysis of gender, ignoring important differences of race and class.

Ideally, to provide a full and adequate reading of texts such as the *Rambo* and *Rocky* films of Sylvester Stallone, one would use textual analysis and a Marxist, feminist, and anti-imperialist perspective to see how ideologies of class, gender and race intersect in the films. For example, one would note that the *Rocky* films provide a fantasy of class transcendence, whereby the White, male working-class fighter becomes wealthy and successful, while at the same time women are inscribed in roles of domesticity in the text, and negative images of both Blacks and of Soviet communists are provided, thus promoting racist and anti-Communist ideologies.

Of course, each reading of a text is still only one possible reading from one critic's **subject position,** no matter how multiperspectival, and may or may not be the reading preferred by audiences (who themselves will be significantly different according to their class, race, gender, ethnicity, sexuality, ideologies and so on). Because there is a split between **textual encoding** and **audience decoding** (see Bobo, Chapter 9, for further elaboration of this key concept in cultural studies), there is always the possibility of a multiplicity of readings of any text of media culture (Hall, 1980b). There are limits to the openness or **polysemic** nature of any text, of course, and textual analysis can explicate the parameters of possible readings. Yet to carry through a full cultural studies analysis, one must also examine how diverse audiences actually read media texts, and attempt to determine what effects they have on audience thought and behavior.

Audience Reception and Use of Media Culture

All texts are subject to multiple readings depending on the perspectives and subject positions of the reader. Members of distinct genders, classes, races, nations, regions, sexual preferences and political ideologies are going to read texts differently, and cultural studies can illuminate why diverse audiences interpret texts differently. It is indeed one of the merits of cultural studies to have focused on audience reception in recent years, and this focus provides one of its major contributions, although there are also some limitations and problems with the standard cultural studies approaches.[7]

A standard way to discover how audiences read texts is to engage in ethnographic research, in an attempt to determine how texts affect audiences and shape their beliefs and behavior. Ethnographic cultural studies have indicated some of the various ways that audiences use and appropriate texts, often to empower themselves. Radway's (1983) study of women's use of Harlequin novels, for example, shows how these books provide escapism for women and could be understood as reproducing traditional women's roles, behavior and attitudes. Yet they can also empower women by promoting fantasies of a different life and may thus inspire revolt against male domination. Or they may enforce, in other audiences, female submission to male domination and trap women in ideologies of romance, in which submission to Prince Charming is seen as the alpha and omega of happiness for women. (See Chapter 23 for a selection from Radway's work.)

John Fiske (1989a, 1989b) suggests that young teenage girls use Madonna as a resource to inspire gestures of independence and fashion rebellion and thus are empowered to "express themselves." Teenagers use video games and music television as an escape from the demands of a disciplinary society. Males use sports as a terrain of fantasy identification, in which they feel empowered as "their" team or star triumphs. Such sports events also generate a form of community, currently being lost in the privatized media and consumer culture of our time. Indeed, fandoms of all sorts, ranging from *Star Trek* fans ("Trekkies") to fans of *Beavis and Butt-Head* or various soap operas, also form communities that enable people to relate to others who share their interests and hobbies.

This emphasis on audience reception and appropriation helps cultural studies overcome the previous one-sided textualist orientations to culture. It also focuses on the actual political effects that texts have and how audiences use texts—sometimes in ways that subvert the intentions of the producers or managers of the cultural industries that supply them, as when stoned hippies laugh at the antidrug scenarios of a cop show such as *Dragnet* (see de Certeau, 1984, for more examples). Audience research can reveal how people are actually using cultural texts and what sort of effects they are having on everyday life. Combining quantitative and qualitative research, new reception studies, including some of the essays in this reader, are providing important contributions into how audiences actually interact with cultural texts (e.g., Brown & Schulze, Chapter 57; Lee & Cho, Chapter 41; see Bobo, Chapter 8, for further elaboration of decoding and audience reception).

Yet there are several problems that I see with reception studies as they have been constituted within cultural studies, particularly in the United

States. First, there is a danger that class will be downplayed as a significant variable that structures audience decoding and use of cultural texts. Cultural studies in England were particularly sensitive to class differences—as well as subcultural differences—in the use and reception of cultural texts, but I have noted several dissertations, books and articles in cultural studies in the United States in which attention to class has been downplayed or is missing altogether. This is not surprising, because a neglect of class as a constitutive feature of culture and society is an endemic deficiency in the American academy in most disciplines.

There is also the reverse danger, however, of exaggerating the constitutive force of class and downplaying, or ignoring, other variables, such as gender or ethnicity. Staiger (1992) notes that Fiske, building on Hartley, lists seven "subjectivity positions" that are important in cultural reception, "self, gender, age-group, family, class, nation, ethnicity," and proposes adding sexual orientation. All of these factors, and no doubt more, interact in shaping how audiences receive and use texts and must be taken into account in studying cultural reception, for audiences decode and use texts according to the specific constituents of their class, race or ethnicity, gender, sexual preferences and so on.

Furthermore, I would warn against a tendency to romanticize the active audience, by claiming that all audiences produce their own meanings and denying that media culture may have powerful manipulative effects. The cultural studies tradition of reception research has distinguished between dominant and oppositional readings (Hall, 1980b, still evident in Fiske's work). "Dominant" readings are those in which audiences appropriate texts in line with the interests of the dominant culture and the ideological intentions of a text, as when audiences feel pleasure in the restoration of male power, law and order, and social stability at the end of a film such as *Die Hard*, after the hero and representatives of authority eliminate the terrorists who had taken over a high-rise corporate headquarters. An "oppositional" reading, by contrast, celebrates the resistance to this reading in audience appropriation of a text; for example, Fiske (1993) observes resistance to dominant readings when homeless individuals in a shelter cheered the destruction of police and authority figures, during repeated viewings of a videotape of *Die Hard*.

Although this is a useful distinction, there is a tendency in cultural studies to celebrate resistance per se without distinguishing between types and forms of resistance (a similar problem resides with indiscriminate celebration of audience pleasure in certain reception studies). For example, resistance to social authority by the homeless evidenced in their viewing of *Die Hard* could serve to strengthen brutal masculist behavior and encourage manifestations of physical violence to solve social problems. Sartre, Fanon and Marcuse, among others, have argued that violence can be either emancipatory, when directed at forces of oppression, or reactionary, when directed at popular forces struggling against oppression. Many feminists, by contrast, see all violence as forms of brute masculist behavior, and many people see it as a problematical form of conflict resolution. Resistance and pleasure cannot therefore be valorized per se as progressive elements of the appropriation of cultural texts, but difficult discriminations must be made as to whether the resistance, oppositional reading or pleasure in a given experience is progressive or reactionary, emancipatory or destructive.

Thus, although emphasis on the audience and reception was an excellent correction to the one-sidedness of purely textual analysis, I believe that in recent years cultural studies has overemphasized reception and textual analysis while underemphasizing the production of culture and its political economy. Indeed, I have a sense that there is a growing trend in cultural studies toward audience reception studies that neglect both production and textual analysis, thus producing populist celebrations of the text and audience pleasure in its use of cultural artifacts. This approach, taken to an extreme, would lose its critical perspective and would lead to a positive gloss on audience experience of whatever is being studied. Such studies also might lose sight of the manipulative and conservative effects of certain types of media culture and thus serve the interests of the cultural industries as they are presently constituted.

A new way, in fact, to study media effects is to use the computer databases that collect references to media texts (such as Dialog or Nexis/Lexis) and to trace the effects of media artifacts, such as Rambo, Madonna, and *Beavis and Butt-Head*, through analysis of references to them in the news media. Previous studies of audience reception research have privileged those ethnographic studies that selected small slices of the vast media audiences. Invariably, such studies are limited, whereas broader effects research can indicate how the most popular artifacts of media culture have a wide range of effects. In a forthcoming book on *Media Culture,* I have done precisely this in reference to a large number of cultural artifacts that clearly influenced behavior (Kellner, in press). Examples include groups of kids and adults who imitated Rambo in various forms of asocial behavior or fans of *Beavis and Butt-Head* who started fires or tortured animals in the modes practiced by the popular MTV cartoon characters. Media effects are complex and controversial, and it is the merit of cultural studies to make their study an important part of its agenda.

TOWARD A CULTURAL STUDIES APPROACH
THAT IS CRITICAL, MULTICULTURAL AND MULTIPERSPECTIVAL

I am proposing that cultural studies itself be multiperspectival, getting at culture from the perspectives of political economy, text analysis and audience reception, as outlined earlier. Textual analysis should use a multiplicity of perspectives and critical methods, and audience reception studies should delineate the multiplicity or subject positions, or perspectives, through which audiences appropriate culture. This requires a multicultural approach that sees the importance of analyzing the dimensions of class, race and ethnicity, gender and sexual preference within the texts of media culture and seeing as well their impact on how audiences read and interpret media culture. I also advocate a critical cultural studies that attacks sexism, racism or bias against specific social groups (e.g., gays, intellectuals, and so on) and that criticizes texts that promote any kind of domination or oppression.

As an example of how considerations of production, textual analysis and audience readings can fruitfully intersect in the sort of cultural studies that I am advocating, let us reflect on the Madonna phenomenon. Madonna first appeared in the moment of Reaganism and embodied the materialistic and consumer-oriented ethos of the 1980s ("Material Girl"). She also appeared in a time of dramatic image proliferation, associated with MTV, fashion fever, and intense marketing of products. Madonna was one of the first MTV music video superstars who consciously crafted images to attract a mass audience. Her early music videos were aimed at teenage girls (the Madonna wanna-be's), but she soon incorporated Black, Hispanic, and other minority audiences with her images of interracial sex and multicultural "family" in her concerts. She also appealed to gay and lesbian audiences, as well as feminist and academic audiences, as her videos became more complex and political (e.g., "Like a Prayer," "Express Yourself," "Vogue," and so on).

Thus Madonna's popularity was in large part a function of her marketing strategies and her production of music videos and images that appealed to diverse audiences. The meanings and effects of her artifacts can best be discerned within the context of their production and reception, which involves discussion of MTV, the music industry, concerts, marketing and the production of images (see, for example, chapters in this volume by Pettegrew, Rose, and hooks). Understanding Madonna's popularity also requires focus on audiences, not just as individuals but as members of specific groups, such as teenage girls, who were empowered in their struggles for individual identity by Madonna, or gays, who were also empowered by her incorporation of alternative images of sexuality within popular mainstream cultural artifacts. Yet appraising the politics and effects of Madonna also requires analysis of how her work might merely reproduce a consumer culture that defines identity in terms of images and consumption.

Thus a cultural studies that is critical and multicultural provides comprehensive approaches to culture that can be applied to a wide variety of artifacts, from pornography to Madonna, from the Persian Gulf war to *Beavis and Butt-Head*. Its comprehensive perspectives encompass political economy, textual analysis and audience research and provide critical and political optics that enable individuals to dissect the meanings, messages and effects of dominant cultural forms. Cultural studies is part of a critical media pedagogy that enables individuals to resist media manipulation and to increase their freedom and individuality. It can empower people to gain sovereignty over their culture and enable them to struggle for alternative cultures and political change. Cultural studies is thus not just another academic fad but can be part of a struggle for a better society and a better life.

NOTES

1. For all boldface terms in this chapter, see Glossary for fuller definitions.

2. For more information on British cultural studies, see Hall (1980a), Johnson (1986/1987), Fiske (1986), O'Connor (1989), Turner (1990), Grossberg (1989), Agger (1992), and the articles collected in Grossberg, Nelson, and Treichler (1992) and During (1992).

3. On the concept of ideology, see Kellner (1978, 1979), the Centre for Contemporary Cultural Studies (1980), Kellner and Ryan (1988), and Thompson (1990).

4. This model was adumbrated in Hall (1980a) and Johnson (1986/1987) and guided much of the early Birmingham work. Around the mid-1980s, however, the Birmingham group began to increasingly neglect the production and political economy of culture (some believe that this was always a problem with their work), and much of their work became more academic, cut off from political struggle. I am thus trying to recapture the spirit of the early Birmingham project, reconstructed for our contemporary moment. For a fuller development of my conception of cultural studies, see Kellner (1992, 1994).

5. The term *political economy* calls attention to the fact that the production and distribution of culture takes place within a specific economic and political system, constituted by relations between the state and economy. For instance, in the United States a capitalist economy dictates that cultural production is governed by laws of the market, but the democratic imperatives of the system mean that there is some regulation of culture by the state. There are often tensions within a given society concerning how many activities should be governed by the imperatives of the market, or economics, alone and how much state regulation or intervention is desirable, to assure a wider diversity of programming and broadcasting, for instance, or the prohibition of phenomena agreed to be harmful, such as cigarette advertising or pornography (see Kellner, 1990.)

6. Susan Jeffords (1989), for instance, interprets the *Rambo* and other "return to Vietnam" films as an attempt at remasculinization, of reaffirmation of male values, after the shame of defeat in Vietnam and threats to male power by women and feminists. The *Rocky* films could also be read as assertions of White male power against Blacks and people of color.

7. Cultural studies that have focused on audience reception include Brunsdon and Morley (1978), Radway (1983), Ang (1985), Morley (1986), and Fiske (1989a, 1989b).

REFERENCES

Agger, B. (1992). *Cultural studies.* London: Falmer.

Ang, I. (1985). *Watching Dallas.* New York: Methuen.

Brunsdon, C., & Morley, D. (1978). *Everyday television: "Nationwide."* London: British Film Institute.

Centre for Contemporary Cultural Studies. (1980). *On ideology.* London: Hutchinson.

de Certeau, M. (1984). *The practice of everyday life.* Berkeley: University of California.

During, S. (1992). *Cultural studies.* New York: Routledge.

Fiske, J. (1986). British cultural studies and television. In R. C. Allen (Ed.), *Channels of discourse* (pp. 245-289). Chapel Hill: University of North Carolina Press.

Fiske, J. (1989a). *Reading the popular.* Boston: Unwin Hyman.

Fiske, J. (1989b). *Understanding popular culture.* Boston: Unwin Hyman.

Fiske, J. (1993). *Power plays, power works.* London: Verso.

Gramsci, A. (1971). *Selections from the prison notebooks.* New York: International.

Grossberg, L. (1989). The formations of cultural studies: An American in Birmingham. *Strategies, 22,* 114-149.

Grossberg, L., Nelson, C., & Treichler, P. (1992). *Cultural studies.* New York: Routledge.

Hall, S. (1980a). Cultural studies and the Centre: Some problematics and problems. In S. Hall et al. (Eds.), *Culture, media, language* (pp. 15-47). London: Hutchinson.

Hall, S. (1980b). Encoding/decoding. In S. Hall et al. (Eds.), *Culture, media, language* (pp. 128-138). London: Hutchinson.

Jeffords, S. (1989). *The remasculinization of America.* Bloomington: University of Indiana Press.

Johnson, R. (1986/1987). What is cultural studies anyway? *Social Text, 16,* 38-80.

Kellner, D. (1978, November/December). Ideology, Marxism, and advanced capitalism. *Socialist Review,* pp. 37-65.

Kellner, D. (1979, May/June). TV, ideology, and emancipatory popular culture. *Socialist Review,* pp. 13-53.

Kellner, D. (1990). *Television and the crisis of democracy.* Boulder, CO: Westview.

Kellner, D. (1992). *The Persian Gulf TV war.* Boulder, CO: Westview.

Kellner, D. (1994). *On cultural studies and society: Identity, politics and media culture between the modern and the postmodern.* New York: Routledge.

Kellner, D. (in press). *Media culture.* New York: Routledge.

Kellner, D., & Ryan, M. (1988). *Camera politica: The politics and ideology of contemporary Hollywood film.* Bloomington: Indiana University Press.

Morley, D. (1986). *Family television.* London: Comedia.

O'Connor, A. (1989). The problem of American cultural studies. *Critical Studies in Mass Communication, 6,* 405-413.

Radway, J. (1983). *Reading the romance.* Chapel Hill: University of North Carolina Press.

Staiger, J. (1992). *Centennial Review, 26*(1).

Thompson, J. (1990). *Ideology and modern culture.* Stanford: Stanford University Press.

Turner, G. (1990). *British cultural studies: An introduction.* New York: Unwin Hyman.

.2

The Whites of Their Eyes

Racist Ideologies and the Media

STUART HALL

. . . We begin by defining some of the terms of the argument. "Racism and the media" touches directly the problem of *ideology*, since the media's main sphere of operations is the production and transformation of ideologies. An intervention in the media's construction of race is an intervention in the *ideological* terrain of struggle. Much murky water has flowed under the bridge provided by this concept of ideology in recent years; and this is not the place to develop the theoretical argument. I am using the term to refer to those images, concepts and premises which provide the frameworks through which we represent, interpret, understand and "make sense" of some aspect of social existence. Language and ideology are not the same—since the same linguistic term ("democracy," for example, or "freedom") can be deployed within different ideological discourses. But language, broadly conceived, is by definition the principal medium in which we find different ideological discourses elaborated.

Three important things need to be said about ideology in order to make what follows intelligible. First, ideologies do not consist of isolated and separate concepts, but in the articulation of different elements into a distinctive set or chain of meanings. In liberal ideology, "freedom" is connected (articulated) with individualism and the free market; in socialist ideology,

NOTE: Excerpts reprinted from *Silver Linings: Some Strategies for the Eighties*, edited by G. Bridges and R. Brunt (Lawrence and Wishart Ltd., London, 1981), by permission of the publisher.

"freedom" is a collective condition, dependent on, not counterposed to, "equality of condition," as it is in liberal ideology. The same concept is differently positioned within the logic of different ideological discourses. One of the ways in which ideological struggle takes place and ideologies are transformed is by articulating the elements differently, thereby producing a different meaning: breaking the chain in which they are currently fixed (e.g., "democratic" = the "Free" West) and establishing a new articulation (e.g., "democratic" = deepening the democratic content of political life). This "breaking of the chain" is not, of course, confined to the head: it takes place through social practice and political struggle.

Second, ideological statements are made by individuals: but ideologies are not the product of individual consciousness or intention. Rather we formulate our intentions *within ideology*. They pre-date individuals, and form part of the determinate social formations and conditions in which individuals are born. We have to "speak through" the ideologies which are active in our society and which provide us with the means of "making sense" of social relations and our place in them. The transformation of ideologies is thus a collective process and practice, not an individual one. Largely, the processes work *unconsciously*, rather than by conscious intention. Ideologies produce different forms of social consciousness, rather than being produced by them. They work most effectively when we are not aware that how we formulate and construct a statement about the world is underpinned by ideological premises; when our formations seem to be simply descriptive statements about how things are (i.e., must be), or of what we can "take-for-granted." "Little boys like playing rough games; little girls, however, are full of sugar and spice" is predicated on a whole set of ideological premises, though it seems to be an aphorism which is grounded, not in how masculinity and femininity have been historically and culturally constructed in society, but in Nature itself. Ideologies tend to disappear from view into the taken-for-granted "naturalised" world of common sense. Since (like gender) race appears to be "given" by Nature, racism is one of the most profoundly "naturalised" of existing ideologies.

Third, ideologies "work" by constructing for their subjects (individual and collective) positions of identification and knowledge which allow them to "utter" ideological truths as if they were their authentic authors. This is not because they emanate from our innermost, authentic and unified experience, but because we find ourselves mirrored in the positions at the centre of the discourses from which the statements we formulate "make sense." Thus the same "subjects" (e.g., economic classes or ethnic groups) can be differently constructed in different ideologies. . . .

Let us look, then, a little more closely at the apparatuses which generate and circulate ideologies. In modern societies, the different media are especially important sites for the production, reproduction and transformation of ideologies. Ideologies are, of course, worked on in many places in society, and not only in the head. . . . But institutions like the media are peculiarly central to the matter since they are, by definition, part of the dominant means of *ideological* production. What they "produce" is, precisely, representations of the social world, images, descriptions, explanations and frames for understanding how the world is and why it works as it is said and shown to work. And, amongst other kinds of ideological labour, the media construct for us a definition of what *race* is, what meaning the imagery of race carries, and what the "problem of race" is understood to be. They help to classify out the world in terms of the categories of race.

The media are not only a powerful source of ideas about race. They are also one place where these ideas are articulated, worked on, transformed and elaborated. We have said "ideas" and "ideologies" in the plural. For it would be wrong and misleading to see the media as uniformly and conspiratorially harnessed to a single, racist conception of the world. Liberal and humane ideas about "good relations" between the races, based on open-mindedness and tolerance, operate inside the world of the media. . . .

It would be simple and convenient if all the media were simply the ventriloquists of a unified and racist "ruling class" conception of the world. But neither a unifiedly conspiratorial media nor indeed a unified racist "ruling class" exist in anything like that simple way. I don't insist on complexity for its own sake. But if critics of the media subscribe to too simple or reductive a view of their operations, this inevitably lacks credibility and weakens the case they are making because the theories and critiques don't square with reality. . . .

Another important distinction is between what we might call "overt" racism and "inferential" racism. By *overt* racism, I mean those many occasions when open and favourable coverage is given to arguments, positions and spokespersons who are in the business of elaborating an openly racist argument or advancing a racist policy or view. . . .

By *inferential* racism I mean those apparently naturalised representations of events and situations relating to race, whether "factual" or "fictional," which have racists premises and propositions inscribed in them as a set of *unquestioned assumptions*. These enable racist statements to be formulated without ever bringing into awareness the racist predicates on which the statements are grounded. . . .

An example of *this* type of racist ideology is the sort of television programme which deals with some "problem" in race relations. It is probably made by a good and honest liberal broadcaster, who hopes to do some good in the world for "race relations" and who maintains a scrupulous balance and neutrality when questioning people interviewed for the programme. The programme will end with a homily on how, if only the "extremists" on *either* side would go away, "normal blacks and whites" would be better able to get on with learning to live in harmony together. Yet every word and image of such programmes are impregnated with unconscious racism because they are all predicated on the unstated and unrecognized assumption that the *blacks* are the *source of the problem*. Yet virtually the whole of "social problem" television about race and immigration—often made, no doubt, by well-intentioned and liberal-minded broadcasters—is precisely predicated on racist premises of this kind. . . .

. . . Recent critics of the literature of imperialism have argued that, if we simply extend our definition of nineteenth-century fiction from one branch of "serious fiction" to embrace popular literature, we will find a second, powerful strand of the English literary imagination to set beside the *domestic* novel: the male-dominated world of imperial adventure, which takes *empire*, rather than *Middlemarch*, as its microcosm. . . . In this period, the very idea of *adventure* became synonymous with the demonstration of the moral, social and physical mastery of the colonisers over the colonised.

Later, this concept of "adventure"—one of the principal categories of modern *entertainment*—moved straight off the printed page into the literature of crime and espionage, children's books, the great Hollywood extravaganzas and comics. There, with recurring persistence, they still remain. Many of these older versions have had their edge somewhat blunted by time. They have been distanced from us, apparently, by our superior wisdom and liberalism. But they still reappear on the television screen, especially in the form of "old movies" (some "old movies," of course, continue to be made). But we can grasp their recurring resonance better if we identify some of the base-images of the "grammar of race."

There is, for example, the familiar *slave-figure:* dependable, loving in a simple, childlike way—the devoted "Mammy" with the rolling eyes, or the faithful fieldhand or retainer, attached and devoted to "his" Master. The best-known extravaganza of all—*Gone With The Wind*—contains rich variants of both. The "slave-figure" is by no means limited to films and programmes *about* slavery. Some "Injuns" and many Asians have come on to the screen in this disguise. A deep and unconscious ambivalence pervades this stereotype. Devoted and childlike, the "slave" is also unreliable, unpredictable and undependable—capable of "turning nasty," or of plotting in a treacherous way, secretive, cunning, cut-throat once his or her Master's or Mistress's back is turned: and inexplicably given to running way into the bush at the slightest opportunity. The whites can never be sure that this childish simpleton—"Sambo"—is not mocking his master's white manners behind his hand even when giving an exaggerated caricature of white refinement.

Another base-image is that of the "native." The good side of this figure is portrayed in a certain primitive nobility and simple dignity. The bad side is portrayed in terms of cheating and cunning, and, further out, savagery and barbarism. Popular culture is still full today of countless savage and restless "natives," and sound-tracks constantly repeat the threatening sound of drumming in the night, the hint of primitive rites and cults. Cannibals, whirling dervishes, Indian tribesmen, garishly got up, are constantly threatening to over-run the screen. They are likely to appear at any moment out of the darkness to decapitate the beautiful heroine, kidnap the children, burn the encampment or threatening to boil, cook and eat the innocent explorer or colonial administrator and his lady-wife. These "natives" always move as an anonymous collective mass—in tribes or hordes. And against them is always counterposed the isolated white figure, alone "out there," confronting his Destiny or shouldering his Burden in the "heart of darkness," displaying coolness under fire and an unshakeable authority—exerting mastery over the rebellious natives or quelling the threatened uprising with a single glance of his steel-blue eyes.

A third variant is that of the "clown" or "entertainer." This captures the "innate" humour, as well as the physical grace of the licensed entertainer—putting on a show for The Others. It is never quite clear whether we are laughing with or at this figure: admiring the physical and rhythmic grace, the open expressivity and emotionality of the "entertainer," or put off by the "clown's" stupidity.

One noticeable fact about all these images is their deep *ambivalence*—the double vision of the white eye through which they are seen. The primitive nobility of the aging tribesman or chief, and the native's rhythmic grace, always contain both a nostalgia for an innocence lost forever to the civilised, and the threat of civilisation being over-run or undermined by the recurrence of savagery, which is always lurking just below the surface; or by an untutored sexuality, threatening to "break out." Both are aspects—the good and the bad sides—of *primitivism*. In these images, "primitivism" is defined by the fixed proximity of such people to Nature.

Is all this so far away as we sometimes suppose from the representation of race which fill the screens today? These *particular* versions may have faded. But their *traces* are still to be observed, reworked in many of the modern and up-dated images. And though they may appear to carry a different meaning, they are often still constructed on a very ancient grammar. Today's restless native hordes are still alive and well and living, as guerilla armies and freedom fighters in the Angola, Zimbabwe or Namibian "bush." Blacks are still the most frightening, cunning and glamorous crooks (and policemen) in New York cop series. They are the fleet-footed, crazy-talking under-men who connect Starsky and Hutch to the drug-saturated ghetto. The scheming villains and their giant-sized bully boys in the world of James Bond and his progeny are still, unusually, recruited from "out there" in Jamaica, where savagery lingers on. The sexually-available "slave girl" is alive and kicking, smouldering away on some exotic TV set or on the covers of paperbacks, though she is now the centre of a special admiration, covered in a sequinned gown and supported by a white chorus line. Primitivism, savagery, guile and unreliability—all "just below the surface"—can still be identified in the faces of black political leaders around the world, cunningly plotting the overthrow of "civilisation." . . .

■3

White Negroes

JAN NEDERVEEN PIETERSE

. . . The interplay of race, class and gender, the main systems of domination, . . . is a well-established theme, but most discussions concern the way these systems intersect rather than the way they interact. Comparisons are rare between racism, classism and sexism in terms of their histories, ideologies, imageries and underlying logic; we are offered a wealth of vignettes but systematic explorations are lacking. However brief an excursion into a large and difficult area, the focus here on images and stereotypes may shed new light. . . .

SITUATIONS: IRISHMEN, CHINESE, JEWS

Statements in which comparisons are made between blacks and other groups, without a reason why being given, seem to be relatively simple; presumably the comparison is in terms of status, treatment or appearance. Thus Chamfort, in the eighteenth century: "The poor are the negroes of Europe." The British in India often referred to Indians as "niggers," mostly on the basis of skin colour. Of a similar nature is the statement . . . by the Belgian socialist leader Emiel Vandervelde, who compared the way the

NOTE: Excerpts reprinted from *White on Black: Images of Blacks in Western Popular Culture*, by Jan Nederveen Pieterse (New Haven, CT: Yale University Press, 1992), by permission of the publisher.

working class was treated with the treatment of negroes.[1] John Lennon said, "Women are the niggers of the world." A little more complex is a statement by Francisco Cabral, superior of the Portuguese Jesuit mission in Japan (1570-81), about the Japanese: "After all, they are Niggers, and their customs are barbarous."[2] So to the pious Portuguese, after a hundred years of Portuguese experience in Africa, the Japanese were put in the same category as Africans.

In some cases comparison of blacks with other groups goes much further. In 1880 the Belgian essayist Gustave de Molinari noted, in a series of articles about Ireland, that England's most important newspapers and magazines "allow no occasion to escape them of treating the Irish as a kind of inferior race—as a kind of white negroes—and a glance in *Punch* is sufficient to show the difference between the plump and robust personification of John Bull and the wretched figure of lean and bony Pat."[3]

English views of Ireland display an interesting zigzag pattern. In the early Middle Ages Ireland was famed as a centre of Christian civilization: several English kings went there to be educated. Ireland's reputation declined, however, as England's interest in conquering and colonizing it increased. In the wake of the Anglo-Norman invasion and after the classic description of Ireland by Gerald of Wales in the twelfth century, which set the tone for later descriptions, Ireland was considered savage and barbarous. Down to the present this notion of the "wilde Irish" has hardly changed, although there have been marked shifts of emphasis. The distinction between Celtic and Anglo-Saxon "races" in the British Isles is one of long standing, but from the mid-nineteenth century onward the British image of the Irish was recast in biological racial terms.[4] In addition, from about 1840, the standard image of the good-natured Irish peasant was revised, becoming that of a repulsive ape-like creature.

> In cartoons and caricatures as well as prose, Paddy began to resemble increasingly the chimpanzee, the orangutan, and, finally, the gorilla. The transformation of peasant Paddy into ape-man or simianized Caliban was completed by the 1860s and 1870s, when for various reasons it became necessary for a number of Victorians to assign Irishmen to a place closer to the apes than the angels.[5]

Irishmen were depicted with low foreheads, prognathous features and an apelike gait by cartoonists such as Sir John Tenniel of *Punch*. In 1862 a satire in *Punch* attacked Irish immigration under the title "The Missing Link": "A creature manifestly between the Gorilla and the Negro is to be met with in some of the lowest districts of London and Liverpool by adventurous explorers. It comes from Ireland, whence it has contrived to migrate; it belongs in fact to a tribe of Irish savages: the lowest species of Irish Yahoo."[6]

What prompted the metamorphosis of Paddy the peasant to Paddy the ape was the stream of Irish immigrants, in the wake of the famines of the 1840s, along with the mounting Irish resistance to British domination. The "Fenian outrages" of the 1860s involved anti-English acts of sabotage and subversion. Thus, English images of the Irish hardened in the context of colonialism, migration and resistance. About this time the first apes were brought to Europe (the first live adult gorilla arrived at the London Zoo in 1860), and as they made their first appearance in zoos, they began to appear in cartoons and as a new metaphor in popular imagery. . . .

. . . What is striking is how consistent the colonizer's cultural politics are, regardless of geography or ethnicity. Like Africans and blacks, the Irish have been referred to as "savages" and likened to "apes," to "women." and to "children," just as the Celts were often described as a "feminine" race, by contrast with the "masculine" Anglo-Saxons. . . .

Cartoons in periodicals such as *Harper's Weekly (A Journal of Civilization)* made the hostile equation of Irishmen with blacks a routine part of American culture.[7]

These comparisons, in England between Irish people and Africans, and in the United States between the Irish and blacks, were made under the heading of race, but this only serves as a reminder that, until fairly recently, the terms "race" and "nation" (or "people") were synonymous. The peoples of Europe, within regions as well as within countries, were viewed as much as rungs on the racial "ladder" as were peoples or "races" outside Europe. Indeed, virtually all the images and stereotypes projected outside Europe in the age of empire had been used first within Europe. However, when they were *re-used* within Europe the repertoire was infused with the imagery of empire, with other, wider logics of exclusion, of which the imperial construction of "race" was one. Thus in 1885 the English physician John Beddoe devised an "index of nigrescence," a formula for identifying a people's racial components. "He concluded that the Irish were darker than the people of eastern and central England, and were closer to the aborigines of the British Isles, who in turn had traces of 'negro' ancestry in their appearances. The British upper classes also regarded their own working class as almost a race apart, and claimed that they had darker skin and hair than themselves."[8]

This profile could be extended to other minorities. An example is the Chinese who entered the western United States in the nineteenth century as a cheap labour force, following in the footsteps of blacks. Imported on a contract basis to work on the railroads, the "coolie" had in common with the black slave that both were perceived as enemies of free labour and republicanism; what ensued has been termed the "Negroization" of the Chinese.

> Racial qualities that had been assigned to blacks became Chinese characteristics. Calling for Chinese exclusion, the editor of the *San Francisco Alta* claimed the Chinese had most of the vices of the African: "Every reason that exists against the toleration of free blacks in Illinois may be argued against that of the Chinese here." Heathen, morally inferior, savage, and childlike, the Chinese were also viewed as lustful and sensual. Chinese women were condemned as a "depraved class" and their depravity was associated with their almost African-like physical appearance. While their complexions approached "fair," one writer observed, their whole physiognomy indicated "but a slight removal

from the African race." Chinese men were denounced as threats to
white women. . . .[9]

Thus virtually the whole repertoire of anti-black prejudice was transferred to the Chinese: projected on to a different ethnic group which did,
however, occupy a similar position in the labour market and in society. The
profile of the new minority was constructed on the model of the already
existing minority.

Americans often drew comparisons between national minorities (blacks
or Native Americans) and peoples overseas. When the US annexed or
colonized Hawaii, the Philippines, Puerto Rico and Cuba at the turn of the
century, the American popular press characterized the native populations
by analogy with either "red Injuns" or blacks. The *Literary Digest* of August
1898 spoke casually of "Uncle Sam's New-Caught Anthropoids."[10] On the
American conquest of the Philippines, Rudyard Kipling, the bard of imperialism, characterized the native inhabitants as "half devil and half child."
The American press regularly presented Filipinos and other peoples *as*
blacks—images which suggest graphically that the sensation of power and
supremacy was the same, whether on the American continent or overseas,
and was being expressed through the same metaphors. Again, it is not
ethnicity, or "race" that governs imagery and discourse, but rather, the
nature of the *political relationship* between peoples which causes a people to
be viewed in a particular light.

A similar dynamic was at work during the Vietnam war. A common
expression among American GIs in Vietnam was "The only good gook is a
dead gook," with "gook" (the term of abuse for Vietnamese) replacing
"nigger" or Indian ("Injun") in the existing formula.[11] The underlying logic
of dehumanizing the enemy by means of stereotyping is the same. These
examples of dehumanization and victimization illustrate what Ron Dellums
has called, in a phrase, the "niggering process."[12] . . .

. . . What racism, classism, sexism all have in common is social inequality:
the key to all the social relations discussed above is the pathos of hierarchy.
While the common denominator is power—the power that arises from a
hierarchical situation and the power required to maintain that situation—it
is also a matter of the anxiety that comes with power and privilege. Existing
differences and inequalities are magnified for fear they will diminish. Stereotypes are reconstructed and reasserted precisely when existing hierarchies
are being challenged and inequalities are or may be lessening. Accordingly,
stereotyping tends to be not merely a matter of domination, but above all,
of humiliation. Different and subordinate groups are not merely described,
they are *debased*, degraded. Perceptions are manipulated in order to enhance
and to magnify social distance. The rhetoric and the imagery of domination
and humiliation permeate society. They concern processes in which we all
take part, as receivers and senders, in the everyday rituals of impression
management, in so far as taking part in society means taking part in some
kind of status-ranking.

As the negative of the denigrating images sketched above, there emerges
the top-dog position, whose profile is approximately as follows: white,
western, civilized, male, adult, urban, middle-class, heterosexual, and so on.

It is this profile that has monopolized the definition of humanity in mainstream western imagery. It is a programme of fear for the rest of the world population.

NOTES

1. Quoted in Vints (1984, p. 26).
2. Boxer (1978, p. 23).
3. Quoted in Curtis (1971, p. 1).
4. A classic source is J. Beddoe, *The Races of Britain* (1885). See MacDougall (1982) and Rich (1986, pp. 13-20).
5. Curtis (1971, p. 2).
6. Curtis (1971, p. 100). See cartoons by Tenniel and others (pp. 55, 56, 57, 58, 59, 60, 62).
7. During a visit to America in 1881, the English historian Edward Freeman wrote: "This would be a great land if only every Irishman would kill a Negro, and be hanged for it. I find this sentiment generally approved—sometimes with the qualification that they want Irish and negroes for servants, not being able to get any other" (Curtis, 1984, p. 58).
8. Curtis (1984, p. 55) and Beddoe (1885).
9. Takaki (1980, pp. 217-218). "The 'Negroization' of the Chinese reached a high point when a magazine cartoon depicted [one of] them as a bloodsucking vampire with slanted eyes, a pigtail, dark skin, and thick lips. White workers made the identification even more explicit when they referred to the Chinese as 'nagurs.' " One may add that there were also differences between the stereotypes of Chinese and blacks.
10. See Drinnon (1980, pp. 276-277) and Jacobs and Landau (1971).
11. Lifton (1973/1985, p. 204).
12. Dellums (1978).

REFERENCES

Beddoe, J. (1885). *The races of Britain.* London.

Boxer, C. R. (1978). *The church militant and Iberian expansion, 1440-1770.* Ann Arbor, MI: Books of Demand.

Curtis, L. P., Jr. (1971). *Apes and angels: The Irishman in victorian caricature.* London: Newton Abbot.

Curtis, L. (1984). *Nothing but the same old story: The roots of Anti-Irish racism.* London.

Dellums, R. V. (1978). *The link between struggles for human rights in the United States and Third World.* Washington, DC.

Drinnon, R. (1980). *Facing west: The metaphysics of Indian-hating and Empire-building.* New York: Schocken.

Jacobs, P., & Landau, S. (1971). *To serve the devil* (2 vols.). New York.

Lifton, R. J. (1985). *Home from the war: Vietnam veterans: Neither victims nor executioners.* Boston: Beacon. (Original work published 1973)

MacDougall, H. A. (1982). *Racial myth in English history.* Montreal: Hannover.

Rich, P. B. (1986). *Race and empire in British politics.* Cambridge.

Takaki, R. T. (1980). *Iron cages: Race and culture in nineteenth-century America.* London: Oxford University Press.

Vints, L. (1984). *Kongo: Made in Belgium.* Leuven.

EDITOR'S NOTE: The original manuscript did not provide publishers for books cited. Publisher's names have been added to references for which we have been able to determine the publisher.

4

Madonna

Plantation Mistress or Soul Sister?

BELL HOOKS

> *Subversion is contextual, historical, and above all social. No matter how exciting the "destabilizing" potential of texts, bodily or otherwise, whether those texts are subversive or recuperative or both or neither cannot be determined by abstraction from actual social practice.*
>
> —Susan Bordo

. . . Once I read an interview with Madonna where she talked about her envy of black culture, where she stated that she wanted to be black as a child. It is a sign of white privilege to be able to "see" blackness and black culture from a standpoint where only the rich culture of opposition black people have created in resistance marks and defines us. Such a perspective enables one to ignore white supremacist domination and the hurt it inflicts *via* oppression, exploitation, and everyday wounds and pains. White folks who do not see black pain never really understand the complexity of black pleasure. And it is no wonder then that when they attempt to imitate the joy in living which they see as the "essence" of soul and blackness, their cultural productions may have an air of sham and falseness that may titillate and even move white audiences yet leave many black folks cold. . . .

For masses of black women, the political reality that underlies Madonna's and our recognition that this is a society where "blondes" not only

---

NOTE: Excerpts reprinted from *Black Looks: Race and Representation,* by bell hooks (Boston: South End Press, 1992), by permission of the publisher.

"have more fun" but where they are more likely to succeed in any endeavor is white supremacy and racism. We cannot see Madonna's change in hair color as being merely a question of aesthetic choice. I agree with Julie Burchill in her critical work *Girls on Film,* when she reminds us: "What does it say about racial purity that the best blondes have all been brunettes (Harlow, Monroe, Bardot)? I think it says that we are not as white as we think. I think it says that Pure is a Bore." I also know that it is the expressed desire of the non-blonde Other for those characteristics that are seen as the quintessential markers of racial aesthetic superiority that perpetuate and uphold white supremacy. In this sense Madonna has much in common with the masses of black women who suffer from internalized racism and are forever terrorized by a standard of beauty they feel they can never truly embody.

Like many black women who have stood outside the culture's fascination with the blonde beauty and who have only been able to reach it through imitation and artifice, Madonna often recalls that she was a working-class white-girl who saw herself as ugly, as outside the mainstream beauty standard. And indeed what some of us like about her is the way she deconstructs the myth of "natural" white girl beauty by exposing the extent to which it can be and is usually artificially constructed and maintained. She mocks the conventional racist defined beauty ideal even as she rigorously strives to embody it. Given her obsession with exposing the reality that the ideal female beauty in this society can be attained by artifice and social construction it should come as no surprise that many of her fans are gay men, and that the majority of non-white men, particularly black men, are among that group. . . .

Certainly no one, not even die-hard Madonna fans, ever insists that her beauty is not attained by skillful artifice. And indeed, a major point of the documentary film *Truth or Dare: In Bed With Madonna* was to demonstrate the amount of work that goes into the construction of her image. Yet when the chips are down, the image Madonna most exploits is that of the quintessential "white girl." To maintain that image she must always position herself as an outsider in relation to black culture. It is that position of outsider that enables her to colonize and appropriate black experience for her own opportunistic ends even as she attempts to mask her acts of racist aggression as affirmation. And no other group sees that as clearly as black females in this society. For we have always known that the socially constructed image of innocent white womanhood relies on the continued production of the racist/sexist sexual myth that black women are not innocent and never can be. Since we are coded always as "fallen" women in the racist cultural iconography we can never, as can Madonna, publicly "work" the image of ourselves as innocent female daring to be bad. Mainstream culture always reads the black female body as sign of sexual experience. In part, many black women who are disgusted by Madonna's flaunting of sexual experience are enraged because the very image of sexual agency that she is able to project and affirm with material gain has been the stick this society has used to justify its continued beating and assault on the black female body. The vast majority of black women in the United States, more concerned with projecting images of respectability than with the idea of female sexual agency and transgression, do not often feel we have the "freedom" to act in rebellious ways in regards to sexuality without being punished. We have only to contrast the life story of Tina Turner with that of Madonna to see the different connotations "wild" sexual agency has when it is asserted by a black female. Being represented publicly as an active sexual being has only recently enabled Turner to gain control over her life and career. For years the public image of aggressive sexual agency Turner projected belied the degree to which she was sexually abused and exploited privately. She was also materially exploited. Madonna's career could not be all that it is if there were no Tina Turner and yet, unlike her cohort Sandra Bernhard, Madonna never articulates the cultural debt she owes black females.

In her most recent appropriations of blackness, Madonna almost always imitates phallic black masculinity. Although I read many articles which talked about her appropriating male codes, no critic seems to have noticed her emphasis on black male experience. In his *Playboy* profile, "Playgirl of the Western World," Michael Kelly describes Madonna's crotch grabbing as "an eloquent visual put-down of male phallic pride." He points out that she worked with choreographer Vince Paterson to perfect the gesture. Even though Kelly tells readers that Madonna was consciously imitating Michael Jackson, he does not contextualize his interpretation of the gesture to include this act of appropriation from black male culture. And in that specific context the groin grabbing gesture is an assertion of pride and phallic domination that usually takes place in an all male context. Madonna's imitation of this gesture could just as easily be read as an expression of envy.

Throughout much of her autobiographical interviews runs a thread of expressed desire to possess the power she perceives men have. Madonna may hate the phallus, but she longs to possess its power. She is always first and foremost in competition with men to see who has the biggest penis. She longs to assert phallic power, and like every other group in this white supremacist society, she clearly sees black men as embodying a quality of maleness that eludes white men. Hence, they are often the group of men she most seeks to imitate, taunting white males with her own version of "black masculinity." When it comes to entertainment rivals, Madonna clearly perceives black male stars like Prince and Michael Jackson to be the standard against which she must measure herself and that she ultimately hopes to transcend. . . .

Eager to see the documentary *Truth or Dare* because it promised to focus on Madonna's transgressive sexual persona, which I find interesting, I was angered by her visual representation of her domination over not white men (certainly not over Warren Beatty or Alek Keshishian), but people of color and white working-class women. I was too angered by this to appreciate other aspects of the film I might have enjoyed. In *Truth or Dare* Madonna clearly revealed that she can only think of exerting power along very traditional, white supremacist, capitalistic, patriarchal lines. That she made people who were dependent on her for their immediate likelihood submit to her will was neither charming nor seductive to me or the other black folks that I spoke with who saw the film. We thought it tragically ironic that

Madonna would choose as her dance partner a black male with dyed blonde hair. Perhaps had he appeared less like a white-identified black male consumed by "blonde ambition" he might have upstaged her. Instead he was positioned as a mirror, into which Madonna and her audience could look and see only a reflection of herself and the worship of "whiteness" she embodies—that white supremacist culture wants everyone to embody. Madonna used her power to ensure that he and the other non-white women and men who worked for her, as well as some of the white subordinates would all serve as the backdrop to her white-girl-makes-good drama. Joking about the film with other black folks, we commented that Madonna must have searched long and hard to find a black female that was not a good dancer, one who would not deflect attention away from her. And it is telling that when the film directly reflects something other than a positive image of Madonna, the camera highlights the rage this black female dancer was suppressing. It surfaces when the "subordinates" have time off and are "relaxing."

As with most Madonna videos, when critics talk about this film they tend to ignore race. Yet no viewer can look at this film and not think about race and representation without engaging in forms of denial. After choosing a cast of characters from marginalized groups—non-white folks, heterosexual and gay, and gay white folks—Madonna publicly describes them as "emotional cripples." And of course in the context of the film this description seems borne out by the way they allow her to dominate, exploit, and humiliate them. Those Madonna fans who are determined to see her as politically progressive might ask themselves why it is she completely endorses those racist/sexist/classist stereotypes that almost always attempt to portray marginalized groups as "defective." Let's face it, by doing this, Madonna is not breaking with any white supremacist, patriarchal *status quo;* she is endorsing and perpetuating it.

Some of us do not find it hip or cute for Madonna to brag that she has a "fascistic side," a side well documented in the film. Well, we did not see any of her cute little fascism in action when it was Warren Beatty calling her out in the film. No, there the image of Madonna was the little woman who grins and bears it. No, her "somebody's got to be in charge side," as she names it, was most expressed in her interaction with those representatives from marginalized groups who are most often victimized by the powerful. Why is it there is little or no discussion of Madonna as racist or sexist in her relation to other women? Would audiences be charmed by some rich white male entertainer telling us he must "play father" and oversee the actions of the less powerful, especially women and men of color? So why did so many people find it cute when Madonna asserted that she dominates the interracial casts of gay and heterosexual folks in her film because they are crippled and she "like[s] to play mother." No, this was not a display of feminist power, this was the same old phallic nonsense with white pussy at the center. And many of us watching were not simply unmoved—we were outraged.

Perhaps it is a sign of a collective feeling of powerlessness that many black, non-white, and white viewers of this film who were disturbed by the display of racism, sexism, and heterosexism (yes, it's possible to hire gay people, support AIDS projects, and still be biased in the direction of phallic patriarchal heterosexuality) in *Truth or Dare* have said so little. Sometimes it is difficult to find words to make a critique when we find ourselves attracted by some aspect of a performer's act and disturbed by others, or when a performer shows more interest in promoting progressive social causes than is customary. We may see that performer as above critique. Or we may feel our critique will in no way intervene on the worship of them as a cultural icon.

To say nothing, however, is to be complicit with the very forces of domination that make "blonde ambition" necessary to Madonna's success. Tragically, all that is transgressive and potentially empowering to feminist women and men about Madonna's work may be undermined by all that it contains that is reactionary and in no way unconventional or new. It is often the conservative elements in her work converging with the *status quo* that has the most powerful impact. For example: Given the rampant homophobia in this society and the concomitant heterosexist voyeuristic obsession with gay lifestyles, to what extent does Madonna progressively seek to challenge this if she insists on primarily representing gays as in some way emotionally handicapped or defective? Or when Madonna responds to the critique that she exploits gay men by cavalierly stating: "What does exploitation mean? . . . In a revolution, some people have to get hurt. To get people to change, you have to turn the table over. Some dishes get broken."

I can only say this doesn't sound like liberation to me. Perhaps when Madonna explores those memories of her white working-class childhood in a troubled family in a way that enables her to understand intimately the politics of exploitation, domination, and submission, she will have a deeper connection with oppositional black culture. If and when this radical critical self-interrogation takes place, she will have the power to create new and different cultural productions, work that will be truly transgressive—acts of resistance that transform rather than simply seduce.

5

The Visibility of Race and Media History

JANE RHODES

> *The Negro, never so much a Negro as since he has been dominated by the whites,*
> *when he decides to prove that he has a culture and to behave like a cultured person,*
> *comes to realize that history points out a well-defined path to him: he must*
> *demonstrate that a Negro culture exists.*
>
> —Frantz Fanon,
> *The Wretched of the Earth* (1963)

The psychiatrist and black revolutionary from Martinque, Frantz Fanon, used the experience of Africans under colonial rule—in this case Algeria—as his model for understanding the racialization of thought and history. But he could just as easily have been describing how American society responded to the existence of Africans, Asians, and indigenous people by erasing their cultures and substituting images that supported a system of racial dominance and control. Over time, these representations of America's subordinate groups nourished the nation's popular culture and helped fuel the rise of mass media. Members of these groups responded, when they could, with images of their own creation, and alternative media to disseminate them. Yet, they could do little to counteract the prevailing definitions of race.

NOTE: Reprinted from *Critical Studies in Mass Communication*, Vol. 20, No. 2, 1993, by permission of the publisher. Copyright by the Speech Communication Association, 1993.

This struggle between the transmission of racist ideology and dogma, and the efforts of oppressed groups to claim control over their own image, is part of the legacy of the American mass media. Racial identity has been—and continues to be—a crucial factor in determining who can produce popular culture, and what messages are created. Yet this story has received minimal attention in a historiography that has focused on the celebration of technological achievement and financial success. This is the darker side of media history; the tale of a national institution encumbered by a racist past. Contemporary discussions about the politics of identity in media production lack relevance unless they are placed in the context of this history.

Twenty years ago, a noted scholar of African-American history proclaimed that "a racist society breeds and needs a racist historiography" to support and reinforce the ideologies of racial superiority (Aptheker, 1971, p. 9). We might extend that concept to suggest that a racist society also requires a racist media to disseminate these values and beliefs to a mass audience. Recent historical studies have begun to explore the manifestations of race in popular novels, the press, and early motion pictures, and they tell us a great deal about the role of the media in American social formation (for example, see Fredrickson, 1971; Saxton, 1990; Van Deburg, 1984). Media historians have lagged far behind in this process, and students of mass communication receive little exposure to this legacy. In this essay I will explore two points of juncture in media history: the emergence of the penny press and the coinciding development of the black press, and the development of early motion pictures and the efforts to form an independent black film movement. Each example demonstrates the centrality of race to media production.

Race has been a popular text of the American mass media since the eighteenth century. Racism, which maintained the superiority of white European settlers over the continent's indigenous people, African slaves, and Asian immigrant workers, was equal to the ideologies of manifest destiny and free enterprise in their impact on the developing nation. Racist stereotypes were an important political and sociological tool for presenting this ideology.

Winthrop Jordan locates the origins of American racial ideas in seventeenth century Britain, where whites sought to account for the physical and cultural differences between themselves and Africans by employing explanations based on religion and mythology. Thus, Negroes were the forever-cursed sons of Ham. Just as the industrial revolution and colonialism fueled British expansionism, religion provided a rationale for the growth of slavery: " . . . to be Christian was to be civilized rather than barbarous, English rather than African, white rather than black" (Jordan, 1974, p. 51). Reginald Horsman finds the beginnings of modern racism in eighteenth-century British intellectuals' claim to an Anglo-Saxon tradition, which explained England's quests for land, power, and cultural superiority. A century later these notions were widely disseminated in books and the press by influential authors such as Thomas Carlyle, who published a tract titled "Occasional Discourse on the Nigger Question." In Carlyle's view, "The Saxons were a race destined for greatness and accomplishment; other races could be viewed as obstacles to progress" (Horsman, 1981, p. 65).

This ideology profoundly influenced American colonists, who sought political independence from Britain but clung to the cultural and ethnic heritage of their forebears. The burgeoning popular culture of the new republic served as a powerful agent of control, encouraging the dominant group to assert their authority and constantly reminding the subordinate groups of their fragile and oppressed status in society. For example, the newly-formed American musical theater of the late eighteenth century created a host of characters that lampooned and stereotyped free and en-slaved blacks. One of the most enduring of these images, introduced in 1795, was Sambo, the vain, pompous, and ignorant darkie whose life revolved around song and dance (Van Deburg, 1984). Sambo was effective in perpetu-ating the myth that blacks were happy with their slave status.

While the nation's cultural discourse reinforced the inferiority of blacks with highly visible stereotypes, the political discourse of early newspapers rendered them invisible except as commodities. Publications both before and after the Revolutionary War relied heavily on advertisements for the sale of slaves, or for the return of runaway slaves, as a source of revenue. Amid the discussions of liberty, free speech, and Jeffersonian democracy there was little consideration of the plight of blacks or Indians in the republic. Indeed, as the penny newspapers took hold in the early nineteenth century, they frequently served the agenda of asserting racial superiority. Alexander Saxton argues that the press almost universally portrayed Indi-ans as savage and barbaric in order to justify westward expansion. The same papers, however, showed ambivalence about slavery, perhaps in response to the growing impact of abolitionism. Yet some of the earliest and most famous newspaper publishers were equally hostile to blacks and frequently employed racist invective. Benjamin Day, founder of the *New York Sun*, constantly fought with his partner because he "was always sticking his damned little Abolitionist articles" in the paper (Saxton, 1990, p. 103). James Gordon Bennett, publisher of the *New York Herald*, regularly used racial stereotypes in his attacks on competitors, one of whom he likened to "a small, decrepit, dying penny paper, owned and controlled by a set of woolly-headed and thick-lipped Negroes" (Kluger, 1986, p. 45). There were opposing voices, of course, such as Horace Greeley, publisher of the *New York Tribune* and an outspoken abolitionist. But his was a minority view in American journalism of the period.

Even the African-American's champion, the abolitionist press, was deeply paternalistic and relied on racist mythologies. While white-owned newspapers such as the *Liberator* provided an early forum for African-American writers, their voice was buried within the rhetoric of abolitionism which cast the slave as childlike and dependent. The image of the slave sup-plicant, kneeling, pleading for freedom, and looking to benevolent whites for salvation, was popularized in abolitionist periodicals (Van Deburg, 1984; Yellin, 1989).

The first African-American newspaper, *Freedom's Journal*, emerged in response to the racist discourse of the nation's press and sought to present a distinct racial identity and agenda. In 1827, after a series of especially vituperative anti-black attacks by several New York City editors, John B.

Russwurm and Samuel E. Cornish collaborated to produce their newspaper in which they hoped to counter the stereotypes that prevailed in American popular culture. "We wish to plead our own cause. Too long have others spoken for us. Too long has the publick been deceived by misrepresentations . . ." they wrote in the first issue. But their efforts at counter-discourse were only marginally successful in ameliorating American racism. The impulse to establish an alternative medium in response to oppression from the mainstream served to improve communication to a smaller audience—in this case, other blacks and white abolitionist supporters. Nordin (1977-1978) suggests *Freedom's Journal* functioned primarily as a medium to develop a sense of fraternity and consciousness for freeborn African Americans. I have come to similar conclusions in my own research on the black press that published in Canada during the 1850s: A prime function of these newspapers was to establish community ties among a fragmented population, and to foster a black nationalist identity (Rhodes, 1989).

Despite their tenacity and courage, black journalists of the antebellum era had little power to transform the racist content of the mainstream media, or to influence public opinion on any large scale. Few whites who were not already converted to the abolitionist cause were persuaded by the black press' efforts to show the best intellectual and social accomplishments of the race. The black press was responsible, in part, for elevating a handful of black activists such as Frederick Douglass to a visible position in the national debate on slavery. But Douglass's success also was due to his ability as an orator and his skill as a power broker in the anti-slavery movement.

Meanwhile, most black newspapers struggled against harassment, financial insolvency, illiteracy, and intergroup squabbles. Of the 40-odd newspapers founded by African Americans before the Civil War, only a handful survived more than two years. And the few that lived on, including *Frederick Douglass' Paper* and the *Christian Recorder,* relied heavily on philanthropic aid or support from larger institutions. Antebellum African-American voices could be heard, on a limited basis, through literature, the press, and the lecture hall. But theirs was a small chorus amid the thunder of American racism.

Racist stereotypes shifted throughout the nineteenth century to coincide with the nation's political and social mood. Scientific theories, particularly social Darwinism, replaced earlier justifications for American racism as separation of the races became codified into law (Saxton, 1990, pp. 369-377). By the 1890s, Jim Crow segregation was reinforced by a system of economic exploitation, political disenfranchisement, and violence targeted at the black population. The motion picture industry was born in an era when the full effects of Redemption—the white southern response to blacks' gains during Reconstruction—had taken hold.

Thus, the pre-Civil War images of the benign and happy slave, such as Sambo, were replaced in popular culture by the more sinister coon or the black brute whose sole aim was raping white women. Black women often were characterized as the complacent servant mammy whose matriarchal loyalty compensated for the black male's lasciviousness and irresponsibility. But promiscuous black women also could be found in the role of a scheming and wicked Jezebel casting her spell over vulnerable men. The sexualization of black stereotypes, especially the preoccupation with black male sexual prowess, fueled the practice of lynching, which rose to epidemic proportions in the early twentieth century (see Wiegman, 1993). These, and other representations, illustrated whites' irrational fears of miscegenation and black liberation, and were employed liberally in early motion pictures.

Silent films borrowed heavily from the racial narratives of the Jim Crow south and the hostile north. Movies such as *The Watermelon Contest* (1890s), *The Wedding and Wooing of a Coon* (1905), and *The Nigger* (1915), ridiculed and debased black life in the crude, slapstick form that had been inherited from minstrel shows and vaudeville (Cripps, 1977). Another tradition inherited from the stage was the use of white actors in blackface to parody black characters; the growing film industry had no intention of employing blacks to portray themselves, even in demeaning roles. Filmmakers joined historians at the turn of the century to produce a particularly racist revision of history that portrayed slavery as a benign institution which befit the black character. For example, Edwin Porter, considered a film pioneer by media historians, brought Harriet Beecher Stowe's novel *Uncle Tom's Cabin* to the screen in 1903. One scholar notes the movie diluted the horrors of slavery, and depicted slaves as "grinning, singing and dancing blacks who apparently love their masters and are even made to appear grateful when sold" (Silk & Silk, 1990, p. 122).

No film in this racist tradition has received more attention than *Birth of a Nation*. In this context, it is useful to consider the legacy of D. W. Griffith's notorious film and the way it is presented in the historiography of mass media (Emery & Emery, 1988; Folkerts & Teeter, 1989). An early film history described Griffith as "the admitted master of the art of the screen" and argued that protests against the film by the NAACP and others actually contributed to its popularity and box-office receipts, rather than causing it any serious injury (Ramsaye, 1926/1986). Today, basic textbooks often gloss over the racist content of the film, while extolling Griffith's excellence as a filmmaker and technical innovator. A new edition of one textbook refers to *Birth of a Nation* as "his brilliant Civil War drama," using terms such as "masterful" to describe Griffith's accomplishments (Dominick, 1993). One video documentary I have used in my introductory classes shows clips from the film that often causes students to gasp and shake their heads in horror at Griffith's sympathetic portrayal of the KKK, and his gross stereotypes of African Americans. In the next breath, however, this teaching aid demonstrates the editing, directing, and other techniques that Griffith is credited with developing. The student is left to decide what Griffith's legacy should be, and his racism is seen as an aberration. The underlying message is that Griffith's contributions to the film industry override his "horrible little prejudices," which are blamed on the fact that he was an unreconstructed Southerner.

Griffith's racism is also presented as an individualized phenomenon—as a solitary interpretation of events that had little relationship to the structures of meaning in American society. In fact, *Birth of a Nation* was part of an era in which historians, led by William Archibald Dunning, reinforced the image of blacks as inferior, slavery as benevolent, and Reconstruction as a failure. It is not surprising, then, that Griffith selected Thomas Dixon's popular novel *The Clansmen*, published in 1905, as the subject for his first epic film. In the novel's introduction, Dixon explained the historical vision that he sought to dramatize:

> How the young South, led by the reincarnated souls of the Clansmen of Old Scotland, went forth under this cover and against overwhelming odds, daring exile, imprisonment, and a felon's death, and saved the life of a people, forms one of the most dramatic chapters in the history of the Aryan race. (1905/1970, p. 2)

Despite the film's financial success, Griffith was frustrated by what he saw as affronts to his right to free speech, and his next major film, *Intolerance* (1916), was an "endeavor to expose the absurdities of public opinion" (Ramsaye, 1926/1986, p. 644).

The African-American response to *Birth of a Nation* helped to launch a campaign to counter Griffith's representations. Black newspapers and periodicals, led by the *Crisis*, which was edited by W.E.B. DuBois, urged their readers to boycott the film and encouraged investment in an independent black film industry. By the 1920s several small black film companies were cranking out low-budget products for both black and white audiences (Bogle, 1973; Cripps, 1977). These companies succeeded in giving black performers their entree into the movies, but like the antebellum black press, they were hampered by insufficient funds and competition from an established and cut-throat film industry. A handful of black producers, perhaps the best known being Oscar Micheaux, fed the "race movie" business through the Depression. But in their clumsy attempts to overcome the racist discourse of American society, these films often relied on trivial or stereotyped themes such as the black gangster, and reinforced white standards of beauty with their use of light-skinned performers. Once again, the structures of racism prevented the broad dissemination of messages contradicting the dominant ideology. Not until World War II was there any concerted effort on the part of the motion picture industry to temper its racial content.

When a historical perspective is applied to the examination of the race, gender, or sexual identity of media producers, it becomes readily apparent that the patterns of earlier generations continue to replicate themselves. Today, the cultural products of African Americans and other subordinate groups are routinely appropriated and commodified by the mainstream, while the originators struggle for an autonomous voice. African-American newspapers falter while hip-hop and rap become part of the middle-class, white American practice. Only one African-American woman, Julie Dash, has produced and directed a full-length feature film that received critical (but not financial) success. These media producers shoulder the burden of satisfying the need for alternative representations in a racist society while being true to their art. But many hold on to the belief in the empowerment and healing that can be accomplished with their work. Says Dash, "I like telling stories and controlling worlds. In my world, black women can do anything. They ride horses and fly from trapezes; they are in the future as well as in the past" (Rule, 1992). Media scholars, take heed; learn this history and incorporate it into the dominant narratives of our discipline before another generation is lost.

REFERENCES

Aptheker, H. (1971). *Afro-American history: The modern era.* New York: Citadel Press.

Bogle, D. (1973). *Toms, coons, mulattoes, mammies, and bucks: An interpretive history of Blacks in American films.* New York: Viking.

Cripps, T. (1977). *Slow fade to Black: The Negro in American film, 1900-1942.* New York: Oxford University Press.

Dixon, T. (1970). *The clansman: An historical romance of the Ku Klux Klan.* Lexington: University of Kentucky Press. (Original work published 1905)

Dominick, J. R. (1993). *The dynamics of mass communication* (3rd ed.). New York: McGraw-Hill.

Emery, M., & Emery, E. (1988). *The press and America: An interpretive history of the mass media* (6th ed.). Englewood Cliffs, NJ: Prentice Hall.

Fanon, F. (1963). *The wretched of the earth.* New York: Grove.

Folkerts, J., & Teeter, D. L. (1989). *Voices of a nation: A history of the media in the United States.* New York: Macmillan.

Fredrickson, G. M. (1971). *The Black image in the White mind: The debate on Afro-American character and destiny, 1817-1914.* New York: Harper & Row.

Horsman, R. (1981). *Race and manifest destiny: The origins of American racial Anglo-Saxonism.* Cambridge, MA: Harvard University Press.

Jordan, W. D. (1974). *The White man's burden: Historical origins of racism in the United States.* New York: Oxford University Press.

Kluger, R. (1986). *The paper: The life and death of the* New York Herald Tribune. New York: Knopf.

Nordin, K. D. (1977-1978). In search of Black unity: An interpretation of the content and function of "Freedom's Journal." *Journalism History, 4*(4), 123-128.

Ramsaye, T. (1986). *A million and one nights: A history of the motion picture through 1925.* New York: Simon & Schuster. (Original work published 1926)

Rhodes, J. (1989, August). *Fugitives and freemen: The role of the abolitionist press in the building of a Black community in Canada West.* Paper presented at the Association for Education in Journalism and Mass Communication Conference, Washington, DC.

Rule, S. (1992, February 12). Director defies the odds, and wins. *New York Times,* pp. C15, C17.

Saxton, A. (1990). *The rise and fall of the White republic: Class, politics and mass culture in nineteenth-century America.* London: Verso.

Silk, C., & Silk, J. (1990). *Racism and anti-racism in American popular culture.* Manchester, UK: Manchester University Press.

Van Deburg, W. L. (1984). *Slavery and race in American popular culture.* Madison: University of Wisconsin Press.

Wiegman, R. (1993). The anatomy of lynching. *Journal of the History of Sexuality, 3,* 445-467.

Yellin, J. F. (1989). *Women and sisters: The antislavery feminists in American culture.* New Haven, CT: Yale University Press.

.6

The Silenced Majority

*Why the Average Working Person Has
Disappeared From American Media and Culture*

BARBARA EHRENREICH

It is possible for a middle-class person today to read the papers, watch television, even go to college, without suspecting that America has any inhabitants other than white-collar people—and, of course, the annoyingly persistent "black underclass." The average American has disappeared—from the media, from intellectual concern, and from the mind of the American middle class. The producers of public affairs talk shows do not blush to serve up four upper-income professionals (all, incidentally, white, male, and conservative) to ponder the minimum wage or the possible need for national health insurance. Never, needless to say, an uninsured breadwinner or an actual recipient of the minimum wage. Working-class people are likely to cross the screen only as witnesses to crimes or sports events, never as commentators or—even when their own lives are under discussion—as "experts."

A quick definition: By "working class" I mean not only industrial workers in hard hats, but all those people who are not professionals, managers, or entrepreneurs; who work for wages rather than salaries; and who spend their working hours variously lifting, bending, driving, monitoring, typing, keyboarding, cleaning, providing physical care for others, loading, unload-

---

NOTE: Reprinted by permission of Barbara Ehrenreich. Excerpts as reprinted in the *Utne Reader*, January/February 1990, from original publication in *Zeta* (now Z) Magazine, September 1989.

ing, cooking, serving, etc. The working class so defined makes up 60 to 70 percent of the U.S. population.

By "middle class" I really mean the "professional middle class," or the "professional-managerial class." This group includes the journalists, professors, media executives, etc. who are responsible, in a day-to-day sense, for what we do or do not see or read about in the media. By this definition, the middle class amounts to no more than 20 percent of the U.S. population.

So when I say the working class is disappearing, I do not mean just a particular minority group favored, for theoretical reasons, by leftists. I mean the American majority. And I am laying the blame not only on the corporate sponsors of the media, but on many less wealthy and powerful people. Media people for example. People who are, by virtue of their lifestyles and expectations, not too different from me, and possibly also you.

The disappearance of the working class reflects—and reinforces—the long-standing cultural insularity of the professional middle class. Compared to, say, a decade ago, the classes are less likely to mix in college (due to the decline of financial aid), in residential neighborhoods (due to the rise in real estate prices), or even in the malls (due to the now almost universal segmentation of the retail industry into upscale and downscale components).

In the absence of real contact or communication, stereotypes march on unchallenged; prejudices easily substitute for knowledge. The most intractable stereotype is of the working class (which is, in imagination, only white) as a collection of reactionaries and bigots—reflected, for example, in the use of the terms "hard hat" or "redneck" as class slurs. Even people who call themselves progressives are not immune to this prejudice.

The truth is that, statistically and collectively, the working class is far more reliably liberal than the professional middle class. It was more, not less, opposed to the war in Vietnam. It is more, not less, disposed to vote for a Democrat for president. And thanks to the careful, quantitative studies of Canadian historian Richard F. Hamilton, we know that the white working class (at least outside the South) is no more racist, and by some measures less so, than the white professional class.

Even deeper-rooted than the stereotype of the hard-hat bigot is the middle-class suspicion that the working class is dumb, inarticulate, and mindlessly loyal to old-fashioned values. In the entertainment media, for example, the working class is usually portrayed by macho exhibitionism (from *Saturday Night Fever* to *Working Girl*) or mental inferiority (*Married, With Children*). Mainstream sociologists have reinforced this prejudice with their emphasis on working class "parochialism," as illustrated by this quote from a 1976 beginning sociology textbook: "The limited education, reading habits and associations isolate the lower class. . . . and this ignorance, together with their class position, makes them suspicious of [the] middle- and upper-class 'experts' and 'do-gooders'. . . ."

Finally, there is a level of prejudice that grows out of middle-class moralism about matters of taste and lifestyle. All privileged classes seek to differentiate themselves from the less-privileged through the ways they dress, eat, entertain themselves, and so on, and tend to see their own choices in these matters as inherently wiser, better, and more aesthetically inspired. In middle-class stereotype, the white working class, for example, is addicted to cigarettes, Budweiser, polyester, and network television. (In part this is true, and it is true in part because Bud is cheaper than Dos Equis and polyester is cheaper than linen.) Furthermore in the middle-class view, polyester and the like is "tacky"—a common code word for "lower class." Health concerns, plus a certain reverence for the "natural" in food and fiber, infuse these middle-class prejudices with a high-minded tone of moral indignation.

But I am alarmed by what seems to me to be the growing parochialism of the professional middle class—living in its own social and residential enclaves, condemned to hear only the opinions of its own members (or, of course, of the truly rich), and cut off from the lives and struggles and insights of the American majority. This middle-class parochialism is insidiously self-reinforcing: The less "we" know about "them," the more likely "we" are to cling to our stereotypes—or forget "them" altogether.

.7

The Meaning of Memory

Family, Class and Ethnicity
in Early Network Television

GEORGE LIPSITZ

THE MEANING OF MEMORY

. . . In the midst of extraordinary social change, television emerged as the most important discursive medium in American culture. As such, it was charged with special responsibilities for making new economic and social relations credible and legitimate to audiences haunted by ghosts from the past. Urban, ethnic, working-class comedies provided one means of addressing the anxieties and contradictions emanating from the clash between the consumer present of the 1950s and collective memory about the 1930s and 1940s.

The consumer consciousness generated by economic and social change in postwar America conflicted with the lessons of historical experience for many middle- and working-class American families. The Great Depression of the 1930s had not only damaged the economy, it had also undercut the political and cultural legitimacy of American capitalism. Herbert Hoover had been a national hero in the 1920s, with his credo of "rugged individualism" forming the basis for a widely shared cultural ideal. But the Depression discredited Hoover's philosophy and made him a symbol of yesterday's

NOTE: Excerpts reproduced by permission of the American Anthropological Association and George Lipsitz. *Cultural Anthropology*, Vol. 1, No. 4, 1986. Not for further distribution.

blasted hopes to millions of Americans. In the 1930s, cultural ideals based on mutuality and collectivity eclipsed the previous decade's individualism, and helped propel massive union organizing drives, anti-eviction movements, and general strikes. President Roosevelt's New Deal attempted to harness and co-opt that grass-roots mass activity in its efforts to restore social order and recapture credibility and legitimacy for the capitalist system.[1] The social welfare legislation of the "Second New Deal" in 1935 went far beyond any measures previously favored by Roosevelt and most of his advisors, but radical action proved necessary if the administration was to contain the upsurge of activism that characterized the decade. Even in the private sector, industrial corporations conceded more to workers than naked power realities necessitated because they feared the political consequences of mass disillusionment with the system.[2]

World War II ended the Depression and brought prosperity, but it did so on a basis even more collective than the New Deal of the 1930s. Government intervention in the wartime economy reached unprecedented levels, bringing material reward and shared purpose to a generation raised on the deprivation and sacrifice of the Depression. In the postwar years, the largest and most disruptive strike wave in American history won major improvements in the standard of living for the average worker, through both wage increases and government commitments to support full employment, decent housing, and expanded educational opportunities. Grass-roots militancy and working-class direct action wrested concessions from a reluctant business and government elite—mostly because the public at large viewed workers' demands as more legitimate than the desires of capital.[3]

Yet the collective nature of working-class mass activity in the postwar era posed severe problems for capital. In sympathy strikes and secondary boycotts, workers placed the interests of their class ahead of their own individual material aspirations. Strikes over safety and job control far outnumbered wage strikes, revealing aspirations to control the process of production that conflicted with the imperatives of capitalist labor-management relations. Mass demonstrations demanding government employment and housing programs indicated a collective political response to problems previously adjudicated on a personal level. Radical challenges to the authority of capital (like the United Auto Workers' 1946 demand during the General Motors strike that wage increases come out of corporate profits rather than from price hikes passed on to consumers) demonstrated a social responsibility and a commitment toward redistributing wealth rare in the history of American labor.[4]

Capital attempted to regain the initiative in the postwar years by making qualified concessions to working-class pressures for redistribution of wealth and power. Rather than paying wage increases out of corporate profits, business leaders instead worked to expand the economy through increases in government spending, foreign trade, and consumer debt. Such expansion could meet the demands of workers and consumers without undermining capital's dominant role in the economy. On the presumption that "a rising tide lifts all boats," business leaders sought to connect working-class aspirations for a better life to policies that ensured a commensurate rise in corporate profits, thereby leaving the distribution of wealth unaffected. Federal defense spending, highway construction programs, and home-loan policies expanded the economy at home in a manner conducive to the interests of capital, while the Truman Doctrine and Marshall Plan provided models for enhanced access to foreign markets and raw materials for American corporations. The Taft-Hartley Act of 1947 banned the class-conscious collective activities most threatening to capital (mass strikes, sympathy strikes, secondary boycotts): the leaders of labor, government, and business accepted as necessary the practice of paying wage hikes for organized workers out of the pockets of consumers and unorganized workers in the form of higher prices.[5]

Commercial network television played an important role in this emerging economy, functioning as a significant new object of consumer purchases as well as an important marketing medium. Sales of sets jumped from three million during the entire decade of the 1940s to over five million *a year* during the 1950s.[6] But television's most important economic function came from its role as an instrument of legitimation for transformations in values initiated by the new economic imperatives of postwar America. For Americans to accept the new world of 1950s consumerism, they had to make a break with the past. The Depression years had helped generate fears about installment buying and excessive materialism, while the New Deal and wartime mobilization had provoked suspicions about individual acquisitiveness and upward mobility. Depression era and wartime scarcities of consumer goods had led workers to internalize discipline and frugality while nurturing networks of mutual support through family, ethnic, and class associations. Government policies after the war encouraged an atomized acquisitive consumerism at odds with the lessons of the past. At the same time, federal home-loan policies stimulated migrations to the suburbs from urban, ethnic, working-class neighborhoods. The entry of television into the American home disrupted previous patterns of family life and encouraged fragmentation of the family into separate segments of the consumer market.[7] The priority of consumerism in the economy at large and on television may have seemed organic and unplanned, but conscious policy decisions by officials from both private and public sectors shaped the contours of the consumer economy and television's role within it.

COMMERCIAL TELEVISION
AND ECONOMIC CHANGE

Government policies during and after World War II shaped the basic contours of home television as an advertising medium. Government-sponsored research and development during the war perfected the technology of home television while federal tax policies solidified its economic base. The government allowed corporations to deduct the costs of advertising from their taxable incomes during the war, despite the fact that rationing and defense production left businesses with few products to market. Consequently, manufacturers kept the names of their products before the public

while lowering their tax obligations on high wartime profits. Their advertising expenditures supplied radio networks and advertising agencies with
the capital reserves and business infrastructure that enabled them to dominate the television industry in the postwar era. After the war, federal antitrust action against the motion-picture studios broke up the "network"
system in movies, while the FCC sanctioned the network system in television. In addition, FCC decisions to allocate stations on the narrow VHF
band, to grant the networks ownership and operation rights over stations
in prime markets, and to place a freeze on the licensing of new stations
during the important years between 1948 and 1952 all combined to guarantee that advertising-oriented programming based on the model of radio
would triumph over theater TV, educational TV, or any other form.[8] Government decisions, not market forces, established the dominance of commercial television, but these decisions reflected a view of the American economy
and its needs which had become so well accepted at the top levels of business
and government that it had virtually become the official state economic
policy.

Fearing both renewed Depression and awakened militancy among workers, influential corporate and business leaders considered increases in consumer spending—of 30% to 50%—to be necessary to perpetuate prosperity
in the postwar era.[9] Defense spending for the Cold War and the Korean
conflict had complemented an aggressive trade policy to improve the state
of the economy, but it appeared that the hope for an ever-expanding economy rested on increased consumer spending fueled by an expansion of
credit.[10] Here, too, government policies led the way, especially with regard
to stimulating credit purchases of homes and automobiles. During World
War II, the marginal tax rate for most wage earners jumped from 4% to 25%,
making the home ownership deduction more desirable. Federal housing-
loan policies favored construction of new single-family, detached suburban
houses over renovation or construction of central-city multi-family units.
Debt-encumbered home ownership in accord with these policies stimulated
construction of 30 million new housing units in just twenty years, bringing
the percentage of homeowning Americans from below 40% in 1940 to more
than 60% by 1960. Mortgage policies encouraging long-term debt and low
down payments freed capital for other consumer purchases, while government highway building policies undermined mass-transit systems and contributed to increased demand for automobiles. Partly as a result of these
policies, consumer spending on private cars averaged $7.5 billion per year
in the 1930s and 1940s, but grew to $22 billion per year in 1950 and almost
$30 billion by 1955.[11]

Business leaders understood the connection between suburban growth
and increased consumer spending. A 1953 article in *Fortune* celebrated the
"lush new suburban market" which "has centered its customs and conventions on the needs of children and geared its buying habits to them."[12] For
the first time in U.S. history, middle-class and working-class families could
routinely expect to own homes or buy new cars every few years. Between
1946 and 1965, residential mortgage debt rose three times as fast as the gross
national product and disposable income. Mortgage debt accounted for just

under 18% of disposable income in 1946, but it grew to almost 55% by 1965.[13] To ensure the eventual payment of current debts, the economy had to generate tremendous growth and expansion, further stimulating the need to increase consumer spending. Manufacturers had to find ways of motivating consumers to buy ever increasing amounts of commodities. Television provided an important means of accomplishing that end.

Television advertised individual products, but it also provided a relentless flow of information and persuasion that placed acts of consumption at the core of everyday life. The physical fragmentation of suburban growth and subsequent declines in motion-picture attendance created an audience more likely to stay at home and to receive entertainment there than ever before. But television also provided a forum for redefining American ethnic, class, and family identities into consumer identities. To accomplish this task effectively, television programs had to address some of the psychic, moral, and political obstacles to consumption among the public at large.

The television and advertising industries knew they had to overcome consumer resistance. Marketing expert and motivational specialist Ernest Dichter observed that "one of the basic problems of this prosperity is to give people that sanction and justification to enjoy it and to demonstrate that the hedonistic approach to life is a moral one, not an immoral one."[14] Dichter later noted the many barriers inhibiting consumer acceptance of unrestrained hedonism, and he called on advertisers "to train the average citizen to accept growth of his country and its economy as *his* growth rather than as a strange and frightening event."[15] One method of encouraging that acceptance, according to Dichter, consisted of identifying new products and styles of consumption with traditional, historically sanctioned practices and behaviors. He noted that such an approach held particular relevance in addressing consumers who had only recently acquired the means to spend freely and who might harbor a lingering conservatism about spending based on their previous experiences.[16] . . .

FAMILY FORMATION AND THE ECONOMY—
THE TELEVISION VIEW

Advertisers incorporated their messages into urban, ethnic, working-class comedies through direct and indirect means. Tensions developed in the programs often found indirect resolutions in commercials. Thus Jeannie MacClennan's search for an American sweetheart in one episode of *Hey Jeannie* set up commercials proclaiming the virtues of Drene shampoo for keeping one prepared to accept last-minute ideas and of Crest toothpaste for producing an attractive smile.[17] Conversations about shopping for new furniture in an episode of *The Goldbergs* directed viewers' attention to furnishings in the Goldberg home provided for the show by Macy's department store in exchange for a commercial acknowledgment.[18]

The content of the shows themselves offered even more direct emphasis on consumer spending. In one episode of *The Goldbergs*, Molly expresses disapproval of her future daughter-in-law's plan to buy a washing machine on the installment plan. "I know Papa and me never bought anything unless we had the money to pay for it," she intones with logic familiar to a generation with memories of the Great Depression. Her son, Sammy, confronts this "deviance" by saying "Listen, Ma, almost everybody in this country lives above their means—and everybody enjoys it." Doubtful at first, Molly eventually learns from her children and announces her conversion to the legitimacy of installment buying, proposing that the family buy two cars in order to "live above our means—the American way." [19] In a subsequent episode, Molly's daughter, Rosalie, assumes the role of ideological tutor to her mother. When planning a move out of their Bronx apartment to a new house in the suburbs, Molly ruminates about where to place her old furniture in her new home. "You don't mean we're going to take all this junk with us into a brand new house?" asks an exasperated Rosalie. With traditionalist sentiment Molly answers, "Junk? My furniture's junk? My furniture that I lived with and loved for twenty years is junk?" But by the end of the episode she accepts Rosalie's argument—even selling off all her old furniture to help meet the down payment on the new house and deciding to buy all new furniture on the installment plan.[20]

Chester A. Riley confronts similar choices about family and commodities in *The Life of Riley*. His wife complains that he only takes her out to the neighborhood bowling alley and restaurant, not to "interesting places." Riley searches for ways to impress her and discovers from a friend that a waiter at the fancy Club Morambo will let them eat first and pay later, for a cost of a dollar per week plus 10% interest. "Ain't that dishonest?" asks Riley. "No, it's usury," his friend replies. Riley does not borrow the money, but he impresses his wife anyway by taking the family out to dinner on the proceeds of a prize that he receives for being the one thousandth customer in a local flower shop. Though we eventually learn that Peg Riley only wanted attention and not an expensive meal, the happy ending of the episode hinges on Riley's restored prestige once he demonstrates his ability to provide a luxury outing for the family.[21]

The same episode of *The Life of Riley* reveals another consumerist element common to this subgenre. When Riley protests that he lacks the money needed to fulfill Peg's desires, she answers that he would have plenty of cash if he didn't spend so much on "needless gadgets." His shortage of funds becomes personal failure caused by incompetent behavior as a consumer. Nowhere do we hear about the size of his paycheck, relations between his union and his employer, or, for that matter, of the relationship between the value of his labor and the wages paid to him by the Stevenson Aircraft Company. Like Uncle David in *The Goldbergs* (who buys a statue of Hamlet shaking hands with Shakespeare and an elk's tooth with the Gettysburg address carved on it), Riley's comic character stems in part from a flaw which might be more justly applied to the entire consumer economy: a preoccupation with "needless gadgets." By contrast, Peg Riley's desire for an evening out is portrayed as reasonable and modest, as reparations due her for the inevitable tedium of housework. The solution to her unhappiness comes from an evening out, rather than from a change in her work circumstance. Even within the home, television elevates consumption over production: production is assumed to be a constant, only consumption can be varied. But more than enjoyment is at stake. Unless Riley can provide Peg with the desired night on the town, he will fail in his obligations as a husband and father.[22] . . .

. . . "Mama's Birthday," broadcast in 1954, delineated the tensions between family loyalty and consumer desire endemic to modern capitalist society. The show begins with Mama teaching Katrin to make Norwegian meatballs, which she used long ago to "catch" Papa. Unimpressed by that accomplishment, Katrin changes the subject and asks Mama what she wants for her birthday. In an answer that locates Mama within the gender roles of the 1950s, she replies, "Well, I think a fine new job for your Papa. You and Dagmar to marry nice young men and have a lot of wonderful children—just like I have. And Nels, well, Nels to become president of the United States."[23] In one sentence Mama sums up the dominant culture's version of legitimate female expectations: success at work for her husband, marriage and childrearing for her daughters, the presidency for her son—and nothing for herself.

But we learn that Mama does have some needs, although we do not hear it from her lips. Her sister, Jenny, asks Mama to attend a fashion show, but Mama cannot leave the house because she has to cook a roast for a guest whom Papa has invited to dinner. Jenny comments that Mama never seems to get out of the kitchen, adding that "it's a shame that a married woman can't have some time to herself." The complaint is a valid one, and we can imagine how it might have resonated for women in the 1950s. The increased availability of household appliances and the use of synthetic fibers and commercially processed food should have decreased the amount of time women spent in housework, but surveys showed that homemakers spent the same number of hours per week (between 51 and 56) doing housework as had been the norm in the 1920s. Advertising and marketing strategies undermined the labor-saving potential of technological changes because they upgraded standards of cleanliness in the home and expanded desires for more varied wardrobes and menus for the average family.[24] In that context, Aunt Jenny would have been justified in launching into a tirade about the division of labor within the Hansen household or about the possibilities for cooperative housework, but network television specializes in less social and more commodified dialogues about problems like housework. Aunt Jenny suggests that her sister's family buy Mama a "fireless cooker," a cast-iron stove, for her birthday. "They're wonderful," she tells them in language borrowed from the rhetoric of advertising. "You just put your dinner inside them, close 'em up, and go wherever you please. When you come back your dinner is all cooked." Papa protests that Mama likes to cook on her woodburning stove, but Jenny dismisses that objection with an insinuation about his motives when she replies, "Well I suppose it *would* cost a little more than you could afford, Hansen."[25]

By identifying a commodity as the solution to Mama's problem, Aunt Jenny unites the inner voice of Mama with the outer voice of the television sponsor. . . . Prodded by their aunt, the Hansen children go shopping and purchase the fireless cooker from a storekeeper who calls the product "the new Emancipation Proclamation—setting housewives free from their old kitchen range."[26] Our exposure to advertising hyperbole should not lead us to miss the analogy here: housework is compared to slavery and the commercial product takes on the aura of Abraham Lincoln. The shopkeeper's appeal convinces the children to pool their resources and buy the stove for Mama. But we soon learn that Papa plans to make a fireless cooker for Mama with his tools. When Mama discovers Papa's intentions, she persuades the children to buy her another gift. Even Papa admits that his stove will not be as efficient as one made in a factory, but Mama nobly affirms that she will like his better because he made it himself. The children use their money to buy dishes for Mama (a gift hardly likely to leave her with less work), and Katrin remembers the episode as Mama's happiest birthday ever.

The stated resolution of "Mama's Birthday" favors traditional values. Mama prefers to protect Papa's pride instead of having a better stove. The product built by a family member has more value than the one sold as a commodity. Yet as was so often the case in these urban, ethnic, working-class comedies, the entire development of the plot leads in the opposite direction. The "fireless cooker" is the star of the episode, setting in motion all the other characters, and it has an unquestioned value, even in the face of Jenny's meddlesome brashness, Papa's insensitivity, and Mama's old-fashioned ideals. Buying a product appears as the true means of changing the unpleasant realities and low status of women's work in the home.

This resolution of the conflict between consumer desires and family roles reflected television's social role as mediator between the family and the economy. . . . The television industry recognized and promoted its privileged place within families in advertisements like the one in *The New York Times* in 1950 that claimed, "Youngsters today need television for their morale as much as they need fresh air and sunshine for their health."[27] Like previous communications media, television sets occupied honored places in family living rooms and helped structure family time; but unlike other previous communications media, television displayed available commodities in a way that transformed home entertainment into a glorified shopping catalog. . . .

NOTES

1. See Romasco (1965) and Bernstein (1968).
2. Berger (1982).
3. Lipsitz (1981).
4. Lipsitz (1981).
5. Lipsitz (1981).
6. *TV Facts* (1980, p. 141).
7. Neilsen ratings epitomize television's view of the family as separate market segments to be addressed independently.
8. Boddy (1986); Allen (1983).
9. Lipsitz (1981, pp. 120-121).
10. Moore and Klein (1962); Jezer (1982).
11. Hartmann (1982, pp. 165-168); Mollenkopf (1983, p. 111).
12. "The Lush New Suburban Market," (1953, p. 128).

13. Stone (1983, p. 122).

14. Quoted in Jezer (1982, p. 127).

15. Dichter (1960, p. 210).

16. Dichter (1960, p. 209).

17. "The Rock and Roll Kid," *Hey, Jeannie,* Academy of Television Arts Collection, University of California, Los Angeles.

18. "The In-Laws," *The Goldbergs (Molly),* Academy of Television Arts Collection, University of California, Los Angeles.

19. "The In-Laws," *The Goldbergs (Molly).*

20. "Moving Day," *The Goldbergs (Molly),* Academy of Television Arts Collection, University of California, Los Angeles.

21. "R228," *Life of Riley,* Academy of Television Arts Collection, University of California, Los Angeles.

22. "R228," *Life of Riley;* "Bad Companions," *The Goldbergs (Molly),* Academy of Television Arts Collection, University of California, Los Angeles.

23. Elizabeth Meehan and Bradford Ropes, "Mama's Birthday," Theater Arts Collection, University Research Library. University of California, Los Angeles.

24. Hartmann (1982, p. 168).

25. Elizabeth Meehan and Bradford Ropes, "Mama's Birthday."

26. Elizabeth Meehan and Bradford Ropes, "Mama's Birthday."

27. Wolfenstein (1951).

REFERENCES

Allen, J. (1983). The social matrix of television: Invention in the United States. In E. A. Kaplan (Ed.), *Regarding television* (pp. 109-119). Los Angeles: University Publications of America.

Berger, H. (1982, March 12). *Social protest in St. Louis.* Paper presented at a Missouri Committee for the Humanities Forum, St. Louis, MO.

Bernstein, B. (1968). The conservative achievements of New Deal reform. In B. Bernstein (Ed.), *Towards a new past.* New York: Vintage.

Boddy, W. (1986). The studios move into prime time: Hollywood and the television industry in the 1950s. *Cinema Journal, 12*(4), 23-27.

Dichter, E. (1960). *The strategy of desire.* Garden City, NY: Doubleday.

Hartmann, S. (1982). *The home front and beyond.* Boston: Twayne.

Jezer, M. (1982). *The dark ages.* Boston: South End Press.

Lipsitz, G. (1981). *Class and culture in cold war America.* Westport, CT: Greenwood.

The lush new suburban market. (1953, November). *Fortune.*

Mollenkopf, J. (1983). *The contested city.* Princeton, NJ: Princeton University Press.

Moore, G., & Klein, P. (1976). *The quality of consumer installment credit.* Washington, DC: National Bureau of Economics Research.

Romasco, A. U. (1965). *The poverty of attendance.* New York: Oxford University Press.

Stone, M. (1983). Housing: The economic crisis. In C. Hartman (Ed.), *America's housing crisis: What is to be done?* New York: Routledge & Kegan Paul.

TV facts. (1980). New York: Facts on File.

Wolfenstein, M. (1951). The emergence of fun morality. *Journal of Social Issues, 7*(4), 15-25.

8

The Color Purple

Black Women as Cultural Readers

JACQUELINE BOBO

. . . *The Color Purple* was a small quiet book when it emerged on the literary scene in 1982. The subject of the book is a young, abused, uneducated Black girl who evolves into womanhood and a sense of her own worth gained by bonding with the women around her. When Alice Walker won the American Book Award and the Pulitzer Prize for Fiction in 1983, the sales of the novel increased to over two million copies, placing the book on the *New York Times* best-seller lists for a number of weeks.[1] Still the book did not have as wide an audience or the impact the film would have. In December 1985 Steven Spielberg's *The Color Purple* exploded with the force of a land-mine on the landscape of cultural production. Many commentators on the film have pointed out that the film created discussion and controversy about the image of Black people in media, the likes of which had not been seen since the films *The Birth of a Nation* (1915) and *Gone With the Wind* (1939).

One of the reasons Alice Walker sold the screen rights was that she understood that people who would not read the book would go to see the film. Walker and her advisers thought that the book's critical message needed to be exposed to a wider audience. The readership for the novel was a very specific one and drastically different from the mass audience toward which the film is directed. However, the film is a commercial venture produced in Hollywood by a white male according to all of the tenets and

NOTE: Excerpts reprinted from *Female Spectators: Looking At Film and Television,* edited by E. Deirdre Pribam (London: Verso, 1988), by permission. © 1988 Verso.

conventions of commercial cultural production in the United States. The manner in which an audience responds to such a film is varied, diverse and complex. I am especially concerned with analysing how Black women have responded.

My aim is to examine the way in which a specific audience creates meaning from a mainstream text and uses the reconstructed meaning to empower themselves and their social group. This analysis will show how Black women as audience members and cultural consumers have connected up with what has been characterized as the "renaissance of Black women writers." [2] The predominant element of this movement is the creation and maintenance of images of Black women that are based upon Black women's constructions, history and real-life experiences.

As part of a larger study I am doing on *The Color Purple* I conducted a group interview with selected Black women viewers of the film.[3] Statements from members of the group focused on how moved they were by the fact that Celie eventually triumphs in the film. One woman talked about the variety of emotions she experienced: "I had different feelings all the way through the film, because first I was very angry, and then I started to feel so sad I wanted to cry because of the way Celie was being treated. It just upset me the way she was being treated and the way she was so totally dominated. But gradually, as time went on, she began to realize that she could do something for herself, that she could start moving and progressing, that she could start reasoning and thinking things out for herself." Another woman stated that she was proud of Celie for her growth: "The lady was a strong lady, like I am. And she hung in there and she overcame."

One of the women in the group talked about the scene where Shug tells Celie that she has a beautiful smile and that she should stop covering up her face. This woman said that she could relate to that part because it made Celie's transformation in the film so much more powerful. At first, she said, everybody who loved Celie [Shug and Nettie], and everyone that Celie loved, kept telling her to put her hand down. The woman then pointed out "that last time that Celie put her hand down nobody told her to put her hand down. She had started coming into her own. So when she grabbed that knife she was ready to use it." This comment refers to the scene in the film at the dinner table, when Celie and Shug are about to leave for Memphis. Mister begins to chastise Celie telling her that she will be back. He says, "You ugly, you skinny, you shaped funny and you scared to open your mouth to people." Celie sits there quietly and takes Mister's verbal abuse. Then she asks him, "Any more letters come?" She is talking about Nettie's letters from Africa that Mister has been hiding from Celie and that Celie and Shug had recently found. Mister replies, "Could be, could be not." Celie jumps up at that point, grabs the knife, and sticks it to Mister's throat.

The woman who found this scene significant continued: "But had she not got to that point, built up to that point [of feeling herself worthwhile], she could have grabbed the knife and turned it the other way for all that it mattered to her. She wouldn't have been any worse off. But she saw herself getting better. So when she grabbed that knife she was getting ready to use it and it wasn't on herself."

Other comments from the women were expressions of outrage at criticisms made against the film. The women were especially disturbed by vicious attacks against Alice Walker and against Black women critics and scholars who were publicly defending the film. One of the women in the interview session commented that she was surprised that there was such controversy over the film: "I had such a positive feeling about it, I couldn't imagine someone saying that they didn't like it." Another said that she was shocked at the outcry from some Black men: "I didn't look at it as being stereotypically Black or all Black men are this way" (referring to the portrayal of the character Mister).

Another related a story that shows how two people can watch the same film and have opposite reactions: "I was thinking about how men felt about it [*The Color Purple*] and I was surprised. But I related it to something that happened to me sometime ago when I was married. I went to see a movie called *Three in the Attic.* I don't know if any of you ever saw it. But I remember that on the way home—I thought it was funny—but my husband was so angry he wouldn't even talk to me on the way home. He said, 'You thought that was funny.' I said that I sure did. He felt it was really hostile because these ladies had taken this man up in the attic and made him go to bed with all of them until he was . . . blue. Because he had been running around with all of these ladies. But he [her husband] was livid because I thought it was funny. And I think now, some men I talked to had a similar reaction to *The Color Purple.* That it was . . . all the men in there were dummies or horrible. And none of the men, they felt, were portrayed in a positive light. And then I started thinking about it and I said, 'well . . . I felt that somebody had to be the hero or the heroine, and in this case it just happened to be the woman.'"

I have found that on the whole Black women have discovered something progressive and useful in the film. It is crucial to understand how this is possible when viewing a work made according to the encoding of dominant ideology. Black women's responses to *The Color Purple* loom as an extreme contrast to those of many other viewers. Not only is the difference in reception noteworthy but Black women's responses confront and challenge a prevalent method of media audience analysis which insists that viewers of mainstream works have no control or influence over a cultural product. Recent developments in media audience analysis demonstrate that there is a complex process of negotiation whereby specific members of a culture construct meaning from a mainstream text that is different from the meanings others would produce. These different readings are based, in part, on viewers' various histories and experiences.

OPPOSITIONAL READINGS

The encoding/decoding model is useful for understanding how a cultural product can evoke such different viewer reactions. The model was developed by the University of Birmingham Centre for Contemporary Cultural Studies, under the direction of Stuart Hall, in an attempt to synthesize various perspectives on media audience analysis and to incorporate theory from sociology and cultural studies. This model is concerned with an understanding of the communication process as it operates in a specific cultural context. It analyses ideological and cultural power and the way in which meaning is produced in that context. The researchers at the Centre felt that media analysts should not look simply at the meaning of a text but should also investigate the social and cultural framework in which communication takes place.[4]

From political sociology, the encoding/decoding model was drawn from the work of Frank Parkin, who developed a theory of meaning systems.[5] This theory delineates three potential responses to a media message: dominant, negotiated or oppositional. A dominant (or preferred) reading of a text accepts the content of the cultural product without question. A negotiated reading questions parts of the content of the text but does not question the dominant ideology which underlies the production of the text. An oppositional response to a cultural product is one in which the recipient of the text understands that the system that produced the text is one with which she/he is fundamentally at odds.[6]

A viewer of a film (reader of a text) comes to the moment of engagement with the work with a knowledge of the world and a knowledge of other texts, or media products. What this means is that when a person comes to view a film, she/he does not leave her/his histories, whether social, cultural, economic, racial, or sexual at the door. An audience member from a marginalized group (people of colour, women, the poor, and so on) has an oppositional stance as they participate in mainstream media. The motivation for this counter-reception is that we understand that mainstream media has never rendered our segment of the population faithfully. We have as evidence our years of watching films and television programmes and reading plays and books. Out of habit, as readers of mainstream texts, we have learned to ferret out the beneficial and put up blinders against the rest.

From this wary viewing standpoint, a subversive reading of a text can occur. This alternative reading comes from something in the work that strikes the viewer as amiss, that appears "strange." Behind the idea of subversion lies a reader-oriented notion of "making strange." [7] When things appear strange to the viewer, she/he may then bring other viewpoints to bear on the watching of the film and may see things other than what the film-makers intended. The viewer, that is, will read "against the grain" of the film.

Producers of mainstream media products are not aligned in a conspiracy against an audience. When they construct a work they draw on their own background, experience and social and cultural milieu. They are therefore under "ideological pressure" to reproduce the familiar.[8] When Steven Spielberg made *The Color Purple* he did not intend to make a film that would be in the mould of previous films that were directed by a successful white director and had an all-Black or mostly Black cast.

Spielberg states that he deliberately cast the characters in *The Color Purple* in a way that they would not carry the taint of negative stereotypes:

> I didn't want to cast traditional Black movie stars, which I thought
> would create their own stereotypes. I won't mention any names be-
> cause it wouldn't be kind, but there were people who wanted to play
> these parts very much. It would have made it seem as if these were the
> only Black people accepted in white world's mainstream. I didn't want
> to do that. That's why I cast so many unknowns like Whoopi Gold-
> berg, Oprah Winfrey, Margaret Avery.[9]

But it is interesting that while the director of the film made a conscious
decision to cast against type, he could not break away from his culturally
acquired conceptions of how Black people are and how they should act.
Barbara Christian, Professor of Afro-American Studies at University of
California, Berkeley, contends that the most maligned figure in the film is
the character Harpo. She points out that in the book he cannot become the
patriarch that society demands he be.[10] Apparently Spielberg could not
conceive of a man uncomfortable with the requirements of patriarchy, and
consequently depicts Harpo as a buffoon. Christian comments that "the
movie makes a negative statement about men who show some measure of
sensitivity to women." The film uses the husband and wife characters,
Harpo and Sofia, as comic relief. Some of the criticisms against the film from
Black viewers concerned Harpo's ineptness in repairing a roof. If the filmmakers have Harpo fall once, it seems they decided that it was even funnier
if he fell three times.

In her *Village Voice* review, Michele Wallace attributed motives other than
comic relief to the film's representations of the couple. Wallace considered
their appearances to be the result of "white patriarchal interventions." She
wrote:

> In the book Sofia is the epitome of a woman with masculine powers,
> the martyr to sexual injustice who eventually triumphs through the
> realignment of the community. In the movie she is an occasion for
> humor. She and Harpo are the reincarnations of Amos and Sapphire;
> they alternately fight and fuck their way to a house full of pickanin-
> nies. Harpo is always falling through a roof he's chronically unable to
> repair. Sofia is always shoving a baby into his arms, swinging her large
> hips, and talking a mile a minute. Harpo, who is dying to marry Sofia
> in the book, seems bamboozled into marriage in the film. Sofia's only
> masculine power is her contentiousness. Encircled by the mayor, his
> wife and an angry mob, she is knocked down and her dress flies up
> providing us with a timely reminder that she is just a woman.[11]

The depiction of Sofia lying in the street with her dress up is almost an exact
replica of a picture published in a national mass-circulation magazine of a
large Black woman lying dead in her home after she had been killed by her
husband in a domestic argument. Coincidence or not, this image among
others in the film makes one wonder about Spielberg's unconscious store of
associations.

BLACK PEOPLE'S
REPRESENTATION IN FILM

While a film-maker draws on her/his background and experience, she/ he also draws on a history of other films. *The Color Purple* follows in the footsteps of earlier films with a Black storyline and/or an all Black cast which were directed by a white male for mass consumption by a white American audience. The criticisms against the film repeatedly invoked the names of such racist films as *The Birth of a Nation* (1915), *Hallelujah* (1929) and *Cabin in the Sky* (1943). One reviewer in the *Village Voice* wrote that *The Color Purple* was "a revisionist *Cabin in the Sky*, with the God-fearing, long-suffering Ethel Waters (read Celie) and the delectable temptress Lena Horne (known as Shug Avery) falling for each other rather than wrestling over the soul of feckless (here sadistic) Eddie Anderson." [12]

According to Donald Bogle in *Toms, Coons, Mulattoes, Mammies and Bucks*, Nina Mae McKinney's character in *Hallelujah* executing "gyrations and groans" and sensuous "bumps and grinds" became a standard for almost every Black "leading lady" in motion pictures, from Lena Horne in *Cabin in the Sky* to Lola Falana in *The Liberation of L. B. Jones*.[13] The corollary of this stereotype can be seen acted out by Margaret Avery as Shug in the juke-joint scenes in *The Color Purple*. Here we see Shug singing in the juke-joint and later leading the "jointers" singing and prancing down the road to her father's church. One viewer of *The Color Purple* wondered, in reference to this scene, if it were obligatory in every film that contained Black actors and actresses that they sing and dance.[14] . . .

Black Women's Response

. . . Barbara Christian relates that the most frequent statement from Black women has been: "Finally, somebody says something about us." [15] This sense of identification with what was in the film would provide an impetus for Black women to form an engagement with the film. This engagement could have been either positive or negative. That it was favourable indicates something about the way in which Black women have constructed meaning from this text.

It would be too easy, I think, to categorize Black women's reaction to the film as an example of "false consciousness"; to consider Black women as cultural dupes in the path of a media barrage who cannot figure out when a media product portrays them and their race in a negative manner. Black women are aware, along with others, of the oppression and harm that comes from a negative media history. But Black women are also aware that their specific experience, as Black people, as women, in a rigid class/caste state, has never been adequately dealt with in mainstream media.

One of the Black women that I interviewed talked about this cultural past and how it affected her reaction to the *The Color Purple:* "When I went to the movie, I thought, here I am. I grew up looking at Elvis Presley kissing on all these white girls. I grew up listening to 'Tammy, Tammy, Tammy.' [She sings the song that Debbie Reynolds sang in the movie of the same name.] And it wasn't that I had anything projected before me on the screen to really give me something that I could grow up to be like. Or even wanted to be. Because I knew I wasn't Goldilocks, you know, and I had heard those stories all my life. So when I got to the movie, the first thing I said was 'God, this is good acting.' And I liked that. I felt a lot of pride in my Black brothers and sisters. . . . By the end of the movie I was totally emotionally drained. . . . The emotional things were all in the book, but the movie just took every one of my emotions. . . . Towards the end, when she looks up and sees her sister Nettie . . . I had gotten so emotionally high at that point . . . when she saw her sister, when she started to call her name and to recognize who she was, the hairs on my neck started to stick up. I had never had a movie do that to me before."

The concept "interpellation" sheds light on the process by which Black women were able to form a positive engagement with *The Color Purple*. Interpellation is the way in which the subject is hailed by the text; it is the method by which ideological discourses constitute subjects and draw them into the text/subject relationship. John Fiske describes "hailing" as similar to hailing a cab. The viewer is hailed by a particular work; if she/he gives a co-operative response to the beckoning, then not only are they constructed as a subject, but the text then becomes a text, in the sense that the subject begins to construct meaning from the work and is constructed by the work.[16]

The moment of the encounter of the text and the subject is known as the "interdiscourse." David Morley explains this concept, developed by Michel Pêcheux, as the space, the specific moment when subjects bring their histories to bear on meaning production in a text.[17] Within this interdiscursive space, cultural competencies come into play. A cultural competency is the repertoire of discursive strategies, the range of knowledge, that a viewer brings to the act of watching a film and creating meaning from a work. As has been stated before, the meanings of a text will be constructed differently depending on the various backgrounds of the viewers. The viewers' position in the social structure determines, in part, what sets of discourses or interpretive strategies they will bring to their encounter with the text. A specific cultural competency will set some of the boundaries to meaning construction.

The cultural competency perspective has allowed media researchers to understand how elements in a viewer's background play a determining role in the way in which she/he interprets a text. Stuart Hall, David Morley and others utilize the theories of Dell Hymes, Basil Bernstein and Pierre Bourdieu for an understanding of the ways in which a social structure distributes different forms of cultural decoding strategies throughout the different sections of the media audience. These understandings are not the same for everyone in the audience because they are shaped by the individual's history, both media and cultural, and by the individual's social affiliations such as race, class, gender, and so on.[18]

As I see it, there can be two aspects to a cultural competency, or the store of understandings that a marginalized viewer brings to interpreting a cultural product. One is a positive response where the viewer constructs something useful from the work by negotiating her/his response, and/or gives a subversive reading to the work. The other is a negative response in which the viewer rejects the work. Both types of oppositional readings are prompted by the store of negative images that have come from prior mainstream media experience; in the case of *The Color Purple*, from Black people's negative history in Hollywood films.

A positive engagement with a work could come from an intertextual cultural experience. This is true, I think, with the way in which Black women constructed meaning from *The Color Purple*. Creative works by Black women are proliferating now. This intense level of productivity is not accidental nor coincidental. It stems from a desire on the part of Black women to construct works more in keeping with their experiences, their history, and with the daily lives of other Black women. And Black women, as cultural consumers, are receptive to these works. This intertextual cultural knowledge is forming Black women's store of decoding strategies for films that are about them. This is the cultural competency that Black women brought to their favourable readings of *The Color Purple*. . . .

NOTES

1. Goldstein (1985, p. 48).
2. Washington (1982, p. 182).
3. I am at present writing a dissertation on Black women's response to the film *The Color Purple*. As part of the study I conducted what will be an ethnography of reading with selected Black women viewers of the film in December 1987 in California. All references to women interviewed come from this study. For a discussion of the issues of readers' response to texts in media audience analysis see Ellen Seiter et al. (1989). See also Seiter's (1981) use of Umberto Eco's open/closed text distinction to examine the role of the woman reader. Seiter uses Eco's narrative theory to argue for the possibility of "alternative" readings unintended by their producers.
4. Morley (1989).
5. Morley (1989, p. 4).
6. Grossberg (1984, p. 403).
7. Christine Gledhill explains the idea of "making strange" in two articles: "Developments in Feminist Film Criticism" (1984) and "Klute 1: A Contemporary Film Noir and Feminist Criticism" (1984).
8. Grossberg (1984, p. 403).
9. Spielberg (1986).
10. Christian (1986).
11. Wallace (1986, p. 25).
12. Hoberman (1985, p. 76).
13. Bogle (1973, p. 31).
14. Salamon (1985, p. 20).
15. Christian (1986).
16. Fiske (1987, p. 258).
17. Morley (1980, p. 164).
18. Morley (1989, p. 4).

REFERENCES

Bogle, D. (1973). *Toms, coons, mulattoes, mammies and bucks: An interpretive history of Blacks in American films.* New York: Viking.

Christian, B. (1986, May 20). *De-visioning Spielberg and Walker: The Color Purple—The novel and the film.* Paper presented at the Center for the Study of Women in Society, University of Oregon, Eugene.

Fiske, J. (1987). British cultural studies and television. In R. C. Allen (Ed.), *Channels of discourse: Television and contemporary criticism.* Chapel Hill: University of North Carolina Press.

Gledhill, C. (1984). Developments in feminist film criticism. In M. E. Doan, P. Mellencamp, & L. Williams (Eds.), *Re-vision: Essays in feminist film criticism.* Frederick, MD: University Publications of America.

Gledhill, C. (1984). Klute I: A contemporary film noir and feminist criticism. In E. A. Kaplan (Ed.), *Women in film noir.* London: British Film Institute.

Goldstein, W. (1985, September 6). Alice Walker on the set of *The Color Purple. Publisher's Weekly.*

Grossberg, L. (1984). Strategies of Marxist cultural interpretation. *Critical Studies in Mass Communication, 1.*

Hoberman, J. (1985, December 24). Color me purple. *Village Voice.*

Morley, D. (1980). Texts, readers, subjects. In S. Hall, D. Hobson, A. Lowe, & P. Willis (Eds.), *Culture, media, language.* London: Hutchinson.

Morley, D. (1989). Changing paradigms in audience studies. In E. Seiter (Ed.), *Rethinking television audiences.* Chapel Hill: University of North Carolina Press.

Salamon, J. (1985, December 18). . . . as Spielberg's film version is released. *Wall Street Journal,* p. 20.

Seiter, E. (1981). Eco's TV guide: The soaps. *Tabloid, 6,* 36-43.

Seiter, E. et al. (1989). Don't treat us like we're so stupid and naive: Towards an ethnography of soap opera viewers. In E. Seiter (Ed.), *Rethinking television audiences.* Chapel Hill: University of North Carolina Press.

Spielberg, S. (1986). *Alice Walker and the Color Purple* [BBC documentary].

Wallace, M. (1986, March 18). Blues for Mr. Spielberg. *Village Voice.*

Washington, M. H. (1982, August). Book review of Barbara Christian's *Black Women Novelists. Signs: Journal of Culture and Society,* p. 1.

9

Out of the Mainstream

Sexual Minorities and the Mass Media

LARRY GROSS

In a society dominated by centralized sources of information and imagery, in which economic imperatives and pervasive values promote the search for large, common-denominator audiences, what is the fate of those groups who for one or another reason find themselves outside the mainstream? Briefly, and it is hardly a novel observation, such groups share a common fate of relative invisibility and demeaning stereotypes. But there are differences as well as similarities in the ways various minorities (racial, ethnic, sexual, religious, political) are treated by the mass media. And given important differences in their life situations, members of such groups experience varying consequences of their mediated images. . . .

Before turning to the discussion of minority audience perspectives, it would be helpful to briefly characterize the role of the mass media, television in particular, in our society.

THE SYSTEM IS THE MESSAGE

First, the economic, political and social integration of modern industrial society allows few communities or individuals to maintain an independent

---

NOTE: Excerpts reprinted from *Gay People, Sex and the Media*, by Michelle A. Wolf and Alfred P. Kielwassen, eds. (Binghamton, NY: Haworth Press, 1991), by permission of the publisher.

integrity. The world is becoming a Leviathan, like it or not, and its nervous system is telecommunications. Our knowledge of the "wide world" is what this nervous system transmits to us. The mass media provide the chief common ground among the different groups that make up a heterogeneous national and international community. Never before have all classes and groups (as well as ages) shared so much of the same culture and the same perspectives while having so little to do with their creation.

Second, representation in the mediated "reality" of our mass culture is in itself power; certainly it is the case that non-representation maintains the powerless status of groups that do not possess significant material or political power bases. That is, while the holders of real power—the ruling class—do not require (or seek) mediated visibility, those who are at the bottom of the various power hierarchies will be kept in their places in part through their relative invisibility. This is a form of what Gerbner and I (1976) have termed symbolic annihilation. Not all interests or points of view are equal; judgements are made constantly about exclusions and inclusions and these judgements broaden or narrow (mostly narrow) the spectrum of views presented.

Third, when groups or perspectives do attain visibility, the manner of that representation will itself reflect the biases and interests of those elites who define the public agenda. And these elites are (mostly) white, (mostly) middle-aged, (mostly) male, (mostly) middle and upper-middle class, and entirely heterosexual (at least in public).

Fourth, we should not take too seriously the presumed differences between the various categories of media messages—particularly in the case of television. News, drama, quiz shows, sports and commercials share underlying similarities of theme, emphasis and value. Even the most widely accepted distinctions (i.e., news vs. fiction programs vs. commercials) are easily blurred. Decisions about which events are newsworthy and about how to present them are heavily influenced by considerations of dramatic form and content (e.g., conflict and resolution) that are drawn from fictional archetypes; and the polished mini-dramas of many commercials reveal a sophisticated mastery of fictional conventions, just as dramatic programs promote a style of consumption and living that is quite in tune with their neighboring commercial messages. More important, the blending of stylistic conventions allows for greater efficacy and mutual support in packaging and diffusing common values.

Fifth, the dominant conventions of our mass media are those of "realism" and psychologically-grounded naturalism. Despite a limited degree of reflexivity which occasionally crops up, mainstream film and television are nearly always presented as transparent mediators of reality which can and do show us how people and places look, how institutions operate; in short, the way it is. These depictions of the way things are, and why, are personified through dramatic plots and characterizations which take us behind the scenes to the otherwise inaccessible backstages of individual motivation, organizational performance and subcultural life.

Normal adult viewers, to be sure, are aware of the fictiveness of media drama: no one calls the police when a character on TV is shot. But we may still wonder how often and to what extent viewers suspend their disbelief in the persuasive realism of the fictional worlds of television and film drama. Even the most sophisticated among us can find many components of our "knowledge" of the real world which derive wholly or in part from fictional representations. And, in a society which spans a continent, in a cosmopolitan culture which spans much of the globe, the mass media provide the broadest common background of assumptions about what things are, how they work (or should work), and why.

Finally, the contributions of the mass media are likely to be especially powerful in cultivating images of groups and phenomena about which there is little first-hand opportunity for learning; particularly when such images are not contradicted by other established beliefs and ideologies. By definition, portrayals of minority groups and "deviants" will be relatively distant from the real lives of a large majority of viewers. . . .

. . . What options and opportunities are available to those groups whose concerns, values and even very existence are belittled, subverted and denied by the mainstream? Can the power of the mass media's central tendencies be resisted; can one can avoid being swept into the mainstream? The answers to such questions depend in large part on which group or segment we are discussing; while many minorities are similarly ignored or distorted by the mass media, not all have the same options for resistance and the development of alternative channels. . . .

HOMOSEXUALS AND TELEVISION: FEAR AND LOATHING

Close to the heart of our cultural and political system is the pattern of roles associated with sexual identity: our conceptions of masculinity and femininity, of the "normal" and "natural" attributes and responsibilities of men and women. And, as with other pillars of our moral order, these definitions of what is normal and natural serve to support the existing social power hierarchy. The maintenance of the "normal" gender role system requires that children be socialized—and adults retained—within a set of images and expectations which limit and channel their conceptions of what is possible and proper for men and for women. The gender system is supported by the mass media treatment of sexual minorities. Mostly, they are ignored or denied—symbolically annihilated; when they do appear they do so in order to play a supportive role for the natural order and are thus narrowly and negatively stereotyped. Sexual minorities are not, of course, unique in this regard (cf. Gross, 1984). However, lesbians and gay men are unusually vulnerable to mass media power; even more so than blacks, national minorities, and women. Of all social groups (except perhaps communists), we are probably the least permitted to speak for ourselves in the mass media. We are also the only group (again, except for communists and, currently, Arab "terrorists") whose enemies are generally uninhibited by the consensus of "good taste" which protects most minorities from the more public displays of bigotry. The reason for this vulnerability lies in large part in our initial isolation and invisibility. . . .

Women are surrounded by other women, people of color by other people of color, etc., and can observe the variety of choices and fates that befall those who are like them. Mass media stereotypes selectively feature and reinforce some of the available roles and images for women, national minorities, people of color, etc.; but they operate under constraints imposed by the audiences' immediate environment. Lesbians and gay men, conversely, are a self-identifying minority. We are assumed (with few exceptions, and these—the "obviously" effeminate man or masculine woman—may not even be homosexual) to be straight, and are treated as such, until we begin to recognize that we are not what we have been told we are, that we are different. But how are we to understand, define and deal with that difference? Here we generally have little to go on beyond very limited direct experience with those individuals who are sufficiently close to the accepted stereotypes that they are labelled publicly as queers, faggots, dykes, etc. And we have the mass media. The mass media play a major role in this process of social definition, and rarely a positive one. In the absence of adequate information in their immediate environment, most people, gay or straight, have little choice other than to accept the narrow and negative stereotypes they encounter as being representative of gay people. . . . But there is more to it than stereotyping. For the most part gay people have been simply invisible in the media. The few exceptions were almost invariably either victims—of violence or ridicule—or villains. As Vito Russo noted recently, "It is not insignificant that out of 32 films with major homosexual characters from 1961 through 1976, 13 feature gays who commit suicide and 18 have the homosexual murdered by another character" (1986, p. 32). . . .

The gay liberation movement emerged in the late 1960s in the United States, spurred by the examples of the black, anti-war, and feminist movements. Consequently, media attention to gay people and gay issues increased in the early 1970s, much of it positive (at least in comparison with previous and continuing heterosexist depictions and discussions), culminating (in the sense of greater media attention—in the pre-AIDS era) in 1973, with the decision by the American Psychiatric Association to delete homosexuality from its "official" list of mental diseases. By the middle 1970s, however, a backlash against the successes of the gay movement began to be felt around the country, most visibly in Anita Bryant's successful campaign to repeal a gay rights ordinance in Dade County, Florida, in 1977. Since then the gay movement and its enemies, mostly among the "new right," have been constant antagonists (right wing fund-raisers acknowledge that anti-homosexual material is their best bet to get money from supporters), and television has often figured in the struggle. But, although the right wing has attacked the networks for what they consider to be overly favorable attention to gay people, in fact gay people are usually portrayed and used in news and dramatic media in ways that serve to reinforce rather than challenge the prevailing images.

Kathleen Montgomery (1981) observed the efforts of the organized gay movement to improve the ways network programmers handle gay characters and themes. In particular she describes the writing and production of a made-for-TV network movie that had a gay-related theme, and involved consultation with representatives of gay organizations. And the result?

> Throughout the process all the decisions affecting the portrayal of gay life were influenced by the constraints which commercial television as a mass medium imposes upon the creation of its content. The fundamental goal of garnering the largest possible audience necessitated that (a) the program be placed in a familiar and successful television genre—the crime-drama, (b) the story focus upon the heterosexual male lead character and his reactions to the gay characters rather than upon the homosexual characters themselves, and (c) the film avoid any overt display of affection which might be offensive to certain segments of the audience. These requirements served as a filter through which the issue of homosexuality was processed, resulting in a televised picture of gay life designed to be acceptable to the gay community and still palatable to a mass audience. (p. 56)

Acceptability to the gay community, in this case, means that the movie was not an attack on our character and a denial of our basic humanity: it could not be mistaken for an expression of our values or perspectives. But of course they weren't aiming at us, either; they were merely trying to avoid arguing with us afterwards. In Vito Russo's (1986) words, "mainstream films about homosexuals are not for homosexuals. They address themselves exclusively to the majority" (p. 32). However, there will inevitably be a great many lesbians and gay men in the audience.

The rules of the mass media game have a double impact on gay people: not only do they mostly show us as weak and silly, or evil and corrupt, but they exclude and deny the existence of normal, unexceptional as well as exceptional lesbians and gay men. Hardly ever shown in the media are just plain gay folks, used in roles which do not center on their deviance as a threat to the moral order which must be countered through ridicule or physical violence. Television drama, in particular, reflects the deliberate use of clichéd casting strategies which preclude such daring innovations. . . .

The situation has only been worsened by the AIDS epidemic. By 1983 nearly all mass media attention to gay men was in the context of AIDS-related stories, and because this coverage seems to have exhausted the media's limited interest in gay people, lesbians became even less visible than before (if possible). AIDS reinvigorated the two major mass media "roles" for gay people: victim and villain. Already treated as an important medical topic, AIDS moved up to the status of "front page" news after Rock Hudson emerged as the most famous person with AIDS. At present AIDS stories appear daily in print and broadcast news—often with little or no new or important content—and the public image of gay men has been inescapably linked with the specter of plague. Television dramatists have presented the plight of (white, middle class) gay men with AIDS, but their particular concern is the agony of the families/friends who have to face the awful truth:

their son (brother, boyfriend, husband, etc.) is, gasp, gay! But, even with AIDS, not too gay, mind you. In the major network made-for-TV movie on AIDS, NBC's *An Early Frost*, a young, rich, white, handsome lawyer is forced out of the closet by AIDS. "We know he is gay because he tells his disbelieving parents so, but his lack of a gay sensibility, politics and sense of community make him one of those homosexuals heterosexuals love" (Weiss, 1986). . . .

Being defined by their "problem," it is no surprise therefore that gay characters have mostly been confined to television's favorite problem-of-the-week-genre, the made-for-TV movie, with a very occasional one-shot appearance of a gay character on a dramatic series (examples include episodes of "Lou Grant," "Medical Center" and "St. Elsewhere," among others). Continuing gay characters tend to be so subtle as to be readily misunderstood by the innocent (as in the case of Sidney in "Love, Sidney," whose homosexuality seemed to consist entirely of crying at the movies and having a photo of his dead lover on the mantlepiece), or confused about their sexuality and never seen in an ongoing romantic relationship (as in the case of the off-again-on-again Steven Carrington in "Dynasty," whose lovers had an unfortunate tendency to get killed). . . .

COLONIZATION:
THE STRAIGHT GAY

There are several categories of response to the mainstream media's treatment of minorities; among them are internalization, subversion, secession and resistance. To begin with, as we've already noted, we are all colonized by the majority culture. Those of us who belong to a minority group may nevertheless have absorbed the values of the dominant culture, even if these exclude or diminish us. We are all aware of the privileging of male-identified attributes in our patriarchal culture, and the dominance of the male perspective in the construction of mass media realities. Similarly, the mass media in the United States offer a white-angled view of the world which is shared with people of color around the world. In a study of Venezuelan children in which they were asked to describe their heroes, the child's hero was North American in 86% of the cases and Venezuelan in only 8%; English-speaking in 82% and Spanish-speaking in 15%; white heroes outnumbered black heroes 11 to 1; and heroes were wealthy in 72% of the cases (Pasquali, 1975).

Sexual minorities are among the most susceptible to internalizing the dominant culture's values because the process of labelling generally occurs in isolation and because:

> We learn to loathe homosexuality before it becomes necessary to acknowledge our own. . . . Never having been offered *positive* attitudes to homosexuality, we inevitably adopt *negative* ones, and it is from these that all our values flow. (Hodges & Hutter, 1977, p. 4)

. . . Gay writer Merle Miller recalled that, "as editor of a city newspaper, he indulged in 'queer-baiting' to conceal his own homosexuality" (Adam, 1978, p. 89). Openly gay actor Michael Kearns

> speaks of a gay agent who makes it a habit to tell "fag jokes" at the close of interviews with new actors. "If an actor laughs, he's signed up; if he doesn't, he isn't." (Hachem, 1987, p. 48)

Working backstage, it would seem, does not exempt one from falling under the spell of the hegemonic values cultivated and reflected by the media. However, as Raymond Williams (1977) has suggested, hegemony "is never either total or exclusive. At any time, forms of alternative or directly oppositional politics and culture exist as significant elements in the society" (p. 111).

RESISTANCE AND OPPOSITION

The most obvious form of resistance, but possibly the most difficult, would be to simply ignore the mass media, and refuse to be insulted and injured by their derogation and denial of one's identity and integrity as a member of a minority group. Unfortunately, although some of us can personally secede from the mass mediated mainstream, or sample from it with great care and selectivity, we cannot thereby counter its effect on our fellow citizens. We cannot even prevent our fellow minority group members from attending to messages which we feel are hostile to their interests (this is, of course, a familiar dilemma for parents who feel that commercial TV is not in the best interests of their children). Given the generally high levels of TV viewing at the lower rungs of the socio-economic ladder, it can be expected that large segments of the population consume media fare that serves to maintain their subordinate status. . . .

. . . Just as racial and ethnic minority groups pay close attention to programs which feature their members, so too gay people will tune in regularly to any program which promises an openly or explicitly lesbian or gay character (or even a favorite performer assumed to be gay). The images and messages they will encounter will not, as we've already noted, provide them with much comfort or support. More typically, they will again be marginalized, trivialized and insulted.

Yet, of course, the determination of a message's value and impact can never be made in the abstract. Just as for some heterosexists *any* mention of gay people is excessive, for many isolated gay people any recognizably gay character may provide some degree of solidarity. As Pete Freer notes,

> . . . the notion of a "negative" representation is difficult precisely because the meanings are not fixed within the text but generated between text and audience. Hence my memories of certain films (e.g., *A Taste of Honey*) that I saw when young, in which the very existence of a

gay character was a positive experience—I recognized myself. The same film, seen today, fills me with horror. Now I know I'm not alone; then I didn't. (1987, p. 62) . . .

SUBVERSION

A second oppositional strategy is the subversion and appropriation of mainstream media, as well as the occasionally successful infiltration. The classic gay (male) strategy of subversion is camp—an ironic stance towards the straight world rooted in a gay sensibility. . . .

. . . The sting can be taken out of oppressive characterizations and the hot air balloons of official morality can be burst with the ironic weapon of camp humor. Most importantly, by self-consciously taking up a position outside the mainstream, if only in order to look back at it, camp cultivates a sense of detachment from the dominant ideology.

> The sense of being different . . . made me feel myself as "outside" the mainstream in fundamental ways—and this does give you a kind of knowledge of the mainstream you cannot have if you are immersed in it. I do not necessarily mean a truer perspective, so much as an aware-ness of the mainstream as a mainstream, and not just the way every-thing and everybody inevitably are; in other words, it denaturalizes normality. This knowledge is the foundation of camp. (Cohen & Dyer, 1980, pp. 177-178)

Camp can also be seen in the appropriation of mainstream figures and products when they are adopted as "cult" objects by marginal groups. Camp cult favorites are often women film stars who can be seen as standing up to the pressures of a male-dominated movie industry and despite all travails remaining in command of their careers (Bette Davis, Joan Crawford, Mae West), or at least struggling back from defeat (Judy Garland, cf. Dyer, 1986). . . .

In Our Own Voice

The ultimate expression of independence for a minority audience strug-gling to free itself from the dominant culture's hegemony is to become the creators and not merely the consumers of media images. In recent years lesbian women and gay men have begun—although with difficulty—to gather the necessary resources with which to tell our own stories. . . .

Since the 1970s a lesbian and gay alternative culture has offered a range of media sources and products—press, music, theatre, pornography—which are unmistakably the product of gay people's sensibility. . . .

In the past decade lesbian and gay filmmakers have been able, with difficulty, to raise the money needed to produce independent documentaries and fictional films which have inaugurated a true alternative channel in the crucial media of movies and television. The pioneering documentary *Word Is Out* (1977), and the more recent Oscar-winning *Life And Times Of Harvey Milk*, among others, represent authentic examples of gay people speaking for ourselves, in our own words; although even here there have been compromises in order to meet the demands of the Public Broadcasting System— the only viable channel for independent documentaries in the United States (cf. Waugh, 1988). And, even more recently, and tentatively, there are the stirrings of lesbian and gay fiction films exhibited through mainstream (art) theatres and becoming accessible to a nationwide gay audience. . . .

Finally, then, the answer to the plight of the marginalized minority audience would seem to lie in the cultivation of alternative channels, even while we continue to press upon the media our claims for equitable and respectful treatment. But neither goal can be easily achieved, and each will require overcoming formidable obstacles.

REFERENCES

Adam, B. (1978). *The survival of domination: Inferiorization and everyday life.* New York: Elsevier.

Cohen, D., & Dyer, R. (1980). The politics of gay culture. In Gay Left Collective (Eds.), *Homosexuality: Power and politics* (pp. 172-186). London: Allison & Busby.

Dyer, R. (1986). *Heavenly bodies: Film stars and society.* New York: St. Martin's.

Freer, P. (1987). AIDS and . . . In G. Hanscombe & M. Humphries (Eds.), *Heterosexuality* (pp. 52-70). London: GMP.

Gerbner, G., & Gross, L. (1976). Living with television. *Journal of Communication, 26*(2), 172-199.

Gross, L. (1984). The cultivation of intolerance. In G. Melischek, K. Rosengren, & J. Stappers (Eds.), *Cultural indicators: An international symposium* (pp. 345-364). Vienna: Austrian Academy of Sciences.

Hachem, S. (1987, March 17). Inside the tinseled closet. *The Advocate,* pp. 42-48.

Hodges, A., & Hutter, D. (1977). *With downcast gays: Aspects of homosexual self-oppression.* Toronto: Pink Triangle Press.

Montgomery, K. (1981). Gay activists and the networks. *Journal of Communication, 31*(3), 49-57.

Pasquali, A. (1975). Latin America: Our image or theirs? In *Getting the message across* (No editor listed). Paris: The *UNESCO* Press.

Russo, V. (1986, April). When the gaze is gay: A state of being. *Film Comment,* pp. 32-34.

Waugh, T. (1988). Minority self-imaging in oppositional film practice: Lesbian and gay documentary. In L. Gross, J. Katz, & J. Ruby (Eds.), *Image ethics: The moral rights of subjects in photography, film and television* (pp. 248-272). New York: Oxford University Press.

Weiss, A. (1986). From the margins: New images of gays in the cinema. *Cineaste, 15*(1), 4-8.

Williams, R. (1977). *Marxism and literature.* Oxford, UK: Oxford University Press.

PART II

You open your mail or read a magazine or newspaper, you walk down the street, you ride the bus or subway, you turn on the radio or TV—what do you find? You are surrounded by advertising, **imagery** in pictures and words designed to sell you products. Advertising is everywhere in our society, but many of us see it as "natural" and don't stop to look at it closely. As Sut Jhally says in "Image-Based Culture" (Chapter 10), which introduces this part: "In the contemporary world, messages about goods are all pervasive—advertising has increasingly filled up the spaces of our daily existence . . . it is the air that we breathe as we live our daily lives." For this reason it is critical that we all develop the ability to analyze not just the advertising imagery itself but also the place of the advertising industry in our society.

In an economy organized around the principles of **capitalism,** the profit motive is the driving force behind the production, distribution and consumption of goods and services. Advertising legitimizes and even sacralizes consumption as a way of life. However, as Robert Goldman's chapter (Chapter 11) argues, the major **commodity** being bought and sold in what Jhally calls "the image commodity system" in which we live is the audience for advertising, segmented along lines of **gender, race, class** (and age). Consequently, any discussion of the role of media within a capitalist economy has to foreground advertising, both as an industry in its own right and, in Jhally's words, as "a discourse through and about objects."

The advertising industry almost entirely finances the U.S. media system. According to Herman (1990), "Newspapers obtain about 75% of their revenues from advertisers, general-circulation magazines about 50%, and broadcasters almost 100%" (pp. 80). It should not be surprising, therefore, to find that corporations that purchase advertising space and time influence the ideological content of all media forms to varying degrees.

One example we have already seen (see Lipsitz, Chapter 7) is the way in which advertising influenced the relocation of the early TV situation comedy from the urban, ethnic, blue-collar home to the suburban home of the White upper-middle class. The world represented in sitcoms is also, not coincidentally, that which we see in ads. Although many of the chapters in this part will be discussing the **representation** of various specific marginalized groups in advertising, it should be remembered that despite other differences, all have a similar class position—all are represented as having plenty of money. Advertising imagery obfuscates the way capitalism creates a class-based society, where only a few can really afford to consume at the level depicted as the ideal in both ads and other media fictions. Moreover, because we never see the structural barriers to the acquisition of wealth in this media world, the implicit message is that one's comparative poverty is the result of personal failing, an idea not incompatible with the **ideology** of the American dream.

This American-dream ideology is racialized as well. Prior to the Civil Rights movement of the 1960s, the media world was virtually all White, although some demeaning **stereotypes** of African Americans, such as Aunt Jemima and the characters on *The Amos and Andy Show* served to reassure White audiences as to the "naturalness" of racial hierarchy. African American audiences and cultural producers have long understood and repeatedly critiqued these historical, overtly **racist** images that were produced by the predominantly White media industries when racial segregation in education, housing and employment was both customary and legal. As a result of the Civil Rights movement, the destruction of legal segregation, the passage of antidiscrimination law and consciousness-raising on issues of racial imagery, there are many more Black characters in mainstream media, including ad texts, than in the past.

There are also more African Americans working as cultural producers within mainstream media industries. In the Cassidy and Katula interview chapter, "The Black Experience in Advertising" (Chapter 12), Thomas Burrell, the owner of a prominent African American advertising firm, talks about his efforts to produce more culturally authentic imagery of the African American community. Burrell's reminiscences suggest the fine line that someone from a marginalized culture must walk when attempting both to create affirmative imagery out of a sense of community responsibility and to "move goods and services, because if we don't do that, then we're not going to be around very long to create any images."

Eliminating racism in advertising imagery is not just a matter of changing the numbers, of course, but also of reexamining and changing the codes and conventions of representation. Both Burrell's experience and Ellen Seiter's chapter in this part (Chapter 13) help make this point. Using the method of qualitative **content analysis** to study racial representation in advertising on children's TV, Seiter found, among other patterns, that "Black children . . . tend to be shown in advertising as passive observers of their white playmates." Seiter's study suggests the way in which the assumptions of White supremacy, even if in more subtle ways than in the past, still inform mainstream images of both Blacks and Whites. Moreover, the racial segmentation of cigarette and alcohol advertising is overtly exploitative and has recently become a significant political issue, as the brief account by Pollay, Lee and Carter-Whitney (Chapter 14) shows.

Gender is a strong focus in most of the chapters in this part on advertising. Along with its closely linked ideology of sexuality, gender is crucial in contemporary advertising, both because advertisers commonly practice market segmentation by gender and because the codes and conventions of advertising images themselves are highly gendered. Following in the tradition of sociologist Erving Goffman's (1976) *Gender Advertisements*, Sut Jhally (Chapter 10) speculates that

> it is because . . . conventions of gender display are so easily recognized by the audience that they figure so prominently in the image system. Also, images having to do with gender strike at the core of individual identity. . . . What better place to choose than an area of life that can be communicated at a glance and that reaches into the core of individual identity.

Advertising images provide culturally sanctioned ideal types of (heterosexual) masculinity and femininity. Recounting her experience seeking advertisers to support *Ms.* magazine in its early days, Gloria Steinem shows us, in "Sex, Lies and Advertising" (Chapter 15), how advertisers targeting women consumers subscribed to very limited notions of what constitutes femininity (i.e., dependency, concern with beauty, fixation on family and nurturance, fear of technology) and, consequently, "feminine" buying patterns. Feminist efforts to redefine gender ideals for advertisers in the 1970s and 1980s met with disbelief, resistance and downright hostility. Steinem's essay reveals the extent to which advertisers also assume the right to control editorial content of the media—citing, among other practices, efforts to censor feature stories that might conflict with the interests of advertisers.

In "Beauty and the Beast of Advertising" (Chapter 16), media activist and feminist Jean Kilbourne helps us see the financial stake that advertisers have in this narrow ideal of femininity that they promote, in beauty product ads in particular. As Kilbourne says, the image of the ideal beautiful woman (young; thin; White or modeled on White facial, skin and hair conventions; coiffed; made up; and with some body areas shaved) is "artificial, and can only be achieved artificially," through the purchase of vast quantities of beauty products. Although the feminist movement took on what Naomi Wolf names "the beauty myth" as one of its early targets, the beauty industries (cosmetics, fashion, diet and cosmetic surgery), using advertising, responded with a multipronged strategy. First, they simply increased the quantity of the commercial beauty images with which women are surrounded. More important, they created a revised beauty ideal that would be more difficult than ever for real women to emulate (e.g., the anorexic-looking "waif" model [Bordo, 1993; Wolf, 1991])—thus increasing the anxiety many girls and women feel about their own appearance. At the same time, many advertising images attempted to **co-opt** and **commodify** the very notion of "women's liberation" itself.

Probably the best known example of this exploitative trend is the long-running Virginia Slims "You've Come A Long Way, Baby," advertising campaign. In "Reading Images Critically" (Chapter 17), Douglas Kellner brings us in close on this familiar effort to associate the lifestyle of a "liberated" woman with smoking. Kellner also examines the "Marlboro Man" campaign begun in the 1950s, which used "the cowboy Western image" as "a familiar icon of masculinity, independence, and ruggedness." In reading the cultural codes of gender informing both sets of images, and in tracing the evolution of these campaigns over time, in relation to changing social developments, Kellner demonstrates "the need to expand [media] literacy . . . in order to survive the onslaught of media images, messages, and spectacles which are inundating our culture."

The Marlboro Man is only one among many advertising images of modern masculinity. Jackson Katz, working within a feminist understanding of how gender is constructed, turns our attention to the range of (heterosexual, White)[1] "masculinities" apparent in advertising imagery (Chapter 18). Katz's essay is part of a growing body of work in academia that analyzes how masculinity is being renegotiated as a result of both feminism and the gay and lesbian movement.

The advertising industry of the 1990s has not been slow to grasp the destabilized or shifting condition of gender ideology in our time nor to co-opt another liberation movement in the service of profit. We have seen that the Virginia Slims campaign was about co-opting the liberation message of feminism and equating liberation with addiction (in Jean Kilbourne's formulation). Similarly, as Danae Clarke's "Commodity Lesbianism" (Chapter 19) points out, when contemporary advertisers court the gay and lesbian market with cryptic visual codes, lesbian style, which has a political meaning in the social world, "becomes commodified as chic when it leaves the political realm and enters the fashion world." This has consequences for both lesbian visibility in the social world and for lesbian identity politics.

At the beginning of this section, Sut Jhally's essay alerts us to the influence of the highly visual, fast-paced contemporary advertising style on other media artifacts. Locked in competition for our attention, advertisers strive to present us with visual imagery that is ever new, striking and even shocking. In the process, the industry's creative personnel increase the visual seductiveness of still photos and the pace and noise level of television commercials in an ever increasing spiral. This frenetic style of quick cutting and visual excess reaches beyond overtly commercial messages into other media culture forms such as MTV, dramatic programming and even news delivery. Advertising's influence on other media forms is both **ideological** and **formal** (or stylistic). Advertising also easily overflows its banks into programming in an advertising-based media system such as ours, in which no information or entertainment format exists in isolation from the messages of the sponsor.

In the last chapter of this section, "Watching the Girls Go Buy," (Chapter 20), which analyzes the appeal for the audience of the "home shopping channel" formats, Mimi White enhances this insight, that advertisements are no longer (if they ever were) just the containable product messages interrupting the shows. Here direct selling of products fuses inextricably with aspects of other media forms, such as talk shows and soap opera. White's piece suggests that the advertising-soaked media of the future will provide just enough semblance of interaction with others in the community of consumers to keep us glued to the set, our credit cards in one hand and our phones in the other.

NOTE

1. Although we are aware of intense discussion about masculinity and race going on among African American academics and intellectuals (e.g., Duneier, 1992; hooks, 1989; Majors & Gordon, 1994; West 1983), we were unable to locate any articles that used advertising images to illuminate these issues.

REFERENCES

Bordo, S. (1993). *Unbearable weight: Feminism, Western culture and the body.* Berkeley: University of California Press.

Duneier, M. (1992). *Slim's table: Race, respectability and masculinity.* Chicago: University of Chicago Press.

Goffman, E. (1976). *Gender advertisements.* New York: Harper.

Herman, E. (1990). Media in the U.S. political economy. In J. Downing, A. Mohammadi, & A. Sreberny-Mohammadi (Eds.), *Questioning the media: A critical introduction* (pp. 75-87). Newbury Park, CA: Sage.

hooks, b. (1989). Feminist focus on men: A comment. In b. hooks, *Talking back: Thinking feminist, thinking Black* (pp. 127-133). Boston: South End Press.

Majors, R., & Gordon, J. (Eds.). (1994). *The American Black male: His present status and his future.* Chicago: Nelson-Hall.

West, C. (1983). *Race matters.* Boston: Beacon.

Wolf, N. (1991). *The beauty myth: How images of beauty are used against women.* New York: Doubleday.

10

Image-Based Culture

Advertising and Popular Culture

SUT JHALLY

Because we live inside the consumer culture, and most of us have done so for most of our lives, it is sometimes difficult to locate the origins of our most cherished values and assumptions. They simply appear to be part of our natural world. It is a useful exercise, therefore, to examine how our culture has come to be defined and shaped in specific ways—to excavate the origins of our most celebrated rituals. For example, everyone in this culture knows a "diamond is forever." It is a meaning that is almost as "natural" as the link between roses and romantic love. However, diamonds (just like roses) did not always have this meaning. Before 1938 their value derived primarily from their worth as scarce stones (with the DeBeers cartel carefully controlling the market supply). In 1938 the New York advertising agency of N. W. Ayers was hired to change public attitudes toward diamonds—to transform them from a financial investment into a *symbol* of committed and everlasting love. In 1947 an Ayers advertising copywriter came up with the slogan "a diamond is forever" and the rest, as they say, is history. As an N. W. Ayers memorandum put it in 1959: "Since 1939 an entirely new generation of young people has grown to marriageable age. To the new generation, a diamond ring is considered a necessity for engagement to virtually everyone." [1]

NOTE: This article appeared in the July 1990 issue and is reprinted with permission from *The World & I*, a publication of the Washington Times Corporation, copyright © 1990.

This is a fairly dramatic example of how the institutional structure of the consumer society orients the culture (and its attitudes, values, and rituals) more and more toward the world of commodities. The marketplace (and its major ideological tool, advertising) is the major structuring institution of contemporary consumer society.

This of course was not always the case. In the agrarian-based society preceding industrial society, other institutions such as family, community, ethnicity, and religion were the dominant institutional mediators and creators of the cultural forms. Their influence waned in the transition to industrial society and then consumer society. The emerging institution of the marketplace occupied the cultural terrain left void by the evacuation of these older forms. Information about products seeped into public discourse. More specifically, public discourse soon became dominated by the "discourse through and about objects." [2]

At first, this discourse relied upon transmitting information about products alone, using the available means of textual communication offered by newspapers. As the possibility of more effective color illustration emerged and as magazines developed as competitors for advertising dollars, this "discourse" moved from being purely text-based. The further integration of first radio and then television into the advertising/media complex ensured that commercial communication would be characterized by the domination of *imagistic* modes of representation.

Again, because our world is so familiar, it is difficult to imagine the process through which the present conditions emerged. In this context, it is instructive to focus upon that period in our history that marks the transition point in the development of an image-saturated society—the 1920s. In that decade the advertising industry was faced with a curious problem—the need to sell increasing quantities of "nonessential" goods in a competitive marketplace using the potentialities offered by printing and color photography. Whereas the initial period of national advertising (from approximately the 1880s to the 1920s) had focused largely in a celebratory manner on the products themselves and had used text for "reason why" advertising (even if making the most outrageous claims), the 1920s saw the progressive integration of people (via visual representation) into the messages. Interestingly, in this stage we do not see representations of "real" people in advertisements, but rather we see representations of people who "stand for" reigning social values such as family structure, status differentiation, and hierarchical authority.

While this period is instructive from the viewpoint of content, it is equally fascinating from the viewpoint of *form;* for while the possibilities of using visual imagery existed with the development of new technologies, there was no guarantee that the audience was sufficiently literate in visual imagery to properly decode the ever-more complex messages. Thus, the advertising industry had to educate as well as sell, and many of the ads of this period were a fascinating combination where the written (textual) material explained the visual material. The consumer society was literally being taught how to read the commercial messages. By the postwar period the education was complete and the function of written text moved away from explaining the visual and toward a more cryptic form where it appears as a "key" to the visual "puzzle."

In the contemporary world, messages about goods are all pervasive— advertising has increasingly filled up the spaces of our daily existence. Our media are dominated by advertising images, public space has been taken over by "information" about products, and most of our sporting and cultural events are accompanied by the name of a corporate sponsor. There is even an attempt to get television commercials into the nations' high schools under the pretense of "free" news programming. As we head toward the twenty-first century, advertising is ubiquitous—it is the air that we breathe as we live our daily lives.

ADVERTISING AND THE GOOD LIFE:
IMAGE AND "REALITY"

I have referred to advertising as being part of "a discourse through and about objects" because it does not merely tell us about things but of how things are connected to important domains of our lives. Fundamentally, advertising talks to us as individuals and addresses us about how we can become *happy*. The answers it provides are all oriented to the marketplace, through the purchase of goods or services. To understand the system of images that constitutes advertising we need to inquire into the definition of happiness and satisfaction in contemporary social life.

Quality of life surveys that ask people what they are seeking in life— what it is that makes them happy—report quite consistent results. The conditions that people are searching for—what they perceive will make them happy—are things such as having personal autonomy and control of one's life, self-esteem, a happy family life, loving relations, a relaxed, tension-free leisure time, and good friendships. The unifying theme of this list is that these things are not fundamentally connected to goods. It is primarily "social" life and not "material" life that seems to be the locus of perceived happiness. Commodities are only *weakly related* to these sources of satisfaction.[3]

A market society, however, is guided by the principle that satisfaction should be achieved via the marketplace, and through its institutions and structures it orients behavior in that direction. The data from the quality of life studies are not lost on advertisers. If goods themselves are not the locus of perceived happiness, then they need to be connected in some way with those things that are. Thus advertising promotes images of what the audience conceives of as "the good life": Beer can be connected with anything from eroticism to male fraternity to the purity of the old West; food can be tied up with family relations or health; investment advice offers early retirements in tropical settings. The marketplace cannot directly offer the real thing, but it can offer visions of it connected with the purchase of products.

Advertising thus does not work by creating values and attitudes out of nothing but by drawing upon and rechanneling concerns that the target audience (and the culture) already shares. As one advertising executive put it: "Advertising doesn't always mirror how people are acting but how they're *dreaming*. In a sense what we're doing is wrapping up your emotions and selling them back to you." Advertising absorbs and fuses a variety of symbolic practices and discourses, it appropriates and distills from an unbounded range of cultural references. In so doing, goods are knitted into the fabric of social life and cultural significance. As such, advertising is not simple manipulation, but what ad-maker Tony Schwartz calls "partipula-tion," with the audience participating in its own manipulation.

What are the consequences of such a system of images and goods? Given that the "real" sources of satisfaction cannot be provided by the purchase of commodities (merely the "image" of that source), it should not be surprising that happiness and contentment appear illusory in contemporary society. Recent social thinkers describe the contemporary scene as a "joyless econ-omy,"[4] or as reflecting the "paradox of affluence."[5] It is not simply a matter of being "tricked" by the false blandishments of advertising. The problem is with the institutional structure of a market society that propels definition of satisfaction *through* the commodity/image system. The modern context, then, provides a curious satisfaction experience—one that William Leiss describes as "an ensemble of satisfactions and dissatisfactions" in which the consumption of commodities mediated by the image-system of advertising leads to consumer uncertainty and confusion.[6] The image-system of the marketplace reflects our desire and dreams, yet we have only the pleasure of the images to sustain us in our actual experience with goods.

The commodity image-system thus provides a particular vision of the world—a particular mode of self-validation that is integrally connected with what one *has* rather than what one *is*—a distinction often referred to as one between "having" and "being," with the latter now being defined through the former. As such, it constitutes a way of life that is defined and structured in quite specific political ways. Some commentators have even described advertising as part of a new *religious* system in which people construct their identities through the commodity form, and in which commodities are part of a supernatural magical world where anything is possible with the pur-chase of a product. The commodity as displayed in advertising plays a mixture of psychological, social, and physical roles in its relations with people. The object world interacts with the human world at the most basic and fundamental of levels, performing seemingly magical feats of enchant-ment and transformation, bringing instant happiness and gratification, cap-turing the forces of nature, and acting as a passport to hitherto untraveled domains and group relationships.[7]

In short, the advertising image-system constantly propels us toward things as means to satisfaction. In the sense that every ad says it is better to buy than not to buy, we can best regard advertising as a *propaganda* system for commodities. In the image-system as a whole, happiness lies at the end of a purchase. Moreover, this is not a minor propaganda system—it is all pervasive. It should not surprise us then to discover that the problem that it poses—how to get more things for everyone (as that is the root to happi-ness)—guides our political debates. The goal of *economic growth* (on which the commodity vision is based) is an unquestioned and sacred proposition of the political culture. As the environmental costs of the strategy of unbridled economic growth become more obvious, it is clear we must, as a society, engage in debate concerning the nature of future economic growth. However, as long as the commodity image-system maintains its ubiquitous presence and influence, the possibilities of opening such a debate are remote. At the very moment we most desperately need to pose new questions within the political culture, the commodity image-system propels us with even greater certainty and persuasion along a path that, unless checked, is destined to end in disaster.

Moreover, this problem will be exponentially compounded in the twenty-first century, as more and more nations (both Third World and "presently existing socialist") reach for the magic of the marketplace to provide the panacea for happiness. One of the most revealing images following the collapse of the Berlin Wall was the sight of thousands of East German citizens streaming into West Berlin on a Sunday (when the shops were closed) to simply stare in rapture and envy at the commodities in the windows. Transnational corporations are licking their lips at the new markets that Eastern Europe and China will provide for their products. Accompanying the products (indeed preceding them, preparing the way) will be the sophisticated messages of global advertising emerging from Madison Avenue. From a global perspective, again at the very moment that there needs to be informed debate about the direction and scope of industrial production, the commodity propaganda system is colonizing new areas and new media, and channeling debate into narrower confines.

THE SPREAD OF
IMAGE-BASED INFLUENCE

While the commodity image-system is primarily about satisfaction, its influence and effect are not limited to that alone. I want to briefly consider four other areas in the contemporary world where the commodity system has its greatest impact. The first is in the area of gender identity. Many commercial messages use images and representations of men and women as central components of their strategy to both get attention and persuade. Of course, they do not use any gender images but images drawn from a narrow and quite concentrated pool. As Erving Goffman has shown, ads draw heavily upon the domain of gender display—not the way that men and women actually behave but the ways in which we think men and women behave.[8] It is because these conventions of gender display are so easily recognized by the audience that they figure so prominently in the image-system. Also, images having to do with gender strike at the core of individual identity; our understanding of ourselves as either male or female (socially defined within this society at this time) is central to our understanding of who we are. What better place to choose than an area of social life that can be communicated at a glance and that reaches into the core of individual identity.

However, we should not confuse these portrayals as true reflections of gender. In advertising, gender (especially for women) is defined almost exclusively along the lines of sexuality. The image-system thus distorts our perceptions and offers little that balances out the stress on sexuality. Advertisers, working within a "cluttered" environment in which there are more and more messages must have a way to break through the attendant noise. Sexuality provides a resource that can be used to get attention and communicate instantly. Within this sexuality is also a powerful component of gender that again lends itself even easier to imagistic representation.

If only one or two advertisers used this strategy, then the image-system would not have the present distorted features. The problem is that the vast majority do so. The iconography of the culture, perhaps more than any previous society, seems to be obsessed with sexuality. The end result is that the commodity is part of an increasingly eroticized world—that we live in a culture that is more and more defined erotically through commodities.

Second, the image-system has spread its influence to the realm of electoral politics. Much has been written (mostly negatively) about the role that television advertising now plays within national electoral politics. The presidency seems most susceptible to "image-politics," as it is the office most reliant on television advertising. The social commentary on politics from this perspective has mostly concerned the manner in which the focus has shifted from discussion of real "issues" to a focus on symbolism and emotionally based imagery.

These debates are too important and complex to be discussed in any depth here, but there is a fundamental point to be made. The evidence suggests that George Bush won the 1988 presidential race because he ran a better ad and public relations campaign. Given the incredible swings in the polls over a relatively short period of time, when media information was the only thing that voters had to go on, it seems to be a conclusion with some substance. The implications of such a conclusion, though, have not really been explored the way they should. The fact that large numbers of people are changing their minds on who to vote for after seeing a thirty-second television commercial says a great deal about the nature of the political culture. It means that politics (for a significant portion of the electorate) is largely conducted on a symbolic realm, and that a notion of politics that is based upon people having a coherent and deep vision of their relationship to the social world is no longer relevant. Politics is not about issues; it is about "feeling good" or "feeling bad" about a candidate—and all it takes to change this is a thirty-second commercial.

The grammar of these images, then, clearly is different to the grammar of verbal or written language. The intrusion of the image-system into the world of electoral politics has meant that the majority of committed voters are held ransom by those who are uncommitted (the undecided or swing votes), and that these groups are influenced differently—and have a different relationship to politics—than those who have an old style view of politics. These huge swings of opinion, based upon information provided by the image-system, suggest that the political culture is incredibly superficial and does not correspond to what we normally think of as "politics."

Third, the commodity image-system is now implicated, due to changes in the way that toys are marketed, in the very structure and experience of children's play. With both children's television programming and commercials oriented around the sale of toys, writers such as Stephen Kline argue that the context within which kids play is now structured around marketing considerations. In consequence, "Children's imaginative play has become the target of marketing strategy, allowing marketers to define the limits of children's imaginations. . . . Play in fact has become highly ritualized—less an exploration and solidification of personal experiences and developing conceptual schema than a rearticulation of the fantasy world provided by market designers. Imaginative play has shifted one degree closer to mere imitation and assimilation." Further, the segmentation of the child audience in terms of both age and gender has led to a situation where parents find it difficult to play with their children because they do not share the marketing fantasy world that toy advertisers have created and where there is a growing divide between boys and girls at play. "Since the marketing targets and features different emotional and narrative elements (action/conflict vs. emotional attachment and maintenance) boys and girls also experience difficulty in playing together with these toys." [9]

Fourth, the visual image-system has colonized areas of life that were previously largely defined (although not solely) by auditory perception and experience. The 1980s has seen a change in the way that popular music commodities (records, tapes, compact discs) are marketed, with a music video becoming an indispensable component of an overall strategy. These videos are produced as commercials for musical commodities by the advertising industry, using techniques learned from the marketing of products. Viewing these videos, there often seems to be little link between the song and the visuals. In the sense that they are commercials for records, there of course does not have to be. Video makers are in the same position as ad makers in terms of trying to get attention for their message and making it visually pleasurable. It is little wonder then that representations involving sexuality figure so prominently (as in the case of regular product advertising). The visuals are chosen for their ability to sell.

Many people report that listening to a song after watching the video strongly effects the interpretation they give to it—the visual images are replayed in the imagination. In that sense, the surrounding commodity image-system works to fix—or at least to limit—the scope of imaginative interpretation. The realm of listening becomes subordinated to the realm of seeing, to the influence of commercial images. There is also evidence suggesting that the composition of popular music is effected by the new video context. People write songs or lines with the vital marketing tool in mind.

SPEED AND FRAGMENTATION:
TOWARD A TWENTY-FIRST-CENTURY CONSCIOUSNESS

In addition to issues connected with the colonization of the commodity image-system of other areas of social life (gender socialization, politics, children's play, popular cultural forms), there are also important broader issues connected with its relation to modes of perception and forms of consciousness within contemporary society. For instance, the commodity information-system has two basic characteristics: reliance on visual modes of representation and the increasing speed and rapidity of the images that constitute it. It is this second point that I wish to focus on here (I will return to the first point at the end of the article).

The visual images that dominate public space and public discourse are, in the video age, not static. They do not stand still for us to examine and linger over. They are here for a couple of seconds and then they are gone. Television advertising is the epitome of this speed-up. There is nothing mysterious in terms of how it arose. As commercial time slots declined from sixty seconds to thirty seconds (and recently to fifteen seconds and even shorter), advertisers responded by creating a new type of advertising—what is called the "vignette approach"—in which narrative and "reason-why" advertising are subsumed under a rapid succession of life-style images, meticulously timed with music, that directly sell feeling and emotion rather than products. As a commercial editor puts it of this new approach: "They're a wonderful way to pack in information: all those scenes and emotions—cut, cut, cut. Also they permit you a very freestyle approach—meaning that as long as you stay true to your basic vignette theme you can usually just drop one and shove in another. They're a dream to work with because the parts are sort of interchangeable."[10]

The speed-up is also a response by advertisers to two other factors: the increasing "clutter" of the commercial environment and the coming of age, in terms of disposable income, of a generation that grew up on television and commercials. The need for a commercial to stand out to a visually sophisticated audience drove the image-system to a greater frenzy of concentrated shorts. Again, sexuality became a key feature of the image-system within this.

The speed-up has two consequences. First, it has the effect of drawing the viewer into the message. One cannot watch these messages casually; they require undivided attention. Intensely pleasurable images, often sexual, are integrated into a flow of images. Watching has to be even more attentive to catch the brief shots of visual pleasure. The space "in between" the good parts can then be filled with other information, so that the commodity being advertised becomes a rich and complex sign.

Second, the speed-up has replaced narrative and rational response with images and emotional response. Speed and fragmentation are not particularly conducive to *thinking*. They induce *feeling*. The speed and fragmentation that characterize the commodity image-system may have a similar effect on the construction of consciousness. In one series of ads for MTV, a teenage boy or girl engages in a continuous monologue of events, characters, feelings, and emotions without any apparent connecting theme. As the video images mirror the fragmentation of thoughts, the ad ends with the plug: "Finally, a channel for the way you *think*." The generalization of this speed/ fragmentation strategy to the entire domain of image culture may in fact mean that this is the form that thought increasingly is taking at the end of the twentieth century.

POLITICAL IMPLICATIONS:
EDUCATION IN AN IMAGE-SATURATED SOCIETY

There really is not much to dispute in the analysis I have offered of the history, character, and consequences the commodity image-system may have. The real question concerning these issue has to do with the political implications that one may draw from this kind of approach. Put simply: Is there a problem with this situation, and if so what precisely is it? Further, what solutions may be offered?

In a provocative recent book, Stuart Ewen offers a clear evaluation of the contemporary image-system. He states it succinctly:

> The danger is this: as the world encourages us to accept the autonomy of images, "the given facts that appear" imply that substance is unimportant, not worth pursuing. Our own experiences are of little consequence, unless they are substantiated and validated by the world of style. In the midst of such charades, the chasm between surface and reality widens; we experience a growing sense of disorientation. . . . For meaningful alternatives to come into being, however, the dominance of surface over substance must be overcome. There must be a reconciliation of surface over substance, a reinvigoration of a politics of substance.[11]

Beneath his insightful analysis and his many examples from different domains, Ewen maintains a relatively simple division: There is a world of "substance" where real power rests and where people live their real lives (the "material" world of "essence") and there is a world of "style" and surface (the evanescent world of "appearances"). In the history of twentieth-century capitalism the world of substance has been hidden and given a false veil by the world of appearances. People have given up control of the real world and immersed themselves in the ultimately illusory world of appearances. Surface has triumphed over substance.

I am less sure than Ewen of the dichotomy that he works with—after all, appearance is the form in which essence reveals itself—but I am convinced that a modern cultural politics must be conducted on the terrain of the image-system. The question is, how is substance (reality) revealed? Given that our understanding of reality is always socially constructed (that "ideology" is present in any system or situation), visual images are the central mode through which the modern world understands itself. Images are the dominant language of the modern world. We are stuck with them. Further, we have to acknowledge the pleasure that such images provide. This is not simply trickery or manipulation—the pleasure is substantive.

I would focus a cultural politics on two related strategies. First, the struggle to reconstruct the existence and meaning of the world of substance has to take place on the terrain of the image-system. In some progressive cultural politics the very techniques associated with the image-system are part of the problem—that is, images themselves are seen as the problem. A struggle over definitions of reality (what else is cultural politics?) needs to use other mediums of communication. I believe such a strategy surrenders the very terrain on which the most effective battles can be fought—the language of the contemporary world.[12]

The second aspect of the strategy centers less on revealing matters of substance (the underlying reality) than on opening up further the analysis of the contemporary image-system, in particular, *democratizing* the image-system. At present the "discourse through and about objects" is profoundly authoritarian—it reflects only a few narrow (mostly corporate) interests. The institutions of the world of substance must be engaged to open up the public discourse to new and varied (and dissenting) voices.

The other set of concerns are connected to issues of *literacy* in an image-saturated society. As Raymond Williams has pointed out, in the early development of capitalism workers were taught to read but not to write. The skills of reading were all that were required to follow orders and to understand the Bible. Contemporary society is in a similar position. While we can read the images quite adequately (for the purposes of their creators) we do not know how to *produce* them. Such skills, or knowledge of the process, must be a prerequisite for functional literacy in the contemporary world. Basic course work in photography and video production should be required in all high schools. Moreover, while messages can be read adequately, most people do not understand *how* the language of images works. Just as knowledge of grammar is considered vital in learning foreign languages, so the grammar of images (how they work) needs to be integrated into the high school curriculum. "Visual literacy" courses should be taken right after the production courses.

Finally, information about the institutional context of the production and consumption of the image-system should be a prerequisite for literacy in the modern world. Advertisements, for example, are the only message forms that are not accompanied by credits in terms of who has produced them. In this sense, movies and television programs have a different status within the image-system in that at least *some* of their process of production is revealed. At minimum, we know that they are made by lots of people!

Ads, on the other hand, simply appear and disappear without any credits. A third set of courses could focus on the political economy of the media and advertising industries. Stripping away the veil of anonymity and mystery would by itself be of great value in demystifying the images that parade before our lives and through which we conceptualize the world and our role within it. As Noam Chomsky puts it (talking about the media in general) in his book *Necessary Illusions:* "Citizens of the democratic societies should undertake a course of intellectual self-defense to protect themselves from manipulation and control, and to lay the basis for meaningful democracy."[13] Such a course of action will not be easy, for the institutional structure of the image-system will work against it. However, the invigoration of democracy depends upon the struggle being engaged.

NOTES

1. See Epstein (1982).
2. This is discussed more fully in Leiss, Kline, and Jhally (1986).
3. See Hirsch (1976).
4. Scitovsky (1976).
5. Hirsch (1976).
6. Leiss (1976).
7. See Jhally (1987) and Kavanaugh (1981).
8. Goffman (1979).
9. Kline (1989, pp. 299, 315).
10. Quoted in Arlen (1981, p. 182).
11. Ewen (1988, p. 271).
12. For more on progressive cultural politics, see Angus and Jhally (1989, Introduction).
13. Chomsky (1989).

REFERENCES

Angus, I., & Jhally, S. (1989). *Cultural politics in contemporary America.* New York: Routledge.

Arlen, M. (1981). *Thirty seconds.* New York: Penguin.

Chomsky, N. (1989). *Necessary illusions: Thought control in democratic societies.* Boston: South End Press.

Epstein, E. (1982). *The rise and fall of diamonds.* New York: Simon & Schuster.

Ewen, S. (1988). *All consuming images: The politics of style in contemporary culture.* New York: Basic Books.

Goffman, E. (1979). *Gender advertisements.* New York: Harper & Row.

Hirsch, F. (1976). *Social limits to growth.* Cambridge, MA: Harvard University Press.

Jhally, S. (1987). *The codes of advertising.* New York: St. Martin's.

Kavanaugh, J. (1981). *Following Christ in a consumer society.* New York: Orbis.

Kline, S. (1989). Limits to the imagination: Marketing and children's culture. In I. Angus & S. Jhally (Eds.), *Cultural politics in contemporary America.* New York: Routledge.

Leiss, W. (1976). *The limits to satisfaction.* Toronto: Toronto University Press.

Leiss, W., Kline, S., & Jhally, S. (1986). *Social communication in advertising.* Toronto: Nelson.

Scitovsky, T. (1976). *The joyless economy.* New York: Oxford University Press.

.11

Constructing and Addressing the Audience as Commodity

ROBERT GOLDMAN

. . . Consider how women are portrayed in ads which market women readers to media buyers. Publications such as *Advertising Age* contain the pictorial flip side of turning women into commodities. They foreground what is usually background or subtext: the political economy of consumer product advertising as it conditions editorial and advertising messages in women's magazines.

Women's magazines prosper as vehicles for advertising messages.[1] These magazines compete for advertising revenue by delivering demographically identified segments of the women's market. When women buy a magazine, they become part of a "package" the magazine has sold to companies that advertise in its pages. Women readers, as potential consumers, are marketed to media buyers just as other goods are sold. Using images of femininity and feminism combined with specific descriptions of purchasing power, household income, age and lifestyle characteristics, women's magazines make their pitch to potential advertisers in the pages of trade journals. A magazine's appeal to readers is putatively based on editorial content; the appeal to advertisers is based on the audience whose attention (and buying power) it can command.

Ads for *SELF, MS.* and *Cosmopolitan* appeared in *Advertising Age*. In each ad, the magazine positions their "product"—the woman reader/consumer.

NOTE: Excerpts reprinted from *Reading Ads Socially,* by Robert Goldman (London: Routledge, 1992), by permission of the publisher.

The commodity sold here is an *audience* of women.[2] The two-page ad for *SELF* magazine features a young woman reclining against a white background.[3] Across the top, the caption reads "HEALTHY, WEALTHY, and WISE." The woman's body is photographically segmented into three corresponding zones, each clothed and accessorized to signify the different spheres of consumption in her life. Hiking boots, wool socks and jeans on her feet and legs signify a healthy outdoors lifestyle. This is spliced to a photo of her mid-section clothed in nylons, a red satin dress and silver bracelets on her sun-tanned arm—all signifiers of a woman of means and sensuality. From the shoulders up she wears a black and white business dress, accessorized with gold jewelry, pen in hand and glasses lying in front of her on an open magazine. This offers a carefully constructed visual representation of marketers' compartmentalized vision of young women.

Note how a magazine that purports to speak from a feminist perspective markets itself to readers and advertisers. The *MS.* pitch to advertisers (Figure 11.1) makes "buying power" the motive for postfeminism.

> WHAT DO YOU CALL A WOMAN WHO'S MADE IT TO THE TOP?
> MS.
> She's a better prospect than ever. Because we've turned the old Ms. upside down to reflect how women are living today. And you're going to love the results.
> The new Ms. is witty and bold, with a large-size format that's full of surprises. Whether it's money, politics, business, technology, clothing trends, humor or late-breaking news—it's up-to-the-minute, it's part of the new Ms. So if you want to reach the top women consumers in America, reach for the phone . . .
> THE NEW MS. AS IMPRESSIVE AS THE WOMAN WHO READS IT.[4]

Pictorially, the new *MS.* woman is literally turned on her head. In a light-hearted moment she reclines over a couch so that a collection of identifiable items spill from her pockets. These include a passport; Tictac breath mints; a child's drawing; calculator; keys; American Express Card; perfume atomizer; gold charm bracelet; a crumpled $100 bill; Anacin; and a business card. These material artifacts signify the mix of interests and accomplishments of the "new 80s women" who look to *MS.* for direction. Each significant *relation* is encoded in commodity-object form.

Though *MS.* is usually cast as the ideological opposite of Helen Gurley Brown's *Cosmopolitan*, note the similarity of their pitch to media buyers. *Cosmopolitan*'s campaign (Figure 11.2) works off the tagline "The power behind the pretty face."[5]

> You assume she likes to get around. To her, that means a new set of wheels. You figure she likes to keep in shape. She knows that includes exercising her mind. The truth is, the Cosmo girl knows more, does more, earns more, spends more.
> THAT'S POWER. THAT'S THE COSMOPOLITAN GIRL.

Figure 11.1 *Ms.*
SOURCE: *Advertising Age*, March 7, 1988, p. S-7.

Behind her back, the Cosmo Girl holds her collection of objects, remarkably comparable to the signifying objects of the *MS.* woman: American Express gold card; make-up brushes; Pan Am World air travel card; Hertz Rent-a-Car card; compact disk (Mozart); portable Sharp calculator; motorcycle helmet; scuba diving mask. Both *MS.* and *Cosmopolitan* represent their "woman" as

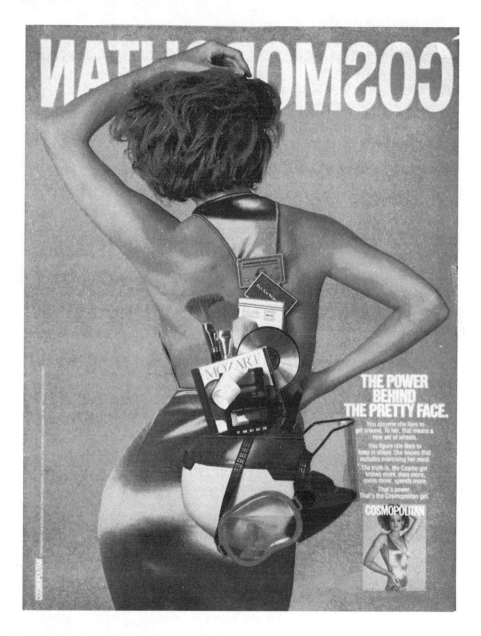

Figure 11.2 *Cosmopolitan.*
SOURCE: *Advertising Age,* November 7, 1987.

a consumer of objects that symbolize the worth of emancipated women—
signifying lifestyle leisure activities, disposable income, professional and
personal roles, concern for appearance and travel.

The Conde Nast package of women's magazines included *Mademoiselle,*
Vogue, Brides, Glamour and *SELF.* Like its competitors, Conde Nast sold women as active leisurers packaged in unabashedly commodity metaphors.[6]

26 MILLION WOMEN IN A PACKAGE.

Critical Mass. 26 million high-gear women readers set wheels in motion, get ideas rolling. Their sources are *Vogue, Glamour, Mademoiselle, Brides* and *Self,* the magazines of the most dynamic force in women's media. The Conde Nast Package of Women. To shift tastes. To drive sales curves uphill, get the particulars on The Conde Nast Women's Package, the Critical Mass.

In Conde Nast's commodified family of women, *Mademoiselle* is the magazine for *Strong women with a weakness for fashion and beauty.* . . .

NOTES

1. The 1987 year-to-date figures through November showed 36,256 ad pages in women's magazines ("Consumer Magazine Ad Linage," 1987).

2. See Smythe (1977). The images assembled in these ads mirror the uncertainty of those who work in advertising about how to speak effectively to women. Advertising "agencies and clients are having trouble appealing to women who work as well as to those who stay home. . . . 'The majority of women out there aren't neatly typecast, so it's very difficult to develop strategies to reach a large number of them.' " See "Despite Less Blatant Sexism" (1985).

3. In *Advertising Age,* March 7, 1988, pp. 30-31.

4. In *Advertising Age,* March 7, 1988, p. S-7.

5. *Cosmopolitan* belongs to the Hearst Group which pushes *"Woman Power."* This is defined as "bring[ing] together 53 million women. And joins the forces of the five best editorial staffs in the business . . . *Cosmopolitan, Good Housekeeping, Harper's Bazaar, Country Living* and *Redbook,* all in one . . . what you can buy like one magazine is actually five of the most powerful *editorial environments* around" (in *Advertising Age,* November 7, 1987).

6. In *Advertising Age,* March 7, 1988, inside cover.

REFERENCES

Consumer magazine ad linage. (1987, November 16). *Advertising Age,* pp. 81-82.

Despite less blatant sexism, ads still insult women. (1985, August 1). *Wall Street Journal,* p. 19.

Smythe, D. (1977). Communications: Blindspot of Western Marxism. *Canadian Journal of Political and Social Theory, 1*(3), 1-27.

The Black Experience in Advertising

An Interview With Thomas J. Burrell

MARSHA CASSIDY

RICHARD KATULA

INTRODUCTION

Thomas J. Burrell is *the* pioneer of advertising aimed at the black consumer. Founder of Burrell Advertising, the largest black-owned advertising agency in the world, Burrell has emerged over the past two decades as a key creative force in the advertising industry, setting the standard for quality ads that address black audiences. . . .

Underlying the Burrell Style are two key concepts: "psychological distance" and "positive realism." Burrell describes "psychological distance" as a feeling of separation between the black consumer and a mainstream product. To overcome the perception that "this product's not for me," his ads associate the product with portrayals of black people at their best—what he calls "positive realism"—"people working productively; people engaging in family life . . . people being well-rounded . . . and thoughtful; people caring about other people; good neighbors, good parents . . . people with dreams and aspirations; people with ambition." In other words, the Burrell Style depicts black people who express the dominant values of American culture, the very values that are directly countered in current pejorative

NOTE: Excerpts reprinted from *Journal of Communications Inquiry*, Vol. 14, No. 1 (1990), by permission of the journal editor and Richard Katula.

93

stereotypes of blacks, like the "lazy ni—er" "the welfare mother," "the irresponsible father," "the ghetto drug-dealer," or "the violent, unemployed youth."

Burrell's "positive realism" fits nicely within the confines of advertising's symbolic system, what Michael Schudson (1984, p. 216) describes in *Advertising: The Uneasy Persuasion* as "capitalist realism." Schudson argues that all of American advertising is "thoroughly optimistic," portraying the social *ideals* of the dominant culture. Advertising "does not claim to picture reality as it is," he says, "but reality as it should be—life and lives worth emulating" (p. 215). But advertising is also a kind of social shorthand. Because it "simplifies" and "typifies," advertising's symbolic system relies upon stereotypical social categories and values (p. 215). As T. E. Perkins (1979) suggests, however, stereotypes can be "laudatory" as well as pejorative. The Burrell strategy, working as it must within advertising's boundaries, emphasizes positive realism to create new laudatory stereotypes of blacks. These portrayals fit safely into the values of the dominant culture and do not threaten it, unlike, for example, Spike Lee's depictions in the film *Do the Right Thing.*

Critics have charged that it is the glossy typification of American social stereotypes that makes advertising a dangerous force, often strengthening a regressive set of social categories. But in an interesting reversal, Burrell's version of "capitalist realism" works as a progressive tool in Burrell's ads, which depict blacks participating in mainstream American culture without foregoing pride in their heritage. . . .

AN INTERVIEW WITH THOMAS J. BURRELL

Question. As a consumer of images, you must watch TV, see billboards, and so on. Do you feel that there has been progress in how minorities are portrayed in our culture? Looking back over the past decades at stereotypical, pejorative images of blacks and other minorities in advertising, do you think there has been progress now that minorities are controlling the images?

Burrell. Oh, there is no doubt that there has been change. I don't know whether it is because minorities are controlling the images, because "control" is a strong term, but I think that there have been changes because of the increasing sensitivity on the part of the majority, or the image makers who are, for the most part, members of the majority, and because of the active way that minorities respond to negative images. Everyone remembers the "Frito Bandito" and an agency cannot get away with that kind of ad any longer. And the Italian gangsters, and so forth—the way they were doing that kind of advertising in the forties, fifties, and sixties—you just can't do that any longer, because these people represent large buying blocks and they are more organized; they're more sensitive to the kind of damage that the projection of those images can inflict. . . .

Question. Would the Crest toothpaste ad that emphasizes the strong father figure be a good example of a Burrell campaign?

Burrell. That is exactly what I was getting ready to talk about—the Crest ad. The entire campaign started with a strategy, a need to take a product that had a low awareness among black consumers. . . . We fit this product into their lives by talking about the thing that's most important to them, *their kids.*

. . . It really comes out of the concept of using the male, the father figure, as the main spokesman in that communication. Because . . . that's the hot button in the black community. For everyone, whether there is a father present—and as you know in many cases there isn't a father present—or where there is, that idealization of the father figure is something that would make the female head-of-household that you're talking to feel very good about the advertisement, the product, and relate to it, because we are sure that she would like to have that male figure in the house. If she already has a male figure in the house, then that's called realism, and that's a *positive realism,* so it works. From the kid's point of view, if they have a father in the house, then, again that's realism. If they don't, it's certainly something that they relate to vicariously . . . So the use of the father was a real key executional variable that we put in, and caring, wanting to be there, and to be a part of this kid's life, was a real emotional hook. . . .

Question. Can you give us the thinking behind the well known "double-dutch" ad, the one in which the black girls are skipping ropes? That ad was quite successful.

Burrell. The thinking behind the "double-dutch" ad was pretty simple and that is that we wanted to show that McDonald's had special sensitivity and insight into the black community and black viewing. Again, it was just a matter of decreasing the psychological distance between this massive entity called McDonald's. We wanted to elicit from the consumer a feeling that, "Yeah, they know me, they know my culture, they know where I came from." And that is why we came up with this traditional custom that exists in the black community. Now, somebody threw me a curve not too long ago, a white woman in Boston—I think she was a reporter—who told me that she used to jump double-dutch when she was a kid in her neighborhood. I had never heard that before. We went under the assumption that double-dutch was a custom that came out of the black community and was fairly much restricted to the black community.

Right now, I think everybody knows double-dutch, but that's an important point. Just because something is practiced in the white community doesn't lessen its impact on the black community if the black community perceives it to be theirs. In other words, in order to be black, an idea doesn't have to be "unwhite."

Question. You have said that it is easier to reach white consumers through black-oriented advertising than it is the other way around. What do you mean?

Burrell. What I mean by that statement is that it is easier for me to sell goods and services through advertising to white consumers because I have been forced and have been compelled to be a student of white culture, because I was born and grew up in a society where I had to know white culture in order to survive. From the time that I was four years old and had to go to the store and deal with the white merchant, I have had to know white society. Similarly, when I came down out of my black neighborhood to work for a white company, I had to understand white society. We live in a white society. We are a minority in a white society, and in order to survive in that society, we have to know it. If I am going to come down and work at Leo Burnett, or wherever else I have to work, I've got to learn how to interact; I've got to understand white culture.

You can be white in America and live your whole life quite fully without ever having to know black culture. You don't ever have to go to a black neighborhood; you never have to know black customs, because when you encounter blacks, you are generally encountering them on your turf, and they are going through the changes. You don't have to go through any changes. So, you can live your whole life as a white person without ever having to know black people and black culture. And many, many people do, and many people who are in the advertising business do, because they move from their suburban enclave to a train full of white people, and they get off and go to a company full of white people, and they have lunch in a restaurant full of white people, and then they may go to a concert that evening full of white people, and they never ever have any kind of meaningful contact with black culture. . . .

Question. Do you feel, as a leader in the black community, and as the owner of the largest black-owned advertising agency in the country, and as a person who creates messages and images that are seen and heard in the entire community, do you feel a certain social consciousness? Do you feel as though you have a responsibility to create a certain image of blacks?

Burrell. Sure, I do feel that. I also feel, however, that our primary objective is to work for the people who pay us. Our primary objective is to move goods and services, because if we don't do that, then we're not going to be around very long to create any images. The fortuitous thing is that the best way to sell products to the black consumer market is through the projection of positive images.

Question. So the two are closely linked together, and you have never had to sacrifice your social conscience for the sake of business?

Burrell. Right. In the overwhelming number of cases, those two things go hand in hand: the projection of positive black images is the best, most effective way to sell goods and services to the black consumer. . . .

Question. Do you get comments from leaders in the black community or leaders in the white community who have been affected by your ads?

Burrell. Absolutely. We certainly have received some tremendously positive kinds of responses. But I have been surprised a couple of times.

There was one ad that we did for Coca-Cola some years ago that really surprised me, because I thought it was really doing a job. There is a custom, an old black custom that goes back to the days of slavery, that when a couple got married, there was a ceremony in which they jumped over a broom. It was a part of that tradition that had continued to exist in some places— where when you jump over a broom it means you are married. So we did a commercial that had a couple getting married, and they were getting married in a traditional style of African-Americans, and I thought it was very touching and very enriching and all those other positive, good things. And we got these letters saying, "I'm offended by that commercial. I'm offended because you're bringing up all this negative imagery. That's something that existed in slavery." I was really hurt by it; I was devastated by it. . . .

Question. Do you believe that, in terms of general market accounts, there is still discrimination against minority-owned agencies?

Burrell. Yes. I think that "discrimination" might suggest that in all cases it is a kind of methodical prejudice that assumes no business with any black people. First of all, to be fair and balanced about it, one of the reasons for it is that black agencies have done such a good job of positioning themselves against the black consumer market that it becomes more difficult for prospective clients to see us in another way. Another reason is, frankly, institutionalized racism, which really makes it difficult for a client to say, "I'm going to give responsibility for all of my business to this black company." This is especially a problem given the nature of client/agency relationships traditionally, and the fact that so much of the selection process, and so much of how agencies and clients work together is based on interpersonal, intercultural kinds of things, and that goes back to the early days where the advertising agency was a clubby kind of place, and it was an extension of the old school days; you do business with your buddies. So there is a lot of cronyism still lingering.

There is also some nepotism, and there's some racism, and those things working together make it rather difficult, although it's changing, because, as you see the advertising business change, it's changing to a more pragmatic, bottom-line, and hard-nosed kind of business. Just look at the change that has taken place in the people-to-billings ratio over the past twenty years. It's just amazing that we are now working with a ratio of one-and-a-half people per million dollar's billings. When I first came into this business, it was about eight-and-a-half people. Much of the extraneous stuff—going out with the guys and having an account person in charge of entertaining the brand manager—a lot of that activity is going by the wayside, and clients are getting more hard-nosed about their bottom line.

So these realities are good for us. They bode well for any agency that can deliver. Eventually, two things are going to happen. Those images of cronyism and so forth are going to be less important; and, of course, at the same time, minorities and blacks are going to become more familiar to the people making those decisions. In the future, we won't be such strangers.

Interviewer. Thank you.

REFERENCES

Perkins, T. E. (1979). Rethinking stereotypes. In M. Barrett et al. (Eds.), *Ideology and cultural production* (pp. 135-159). New York: St. Martin's.

Schudson, M. (1984). *Advertising: The uneasy persuasion: Its dubious impact on American society.* New York: Basic Books.

.13

Different Children, Different Dreams

Racial Representation in Advertising[1]

ELLEN SEITER

THE GEOGRAPHY OF WHITENESS

Let me begin with a discussion of white babies in mass-market advertising and by calling attention to those advertisements where children of color never appear. Tessa Perkins (1979) has argued that you must look at stereotypes of dominant groups to understand the latent content of stereotypes of oppressed groups. Positive, laudatory stereotypes about white men, for example, may be as persistent as pejorative stereotypes of Black women. The association of reasoned authority with white men is as strong as the association of heightened sexuality with Black women. Positive stereotypes are as important as negative ones in defining the field of what the media communicate to us about race. As Hazel Carby has put it, "Stereotypes only appear to exist in isolation while actually depending on a nexus of figurations which can be explained only in relation to each other" (Carby, 1987, p. 20).

Dreams of a great and inevitable destiny begin at infancy for whites as seen in print advertising. Their preciousness is underscored by allusions to their future economic value. A Johnson advertisement shows a bare white buttocks under the headline, "One day this little bottom may sit on the board of directors. Today it needs Johnson's." (The girl's version of the advertisement reads "One day this soft hair may be colored and permed," across the

NOTE: Excerpts reprinted from *Journal of Communication Inquiry*, Vol. 14, No. 1 (1990), by permission of the journal editor and Ellen Seiter.

forehead of a blonde, blue-eyed girl in extreme close-up: a typical example of the strenuous gender identification of all children in advertisements.) "Power Play" reads the bold headline over a picture of a blonde, grimacing boy ruggedly dressed in flannel shirt, jeans and thermal undershirt; as he drives his *Power Wheels*. Playskool advertises "Alphie II My first Computer," with a picture of a red-haired boy, gazing directly into the camera, above the line "We've got a Genius for Making Learning Fun." In a two-page advertisement for the Socrates "Educational Video System," a smiling blonde boy holds up his test with an A plus marked prominently in red, the opposite page reads, " 'Pay attention to the young and make them just as good as possible'—Socrates." The preoccupation with children's intelligence and achievement spills over into all product categories: "Kids are brighter than they used to be" promises Vivid bleach, above three fashionably dressed and smiling white kids. . . .

One of the most common stereotypes of white infants and small children in advertising is the go-getter. The go-getter is not a stereotype available for the representation of Black children, who tend to be shown in advertising as passive observers of their white playmates. If Black children were pictured in the same aggressive postures used for white boys, the available stereotype with which they are likely to be associated by whites is the "pushy" Black or the hoodlum. Thus the same set of behaviors, descriptively speaking, can be negatively or positively evaluated in racial stereotypes.

When I began looking for children in commercials, I was struck by the remarkable stability of images of white children, how often blondes were cast in commercials, and how similar they all looked. It is because "a dominant group's position is relatively stable and unproblematic" that images of blonde children seem to have remained largely unchanged for a century (Perkins, 1979, p. 148). It is very difficult for whites to see how whiteness *as a norm* informs all media representation, "as if it is the natural, inevitable, ordinary way of being human," Richard Dyer explains (1988, p. 44).

> "White is not anything really, not an identity, not a particularizing quality, because it is everything—white is no color because it is all colors. This property of whiteness to be everything and nothing, is the source of its representational power. . . ." (Dyer, 1988, p. 45)

This is why it is easy to pick out children of color in advertisements, but harder to see their absence in all-white commercials. The perspective of whiteness makes it impossible to see difference within minority groups. Overwhelmingly, advertisers use a single Black to signify "minority," while whites are portrayed as endlessly varied, individual, even quirky and idiosyncratic.[2] Advertisers utterly fail to register the tremendous range of differences *among* Hispanics, *among* Blacks, *among* Asians, *among* American Indians.

"The invisibility of whiteness," writes Richard Dyer (1988), "masks whiteness itself as a category." One of the most opaque masks of whiteness is the code of "nostalgia." Norman Rockwell's illustrations made a comeback in 1989 commercials to sell breakfast cereal and station wagons, and they offer a good example of the representation of whiteness as innocence. Rockwell's work epitomizes many aspects of the nostalgic myth of America: small town, parents and children together, naughtiness in boys, flirtatiousness in girls, the institutions of school, church, Boy Scouts—everyone is white.

The classroom is a favorite location for the nostalgia motif. The set design—bathed in yellow light, flag in the front of the class and globe on the teacher's desk—places the classroom in a mythical and decidedly preintegration past. This is made explicit in a US West commercial where the music classroom of the past (bathed in soft white light, resembling an illustration from Laura Ingalls Wilder's *Little House on the Prairie*) gives way to the "modern" classroom where the music teacher, an Asian woman, instructs via a video monitor. It is the white girl, center frame, who performs for the teacher. The Asian girl seated next to her listens silently, politely.[3] In a commercial for Eggo waffles, the classroom is visually the same as the room in the US West "flashback," and again every face is white. A boy gets up in front of the class to explain his "invention"—he has remodelled his toaster to prevent his brother from stealing his waffles—displaying the smartness and ingenuity of young white boys.

When television commercials are set in the home, in the domestic sphere, we can predict with certainty that only white children will be shown. Whenever commercials take place at the kitchen table, or on the front porch, whites are pictured alone. White children may be pictured with Black children playing in public (albeit in a restricted set of locations, as I shall describe below) but whenever the parents or grandparents are present, if the space is personal, intimate, familial, scenes are totally segregated by race. Children of color are orphaned on television commercials, excluded from the loving grasp of parents, restricted to token membership in a peer group, relegated to the status of "neighborhood kids" as Mattel named one of its multi-racial ensembles of dolls. . . .

In general market-advertising, African-American children never appear in the space of domestic fantasies, never share in these utopian visions of "home." When a scene takes place in the kitchen or on the front porch or in the old-fashioned classroom, no children of color appear. Instead, advertisers set minority images against a very different set of backdrops. They usually take place out-of-doors, on city streets, or in the negative space of a photography studio set.[4] Thus Black children—the most visible minorities on television commercials—are permanently outside of the golden, homey glow of television's fantasy of fantasy, safety and love.

EXPLORATION AND DISCOVERY

. . . Casting, camerawork, and direction work together with storyline to create stereotypes in children's advertising. Advertisements often fall into a limited number of genres, which are linked to product categories. On Saturday morning television, the "adventure" genre often serves as a metaphor for the consumer's discovery of new food products through advertising.

Scenes are coded for instant recognition: jungles, tents, camping gear, forests, and children wearing pith helmets, khakis, and ammunition belts. Movies such as *Indiana Jones* have, of course, done much to resurrect and revitalize the treasure hunt in remote, exotic, "Third World" locations (see Marchetti, 1989).

As Stuart Hall reminds us "New forms of ideological struggle can bring old 'traces' to life" (Hall, 1981, p. 34). Adventure stories neutralize the historical meaning of such exploits—the violent domination of natives by whites. Although the violent racism of exploration is repressed, the basic roles are reenacted. White boys are always cast as the adventurous, courageous "explorers"; while children of color are either excluded altogether, or are represented as passive, primitive, and ignorant. In a Nestlé's Quik cartoon, two children in search of a schoolhouse, accompanied by a rabbit and polar bear as their guides, suffer an avalanche, then head into a diner for a spot of hot chocolate. A smiling Eskimo, so much a caricature that his eyes are drawn by straight lines, speechlessly and smilingly serves them. Silent, smiling, and in the background, this is the only Native American child I found on contemporary television commercials from 1988-1990. . . .

Fanciful "exotic" adults populate live action advertisements also. In a Honeycomb commercial, the white children are visited by a magical strong man genie: a well-muscled shirtless Black man, turbanned, covered with jewelry. He is shot in extreme close up to emphasize his huge size, and he appears and disappears according to the children's whim. An inscrutable Asian man, "The Wisdom Tooth," recommends Crest toothpaste. An Indian man sings in English about potato chips baked by "Pequenos Keebleros," animated Keebler elves. In a commercial for trash bags, a group of aged American Indians watch over children dressed in scouting uniforms as they pick up trash on a hillside. In close up, the chief nods approvingly then literally "vanishes," optically dissolving from the picture. "Leave the land as you found it," is the voice over's message. Thus, minority adults are relegated to the roles of supernatural companions and helpers, playing roles very similar to those of animated animal figures. Their representations are fixed in "orientalist" fairy tales (Said, 1978). Again, we need only re-cast these advertisements with a middle aged white man in any of these parts to recognize the racial problematic implicit in these images.

TOGETHER ON SATURDAY MORNING

A spot that launched the Nabisco cookie, Teddy Grahams, typifies the representation of white and black children together. This commercial, in thirty and fifteen second versions, has had a great deal of air play, both on Saturday morning and in the "early fringe" weekday slots. It has been shown hundreds of times during many different time periods, during and outside of Saturday morning. Three adult-sized Teddy Bears sing a version of Elvis's "Teddy Bear" ("I wanna be your Teddy Graham"). They perform on a glittery stage, wearing fashion sunglasses and holding microphones. Three children join them on stage: a white boy and girl and a black boy. (The children syntagmatically represent the three varieties of teddy grahams, chocolate, vanilla and cinnamon). As the children pop up behind the white piano that one of the bear musicians plays, eat cookies, and crowd into the spotlight, the Black boy is partially obscured from view by the piano or nearly pushed out of the frame by the other kids.

This commercial exemplifies many of the rules which seem to govern the representation of children of color in Saturday morning commercials. First, they are always outnumbered by whites. Most often three children are pictured—two whites and one African-American (white boy in center, Black boy on left, white girl on right, as in the Teddy Grahams commercial). Children of color are pictured singly on commercials, if at all. The minority child is seen left screen—the least dynamic portion of the frame according to design theory. The Black child is not given a speaking part and is seen mainly in group shots with white children, only once alone and never in facial close up. Like most Black models, the boy has been directed to smile broadly and act clownish, manic. (Sadness, frustration, or complaint are the prerogatives of whites.) These rules govern the representation of children in commercials across a broad range of advertising styles and narratives.

Through casting, advertising glorifies white features, "good hair," light skin. Black feminists have described the oppressiveness of this beauty standard: to look as much like whites as possible. Toni Morrison (1970) has described a child's point of view in *The Bluest Eye*. This tyranny of physical type is strongest in the representation of Black girls. When advertising the most feminine toys: baby dolls, modelling clay flowers, kitchens, toy commercials use white models. When girls are really being middle-class girls—wearing long hair and traditional, pastel dresses, playing with dolls and flowers—they are always *white* girls. This is an extension of the taboo against representing children of color in the domestic space. Commercials such as those for "Bouncin' Babies" and "Fantastic Flower Basket" are typical of this genre. Merchandising as well as advertising excludes Black girls from the most strictly gender-coded types of play. An exception here is Mattel, which markets Black and Hispanic product lines extensively. In television commercials for a new "Style Magic," one African-American and two white girls appear together. Here the girls marvel over the voluptuous curly blonde hair of Barbie. It is unusual that the Black girl is given the largest speaking part, exclaiming over the fun of Barbie, enthusiastically describing her attributes. But the Black version of the doll is seen only in long shot, and is never admired or played with by the Black girl. In the final shot, the Black girl stands behind a seated white girl, fixing her hair.

But it would be a mistake to represent advertisers as monolithic in their racism; they are too fashion sensitive, too anxious to please as large a market as possible. Advertisers also negotiate, and revise the codes of racial representation. As Stuart Hall points out:

> The media are not only a powerful source of ideas about race. They are also one place where these ideas are articulated, worked on, transformed and elaborated. We have said "ideas" and "ideologies" in the plural. For it would be wrong and misleading to see the media as

uniformly and conspiratorially harnessed to a single, racist conception of the world. (Hall, 1981, p. 35)

This may happen more frequently in advertising using children because of the advertiser's growing consciousness of minority parents as a market. If we reach into our media memory for pictures of black and white children together, the images that come to mind are from educational children's programming such as *Sesame Street. Mister Rogers* books are one of the few places where parents and children of color are seen together. But integrated advertisements do exist, especially in publications such as *Parents* and *Working Mother* magazine. In fact, groups of children are much more frequently integrated than are groups of adults in advertising. Black children under 10 or so are coded as less threatening to the white audience than adolescents or adults (as in *The Cosby Show* or *Diff'rnt Strokes*), and most advertisers are interested in attracting the Black market if they can do so without offending the white one. In contrast to the semiotically rich associations of the "nostalgia" sets featuring white children, integrated advertisements often appear "contextless" set neither in a classroom, nor a playground, nor the park—and never in someone's home. . . .

Most commercials which use African-American children today feature a rap theme and/or some reference to sports. The presence of African-American children in a commercial is used to define the product as "cool," modern, up-to-the-minute. They are set up as more lively, more cool, more fashionable, more with-it than whites. Thus, their presence verifies the product's fashionability. This also means that we are most likely to see Blacks in advertisements for the trendiest products. It is one of the contradictory and compensatory aspects of Black stereotyping that they are presented as enviable for their greater vivacity and looseness. But by making these qualities the *exclusive* domain of Blacks the representation is ambiguous, suggesting by default that these qualities—though perhaps more fun—are not to be valued in the long run. . . . Black children are routinely granted the authority of a privileged relation to sports and music. For example, Black children appear in nearly all the advertisements for infant sports shoes, thus emphasizing their presumably "inborn" athletic ability. A television commercial for Apple Jacks uses a rap soundtrack and a basketball game to envision the "teamwork" of whites and Blacks playing together. One of the Black boys makes the final slam dunk of the cereal box at the end: the only starring role repeatedly offered to Black boys. In a commercial for "Pocket Rockers," top-forty singles on miniature cassettes, a Black girl is given center stage, flanked by her white playmates as they dance down the street. Achievement in sports and in music are obviously a proud and valuable aspect of Black culture. But in advertising they are distorted because they appear not as aspects of culture but as innate, natural talents. They are the only arenas for achievement and ambition allowed Black children.

To understand the significance of this, we must return to the representation of white children. Cultivation of learning and creativity are the qualities advertisers associate with white children. It is especially significant that toy advertising that makes particular claims for developing creativity have only white actors. The commercial for Ohio Art's ZAKS (a lego-like building toy) features a rap soundtrack: but only whites play in the advertisements. The same is true of the new series of PlayDoh commercials. McDonald's has run a couple of Saturday morning advertisements where the link to the future is made explicit. In the first, "Report Card," a group of children is seen at school opening their report cards. The white children have a range of reactions—joy, excitement, fainting, grief. But the single Black boy is seen opening the card and rapidly closing it, in a quick shot in which his reaction is open to a variety of readings (shock? relief?). The kids then head off to McDonald's to recuperate. The Black boy joins them at the table, but he is seen only from the back in an over-the-shoulder-shot. A second advertisement, "Big Dreams," features a group of children discussing what they want to be when they grow up. A girl says, giggling, "I want to be a lawyer, or maybe a fashion designer." A song describes three of the dreams in flashback/fantasies—to be a dancer, rock-n-roller, rodeo rider. When we cut back to the scene at the table, two Black girls are briefly shown, moving in and out of frame, slightly out of focus.[5] They are not given speaking parts. The range of possibilities discussed by the kids: from Aerospace engineer, to "Electrocardiogramtechnologist" are the province of the white kids. "Tomorrow belongs to you," advertising tells white children over and over again. . . .

TARGET MARKETS

Minority-owned agencies have stressed the need for targeted research and specialized appeals, explaining the inappropriateness—often the offensiveness—of many of advertising's messages for Hispanic and Black audiences. The most successful of these has been the Burrell agency of Chicago—although interest in the Black market which peaked in the late 1970s has somewhat dissipated. Increasingly, clients find the need for Spanish-language advertising easier to understand than the need for specifically Black advertising. Because Spanish-language advertisements appear in specialty media, clients do not worry about negative associations that might turn white consumers away from their products. These agencies are the most important force for change in minority images in advertising—perhaps in broadcast television—today. Their job is a very difficult one; they are obliged to convince advertisers of the special needs of the target markets in which they specialize, and in doing so, they also confirm white advertisers' preconceptions about the unsuitability of this work for white audiences.

The work of the Burrell agency exemplifies the constraints and the achievements of minority-owned advertising agencies. Here I would like to consider some features of their work in order to discuss of the problem of the positive minority image in advertising. Black agencies like Burrell have stressed the need to offer representations of the intact nuclear family.[6] They have highlighted the emotional appeal of the Black father's involvement with his children, as in a Gerber "First Foods" spot, where the mother's voice, off screen, speaks over images of father feeding his infant daughter.

"I love to watch Rachel with her Daddy. He's really involved with his little girl." The work of the Burrell agency approaches Black mothers as consumers very differently from the way that white advertisers approach white mothers. (Many advertisers still prefer to treat most white women as full-time homemakers, "New Traditionalists," as *Ladies Home Journal* promises.)

The Burrell approach is grounded in the recognition of—and the attempt to exploit—problems facing working mothers: scarcity of time, anxiety over children, guilt over the impossibility of fulfilling multiple role expectations. Burrell has promoted a different attitude towards women working outside the home. The agency has tried to educate its clients about African-American women, as Sarah Burroughs explains: "Clients want to portray black working women as a neat new female thing. That isn't true among black women. My mother worked, her mother worked, I grew up assuming that I would work" (Gadsden, 1985, p. 20).

In a series of advertisements for McDonald's, the "you deserve a break today" theme is tied directly to the strains experienced by working mothers. In one spot, a grandmother waits impatiently for her daughter-in-law to get up on Sunday to make breakfast for the whole family before church. A trip to McDonald's—with several kids, the mother, father, and grandmother—satisfies everyone, relieves the strain on the mother, and gets them to church on time. In "Special Delivery," a girl sings about the rush of the morning, as Dad leaves early and mother and daughter move hurriedly in the morning to get ready for work and school. Mother makes the bed while the girl dresses. Mother and daughter drive through McDonald's, then drop off breakfast for the father, who is already on the street delivering mail. In "Jimmy," a tired mother picks up her three-year-old from daycare, then dozes on the bus a they ride home. Meeting father at McDonald's after work saves her from cooking dinner and gives the boy an outlet for his energy. In "First Glasses," a Black girl is the center of the story about her adjustment to new eyeglasses and fending off her brother's teasing. A spot for Crest centers on a boy's performance in a school musical piece and his father's ability to leave work early enough to make it to the show on time. Here we find images of devoted, concerned parents, with children the center of their world. We find an acknowledgement of the hardships for working mothers, separated from their children during the day, orchestrating the family's different schedules. We find images of different kinds of families: extended families grandparents involved with the children. Songs speak lovingly about hard changes, about time going by fast, about special moments. These images hint at a "different culture when children understand maturely the kinds of burdens the parents, especially the mother carries" (Joseph, 1981, p. 95).

The search for "positive images" is limited by ideology, a set of relations which include hierarchies based in class and gender. The work of the Burrell agency certainly offers more desirable images of African-American children than those offered in white advertisements. But the efforts of minority agencies are circumscribed by ideology and by the worry over offending white audiences. In focusing on the family in these commercials, they both answer and replicate the dominant media construction of minorities as a "problem." Since the Moynihan report of the 1960s, the media have explained the problem with Blacks as deriving from the absence of the father and the female-headed household (the Black matriarch). As many Black sociologists and feminists have explained, this thesis, which has been remarkably durable as an ideological construct, denies the possibility that Black poverty is created through white economic privilege (hooks, 1981, pp. 51-86). The history of slavery, the grossly inferior public education system, and employment discrimination vanish and the Black family is the source of the problem. These commercials "answer" the negative Black images produced by whites by picturing the Black middle-class family—with father present. But the terms of the representation are the same; we simply have the positive rather than the negative version of the stereotype. These issues have been heard in the debate over *The Cosby Show,* the object of great suspicion (by white leftists) and wonder (by industry workers) because of its enormous popularity with whites and Blacks. While it has "normalized" the Black family, *Cosby* has been vigorously attacked for its upper-middle-classness, its materialism, its conspicuous consumption, its adoption of conventions from white family sitcoms (see Miller, 1988).

The Burrell commercials do what advertising does best: provide celebratory, utopian, unabashedly sentimental pictures of the family. They are important as an intervention, as an antidote, to the white advertising I have described here. But there is no such thing as a free lunch. The African-American community has had to badger McDonald's to purchase advertising time on Black-owned stations. Their huge profits are substantially due to Black consumers (and to Black employees). These "best" images of the Black family advertise a product indisputably dangerous to a community at risk of high blood pressure and heart disease.

It is within this field of cultural, ideological, and economic contradictions that minority images in advertising need to be understood, judged, discussed, protested against. One of the ironies of the media under capitalism is that because advertising links its products to utopian ideals, commercials offer us a rare glimpse of people of color starring in their own stories of emotion and intensity. Such stories are rarely found on regular television programs, or in advertising for white audiences. It may be useful to consider Terry Lovell's (1983) suggestion that we differentiate between the use-value of a commercial for the consumer, and its utility for the advertiser. When commercials lead to a consumer purchase, or when they secure ideological assent, they have fulfilled one kind of value; but this is by no means assured. In the meantime their use-value is up to the audience, which can make of them what they like. Commercials such as those of the Burrell agency may offer more to African-American children than anything else on television. . . .

NOTES

1. This paper is based on a book chapter from *Sold Separately: Aspects of Children's Consumer Culture.* Winchester, MA, and London: Unwin Hyman, 1993.

2. Jews are an ideologically crucial exclusion here. Whiteness is Christian, usually WASP. One of the marks of anti-semitism is the obliteration of Jews from advertising images. Totally

assimilated Jews do appear on some popular dramatic television shows, such as *LA Law* and *Thirtysomething*.

3. Since the 1940s, Asians have been represented as a "Model Minority," a stereotype that is defined primarily by the fact that Asians are seen as different from and more desirable than African-Americans. Asian children usually conform to this model minority stereotype. Currently, the model minority stereotype seems to be undergoing a process of re-evaluation, and is now taking on the negative connotations of "drudge." The Asian student as drudge is seen as an "unfair" competitor with whites college students (see Fong, 1989).

4. I have discussed the various connotations of this type of set as seen in *The Cosby Show* title sequences in Seiter (1987).

5. This imitation documentary style (handheld camera, imperfect framing, loss of focus) is frequently used to pan quickly past children of color. It is a way of signalling their presence, while "accidentally" passing them over.

6. See "Black-and-White Magic in Chicago" (1985); "Chicago: Windy, Toddling, and Black!" (1986); "The Burrell Style" (1985).

REFERENCES

Black-and-White magic in Chicago. (1985, September 2). *Fortune.*

The Burrell style. (1985, December 19). *Advertising Age.*

Carby, H. (1987). *Reconstructing womanhood: The emergence of the Afro-American woman novelist.* New York: Oxford.

Chicago: Windy, toddling, and Black! (1986, February). *Madison Avenue,* pp. 39-43.

Dyer, R. (1988). White. *Screen, 29*(4), 44-65.

Fong, C. (1989). *The model minority and shifts in the images of Chinese Americans, 1800-1930.* Unpublished doctoral dissertation, University of Oregon, Eugene.

Gadsden, S. (1985, December 12). Seeking the right tack in talking to Blacks. *Advertising Age,* pp. 18-20.

Hall, S. (1981). The whites of their eyes: Racist ideologies and the media. In G. Bridges & R. Brunt (Eds.), *Silver linings* (pp. 28-52). London: Lawrence & Wishart.

hooks, b. (1981). *Ain't I a woman: Black women and feminism.* Boston: South End Press.

Joseph, G. I. (1981). Black mothers and daughters: Their roles and functions in American society. In J. Lewis & J. Lewis (Eds.), *Common differences.* Boston: South End Press.

Lovell, T. (1983). *Pictures of reality: Aesthetics, politics, pleasure.* London: BFI.

Marchetti, G. (1989). Action-adventure as ideology. In I. Angus & S. Jhally (Eds.), *Cultural politics in contemporary America* (pp. 182-197). New York: Routledge.

Miller, M. C. (1988). Cosby knows best. In M. C. Miller, *Boxed in* (pp. 69-78). Boston: Northeastern University Press.

Morrison, T. (1970). *The bluest eye.* New York: Washington Square Press.

Perkins, T. E. (1979). Rethinking stereotypes. In M. Barrett et al. (Eds.), *Ideology and cultural production* (pp. 135-159). New York: St. Martin's.

Said, E. (1978). *Orientalism.* London: Routledge & Kegan Paul.

Seiter, E. (1987). Semiotics and television. In R. C. Allen (Ed.), *Channels of discourse* (pp. 17-41). Chapel Hill: University of North Carolina Press.

.14

Separate, But Not Equal

Racial Segmentation in Cigarette Advertising

RICHARD W. POLLAY

JUNG S. LEE

DAVID CARTER-WHITNEY

CIGARETTE SEGMENTATION

. . . Research has shown that the cigarette industry focuses considerable efforts toward specific target segments, such as blue collar women, ambitious Hispanics or urban blacks. Gender or race is unlikely to be the only basis for segmentation, as these examples with their social class and personality qualifiers suggest. Also, it is likely that other brands and programs in the U.S., like those of their Canadian subsidiaries, are aimed at segments defined with terms like "young starters," "pre-quitters," or "ostriches." These segments are seen by the industry, respectively, as the most important in the long run, the largest, and the least in need of advertising reassurance (Pollay, 1990). Women, long the target for "slim" brands such as Virginia Slims, Eve, More and Capri, were recently offered new products such as SuperSlims, Style, and a scented Chelsea (Dagnoli, 1989; Waldman, 1989). Dakota is a new brand aimed at the "virile female," working class woman

NOTE: Excerpts reprinted from *Journal of Advertising*, Vol. 21, No. 1 (1992), by permission of the publisher.

who enjoy events like drag races, wrestling, tractor pulls, or shooting pool in bars (Gallagher, 1990). Brands such as Rio and Dorado are targeted at Hispanics, making Philip Morris the single biggest advertiser in Hispanic media, with R. J. Reynolds not far behind (Levin, 1988, p. 14; Maxwell & Jacobson, 1989).

Black magazines, like those for Hispanics or youth, have been receiving an increasing number of cigarette ads since at least 1965 (Schooler & Basil, 1990). Magazines in the aggregate enjoyed a nearly six-fold surge of cigarette ad income during the 1970s after the firms voluntarily withdrew from radio and TV to terminate the FCC mandated Fairness Doctrine messages of the Cancer Society and others (Arbogast, 1986; Feinberg, 1971). (The idea that "they were booted off" radio and TV is a misunderstanding common enough to be shared by a reviewer. The Fairness Doctrine was withstanding industry challenge, being upheld by the U.S. Court of Appeals. A bill renewing the 1965 package warning law, and pre-empting FTC and FCC initiatives with respect to cigarette advertising, passed the House in June 1969. Joseph F. Cullman III, the President of Philip Morris and Chairman of the Tobacco Institute, surprised many when he announced in a July Senate hearing that the industry would voluntarily discontinue all broadcast advertising effective Dec. 31, if granted immunity from anti-trust laws and released from forward contracts with the networks. The legislation blocking backsliding on this promised self regulation passed Congress in March 1970, eight months later. For detail, see the legislative history [P.L. 91-222, 2652ff]. Broadcast cigarette ads stopped after the January 1, 1971 end of season football games.)

Ethnic markets for cigarettes are reached today primarily with outdoor, point of sale, transit, taxi-top, bus shelter, and other "street" advertising. Black neighborhoods have particularly high densities of billboards, and a higher fraction of these are for tobacco and alcohol ads than is true for billboards in general (Schooler & Basil, 1990). *Marketing and Media Decisions* reported that the top ten outdoor advertisers were all cigarette brands (U.S. House of Representatives, 1986, pp. 772-773). This intense targeting of the ethnic neighborhoods motivated one priest, Rev. Michael Pfleger, to paint over brand names on some of 118 billboards within ten blocks of his Chicago school. This act of civil disobedience led to criminal charges, a trial and an ultimate acquittal (Castro, 1990; Duff, 1991). The anonymous Mandrake and New York's Rev. Calvin Butts have engaged in similar protests (Wildavsky, 1990). Handbooks are available to concerned citizens with plans of action to fight against billboards and ethnic targeting (McMahon & Taylor, 1990). In response to ethnic protests, Philip Morris now trains its staff with a professional actress role playing an intruder disrupting ethnic promotional events screaming "You are killing my people" (STAT, 1991).

More publicly, Philip Morris fights ethnic and other attacks on their advertising and promotional activities with a travelling exhibit and large advocacy ad campaign that champions the Bill of Rights, particularly "Free Speech." This campaign, like other cigarette advertising, also uses black endorsers: Benjamin Brooks, the Executive Director of the NAACP; James Earl Jones, an actor; Barbara Jordan, a former Congresswoman; and Judith

Jamieson, the Artistic Director of the Alvin Ailey Dance Company, a regular recipient of funds from Philip Morris. The black community has enjoyed Kool Jazz Festivals and Achiever Awards, More's sponsorship of *Ebony's* travelling fashion shows, and Philip Morris' patronage of the arts. Sponsorship and support is also extended to groups such as the United Negro College Fund, the National Association for the Advancement of Colored People (NAACP), the National Black Caucus of State Legislators, and the National Urban League, which receives an estimated $4 million plus annually from cigarette companies (Assael, 1990; Williams, 1987). . . .

REFERENCES

Arbogast, R. (1986). A proposal to regulate the manner of tobacco advertising. *Journal of Health Politics, Policy and Law, 11*(3), 393-422.

Assael, S. (1990, January 29). Why big tobacco woos minorities. *Adweek's Marketing Week,* pp. 21-30.

Castro, J. (1990, April 23). Volunteer vice squad. *Time,* pp. 60-61.

Dagnoli, J. (1989, February 6). RJR's Chelsea. *Advertising Age,* pp. 3ff.

Duff, C. (1991, July 5). Priest who defaced billboards acquitted. *Wall Street Journal.*

Feinberg, B. (1971). Content analysis shows cigarette advertising up twofold in fourteen magazines. *Journalism Quarterly, 48*(3), 539-542.

Gallagher, J. E. (1990, March 5). Under fire from all sides. *Time,* pp. 41.

Kessler, L. (1989). Women's magazines' coverage of smoking. Related health hazards. *Journalism Quarterly, 66,* 316-322f.

Levin, M. (1988, Spring). The tobacco industry's strange bedfellows. *Business and Society Review, 65,* 11-17.

Maxwell, B., & Jacobson, M. (1989). *Marketing disease to Hispanics.* Washington, DC: Center for Science in the Public Interest.

McMahon, E. T., & Taylor, P. A. (1990). *Citizen's action handbook on alcohol and tobacco billboard advertising.* Washington, DC: Center for Science in the Public Interest.

Pollay, R. W. (1990). *The functions and management of cigarette advertising* (Working paper, Faculty of Commerce, University of British Columbia, Canada, History of Advertising Archives, for Quebec Superior Court, Imperial Tobacco Limitee & RJR-Macdonald Inc. c. Le Procurer General du Canada).

Schooler, C., & Basil, M. D. (1990, June). *Alcohol and cigarette advertising on billboards: Targeting with social cues.* Paper presented at the International Communication Association Conference, Dublin, Ireland.

STAT. (1991, May 4). The new money changers at Phillip Morris. *STAT (Stop Teenage Addiction to Tobacco) News.*

U.S. House of Representatives (1986). *Advertising of tobacco products* (Hearings, Committee on Energy and Commerce, Subcommittee on Health and the Environment, July 18 and August 1, 1986. Serial No. 99-167). Washington, DC: Government Printing Office.

Waldman, P. (1989, December 19). Tobacco firms try soft, feminine sell. *Wall Street Journal,* pp. B1ff.

Wildavsky, B. (1990, August 29). Tilting at billboards: Butts vs. butts. *New Republic,* pp. 19-20.

Williams, L. (1987, January 17). Blacks debate the influences of tobacco industry. *New York Times,* pp. 1ff.

.15

Sex, Lies and Advertising

GLORIA STEINEM

. . . When *Ms.* began, we didn't consider *not* taking ads. The most important reason was keeping the price of a feminist magazine low enough for most women to afford. But the second and almost equal reason was providing a forum where women and advertisers could talk to each other and improve advertising itself. After all, it was (and still is) as potent a source of information in this country as news or TV and movie dramas.

We decided to proceed in two stages. First, we would convince makers of "people products" used by both men and women but advertised mostly to men—cars, credit cards, insurance, sound equipment, financial services, and the like—that their ads should be placed in a women's magazine. Since they were accustomed to the division between editorial and advertising in news and general interest magazines, this would allow our editorial content to be free and diverse. Second, we would add the best ads for whatever traditional "women's products" (clothes, shampoo, fragrance, food, and so on) that surveys showed *Ms.* readers used. But we would ask them to come in *without* the usual quid pro quo of "complementary copy."

We knew the second step might be harder. Food advertisers have always demanded that women's magazines publish recipes and articles on entertaining (preferably ones that name their products) in return for their ads: clothing advertisers expect to be surrounded by fashion spreads (especially

---

NOTE: Excerpts reprinted from *Ms.*, July/August 1990, by permission of Gloria Steinem.

ones that credit their designers); and shampoo, fragrance, and beauty products in general usually insist on positive editorial coverage of beauty subjects, plus photo credits besides. That's why women's magazines look the way they do. But if we could break this link between ads and editorial content, then we wanted good ads for "women's products," too. . . .

I thought then that our main problem would be the imagery in ads themselves. Carmakers were still draping blondes in evening gowns over the hoods like ornaments. Authority figures were almost always male, even in ads for products that only women used. Sadistic, he-man campaigns even won industry praise. (For instance, *Advertising Age* had hailed the infamous Silva Thin cigarette theme. "How to Get a Woman's Attention: Ignore Her," as "brilliant.") Even in medical journals, tranquilizer ads showed depressed housewives standing beside piles of dirty dishes and promised to get them back to work.

Obviously, *Ms.* would have to avoid such ads and seek out the best ones—but this didn't seem impossible. *The New Yorker* had been selecting ads for aesthetic reasons for years, a practice that only seemed to make advertisers more eager to be in its pages. *Ebony* and *Essence* were asking for ads with positive black images, and though their struggle was hard, they weren't being called unreasonable. . . .

. . . The fact that *Ms.* was asking companies to do business in a different way meant our saleswomen had to make many times the usual number of calls—first to convince agencies and then client companies besides—and to present endless amounts of research. I was often asked to do a final ad presentation, or see some higher decision-maker, or speak to women employees so executives could see the interest of women they worked with. That's why I spent more time persuading advertisers than editing or writing for *Ms.* and why I ended up with an unsentimental education in the seamy underside of publishing that few writers see (and even fewer magazines can publish).

Let me take you with us through some experiences, just as they happened:

- Cheered on by early support from Volkswagen and one or two other car companies, we scrape together time and money to put on a major reception in Detroit. We know U.S. carmakers firmly believe that women choose the upholstery, not the car, but we are armed with statistics and reader mail to prove the contrary: a car is an important purchase for women, one that symbolizes mobility and freedom.

But almost nobody comes. We are left with many pounds of shrimp on the table, and quite a lot of egg on our face. We blame ourselves for not guessing that there would be a baseball pennant play-off on the same day, but executives go out of their way to explain they wouldn't have come anyway. Thus begins ten years of knocking on hostile doors, presenting endless documentation, and hiring a full-time saleswoman in Detroit: all necessary before *Ms.* gets any real results.

This long saga has a semihappy ending: foreign and, later, domestic carmakers eventually provided *Ms.* with enough advertising to make cars one of our top sources of ad revenue. Slowly, Detroit began to take the women's market seriously enough to put car ads in other women's magazines, too, thus freeing a few pages from the hothouse of fashion-beauty-food ads.

But long after figures showed a third, even a half, of many car models being bought by women, U.S. makers continued to be uncomfortable addressing women. Unlike foreign carmakers, Detroit never quite learned the secret of creating intelligent ads that exclude no one, and then placing them in women's magazines to overcome past exclusion. (*Ms.* readers were so grateful for a routine Honda ad featuring rack and pinion steering, for instance, that they sent fan mail.) Even now, Detroit continues to ask, "Should we make special ads for women?" Perhaps that's why some foreign cars still have a disproportionate share of the U.S. women's market.

• In the *Ms.* Gazette, we do a brief report on a congressional hearing into chemicals used in hair dyes that are absorbed through the skin and may be carcinogenic. Newspapers report this too, but Clairol, a Bristol-Myers subsidiary that makes dozens of products—a few of which have just begun to advertise in *Ms.*—is outraged. Not at newspapers or newsmagazines, just at us. It's bad enough that *Ms.* is the only women's magazine refusing to provide the usual "complementary" articles and beauty photos, but to criticize one of their categories—*that* is going too far.

We offer to publish a letter from Clairol telling its side of the story. In an excess of solicitousness, we even put this letter in the Gazette, not in Letters to the Editors where it belongs. Nonetheless—and in spite of surveys that show *Ms.* readers are active women who use more of almost everything Clairol makes than do the readers of any other women's magazine—*Ms.* gets almost none of these ads for the rest of its natural life.

Meanwhile, Clairol changes its hair coloring formula, apparently in response to the hearings we reported.

• Our saleswomen set out early to attract ads for consumer electronics: sound equipment, calculators, computers, VCRs, and the like. We know that our readers are determined to be included in the technological revolution. We know from reader surveys that *Ms.* readers are buying this stuff in numbers as high as those of magazines like *Playboy;* or "men 18 to 34," the prime targets of the consumer electronics industry. Moreover, unlike traditional women's products that our readers buy but don't need to read articles about, these are subjects they want covered in our pages. There actually *is* a supportive editorial atmosphere.

"But women don't understand technology," say executives at the end of ad presentations. "Maybe not," we respond, "but neither do men—and we all buy it."

"If women *do* buy it," say the decision-makers, "they're asking their husbands and boyfriends what to buy first." We produce letters from *Ms.* readers saying how turned off they are when salesmen say things like "Let me know when your husband can come in."

After several years of this, we get a few ads for compact sound systems. Some of them come from JVC, whose vice president, Harry Elias, is trying to convince his Japanese bosses that there is something called a women's market. At his invitation, I find myself speaking at huge trade shows in Chicago and Las Vegas, trying to persuade JVC dealers that showrooms don't have to be locker rooms where women are made to feel unwelcome. But as it turns out, the shows themselves are part of the problem. In Las Vegas, the only women around the technology displays are seminude models serving champagne. In Chicago, the big attraction is Marilyn Chambers, who followed Linda Lovelace of *Deep Throat* fame as Chuck Traynor's captive and/or employee. VCRs are being demonstrated with her porn videos.

In the end, we get ads for a car stereo now and then, but no VCRs; some IBM personal computers, but no Apple or Japanese ones. We notice that office magazines like *Working Woman* and *Savvy* don't benefit as much as they should from office equipment ads either. In the electronics world, women and technology seem mutually exclusive. It remains a decade behind even Detroit.

• Because we get letters from little girls who love toy trains, and who ask our help in changing ads and box-top photos that feature little boys only, we try to get toy-train ads from Lionel. It turns out that Lionel executives *have* been concerned about little girls. They made a pink train, and were surprised when it didn't sell.

Lionel bows to consumer pressure with a photograph of a boy *and* a girl—but only on some of their boxes. They fear that, if trains are associated with girls, they will be devalued in the minds of boys. Needless to say, *Ms.* gets no train ads, and little girls remain a mostly unexplored market. By 1986, Lionel is put up for sale.

But for different reasons, we haven't had much luck with other kinds of toys either. In spite of many articles on child-rearing: an annual listing of nonsexist, multi-racial toys by Letty Cottin Pogrebin; Stories for Free Children, a regular feature also edited by Letty; and other prizewinning features for or about children, we get virtually no toy ads. Generations of *Ms.* saleswomen explain to toy manufacturers that a larger proportion of *Ms.* readers have preschool children than do the readers of other women's magazines, but this industry can't believe feminists have or care about children.

• When *Ms.* begins, the staff decides not to accept ads for feminine hygiene sprays or cigarettes: they are damaging and carry no appropriate health warnings. Though we don't think we should tell our readers what to do, we do think we should provide facts so they can decide for themselves. Since the antismoking lobby has been pressing for health warnings on cigarette ads, we decide to take them only as they comply.

Philip Morris is among the first to do so. One of its brands, Virginia Slims, is also sponsoring women's tennis and the first national polls of women's opinions. On the other hand, the Virginia Slims theme, "You've come a long way, baby," has more than a "baby" problem. It makes smoking a symbol of progress for women.

We explain to Philip Morris that this slogan won't do well in our pages, but they are convinced its success with some women means it will work with *all* women. Finally, we agree to publish an ad for a Virginia Slims calendar as a test. The letters from readers are critical—and smart. For instance: Would you show a black man picking cotton, the same man in a Cardin suit, and symbolize the antislavery and civil rights movements by smoking? Of course not. But instead of honoring the test results, the Philip Morris people seem angry to be proven wrong. They take away ads for *all* their many brands.

This costs *Ms.* about $250,000 the first year. After five years, we can no longer keep track. Occasionally, a new set of executives listens to *Ms.* saleswomen, but because we won't take Virginia Slims, not one Philip Morris product returns to our pages for the next 16 years.

Gradually, we also realize our naiveté in thinking we *could* decide against taking cigarette ads. They became a disproportionate support of magazines the moment they were banned on television, and few magazines could compete and survive without them: certainly not *Ms.*, which lacks so many other categories. By the time statistics in the 1980s showed that women's rate of lung cancer was approaching men's, the necessity of taking cigarette ads has become a kind of prison.

• General Mills, Pillsbury, Carnation, DelMonte, Dole, Kraft, Stouffer, Hormel, Nabisco: you name the food giant, we try it. But no matter how desirable the *Ms.* readership, our lack of recipes is lethal.

We explain to them that placing food ads *only* next to recipes associates food with work. For many women, it is a negative that works *against* the ads. Why not place food ads in diverse media without recipes (thus reaching more men, who are now a third of the shoppers in supermarkets anyway), and leave the recipes to specialty magazines like *Gourmet* (a third of whose readers are also men)?

These arguments elicit interest, but except for an occasional ad for a convenience food, instant coffee, diet drinks, yogurt, or such extras as avocados and almonds, this mainstay of the publishing industry stays closed to us. Period.

• Traditionally, wines and liquors didn't advertise to women: men were thought to make the brand decisions, even if women did the buying. But after endless presentations, we begin to make a dent in this category. Thanks to the unconventional Michel Roux of Carillon Importers (distributors of Grand Marnier, Absolut Vodka, and others), who assumes that food and drink have no gender, some ads are leaving their men's club.

Beermakers are still selling masculinity. It takes *Ms.* fully eight years to get its first beer ad (Michelob). In general, however, liquor ads are less stereotyped in their imagery—and far less controlling of the editorial content around them—than are women's products. But given the underrepresentation of other categories, these very facts tend to create a disproportionate number of alcohol ads in the pages of *Ms.* This in turn dismays readers worried about women and alcoholism.

• We hear in 1980 that women in the Soviet Union have been producing feminist *samizdat* (underground, self-published books) and circulating them throughout the country. As punishment, four of the leaders have been exiled. Though we are operating on our usual shoestring, we solicit individual contributions to send Robin Morgan to interview these women in Vienna.

The result is an exclusive cover story that includes the first news of a populist peace movement against the Afghanistan occupation, a prediction of *glasnost* to come, and a grass-roots, intimate view of Soviet women's lives. From the popular press to women's studies courses, the response is great. The story wins a Front Page award.

Nonetheless, this journalistic coup undoes years of efforts to get an ad schedule from Revlon. Why? Because the Soviet women on our cover *are not wearing makeup.*

• Four years of research and presentations go into convincing airlines that women now make travel choices and business trips. United, the first airline to advertise in *Ms.*, is so impressed with the response from our readers that one of its executives appears in a film for our ad presentations. As usual, good ads get great results.

But we have problems unrelated to such results. For instance: because American Airlines flight attendants include among their labor demands the stipulation that they could choose to have their last names preceded by "Ms." on their name tags—in a long-delayed revolt against the standard, "I am your pilot, Captain Rothgart, and this is your flight attendant, Cindy Sue"—American officials seem to hold the magazine responsible. We get no ads.

There is still a different problem at Eastern. A vice president cancels subscriptions for thousands of copies on Eastern flights. Why? Because he is offended by ads for lesbian poetry journals in the *Ms.* Classified. A "family airline," as he explains to me coldly on the phone, has to "draw the line somewhere."

It's obvious that *Ms.* can't exclude lesbians and serve women. We've been trying to make that point ever since our first issue included an article by and about lesbians, and both Suzanne Levine, our managing editor, and I were lectured by such heavy hitters as Ed Kosner, then editor of *Newsweek* (and now of *New York Magazine*), who insisted that *Ms.* should "position" itself *against* lesbians. But our advertisers have paid to reach a guaranteed number of readers, and soliciting new subscriptions to compensate for Eastern would cost $150,000, plus rebating money in the meantime.

Like almost everything ad-related, this presents an elaborate organizing problem. After days of searching for sympathetic members of the Eastern board, Frank Thomas, president of the Ford Foundation, kindly offers to call Roswell Gilpatrick, a director of Eastern. I talk with Mr. Gilpatrick, who calls Frank Borman, then the president of Eastern. Frank Borman calls me to say that his airline is not in the business of censoring magazines: *Ms.* will be returned to Eastern flights. . . .

• Women of color read *Ms.* in disproportionate numbers. This is a source of pride to *Ms.* staffers, who are also more racially representative than the editors of other women's magazines. But this reality is obscured by ads filled with enough white women to make a reader snowblind.

Pat Carbine remembers mostly "astonishment" when she requested African American, Hispanic, Asian, and other diverse images. Marcia Ann Gillespie, a *Ms.* editor who was previously the editor in chief of *Essence*, witnesses ad bias a second time: having tried for *Essence* to get white advertisers to use black images (Revlon did so eventually, but L'Oréal, Lauder, Chanel, and other companies never did), she sees similar problems getting integrated ads for an integrated magazine. Indeed, the ad world often creates black and Hispanic ads only for black and Hispanic media. In an exact parallel of the fear that marketing a product to women will endanger its appeal to men, the response is usually, "But your [white] readers won't identify."

In fact, those we are able to get—for instance, a Max Factor ad made for *Essence* that Linda Wachner gives us after she becomes president—is praised by white readers, too. But there are pathetically few such images.

• By the end of 1986, production and mailing costs have risen astronomically, ad income is flat, and competition for ads is stiffer than ever. The 60/40 preponderance of edit over ads that we promised to readers becomes 50/50; children's stories, most poetry, and some fiction are casualties of less space: in order to get variety into limited pages, the length (and sometimes the depth) of articles suffers; and, though we do refuse most of the ads that would look like a parody in our pages, we get so worn down that some slip through. . . . Still, readers perform miracles. Though we haven't been able to afford a subscription mailing in two years, they maintain our guaranteed circulation of 450,000.

Nonetheless, media reports on *Ms.* often insist that our unprofitability must be due to reader disinterest. The myth that advertisers simply follow readers is very strong. Not one reporter notes that other comparable magazines our size (say, *Vanity Fair* or *The Atlantic*) have been losing more money in one year than *Ms.* has lost in 16 years. No matter how much never-to-be-recovered cash is poured into starting a magazine or keeping one going, appearances seem to be all that matter. (Which is why we haven't been able to explain our fragile state in public. Nothing causes ad-flight like the smell of nonsuccess.)

My healthy response is anger. My not-so-healthy response is constant worry. Also an obsession with finding one more rescue. There is hardly a night when I don't wake up with sweaty palms and pounding heart, scared that we won't be able to pay the printer or the post office; scared most of all that closing our doors will hurt the women's movement.

Out of chutzpah and desperation, I arrange a lunch with Leonard Lauder, president of Estée Lauder. With the exception of Clinique (the brainchild of Carol Phillips), none of Lauder's hundreds of products has been advertised in *Ms.*. A year's schedule of ads for just three or four of them could save us. Indeed, as the scion of a family-owned company whose ad practices are followed by the beauty industry, he is one of the few men who could liberate many pages in all women's magazines just by changing his mind about "complementary copy."

Over a lunch that costs more than we can pay for some articles, I explain the need for his leadership. I also lay out the record of *Ms.*: more literary and journalistic prizes won, more new issues introduced into the mainstream, new writers discovered, and impact on society than any other magazine: more articles that became books, stories that became movies, ideas that became television series, and newly advertised products that became profitable: and, most important for him, a place for his ads to reach women who aren't reachable through any other women's magazine. Indeed, if there is one constant characteristic of the ever-changing *Ms.* readership, it is their impact as leaders. Whether it's waiting until later to have first babies, or pioneering PABA as sun protection in cosmetics, *whatever* they are doing today, a third to a half of American women will be doing three to five years from now. It's never failed.

But, he says, *Ms.* readers are not *our* women. They're not interested in things like fragrance and blush-on. If they were, *Ms.* would write articles about them.

On the contrary, I explain, surveys show they are more likely to buy such things than the readers of, say, *Cosmopolitan* or *Vogue*. They're good customers because they're out in the world enough to need several sets of everything: home, work, purse, travel, gym, and so on. They just don't need to read articles about these things. Would he ask a men's magazine to publish monthly columns on how to shave before he advertised Aramis products (his line for men)?

He concedes that beauty features are often concocted more for advertisers than readers. But *Ms.* isn't appropriate for his ads anyway, he explains. Why? Because Estée Lauder is selling "a kept-woman mentality."

I can't quite believe this. Sixty percent of the users of his products are salaried, and generally resemble *Ms.* readers. Besides, his company has the appeal of having been started by a creative and hardworking woman, his mother, Estée Lauder.

That doesn't matter, he says. He knows his customers, and they would *like* to be kept women. That's why he will never advertise in *Ms.*

In November 1987, by vote of the Ms. Foundation for Education and Communication (*Ms.*'s owner and publisher, the media subsidiary of the Ms. Foundation for Women), *Ms.* was sold to a company whose officers, Australian feminists Sandra Yates and Anne Summers, raised the investment money in their country that *Ms.* couldn't find in its own. They also started *Sassy* for teenage women.

In their two-year tenure, circulation was raised to 550,000 by investment in circulation mailings, and, to the dismay of some readers, editorial features on clothes and new products made a more traditional bid for ads. Nonetheless, ad pages fell below previous levels. In addition, *Sassy*, whose fresh voice and sexual frankness were an unprecedented success with young readers, was targeted by two mothers from Indiana who began, as one of them put it, "calling every Christian organization I could think of." In response to this controversy, several crucial advertisers pulled out.

Such links between ads and editorial content was a problem in Australia, too, but to a lesser degree. "Our readers pay two times more for their magazines," Anne explained, "so advertisers have less power to threaten a magazine's viability."

"I was shocked," said Sandra Yates with characteristic directness. "In Australia, we think you have freedom of the press—but you don't."

Since Anne and Sandra had not met their budget's projections for ad revenue, their investors forced a sale. In October 1989, *Ms.* and *Sassy* were bought by Dale Lang, owner of *Working Mother, Working Woman,* and one of the few independent publishing companies left among the conglomerates. In response to a request from the original *Ms.* staff—as well as to reader letters urging that *Ms.* continue, plus his own belief that *Ms.* would benefit his other magazines by blazing a trail—he agreed to try the ad-free, reader-supported *Ms.* you hold now and to give us complete editorial control. . . .

16

Beauty and the Beast of Advertising

JEAN KILBOURNE

"You're a Halston woman from the very beginning," the advertisement proclaims. The model stares provocatively at the viewer, her long blonde hair waving around her face, her bare chest partially covered by two curved bottles that give the illusion of breasts and a cleavage.

The average American is accustomed to blue-eyed blondes seductively touting a variety of products. In this case, however, the blonde is about five years old.

Advertising is an over $130 billion a year industry and affects all of us throughout our lives. We are each exposed to over 1500 ads a day, constituting perhaps the most powerful educational force in society. The average adult will spend one and one-half years of his/her life watching television commercials. But the ads sell a great deal more than products. They sell values, images and concepts of success and worth, love and sexuality, popularity and normalcy. They tell us who we are and who we should be. Sometimes they sell addictions.

Advertising is the foundation and economic lifeblood of the mass media. The primary purpose of the mass media is to deliver an audience to advertisers.

Adolescents are particularly vulnerable, however, because they are new and inexperienced consumers and are the prime targets of many advertise-

NOTE: Reprinted with permission from *Media&Values* (Winter 1989), published by the Center for Media and Values, Los Angeles.

ments. They are in the process of learning their values and roles and developing their self-concepts. Most teenagers are sensitive to peer pressure and find it difficult to resist or even question the dominant cultural messages perpetuated and reinforced by the media. Mass communication has made possible a kind of nationally distributed peer pressure that erodes private and individual values and standards.

But what does society, and especially teenagers, learn from the advertising messages that proliferate in the mass media? On the most obvious level they learn the stereotypes. Advertising creates a mythical, WASP-oriented world in which no one is ever ugly, overweight, poor, struggling or disabled either physically or mentally (unless you count the housewives who talk to little men in toilet bowls). And it is a world in which people talk only about products.

HOUSEWIVES OR SEX OBJECTS

The aspect of advertising most in need of analysis and change is the portrayal of women. Scientific studies and the most casual viewing yield the same conclusion: Women are shown almost exclusively as housewives or sex objects.

The housewife, pathologically obsessed by cleanliness and lemon-fresh scents, debates cleaning products and worries about her husband's "ring around the collar."

The sex object is a mannequin, a shell. Conventional beauty is her only attribute. She has no lines or wrinkles (which would indicate she had the bad taste and poor judgment to grow older), no scars or blemishes—indeed, she has no pores. She is thin, generally tall and long-legged, and, above all, she is young. All "beautiful" women in advertisements (including minority women), regardless of product or audience, conform to this norm. Women are constantly exhorted to emulate this ideal, to feel ashamed and guilty if they fail, and to feel that their desirability and lovability are contingent upon physical perfection.

CREATING ARTIFICIALITY

The image is artificial and can only be achieved artificially (even the "natural look" requires much preparation and expense). Beauty is something that comes from without: more than one million dollars is spent every hour on cosmetics. Desperate to conform to an ideal and impossible standard, many women go to great lengths to manipulate and change their faces and bodies. A woman is conditioned to view her face as a mask and her body as an object, as *things* separate from and more important than her real self, constantly in need of alteration, improvement, and disguise. She is made to feel dissatisfied with and ashamed of herself, whether she tries to achieve "the look" or not. Objectified constantly by others, she learns to objectify

Promises! Promises!

"The promise of the commercial is not just 'You will have pleasure if you buy our product,' but also (and perhaps more important), 'You will be happy because people will envy you if you have this product.' The spectator of the commercial imagines herself transformed by the product into an object of envy for others—an envy which will justify her loving herself. The commercial image steals her love of herself as she is, and offers it back to her for the price of the product."

—John Berger

Sexist Advertisements:
How to See Through the Soft Sell

Everyone has seen blatantly offensive advertisements that portray women as sexual toys or victims of violence. Such irresponsible advertising has rightly touched off cries of protest and organized action. The following are some of the more subtle ways advertising reinforces cultural values of subservience, domination and inequality between the sexes.

1. **Superiority.** Three common tactics used to establish superiority are size, attention and positioning. . . . Both men and women in [a] Hanes ad appear subservient because of their positions below and behind their partners. The Gable Film Festival poster lends historical reference to the stereotype that women . . . fawn over men yet cannot hold their attention.

2. **Dismemberment.** Women's bodies are often dismembered and treated as separate parts, perpetuating the concept that a woman's body is not connected to her mind and emotions. The hidden message: If a woman has great legs, who cares who she is?

3. **Clowning.** Shown alone in ads, men are often portrayed as secure, powerful and serious. By contrast, women are pictured as playful clowns, perpetuating the attitude that women are childish and cannot be taken seriously.

4. **Canting.** People in control of their lives stand upright, alert and ready to meet the world. In contrast, the bending of body parts conveys unpreparedness, submissiveness and appeasement. [A] Capri ad further exemplifies head and body canting. The woman appears off-balance, insecure and weak. Her upraised hand in front of her face also conveys shame or embarrassment.

5. **Dominance/Violence.** The tragic abuse-affection cycle that many women are trapped in is too often glorified in advertising. . . .

—Research by Media&Values intern Barbie White
from Erving Goffman's Gender Advertisements,
Harper Colophon Books (1979).

herself. (It is interesting to note that one in five college-age women have an eating disorder).

"When *Glamour* magazine surveyed its readers in 1984, 75 percent felt too heavy and only 15 percent felt just right. Nearly half of those who were actually underweight reported feeling too fat and wanting to diet. Among a sample of college women, 40 percent felt overweight when only 12 percent actually were too heavy," according to Rita Freedman in her book *Beauty Bound.*

There is evidence that this preoccupation with weight begins at ever-earlier ages for women. According to a recent article in *New Age Journal*, "even grade-school girls are succumbing to stick-like standards of beauty enforced by a relentless parade of wasp-waisted fashion models, movie stars and pop idols." A study by a University of California professor showed that nearly 80 percent of fourth-grade girls in the Bay Area are watching their weight.

A recent *Wall Street Journal* survey of students in four Chicago-area schools found that more than half the fourth-grade girls were dieting and three-quarters felt they were overweight. One student said, "We don't expect boys to be that handsome. We take them as they are." Another added, "But boys expect girls to be perfect and beautiful. And skinny."

Dr. Steven Levenkrom, author of *The Best Little Girl in the World,* the story of an anorexic, says his blood pressure soars every time he opens a magazine and finds an ad for women's fashions. "If I had my way," he said, "every one of them would have to carry a line saying, 'Caution: This model may be hazardous to your health.' "

Women are also dismembered in commercials, their bodies separated into parts in need of change or improvement. If a woman has "acceptable" breasts, then she must also be sure that her legs are worth watching, her hips slim, her feet sexy, and that her buttocks look nuder under her clothes ("like I'm not wearin' nothin' "). This image is difficult and costly to achieve and impossible to maintain—no one is flawless and everyone ages. Growing older is the great taboo. Women are encouraged to remain little girls ("because innocence is sexier than you think"), to be passive and dependent, never to mature. The contradictory message—"sensual, but not too far from innocence"—places women in a double bind: somehow we are supposed to be both sexy and virginal, experienced and naive, seductive and chaste. The disparagement of maturity is, of course, insulting and frustrating to adult women, and the implication that little girls are seductive is dangerous to real children.

INFLUENCING SEXUAL ATTITUDES

Young people also learn a great deal about sexual attitudes from the media and from advertising in particular. Advertising's approach to sex is pornographic: it reduces people to objects and de-emphasizes human contact and individuality. This reduction of sexuality to a dirty joke and of people to objects is the real obscenity of the culture. Although the sexual sell, overt and subliminal, is at a fevered pitch in most commercials, there is at the same time a notable absence of sex as an important and profound human activity.

There have been some changes in the images of women. Indeed, a "new woman" has emerged in commercials in recent years. She is generally presented as superwoman, who manages to do all the work at home and on the job (with the help of a product, of course, not of her husband or children or friends), or as the liberated woman, who owes her independence and self-esteem to the products she uses. These new images do not represent any real progress but rather create a myth of progress, an illusion that reduces complex sociopolitical problems to mundane personal ones.

Advertising images do not cause these problems, but they contribute to them by creating a climate in which the marketing of women's bodies—the sexual sell and dismemberment, distorted body image ideal and children as sex objects—is seen as acceptable.

This is the real tragedy, that many women internalize these stereotypes and learn their "limitations," thus establishing a self-fulfilling prophecy. If one accepts these mythical and degrading images, to some extent one actualizes them. By remaining unaware of the profound seriousness of the ubiquitous influence, the redundant message and the subliminal impact of advertisements, we ignore one of the most powerful "educational" forces in the culture—one that greatly affects our self-images, our ability to relate to each other, and effectively destroys awareness and action that might help to change that climate.

17

Reading Images Critically

Toward a Postmodern Pedagogy[1]

DOUGLAS KELLNER

. . . I will make some proposals that concern developing *critical media literacy* and the development of competencies in reading images critically, concentrating on some examples from print advertisements. These examples pose in a provocative way the need to expand literacy and cognitive competencies in order to survive the onslaught of media images, messages, and spectacles which are inundating our culture. The goal will be to teach a critical media literacy which will empower individuals to become more autonomous agents, able to emancipate themselves from contemporary forms of domination and able to become more active citizens, eager and competent to engage in processes of social transformation. . . .

READING ADVERTISEMENTS CRITICALLY

As a test case for a critical pedagogy of images, I will take advertising, that prolific and potent source of cultural imagery. Elsewhere, I develop a general theory of advertising and fashion, and review new critical perspectives on advertising (Harms & Kellner, in press; Kellner, in press a). Here I will focus on developing tools to decipher, interpret, and criticize those ubiquitous advertising images that saturate our culture. The phenomenon

---

NOTE: Excerpts reprinted with permission from the Trustees of Boston University. *Journal of Education,* Vol. 170, No. 3, 1988.

of advertising and importance of learning to read advertisements critically is far from trivial, as U.S. society invests over $102 billion a year into advertising, fully two percent of our gross national product, far more money than in education (Association of National Advertisers, 1988, p. 4). This is a crime and a national scandal which alone should concern educators. . . .

Symbolic Images in Virginia Slims and Marlboro Ads

In order to provide an introduction to reading the symbolic images of ads critically, I shall examine some print ads which are readily available for scrutiny and which lend themselves to critical analysis. Print ads are an important section of the advertising world with about fifty percent of advertising revenues going to various print media, while twenty-two percent is expended on television advertising (Association of National Advertisers, 1988, p. 4). Although apologists for the advertising industry claim that advertising is predominantly informative, careful scrutiny of magazine, television, and other imagistic ads indicate that it is overwhelmingly persuasive and symbolic and that its images not only attempt to sell the product by associating it with certain socially desirable qualities, but they sell as well a worldview, a lifestyle, and value system congruent with the imperatives of consumer capitalism.

To illustrate this point, let us look, first, at two cigarette ads: a 1981 Marlboro ad aimed primarily at male smokers and a 1983 Virginia Slims ad which tries to convince women that it is cool to smoke and that the product being advertised is perfect for the "modern" woman.[2] Corporations like the tobacco industry undertake campaigns to associate their product with positive and desirable images and gender models. Thus in the 1950s, Marlboro undertook a campaign to associate its cigarette with masculinity, associating smoking its product with being a "real man." Marlboro had been previously packaged as a milder women's cigarette, and the "Marlboro Man" campaign was an attempt to capture the male cigarette market with images of archetypically masculine characters. Since the cowboy Western image provided a familiar icon of masculinity, independence, and ruggedness, it was the preferred symbol for the campaign. Subsequently, the Marlboro Man became a part of American folklore and a readily identifiable cultural symbol.

Such symbolic images in advertising attempt to create an association between the products offered and socially desirable and meaningful traits in order to produce the impression that if one wants to be a certain type of person, for instance, to be a "real man," then one should buy Marlboro cigarettes. Consequently, for decades Marlboro used the cowboy figure as the symbol of masculinity and the center of their ads. In a postmodern image culture, individuals get their very identity from these figures; thus advertising becomes an important and overlooked mechanism of socialization as well as manager of consumer demand.

Ads form textual systems with basic components which are interrelated in ways that positively position the product. The main components of the classical Marlboro ad is its conjunction of nature, the cowboy, horses, and the cigarette. This system associates the Marlboro cigarette with masculinity, power, and nature . . . In one recent ad, a cowboy is a relatively small figure, dwarfed by the images of snow, trees, and sky. Whereas in earlier Marlboro ads, the Marlboro Man loomed largely in the center of the frame, now images of nature are highlighted. Why this shift?

All ads are social texts which respond to key developments during the period in which they appear. During the 1980s, media reports concerning the health hazard of cigarettes became widespread—a message was high-lighted in the mandatory box at the bottom of the ad that read "The Surgeon General Has Determined That Cigarette Smoking Is Dangerous to Your Health." As a response to this attack, the Marlboro ads now feature images of clean, pure, wholesome nature, as if it were "natural" to smoke cigarettes, as if cigarettes were a healthy natural product, an emanation of benign and healthy nature. The ad, in fact, hawks Marlboro Lights and one of the captions describes it as a "low tar cigarette." The imagery is itself light, white, green, snowy, and airy. Through the process of metonomy, or contigu-ous association, the ad tries to associate the cigarettes with light, natural, healthy snow, horses, the cowboy, trees, and sky, as if they were all related natural artifacts, sharing the traits of nature, thus covering over the fact that cigarettes are an artificial, synthetic product, full of dangerous pesticides, preservatives, and other chemicals.[3]

. . . The Marlboro ad also draws on images of tradition (the cowboy), hard work . . . (this cowboy is doing some serious work), caring for animals, and other desirable traits, as if smoking were a noble activity, metonomically equivalent to these other positive social activities. The images, texts, and product shown in the ad thus provide a symbolic construct which tries to cover and camouflage contradictions between the heavy work and the light cigarette, between the natural scene and the artificial product, between the cool and healthy outdoors scene and the hot and unhealthy activity of smoking, and the rugged masculinity of the Marlboro Man and the Light cigarette, originally targeted at women. In fact, this latter contradiction can be explained by the marketing ploy of suggesting to men that they can be both highly masculine, like the Marlboro Man, and smoke a supposedly healthier cigarette, while also appealing to macho women who might enjoy smoking a "man's" cigarette which is also lighter and healthier as women's cigarettes are supposed to be.

A 1983 Virginia Slims ad also attempts to associate its product with socially desired traits and offers subject positions with which women can identify. The Virginia Slims textual system classically includes a vignette at the top of the ad with a picture underneath of the Virginia Slims woman next to the prominently displayed package of cigarettes. . . . The top of the ad features a framed box that contains the narrative images and message, which is linked to the changes in the situation of women portrayed through a contrast with the modern woman below. The caption under the boxed image of segregated male and female exercise classes in 1903 contains the familiar Virginia Slims slogan "You've come a long way baby." The caption, linked to the Virginia Slims woman, next to the package of cigarettes, connotes a message of progress, metonomically linking Virginia Slims to the progres-sive woman and modern living. In this ad, it is the linkages and connections between the parts that establish the message which associates Virginia Slims with progress. The ad tells women that it is progressive and socially acceptable to smoke, and it associates Virginia Slims with modernity, social progress, and the desired social trait of slimness.

In fact, Lucky Strike carried out a successful advertising campaign in the 1930s which associated smoking with weight reduction ("Reach for a Lucky instead of a sweet!"), and Virginia Slims plays on this tradition, encapsulated in the very brand name of the product. Note too that the cigarette is a "Lights" variety and that, like the Marlboro ad, it tries to associate its product with health and well-being. The pronounced smile on the woman's face also tries to associate the product with happiness and self-contentment, struggling against the association of smoking with guilt and dangers to one's health. The image of the slender woman, in turn, associated with slimness and lightness, not only associates the product with socially desirable traits, but in turn promotes the ideal type of femininity.

. . . A 1988 Virginia Slims ad, in fact, reveals a considerable transformation in its image of women during the 1980s and a new strategy to persuade women that it is all right and even progressive and ultramodern to smoke. This move points to shifts in the relative power between men and women and discloses new subject positions for women validated by the culture industries.

Once again the sepia-colored framed box at the top of the ad contains an image of a woman serving her man in 1902; the comic pose and irritated look of the woman suggests that such servitude is highly undesirable and its contrast with the Virginia Slims woman (who herself now wears the leather boots and leather gloves and jacket as well) suggests that women have come a long way while the ever-present cigarette associates a woman's right to smoke in public with social progress. This time the familiar "You've come a long way, baby" is absent, perhaps because the woman pictured would hardly tolerate being described as baby and because indeed women's groups had been protesting the sexist and demeaning label in the slogan. We note, too, the transformation of the image of the woman in the Virginia Slims ad. No longer the smiling, cute, and wholesome potential wife of the earlier ad, she is now more threatening, more sexual, less wifely, and more masculine. The sunglasses connote the distance from the male gaze which she wants to preserve and the leather jacket with the military insignia connotes that she is equal to men, able to carry on a masculine role, and is stronger and more autonomous than women of the past.

The 1988 ad is highly anti-patriarchal and even expresses hostility toward men with an overweight man with glasses and handle bar mustache looking slightly ridiculous while it is clear that the woman is being held back by ridiculous fashion and intolerable social roles. The new Virginia Slims woman, however, who completely dominates the scene, is the epitome of style and power. This strong woman can easily take in hand and enjoy the phallus, i.e., the cigarette as the sign of male power accompanied by the male dress and military insignia, and serve as an icon of female glamour as well. This ad links power, glamour, and sexuality and offers a model of female power, associated with the cigarette and smoking. Ads work in part by generating dissatisfaction and by offering images of transformation, of a "new you." This particular ad promotes dissatisfaction with traditional images and presents a new image of a more powerful woman, a new lifestyle and identity for the Virginia Slims smoker.

Although "Lights" and "Ultra Lights" continue to be the dominant Virginia Slims types, the phrase does not appear as a highlighted caption as it used to appear and the package does not appear either. No doubt this "heavy" woman contradicts the light image and the ad seems to want to connote power and (a dubious) progress for women rather than slimness or lightness. Yet the woman's teased and flowing blonde hair, her perfect teeth which form an obliging smile, and, especially her crotch positioned in the ad in a highly suggestive and inviting fashion code her as a symbol of beauty and sexuality, albeit more autonomous and powerful. In these ways, the images associate the products advertised with certain socially desirable traits and convey messages concerning the symbolic benefits accrued to those who consume the product. . . .

IMPLICATIONS FOR EDUCATION AND PUBLIC POLICY

I indicated that in 1988 more than $102 billion or roughly two percent of the U.S. gross National Product was spent on advertising. Advertising expenditures in 1950 were about $6.5 billion a year while by 1970 $40 billion a year was squandered, and by 1980 $56 billion was wasted. Advertising expenditure almost doubled from 1980 to 1986, pointing to an alarming expansion of advertising during the 1980s. When one considers that an equal amount of money is spent on design, packaging, marketing, and product display, one grasps that a prodigious amount of money is expended on advertising and marketing. For example, only eight cents of the cosmetics sales dollar goes to pay for ingredients; the rest goes to packaging, promotion, and marketing (Goldman, 1987, p. 697). Consequently, consumer capitalism constitutes a tremendous waste of resources, and forces consumers to pay high prices for products that they are induced to think that they need for success, popularity, self-esteem, and other socially desirable qualities.

This vicious process of waste and manipulation during an age of growing scarcity of resources is a national scandal and raises the question of what can be done to combat the excesses of consumer capitalism. Such questions make advertising a public policy issue and a contested terrain subject to critique and [to] struggle with. The question of cigarette advertising immediately raises the issue of whether all cigarette advertising should be banned, as television cigarette advertising was banned in the 1970s. The very fact of cigarettes, a highly addictive and potentially dangerous uncontrolled substance, raises questions concerning how to deal with this public health menace. While the Surgeon General has been helping to publicize the dangers of cigarette smoking, surely stronger actions could be taken.

In the light of the massive federal deficit, heavy user taxes on cigarettes, alcohol, and other "sin" products might, in conjunction with a public health campaign, reduce the harmful effects of cigarette smoking, drinking, drug use, and so on. Considering the social effects of advertising also raises the issue of whether advertising should be subject to taxation; currently, it is written off by corporations as a business expense, thus passing off advertising expenses to the taxpayer, as well as the consumer. Congress could also consider disallowing tax writeoffs for advertising and could also tax advertising expenditures and advertising agencies at a higher rate, given the dubious impact of advertising on U.S. society and the massive waste of resources, talent, and human energies.[4] At the very least television advertising could be taxed as could print advertising for cigarettes, alcohol, and other socially undesirable products. The question of advertising also raises the question of the effects of advertising on our media system and whether a commercial media system really provides the best model.[5] . . .

NOTES

1. For Henry Giroux with respect and affection.

2. The method of reading ads and interpretation of advertising which follows is indebted to the work of Robert Goldman (1987, in press). See also John Berger (1973) and Judith Williamson (1978) for excellent pedagogical introductions to reading advertisements critically.

3. The tobacco leaf is (for insects) one of the most sweet and tasty of all plants—and therefore it requires a large amount of pesticides to keep insects from devouring it. Cigarette makers use chemicals to give a distinctive smell and taste to the product and use preservatives to keep it from spoiling. Other chemicals are used to regulate the burning process and to filter out tars and nicotine. While these latter ingredients are the most publicized dangers in cigarette smoking, actually the pesticides, chemicals, and preservatives may well be more deadly. Scandalously, cigarettes are one of the most unregulated products in the U.S. consumer economy (European countries, for example, carefully regulate the pesticides used in tobacco growing and the synthetics used in cigarette production). Government-sponsored experiments on the effects of cigarette smoking also use generic cigarettes, which may not have the chemicals and preservatives of name brands; thus no really scientifically accurate major survey on the dangers of cigarette smoking has ever been done by the U.S. government. The major media, many of which are part of conglomerates with heavy interests in the tobacco industry, or which depend on cigarette advertising for revenue, have never really undertaken to expose to the public the real dangers concerned with cigarette smoking and the scandalous neglect of this issue by government and media in the United States. Cigarette addiction is thus a useful object lesson in the unperceived dangers and destructive elements of the consumer society and the ways these dangers are covered over. (My own information on the cigarette industry derives from an *Alternative Views* television interview which Frank Morrow and I did with Bill Drake on the research which will constitute his forthcoming book.)

4. For an interesting revelation of how the advertising world itself is worried about forthcoming taxes on their product, see "What's Ahead? Read My Lips: Taxes," *Advertising Age*, Nov. 7, 1988, p. 1.

5. Further explorations of what can be done about advertising can be found in Harms and Kellner (in press) and in my forthcoming book *Television, Politics, and Society: Toward a Critical Theory of Television* (Kellner, in press b).

REFERENCES

Association of National Advertisers. (1988). *The role of advertising in America*. New York: Author.

Berger, J. (1973). *Ways of seeing*. New York: Viking.

Goldman, R. (1987). Marketing fragrances: Advertising and the production of commodity signs. *Theory, Culture & Society, 4,* 691-725.

Goldman, R. (in press). The mortise and the frame. *Critical Studies in Mass Communication.*

Harms, J., & Kellner, D. (in press). *New theoretical perspectives on advertising.*

Kellner, D. (in press a). Fashion, advertising, and the consumer society. In *Radical perspectives on mass communications and culture.* Newbury Park, CA: Sage.

Kellner, D. (in press b). *Television, politics, and society: Toward a critical theory of television.* Boulder, CO: Westview.

Williamson, J. (1978). *Decoding advertisements.* London: Marion Boyer.

18

Advertising and the Construction of Violent White Masculinity

JACKSON KATZ

Violence is one of the most pervasive and serious problems we face in the United States. Increasingly, academics, community activists and politicians have been paying attention to the role of the mass media in producing, reproducing and legitimating this violence.[1]

Unfortunately, however, much of the mainstream debate about the effects of media violence on violence in the "real" world fails to include an analysis of gender. Although, according to the Federal Bureau of Investigation (1992), approximately 90% of violent crime is committed by males, magazine headline writers talk about "youth" violence and "kids'" love affair with guns. It is unusual even to hear mention of "masculinity" or "manhood" in these discussions, much less a thorough deconstruction of the gender order and the way that cultural definitions of masculinity and femininity might be implicated. Under these conditions, a class-conscious discussion of masculine gender construction is even less likely.

There is a glaring absence of a thorough body of research into the power of cultural images of masculinity. But this is not surprising. It is in fact consistent with the lack of attention paid to other dominant groups. Discussions about racial representation in media, for example, tend to focus on African Americans, Asians or Hispanics, and not on Anglo Whites.[2] Writing about the representation of Whiteness as an ethnic category in mainstream film, Richard Dyer (1988, cited in Hanke, 1992) argues that "white power secures its dominance by seeming not to be anything in particular;" "Whiteness" is constructed as the norm against which nondominant groups are defined as "other." Robert Hanke (1992), in an article about hegemonic masculinity in transition, argues that masculinity, like Whiteness, "does not appear to be a cultural/historical category at all, thus rendering invisible the privileged position from which (white) men in general are able to artic- ulate their interests to the exclusion of the interests of women, men and women of color, and children" (p. 186).

There has been some discussion, since the mid-1970s, of the ways in which cultural definitions of White manhood have been shaped by stereo- typical representations in advertising. One area of research has looked at the creation of modern masculine archetypes such as the Marlboro Man. But there has been little attention, in scholarship or antiviolence activism, paid to the relationship between the construction of violent masculinity in what Sut Jhally (1990) refers to as the "commodity image-system" of advertising and the pandemic of violence committed by boys and men in the homes and streets of the United States.

This chapter is an attempt to sketch out some of the ways in which hegemonic constructions of masculinity in mainstream magazine advertis- ing normalize male violence. Theorists and researchers in profeminist soci- ology and men's studies in recent years have developed the concept of *masculinities*, as opposed to *masculinity*, to more adequately describe the complexities of male social position, identity and experience. At any given time, the class structure and gender order produce numerous masculinities stratified by socioeconomic class, racial and ethnic difference and sexual orientation. The central delineation is between the hegemonic, or dominant, masculinity (generally, White and middle-class) and the subordinated mas- culinities.

But although there are significant differences between the various mas- culinities, in patriarchal culture, violent behavior is typically gendered male. This doesn't mean that all men are violent but that violent behavior is con- sidered masculine (as opposed to feminine) behavior. This masculine gen- dering of violence in part explains why the movie *Thelma and Louise* touched such a chord: Women had appropriated, however briefly, the male preroga- tive for, and identification with, violence.

One need not look very closely to see how pervasive is the cultural imagery linking various masculinities to the potential for violence. One key source of constructions of dominant masculinity is the movie industry, which has introduced into the culture a seemingly endless stream of violent male icons. Tens of millions of people, disproportionately male and young, flock to theaters and rent videocassettes of the "action-adventure" (a Holly- wood euphemism for *violent*) films of Arnold Schwarzenegger, Sylvester Stallone, Bruce Willis, et al.

These cultural heroes rose to prominence in an era, the mid-to-late 1970s into the 1980s, in which working-class White males had to contend with increasing economic instability and dislocation, the perception of gains by people of color at the expense of the White working class, and a women's movement that overtly challenged male hegemony. In the face of these pressures, then, it is not surprising that White men (especially but not exclusively working-class) would latch onto big, muscular, violent men as cinematic heroes. For many males who were experiencing unsettling changes, one area of masculine power remained attainable: physical size and strength and the ability to use violence successfully.

Harry Brod (1987) and other theorists have argued that macro changes in postindustrial capitalism have created deep tensions in the various masculinities. For example, according to Brod,

> Persisting images of masculinity hold that "real men" are physically strong, aggressive, and in control of their work. Yet the structural dichotomy between manual and mental labor under capitalism means that no one's work fulfills all these conditions.
>
> Manual laborers work for others at the low end of the class spectrum, while management sits at a desk. Consequently, while the insecurities generated by these contradictions are personally dissatisfying to men, these insecurities also impel them to cling all the more tightly to sources of masculine identity validation offered by the system. (p. 14)

One way that the system allows working class men (of various races) the opportunity for what Brod refers to as "masculine identity validation" is through the use of their body as an instrument of power, dominance and control. For working-class males, who have less access to more abstract forms of masculinity-validating power (economic power, workplace authority), the physical body and its potential for violence provide a concrete means of achieving and asserting "manhood."

At any given time, individual as well as groups of men are engaged in an ongoing process of creating and maintaining their own masculine identities. Advertising, in a commodity-driven consumer culture, is an omnipresent and rich source of gender ideology. Contemporary ads are filled with images of "dangerous"-looking men. Men's magazines and mainstream newsweeklies are rife with ads featuring violent male icons, such as uniformed football players, big-fisted boxers and leather-clad bikers. Sports magazines aimed at men, and televised sporting events, carry millions of dollars worth of military ads. In the past decade, there have been hundreds of ads for products designed to help men develop muscular physiques, such as weight training machines and nutritional supplements.

Historically, use of gender in advertising has stressed difference, implicitly and even explicitly reaffirming the "natural" dissimilarity of males and females. In late 20th century U.S. culture, advertising that targets young White males (with the exception of fashion advertising, which often features more of an androgynous male look) has the difficult task of stressing gender difference in an era characterized by a loosening of rigid gender distinctions. Stressing gender difference in this context means defining masculinity in opposition to femininity. This requires constantly reasserting what is masculine and what is feminine. One of the ways this is accomplished, in the image system, is to equate masculinity with violence (and femininity with passivity).

The need to differentiate from the feminine by asserting masculinity in the form of power and aggression might at least partially account for the high degree of male violence in contemporary advertising, as well as in video games, children's toys, cartoons, Hollywood film and the sports culture.

By helping to differentiate masculinity from femininity, images of masculine aggression and violence—including violence against women—afford young males across class a degree of self-respect and security (however illusory) within the more socially valued masculine role.

VIOLENT WHITE MASCULINITY
IN ADVERTISING

The appeal of violent behavior for men, including its rewards, is coded into mainstream advertising in numerous ways: from violent male icons (such as particularly aggressive athletes or superheroes) overtly threatening consumers to buy products, to ads that exploit men's feelings of not being big, strong or violent enough by promising to provide them with products that will enhance those qualities. These codes are present in television and radio commercials as well, but this chapter focuses on mainstream American magazine ads (*Newsweek, People, Sports Illustrated*, etc.), from the early 1990s.

Several recurring themes in magazine advertising targeting men help support the equation of White masculinity and violence. Among them are violence as genetically programmed male behavior, the use of military and sports symbolism to enhance the masculine appeal and identification of products, the association of muscularity with ideal masculinity, and the equation of heroic masculinity with violent masculinity. Let us now consider, briefly, each of these themes.

Violence as Genetically Programmed Male Behavior. One way that advertisers demonstrate the "masculinity" of a product or service is through the use of violent male icons or types from popular history. This helps to associate the product with manly needs and pursuits that presumably have existed from time immemorial. It also furthers the ideological premise, disguised as common sense, that men have always been aggressive and brutal, and that their dominance over women is biologically based. "Historical" proof for this is shown in a multitude of ways.

An ad for the Chicago Mercantile Exchange, an elite financial institution, depicts a medieval battlefield where muscle-bound toy figurines, accompanied by paradoxically muscular skeleton men, prepare to engage in a sword fight. They might wear formal suits and sit behind desks, the ad implies, but the men in high finance (and those whose money they manage) are actually rugged warriors. Beneath the veneer of wealth and class privilege, *all* men are really brutes. The text reads: "How the Masters of the Universe Overcame the Attack of the Deutschmarks."

An ad for Trojan condoms features a giant-sized Roman centurion, in full uniform, muscles rippling, holding a package of condoms as he towers over the buildings of a modern city. Condom manufacturers know that the purchase and use of condoms by men can be stressful, partially because penis size, in popular Western folklore, is supposedly linked to virility. One way to assuage the anxieties of male consumers is to link the product with a recognizably violent (read: masculine) male archetype. It is no coincidence that the two leading brands of condoms in the United States are named for ancient warriors and kings (Trojan and Ramses).

Sometimes products with no immediately apparent connection to gender or violence nonetheless make the leap. An ad for Dell computers, for example, shows a painting of a group of White cowboys on horseback shooting at mounted Indians who are chasing them. The copy reads "Being Able to Run Faster Could Come in Real Handy." The cowboys are foregrounded and the viewers are positioned to identify with them against the Indian "other." The cowboys' violence is depicted as defensive, a construction that was historically used to justify genocide. The ad explains that "you never know when somebody (read: Indians, Japanese business competitors) is going to come around the corner and surprise you." It thus masculinizes the White middle-class world of the computer business by using the violent historical metaphor of cowboys versus Indians.

An even more sinister use of historical representations involves portraying violence that would not be acceptable if shown in contemporary settings. Norwegian Cruise Line, for example, in an ad that ran in major newsweekly magazines, depicted a colorful painting of a scene on a ship's deck, set sometime in the pirate era, where men, swords drawn, appear simultaneously to be fighting each other while a couple of them are carrying off women. The headline informs us that Norwegian is the "first cruise line whose entertainment doesn't revolve around the bar."

It is highly doubtful that the cruise line could have set what is clearly a rape or gang rape scenario on a modern ship. It would no doubt have prompted feminist protests about the company's glorification of the rape of women. Controversy is avoided by depicting the scene as historical.[3] But Norwegian Cruise Line, which calls itself "The Pleasure Ships," in this ad reinforces the idea that rape is a desirable male pastime. Whether intentional or not, the underlying message is that real men (pirates, swashbucklers) have always enjoyed it.

The Use of Military and Sports Symbolism to Enhance the Masculine Identification and Appeal of Products. Advertisers who want to demonstrate the unquestioned manliness of their products can do so by using one of the two key subsets in the symbolic image system of violent masculinity: the military and sports. Uniformed soldiers and players, as well as their weapons and gear, appear frequently in ads of all sorts. Many of the Camel Smooth Character cartoon ads, for example, display submarines surfacing or fighter jets streaking by as Joe Camel stands confidently in the foreground. One ad features Joe Camel himself wearing an air force bomber pilot's jacket. The message to the young boys and adolescent males targeted by the campaign is obvious: Violence (as signified by the military vehicles) is cool and suave. The sexy blond woman gazing provocatively at the James Bond-like camel provides female ratification of Joe's masculinity.

Ads for the military itself also show the linkage between masculinity and force. The U.S. military spends more than $100 million annually on advertising. Not surprisingly, armed services advertisements appear disproportionately on televised sporting events and in sports and so-called men's magazines. Military ads are characterized by exciting outdoor action scenes with accompanying text replete with references to "leadership," "respect," and "pride." Although these ads sometimes promote the educational and financial benefits of military service, what they're really selling to young working-class males is a vision of masculinity—adventurous, aggressive and violent—that provides men of all classes with a standard of "real manhood" against which to judge themselves.

Boxers and football players appear in ads regularly, promoting products from underwear to deodorants. Sometimes the players are positioned simply to sanction the masculinity of a product. For example, an ad for Bugle Boy clothing depicts a clean-cut young White man, dressed in Bugle Boy jeans and posed in a crouching position, kneeling on a football. Standing behind him, inexplicably, is a large, uniformed football player flexing his muscles. The only copy says, in bold letters, "Bugle Boy Men." It seems reasonable to infer that the goal of this ad was to shore up the masculine image of a product whose name (Bugle Boy) subverts its macho image. The uniformed football player, a signifier of violent masculinity, achieves this task by visually transmitting the message: Real men wear Bugle Boy.

Advertisers know that using high-profile violent male athletes can help to sell products, such as yogurt and light beer, that have historically been gendered female. Because violence establishes masculinity, if these guys (athletes) use traditionally "female" products, they don't lose their masculinity. Rather, the masculinity of the product—and hence the size of the potential market—increases. Miller Brewing Company proved the efficacy of this approach in their long-running television ad campaign for Lite beer. The Miller Lite campaign, which first appeared in the early 1970s, helped bring Miller to the top of the burgeoning light beer market and is often referred to as the most successful TV ad campaign in history.

The Association of Muscularity With Ideal Masculinity. Men across socioeconomic class and race might feel insecure in their masculinity, relatively powerless or vulnerable in the economic sphere and uncertain about how to respond to the challenges of women in many areas of social relations. But, in general, males continue to have an advantage over females in the area of physical size and strength. Because one function of the image system is to legitimate and reinforce existing power relations, representations that equate masculinity with the qualities of size, strength and violence thus become more prevalent.

The anthropologist Alan Klein (1993)[4] has looked at how the rise in popularity of bodybuilding is linked to male insecurity. "Muscles," he argues, "are about more than just the functional ability of men to defend home and hearth or perform heavy labor. Muscles are markers that separate men from each other and, most important perhaps, from women. And while he may not realize it, every man—every accountant, science nerd, clergyman, or cop—is engaged in a dialogue with muscles" (p. 16).

Advertising is one area of the popular culture that helps feed this "dialogue." Sports and other magazines with a large male readership are filled with ads offering men products and services to enhance their muscles. Often these ads explicitly equate muscles with violent power, as in an ad for a Marcy weight machine that tells men to "Arm Yourself" under a black and white photograph of a toned, muscular White man, biceps and forearms straining, in the middle of a weight lifting workout. The military, too, offers to help men enhance their bodily prowess. An ad for the Army National Guard shows three slender young men, Black and White, working out, over copy that reads "Get a Part-Time Job in Our Body Shop."

The discourse around muscles as signifiers of masculine power involves not only working-class men but also middle- and upper-class males. This is apparent in the male sports subculture, where size and strength are valued by men across class and racial boundaries. But muscularity as masculinity is also a theme in advertisements aimed at upper-income males. Many advertisers use images of physically rugged or muscular male bodies to masculinize products and services geared to elite male consumers. An ad for the business insurance firm Brewer and Lord uses a powerful male body as a metaphor for the more abstract form of (financial) power. The ad shows the torso of a muscular man curling a barbell, accompanied by a headline that reads "the benefits of muscle defined." The text states that "the slow building of strength and definition is no small feat. In fact, that training has shaped the authority that others see in you, as well."

Saab, targeting an upscale, educated market, bills itself as "the most intelligent car ever built." But in one ad, they call their APC Turbo "the muscle car with a social conscience"—which signals to wealthy men that by driving a Saab they can appropriate the working-class tough guy image associated with the concept of a "muscle car" while making clear their more privileged class position.

The Equation of Heroic Masculinity With Violent Masculinity. The cultural power of Hollywood film in the construction of violent masculinity is not limited to the movies themselves. In fact, many more people see the advertising for a given film than see the film itself.

Advertising budgets for major Hollywood releases typically run in the millions of dollars. Larger-than-life billboards enhance the heroic stature of the icons. Movie ads appear frequently on prime time TV and daily in newspapers and magazines. Not surprisingly, these ads highlight the movies' most violent and sexually titillating scenes.

Violence on-screen, like that in real life, is perpetrated overwhelmingly by males. Males constitute the majority of the audience for violent films, as well as violent sports such as football and hockey. It is important to note, then, that what is being sold is not just "violence," but rather a glamorized form of violent masculinity.

Guns are an important signifier of virility and power and hence are an important part of the way violent masculinity is constructed and then sold to audiences. In fact, the presence of guns in magazine and newspaper ads is crucial in communicating the extent of a movie's violent content. Because so many films contain explicit violence, images of gun-toting macho males (police detectives, old west gunslingers, futuristic killing machines) pervade the visual landscape.

CONCLUSION

Recent research in sociology, media and cultural studies strongly suggests that we need to develop a much more sophisticated approach to understanding cultural constructions of masculinity. Feminists, who have been at the forefront in studying the social construction of gender, have, historically, focused on images and representations of women. Clearly we need a similarly intensive examination of the representation of men—particularly in light of the crisis of men's violence in our society.

This chapter focuses attention on constructions of violent White masculinity in mainstream magazine advertising. But we need also to examine critically a number of other areas where violent masculinities are produced and legitimated: comic books, toys, the sports culture, comedy, interactive video, music video, pornography. This will help us to understand more fully the links between the construction of gender and the prevalence of violence, which might then lead to effective antiviolence interventions.

NOTES

1. *Violence* refers to immediate or chronic situations that result in injury to the psychological, social or physical well-being of individuals or groups. For the purpose of this chapter, I will use the American Psychological Association's (APA) more specific definition of interpersonal violence. Although acknowledging the multidimensional nature of violence, the APA Commission on Violence and Youth defines interpersonal violence as "behavior by persons against persons that threatens, attempts, or completes intentional infliction of physical or psychological harm" (APA, 1993, p. 1).

2. Although hegemonic constructions of masculinity affect men of all races, there are important variables due to racial differences. Because it is not practical to do justice to these variables in a chapter of this length, and because the vast majority of images of men in mainstream magazine advertisements are of White men, for the purpose of this chapter, I will focus on the constructions of various White masculinities.

3. Some feminist groups did protest the ad, such as the Cambridge, Massachusetts-based group Challenging Media Images of Women. But the protests never reached a wide audience and had no discernible effect.

4. The article cited here was excerpted from Klein's book *Little Big Men: Bodybuilding Subculture and Gender Construction* (Albany: State University of New York Press, 1993).

REFERENCES

American Psychological Association. (1993). *Violence and youth: Psychology's response.* Washington, DC: Author.

Brod, H. (Ed.). (1987). *The making of masculinities: The new men's studies.* Boston: Allen & Unwin.

Federal Bureau of Investigation. (1992). *Uniform crime reports.* Washington, DC: Author.

Hanke, R. (1992). Redesigning men: Hegemonic masculinity in transition. In S. Craig (Ed.), *Men, masculinity and the media* (pp. 185-198). Newbury Park, CA: Sage.

Jhally, S. (1990, July). Image-based culture: Advertising and popular culture. *The World and I,* pp. 508-519.

Klein, A. (1993, January). Little big men. *Northeastern University Magazine,* p. 14-19.

.19

Commodity Lesbianism

DANAE CLARK

> *A commodity appears, at first sight, a very trivial thing, and easily understood. Its analysis shows that it is, in reality, a very queer thing . . .*
>
> Karl Marx, *Capital*[1]

. . . Analyses of female consumerism join a substantial body of other feminist work that "assumes, but leaves unwritten, a heterosexual context for the subject" and thus contributes to the continued invisibility of lesbians.[2]

But lesbians too are consumers. Like heterosexual women they are major purchasers of clothing, household goods and media products. Lesbians have not, however, been targeted as a separate consumer group within the dominant configuration of capitalism, either directly through the mechanism of advertising or indirectly through fictional media representations; their relation to consumerism is thus necessarily different. . . .

DIVIDING THE CONSUMER PIE

Lesbians have not been targeted as consumers by the advertising industry for several historical reasons. First, lesbians as a social group have not

NOTE: Excerpts reprinted from *Camera Obscura*, Vol. 25 (1991), by permission of Indiana University Press.

been economically powerful; thus, like other social groups who lack substantial purchasing power (for example, the elderly), they have not been attractive to advertisers. Second, lesbians have not been easily identifiable as a social group anyway. According to the market strategies commonly used by advertisers to develop target consumer groups, four criteria must be met. A group must be: (1) identifiable, (2) accessible, (3) measurable, and (4) profitable.[3] In other words, a particular group must be "knowable" to advertisers in concrete ways. Lesbians present a problem here because they exist across race, income and age (three determinants used by advertisers to segment and distinguish target groups within the female population). To the extent that lesbians are not identifiable or accessible, they are not measurable and, therefore, not profitable. The fact that many lesbians prefer not to be identified because they fear discrimination poses an additional obstacle to targeting them. Finally, most advertisers have had no desire to identify a viable lesbian consumer group. Advertisers fear that by openly appealing to a homosexual market their products will be negatively associated with homosexuality and will be avoided by heterosexual consumers.[4] Thus, although homosexuals (lesbians and gay men) reputedly comprise 10% of the overall U.S. market population—and up to 20-22% in major urban centers such as New York and San Francisco—advertisers have traditionally stayed in the closet when it comes to peddling their wares.[5]

Recently, however, this trend has undergone a visible shift—especially for gay men. According to a 1982 review in *The New York Times Magazine* called "Tapping the Homosexual Market," several of today's top advertisers are interested in "wooing . . . the white, single, well-educated, well-paid man who happens to be homosexual."[6] This interest, prompted by surveys conducted by *The Advocate* between 1977 and 1980 that indicated that 70% of their readers aged 20-40 earned incomes well above the national median, has led companies such as Paramount, Seagram, Perrier, and Harper & Row to advertise in gay male publications like *Christopher Street* and *The Advocate*.[7] Their ads are tailored specifically for the gay male audience. Seagram, for example, ran a "famous men of history" campaign for Boodles Gin that pictured men "purported to be gay."[8]

A more common and more discreet means of reaching the gay male consumer, however, is achieved through the mainstream (predominately print) media. As one marketing director has pointed out, advertisers "really want to reach a bigger market than just gays, but [they] don't want to alienate them" either.[9] Thus, advertisers are increasingly striving to create a dual marketing approach that will "speak to the homosexual consumer in a way that the straight consumer will not notice.[10] As one observer explains:

> It used to be that gay people could communicate to one another, in a public place, if they didn't know one another, only by glances and a sort of *code behavior* . . . to indicate to the other person, but not to anybody else, that you, too, were gay. Advertisers, if they're smart, can do that too (emphasis added).[11]

One early example of this approach was the Calvin Klein jeans series that featured "a young, shirtless blond man lying on his stomach" and, in another ad, "a young, shirtless blond man lying on his side, holding a blue-jeans jacket." According to Peter Frisch, a gay marketing consultant, one would "have to be comatose not to realize that it appeals to gay men" (I presume he is referring to the photographs' iconographic resemblance to gay pornography).[12] Calvin Klein marketing directors, however, denied any explicit gay element:

> We did not try *not to* appeal to gays. We try to appeal, period. With healthy, beautiful people. If there's an awareness in that community of health and grooming, they'll respond to the ads.[13]

This dual marketing strategy has been referred to as "gay window advertising."[14] Generally, gay window ads avoid explicit references to heterosexuality by depicting only one individual or same-sexed individuals within the representational frame. In addition, these models bear the signifiers of sexual ambiguity or androgynous style. But "gayness" remains in the eye of the beholder: gays and lesbians can read into an ad certain subtextual elements that correspond to experiences with or representations of gay/lesbian subculture. If heterosexual consumers do not notice these subtexts or subcultural codes, then advertisers are able to reach the homosexual market along with the heterosexual market without ever revealing their aim. . . .

. . .Lesbians have a long tradition of resisting dominant cultural definitions of female beauty and fashion as a way of separating themselves from heterosexual culture politically and as a way of signaling their lesbianism to other women in their subcultural group. This resistance to or reformulation of fashion codes thus distinguished lesbians from straight women at the same time that it challenged patriarchal structures. As Arlene Stein explains in a recent article on style in the lesbian community:

> Lesbian-feminist anti-style was an emblem of refusal, an attempt to strike a blow against the twin evils of capitalism and patriarchy, the fashion industry and the female objectification that fueled it. The flannel-and-denim look was not so much a style as it was anti-style— an attempt to replace the artifice of fashion with a supposed naturalness, free of gender roles and commercialized pretense.[15]

Today, however, many lesbians, particularly younger, urban lesbians, are challenging this look, exposing the constructedness of "natural" fashion, and finding a great deal of pleasure in playing with the possibilities of fashion and beauty.

This shift, which is not total and certainly not without controversy, can be attributed to a number of factors. First of all, many lesbians are rebelling against a lesbian-feminist credo of political correctness that they perceive as stifling. As a *Village Voice* writer observes:

> A lesbian can wag her fingers as righteously as any patriarchal puritan, defining what's acceptable according to what must be ingested, worn, and especially desired. . . . In a climate where a senator who doesn't like a couple of photographs tries to do away with the National Endowment for the Arts, censorious attacks within the lesbian community begin to sound a lot like fundamentalism. . . . They amount to a policing of the lesbian libido.[16]

Stein thus notes that while the old-style, politically correct(ing) strain of lesbian feminism is on the wane, "life style" lesbianism is on the rise. Lifestyle lesbianism is a recognition of the "diverse subcultural pockets and cliques—corporate dykes, arty dykes, dykes of color, clean and sober dykes—of which political lesbians are but one among many."[17] But it may also be a response to the marketing strategies of consumer culture.

The predominate research trend in U.S. advertising for the past two decades has been VALS (values and life styles) research. By combining information on demographics (sex, income, educational level), buying habits, self-image, and aspirations, VALS research targets and, in the case of yuppies, effectively *creates* consumer lifestyles that are profitable to advertisers.[18] Given lesbian-feminism's countercultural, anti-capitalist roots, it is not surprising that lesbians who "wear" their lifestyles or flaunt themselves as "material girls" are often criticized for trading in their politics for a self-absorbed materialism. But there is more to "lipstick lesbians" or "style nomads" than a freewheeling attitude toward their status as consumers or a boredom with the relatively static nature of the "natural look" (fashion, after all, implies change). Fashion-conscious dykes are rebelling against the idea that there is a clear one-to-one correspondence between fashion and identity. As Stein explains:

> You can dress as a femme one day and a butch the next. You can wear a crew-cut along with a skirt. Wearing high heels during the day does not mean you're a femme at night, passive in bed, or closeted on the job.[19]

Seen in this light, fashion becomes an assertion of personal freedom as well as political choice. . . .

. . . In fashion magazines such as *Elle* and *Mirabella,* and in mail-order catalogs such as *Tweeds, J. Crew* and *Victoria's Secret,* advertisers (whether knowingly or not) are capitalizing upon a dual market strategy that packages gender ambiguity and speaks, at least indirectly, to the lesbian consumer market. The representational strategies of gay window advertising thus offer what John Fiske calls "points of purchase" or points of identification that allow readers to make sense of cultural forms in ways that are meaningful or pleasurable to them.[20] The important question here is how these consumer points of purchase become involved in lesbian notions of identity, community, politics, and fashion.

WHEN DYKES GO SHOPPING . . .

In a recent issue of *Elle* a fashion layout entitled "Male Order" shows us a model who, in the words of the accompanying ad copy, represents "the zenith of masculine allure." In one photograph the handsome, short-haired model leans against the handlebars of a motorcycle, an icon associated with bike dyke culture. Her man-styled jacket, tie, and jewelry suggest a butch lesbian style that offers additional points of purchase for the lesbian spectator. In another photograph from the series, the model is placed in a more neutral setting, a cafe, that is devoid of lesbian iconography. But because she is still dressed in masculine attire and, more importantly, exhibits the "swaggering" style recommended by the advertisers, the model incorporates aspects of lesbian style. Here, the traditional "come on" look of advertising can be read as the look or pose of a cruising dyke. Thus, part of the pleasure that lesbians find in these ads might be what Elizabeth Ellsworth calls "lesbian verisimilitude," or the representation of body language, facial expression, and general appearance that can be claimed and coded as "lesbian" according to current standards of style within lesbian communities.[21]

. . . Because lesbians (as members of a heterosexist culture) have been taught to read the heterosexual possibilities of representations, the "straight" reading is never entirely erased or replaced. Lesbian readers, in other words, know that they are not the primary audience for mainstream advertising, that androgyny is a fashionable and profitable commodity, and that the fashion models in these ads are quite probably heterosexual. In this sense, the dual approach of gay window advertising can refer not only to the two sets of readings formulated by homosexuals and heterosexuals, but to the dual or multiple interpretations that exist *within* lesbian reading formations. . . .

Another aspect of reading that must be considered is the pleasure derived from seeing the dominant media "attempt, but fail, to colonize 'real' lesbian space."[22] Even in representations that capitalize upon sexual ambiguity there are certain aspects of lesbian subculture that remain (as yet) inaccessible or unappropriated. By claiming this unarticulated space as something distinct and separable from heterosexual (or heterosexist) culture, lesbian readers are no longer outsiders, but insiders privy to the inside jokes that create an experience of pleasure and solidarity with other lesbians "in the know." Thus, as Ellsworth notes, lesbians "have responded to the marginalization, silencing and debasement" found in dominant discourse "by moving the field of social pleasures . . . to the center of their interpretive activities" and reinforcing their sense of identity and community.[23]

This idea assumed concrete dimensions for me during the course of researching and presenting various versions of this paper. Lesbians across the country were eager to talk about or send copies of advertisements that had "dyke appeal" (and there was a good deal of consensus over how that term was interpreted). A number of lesbians admitted to having an interest in *J. Crew* catalogs because of a certain model they looked forward to seeing each month. Another woman told me of several lesbians who work for a major fashion publication as if to reassure me that gay window fashion photography is not an academic hallucination or a mere coincidence. Gossip, hearsay and confessions are activities that reside at the center of lesbian interpretive communities and add an important discursive dimension to lesbians' pleasure in looking.

This conception of readership is a far cry from earlier (heterosexist) feminist analyses of advertising that argued that "advertisements help to endorse the powerful male attitude that women are passive bodies to be endlessly looked at, waiting to have their sexual attractiveness matched with *active* male sexual desire," or that women's relation to advertisements can only be explained in terms of anxiety or "narcissistic damage."[24] These conclusions were based on a conspiracy theory that placed ultimate power in the hands of corporate patriarchy and relegated no power or sense of agency to the female spectator. Attempts to modify this position, however, have created yet another set of obstacles around which we must maneuver with caution. For in our desire and haste to attribute agency to the spectator and a means of empowerment to marginal or oppressed social groups, we risk losing sight of the interrelation between reading practices and the political economy of media institutions.

In the case of gay window advertising, for example, appropriation cuts both ways. While lesbians find pleasure (and even validation) in that which is both accessible and unarticulated, the advertising industry is playing upon a material and ideological tension that simultaneously appropriates aspects of lesbian subculture and positions lesbian reading practices in relation to consumerism. As John D'Emilio explains: "This dialectic—the constant interplay between exploitation and some measure of autonomy— informs all of the history of those who have lived under capitalism."[25] According to D'Emilio's argument that capitalism and the institution of wage labor have created the material conditions for homosexual desire and identity, gay window advertising is a logical outgrowth of capitalist development, one which presumably will lead to more direct forms of marketing in the future. But the reasons behind this development can hardly be attributed to a growing acceptance of homosexuality as a legitimate lifestyle. Capitalist enterprise creates a tension: materially it "weakens the bonds that once kept families together," but ideologically it "drives people into heterosexual families." Thus, "while capitalism has knocked the material foundations away from family life, lesbians, gay men, and heterosexual feminists have become the scapegoats for the social instability of the system."[26] The result of this tension is that capitalists welcome homosexuals as consuming subjects but not as social subjects. Or, as David Ehrenstein remarks, "the market is there for the picking, and questions of 'morality' yield ever so briefly to the quest for capital."[27] . . .

In an era of "outing" (the practice of forcing gay and lesbian public figures to come out of the closet as a way to confront heterosexuals with our ubiquity as well as our competence, creativity or civicmindedness), gay window advertising can be described as a practice of "ining." In other words this type of advertising invites us to look *into* the ad to identify with elements of style, invites us *in* as consumers, invites us to be part of a fashionable "*in* crowd," but negates an identity politics based on the act of "coming out."

Indeed, within the world of gay window advertising, there is no lesbian community to come out to, no lesbian community to identify with, no indication that lesbianism or "lesbian style" is a political issue. This stylization furthermore promotes a liberal discourse of choice that separates sexuality from politics and connects them both with consumerism. Historically, this advertising technique dates back to the 1920s, as Roland Marchand explains:

> The compulsion of advertising men to relegate women's modernity to the realm of consumption and dependence found expression not only in pictorial styles but also in tableaux that sought to link products with the social and political freedoms of the new woman. Expansive rhetoric that heralded women's march toward freedom and equality often concluded by proclaiming their victory only in the narrower realm of consumer products.[28]

Just as early twentieth-century advertisers were more concerned about women's votes in the marketplace than their decisions in the voting booth, contemporary advertisers are more interested in lesbian consumers than lesbian politics. Once stripped of its political underpinnings, lesbianism can be represented as a style of consumption linked to sexual preference. Lesbianism, in other words, is treated as merely a sexual style that can be chosen—or not chosen—just as one chooses a particular mode of fashion for self-expression.

But within the context of consumerism and the historical weight of heterosexist advertising techniques, "choice" is regulated in determinate ways. For example, gay window advertising appropriates lesbian subcultural style, incorporates its features into commodified representations, and offers it back to lesbian consumers in a packaged form cleansed of identity politics. In this way, it offers lesbians the opportunity to solve the "problem" of lesbianism: by choosing to clothe oneself in fashionable ambiguity, one can pass as "straight" (in certain milieux) while still choosing lesbianism as a sexual preference; by wearing the privilege of straight culture, one can avoid political oppression. Ironically, these ads also offer heterosexual women an alternative as well. As Judith Williamson notes, "[t]he bourgeois always wants to be in disguise, and the customs and habits of the oppressed seem so much more fascinating than his (sic) own."[29] Thus, according to Michael Bronski, "when gay sensibility is used as a sales pitch, the strategy is that gay images imply distinction and non-conformity, granting straight consumers a longed-for place outside the humdrum mainstream."[30] The seamless connections that have traditionally been made between heterosexuality and consumerism are broken apart to allow straight and lesbian women alternative choices. But these choices, which result in a rearticulated homogenized style, deny the differences among women as well as the potential antagonisms that exist between straight and lesbian women over issues of style, politics, and sexuality. As Williamson might explain, "femininity needs the 'other' in order to function . . . even as politically [it] seek[s] to eliminate it."[31]

Similar contradictions and attempts at containment occur within the discourses surrounding women's bodybuilding. As Laurie Schulze notes, "The deliberately muscular woman disturbs dominant notions of sex, gender, and sexuality, and any discursive field that includes her risks opening up a site of contest and conflict, anxiety and ambiguity."[32] Thus, within women's fashion magazines, bodybuilding has been recuperated as a normative ideal of female beauty that promotes self-improvement and ensures attractiveness to men. This discourse

> also assures women who are thinking about working out with weights that they need not fear a loss of privilege or social power; despite any differences that may result from lifting weights, they will still be able to "pass."[33]

The assurances in this case are directed toward heterosexual women who fear that bodybuilding will bring the taint of lesbianism. The connection between bodybuilding and lesbianism is not surprising, says Schulze, for "the ways in which female bodybuilders and lesbians disturb patriarchy and heterosexism . . . draw very similar responses from dominant culture."[34] Both the muscular female and the butch lesbian are accused of looking like men or wanting to be men. As Annette Kuhn puts it, "Muscles are rather like drag."[35] Lesbian style, too, tends toward drag, masquerade and the confusion of gender. Thus, both are subjected to various forms of control that either refuse to accept their physical or sexual "excesses" or otherwise attempt to domesticate their threat and fit them into the dominant constructions of feminine appearances and roles.

Both bodybuilders and lesbians, in other words, are given opportunities to "pass" in straight feminine culture. For bodybuilders, this means not flexing one's muscles while walking down the street or, in the case of competitive bodybuilders, exhibiting the signs of conventional feminine style (for example, makeup, coiffed hair and string bikinis) while flexing on stage.[36] For lesbians, as discussed earlier, this means adopting more traditionally feminine apparel or the trendy accoutrements of gender ambiguity. But within these passing strategies are embodied the very seeds of resistance. As Schulze argues, muscle culture is a "terrain of resistance/ refusal" as well as a "terrain of control."[37] It's simply a matter of how much muscle a woman chooses to flex. Within bodybuilding subculture, flexing is encouraged and admired; physical strength is valorized as a new form of femininity. Lesbians engage in their own form of "flexing" within lesbian subcultures (literally so for those lesbians who also pump iron) by refusing to pass as straight. . . .

Ironically, now that our visibility is growing, lesbians have become the target of "capitalism's constant search for new areas to colonize."[38] This consideration must remain central to the style debates. For lesbians are not simply forming a new relationship with the fashion industry, *it* is attempting to forge a relationship with us. This imposition challenges us and is forcing us to renegotiate certain aspects of identity politics. (I can't help but think, for example, that the fashion controversy may not be about "fashion" at all but has more to do with the fact that it is the femmes who are finally asserting themselves.) In the midst of this challenge, the butch-femme aesthetic will undoubtedly undergo realignment. We may also be forced to reconsider the ways in which camp can function as a form of resistance. For once "camp" is commodified by the culture industry, how do we continue to camp it up? . . .

NOTES

1. Marx (1970, p. 71).
2. Case (1988-1989, p. 56).
3. Astroff (1989).
4. Stabiner (1982, p. 80).
5. Stabiner (1982, p. 79).
6. Stabiner (1982, p. 34).
7. Stabiner (1982, p. 34).
8. Stabiner (1982, p. 75).
9. Stabiner (1982, p. 81).
10. Stabiner (1982, p. 80).
11. Stabiner (1982, p. 80).
12. Stabiner (1982, p. 81).
13. Stabiner (1982, p. 81).
14. Stabiner (1982, p. 80).
15. Stein (1989, p. 37).
16. Solomon (1990, p. 40).
17. Stein (1989, p. 39).
18. Wilson (1989, p. 279).
19. Stein (1989, p. 38).
20. Fiske (1988, p. 247).
21. Ellsworth (1986, p. 54).
22. Ellsworth (1986, p. 54).
23. Ellsworth (1986, p. 54).
24. Root (1984); Coward (1985, p. 80).
25. D'Emilio (1983, p. 102).
26. D'Emilio (1993, p. 109).
27. Ehrenstein (1980, p. 62).
28. Marchand (1985, p. 186).
29. Williamson (1986, p. 116).
30. Bronski (1984. p. 187).
31. Williamson (1986, pp. 109, 112).
32. Schulze (1990, p. 59).
33. Schulze (1990, p. 63).
34. Schulze (1990, p. 73).
35. Kuhn (1989, p. 56).
36. Schulze (1990, p. 68).
37. Schulze (1990, p. 67).
38. Williamson (1986, p. 116).

REFERENCES

Astroff, R. (1989). *Commodifying cultures: Latino ad specialists as cultural brokers.* Paper presented at the 7th International Conference on Culture and Communication, Philadelphia, PA.

Bronski, M. (1984). *Culture clash: The making of gay sensibility.* Boston: South End Press.

Case, S.-E. (1988-1989). Towards a butch-femme aesthetic. *Discourse, 11*(1).

Coward, R. (1985). *Female desires.* New York: Grove.

D'Emilio, J. (1983). Capitalism and gay identity. In A. Snitow, C. Stansell, & S. Thompson (Eds.), *Powers of desire: The politics of sexuality.* New York: Monthly Review Press.

Ehrenstein, D. (1980). Within the pleasure principle or irresponsible homosexual propaganda. *Wide Angle, 4*(1).

Ellsworth, E. (1986). Illicit pleasures: Feminist spectators and *Personal Best. Wide Angle, 8*(2).

Fiske, J. (1988). Critical response: Meaningful moments. *Critical Studies in Mass Communications, 5.*

Kuhn, A. (1989). The body and cinema: Some problems for feminism. *Wide Angle, 11*(4).

Marchand, R. (1985). *Advertising the American dream.* Berkeley: University of California Press.

Marx, K. (1970). *Capital* (Vol. 1). London: Lawrence & Wishart.

Root, J. (1984). *Pictures of women.* London: Pandora.

Schulze, L. (1990). On the muscle. In J. Gaines & C. Herzog (Eds.), *Fabrications: Costume and the female body.* New York: Routledge.

Solomon, A. (1990, June 26). Dykotomies: Scents and sensibility in the lesbian community. *Village Voice.*

Stabiner, K. (1982, May 2). Tapping the homosexual market. *The New York Times Magazine.*

Stein, A. (1989). All dressed up, but no place to go? Style wars and the new lesbianism. *OUT/LOOK, 1*(4).

Williamson, J. (1986). Woman is an island: Femininity and colonization. In T. Modleski (Ed.), *Studies in entertainment: Critical Approaches to mass culture.* Bloomington: Indiana University Press.

Wilson, S. L. (1989). *Mass media/mass culture.* New York: Random House.

Watching the Girls Go Buy

Shop-at-Home Television

MIMI WHITE

There's something oddly intriguing, and at times even hypnotic, about home-shopping shows. Yet, home shopping is tacky, ghastly, vulgar, and boring. Those are easy judgments to make. The real question is why people tune in—including, apparently, some viewers who never buy anything.

—Mark N. Vamos, *Business Week*

. . . A closer look at the phenomenon of shop-at-home broadcasting helps to clarify how television can exist, and even prosper, in the absence of conventional programming. This inquiry into the Home Shopping Network (HSN) has the potential to call many basic assumptions about the television apparatus into question. At the same time, it contributes to an understanding of the minimal requirements of programmatic representation within the contemporary formation of television as an apparatus of consumer culture. Pleasure seems to persist in the absence of conventional entertainment and information programs, as television shopping extends and exacerbates the ideological keystones of commercial television, even while it challenges all familiar theories of the television apparatus derived therefrom. In this light, it is striking that the Home Shopping Network appeals to its viewer-shoppers as members of a community, indeed a family, of consumers connected through exchanges of confessions and testimonials between program hosts and call-in purchasers, constructing a therapeutic discourse of consumption.

In the process of selling its products, HSN provides appropriate terms and guidelines for its own use by the viewer, with a particular emphasis on the female as the ideal consumer and on domestic space as the ideal site of consumption. Indeed, since both a television and a telephone are necessary to shop with HSN, the home is very nearly the only location from which one can shop. The very networks of exchange set in place by the home shopping transaction include not only the viewer and the television but also the telephone and consumer credit industries. . . .

Based in Clearwater, Florida, HSN was started in 1977 as a radio sales program. In 1982 it began selling products on the local cable system, and it expanded to a national scale in July 1985. Since then, HSN has purchased twelve broadcasting stations to assure nationwide major-market coverage and to include markets not covered by cable.[1] HSN provides twenty-four-hour-a-day programming in the form of television marketing via two services, HSN I and HSN II. These services are programmed respectively on the twelve broadcast stations owned and operated by the network and on cable systems across the country. HSN also sells its service to other stations to be aired in particular dayparts, especially in the late-night and early-morning fringe. As an owner of so many stations, and an originator and seller of programming, however unorthodox, HSN might legitimately be considered the fifth "commercial network" in the United States, behind ABC, CBS NBC, and the Fox Broadcasting System.[2]

HSN provides its shop-at-home services under the name of the Home Shopping Club (HSC)—the corporate "network" identity thus distinguished from its programming—which individuals can join with the purchase of any product. The club offers items for purchase one at a time, and the items can be bought only while they are displayed on the television screen.[3] Usually, between five and fifteen items are displayed each hour, though during special "bargathon" close-out sessions, merchandise comes on and goes off far more quickly. Conversely, on occasions when guests appear with the host—for example, athletes paired with the selling of sports memorabilia—products often move on and off screen at a slower pace. Items appear in a random and unpredictable order, though sales hosts usually hint at the kinds of things they will be presenting in the next few hours. Special segments feature only clothing or jewelry for one to five hours at a time. The day is subdivided into program segments according to the individual sales hosts, who introduce and describe each item and talk with call-in purchasers.

The program uses a limited and highly regularized repertoire of images, with particular emphasis on the close-up product shot. Each item is shown in a series of tight shots that may go on for several minutes at a time. All products are shown with a column on the left side of the screen indicating the "retail" price and the HSC discount, as well as the toll-free number to call for purchase. Occasionally additional text appears in the upper right-hand corner of the screen or as a crawl along the bottom edge or under the identifying label at the top of the screen. This text provides additional information about the product being presented (e.g., 15 rubies, 1.25 carats) or urges the viewer to use "Tootie," the computerized sales system, for making a purchase. . . .

The unceasing flow of items presented in this way conveys the impression of a plentitude of goods and immense variety. However, the regular viewer quickly learns that certain kinds of products tend to dominate Home Shopping Club sales. These include jewelry, collectibles, clothing, and small electric appliances. . . . In the category of clothing, outfits for women, often including larger women's sizes, are the most frequent offerings. . . .

. . . All HSC viewers are also addressed and presented as knowledgeable and informed shoppers in general. In conversations between program hosts and shoppers there is a constant dialogue about the quality and value of the products being sold: and viewers always seem to know the "retail price" of any object. In this regard the program projects its viewers as experts who fully understand the larger world of consumerism and the merchandise that circulates within it. Thus, if the program offers the image of a working-class taste culture, the subjects who populate this culture are constructed as discerning, active, and educated consumers. In this sense the program makes working-class taste culture visible and available to its audiences in order to celebrate it, perhaps more readily and directly than most other forms of television programming.

At the same time the programming plays to the vanity of those who recognize their ostensible superiority to this culture. This further begins to account for viewers who may watch without actually buying anything. For, at an extreme, one can envision the Home Shopping Club viewer as a cross-class voyeur, engaged by the pleasures of consumerist slumming. In promoting these positions as potential viewing stances—celebrating working-class taste culture, promoting the image of educated consumers, and providing an image of working-class taste culture and its participants as inferior "others"—the program itself is complicit in devaluing the very taste culture it also constructs. . . .

With its bargain-basement production values, random order of sales, and limited purchase time, the Home Shopping Club begins to define the constraining contours of the mode of consumption appropriate to its own success. The strategies for presenting products encourages continual, semi-attentive viewing to ensure that one gets the best products the club has to offer. Since viewers can never know for certain when a particular item will be offered for sale, they are challenged to watch as much as possible if they are interested in buying. The phone calls from viewers provide substantiating evidence—by means of a continuous auditory representation of random typical buyers—that the club's most avid shoppers are equally avid viewers who are fully tuned in to the patterns of reception and watching that will encourage their own consuming habits. The phone-in buyers who talk to the sales hosts routinely mention that they turned on the club as soon as they got home from work; that they have been waiting and watching—for days, weeks, or months—for a particular item to (re)appear; or, quite simply, that they now do all their shopping with the club. . . .

. . . Scrupulous attention to distinctive detail contributes to repeated consumption and extended accumulation by promoting difference and completeness as two complementary categories of concern for educated consumers. For with a newly acquired understanding of refined detail, viewers may come to recognize the value of having one of each kind of gold chain, different gemstones in the same ring design, or the same gemstone in a range of different cuts. Viewers are also encouraged to assemble full sets because collections are valuable in and of themselves. A viewer may already have the three-carat cubic zirconia ring, appropriate for everyday wear; but the five-carat version is just the thing for an elegant evening on the town. And if you have just ordered the cubic zirconia sapphire earrings for your daughter, wouldn't it be nice to get her the matching pendant? This Capodimonte candlestick, with eleven petals, in the white, with pink accents, will perfectly complement the Capodimonte basket with the three flowers ordered last month. And now HSC is offering a curio cabinet, ideal for displaying the clowns, or perhaps the lead crystal animals, you have been accumulating through the club.

The emphasis on distinguishing minutiae as a reason to possess a particular item works hand in hand with appeals to the collector's mentality, to the pleasure and value of accumulation for its own sake. Connoisseurship is constructed as a strategy of discrimination among products to isolate what is unique to one, at the same time that it encourages collections by the amassing of lots of objects whose distinctiveness lies in small details. . . .

. . . The club fosters a sense of familiarity between sales hosts and their audience, mimicking the perceived value of personal service promoted by finer department stores. This familiarity is extended when certain hosts attract repeat calls from specific viewers who come to function as shopper-fans. At times, hosts come to recognize callers by their voices or by the way they initiate a phone call. Thus a caller may begin by saying "Hi handsome," and the host will respond, "Oh, Ann. Hello." In such cases program hosts may even remember that the caller previously purchased the item on display and is therefore calling with a shopper's testimonial to confirm the value of the item.[4]

All callers identify themselves by first name and location, and are asked questions from an established litany: What made you decide to buy this item? For whom are you shopping? How long have you shopped with the club? What else have you bought today? Have you enjoyed your club merchandise? The formal patterns of talk that inform these calls are similar to the visual patterns engaged in presenting items for sale. In this sense the calls provide something of an audio model of connoisseurship and accumulation; they are distinctive and personalized only within highly repetitive and formulaic boundaries. One call after another expresses the same thing: enthusiasm for a product, often accompanied by a desire for the host to give an affirming ritual toot on the bicycle horn, and so on. This is in part due to the host's questions that orient the responses from shoppers. But callers frequently launch into a lengthy spiel on the beauty of a particular ring, or praise a great bargain on a brass lamp, with little prompting. In such instances viewer-shoppers participate in the ritual of shopping through

Home Shopping Club. Those who are willing to speak on the air readily assume the position of shopping enthusiasts and experts in terms appropriate to the culture of HSC. . . .

Hosts specifically appeal to callers as regional experts who can testify to the quality of club merchandise and are familiar with the consumer market in general. Customers are routinely asked if they have priced a given item in their area, and how much the item would sell for in a retail store. Inevitably, club members insist that even the retail price proposed by HSC is too low, assuring that the discount price is even more of a bargain than it seemed at first. In the process, callers become sales hosts, if only provisionally, encouraging others to participate in the process of shopping with the club. . . .

. . . Buyers often mention prior conversations with a host that took place weeks, or even months, earlier, just as hosts may recall shoppers they have spoken with previously. And callers regularly confess to spending large amounts of money on club merchandise. Usually this is conveyed as a customer eagerly describes other dolls, jewelry, music boxes, or Capodimonte arrangements already ordered—or lists a range of items purchased that very day.

In one instance, a woman called in with a testimonial for a ring that she already owned—a small sapphire surrounded by even smaller diamonds, costing several hundred dollars. She went on to discuss her buying habits, noting that she had "worn out" all of her credit cards, her phrase for spending up to the assigned credit limit, shopping with the club. However, her husband had seen the ring on the screen and told her about it so that she could call in and share her satisfaction with other viewers and potential buyers. She was also wondering if the host was going to be offering the same ring in the amethyst. For she had ordered it the previous week, unfortunately on one of the "worn out" credit cards, so the order did not go through. Her husband had discovered another credit card since then, and she was still hoping to get the ring in the amethyst. Throughout the call the host responded with support and enthusiasm. "What a nice husband! I'm so glad you enjoy shopping with the club!"

At times like these, the comments by the hosts are subject to being read ironically. Certainly the remarks by the host in this particular case seem somewhat incommensurate with the narrative recounted by the caller, and the encouragement somewhat hollow. Indeed, in the most general sense, the relentless good cheer, loud volume, and arch-enthusiasm of the hosts open the way to variable interpretation. In the hosts' very tone, one may detect a hint of derision or insincerity in almost all of what they say. This is in fact one of the main ways in which the programming can be said not only to construct a forthright image of a certain working-class taste culture but simultaneously to criticize it. On rare occasions, this undertone of derision and insincerity erupts overtly in the comments or reactions of the hosts, establishing a critical distance between the hosts on the one hand and the products they promote and the people who buy them on the other.

For example, in midsummer one of the hosts was selling a music box with an animal design. When the production staff finally figured out how to get it to play in a demonstration, the tune was a Christmas song. This provoked an outburst of hysterical laughter on the part of the host, which lasted for over five minutes, extending into the presentation of the next item for sale. She was so taken aback by the Christmas jingle in a generic-designed music box being sold in July that she could not control herself. When a woman shopper called in with a testimonial about the music box that she had previously purchased, the host's laughter persisted throughout the call and seemed particularly derisive, insofar as it suggested that the music box was a ridiculous item and could not be taken seriously. Yet such overt demonstrations challenging the value and charm of club merchandise on the part of sales hosts are rare. And any suggestion of substantial critical distance and negative valuation of the products is left to be read in the far more ambiguous displays of excessive affect that are more typical of the hosts. . . .

. . . The testimonials and endorsements of repeat buyers indicate a community of highly satisfied customers. Over and over again HSC viewers hear of consummated desires. The air ionizer has made people sleep better, be more relaxed, and be less susceptible to colds. People have received endless, and envious, compliments on a ring; and no one can tell the difference between the cubic zirconia diamond and the "real thing." Viewer-shoppers become so well versed with the club's codes and routines that hosts barely have to ask questions to provoke perfect responses from callers. One man, buying a porcelain bridal doll, explains with almost no prompting that he is getting it for his wife who has been wanting a bridal doll, that this one is just beautiful, and that his wife has been collecting dolls "ever since you've been offering them on the club."

Moreover, with its unending stock of costume jewelry, collectibles, and decorative *objects,* the club represents its target viewer-consumers as prevailingly working-class women. While fishing rods, hand drills, and attaché cases are included in the club inventory, they do not begin to compete with the female-oriented consumer products in sheer volume or variety. This fact is confirmed by phone calls, which are overwhelmingly from women buyers. . . .

The club represents the exemplary viewer-consumers that have made it successful as members of a larger community of desire that everyone can join. Anyone can share equally in the taste culture, the bargains, and perhaps the consumer debt that the club promotes. Viewer-shoppers are applauded for acting to fulfill their desires through a process of accumulation that will never be complete because there is always another Capodimonte piece, music box, or household gadget to be purchased. There is always another occasion that warrants a gift for a spouse, relative, friend, or even oneself. With their personal phone calls and cheery enthusiasm, the sales hosts are incorporated into the domestic and social circles that are the context for the ever-expanding consuming possibilities offered by HSC. Individual purchases are constantly (re)defined in terms of extended networks of familial relations. Even if a caller buys something for herself, it is going to contribute to the beauty or comfort of the home, or the purchase is possible because of the generosity of a husband who granted the use of yet another credit card. Moreover, once something is purchased, a daughter, uncle, or out-of-town friend who sees it will surely want to own one too. This encourages viewers to continue to watch and wait for items to reappear on the Home Shopping Club, so they can be ordered again.

With consumption literally based in the home, the female consumer—situated in these familial and social networks—becomes the focus for regenerating consuming desires. HSC offers a therapeutic discourse that circulates in relation to the family, home and consumerism. The Home Shopping Club's strategies for representing patterns of consumption and its modes of address aid and abet this process. The pleasures of consumption and accumulation for their own sakes combine with the possibility of recognizing that, and how, consuming habits connect viewer-shoppers to a larger community of desire, national in scope but brought together by the club. The viewer-shopper is not isolated in the home. On the contrary, shopping from the home with the club may be more personal and community-oriented than an afternoon at the local shopping mall. For here the viewer shares the experience with a host, who may even remember the last time she called, and with other shoppers who are part of the common culture of shop-at-home consumption.

The Home Shopping Club and its parent, the Home Shopping Network, represent the pleasures of buying in the very process of selling their merchandise. Their program constantly reconfirms the value of staying home and watching television—HSC in particular—as the best way to secure familial and communal relations; it also validates the position of women as the center of these relations. Thus the history of twentieth-century consumer culture is positively reinforced for a contemporary generation of participants. With these emphases, conventional forms of entertainment and information programming are not necessary as the alibi or lure that situates all viewers as virtual subjects of consumption. In the world according to HSC, the television apparatus affords direct participation in the pleasures of personal and economic exchange to consolidate the family as the subject of an improved standard of living, while more conventional television programming offers these pleasures only in more vicarious forms.

NOTES

1. All of the stations owned by HSN are UHF. As HSN was growing, federal regulations regarding broadcast station ownership allowed a single entity (individual, partnership, or corporation) to own twelve AM radio, twelve FM radio, and twelve television outlets. The total audience reached by any set of twelve television stations was not allowed to exceed 25 percent of the nationwide audience. However, an exception was made for UHF TV on the principle that UHF (channels 14-83) signals tend to be weaker than, and thus not to travel as far as, VHF (channels 2-13) signals. In recognition of this signal imbalance and attendant implications of smaller audiences, UHF audiences were figured at 50 percent of the total toward the nationwide 25 percent quota. In other words, with UHF stations, only half of the audience in the market is counted. Theoretically, an all-UHF network with twelve television stations could broadcast to half of the television viewing audience in the United States. The rules regarding station ownership are subject to periodic review and revision. It is also important to note that on its broadcast stations, HSN includes regular public service programs several times a day, running as long as fifteen minutes, as part of the requirements for holding a broadcast license.

2. In the fall of 1987, HSN offered a syndicated variant of its service, the Home Shopping Overnight Service; see "Home Shopping Hits Syndication" (1987).

3. In a *TV Guide* review of a number of different shop-at-home television services, HSN is criticized for this "high pressure" tactic (Feldon, 1987).

4. Most likely, hosts are given the name of repeat callers as the call is switched to them by the sales operator, but this is unacknowledged on the air.

REFERENCES

Feldon, L. (1987, July 4). Join this home shopping expedition. *TV Guide*, pp. 30-32.
Home shopping hits syndication. (1987, May 4). *Broadcasting*, p. 59.

PART III

MODES OF SEXUAL REPRESENTATION 1: ROMANCE NOVELS AND SLASHER FILMS

One of the aims of **cultural studies** as informed by **feminist criticism** is to make us question the traditional distinction made, in our educational institutions and in our lives as cultural consumers, between "serious reading," "good literature" or "high art," on the one hand and, on the other, "popular trash," cultural "junk" or "escapist entertainment." It is not that there are no significant differences to be observed between, for example, 17th-century European oil paintings and 20th-century American van paintings. But cultural studies talks about the differences in a less elitist, aesthetic-oriented way than does much traditional literary and art criticism.

Rather than arrange cultural artifacts on a hierarchical scale from "higher" to "lower" forms, rejecting popular and mass-produced forms as unworthy of the same attention as "great art," cultural studies assumes that all **artifacts** that audiences consume are potentially of equal significance and interest to students of society and culture. Those types or **genres** that continue to be despised or laughed at (even by their own consumers)—for example, tabloids, comic books and soap operas—can tell us as much about our lives in our particular social world as those that are revered, such as grand opera or epic poems. One of the advantages of taking this approach is that we gain access to cultural artifacts important to the psychological survival of groups marginalized on the basis of their race, class, gender and age.

In the case of the **women's genres** (women-targeted mass cultural forms, such as the soap opera, Gothic novel and Harlequin romance), Tania Modleski (1982) argued that

161

even the contemporary mass produced narratives for women contain elements of protest and **resistance** underneath highly "orthodox" plots. If the popular-culture heroine and the feminist choose utterly different ways of overcoming their dissatisfaction, they at least have in common the dissatisfaction. (pp. 25-26)

The very popularity of such forms must be understood as showing that

they speak to very real problems and tensions in women's lives. The narrative strategies which have evolved for smoothing over these tensions can tell us much about how women have managed not only to live in oppressive circumstances but to invest their situations with some degree of dignity. (pp. 14-15)

In this chapter, we've linked together two types of "escapist entertainment" that at first glance seem to be very different—books ostensibly about romance, targeting women, and films ostensibly about violence, targeting adolescents. But we think there are good reasons for looking at them together. Until relatively recently, both were ignored by traditional criticism, in part because their target audiences—women and adolescents—were not taken seriously as cultural consumers. Both genres are highly formulaic and thus allow us to consider the appeal of "formula fiction," which repeats the same highly predictable narrative pattern over and over, to its consumers. Both raise intriguing questions about sexual **representation** and **gender,** as well. Both lure the consumer with promises of bodily arousal, sexual and otherwise; and although both seem at first merely to trade on or reinforce reactionary gender imagery, contemporary feminist critics of both of these forms argue that we need to take a second look at what is going on with gender.

When we first attempt to take such forms seriously, we may find their apparent narrative content repellent, particularly from a feminist sociological perspective. Romance novels and slasher novels appear to have in common the presentation of women as passive victims of sadistic male victimizers. This is most obvious in the narrative formula of the slasher, where a sequence of females (and males as well) cower and attempt to run away as they are threatened, tortured, mutilated and ultimately murdered by a seemingly indestructible and "psychotic" male with a fearsome weapon. Although depicting male violence less threateningly, perhaps, the traditional romance novel formula insists that "the reader must be aware that the hero is free to do with the heroine as he likes," as Marilyn Lowery (1983), in *How to Write Romance Novels That Sell* candidly tells us.

Not surprisingly, then, the first feminist mode of critique of such formulas tended to assume that these forms simply conveyed negative **gender stereotyping** that would directly reinforce lessons from elsewhere in the culture equating masculinity with action and femininity with passivity and make male domineering and violence against women seem erotic. It was assumed that male and female cultural consumers would uncritically absorb these ideas of exaggerated gender differences, the consumer identifying directly and unproblematically with fictional characters of the same sex.[1]

A very influential step toward a more complex understanding of how gender **ideology** is constructed through and by popular mass-marketed fictions was taken in filmmaker/film critic Laura Mulvey's (1975) influential essay, "Visual Pleasure and Narrative Cinema," which dramatically altered the course of future feminist cultural criticism. Mulvey made a complex theoretical argument in this essay about the way traditional Hollywood narrative film gives its spectators pleasure, drawing heavily on **psychoanalytic theory** about how males and females develop and sustain gender identity. Before we summarize Mulvey's argument briefly, a comment about the potential contributions of psychoanalysis to the study of media culture, and in particular formula fiction texts, is in order.

Psychoanalysis has been an important framework for some literary critics, and for many film critics, in recent years, because of its potential usefulness in explaining the role of emotion, fantasies and motivations not readily accessible to our conscious minds, as they influence our relationship to the popular cultural texts we consume and our behavior as readers and audiences. (The role of feeling and the unconscious is assumed to be especially dominant in the context of film viewing, which some critics claim produces a childlike state of receptivity in the audience sitting in a dark theater, immersed in a dreamlike sequence of moving picture and sound.)

In a tradition stemming originally from Freud, but modified considerably by, among others, French psychoanalytic philosophers Jacques Lacan, Julia Kristeva and Luce Irigaray, feminist psychoanalytic critics seek to explain how males and females, growing up in families within a patriarchal culture and society, emerge as adults with very different relationships to our culture's entire symbolic system—including its language and its media imagery.[2] They argue that as part of the process of separating from the mother in infancy and acquiring a gendered sense of self, male and female children enter into and employ our culture's symbolic systems and find very different messages about themselves embedded there. Because everything in the dominant culture's symbolic system, including the vocabulary and grammar of languages and narratives, communicates the high prestige of masculinity, the male child's process of separating from the mother and "the feminine," through identifying with the "phallic" (or masculine) symbolic order of culture, seems relatively unproblematic on the surface (but anxieties remain). Conversely, the girl child's discovery on entering the cultural realm is that femininity is signified or symbolized everywhere by "lack" or "absence."

It is within this framework, and in dialogue with other film critics influenced by psychoanalysis such as Christian Metz, that Mulvey (1975) developed the influential idea that the spectator of a classic mainstream narrative film, no matter what his or her actual biological sex, is offered only a "masculine **subject position**" from which to experience the fantasy/fiction. This is partly as a result of a narrative structure (plot) that works to invite identification with the active male protagonist, rather than with the passive female object of male desire in the plot. However, Mulvey also theorized that the film's very *formal* techniques, including its visual images, point-of-view shots and editing conventions, guide the viewer's eye to identify with the controlling **male gaze** of the (male) protagonist of the plot. The male gaze (of both protagonist and film viewer) objectifies the female within the film's narrative. Even the female viewer must adopt the objectifying gaze if she is to receive the voyeuristic pleasure[3] offered by the film. Mulvey urged filmmakers to begin to "break down" traditional cinematic *codes* to challenge the voyeuristic pleasure such mainstream narrative film provides, and many feminist filmmakers have produced innovative work in response to this challenge.

The theoretical niceties of Mulvey's essay and the subsequent outpouring of feminist film analysis centering on questions of how and whether a "female gaze" is possible in narrative film are beyond the scope of an introductory reader like this one. Moreover, we, the two editors of this collection, admit candidly that we tend to side with those critics of a Freudian-based psychoanalytic—even as modified by a feminist perspective—who have argued that (especially in U.S. film studies) it is problematically ahistorical and apparently not possible to account for the real (historical) viewer's actual **gendered subjectivity**, as reflected by class, race, sexuality and other aspects of social experience (e.g., Diawara, 1988; Gaines, 1988; Mayne, 1993a, 1993b; Stacey, 1990). Others argue that Freudian-based psychoanalytic theory of the gendering process is at least potentially politically reactionary in its implications (Gaines, 1990).

Nevertheless, Mulvey's (1975) essay must be acknowledged as providing the basis for the prominence of gender considerations in almost 10 years of feminist film criticism and filmmaking practice. Recent feminist film theorists now energetically explore the idea that popular film texts may offer **negotiated** or even multiple **subject positions** (Erens, 1990; Gamman & Marshment, 1989; Gledhill, 1988; Mayne, 1993a, 1993b; Penley, 1988). This concept is better suited to help us understand how a wide variety of consumers of various social identities make sense of and derive pleasure from film narratives—including lesbians and gay men, who have offered a particularly strong critique of the potentially erroneous assumptions of psychoanalysis about the relationship of gender identity to sexual desire.

Cultural studies, then, drawing on these recent advances in film theory, has seen formulaic texts as more complex and nuanced than early feminist critics assumed them to be. Just as gender itself is no longer assumed to be a fixed construct (see introduction to Part I), it can no longer be assumed that the cultural text forces the audience or cultural consumer to adopt a fixed-gender subject position. The chapters we have selected for this part highlight these more contemporary and sophisticated ways of thinking about gender and show both the challenge and intellectual excitement of taking these "escapist entertainment" forms seriously.

Carol Clover's study, "Her Body, Himself: Gender in the Slasher Film," (Chapter 21) draws on feminist film criticism's newer concept of unstable or ambiguously gendered subject positions. Clover notes that there is already a body of work suggesting that women viewers can identify with masculine protagonists of film narrative. She asks whether the male adolescent viewer of the slasher film may not be invited by the film's narrative and cinematic codes to identify with a nominally female protagonist, the "final girl" who triumphs in the end over the equally fluidly gendered psychopath. This type of analysis asks us to reconsider the assumption on which much of the public concern about the popularity of the slasher film is based, namely, "that the sexes are what they seem; that screen males represent the Male and screen females the Female; that this identification along gender lines authorizes impulses toward sexual violence in males and encourages impulses toward victimization in females." We have also included an example of the recent journalistic presentation of public concern over the violence in the slasher film, "Do Slasher Films Breed Real-Life Violence?" by Alison Bass (Chapter 22), to afford students the opportunity of comparing and contrasting two different ways of conceptualizing the relationships between sex, gender and violence in these films.

As noted earlier, Mulvey's (1975) essay theorized the masculinized spectator position on the example of the mainstream Hollywood cinema, with its classic "realistic" narrative of male activity and heroism. But what happens to the spectator position in a text aimed at women and that invites identification with a female protagonist? Within film studies, such questions led to much interesting work on melodrama and **the woman's film** (Byars, 1993; Erens, 1990; Kuhn, 1982). But these concerns have also influenced the study of formula literature targeting women.

The romance novel has received considerable feminist attention as one example of what has been called "the women's genre"—a type of cultural artifact historically aimed at and primarily consumed by women. Depending on one's particular brand of feminist politics, one's critical theory and one's attitude toward the targeted audience, the romance novel formula can be read as reinforcing **patriarchal** values and as expressing (and rewarding) female **resistance** to the devaluation of the feminine in mainstream culture—or as both simultaneously.

One of the first feminist theorists to analyze the traditional Harlequin romance formula in terms of the power dynamics between the two main characters, Ann Snitow also points out (Chapter 23) the heroine's sexual arousal and asks provocatively whether romance novels should be seen as a form of "pornography for women"—that is, a less explicit and visual text than that aimed at male consumers but one that still aims to eroticize male domination, for a specifically female audience. Her essay thus explores the possibilities of this woman's genre as a traditional mode of sexual representation that constructs a distinctly "feminine" sexuality: "In romanticized sexuality, the pleasure lies in the distance itself. Waiting, anticipation, anxiety—these represent the high point of sexual experience." Snitow is careful to dissociate her argument from biological determinism:

> Female sexuality, a rare subject in all but the most recent writing, is not doomed to be what the Harlequins describe. Nevertheless, some of the barriers that hold back female sexual feeling are acknowledged and finally circumvented quite sympathetically in these novels. They are

sex books for people who have plenty of good reasons for worrying about sex.

Snitow's essay takes the romance novel form seriously and provides one possible explication of its **textual codes**,[4] but as Kellner's discussion of textual analysis (Chapter 1) reminds us, no single textual critic's view, no matter how subtle and compelling, can tell us how real-world audiences interact with the form. Janice Radway's **ethnographic research** into the **audience reception** of romance novels, "Women Read the Romance: The Interaction of Text and Context" (Chapter 24) begins to add this dimension, bringing forward women's own interpretations of the role of romance reading in their lives as wives and mothers. Radway shows how one specific group of White working-class[5] women negotiate with the genre, both in terms of the books they select and in terms of the way they actually read the texts and appropriate its meanings. Radway acknowledges that "Romance reading . . . can function as a kind of training for the all-too-common task of reinterpreting a spouse's unsettling actions as the signs of passion, devotion, and love." Yet she sees in their selection of certain books as favorites, and rejection of others, their active tendency to critique certain patriarchal masculine behaviors, substituting an ideal of the "nurturant" male that may be missing in their own family lives. Through the act of reading itself, this group of women romance readers escaped temporarily from familial demands on their time, and Radway interprets this action as potential resistance to the patriarchal restrictions of their lives. Although encouraging respect for women's own experiences as cultural consumers, however, Radway warns against confusing modes of resistance that reside in textual consumption with a more real-world resistance, which might take the form of organized protest against the patriarchal abuses women meet in real life.

Romance readers sometimes aspire to move from fandom into the realm of romance novel production, moved not only by love of the form but also by the knowledge that a few "high-end" romance writers, such as Danielle Steele, "are millionaires a few times over" (Linden & Rees, 1992). Marilyn Lowery (1983), a romance writer and author of *How to Write Romance Novels That Sell*, one of many such how-to-write-romance guides, makes it seem a simple matter for the reader to have success as a romance writer, by following the well-known formula, with all its minor variations to fit different target audience tastes (Chapter 25). However, a career as a romance novel writer is far from a glamorous, liberating force in the lives of most of those who write in that genre.

Pollack's chapter "Romance Slaves of Harlequin" (Chapter 26), reveals the degree to which the women who actually write for Harlequin Enterprises, the Canadian-based corporation that controls 80% of the "series romance" market, are constrained by the conditions of their employment in what is virtually a literary sweatshop. They must abide by the formulas as set by the corporation, and this control is enforced by the corporate ownership of the writer's pen name. As with the advertisers' high-handed practices with "women's magazines" analyzed by Gloria Steinem (Chapter 15), the assumption seems to be that because they are confined in a traditionally feminine sphere, the cultural producers will not have the assertiveness or financial resources to protest such treatment. In this context, it is worth noting the formation of a new organization representing romance writers' labor interests and willing to challenge Harlequin's pseudonym ownership policy. As this example shows, by demystifying the nature of media imagery production, simply working as an individual in a media industry does not bring an appreciable degree of control over the nature of the cultural products.

NOTES

1. For a more extensive and detailed discussion of different schools of feminist criticism and their different approaches to critiquing media imagery, see E. Ann Kaplan (1987).

2. In this summary, we draw, with thanks, on discussions by E. Ann Kaplan (1987) and Sandy Flitterman-Lewis (1987). For a more recent application of a feminist psychoanalytic perspective to film studies, see Jackie Byars (1993).

3. According to this Freudian-influenced theory, the voyeuristic pleasure of the (male) viewer derives from the film's ability to offer a symbolic containment of the threat of femininity.

4. Snitow's provocative and influential essay describes the Harlequin formula as it existed in the early 1970s. A more recent study of the Harlequin romance by Leslie Rabine (1985) argues that Harlequin's updating of the formula to respond "to the specific needs of working women" helps account for its dramatic growth in popularity in the 1980s. Krantz's (1992) collection of essays by romance novel writers includes an interesting piece by writer Linda Barlow (1992), who argues that the brooding hero is an aspect of the heroine's own divided psyche, with which she is reconciled in the end.

5. Although Radway herself identifies the romance readers as "middle-class," if we use her own information on their income and occupational and educational status, they would be seen as "working class" according to Barbara Ehrenreich's class typology (Chapter 6).

REFERENCES

Barlow, L. (1992). The androgynous writer: Another point of view. In J. N. Krentz (Ed.), *Dangerous men and adventurous women* (pp. 45-52). Philadelphia: University of Pennsylvania Press.

Byars, J. (1993). *All that Hollywood allows: Re-reading gender in 1950s melodrama.* New York: Routledge.

Diawara, M. (1988). Black spectatorship: Problems of identification and resistance. *Screen, 29*(4), 66-81.

Erens, P. (Ed.). (1990). *Issues in feminist film criticism.* Bloomington: Indiana University Press.

Flitterman-Lewis, S. (1987). Psychoanalysis, film and television. In R. C. Allen (Ed.), *Channels of discourse: Television and contemporary criticism* (pp. 172-210). Chapel Hill: University of North Carolina Press.

Gaines, J. (1990). Women and representation: Can we enjoy alternative pleasure? In P. Erens (Ed.), *Issues in feminist film criticism.* Bloomington: Indiana University Press.

Gaines, J. (1988, Autumn). White privilege and looking relations: Race and gender in feminist film theory. *Screen, 29.*

Gamman, L., & Marshment, M. (Eds.). (1989). *The female gaze: Women as viewers of popular culture.* London: Women's Press.

Gledhill, C. (1988). Pleasurable negotiations. In D. Pribam (Ed.), *Female spectators: Looking at film and television* (pp. 64-68). London: Verso.

Kaplan, E. A. (1987). Feminist criticism and television. In R. C. Allen (Ed.), *Channels of discourse: Television and contemporary criticism.* Chapel Hill: University of North Carolina Press.

Krentz, J. A. (1992). *Dangerous men and adventuresome women.* Philadelphia: University of Pennsylvania Press.

Kuhn, A. (1982). *Women's pictures: Feminism and cinema.* New York: Routledge & Kegan Paul.

Lowery, M. M. (1983). *How to write romance novels that sell.* New York: Rawson.

Linden, D. W., & Rees, M. (1992, July 6). I'm hungry but not for food. *Forbes.*

Mayne, J. (1993a). *Cinema and spectatorship.* New York: Routledge.

Mayne, J. (1993b). White spectatorship and genre-mixing. In J. Mayne, *Cinema and spectatorship.* New York: Routledge.

Modleski, T. (1982). *Loving with a vengeance: Mass-produced fantasies for women.* New York: Methuen.

Mulvey, L. (1975). Visual pleasure and narrative cinema. *Screen, 16*(3).

Penley, C. (Ed.). *Feminism and film theory.* New York: Routledge.

Rabine, L. W. (1985). Romance in the age of electronics: Harlequin enterprises. *Feminist Studies, 11*(1), 39-60.

Stacey, J. (1990). Desperately seeking difference. In P. Erens (Ed.), *Issues in feminist film criticism* (pp. 365-379). Bloomington: Indiana University Press.

.21

Her Body, Himself

Gender in the Slasher Film

CAROL J. CLOVER

. . . It is a rare Hollywood film that does not devote a passage or two—a car chase, a sex scene—to the emotional/physical excitement of the audience. But horror and pornography are the only two genres specifically devoted to the arousal of bodily sensation. They exist solely to horrify and stimulate, not always respectively, and their ability to do so is the sole measure of their success: they "prove themselves upon our pulses."[1] Thus in horror-film circles, "good" means scary, specifically in a bodily way (ads promise shivers, chills, shudders, tingling of the spine; Lloyds of London insured audiences of *Macabre* against death by fright);[2] and *Hustler's Erotic Film Guide* ranks pornographic films according to the degree of erection they produce (one film is ranked a "pecker popper," another "limp"). The target is in both cases the body, our witnessing body. But *what* we witness is also the body, another's body, in experience: the body in sex and the body in threat. The terms "flesh film" ("skin flicks") and "meat movies" are remarkably apt. . . .

. . . Students of folklore or early literature recognize in the slasher film the hallmarks of oral story: the free exchange of themes and motifs, the archetypal characters and situations, the accumulation of sequels, remakes, imitations. This is a field in which there is in some sense no original, no real or right text, but only variants; a world in which, therefore, the meaning of

NOTE: Excerpts reprinted from *Misogyny, Misandry, and Misanthropy*, edited by R. Howard Bloch and Frances Ferguson (Berkeley: University of California Press, 1989), by permission of the University of California Press.

the individual example lies outside itself. The "art" of the horror film, like the "art" of pornography, is to a very large extent the art of rendition, and it is understood as such by the competent audience.[3] A particular example may have original features, but its quality as a horror film lies in the ways it delivers the cliché. James B. Twitchell rightly recommends an

> ethnological approach, in which the various stories are analyzed as if no one individual telling really mattered. . . . You search for what is stable and repeated; you neglect what is "artistic" and "original." . . . The critic's first job in explaining the fascination of horror is not to fix the images at their every appearance but, instead, to trace their migrations to the audience and, only then, try to understand why they have been crucial enough to pass along.[4] . . .

What makes horror "crucial enough to pass along" is, for critics since Freud, what has made ghost stories and fairy tales crucial enough to pass along: its engagement of repressed fears and desires and its reenactment of the residual conflict surrounding those feelings. Horror films thus respond to interpretation, as Robin Wood puts it, as "at once the personal dreams of their makers and the collective dreams of their audiences—the fusion made possible by the shared structures of a common ideology."[5] And just as attacker and attacked are expressions of the same self in nightmares, so they are expressions of the same viewer in horror film. Our primary and acknowledged identification may be with the victim, the adumbration of our infantile fears and desires, our memory sense of ourselves as tiny and vulnerable in the face of the enormous Other; but the Other is also finally another part of ourself, the projection of our repressed infantile rage and desire (our blind drive to annihilate those toward whom we feel anger, to force satisfaction from those who stimulate us, to wrench food for ourselves if only by actually devouring those who feed us) that we have had in the name of civilization to repudiate. . . .

THE SLASHER FILM

The immediate ancestor of the slasher film is Hitchcock's *Psycho* (1960). Its elements are familiar: the killer is the psychotic product of a sick family, but still recognizably human; the victim is a beautiful, sexually active woman; the location is not-home, at a Terrible Place; the weapon is something other than a gun; the attack is registered from the victim's point of view and comes with shocking suddenness. None of these features is original, but the unprecedented success of Hitchcock's particular formulation, above all the sexualization of both motive and action, prompted a flood of imitations and variations. In 1974, a film emerged that revised the *Psycho* template to a degree and in such a way as to mark a new phase: *The Texas Chain Saw Massacre* (Tobe Hooper). Together with *Halloween* (John Carpenter, 1978), it engendered a new spate of variations and imitations.

The plot of *Texas Chain Saw* is simple enough: five young people are driving through Texas in a van; they stop off at an abandoned house and are murdered one by one by the psychotic sons of a degenerate local family; the sole survivor is a woman. The horror, of course, lies in the elaboration. Early in the film the group picks up a hitchhiker, but when he starts a fire and slashes Franklin's arm (having already slit open his own hand), they kick him out. The abandoned house they subsequently visit, once the home of Sally's and Franklin's grandparents, turns out to be right next door to the house of the hitchhiker and his family: his brother Leatherface; their father; an aged and only marginally alive grandfather; and their dead grandmother and her dog, whose mummified corpses are ceremonially included in the family gatherings. Three generations of slaughterhouse workers, once proud of their craft but now displaced by machines, have taken up killing and cannibalism as a way of life. Their house is grotesquely decorated with human and animal remains—bones, feathers, hair, skins. The young people drift apart in their exploration of the abandoned house and grounds and are picked off one by one by Leatherface and Hitchhiker. Last is Sally. The others are attacked and killed with dispatch, but Sally must fight for her life, enduring all manner of horrors through the night. At dawn she manages to escape to the highway, where she is picked up by a passing trucker.

Likewise the nutshell plot of *Halloween*: a psychotic killer (Michael) stalks a small town on Halloween and kills a string of teenage friends, one by one; only Laurie survives. The twist here is that Michael has escaped from the asylum in which he has been incarcerated since the age of six, when he killed his sister minutes after she and her boyfriend parted following an illicit interlude in her parents' bed. That murder, in flashback, opens the film. It is related entirely in the killer's first person (I-camera) and only after the fact is the identity of the perpetrator revealed. Fifteen years later, Michael escapes his prison and returns to kill Laurie, whom he construes as another version of his sister (a sequel clarifies that she is in fact his *younger* sister, adopted by another family at the time of the earlier tragedy). But before Michael gets to Laurie, he picks off her high school friends: Annie, in a car on her way to her boyfriend's; Bob, going to the kitchen for a beer after sex with Lynda; Lynda, talking on the phone with Laurie and waiting for Bob to come back with the beer. At last only Laurie remains. When she hears Lynda squeal and then go silent on the phone, she leaves her own babysitting house to go to Lynda's. Here she discovers the three bodies and flees, the killer in pursuit. The remainder of the film is devoted to the back-and-forth struggle between Laurie and Michael. Again and again he bears down on her, and again and again she either eludes him (by running, hiding, breaking through windows to escape, locking herself in) or strikes back (once with a knitting needle, once with a hanger). In the end, Doctor Loomis (Michael's psychiatrist in the asylum) rushes in and shoots the killer (though not so fatally as to prevent his return in the sequels).

Before we turn to an inventory of generic components, let us add a third, more recent example: *The Texas Chain Saw Massacre II*, from 1986. The slaughterhouse family (now named the Sawyers) is the same, though older and, owing to their unprecedented success in the sausage business, richer.[6] When Mr. Sawyer begins to suspect from her broadcasts that a disk jockey named Stretch knows more than she should about one of their recent crimes, he dispatches his sons Leatherface and Chop Top (Hitchhiker in Part One) to the radio station late at night. There they seize the technician and corner Stretch. At the crucial moment, however, power fails Leatherface's chainsaw. As Stretch cowers before him, he presses the now still blade up along her thigh and against her crotch, where he holds it unsteadily as he jerks and shudders in what we understand to be orgasm. After that the sons leave. The intrepid Stretch, later joined by a Texas Ranger (Dennis Hopper), tracks them to their underground lair outside of town. Tumbling down the Texas equivalent of a rabbit hole, Stretch finds herself in the subterranean chambers of the Sawyer operation. Here, amidst all the slaughterhouse paraphernalia, the Sawyers live and work. The walls drip with blood. Like the decrepit mansion of Part One, the residential parts of the establishment are quaintly decorated with human and animal remains. After a long ordeal at the hands of the Sawyers, Stretch manages to scramble up through a culvert and beyond that up onto a nearby pinnacle, where she finds a chainsaw and wards off her final assailant. The Texas Ranger evidently perishes in a grenade explosion underground, leaving Stretch the sole survivor. . . .

Killer. The psychiatrist at the end of *Psycho* explains what we had already guessed from the action: that Norman Bates had introjected his mother, in life a "clinging, demanding woman," so completely that she constituted his other, controlling self. Not Norman but "the mother half of his mind" killed Marion—*had* to kill Marion—when he (the Norman half) found himself aroused by her. The notion of a killer propelled by psychosexual fury, more particularly a male in gender distress, has proved a durable one, and the progeny of Norman Bates stalk the genre up to the present day. Just as Norman wears his mother's clothes during his acts of violence and is thought, by the screen characters and also, for a while, by the film's spectators, to *be* his mother, so the murderer in the *Psycho*-imitation *Dressed to Kill* (Brian De Palma, 1980), a transvestite psychiatrist, seems until his unveiling to be a woman; like Norman, he must kill women who arouse him sexually. . . . Like Norman Bates, whose bedroom still displays his childhood toys, Hitchhiker/Chop Top and Leatherface are permanently locked in childhood. Only when Leatherface "discovers" sex in Part Two does he lose his appetite for murder. In *Motel Hell*, a sendup of modern horror with special reference to *Psycho* and *Texas Chain Saw I*, we are repeatedly confronted with a portrait of the dead mother, silently presiding over all manner of cannibalistic and incestuous doings on the part of her adult children. . . .

Even killers whose childhood is not immediately at issue and who display no overt gender confusion are often sexually disturbed. The murderer in *Nightmare on Elm Street* is an undead child molester. The killer in *Slumber Party Massacre* says to a young woman he is about to assault with a power drill: "Pretty. All of you are very pretty. I love you. Takes a lot of love for a person to do this. You know you want it. You want it. Yes." When she grasps the psychodynamics of the situation in the infamous crotch episode of *Texas Chain Saw II*, Stretch tries a desperate gambit: "You're really good, you really are good," she repeats; and indeed, immediately after ejaculation Leatherface becomes palpably less interested in his saw. The parodic *Motel Hell* spells it out. "His pecker don't work; you'll see when he takes off his overalls—it's like a shrivelled prune," Bruce says of his killer-brother Vincent when he learns of Terry's plans to marry him. Terry never does see, for on her wedding night he attempts (needless to say) not sex but murder. Actual rape is practically nonexistent in the slasher film, evidently on the premise—as the crotch episode suggests—that violence and sex are not concomitants but alternatives, the one as much a substitute for and a prelude to the other as the teenage horror film is a substitute for and a prelude to the "adult" film (or the meat movie a substitute for and prelude to the skin flick).[7] When Sally under torture (*Texas Chain Saw I*) cries out "I'll do anything you want," clearly with sexual intention, her assailants respond only by mimicking her in gross terms; she has profoundly misunderstood the psychology. . . .

In films of the *Psycho* type (*Dressed to Kill, Eyes of Laura Mars*), the killer is an insider, a man who functions normally in the action until, at the end, his other self is revealed. *Texas Chain Saw* and *Halloween* introduced another sort of killer: one whose only role is that of killer and one whose identity as such is clear from the outset. Norman may have a normal half, but these killers have none. They are emphatic misfits and emphatic outsiders. Michael is an escapee from a distant asylum; Jason subsists in the forest; the Sawyer sons live a bloody subterranean existence outside of town. Nor are they clearly seen. We catch sight of them only in glimpses—few and far between in the beginning, more frequent toward the end. They are usually large, sometimes overweight, and often masked. In short, they may be recognizably human, but only marginally so, just as they are only marginally visible—to their victims and to us, the spectators. In one key aspect, however, the killers are superhuman: their virtual indestructibility. Just as Michael (in *Halloween*) repeatedly rises from blows that would stop a lesser man, so Jason (in the *Friday the Thirteenth* films) survives assault after assault to return in sequel after sequel. Chop Top in *Texas Chain Saw II* is so called because of a metal plate implanted in his skull in repair of a head wound sustained in the truck accident in Part One. It is worth noting that the killers are normally the fixed elements and the victims the changeable ones in any given series.

Terrible Place. The Terrible Place, most often a house or tunnel, in which the victims sooner or later find themselves is a venerable element of horror. The Bates mansion is just one in a long list of such places—a list that continues, in the modern slasher, with the decaying mansion of *Texas Chain Saw I*, the abandoned and haunted mansion of *Hell Night*, the house for sale but unsellable in *Halloween* (also a point of departure for such films as *Rosemary's Baby* and *Amityville Horror*), and so on. What makes these houses terrible is not just their Victorian decrepitude but the terrible families—murderous, incestuous, cannibalistic—that occupy them. . . . Into such houses unwitting victims wander in film after film, and it is the conventional task of the genre to register in close detail those victims' dawning understanding, as they survey the visible evidence, of the human crimes and perversions that have transpired there. That perception leads directly to the perception of their own immediate peril. . . .

The house or tunnel may at first seem a safe haven, but the same walls that promise to keep the killer out quickly become, once the killer penetrates them, the walls that hold the victim in. A phenomenally popular moment in post-1974 slashers is the scene in which the victim locks herself in (a house, room, closet, car) and waits with pounding heart as the killer slashes, hacks, or drills his way in. The action is inevitably seen from the victim's point of view; we stare at the door (wall, car roof) and watch the surface break with first the tip and then the shaft of the weapon. In Hitchcock's *The Birds*, it is the birds' beaks we see penetrating the door. The penetration scene is commonly the film's pivotal moment; if the victim has up to now simply fled, she has at this point no choice but to fight back.

Weapons. In the hands of the killer, at least, guns have no place in slasher films. Victims sometimes avail themselves of firearms, but like telephones, fire alarms, elevators, doorbells, and car engines, guns fail in the squeeze. In some basic sense, the emotional terrain of the slasher film is pretechnological. The preferred weapons of the killer are knives, hammers, axes, icepicks, hypodermic needles, red hot pokers, pitchforks, and the like. . . . The sense is clearer if we include marginal examples like *Jaws* and *The Birds*, as well as related werewolf and vampire genres. Knives and needles, like teeth, beaks, fangs, and claws, are personal, extensions of the body that bring attacker and attacked into primitive, animalistic embrace.[8] In *I Spit on Your Grave*, the heroine forces her rapist at gunpoint to drop his pants, evidently meaning to shoot him in his genitals. But she changes her mind, invites him home for what he all too readily supposes will be a voluntary follow-up of the earlier gang rape. Then, as they sit together in a bubble bath, she castrates him with a knife. If we wondered why she threw away the pistol, now we know: all phallic symbols are not equal, and a hands-on knifing answers a hands-on rape in a way that a shooting, even a shooting preceded by a humiliation, does not.[9] . . .

Victims. . . . A classic publicity poster for *Psycho* shows Janet Leigh with a slightly uncomprehending look on her face sitting on the bed, dressed in a bra and half-slip, looking backward in such a way as to outline her breasts. If it is the task of promotional materials to state in one image the essence of a film, those breasts are what *Psycho* is all about.

In the slasher film, sexual transgressors of both sexes are scheduled for early destruction. The genre is studded with couples trying to find a place beyond purview of parents and employers where they can have sex, and immediately afterward (or during) being killed. The theme enters the tradition with the Lynda-Bob subplot of *Halloween*. Finding themselves alone in a neighborhood house, Lynda and Bob make hasty use of the master bedroom. Afterward, Bob goes downstairs for a beer. In the kitchen he is silently dispatched by the killer, Michael, who then covers himself with a sheet (it's

Halloween), dons Bob's glasses, and goes upstairs. Supposing the bespectacled ghost in the doorway to be Bob, Lynda jokes, bares her breasts provocatively, and finally, in irritation at "Bob's" stony silence, dials Laurie on the phone. Now the killer advances, strangling her with the telephone cord, so that what Laurie hears on the other end are squeals she takes to be orgasmic. *Halloween II* takes the scene a step further. Here the victims are a nurse and orderly who have sneaked off for sex in the hospital therapy pool. The watching killer, Michael again, turns up the thermostat and, when the orderly goes to check it, kills him. Michael then approaches the nurse from behind (she thinks it's the orderly) and strokes her neck. Only when he moves his hand toward her bare breast and she turns around and sees him does he kill her. . . .

. . . Even in films in which males and females are killed in roughly even numbers, the lingering images are inevitably female. The death of a male is always swift; even if the victim grasps what is happening to him, he has no time to react or register terror. He is dispatched and the camera moves on. The death of a male is moreover more likely than the death of a female to be viewed from a distance, or viewed only dimly (because of darkness or fog, for example), or indeed to happen offscreen and not be viewed at all. The murders of women, on the other hand, are filmed at closer range, in more graphic detail, and at greater length. The pair of murders at the therapy pool in *Halloween II* illustrates the standard iconography. We see the orderly killed in two shots: the first at close range in the control room, just before the stabbing, and the second as he is being stabbed, through the vapors in a medium long shot; the orderly never even sees his assailant. The nurse's death, on the other hand, is shot entirely in medium closeup. The camera studies her face as it registers first her unwitting complicity (as the killer strokes her neck and shoulders from behind), then apprehension, and then, as she faces him, terror; we see the knife plunge into her repeatedly, hear her cries, and watch her blood fill the therapy pool. . . .

Final Girl. The image of the distressed female most likely to linger in memory is the image of the one who did not die: the survivor, or Final Girl. She is the one who encounters the mutilated bodies of her friends and perceives the full extent of the preceding horror and of her own peril; who is chased, cornered, wounded; whom we see scream, stagger, fall, rise, and scream again. She is abject terror personified. If her friends knew they were about to die only seconds before the event, the Final Girl lives with the knowledge for long minutes or hours. She alone looks death in the face; but she alone also finds the strength either to stay the killer long enough to be rescued (ending A) or to kill him herself (ending B). She is inevitably female. In Schoell's words: "The vast majority of contemporary shockers, whether in the sexist mold or not, feature climaxes in which the women fight back against their attackers—the wandering humorless psychos who populate these films. They often show more courage and levelheadedness than their cringing male counterparts."[10] Her scene occupies the last ten to twenty minutes (thirty in the case of *Texas Chain Saw I*) and constitutes the film's emphatic climax. . . .

. . . The Final Girl of the slasher film is presented from the outset as the main character. The practiced viewer distinguishes her from her friends minutes into the film. She is the girl scout, the bookworm, the mechanic. Unlike her girlfriends (and Marion Crane) she is not sexually active. Laurie (*Halloween*) is teased because of her fears about dating, and Marti (*Hell Night*) explains to the boy with whom she finds herself sharing a room that they will have separate beds. . . . The Final Girl is also watchful to the point of paranoia; small signs of danger that her friends ignore she takes in and turns over. Above all she is intelligent and resourceful in extreme situations. Thus Laurie even at her most desperate, cornered in a closet, has the wit to grab a hanger from the rack and bend it into a weapon; Marti can hot-wire her getaway car, the killer in pursuit; and the psych major of *Friday the Thirteenth II*, on seeing the enshrined head of Mrs. Voorhees, can stop Jason in his tracks by assuming a stridently maternal voice. Finally, although she is always smaller and weaker than the killer, she grapples with him energetically and convincingly.

The Final Girl is boyish, in a word. Just as the killer is not fully masculine, she is not fully feminine—not, in any case, feminine in the ways of her friends. Her smartness, gravity, competence in mechanical and other practical matters, and sexual reluctance set her apart from the other girls and ally her, ironically, with the very boys she fears or rejects, not to speak of the killer himself. Lest we miss the point, it is spelled out in her name: Stevie, Marti, Terry, Laurie, Stretch, Will. Not only the conception of the hero in *Alien* and *Aliens* but also her name, Ripley, owes a clear debt to slasher tradition.

With the introduction of the Final Girl, then, the *Psycho* formula is radically altered. . . . *Psycho*'s detective plot, revolving around a revelation, yields in the modern slasher film to a hero plot, revolving around the main character's struggle with and eventual triumph over evil. But for the femaleness, however qualified, of that main character, the story is a standard one of tale and epic. . . .

THE BODY

On the face of it, the relation between the sexes in slasher films could hardly be clearer. The killer is with few exceptions recognizably human and distinctly male; his fury is unmistakeably sexual in both roots and expression; his victims are mostly women, often sexually free and always young and beautiful ones. . . . The case could be made that the slasher films available at a given neighborhood video rental outlet recommend themselves to censorship under the Dworkin-MacKinnon guidelines at least as readily as the hard-core films the next section over, at which that legislation is aimed; for if some victims are men, the argument goes, most are women, and the women are brutalized in ways that come too close to real life for comfort. . . .

It is, of course, "on the face of it" that most of the public discussion of film takes place—from the Dworkin-MacKinnon legislation to Siskel's and Ebert's reviews to our own talks with friends on leaving the movie house. Underlying that discussion is the assumption that the sexes are what they seem; that screen males represent the Male and screen females the Female; that this identification along gender line authorizes impulses toward sexual violence in males and encourages impulses toward victimization in females. In part because of the massive authority cinema by nature accords the image, even academic film criticism has been slow—slower than literary criticism—to get beyond appearances. Film may not appropriate the mind's eye, but it certainly encroaches on it; the gender characteristics of a screen figure are a visible and audible given for the duration of the film. To the extent that the possibility of cross-gender identification has been entertained, it has been in the direction female-with-male. Thus some critics have wondered whether the female viewer, faced with the screen image of a masochistic/narcissistic female, might not rather elect to "betray her sex and identify with the masculine point of view." [11] The reverse question—whether men might not also, on occasion, elect to betray their sex and identify with screen females—has scarcely been asked, presumably on the assumption that men's interests are well served by the traditional patterns of cinematic representation. Then too there is the matter of the "male gaze." As E. Ann Kaplan sums it up: "Within the film text itself, men gaze at women, who become objects of the gaze; the spectator, in turn, is made to identify with this male gaze, and to objectify the women on the screen; and the camera's original 'gaze' comes into play in the very act of filming." [12] But if it is so that all of us, male and female alike, are by these processes "made to" identify with men and "against" women, how are we then to explain the appeal to a largely male audience of a film genre that features a female victim-hero? . . .

A figurative or functional analysis of the slasher begins with the processes of point of view and identification. The male viewer seeking a male character, even a vicious one, with whom to identify in a sustained way has little to hang on to in the standard example. On the good side, the only viable candidates are the schoolmates or friends of the girls. They are for the most part marginal, undeveloped characters; more to the point, they tend to die early in the film. If the traditional horror film gave the male spectator a last-minute hero with whom to identify, thereby "indulging his vanity as protector of the helpless female," [13] the slasher eliminates or attenuates that role beyond any such function; indeed, would-be rescuers are not infrequently blown away for their efforts, leaving the girl to fight her own fight. Policemen, fathers, and sheriffs appear only long enough to demonstrate visible incomprehension and incompetence. On the bad side, there is the killer. The killer is often unseen, or barely glimpsed, during the first part of the film, and what we do see, when we finally get a good look, hardly invites immediate or conscious empathy. He is commonly masked, fat, deformed, or dressed as a woman. Or "he" *is* a woman: woe to the viewer of *Friday the Thirteenth I* who identifies with the male killer only to discover, in the film's final sequences, that he was not a man at all but a middle-aged woman. In either case, the killer is himself eventually killed or otherwise evacuated from the narrative. No male character of any stature lives to tell the tale.

The one character of stature who does live to tell the tale is of course female. The Final Girl is introduced at the beginning and is the only character to be developed in any psychological detail. We understand immediately from the attention paid it that hers is the main story line. She is intelligent, watchful, level-headed; the first character to sense something amiss and the only one to deduce from the accumulating evidence the patterns and extent of the threat; the only one, in other words, whose perspective approaches our own privileged understanding of the situation. We register her horror as she stumbles on the corpses of her friends; her paralysis in the face of death duplicates those moments of the universal nightmare experience on which horror frankly trades. When she downs the killer, we are triumphant. She is by any measure the slasher film's hero. This is not to say that our attachment to her is exclusive and unremitting, only that it adds up, and that in the closing sequence it is very close to absolute.

An analysis of the camerawork bears this out. Much is made of the use of the I-camera to represent the killer's point of view. In these passages— they are usually few and brief, but powerful—we see through his eyes and (on the sound track) hear his breathing and heartbeat. His and our vision is partly obscured by bushes or windowblinds in the foreground. By such means we are forced, the argument goes, to identify with the killer. In fact, however, the relation between camera point of view and the processes of viewer identification are poorly understood; the fact that Steven Spielberg can stage an attack in *Jaws* from the shark's point of view (underwater, rushing upward toward the swimmer's flailing legs) or Hitchcock an attack in *The Birds* from the birds-eye perspective (from the sky, as they gather to swoop down on the streets of Bodega Bay) would seem to suggest either that the viewer's identificatory powers are unbelievably elastic or that point-of-view shots can sometimes be pro forma.[14] But let us for the moment accept the equation point of view = identification. We are linked, in this way, with the killer in the early part of the film, usually before we have seen him directly and before we have come to know the Final Girl in any detail. Our closeness to him wanes as our closeness to the Final Girl waxes—a shift underwritten by story line as well as camera position. By the end, point of view is hers: we are in the closet with her, watching with her eyes the knife blade stab through the door; in the room with her as the killer breaks through the window and grabs at her; in the car with her as the killer stabs through the convertible top, and so on. With her, we become if not the killer of the killer then the agent of his expulsion from the narrative vision. If, during the film's course, we shifted our sympathies back and forth, and dealt them out to other characters along the way, we belong in the end to the Final Girl; there is no alternative. When Stretch eviscerates Chop Top at the end of *Texas Chain Saw II*, she is literally the only character left alive, on either side.

Audience response ratifies this design. Observers unanimously stress the readiness of the "live" audience to switch sympathies in midstream, siding now with the killer and now, and finally, with the Final Girl. As Schoell, whose book on shocker films wrestles with its own monster, "the feminists," puts it:

> Social critics make much of the fact that male audience members cheer on the misogynous misfits in these movies as they rape, plunder, and murder their screaming, writhing female victims. Since these same

critics walk out of the moviehouse in disgust long before the movie is over, they don't realize that these same men cheer on (with renewed enthusiasm, in fact) the heroines, who are often as strong, sexy, and independent as the [earlier] victims, as they blow away the killer with a shotgun or get him between the eyes with a machete. All of these men are said to be identifying with the maniac, but they enjoy *his* death throes the most of all, and applaud the heroine with admiration.[15]

What filmmakers seem to know better than film critics is that gender is less a wall than a permeable membrane.[16]

No one who has read "Red Riding Hood" to a small boy or participated in a viewing of, say, *Deliverance* (an all-male story that women find as gripping as men) or, more recently, *Alien* and *Aliens,* with whose space-age female Rambo, herself a Final Girl, male viewers seem to engage with ease, can doubt the phenomenon of cross-gender identification.[17] . . .

Nor is the gender of the principals as straightforward as it first seems. The killer's phallic purpose, as he thrusts his drill or knife into the trembling bodies of young women, is unmistakeable. At the same time, however, his masculinity is severely qualified: he ranges from the virginal or sexually inert to the transvestite or transsexual, is spiritually divided ("the mother half of his mind") or even equipped with vulva and vagina. Although the killer of *God Told Me To* is represented and taken as a male in the film text, he is revealed, by the doctor who delivered him, to have been sexually ambiguous from birth: "I truly could not tell whether that child was male or female; it was as if the sexual gender had not been determined . . . as if it were being developed."[18] . . . To the extent that the monster is constructed as feminine, the horror film thus expresses female desire only to show how monstrous it is.[19] The intention is manifest in *Aliens,* in which the Final Girl, Ripley, is pitted in the climactic scene against the most terrifying "alien" of all: an egg-laying Mother.

Nor can we help noticing the "intrauterine" quality of the Terrible Place, dark and often damp, in which the killer lives or lurks and whence he stages his most terrifying attacks. . . . It is the exceptional film that does not mark as significant the moment that the killer leaps out of the dark recesses of a corridor or cavern at the trespassing victim, usually the Final Girl. Long after the other particulars have faded, the viewer will remember the images of Amy assaulted from the dark halls of a morgue (*He Knows You're Alone*), Sally or Stretch facing dismemberment in the ghastly dining room or underground labyrinth of the slaughterhouse family (*Texas Chain Saw I-II*), or Melanie trapped in the attic as the savage birds close in (*The Birds*). In such scenes of convergence the Other is at its bisexual mightiest, the victim at her tiniest, and the component of sadomasochism at its most blatant.

The gender of the Final Girl is likewise compromised from the outset by her masculine interests, her inevitable sexual reluctance (penetration, it seems, constructs the female), her apartness from other girls, sometimes her name. At the level of the cinematic apparatus, her unfemininity is signaled clearly by her exercise of the "active investigating gaze" normally reserved for males and hideously punished in females when they assume it themselves; tentatively at first and then aggressively, the Final Girl looks *for* the killer, even tracking him to his forest hut or his underground labyrinth, and then *at* him, therewith bringing him, often for the first time, into our vision as well.[20] When, in the final scene, she stops screaming, looks at the killer, and reaches for the knife (sledge hammer, scalpel, gun, machete, hanger, knitting needle, chainsaw), she addresses the killer on his own terms. To the critics' objection that *Halloween* in effect punished female sexuality, director John Carpenter responded:

> They [the critics] completely missed the boat there, I think. Because if you turn it around, the one girl who is the most sexually uptight just keeps stabbing this guy with a long knife. She's the most sexually frustrated. She's the one that killed him. Not because she's a virgin, but because all that repressed energy starts coming out. She uses all those phallic symbols on the guy. . . . She and the killer have a certain link: sexual repression.[21]

For all its perversity, Carpenter's remark does underscore the sense of affinity, even recognition, that attends the final encounter. But the "certain link" that puts killer and Final Girl on terms, at least briefly, is more than "sexual repression." It is also a shared masculinity, materialized in "all those phallic symbols"—and it is also a shared femininity, materialized in what comes next (and what Carpenter, perhaps significantly, fails to mention): the castration, literal or symbolic, of the killer at her hands. His eyes may be put out, his hand severed, his body impaled or shot, his belly gashed, or his genitals sliced away or bitten off. The Final Girl has not just manned herself; she specifically unmans an oppressor whose masculinity was in question to begin with. By the time the drama has played itself out, darkness yields to light (often as day breaks) and the close quarters of the barn (closet, elevator, attic, basement) give way to the open expanse of the yard (field, road, lakescape, cliff). With the Final Girl's appropriation of "all those phallic symbols" comes the quelling, the dispelling, of the "uterine" threat as well. Consider again the paradigmatic ending of *Texas Chain Saw II*. From the underground labyrinth, murky and bloody, in which she faced saw, knife, and hammer, Stretch escapes through a culvert into the open air. She clambers up the jutting rock and with a chainsaw takes her stand. When her last assailant comes at her, she slashes open his lower abdomen—the sexual symbolism is all too clear—and flings him off the cliff. Again, the final scene shows her in extreme long shot, standing on the pinnacle, drenched in sunlight, buzzing chainsaw held overhead.

The tale would indeed seem to be one of sex and parents. . . . When the Final Girl stands at last in the light of day with the knife in her hand, she has delivered herself into the adult world. Carpenter's equation of the Final Girl with the killer has more than a grain of truth. The killers of *Psycho, The Eyes of Laura Mars, Friday the Thirteenth II-VI,* and *Cruising,* among others, are explicitly figured as sons in the psychosexual grip of their mothers (or fathers, in the case of *Cruising*). The difference is between past and present and between failure and success. The Final Girl enacts in the present, and successfully, the parenticidal struggle that the killer himself enacted unsuccessfully in his own past—a past that constitutes the film's backstory. She is what the killer once was; he is what she could become should she fail in her battle for sexual selfhood. "You got a choice, boy," says the tyrannical father of Leatherface in *Texas Chain Saw II*, "sex or the saw; you never know about sex, but the saw—the saw is the family."

But the tale is no less one of maleness. If the early experience of the oedipal drama can be—is perhaps ideally—enacted in female form, the achievement of full adulthood requires the assumption and, apparently, brutal employment of the phallus. The helpless child is gendered feminine; the autonomous adult or subject is gendered masculine; the passage from childhood to adulthood entails a shift from feminine to masculine. It is the male killer's tragedy that his incipient femininity is not reversed but completed (castration) and the Final Girl's victory that her incipient masculinity is not thwarted but realized (phallicization). When De Palma says that female frailty is a predicate of the suspense genre, he proposes, in effect, that the lack of the phallus, for Lacan the privileged signifier of the symbolic order of culture, is itself simply horrifying, at least in the mind of the male observer. Where pornography (the argument goes) resolves that lack through a process of fetishization that allows a breast or leg or whole body to stand in for the missing member, the slasher film resolves it either through eliminating the woman (earlier victims) or reconstituting her as masculine (Final Girl). The moment at which the Final Girl is effectively phallicized is the moment that the plot halts and horror ceases. Day breaks, and the community returns to its normal order. . . .

If the slasher film is "on the face of it" a genre with at least a strong female presence, it is in these figurative readings a thoroughly strong male exercise, one that finally has very little to do with femaleness and very much to do with phallocentrism. Figuratively seen, the Final Girl is a male surrogate in things oedipal, a homoerotic stand-in, the audience incorporate; to the extent she "means" girl at all, it is only for purposes of signifying phallic lack, and even that meaning is nullified in the final scenes. Our initial question—how to square a female victim-hero with a largely male audience—is not so much answered as it is obviated in these readings. The Final Girl is (apparently) female not despite the maleness of the audience, but precisely because of it. The discourse is wholly masculine, and females figure in it only insofar as they "read" some aspect of male experience. To applaud the Final Girl as a feminist development, as some reviews of *Aliens* have done with Ripley, is, in light of her figurative meaning, a particularly grotesque expression of wishful thinking.[22] She is simply an agreed-upon fiction, and the male viewer's use of her as a vehicle for his own sadomasochistic fantasies an act of perhaps timeless dishonesty. . . .

NOTES

1. Marcus (1964, p. 278).
2. Castle (1978).

3. As Dickstein (1980) puts it, "The 'art' of horror film is a ludicrous notion since horror, even at its most commercially exploitative, is genuinely subcultural like the wild child that can never be tamed, or the half-human mutant who appeals to our secret fascination with deformity and the grotesque" (p. 34).

4. Twitchell (1985, p. 84).

5. Wood (1978, p. 26). In Wes Craven's *Nightmare on Elm Street,* it is the nightmare itself, shared by the teenagers who live on Elm Street, that is fatal. One by one they are killed by the murderer of their collective dream. The one girl who survives does so by first refusing to sleep and then, at the same time that she acknowledges her parents' inadequacies, by conquering the feelings that prompt the deadly nightmare. See, as an example of the topic dream/horror, White (1971).

6. The development of the human-sausage theme is typical of the back-and-forth borrowing in low horror. *Texas Chain Saw Massacre I* hints at it; *Motel Hell* turns it into an industry ("Farmer Vincent's Smoked Meats: This is It!" proclaims a local billboard); and *Texas Chain Saw Massacre II* expands it to a statewide chili-tasting contest.

7. "The release of sexuality in the horror film is always presented as perverted, monstrous, and excessive, both the perversion and the excess being the logical outcome of repressing. Nowhere is this carried further than in *Texas [Chain Saw] Massacre [I].* Here sexuality is totally perverted from its functions, into sadism, violence, and cannibalism. It is striking that there is no suggestion anywhere that Sally is the object of an overtly sexual threat; she is to be tormented, killed, dismembered, and eaten, but not raped" (Wood, 1978, p. 31).

8. Kaminsky (1977, p. 107).

9. The shower sequence in *Psycho* is probably the most echoed scene in all of film history. The bathtub scene in *I Spit on Your Grave* (not properly speaking a slasher, though with a number of generic affinities) is to my knowledge the only effort to reverse the terms.

10. Further: "Scenes in which women whimper helplessly and do nothing to defend themselves are ridiculed by the audience, who find it hard to believe that anyone—male or female—would simply allow someone to kill them with nary a protest" (Schoell, 1985, pp. 55-56).

11. Bovenschen (1977, 114). See also Doane (1980).

12. Kaplan (1983, p. 15). The discussion of the gendered "gaze" is lively and extensive. See above all Mulvey (1975), reprinted in Mast and Cohen (1985, pp. 803-816); also Gledhill (1978), reprinted in Mast and Cohen (1985, pp. 817-845).

13. Wood (1983, p. 64).

14. The locus classicus in this connection is the view-from-the-coffin shot in Carl Dreyer's *Vampyr,* in which the I-camera sees through the eyes of a dead man. See Nash (1976, pp. 32-33). The 1987 remake of *The Little Shop of Horrors* (itself originally a low-budget horror film, made the same year as *Psycho* in two days) lets us see the dentist from the proximate point of view of the patient's tonsils.

15. Two points in this paragraph deserve emending. One is the suggestion that rape is common in these films; it is in fact virtually absent, by definition (see note 7 above). The other is the characterization of the Final Girl as "sexy." She may be attractive (though typically less so than her friends), but she is with few exceptions sexually inactive. For a detailed analysis of point-of-view manipulation, together with a psychoanalytic interpretation of the dynamic, see Neale (1981).

16. Wood (1978) is struck by the willingness of the teenaged audience to identify "against" itself, with the forces of the enemy of youth. "Watching it [*Texas Chain Saw Massacre I*] recently with a large, half-stoned youth audience, who cheered and applauded every one of Leatherface's outrages against their representatives on the screen, was a terrifying experience" (p. 32).

17. "I really appreciate the way audiences respond," Gail Anne Hurd, producer of *Aliens,* is reported to have said. "They buy it. We don't get people, even rednecks, leaving the theater saying, 'That was stupid. No woman would do that.' You don't have to be a liberal ERA supporter to root for Ripley" (as reported in the *San Francisco Examiner Datebook,* August 10, 1986, p. 19). *Time* (July 28, 1986, p. 56), suggests that Ripley's maternal impulses (she squares off against the worst aliens of all in her quest to save a little girl) give the audience "a much stronger rooting interest in Ripley, and that gives the picture resonances unusual in a popcorn epic."

18. Further, "When she [the mother] referred to the infant as a male, I just went along with it. Wonder how that child turned out—male, female, or something else entirely?" The birth is understood to be parthenogenetic, and the bisexual child, literally equipped with both sets of genitals, is figured as the reborn Christ.

19. Williams (1985, p. 90). Williams's emphasis on the phallic leads her to dismiss slasher killers as a "non-specific male killing force" and hence a degeneration in the tradition. "In these films the recognition and affinity between woman and monster of classic horror film gives way to pure identity: she *is* the monster, her mutilated body is the only visible horror" (p. 96). This analysis does not do justice to the obvious bisexuality of slasher killers, nor does it take into account the new strength of the female victim. The slasher film may not, in balance, be more subversive than traditional horror, but it is certainly not less so.

20. "The woman's exercise of an active investigating gaze can only be simultaneous with her own victimization. The place of her specularization is transformed into the locus of a process of seeing designed to unveil an aggression against itself" (Doane, 1984, p. 72).

21. John Carpenter interviewed by Todd McCarthy (1980).

22. This would seem to be the point of the final sequence of Brian De Palma's *Blow Out*, in which we see the boyfriend of the victim-hero stab the killer to death but later hear the television announce that the woman herself vanquished the killer. The frame plot of the film has to do with the making of a slasher film ("Co-Ed Frenzy"), and it seems clear that De Palma means his ending to stand as a comment on the Final Girl formula of the genre. De Palma's (and indirectly Hitchcock's) insistence that only men can kill men, or protect women from men, deserves a separate essay.

REFERENCES

Bovenschen, S. (1977). Is there a feminine aesthetic? *New German Critique, 10.*

Castle, W. (1978). *Step right up! I'm gonna scare the pants off America.* New York: F & W Inc.

Dickstein, M. (1980). The aesthetics of fright. *American Film, 5.*

Doane, M. A. (1980). Misrecognition and identity. *Cine-Tracts, 11,* 25-32.

Doane, M. A. (1984). The woman's film. In M. A. Doane, P. Mellencamp, & L. Williams (Eds.), *Re-vision: Essays in feminist film criticism.* Los Angeles: American Film Institute.

Gledhill, C. (1978). Recent developments in feminist criticism. *Quarterly Review of Film Studies.* Reprinted in G. Mast & M. Cohen (Eds.). *Film theory and criticism: Introductory readings* (3rd ed., 1985). New York: Oxford University Press.

Kaminsky, S. (1977). *American film genres: Approaches to a critical theory of popular film.* Chicago: Nelson-Hall.

Kaplan, E. A. (1983). *Women and film: Both sides of the camera.* London: Methuen.

Marcus, S. (1964). *The other Victorians: A study of sexuality and pornography in mid-nineteenth-century England.* New York.

Mast, G., & Cohen, M. (1985). *Film theory and criticism: Introductory readings* (3rd ed.). New York: Oxford University Press.

McCarthy, T. (1980). Trick and treat [interview with John Carpenter]. *Film Comment, 16,* 23-24.

Mulvey, L. (1975). Visual pleasure and narrative cinema. *Screen, 16*(3), 6-18.

Nash, M. (1976). *Vampyr* and the fantastic. *Screen, 17.*

Neale, S. (1981, Spring). *Halloween:* Suspense, aggression and the look. *Framework, 14,* 25-29.

Schoell, W. (1985). *Stay out of the shower.* New York: Barricade.

Twitchell, J. B. (1985). *Dreadful pleasures: An anatomy of modern horror.* New York: Oxford University Press.

White, D. L. (1971). The poetics of horror. *Cinema Journal, 10,* 1-18.

Williams, L. (1984). When the woman looks. In M. A. Doane, P. Mellencamp, &
    L. Williams (Eds.), *Re-vision: Essays in feminist film criticism.* Los Angeles: Ameri-
    can Film Institute.
Wood, R. (1978). Return of the repressed. *Film Comment, 14*(4), 25-30.
Wood, R. (1983). Beauty bests the beast. *American Film, 8*(10), 63-65.

Do Slasher Films
Breed Real-Life Violence?

ALISON BASS

A month before Rod Matthews bludgeoned a 14-year-old classmate to death, he watched a videotape docudrama that portrays a series of brutal killings. At Matthews' murder trial earlier this year, a psychiatrist testified that the *Faces of Death* video may have inspired the 15-year-old Canton youth to "see what it was like to kill someone."

Police in Greenfield believe that Mark Branch, suspected of having stabbed an 18-year-old female college student to death, may have been similarly inspired. Police found dozens of extremely violent films, including *Faces of Death*, in the 19-year-old's home, along with a machete and goalie masks like those used by Jason, the gruesome film character in the horror movie series, *Friday the 13th*. Branch hanged himself a few days after the murder.

Researchers, police and parents' groups are increasingly disturbed by such cases and by a mounting body of psychological research showing that young men exposed to extremely violent films become more accepting of violence and more callous toward the real-life victims of sexual violence.

One of the latest and most compelling studies shows that college-age men exposed to just a few of these "slasher" films are more likely than other

---

NOTE: Reprinted courtesy of *The Boston Globe*, "Sci-Tech: Science, Health, Technology" section, *The Boston Globe*, December 19, 1988.

men to believe that the victim of an actual rape deserved what she got. They are also less likely to want the rapist to be punished.

"We all have a natural aversion to violence, but these studies show that with constant exposure to violence, that aversion goes away," said Daniel G. Linz, a psychologist at the University of California, Santa Barbara, and co-author of the newest study, published last month in the *Journal of Personality and Social Psychology.*

"What's more important is that this desensitization appears to carry over into judgements about the victims of violence in real-life situations."

Despite the growing weight of this evidence, extremely violent films are more readily available than ever before to teenagers and young children. Converted into videos and stocked by virtually every video store worth its profit margin, such films are regularly sought out by children as young as 10 or 11.

In fact, the preteen set (ages 11 to 14) rent violent horror films in higher numbers than any other age group in the United States, according to Ronnie Gunnerson, editor of Video Marketing Newsletter in Los Angeles.

Although most of these videos are rated "R" (restricted) and are supposedly off limits to youths under 17, they are easily obtained by younger teenagers, who either rent them from video stores that don't check IDs or get them through older friends, siblings or unsuspecting parents.

Rod Matthews got his older sister to rent "Faces of Death" for him.

"It's becoming a popular party game among junior high kids to see how much they can watch of *Faces of Death* before they become physically nauseated," said Ronald G. Slaby, a psychologist and expert on aggression at the Harvard Graduate School of Education.

Recent surveys show that extremely violent horror films such as the *Friday the 13th* and *Nightmare on Elm Street* series are particular favorites of children aged 11 to 13. Both feature grisly scenes of violence against passive female victims, and one of them is the basis for a less gory television show, *Freddy's Dreams.*

"We're talking about saturation levels that were heretofore unknown," said Linz. "Kids today can see any number of slasher films on video because most video outlets are not particularly vigilant about kids getting hold of R-rated material. And parents are simply not aware of the level of sexualized violence in these films."

Researchers say that teenage boys in particular may be drawn to these films as a way of demonstrating their machismo during the awkward time of transition from boyhood to manhood.

Although there is little data on how these films affect the way children view violence—it is difficult to do research on minors—research on young adults allows psychologists to make some educated guesses about the impact on younger viewers.

Linz and others have been studying the effect of film violence since the late 1970s. One of the first studies, by psychologists at the University of California, Los Angeles, found that young men exposed to popular films like *Getaway* and *Swept Away,* which combine sex and violence, were more accepting of violence toward women than those who had seen other types of films.

A larger percentage of these men also said they might try to force women into sexual acts against their will, as long as they were assured of not being caught, says Neil Malamuth, a professor of psychology and communications who conducted the studies.

COLLEGE-AGE MALES STUDIED

In the mid-1980s, Linz and his colleagues at Santa Barbara corroborated Malamuth's findings in larger studies of college-age men who were exposed to even more graphic violence in films like *Texas Chainsaw Massacre, Friday the 13th, Part 2* and *Toolbox Murders*. The Santa Barbara researchers also had their subjects watch a video of an actual rape trial and then questioned them about their attitudes toward violence and women after they had been exposed to a steady diet of slasher films.

They found the same results: The men who had seen the sexually violent films were more accepting of the violence they saw and more callous about the injuries to the rape victim in the trial they witnessed. They were also less likely to want the rapist to be severely punished.

In the latest study, the Santa Barbara researchers exposed college-age men to three types of films: the sexually violent films they had previously studied; X-rated, sexually explicit but nonviolent films like *Debbie Does Dallas*, and R-rated, nonviolent party films aimed at the teen market, such as *Porky's*.

When they compared the attitudes of all three groups, the psychologists discovered that exposure to the nonviolent X- or R-rated films did not produce the callous attitudes toward violence that exposure to slasher films had provoked. These results seem to reinforce other findings that if no violence surrounds the sex, sexually explicit films do not appear to make viewers more callous toward victims of violent crime.

MESSAGES OF VIOLENCE

"It appears that messages of sexual violence are what causes these changes in attitude, not the sexual explicitness per se," said Malamuth.

Even though Edwin Meese, then the US attorney general, focused on the evils of sexually explicit pornography in a controversial 1966 report, the report itself concluded that the greatest area of concern lies with sexually violent materials: " . . . with respect to sexually violent materials, the evidence is strongest . . . and the consequent harms of rape and other forms of sexual violence are hardly ones that this or any other society can take lightly."

Researchers suspect some sexually violent behavior may be the product of long-term exposure to violent movies. Many believe that the effects of these films may be even more pronounced on children than on young adults, and although there is little hard data, psychologists offer a number of compelling reasons why.

Not only are children more impressionable than adults, they say, but youngsters who have had no real-life experience with violence or sex are more likely to believe what they see.

"People without real-world experience with violence are more likely to accept as real the fictionalized portrayal of violence on television and film and buy into the idea that there is no suffering or agony attached to that violence," Slaby said.

Further complicating the situation is the fact that many of the most gruesome videos purport to show real-life events, including outlawed "snuff" films that claim to show actual women being hacked to pieces in front of the camera. Slaby believes such claims are usually bogus, but they make it all the more difficult for young viewers to separate fantasy from reality, he says.

"We know from other studies that the person least likely to make clear distinctions between reality and fantasy is the one most likely to act on what he sees in films," Slaby says.

DISTORTED REALITY

Slasher films further distort reality by intermingling violence with erotic images.

"For many of the younger kids, these films are their first introduction to sex, and it's a negative, distorted introduction," says Patty Carlan, a teacher at Boston English High School and member of the Junior League of Boston, a volunteer social group. "The victim is always a woman and it always looks like she's asking for it. Now what does that say to these kids?"

Carlan and other Junior League volunteers have been campaigning for years for more precise labelling of extremely violent films and for enforceable state laws to prohibit the sale or rental of explicitly violent films to youths under 17. The problem, they say, is that many parents don't realize the extent of violence in horror films. They note, for instance, that the "R" rating applies to both a film with two cursewords and a video that shows a naked woman being raped and slashed to pieces with a chainsaw. *Beverly Hill Cops II* is "R" rated; so is *Texas Chainsaw Massacre*.

The Junior League and parent groups have asked the Motion Picture Association of America to add the letter "V" for violence to its "R" rating. They have also recommended that "S" be added for explicit sex, "L" for obscene language and "N" for nudity, so parents can tell why a film has been restricted.

The Motion Picture Association of America has refused, saying the changes aren't needed and would make the system too complicated.

Parent groups have also campaigned for stiffer penalties for selling or renting violent videos to minors. The Junior League of Boston has been trying for four years to get the legislature to pass a law prohibiting the sale or rental of explicitly violent films to youths under age 17, with a $50 fine for violations. The bill makes it out of committee each year but dies on the floor, Carlan says.

"You have to wonder what the legislature is thinking about," Carlan says. "The majority of video stores couldn't care less about what they rent to kids. They don't want to lose sales."

In a recent survey of 400 11- to 13-year-olds at the Middle School West in Salem, the Junior League found that fully half of the movies and videos they had seen were violent R-rated films.

Psychologists say there are a number of reasons why teenagers, especially young boys, are attracted to these films. Many teenage boys, uncomfortably aware of their own burgeoning sexual urges, are obsessed with sex. On the verge of manhood, they are also sensitive to any insinuation that they might not be "man enough" to handle an experience.

They may use graphically violent films to demonstrate machismo to their peers, researchers say. Recent studies also suggest they use these films to reinforce cultural stereotypes.

One study revealed that young boys watching slasher films with a mixed group of friends are delighted when their girl friends show fear or disgust. And the girls seem most attracted to the boys who register the least amount of fear or anxiety.

Slaby suspects gory films are also popular because teenagers have become desensitized to the routine violence they see on television and want something even more exciting.

Carlan, a former elementary school teacher, agrees. She recalls the time she asked her third grade class if anybody could tell her about the Boston massacre in Revolutionary War times.

"One little kid piped up and told me all about the Texas Chainsaw Massacre," Carlan says. "And he went on in great detail about how the lady gets chopped in half with a buzzsaw. These kids can't tell you what the Boston massacre was, but they sure can tell you about the chainsaw massacre."

.23

Mass Market Romance

Pornography for Women Is Different

ANN BARR SNITOW

. . . What is the Harlequin romance formula? The novels have no plot in the usual sense. All tension and problems arise from the fact that the Harlequin world is inhabited by two species incapable of communicating with each other, male and female. In this sense these Pollyanna books have their own dream-like truth: our culture produces a pathological experience of sex difference. The sexes have different needs and interests, certainly different experiences. They find each other utterly mystifying.

Since all action in the novels is described from the female point of view, the reader identifies with the heroine's efforts to decode the erratic gestures of "dark, tall and gravely handsome"[1] men, all mysterious strangers or powerful bosses. In a sense the usual relationship is reversed: woman is subject, man, object. There are more descriptions of his body than of hers ("Dark trousers fitted closely to lean hips and long muscular legs . . .") though her clothes are always minutely observed. He is the unknowable other, a sexual icon whose magic is maleness. The books are permeated by phallic worship. Male is good, male is exciting, without further points of reference. Cruelty, callousness, coldness, menace, etc. are all equated with maleness and treated as a necessary part of the package: "It was an arrogant remark, but Sara had long since admitted his arrogance as part of his attraction."[2] She, on the other hand, is the subject, the one whose thoughts

NOTE: Excerpts reprinted from *Radical History Review* (Summer 1979), by permission of Cambridge University Press and Ann Barr Snitow.

the reader knows, whose constant re-evaluation of male moods and actions make up the story line.

The heroine is not involved in any overt adventure beyond trying to respond appropriately to male energy without losing her virginity. Virginity is a given here; sex means marriage and marriage, promised at the end, means, finally, there can be sex.

While the heroine waits for the hero's next move, her time is filled by tourism and by descriptions of consumer items: furniture, clothes, and gourmet foods. In *Writers Market* (1977) Harlequin Enterprises stipulate: "Emphasis on travel." (The exception is the occasional hospital novel. Like foreign places, hospitals offer removal from the household, heightened emotional states, and a supply of strangers.) Several of the books have passages that probably come straight out of guide books, but the *particular* setting is not the point, only that it is exotic, a place elsewhere.[3]

More space is filled by the question of what to wear. "She rummaged in her cases, discarding item after item, and eventually brought out a pair of purple cotton jeans and a matching shift. They were not new. She had bought them a couple of years ago. But fortunately her figure had changed little, and apart from a slight shrinkage in the pants which made them rather tighter than she would have liked, they looked serviceable."[4] Several things are going on here: the effort to find the right clothes for the occasion, the problem of staying thin, the problem of piecing together outfits from things that are not new. Finally, there is that shrinkage, a signal to the experienced Harlequin reader that the heroine, innocent as her intent may be in putting on jeans that are a little too tight, is wearing something revealing and will certainly be seen and noted by the hero in this vulnerable, passive act of self exposure. (More about the pornographic aspects later. In any other titillating novel one would suspect a pun when tight pants are "serviceable" but in the context of the absolutely flat Harlequin style one might well be wrong. More, too, about this style later on.)

Though clothes are the number one filler in Harlequins, food and furniture are also important and usually described in the language of women's magazines:[5] croissants are served hot and crispy and are "crusty brown,"[6] while snapper is "filleted, crumbed and fried in butter" and tomato soup is "topped with grated cheese and parsley"[7] (this last a useful, practical suggestion anyone could try).

Harlequins revitalize daily routines by insisting that a woman combing her hair, a woman reaching up to put a plate on a high shelf (so that her knees show beneath the hem, if only there were a viewer), a woman doing what women do all day, is in a constant state of potential sexuality. You never can tell when you may be seen and being seen is a precious opportunity. Harlequin romances alternate between scenes of the hero and heroine together in which she does a lot of social lying to save face, pretending to be unaffected by the hero's presence while her body melts or shivers, and scenes in which the heroine is essentially alone, living in a cloud of absorption, preparing mentally and physically for the next contact.

The heroine is alone. Sometimes there is another woman, a competitor who is often more overtly aware of her sexuality than the heroine, but she is a shadow on the horizon. Sometimes there are potentially friendly females living in the next bungalow or working with the patient in the next bed, but they, too, are shadowy, not important to the real story which consists entirely of an emotionally isolated woman trying to keep her virginity and her head when the only person she ever really talks to is the hero, whose motives and feelings are unclear: "She saw his words as a warning and would have liked to know whether he meant [them] to be."[8]

The heroine gets her man at the end, first, because she is an old-fashioned girl (this is a code for no premarital sex) and, second, because the hero gets ample opportunity to see her perform well in a number of female helping roles. In the course of a Harlequin romance, most heroines demonstrate passionate motherliness, good cooking, patience in adversity, efficient planning, and a good clothes sense, though these are skills and emotional capacities produced in emergencies, and are not, as in real life, a part of an invisible, glamorless work routine.

Though the heroines are pliable (they are rarely given particularized character traits; they are all Everywoman and can fit in comfortably with the lifestyle of the strong willed heroes be they doctors, lawyers, or marine biologists doing experiments on tropical islands), it is still amazing that these novels end in marriage. After one hundred and fifty pages of mystification, unreadable looks, "hints of cruelty"[9] and wordless coldness, the thirty page denouement is powerless to dispell the earlier impression of menace. Why should this heroine marry this man? And, one can ask with equal reason, why should this hero marry this woman? These endings do not ring true, but no doubt this is precisely their strength. A taste for psychological or social realism is unlikely to provide a Harlequin reader with a sustaining fantasy of rescue, of glamour, or of change. The Harlequin ending offers the impossible. It is pleasing to think that appearances are deceptive, that male coldness, absence, boredom, etc. are not what they seem. The hero *seems* to be a horrible roue; he *seems* to be a hopeless, moody cripple; he *seems* to be cruel and unkind; or he *seems* to be indifferent to the heroine and interested only in his work; but always, at the end, a rational explanation of all this appears. In spite of his coldness or preoccupation, the hero really loves the heroine and wants to marry her.

In fact, the Harlequin formula glorifies the distance between the sexes. Distance becomes titillating. The heroine's sexual inexperience adds to this excitement. What is this thing that awaits her on the other side of distance and mystery? Not knowing may be more sexy than finding out. Or perhaps the heroes are really fathers—obscure, forbidden objects of desire. Whatever they are, it is more exciting to wonder about them than to know them. In romanticized sexuality the pleasure lies in the distance itself. Waiting, anticipation, anxiety—these represent the high point of sexual experience.

Perhaps there is pleasure, too, in returning again and again to that breathless, ambivalent, nervous state *before* certainty or satiety. In so far as women's great adventure, the one they are socially sanctioned to seek, is romance, adventurousness takes women always back to the first phase in love. Unlike work, which holds out the possible pleasures of development, of the exercise of faculties, sometimes even of advancement, the Harlequin form of romance depends on the heroine's being in a state of passivity, of not knowing. Once the heroine knows the hero loves her, the story is over. Nothing interesting remains. Harlequin statements in *Writers Market* stress "upbeat ending essential here" (1977). Here at least is a reliable product that reproduces for women the most interesting phase in the love/marriage cycle and knows just when to stop. . . .

ARE HARLEQUIN ROMANCES PORNOGRAPHY?

She had never felt so helpless or so completely at the mercy of another human being . . . a being who could snap the slender column of her body with one squeeze of a steel clad arm.

No trace of tenderness softened the harsh pressure of his mouth on hers . . . there was only a savagely punishing intentness of purpose that cut off her breath until her senses reeled and her body sagged against the granite hardness of his. He released her wrists, seeming to know that they would hang helplessly at her sides, and his hand moved to the small of her back to exert a pressure that crushed her soft outlines to the unyielding dominance of his and left her in no doubt as to the force of his masculinity.[10]

In an unpublished talk,[11] critic Peter Parisi has hypothesized that Harlequin romances are essentially pornography for people ashamed to read pornography. In his view, sex is these novels' real *raison d'etre,* while the romance and the promised marriage are primarily salves to the conscience of readers brought up to believe that sex without love and marriage is wrong. Like me, Parisi sees the books as having some active allure. They are not just escape; they also offer release, as he sees it, specifically sexual release.

This is part of the reason why Harlequins, so utterly denatured in most respects, can powerfully command such a large audience. I want to elaborate here on Parisi's definition of *how* the books are pornography and, finally, to modify his definition of what women are looking for in a sex book.

Parisi sees Harlequins as a sort of poor woman's D. H. Lawrence. The body of the heroine is alive and singing in every fiber; she is overrun by a sexuality that wells up inside her and that she cannot control. ("The warmth of his body close to hers was like a charge of electricity, a stunning masculine assault on her senses that she was powerless to do anything about."[12]) The issue of control arises because, in Parisi's view, the reader's qualms are allayed when the novels invoke morals, then affirm a force, sexual feeling, strong enough to over-ride those morals. He argues further that morals in a Harlequin are secular; what the heroine risks is a loss of social face, of reputation. The books uphold the values of their readers who share this fear of breaking social codes, but behind these reassuringly familiar restraints they celebrate a wild, eager sexuality which flourishes and is finally affirmed in "marriage" which Parisi sees as mainly a code word for "fuck."

Parisi is right: *every* contact in a Harlequin romance is sexualized:

Sara feared he was going to refuse the invitation and simply walk off. It seemed like an eternity before he inclined his head in a brief, abrupt acknowledgement of acceptance, then drew out her chair for her, his hard fingers brushing her arm for a second, and bringing an urgent flutter of reaction from her pulse.[13]

Those "hard fingers" are the penis; a glance is penetration; a voice can slide along the heroine's spine "like a sliver of ice." The heroine keeps struggling for control but is constantly swept away on a tide of feeling. Always, though, some intruder or some "nagging reminder" of the need to maintain appearances stops her. "His mouth parted her lips with bruising urgency and for a few delirious moments she yielded to her own wanton instincts." But the heroine insists on seeing these moments as out of character: She "had never thought herself capable of wantonness, but in Carlo's arms she seemed to have no inhibitions."[14] Parisi argues that the books' sexual formula allows both heroine and reader to feel wanton again and again while maintaining their sense of themselves as not that sort of women.

I agree with Parisi that the sexually charged atmosphere that bathes the Harlequin heroine is essentially pornographic (I use the word pornographic as neutrally as possible here, not as an automatic pejorative). But do Harlequins actually contain an affirmation of female sexuality? The heroine's condition of passive receptivity to male ego and male sexuality is exciting to readers, but this is not necessarily a free or deep expression of the female potential for sexual feeling. Parisi says the heroine is always trying to humanize the contact between herself and the apparently under-socialized hero, "trying to convert rape into love making." If this is so, then she is engaged on a social as well as a sexual odyssey. Indeed, in women, these two are often joined. Is the project of humanizing and domesticating male sexual feeling an erotic one? What is it about this situation that arouses the excitement of the anxiously vigilant heroine and of the readers who identify with her?

In the misogynistic culture in which we live, where violence towards women is a common motif, it is hard to say a neutral word about pornography either as a legitimate literary form or as a legitimate source of pleasure. Women are naturally overwhelmed by the woman-hating theme so that the more universal human expression sometimes contained by pornography tends to be obscured for them.

In recent debates, sex books that emphasize both male and female sexual feelings as a sensuality that can exist without violence are being called "erotica" to distinguish them from "pornography."[15] This distinction blurs more than it clarifies the complex mixture of elements that make up sexuality. "Erotica" is soft core, soft focus; it is gentler and tenderer sex than that depicted in pornography. Does this mean true sexuality is diffuse while only perverse sexuality is driven, power hungry, intense, and selfish? I cannot accept this particular dichotomy. It leaves out too much of what is infantile in sex—the reenactment of early feelings, the boundlessness and omnipotence of infant desire and its furious gusto. In pornography all things tend in one direction, a total immersion in one's own sense experience, for which one paradigm must certainly be infancy. For adults this totality, the total sexualization of everything, can only be a fantasy. But does the fact that it cannot be actually lived mean this fantasy must be discarded? It is a memory, a legitimate element in the human lexicon of feelings.

In pornography, the joys of passivity, of helpless abandonment, of response without responsibility are all endlessly repeated, savored, minutely described. Again this is a fantasy often dismissed with the pejorative "masochistic" as if passivity were in no way a pleasant or a natural condition.

Yet another criticism of pornography is that it presents no recognizable, delineated characters. In a culture where women are routinely objectified it is natural and progressive to see as threatening any literary form that calls dehumanization sexual. Once again, however, there is a more universally human side to this aspect of pornography. Like a lot of far more respectable twentieth century art, pornography is not about personality but about the explosion of the boundaries of the self. It is a fantasy of an extreme state in which all social constraints are overwhelmed by a flood of sexual energy. Think, for example, of all the pornography about servants fucking mistresses, old men fucking young girls, guardians fucking wards. Class, age, custom—all are deliciously sacrificed, dissolved by sex.

Though pornography's critics are right—pornography *is* exploitation— it is exploitation of *everything*. Promiscuity by definition is a breakdown of barriers. Pornography is not only a reflector of social power imbalances, sexual pathologies, etc., but it is also all those imbalances run riot, run to excess, sometimes explored *ad absurdum*, exploded. Misogyny is one content of pornography; another content is a universal infant desire for complete, immediate gratification, to rule the world out of the very core of passive helplessness.

In a less sexist society, there might be a pornography that is exciting, expressive, interesting, even, perhaps, significant as a form of social rebellion, all traits which, in a sexist society, are obscured by pornography's present role as escape valve for hostility towards women, or as metaphor for fiercely guarded power hierarchies, etc. Instead, in a sexist society, we have two pornographies, one for men, one for women. They both have, hiding within them, those basic human expressions of abandonment I have described. The pornography for men enacts this abandonment on women as objects. How different is the pornography for women, in which sex is bathed in romance, diffused, always implied rather than enacted at all! This pornography is the Harlequin romance.

I described above the oddly narrowed down, denatured world presented in Harlequins. Looking at them as pornography obviously offers a number of alternative explanations for these same traits: the heroine's passivity becomes sexual receptivity and, though I complained earlier about her vapidity, in pornography no one need have a personality. Joanna Russ observed about the heroines of gothic romances something true of Harlequin heroines as well: they are loved as babies are loved, simply because they exist.[16] They have no particular qualities, but pornography by-passes this limitation and reaches straight down to the infant layer where we all imagine ourselves the center of everything by birthright and are sexual beings without shame or need for excuse.

Seeing Harlequins as pornography modifies one's criticism of their selectivity, their know-nothing narrowness. In so far as they are essentially pornographic in intent, their characters have no past, no context; they live only in the eternal present of sexual feeling, the absorbing interest in the erotic sex object. In so far as the books are written to elicit sexual excitation, they can be completely closed, repetitive circuits always returning to the moment of arousal when the hero's voice sends "a velvet finger"[17] along the spine of the heroine. In pornography, sex is the whole content; there need be no serious other.

Read this way, Harlequins are benign if banal sex books, but sex books for women have several special characteristics not included in the usual definitions of the genre pornography. In fact, a suggestive, sexual atmosphere is not so easy to establish for women as it is for men. A number of conditions must be right.

In *The Mermaid and the Minotaur*, an extraordinary study of the asymmetry of male and female relationships in all societies where children are primarily raised by women, Dorothy Dinnerstein discusses the reasons why women are so much more dependent than men on deep personal feeling as an ingredient, sometimes a precondition, for sex. Beyond the obvious reasons, the seriousness of sex for the partner who can get pregnant, the seriousness of sex for the partner who is economically and socially dependent on her lover, Dinnerstein adds another, psychological reason for women's tendency to emotionalize sex. She argues that the double standard (male sexual freedom, female loyalty to one sexual tie) comes from the asymmetry in the way the sexes are raised in infancy. Her argument is too complex to be entirely recapitulated here but her conclusion seems crucial to our understanding of the mixture of sexual excitement and anti-erotic restraint that characterizes sexual feeling in Harlequin romances:

> Anatomically, coitus offers a far less reliable guarantee of orgasm—or indeed of any intense direct local genital pleasure—to woman than to man. The first-hand coital pleasure of which she is capable more often requires conditions that must be purposefully sought out. Yet it is woman who has less liberty to conduct this kind of search: . . . societal and psychological constraints . . . leave her less free than man to explore the erotic resources of a variety of partners, or even to affirm erotic impulse with any one partner. These constraints also make her less able to give way to simple physical delight without a sense of total self-surrender—a disability that further narrows her choice of partners, and makes her still more afraid of disrupting her rapport with any one partner by acting to intensify the delight, that is, by asserting her own sexual wishes . . .

What the double standard hurts in women (to the extent that they genuinely, inwardly, bow to it) is the animal center of self-respect: the brute sense of bodily prerogative, of having a right to one's bodily feelings. Fromm made this point very clearly when he argued, in *Man for Himself,* that socially imposed shame about the body serves the function of keeping people submissive to societal authority by weakening in them some inner core of individual authority. . . . On the whole . . . the female burden of genital deprivation is carried meekly, invisibly. Sometimes it cripples real interest in sexual interaction, but often it does not: indeed, it can deepen a woman's need for the emotional rewards of carnal contact. What it most reliably cripples is human pride.[18]

This passage gives us the theoretical skeleton on which the titillations of the Harlequin formula are built. In fact, the Harlequin heroine cannot afford to be only a mass of responsive nerve endings. In order for her sexuality, and the sexuality of the novels' readers, to be released, a number of things must happen that have little to do directly with sex at all. Since she cannot seek out or instruct the man she wants, she must be in a state of constant passive readiness. Since only one man will do, she has the anxiety of deciding, "Is this *the* one?" Since an enormous amount of psychic energy is going to be mobilized in the direction of the man she loves, the man she sleeps with, she must feel sure of him. A one night stand won't work; she's only just beginning to get her emotional generators going when he's already gone. And orgasm? It probably hasn't happened. She couldn't tell him she wanted it and couldn't tell him *how* she wanted it. If he's already gone, there is no way for her erotic feeling for him to take form, no way for her training of him as a satisfying lover to take place.

Hence the Harlequin heroine has a lot of things to worry about if she wants sexual satisfaction. Parisi has said that these worries are restraints there merely to be deliciously over-ridden, but they are so constant an accompaniment to the heroine's erotic feelings as to be, under present conditions, inseparable from them. She feels an urge towards deep emotion; she feels anxiety about the serious intentions of the hero; she role plays constantly, presenting herself as a nurturant, passive, receptive figure; and all of this is part of sex to her. Certain social configurations feel safe and right and are real sexual cues for women. The romantic intensity of Harlequins— the waiting, fearing, speculating—are as much a part of their functionings as pornography for women as are the more overtly sexual scenes.

Nor is this just a neutral difference between men and women. In fact, as Dinnerstein suggests, the muting of spontaneous sexual feeling, the necessity which is socially forced on women of channeling their sexual desire, is in fact a great deprivation. In *The Mermaid and the Minotaur* Dinnerstein argues that men have a number of reasons, social and psychological, for discomfort when confronted by the romantic feeling and the demand for security that so often accompany female sexuality. For them growing up and being male both mean cutting off the passionate attachment and dependence on woman, on mother. Women, potential mother figures themselves, have less need to make this absolute break. Men also need to pull away from that inferior category, Woman. Women are stuck in it and naturally romanticize the powerful creatures they can only come close to through emotional and physical ties.

The Harlequin formula perfectly reproduces these differences, these tensions, between the sexes. It depicts a heroine struggling, against the hero's resistance, to get the right combination of elements together so that, for her, orgasmic sex can at last take place. The shape of the Harlequin sexual fantasy is designed to deal women the winning hand they cannot hold in life: a man who is romantically interesting—hence, distant, even frightening—while at the same time he is willing to capitulate to her needs just enough so that she can sleep with him not once but often. His intractability is exciting to her, a proof of his membership in a superior class of beings but, finally, he must relent to some extent if her breathless anticipation, the foreplay of romance, is to lead to orgasm.

Clearly, getting romantic tension, domestic security, and sexual excitement together in the same fantasy in the right proportions is a delicate balancing act. Harlequins lack excellence by any other measure, but they are masterly in this one respect. In fact, the Harlequin heroine is in a constant fever of anti-erotic anxiety, trying to control the flow of sexual passion between herself and the hero until her surrender can be on her own terms. If the heroine's task is "converting rape into love-making," she must somehow teach the hero to take time, to pay attention, to feel, while herself remaining passive, undemanding, unthreatening. This is yet another delicate miracle of balance which Harlequin romances manage quite well. How do they do it?

The underlying structure of the sexual story goes something like this:

1. The man is hard (a walking phallus).

2. The woman likes this hardness.

3. But, at the outset, this hardness is *too hard*. The man has an ideology that is anti-romantic, anti-marriage. In other words, he will not stay around long enough for her to come, too.

4. Her final release of sexual feeling depends on his changing his mind, but *not too much*. He must become softer (safer, less likely to leave altogether) but not too soft. For good sex, he must be hard, but this hardness must be *at the service of the woman*.

The following passage from Anne Mather's *Born Out of Love* is an example:

His skin was smooth, more roughly textured than hers, but sleek and flexible beneath her palms, his warmth and maleness enveloping her and making her overwhelmingly aware that only the thin material of the culotte suit separated them. He held her face between his hands, and his hardening mouth was echoed throughout the length and breadth of his body. She felt herself yielding weakly beneath him, and his hand slid from her shoulder, across her throat to find the zipper at the front of her suit, impelling it steadily downward.

"No, Logan," she breathed, but he pulled the hands with which she might have resisted him around him, arching her body so that he could observe her reaction to the thrusting aggression of his with sensual satisfaction.

"No?" he probed with gentle mockery, his mouth seeking the pointed fullness of her breasts now exposed to his gaze. "Why not? It's what we both want, don't deny it." . . .

Somehow Charlotte struggled up from the depth of a sexually-induced lethargy. It wasn't easy, when her whole body threatened to betray her, but his words were too similar to the words he had used to her once before, and she remembered only too well what had happened next. . . .

She sat up quickly, her fingers fumbling with the zipper, conscious all the while of Logan lying beside her, and the potent attraction of his lean body. God, she thought unsteadily, what am I doing here? And then, more wildly: Why am I leaving him? *I want him!* But not on his terms, the still small voice of sanity reminded her, and she struggled to her feet.[19]

In these romantic love stories, sex on a woman's terms is romanticized sex. Romantic sexual fantasies are contradictory. They include both the desire to be blindly ravished, to melt, and the desire to be spiritually adored, saved from the humiliation of dependence and sexual passivity through the agency of a protective male who will somehow make reparation to the woman he loves for her powerlessness.

Harlequins reveal and pander to this impossible fantasy life. Female sexuality, a rare subject in all but the most recent writing, is not doomed to be what the Harlequins describe. Nevertheless, some of the barriers that hold back female sexual feelings are acknowledged and finally circumvented quite sympathetically in these novels. They are sex books for people who have plenty of good reasons for worrying about sex.

While there is something wonderful in the heroine's insistence that sex is more exciting and more momentous when it includes deep feeling, she is fighting a losing battle as long as she can only define deep feeling as a mystified romantic longing on the one hand, and as marriage on the other. In Harlequins the price for needing emotional intimacy is that she must passively wait, must anxiously calculate. Without spontaneity and aggression, a whole set of sexual possibilities is lost to her just as, without emotional depth, a whole set of sexual possibilities is lost to men.

Though one may dislike the circuitous form of sexual expression in Harlequin heroines, a strength of the books is that they insist that good sex for women requires an emotional and social context that can free them from constraint. If one dislikes the kind of social norms the heroine seeks as her sexual preconditions, it is still interesting to see sex treated not primarily as a physical event at all but as a social drama, as a carefully modulated set of psychological possibilities between people. This is a mirror image of much writing more commonly labeled pornography. In fact one can't resist speculating that equality between the sexes as child rearers and workers might well bring personal feeling and abandoned physicality together in wonderful combinations undreamed of in either male or female pornography as we know it.

The ubiquity of the books indicates a central truth: romance is a primary category of the female imagination. The women's movement has left this fact of female consciousness largely untouched. While most serious women *novelists* treat romance with irony and cynicism, most women do not. Harlequins may well be closer to describing women's hopes for love than the work of fine women novelists. Harlequins eschew irony; they take love straight. Harlequins eschew realism; they are serious about fantasy and escape. In spite of all the audience manipulations inherent in the Harlequin formula, the connection between writer and reader is tonally seamless; Harlequins are respectful, tactful, friendly towards their audience. The letters that pour in to their publishers speak above all of involvement, warmth, human values. The world that can make Harlequin romances appear warm is indeed a cold, cold place.

NOTES

1. Lindsay (1977, p. 10).
2. Stratton (1977, pp. 56, 147).
3. Here is an example of this sort of travelogue prose: "There was something to appeal to all age groups in the thousand-acre park in the heart of the city—golf for the energetic, lawn bowling for the more sedate, a zoo for the children's pleasure, and even secluded walks through giant cedars for lovers—but Cori thought of none of these things as Greg drove to a parking place bordering the Inlet" (Graham, 1976, p. 25).
4. Mather (1977, p. 42).
5. See Russ (1973).
6. Mather (1977, p. 42).
7. Clair (1978, p. 118).
8. Lindsay (1977, p. 13.
9. Stratton (1977, p. 66). The adjectives "cruel" and "satanic" are commonly used for heroes.
10. Graham (1976, p. 63).
11. Delivered, April 6, 1978, Livingston College, Rutgers University.
12. Stratton (1977, p. 132).
13. Stratton (1977, p. 112).
14. Stratton (1977, pp. 99, 102, 139).
15. See Gloria Steinem (1978) and other articles in the November 1978 issue of *Ms.* An unpublished piece by Brigitte Frase, "From Pornography to Mind-Blowing," MLA talk, 1978, strongly presents my own view that this debate is specious. See also Susan Sontag's "The Pornographic Imagination," in *Styles of Radical Will* and the Jean Paulhan preface to *Story of O,* "Happiness in Slavery."
16. Russ (1973, p. 679).
17. Stratton (1977, p. 115).
18. Dinnerstein (1976, pp. 73-75).
19. Mather (1977, pp. 70-72).

REFERENCES

Clair, C. (1978). *A streak of gold.* Toronto: Harlequin.

Dinnerstein, D. (1976). *The mermaid and the minotaur: Sexual arrangements and human malaise.* New York: Harper & Row.

Graham, E. (1976). *Mason's ridge.* Toronto: Harlequin.

Lindsay, R. (1977). *Prescription for love.* Toronto: Harlequin.

Mather, A. (1977). *Born out of love.* Toronto: Harlequin.

Russ, J. (1973). Somebody's trying to kill me and I think it's my husband: The modern gothic. *Journal of Popular Culture, 6*(4), 666-691.

Sontag, S. (1991). The pornographic imagination. In S. Sontag, *Styles of radical will.* New York: Doubleday.

Steinem, G. (1978, November). Erotica and pornography: A clear and present difference. *Ms.*

Stratton, R. (1977). *The sign of the ram.* Toronto: Harlequin.

24

Women Read the Romance

The Interaction of Text and Context

JANICE A. RADWAY

. . . The interpretation of the romance's cultural significance offered here has been developed from a series of extensive ethnographic-like interviews with a group of compulsive romance readers in a predominantly urban, central midwestern state among the nation's top twenty in total population.[1] I discovered my principal informant and her customers with the aid of a senior editor at Doubleday whom I had been interviewing about the publication of romances. Sally Arteseros told me of a bookstore employee who had developed a regular clientele of fifty to seventy-five regular romance readers who relied on her for advice about the best romances to buy and those to avoid. When I wrote to Dot Evans, as I will now call her, to ask whether I might question her about how she interpreted, categorized, and evaluated romantic fiction, I had no idea that she had also begun to write a newsletter designed to enable bookstores to advise their customers about the quality of the romances published monthly. She has since copyrighted this newsletter and incorporated it as a business. Dot is so successful at serving the women who patronize her chain outlet that the central office of this major chain occasionally relies on her sales predictions to gauge romance distribution throughout the system. Her success has also brought her to the attention of both editors and writers for whom she now reads manuscripts and galleys.

NOTE: Excerpts reprinted from *Feminist Studies*, Vol. 9, No. 1 (1983), by permission of the publisher, FEMINIST STUDIES, Inc., Women's Studies Program, University of Maryland, College Park, MD.

My knowledge of Dot and her readers is based on roughly sixty hours of interviews conducted in June 1980, and February 1981. I have talked extensively with Dot about romances, reading, and her advising activities as well as observed her interactions with her customers at the bookstore. I have also conducted both group and individual interviews with sixteen of her regular customers and administered a lengthy questionnaire to forty-two of these women. Although not representative of all women who read romances, the group appears to be demographically similar to a sizable segment of that audience as it has been mapped by several rather secretive publishing houses.

Dorothy Evans lives and works in the community of Smithton, as do most of her regular customers. A city of about 112,000 inhabitants, Smithton is located five miles due east of the state's second largest city, in a metropolitan area with a total population of over 1 million. Dot was forty-eight years old at the time of the survey, the wife of a journeyman plumber, and the mother of three children in their twenties. She is extremely bright and articulate and, while not a proclaimed feminist, holds some beliefs about women that might be labeled as such. Although she did not work outside the home when her children were young and does not now believe that a woman needs a career to be fulfilled, she feels women should have the opportunity to work and be paid equally with men. Dot also believes that women should have the right to abortion, though she admits that her deep religious convictions would prevent her from seeking one herself. She is not disturbed by the Equal Rights Amendment and can and does converse eloquently about the oppression women have endured for years at the hands of men. Despite her opinions, however, she believes implicitly in the value of true romance and thoroughly enjoys discovering again and again that women can find men who will love them as they wish to be loved. Although most of her regular customers are more conservative than Dot in the sense that they do not advocate political measures to redress past grievances, they are quite aware that men commonly think themselves superior to women and often mistreat them as a result.

In general, Dot's customers are married, middle-class mothers with at least a high school education.[2] More than 60 percent of the women were between the ages of twenty-five and forty-four at the time of the study, a fact that duplicates fairly closely Harlequin's finding that the majority of its readers is between twenty-five and forty-nine.[3] Silhouette Books has also recently reported that 65 percent of the romance market is below the age of 40.[4] Exactly 50 percent of the Smithton women have high school diplomas, while 32 percent report completing at least some college work. Again, this seems to suggest that the interview group is fairly representative, for Silhouette also indicates that 45 percent of the romance market has attended at least some college. The employment status and family income of Dot's customers also seem to duplicate those of the audience mapped by the publishing houses. Forty-two percent of the Smithton women, for instance, work part-time outside the home. Harlequin claims that 49 percent of its audience is similarly employed. The Smithton women report slightly higher incomes than those of the average Harlequin reader (43 percent of the Smithton women have incomes of $15,000 to $24,999, 33 percent have incomes of $25,000 to $49,999—the average income of the Harlequin reader is $15,000 to $20,000), but the difference is not enough to change the general sociological status of the group. . . .

When asked why they read romances, the Smithton women overwhelmingly cite escape or relaxation as their goal. They use the word "escape," however, both literally and figuratively. On the one hand, they value their romances highly because the act of reading them literally draws the women away from their present surroundings. Because they must produce the meaning of the story by attending closely to the words on the page, they find that their attention is withdrawn from concerns that plague them in reality. One woman remarked with a note of triumph in her voice: "My body may be in that room, but I'm not!" She and her sister readers see their romance reading as a legitimate way of denying a present reality that occasionally becomes too onerous to bear. This particular means of escape is better than television viewing for these women, because the cultural value attached to books permits them to overcome the guilt they feel about avoiding their responsibilities. They believe that reading of any kind is, by nature, educational.[5] They insist accordingly that they also read to learn.[6]

On the other hand, the Smithton readers are quite willing to acknowledge that the romances which so preoccupy them are little more than fantasies or fairy tales that always end happily. They readily admit in fact that the characters and events discovered in the pages of the typical romance do not resemble the people and occurrences they must deal with in their daily lives. On the basis of the following comments, made in response to a question about what romances "do" better than other novels available today, one can conclude that it is precisely the unreal, fantastic shape of the story that makes their literal escape even more complete and gratifying. Although these are only a few of the remarks given in response to the undirected question, they are representative of the group's general sentiment.

> Romances hold my interest and do not leave me depressed or up in the air at the end like many modern day books tend to do. Romances also just make me feel good reading them as I identify with the heroines.

> The kind of books I mainly read are very different from everyday living. That's why I read them. Newspapers, etc., I find boring because all you read is sad news. I can get enough of that on TV news. I like stories that take your mind off everyday matters.

> Different than everyday life.

> Everyone is always under so much pressure. They like books that let them escape.

> Because it is an escape and we can dream. And pretend that it is our life.

I'm able to escape the harsh world a few hours a day.

It is a way of escaping from everyday living.

They always seem an escape and they usually turn out the way you wish life really was.

I enjoy reading because it offers me a small vacation from everyday life and an interesting and amusing way to pass the time.

These few comments all hint at a certain sadness that many of the Smithton women seem to share because life has not given them all that it once promised. A deep-seated sense of betrayal also lurks behind their deceptively simple expressions of a need to believe in a fairy tale. Although they have not elaborated in these comments, many of the women explained in the interviews that despite their disappointments, they feel refreshed and strengthened by their vicarious participation in a fantasy relationship where the heroine is frequently treated as they themselves would most like to be loved.

This conception of romance reading as an escape that is both literal and figurative implies flight from some situation in the real world which is either stifling or overwhelming, as well as a metaphoric transfer to another, more desirable universe where events are happily resolved. Unashamed to admit that they like to indulge in temporary escape, the Smithton women are also surprisingly candid about the circumstances that necessitate their desire. When asked to specify what they are fleeing from, they invariably mention the "pressures" and "tensions" they experience as wives and mothers. Although none of the women can cite the voluminous feminist literature about the psychological toll exacted by the constant demand to physically and emotionally nurture others, they are nonetheless eloquent about how draining and unrewarding their duties can be.[7] When first asked why women find it necessary to escape, Dot gave the following answer without once pausing to rest:

As a mother, I have run 'em to the orthodontist, I have run 'em to the swimming pool. I have run 'em to baton twirling lessons. I have run up to school because they forgot their lunch. You know, I mean really. And you do it. And it isn't that you begrudge it. That isn't it. Then my husband would walk in the door and he'd say, "Well, what did you do today?" You know, it was like, "Well, tell me how you spent the last eight hours, because I've been out working." And I finally got to the point where I would say, "Well, I read four books, and I did the wash and got the meal on the table and the beds are all made and the house is tidy." And I would get defensive like, "So what do you call all this? Why should I have to tell you because I certainly don't ask you what you did for eight hours, step by step."

But their husbands do do that. We've compared notes. They hit the house and it's like "Well, all right, I've been out earning a living.

Now what have you been doin' with your time?" And you begin to
be feeling, "Now, really, why is he questioning me?"

Romance reading, as Dot herself puts it, constitutes a temporary "declaration of independence" from the social roles of wife and mother. By placing
the barrier of the book between themselves and their families, these women
reserve a special space and time for themselves alone. As a consequence,
they momentarily allow themselves to abandon the attitude of total self-
abnegation in the interest of family welfare which they have so dutifully
learned is the proper stance for a good wife and mother. Romance reading
is both an assertion of deeply felt psychological needs and a means for satisfying those needs. Simply put, these needs arise because no other member
of the family, as it is presently constituted in this still-patriarchal society, is
yet charged with the affective and emotional reconstitution of a wife and
mother. If she is depleted by her efforts to care for others, she is nonetheless
expected to restore and sustain herself as well. As one of Dot's customers
put it, "You always have to be a Mary Poppins. You can't be sad, you can't
be mad, you have to keep everything bottled up inside."

Nancy Chodorow has recently discussed this structural peculiarity of the
modern family and its impact on the emotional lives of women in her
influential book, *The Reproduction of Mothering*,[8] a complex reformulation of
the Freudian theory of female personality development. Chodorow maintains that women often continue to experience a desire for intense affective
nurturance and relationality well into adulthood as a result of an unresolved
separation from their primary caretaker. It is highly significant, she argues,
that in patriarchal society this caretaker is almost inevitably a woman. The
felt similarity between mother and daughter creates an unusually intimate
connection between them which later makes it exceedingly difficult for the
daughter to establish autonomy and independence. Chodorow maintains,
on the other hand, that because male children are also reared by women,
they tend to separate more completely from their mothers by suppressing
their own emotionality and capacities for tenderness which they associate
with mothers and femininity. The resulting asymmetry in human personality, she concludes, leads to a situation where men typically cannot fulfill all
of a woman's emotional needs. As a consequence, women turn to the act of
mothering as a way of vicariously recovering that lost relationality and
intensity.

My findings about Dot Evans and her customers suggest that the vicarious pleasure a woman receives through the nurturance of others may not be
completely satisfying, because the act of caring for them also makes tremendous demands on a woman and can deplete her sense of self. In that case,
she may well turn to romance reading in an effort to construct a fantasy-
world where she is attended, as the heroine is, by a man who reassures her
of her special status and unique identity.

The value of the romance may have something to do, then, with the fact
that women find it especially difficult to indulge in the restorative experience of visceral regression to an infantile state where the self is cared for
perfectly by another. This regression is so difficult precisely because women

have been taught to believe that men must be their sole source of pleasure. Although there is nothing biologically lacking in men to make this ideal pleasure unattainable, as Chodorow's theories tell us, their engendering and socialization by the patriarchal family traditionally masks the very traits that would permit them to nurture women in this way. Because they are encouraged to be aggressive, competitive, self-sufficient, and unemotional, men often find sustained attention to the emotional needs of others both unfamiliar and difficult. While the Smithton women only minimally discussed their husbands' abilities to take care of them as they would like, when they commented on their favorite romantic heroes they made it clear that they enjoy imagining themselves being tenderly cared for and solicitously protected by a fictive character who inevitably proves to be spectacularly masculine and unusually nurturant as well.[9]

Indeed, this theme of pleasure recurred constantly in the discussions with the Smithton women. They insisted repeatedly that when they are reading a romance, they feel happy and content. Several commented that they particularly relish moments when they are home alone and can relax in a hot tub or in a favorite chair with a good book. Others admitted that they most like to read in a warm bed late at night. Their association of romances with contentment, pleasure, and good feelings is apparently not unique, for in conducting a market research study, Fawcett discovered that when asked to draw a woman reading a romance, romance readers inevitably depict someone who is exaggeratedly happy.[10]

The Smithton group's insistence that they turn to romances because the experience of reading the novels gives them hope, provides pleasure, and causes contentment raises the unavoidable question of what aspects of the romantic narrative itself could possibly give rise to feelings such as these. How are we to explain, furthermore, the obvious contradiction between this reader emphasis on pleasure and hope, achieved through vicarious appreciation of the ministrations of a tender hero, and the observations of the earlier critics of romances that such books are dominated by men who at least temporarily abuse and hurt the women they purportedly love? In large part, the contradiction arises because the two groups are not reading according to the same interpretive strategies, neither are they reading nor commenting on the same books. Textual analyses like those offered by Douglas, Modleski, and Snitow are based on the common assumption that because romances are formulaic and therefore essentially identical, analysis of a randomly chosen sample will reveal the meaning unfailingly communicated by every example of the genre. This methodological procedure is based on the further assumption that category readers do not themselves perceive variations within the genre, nor do they select their books in a manner significantly different from the random choice of the analyst.

In fact, the Smithton readers do not believe the books are identical, nor do they approve of all the romances they read. They have elaborated a complex distinction between "good" and "bad" romances and they have accordingly experimented with various techniques that they hoped would enable them to identify bad romances before they paid for a book that would only offend them. Some tried to decode titles and cover blurbs by looking

for key words serving as clues to the book's tone; others refused to buy
romances by authors they didn't recognize; still others read several pages
including the ending before they bought the book. Now, however, most of the
people in the Smithton group have been freed from the need to rely on these
inexact predictions because Dot Evans shares their perceptions and evalu-
ations of the category and can alert them to unusually successful romantic
fantasies while steering them away from those they call "disgusting perversions."

When the Smithton readers' comments about good and bad romances
are combined with the conclusions drawn from an analysis of twenty of their
favorite books and an equal number of those they classify as particularly
inadequate, an illuminating picture of the fantasy fueling the romance-
reading experience develops.[11] To begin with, Dot and her readers will not
tolerate any story in which the heroine is seriously abused by men. They
find multiple rapes especially distressing and dislike books in which a
woman is brutally hurt by a man only to fall desperately in love with him
in the last four pages. The Smithton women are also offended by explicit sexual description and scrupulously avoid the work of authors like Rosemary
Rogers and Judith Krantz who deal in what they call "perversions" and
"promiscuity." They also do not like romances that overtly perpetuate the
double standard by excusing the hero's simultaneous involvement with
several women. They insist, one reader commented, on "one woman—one
man." They also seem to dislike any kind of detailed description of male
genitalia, although the women enjoy suggestive descriptions of how the
hero is emotionally aroused to an overpowering desire for the heroine. Their
preferences seem to confirm Beatrice Faust's argument in *Women, Sex, and
Pornography* that women are not interested in the visual display characteristic of male pornography, but prefer process-oriented materials detailing the development of deep emotional connection between two individuals.[12]

According to Dot and her customers, the quality of the *ideal* romantic
fantasy is directly dependent on the character of the heroine and the manner
in which the hero treats her. The plot, of course, must always focus on a series
of obstacles to the final declaration of love between the two principals.
However, a good romance involves an unusually bright and determined
woman and a man who is spectacularly masculine, but at the same time
capable of remarkable empathy and tenderness. Although they enjoy the
usual chronicle of misunderstandings and mistakes which inevitably leads
to the heroine's belief that the hero intends to harm her, the Smithton readers
prefer stories that combine a much-understated version of this continuing
antagonism with a picture of a gradually developing love. They most wish
to participate in the slow process by which two people become acquainted,
explore each other's foibles, wonder about the other's feelings, and eventually "discover" that they are loved by the other.

In conducting an analysis of the plots of the twenty romances listed as
"ideal" by the Smithton readers, I was struck by their remarkable similarities
in narrative structure. In fact, all twenty of these romances are very tightly
organized around the evolving relationship between a single couple com-

posed of a beautiful, defiant, and sexually immature woman and a brooding, handsome man who is also curiously capable of soft, gentle gestures. Although minor foil figures are used in these romances, none of the ideal stories seriously involves either hero or heroine with one of the rival characters.[13] They are employed mainly as contrasts to the more likable and proper central pair or as purely temporary obstacles to the pair's delayed union because one or the other mistakenly suspects the partner of having an affair with the rival. However, because the reader is never permitted to share this mistaken assumption in the ideal romance, she knows all along that the relationship is not as precarious as its participants think it to be. The rest of the narrative in the twenty romances chronicles the gradual crumbling of barriers between these two individuals who are fearful of being used by the other. As their defenses against emotional response fall away and their sexual passion rises inexorably, the typical narrative plunges on until the climactic point at which the hero treats the heroine to some supreme act of tenderness, and she realizes that his apparent emotional indifference was only the mark of his hesitancy about revealing the extent of his love for and dependence upon her.

The Smithton women especially like romances that commence with the early marriage of the hero and heroine for reasons of convenience. Apparently, they do so because they delight in the subsequent, necessary chronicle of the pair's growing awareness that what each took to be indifference or hate is, in reality, unexpressed love and suppressed passion. In such favorite romances as *The Flame and the Flower, The Black Lyon, Shanna,* and *Made For Each Other* the heroine begins marriage thinking that she detests and is detested by her spouse. She is thrown into a quandary, however, because her partner's behavior vacillates from indifference, occasional brusqueness, and even cruelty to tenderness and passion. Consequently, the heroine spends most of her time in these romances, as well as in the others comprising this sample, trying to read the hero's behavior as a set of signs expressing his true feelings toward her. The final outcome of the story turns upon a fundamental process of reinterpretation, whereby she suddenly and clearly sees that the behavior she feared was actually the product of deeply felt passion and a previous hurt. Once she learns to reread his past behavior and thus to excuse him for the suffering he has caused her, she is free to respond warmly to his occasional acts of tenderness. Her response inevitably encourages him to believe in her and finally to treat her as she wishes to be treated. When this reinterpretation process is completed in the twenty ideal romances, the heroine is always tenderly enfolded in the hero's embrace and the reader is permitted to identify with her as she is gently caressed, carefully protected, and verbally praised with words of love.[14] At the climactic moment (pp. 201-202) of *The Sea Treasure,* for example, when the hero tells the heroine to put her arms around him, the reader is informed of his gentleness in the following way:

> She put her cold face against his in an attitude of surrender that moved him to unutterable tenderness. He swung her clear of the encroaching water and eased his way up to the next level, with painful slow-

ness. . . . When at last he had finished, he pulled her into his arms and held her against his heart for a moment. . . . Tenderly he lifted her. Carefully he negotiated the last of the treacherous slippery rungs to the mine entrance. Once there, he swung her up into his arms, and walked out into the starlit night.

    The cold air revived her, and she stirred in his arms.

    "Dominic?" she whispered.

    He bent his head and kissed her.

    "Sea Treasure," he whispered.

    Passivity, it seems, is at the heart of the romance-reading experience in the sense that the final goal of the most valued romances is the creation of perfect union in which the ideal male, who is masculine and strong, yet nurturant, finally admits his recognition of the intrinsic worth of the heroine. Thereafter, she is required to do nothing more than exist as the center of this paragon's attention. Romantic escape is a temporary but literal denial of the demands these women recognize as an integral part of their roles as nurturing wives and mothers. But it is also a figurative journey to a utopian state of total receptiveness in which the reader, as a consequence of her identification with the heroine, feels herself the passive *object* of someone else's attention and solicitude. The romance reader in effect is permitted the experience of feeling cared for, the sense of having been affectively reconstituted, even if both are lived only vicariously.

    Although the ideal romance may thus enable a woman to satisfy vicariously those psychological needs created in her by a patriarchal culture unable to fulfill them, the very centrality of the rhetoric of reinterpretation to the romance suggests also that the reading experience may indeed have some of the unfortunate consequences pointed to by earlier romance critics.[15] Not only is the dynamic of reinterpretation an essential component of the plot of the ideal romance, but it also characterizes the very process of constructing its meaning because the reader is inevitably given more information about the hero's motives than is the heroine herself. Hence, when Ranulf temporarily abuses his young bride in *The Black Lyon* the reader understands that what appears as inexplicable cruelty to Lyonene, the heroine, is an irrational desire to hurt her because of what his first wife did to him.[16] It is possible that in reinterpreting the hero's behavior before Lyonene does, the Smithton women may be practicing a procedure which is valuable to them precisely because it enables them to reinterpret their own spouse's similar emotional coldness and likely preoccupation with work or sports. In rereading this category of behavior, they reassure themselves that it does not necessarily mean that a woman is not loved. Romance reading, it would seem, can function as a kind of training for the all-too-common task of reinterpreting a spouse's unsettling actions as the signs of passion, devotion, and love.

    If the Smithton women are indeed learning reading behaviors that help them to dismiss or justify their husbands' affective distance, this procedure is probably carried out on an unconscious level. In any form of cultural or anthropological analysis in which the subjects of the study cannot reveal all the complexity or covert significance of their behavior, a certain amount of speculation is necessary. The analyst, however, can and should take account of any other observable evidence that might reveal the motives and meanings she is seeking. In this case, the Smithton readers' comments about bad romances are particularly helpful.

In general, bad romances are characterized by one of two things: an unusually cruel hero who subjects the heroine to various kinds of verbal and physical abuse, or a diffuse plot that permits the hero to become involved with other women before he settles upon the heroine. Since the Smithton readers will tolerate complicated subplots in some romances if the hero and heroine continue to function as a pair, clearly it is the involvement with others rather than the plot complexity that distresses them. When asked why they disliked these books despite the fact that they all ended happily with the hero converted into the heroine's attentive lover, Dot and her customers replied again and again that they rejected the books precisely because they found them unbelievable. In elaborating, they insisted indignantly that *they* could never forgive the hero's early transgressions and they see no reason why they should be asked to believe that the heroine can. What they are suggesting, then, is that certain kinds of male behavior associated with the stereotype of male machismo can never be forgiven or reread as the signs of love. They are thus not interested *only* in the romance's happy ending. They want to involve themselves in a story that will permit them to enjoy the hero's tenderness *and* to reinterpret his momentary blindness and cool indifference as the marks of a love so intense that he is wary of admitting it. Their delight in both these aspects of the process of romance reading and their deliberate attempt to select books that will include "a gentle hero" and "a slight misunderstanding" suggest that deeply felt needs are the source of their interest in both components of the genre. On the one hand, they long for emotional attention and tender care; on the other, they wish to rehearse the discovery that a man's distance can be explained and excused as his way of expressing love.

It is easy to condemn this latter aspect of romance reading as a reactionary force that reconciles women to a social situation which denies them full development, even as it refuses to accord them the emotional sustenance they require. Yet to identify romances with this conservative moment alone is to miss those other benefits associated with the act of reading as a restorative pastime whose impact on a beleaguered woman is not so simply dismissed. If we are serious about feminist politics and committed to reformulating not only our own lives but those of others, we would do well not to condescend to romance readers as hopeless traditionalists who are recalcitrant in their refusal to acknowledge the emotional costs of patriarchy. We must begin to recognize that romance reading is fueled by dissatisfaction and disaffection, not by perfect contentment with woman's lot. Moreover, we must also understand that some romance readers' experiences are not strictly congruent with the set of ideological propositions that typically legitimate patriarchal marriage. They are characterized, rather, by a sense of longing caused by patriarchal marriage's failure to address all their needs.

In recognizing both the yearning and the fact that its resolution is only a vicarious one not so easily achieved in a real situation, we may find it possible to identify more precisely the very limits of patriarchal ideology's success. Endowed thus with a better understanding of what women want, but often fail to get from the traditional arrangements they consciously support, we may provide ourselves with that very issue whose discussion would reach many more women and potentially raise their consciousnesses about the particular dangers and failures of patriarchal institutions. By helping romance readers to see why they long for relationality and tenderness and are unlikely to get either in the form they desire if current gender arrangements are continued, we may help to convert their amorphous longing into a focused desire for specific change. . . .

NOTES

1. All information about the community has been taken from the 1970 U.S. Census of the Population *Characteristics of the Population,* U.S. Department of Commerce, Social and Economic Statistics Administration, Bureau of the Census, May 1972. I have rounded off some of the statistics to disguise the identity of the town.

2. See the following table.

Table 24.1 Select Demographic Data: Customers of Dorothy Evans

Category	Responses	Number	%
Age	(42) Less than 25	2	5
	25-44	26	62
	45-54	12	28
	55 and older	2	5
Marital Status	(40) Single	3	8
	Married	33	82
	Widowed/separated	4	10
Parental Status	(40) Children	35	88
	No children	4	12
Age at Marriage	Mean-19.9		
	Median-19.2		
Educational Level	(40) High school diploma	21	53
	1-3 years of college	10	25
	College degree	8	20
Work Status	(40) Full or part time	18	45
	Child or home care	17	43
Family Income	(38) $14,999 or below	2	5
	15,000-24,999	18	47
	25,000-49,999	14	37
	50,000 +	4	11
Church Attendance	(40) Once or more a week	15	38
	1-3 times per month	8	20
	A few times per year	9	22
	Not in two (2) years	8	20

Note: (40) indicates the number of responses per questionnaire category. A total of 42 responses per category is the maximum possible. Percent calculations are all rounded to the nearest whole number.

3. Quoted by Brotman (1980). All other details about the Harlequin audience have been taken from Brotman's article. Similar information was also given by Harlequin to Margaret Jensen (1980), whose dissertation, *Women and Romantic Fiction: A Case Study of Harlequin Enterprises, Romances, and Readers,* is the only other study I know of to attempt an investigation of romance readers. Because Jensen encountered the same problems in trying to assemble a representative sample, she relied on interviews with randomly selected readers at a used bookstore. However, the similarity of her findings to those in my study indicates that the lack of statistical representativeness in the case of real readers does not necessarily preclude applying those readers' attitudes and opinions more generally to a large portion of the audience for romantic fiction.

4. See Brotman (1980). All other details about the Silhouette audience have been drawn from Brotman's article. The similarity of the Smithton readers to other segments of the romance audience is explored in greater depth in my book (Radway, 1984). However, the only other available study of romance readers which includes some statistics, Peter H. Mann's (1969) *The Romantic Novel: A Survey of Reading Habits,* indicates that the British audience for such fiction has included in the past more older women as well as younger, unmarried readers than are represented in my sample. However, Mann's survey raises suspicions because it was sponsored by the company that markets the novels and because its findings are represented in such a polemical form. For an analysis of Mann's work, see Jensen (1980, pp. 389-392).

5. The Smithton readers are not avid television watchers. Ten of the women, for instance, claimed to watch television less than three hours per week. Fourteen indicated that they watch four to seven hours a week, while eleven claimed eight to fourteen hours of weekly viewing. Only four said they watch an average of fifteen to twenty hours a week, while only one admitted viewing twenty-one or more hours a week. When asked how often they watch soap operas, twenty-four of the Smithton women checked "never," five selected "rarely," seven chose "sometimes," and four checked "often." Two refused to answer the questions.

6. The Smithton readers' constant emphasis on the educational value of romances was one of the most interesting aspects of our conversations, and chapter 3 of *Reading the Romance* (Radway, 1984) discusses it in depth. Although their citation of the instructional value of romances to a college professor interviewer may well be a form of self-justification, the women also provided ample evidence that they do in fact learn and remember facts about geography, historical customs, and dress from the books they read. Their emphasis on this aspect of their reading, I might add, seems to betoken a profound curiosity and longing to know more about the exciting world beyond their suburban homes.

7. For material on housewives' attitudes toward domestic work and their duties as family counselors, see Oakley (1975a, 1975b); see also Komorovsky (1967) and Lopata (1971).

8. Chodorow (1978). I would like to express my thanks to Sharon O'Brien for first bringing Chodorow's work to my attention and for all those innumerable discussions in which we debated the merits of her theory and its applicability to women's lives, including our own.

9. After developing my argument that the Smithton women are seeking ideal romances which depict the generally tender treatment of the heroine, I discovered Beatrice Faust's (1981) *Women, Sex, and Pornography: A Controversial Study* in which Faust points out that certain kinds of historical romances tend to portray their heroes as masculine, but emotionally expressive. Although I think Faust's overall argument has many problems, not the least of which is her heavy reliance on hormonal differences to explain variations in female and male sexual preferences, I do agree that some women prefer the detailed description of romantic love and tenderness to the careful anatomical representations characteristic of male pornography.

10. Maryles (1979, p. 69).

11. Ten of the twenty books in the sample for the ideal romance were drawn from the Smithton group's answers to requests that they list their three favorite romances and authors. . . . Because I did not include a formal query in the questionnaire about particularly bad romances, I drew the twenty titles from oral interviews and from Dot's newsletter reviews. . . .

12. See Faust (1981), passim.

13. There are two exceptions to this assertion. Both *The Proud Breed* by Celeste DeBlasis and *The Fulfillment* by LaVyrle Spencer detail the involvement of the principal characters with other individuals. Their treatment of the subject, however, is decidedly different from that typically found in the bad romances. Both of these books are highly unusual in that they begin by detailing the extraordinary depth of the love shared by hero and heroine, who marry early

in the story. The rest of each book chronicles the misunderstandings that arise between heroine and hero. In both books the third person narrative always indicates very clearly to the reader that the two are still deeply in love with each other and are acting out of anger, distrust, and insecurity.

14. In the romances considered awful by the Smithton readers, the reinterpretation takes place much later in the story than in the ideal romances. In addition, the behavior that is explained away is more violent, aggressively cruel, and obviously vicious. Although the hero is suddenly transformed by the heroine's reinterpretation of his motives, his tenderness, gentleness, and care are not emphasized in the "failed romances" as they are in their ideal counterparts.

15. Modleski (1980) has also argued that "the mystery of male motives" is a crucial concern in all romantic fiction (p. 439). Although she suggests, as I will here, that the process through which male misbehavior is reinterpreted in a more favorable light is a justification or legitimation of such action, she does not specifically connect its centrality in the plot to a reader's need to use such a strategy in her own marriage. While there are similarities between Modleski's analysis and that presented here, she emphasizes the negative, disturbing effects of romance reading on readers. In fact, she claims, the novels "end up actually intensifying conflicts for the reader" (p. 445) and cause women to "reemerge feeling . . . more guilty than ever" (p. 447). While I would admit that romance reading might create unconscious guilt, I think it absolutely essential that any explanation of such behavior take into account the substantial amount of evidence indicating that women not only *enjoy* romance reading, but feel replenished and reconstituted by it as well.

16. Deveraux (1980, p. 66).

REFERENCES

Brotman, B. (1980, June 2). Ah, romance! Harlequin has an affair for its readers. *Chicago Tribune.*

Chodorow, N. (1978). *The reproduction of mothering: Psychoanalysis and the sociology of gender.* Berkeley: University of California Press.

Deveraux, J. (1980). *The black lyon.* New York: Avon.

Faust, B. (1981). *Women, sex and pornography: A controversial study.* New York: MacMillan.

Jensen, M. (1980). *Women and romantic fiction: A case study of Harlequin Enterprises, romances, and readers.* Unpublished doctoral dissertation, McMaster University, Ontario.

Komorovsky, M. (1967). *Blue collar marriage.* New York: Vintage.

Lopata, H. Z. (1971). *Occupation: Housewife.* New York: Oxford University Press.

Mann, P. H. (1969). *The romantic novel: A survey of reading habits.* London: Mills & Boon.

Maryles, D. (1979, September 3). Fawcett launches romance imprint with brand marketing techniques. *Publishers Weekly,* pp. 69-70.

Modleski, T. (1980). The disappearing act: A study of Harlequin romances. *Signs, 5,* 435-448.

Oakley, A. (1975a). *The sociology of housework.* New York: Pantheon.

Oakley, A. (1975b). *Woman's work: The housewife, past and present.* New York: Pantheon.

Radway, J. (1984). *Reading the romance: Women, patriarchy and popular literature.* Chapel Hill: University of North Carolina Press.

25

The Traditional Romance Formula

MARILYN M. LOWERY

Romances are based on a traditional formula, which has many variations:

1. A girl, our heroine, meets a man, our hero, who is above her socially and who is wealthy and worldly.
2. The hero excites the heroine but frightens her sexually.
3. She is usually alone in the world and vulnerable.
4. The hero dominates the heroine, but she is fiery and sensual, needing this powerful male.
5. Though appearing to scorn her, the hero is intrigued by her and pursues her sexually.
6. The heroine wants love, not merely sex, and sees his pursuit as self-gratification.
7. The two clash in verbal sparring.
8. In holding to her own standards, the heroine appears to lose the hero. She does not know he respects her.

NOTE: Excerpts reprinted from *How to Write Romance Novels That Sell,* by Marilyn M. Lowery (New York: Rawson Associates, 1983), by permission of Rawson Associates, an imprint of Macmillan Publishing Company. Copyright © 1983, Marilyn M. Lowery.

9. A moment of danger for either main character results in the realization on the part of the hero or heroine that the feeling between them is true love.

10. A last-minute plot twist threatens their relationship.

11. The two finally communicate and admit their true love, which will last forever.

Why is the reader fascinated by this formula? It tells her that she can have the romance she was brought up to believe in; that her life can be exciting and happy; that she is desirable sexually; that true love lasts forever.

The novels also fulfill her sexual fantasies. Throughout each romance she can imagine taming a devilish man who first lusts for her, then respects and loves her. She doesn't mind knowing the outcome of the plot. In fact, she wants to. It's the satisfying ending she wants to believe in. The formula is unbeatable.

FIRST STEP—THE TIP SHEET

Each publisher has a different approach to the category, so you as a writer must send a self-addressed, stamped envelope (SASE) to the publisher of your choice, asking for a tip sheet that will give you that publisher's requirements. Your letter will be addressed to the editor of that particular series, for example: Editor, Candlelight Ecstasy Books, Dell Publishing Company, etc. You can get the publishers' addresses either from the reference book *Literary Market Place (LMP)* in your library or from the current *Writer's Market* in your local bookstore.

A good tip sheet will tell you the requirements for a certain publisher. Some sheets are much more detailed than others. If, for instance, you want to write a Gothic romance, you will be told to omit the occult, or to use the occult, or to have any ghostly happenings explained away logically. The ages of the hero and heroine will be specified. You will be told what type of heroine is desired and whether first- or third-person point of view is preferred. If a second man or woman is to figure in the story, you will be informed of this and the role that character will play. The location, in general, will be suggested, as will the amount of sex that is permissible. Finally, you will learn the precise number of words your story is to be. Since each editor's needs vary, the tip sheet is essential to the writer.

Most publishing companies put out a tip sheet for each romance line they handle. Some editors of contemporary lines say that tip sheets are a thing of the past. They prefer to *tell* authors what they want or to send "guidelines." Don't be dismayed. No matter what form the requirements take, formula romances are just that. Discarding tip sheets and pretending no formula exists or calling the novels "mini-mainstream" does not make blockbusters out of series romances. . . .

THE HEROINE'S IDENTITY

Who will your heroine be? How old is she? What is her status—orphan, governess, actress, president of a firm? What goal in life is she working toward, or what problem is she trying to sort through? This goal or problem helps to give her an identity and an interest other than the hero. She is a cheerful, spunky person, quite all right without the hero; but he enters, he adds perfection. To appear strong, she must start with a life outside that with the hero, and her goal must not be to find him.

If the heroine has been widowed or divorced, the pain of that experience should usually be out of the way. If the former husband is in the picture, she is over her love for him and feels some other emotion, such as pity. The reader does not want to be reminded of "lost love" but rather of "new love."

An old lover or even the villain, who has earlier raped the heroine, may have affected her psychologically; and sexual tension may result as the hero tries to overcome her resistance. However, the heroine usually is readily able to put a past romance or rape from her mind and approach the future in high spirits.

THE HEROINE'S VULNERABILITY

The heroine of most romances is vulnerable. She is often much smaller than the hero, tiny against his massive frame. If she is tall, like some of Georgette Heyer's Regency heroines, he is usually taller. The suggestion is always present that he could, if he so desired, rape her; that she is in his power.

A hero is rarely short, but Anne McCaffrey in *Ring of Fear* has been able to portray a short hero who is masculine and masterful:

> I was close enough now to see the light dusting of black hair on his tanned arms and across the muscular plane of his chest, making a thin line down the ridge of the diaphragm muscles, disappearing into the excuse for a bikini he was wearing, which barely covered nature's compensation for his lack of stature.
>
> There was a satisfied expression in his eyes when I jerked mine back from where propriety decreed a well-bred miss ought not to look. He looked suddenly so knowing, so smug, that he was no longer an *objet d'art*, but man, male, masculine. . . .

He soon shows that he is able to rape her if he wishes.

To add to the drama of the heroine's vulnerability, she usually is alone in the world, with few people to depend upon. Also, few people, if any, would ask questions if she were to disappear. This isolation creates suspense.

In Kay Thorpe's *Lord of La Pampa* (Harlequin Presents), the blond heroine from England has not made connections with her dance troupe in Argentina. She signs on as a cocktail waitress, only to learn that she is expected to entertain the men more intimately. The hero rescues her by buying her time then asks her to marry him so he can collect his rightful inheritance. She is alone in the world. What can she do? He reminds her that the nightclub owner has taken her on his payroll:

> " . . . he will expect suitable return. Should it be denied him he may find other ways of extracting a profit. You have heard of the white slave traffic?"

Giving the heroine no choice in the matter keeps the reader sympathetic toward her. The sexual undertones of this scene are obvious, and it is dramatic to think she has just been saved only to be victimized.

If the heroine has a supportive family, its members are usually geographically remote, making it easier for the hero to hire or abduct or marry the heroine. The family may simply be financially unable to help the daughter, as in Richardson's *Pamela* in which the parents lack power to confront the gentleman abductor.

The youthfulness of the heroine can also add to her vulnerability. To the hero's thirty or thirty-five, she can be as young as seventeen, too young to have had a past. This age difference helps to ensure that she is a virgin, and the suggestion is that she is therefore more desirable and, again, more vulnerable.

In some romances, especially contemporaries such as Dell's Candlelight Ecstasy line, the heroine is not a virgin. This fact does not mean that she has experienced the ultimate in love. Her earlier sexual experiences could have been unsatisfactory because of a lack in the husband or lover. Even if her sexual experiences have been satisfactory, no man's lovemaking can compare to that of the hero. . . .

THE COMPLEX HERO

The setting and the heroine help to dictate who the hero will be, and he comes rapidly onto the scene. Though he is usually about ten years older than the heroine, this does not always need to be the case. In Jocelyn Day's *Glitter Girl* (Jove Second Chance at Love), the hero and heroine were in school together and knew each other well before the heroine married a wealthy man and moved away. Now she is back in town, where her first love has become financially successful. But does he trust her to love him for himself rather than for his wealth? Here their similar age is effective.

In period pieces, an age difference is more natural than in a contemporary story. Also, in the Harlequin Romance type of story, the young innocent needs someone older on whom to depend. In the racier contemporary, an age difference is no longer necessary. The heroine portrayed as older is more likely to have a career and is less likely to need an older man to direct her. Today, the two leads can come together as equals.

That the hero is wealthy is never what basically attracts the heroine. But, let's face it, a rich man is the man he is because he has had the power to make money, so that power drive is part of what attracts her.

The hero is a combination of Mr. Darcy in *Pride and Prejudice* and Rhett Butler in *Gone With the Wind*. He appears proud, disdainful, certainly sure of himself, strong, and virile. His outer demeanor cloaks a man who is complex and, most important, loving. But his gentle nature has been carefully masked, perhaps because life has jaded him, perhaps because he carries a deep hurt from the past. Here is mystery.

The chemical reaction between hero and heroine is at once apparent to the reader. Laura London describes Katie's meeting the hero in *The Bad Baron's Daughter* (Dell Candlelight Regency):

> He was the most attractive man Katie had ever seen. Once, as a little girl, when Katie's father had been teaching her how to ride, typically on far too large and temperamental a horse for her tiny size, he had sent her to jump a five-barred gate. The horse had refused, sending Katie flying to the ground with a force that drove the air from her lungs. She felt that same breathless confusion now, as the crowd parted to allow her a clear line of sight.

The sensuality of the horse imagery adds to the power of the description.

At this stage of a story, the hero and heroine feel worlds apart. He looks down on her as an utter innocent—or a schemer, for such goodness cannot possibly ring true to him. She, on the other hand, sees the hero as one who scorns her for her youth or lack of position, or some other reason of which she is unaware.

His scorn for her is apparent mainly through his smiles, which are *mocking, caustic, ironic, sardonic, superior,* and/or *frustrating.* His sensuous lips are continually curling into one of the above. However, you needn't always define the smile. When Thomas in *The Reluctant Duke* comes to propose to Catherine, he cannot help noticing her younger sister, Julia:

> While this exchange was going on, the Duke raised his quizzing glass to look more closely at this younger sister who appeared so lively. The mother thought she caught a slight smile on his lips, but what it meant she could not tell.

As the romance progresses, the heroine often depends upon the hero, whether wishing to or not. If she is in danger, she is sometimes saved in spite of herself. She usually sees *him* as the danger and often sees another man as the one who can help her. That she has the situation reversed is obvious to the reader.

How can the reader trust the hero, even though the heroine does not? Obviously, we can recognize him anywhere. The more sadistic he acts, the more certain we are that there is a heart of gold (not to mention a bank account) beneath the surface. . . .

No matter how she reacts, the hero must save her from some unfortunate situation, such as a fire or other accident, or he might save her from her own misconceptions. Sometimes he saves her from both. Often, she saves *him* at some point in the story. . . .

RAPE AND NEAR-RAPE

The most innocent of romances implies that the hero, if he so desires, can rape the heroine. The reader must be aware that the hero is free to do with the heroine as he likes. His size in comparison to hers helps to remind us that he is in control. That he doesn't take advantage of her characterizes him and shows how truly he loves her.

Often the two are entirely alone, as in Barbara Cartland's *Touch a Star* (Jove). During an elaborate Venetian party, the hero takes the heroine to a deserted island on his estate. No help would be forthcoming were she to need it. So the setting in itself creates some suspense while adding to the reader's sexual fantasy.

In Kathleen E. Woodiwiss's *Ashes in the Wind* the heroine, Alaina, fears the hero. "They were in the house alone, and there was no one to stop him if he chose to take her again." Notice that their situation is spelled out for us.

In most romances there is a touch of sadomasochism. The plot in which the husband or lover rapes his wife or loved one and she enjoys it is not uncommon. Woodiwiss gives us such a scene in *Ashes in the Wind*, in which the hero, Cole Latimer, intoxicated, ravishes Alaina, who makes an unsuccessful attempt to stop him. That she desires him, too, is evident. Moreover, since Cole is drunk, he is not in complete control of his actions. This intoxication is a way of including him in a rape scene and minimizing his responsibility so that the heroine—and readers—can remain sympathetic to him. Moreover, we do not blame the heroine for losing her virtue.

Another familiar plot is one in which the hero holds the heroine captive with the constant threat of rape, a threat that she, while claiming to abhor, actually finds exciting, even fascinating. Violet Winspear in *Palace of the Pomegranate* (Harlequin Presents) goes so far as to have her heroine whisked across the Persian sands by the mysterious Kharim Khan. In one scene, after undressing the heroine so she will not get a desert chill, and roughly drying her with a towel, he says:

> "You deserve the taste of the whip, my little filly, rather than petting—but come, why be shy with me any more? I know how beautiful you are, and you know that I don't intend to let you go. Be kissed instead of bruised. It is far more pleasant, for you, for me."

As he caresses her, she fights back "with all the desperation of a little animal." This fiery spirit fascinates the hero; and out of such tauntings and strugglings comes an ending of true and lasting love. It is just such animal imagery and the idea that the hero loves the heroine because she is beautiful that cause some to condemn the romance as degrading to women and others to read romances.

Near-rapes by the wrong man are also described in a sensuous manner, but he is described in far different terms than is the hero. The villain's breath is disgusting and his kisses wet in Granbeck's *Maura:*

> His weight was overpowering. She was thrown back to the bed and he fell on her, pinning her arms. His mouth searched wetly. When his lips brushed her cheek, she twisted away. His sour breath sickened her and the intimacy of his body on hers was obscene.

When it is the hero who is drunk and rapes the heroine, Woodiwiss writes about "the brandy taste of his mouth." The touch of the hero's body is desirable even though feared.

The reader must not feel disgusted by the actual rape scene. Early in the "bodice-ripper" romance plot, the heroine is usually raped by the hero; and we must remain sympathetic with both characters. In such scenes, the writer must be especially careful to motivate the actions of the two. These rapes are more acts of passion than of violence, and we mustn't feel as we would while reading about an actual rape.

Though the reader feels good about the scene, the heroine feels guilt and anger. Her emotions make her at odds with the hero, who has caused her to lose control. She will show him she doesn't need him (since she has just shown him that she does). Her pride has been hurt. She also has been reminded of feelings she has not been aware of or has been repressing. Now her confusion of feelings is uppermost in her mind, and she resents the one who has caused such doubt.

AROUSING THE READER

Romance writers use strong adjectives and verbs to draw the reader into the love scene. As you write, try adjectives such as *burning, hungering, throbbing, exploding,* or *scalding.* Forget the verb *to be.* Instead, try verbs that convey action or emotion such as *plunged, stroked, caressed, quivered, writhed, pressed, searched, arched,* and *moaned,* to name a few.

When passion subsides and contentment follows, the pace slows and less dynamic verbs take the place of explosive ones. Pacing is important in sex scenes. You as writer may move from short, abrupt sentences to lyrical metaphors to slower-paced moments in which the couple can languorously enjoy each other.

Breathless interjections can lend immediacy as in Charlotte Lamb's *Duel of Desire* (Harlequin Presents):

> He paused, his breathing rapid and harsh. "Did I hurt you? Darling, did I hurt you?"
>
> "No, oh, no," she whispered. Her hands pressed him down to her. "Oh, Alex, darling, I want you so much . . ."

He groaned, his body trembling violently. "Deb. . . . Oh, God, Deb,
I love you like hell . . ."

You will learn to allot little time to sex scenes with a woman other than
the heroine, and your adjectives in such scenes will not be flattering. She will
sound sensuous but not as desirable as the heroine because of your adjectives and verbs. In Granbeck's *Maura* Beau makes love to Irene:

Then they were together, hands exploring, mouths tasting, until their
bodies met in passion. She clawed at his flesh and writhed, to meet
his body. His hard muscles moved under her hands and his mouth
stopped her cries until all thoughts were blanketed by exploding
pleasure.

Similarly, when the wrong man makes love to the heroine, you will
remember to give him less space and see that his sexual prowess does not
compare to that of the hero. . . .

26

What's in a Pseudonym?

Romance Slaves of Harlequin

RICHARD POLLAK

For the hundreds of women yearning to burst into print as writers of romance fiction, Harlequin Enterprises thoughtfully supplies guidelines with some helpful hints. One of them is that the plots of these paperback passionaries "should not be too grounded in harsh realities." Before counting their royalties, however, would-be-authors might want to look into the harsh realities of dealing with Harlequin—in particular its insistence that writers use pseudonyms.

Ostensibly, these pen names merely give the romance novel an extra fillip of mystery and titillation, like the titles (*Savage Promise; Creole Fires*) and the covers depicting bodice-bursting maidens gazing amorously into the eyes of hunks in various states of dress and undress. In fact, the pseudonym requirement is a Harlequin ploy aimed at keeping its stable of writers strictly tethered to the corporate hitching post. "Today," says Anita Diamant, a New York literary agent who represents some twenty romance writers, "I can't get a contract from [Harlequin] unless the author agrees to select a pseudonym."

Once a writer signs the contract, Harlequin takes the position that the pseudonym belongs to the company, something it could never do if the author wrote under her real name. Harlequin, a subsidiary of Canada's billion-dollar Torstar media conglomerate, has almost 1,000 writers here and

---

NOTE: Reprinted from *The Nation* (March 16, 1992), by permission of the publisher. © The Nation Company, Inc.

abroad churning out about sixty novels a month. Since Harlequin Enterprises controls an estimated 80 percent of the romance fiction market, these women challenge the company at considerable risk.

Not long ago, one agent pressed Harlequin on what in recent months has become the most contentious aspect of the pseudonym issue: reversion of rights. Most publishers, once a book is out of print, routinely allow the rights to revert to the author after a number of months. But, except in a very few cases, Harlequin Enterprises has refused to grant reversion of rights unless the author agrees not to use her pseudonym at another publisher, thus denying her the beginning power the pen name may have gained because of the popularity of her books.

When the agent threatened to complain publicly about Harlequin's tactics, the company said it would cancel all Harlequin books with that agent. When the agent persisted, the company terminated the contracts of several of the agent's authors, whose manuscripts had been accepted and who were due to be paid. Harlequin also told the agent that all other agency authors would be frozen out from then on. The agent "was practically in tears," recalls Maria Pallante, a lawyer and assistant director of The Authors Guild, which is investigating Harlequin's pseudonym practices. Pallante said she has talked with some two dozen romance writers and their agents and "there has been a shocking level of fear."

Such is the climate of fear engendered by Harlequin's clout that no one is willing to talk about the company except on deep background. So pray indulge me, reader, if I invent a composite heroine whose plight, I assure you, is representative of many romance authors. Her real name doesn't matter because it doesn't sell books. Under the pen name Desirée Halston, she has written some fifty successful romances for a publisher that, on advice of counsel, I shall call Slapstick Press. Her *oeuvre* includes such shopping-mall blockbusters as *Hot, Stolen Kisses, Fire and Ice, Desert Lust, Secrets of the Casbah* and *Savage Passion*.

Her career is one of those success stories that inspire hundreds of ambitious writers everywhere. But even a star like Desirée, with her considerable bargaining power, learns that she who challenges the company does so at her peril.

Desirée's sin is to request that the rights to twenty-five of her books revert to her. An innocent enough demand, one might think. They're all out of print, so the company's not doing anything with them. But Slapstick adamantly refuses. At first it is avuncular: Why, we know what's best for your career, little lady. But spunky Desirée refuses to back down. So then the company ripples its muscles, like one of her beefy heroes, and launches a series of escalating threats. The message is clear: Unless she knuckles under she will never publish with Slapstick again. Furthermore, if she moves to another publisher, she is forbidden to take her pseudonym with her. The name Desirée Halston would live on—on Slapstick books written by another writer.

Such, at least, is the fate that awaits a Slapstick author who dares cross the street to another publisher. Usually, however, says a source familiar with other such cases in real life, the company has only to threaten the rebellious writers with termination and they cave in immediately.

Harlequin—like Zebra, Avon, Dell, Bantam and other smaller players in the romance field—pays advances ranging from $2,000 to $3,000 to beginners to around $15,000 for established writers. If a book sells, an author can earn as much as $40,000 in royalties. But in most cases, that's all. Almost all romance fiction comes off the racks after a month to make way for the next wave of desire. Romance writers who want to bring in a six-figure income must turn out at least three successful books a year, and a few do.

The heroines of this genre are women like Heather Graham, who has written sixty books in the past nine years (most recently, *Damsel in Distress* and *Bride of the Wild*). She uses her own name when writing for Dell, the pseudonym Shannon Drake at Avon and the pen name Heather Graham Pozzessere for Harlequin's Silhouette series. In 1982, when Graham began writing romances, she, her husband and their five small children were jammed into a frame house near the Miami airport. Graham began spending five to eight hours a day at the word processor, and now the family owns a large home in Coral Gables, Florida, and a mansion near Worcester, Massachusetts, a Greek Revival with twelve rooms, woodburning fireplaces and two ballrooms.

Despite this romantic journey, Graham and others like her remain largely invisible outside their own literary subculture. Romance fiction is sold mostly on newsstands or by mail order, rather than in bookstores, and *The New York Times*'s and other best-seller lists disdain the genre, though it accounts for 35 percent of all paperback sales. So the great dream of most women writers in the field is to make the leap to what the publishing trade calls "women's fiction," to write longer, hard-cover books and become the next Danielle Steel, who started out writing romance fiction and now can usually be found near or at the top of the best-seller ladder. "Danielle reportedly pulls down an income of $25 million," observes *Romantic Times* in its March issue. "She makes this money writing in a little closet of a room, wearing a jogging suit and her diamonds."

Romantic Times is a monthly valentine to the women writing or reading romance fiction, a compendium of advertisements and reviews, interlarded with gossip ("Sylvie Sommerfield had a fire in her living room. . . . By the way, BITTERSWEET, Sylvie's latest Warner release, is selling well") and fanzine profiles of successful authors like Heather Graham, complete with bibliographies and addresses for fan mail. From April 30 through May 4, the faithful will gather in Savannah, Georgia, for *R.T.*'s tenth annual booklovers' convention. There will be the usual how-to panels ("Indians to Know and Love: The Writing of an Indian Romance"), but given the current controversy, perhaps the most useful session will be on handling legal clauses in contracts.

Harlequin gained its lock on the romance market largely because the antitrust division of the Reagan Justice Department looked the other way in 1985 while the Canadians embraced Simon & Schuster's Silhouette Books. In 1990 Harlequin Enterprises grossed $302 million in sales and almost $50 million in operating profits from its two smoothly meshed pulp mills, selling

194 million books in some 100 markets worldwide and in more than twenty languages. This year, the company has launched a twelve-title series aimed at palpitating hearts in Europe's Common Market, with each book set in a different country. ("Yes," *The Economist* was moved to note, "even Belgium.")

But it is not only Harlequin's worldwide reach and near monopoly that give it sway over its authors. The company knows—and so do its writers—that there are plenty of unpublished women (and a few men) breathless for a chance to see their passionate prose in print, to see their pseudonyms on a Harlequin series, whether in the demure Romance line (in which writers are told to avoid "explicit sexual description") or the racier Temptation books ("love scenes should be highly erotic, realistic and fun").

Many of these would-be authors, and some published ones, belong to Romance Writers of America, which has about 4,000 members. The R.W.A. board appears unwilling to challenge Harlequin on the pseudonym issue, in part, possibly, because board members get special treatment from Harlequin's editors. This coziness has angered some state chapters and prompted letters to the board and to The Authors Guild complaining that members' opposition to Harlequin's pseudonym policy is not being represented by the board.

Novelists Inc., which represents about 300 established romance writers and was formed in 1989 because R.W.A. wasn't addressing the needs of the published writers, is squarely behind the guild's investigation of Harlequin's pseudonym tactics. So are two high-profile writers, who have enough courage—and money—at least to hire lawyers to try to protect their pen names, but who nonetheless remain fearful of going public at this stage in the battle.

Harlequin maintains it is the company that promotes and sustains the pseudonyms and that if authors were allowed to take their pen names to another publisher, Harlequin would lose money and its carefully nurtured market would dry up. Whether this is true or not, The Authors Guild's position is essentially, "So what? That's the market in action." Pallante, a guild lawyer, points out that other publishers take the same risk every day with their authors who use pen names. If Stephen King decided to move from Viking to, say, Random House, he doubtless would have no trouble taking his pseudonym, Richard Bachman, with him.

Harlequin has threatened to convert its contracts to "work for hire" if its authors keep making a fuss over pseudonyms. As matters now stand, authors own the copyrights on their books and receive royalties of 6 percent on sales. But under work-for-hire agreements, writers would be paid a flat fee for their manuscripts, would not own the copyright and would get no royalties, however well their books sold. Some romance writers and their agents think that Harlequin has wanted to move to work-for-hire agreements for some time, and that the current hard line on pseudonyms is just part of that larger strategy. Harlequin would not comment on this or any other aspect of the pseudonym controversy. "We are not prepared to use *The Nation* as our method of communication to the author community," explained Bernard Stevenson, vice president for administration and legal affairs.

The Authors Guild has yet to decide on what action, if any, it will take in the Harlequin matter. Among the courses of action it could pursue are: complaining to the Federal Trade Commission that Harlequin is indulging in unfair trade practices made possible by its near monopoly in the market-place; asking the Justice Department's antitrust division to reexamine the 1985 Silhouette merger that created the romance powerhouse in the first place; or mounting a test case by getting an author whose rights are reverting to sue Harlequin. Any of the approaches is likely to produce a protracted and expensive fight, so a peaceful resolution would seem preferable.

Meanwhile, Harlequin is busily preparing a new line of romance mysteries, to be called Silhouette Shadows. The guidelines sheet suggests they might begin: "In an empty house, the air thick with darkness, a woman waits alone. Her heart beats faster as she hears the creaking of the front door, and then a man's voice, soft with menace, calls out . . ."

Work for hire?

PART IV

MODES OF SEXUAL REPRESENTATION 2: PORNOGRAPHY

pornography. n. *[Gr. porne, prostitute and graphein, to write.] 1. originally, a description of prostitutes and their trade. 2. writings, pictures, etc. intended to arouse sexual desire.*

Webster's New Twentieth Century Dictionary
(2nd ed., 1962)

Pornography, then, is verbal or pictorial material which represents or describes sexual behavior that is degrading or abusive to one or more of the participants in such a way as to endorse the degradation. Behavior that is degrading or abusive includes physical harm and abuse and physical or psychological coercion. In addition, behavior which ignores or devalues the real interests, desires, and experiences of one or more of the participants in any way is degrading. Finally, that a person has chosen or consented to be harmed, abused or subjected to coercion does not alter the degrading character of such behavior. (Longino, 1980. p. 29)

Perhaps one could simply say that erotica is about sexuality, but pornography is about power and sex-as-weapon—in the same way we have come to understand that rape is about violence and not really about sexuality at all. (Steinem, 1978, p. 38)

Pornography refers to any literature or film (or other art-technological form) that describes or depicts sexual organs, preludes to sexual activity, or sexual activity (or related organs and activities) in such a way as to produce sexual arousal in the user or the viewer; and this effect in the viewer is either the effect intended by both producer and consumer or a very likely effect in the absence of direct intentions. (Soble, 1986, pp. 8-9)

[Pornography is] the graphic sexually explicit subordination of women through pictures and/or words, that also includes one or more of the following: (a) women are presented dehumanized as sexual objects, things, or commodities; or (b) women are presented as sexual objects who enjoy humiliation or pain; or (c) women are presented as sexual objects experiencing sexual pleasure in rape, incest, or other sexual assault; or (d) women are presented as sexual objects tied up or cut up or mutilated or bruised or physically hurt; or (e) women are presented in postures or positions of sexual submission, servility or display; or (f) women's body parts—including but not limited to vaginas, breasts, or buttocks—are exhibited such that women are reduced to those parts; or (g) women are presented being penetrated by objects or animals; or (h) women are presented in scenarios of degradation, humiliation, injury, torture, shown as filthy or inferior, bleeding, bruised or hurt in a context that makes these conditions sexual. The use of men, children or transsexuals in the place of women shall also be deemed to be pornography for purposes of this definition. (MacKinnon, 1993, p. 121)

Pornography. 1. Pictures, writing or other material that is sexually explicit and sometimes equates sex with power and violence. 2. The presentation or production of this material (*American Heritage Dictionary*, 3rd ed., 1992).

As this shifting set of definitions suggests, pornography may be the most difficult media form to define. It is certainly one of the most difficult to analyze and discuss dispassionately. For some feminists, as a matter of fact, encouraging dispassionate discussion of pornography is part of the problem of pornography's broad social acceptance, especially by liberal cultural elites in our contemporary world.

We, the two editors of this volume, differ in our approaches to pornography, but we hope to make this difference work to the advantage of the readers, both teachers and students.

As teachers, we have found that although pornography is undoubtedly a difficult subject for classroom discussion, most students find the topic highly interesting and important personally as well as intellectually and are happy to have a selection of thought-provoking readings such as the ones included in this chapter to help organize and contextualize the discussion. We recommend deferring the study of pornography until after doing substantial work on advertising (and perhaps MTV) imagery, because it is important to see pornography as a form of **representation** that informs and is informed by other media representations of women. Rather than reliance on documentary film essays on pornography, which allow for less interaction, we recommend the use of slides, seen and discussed in detail and at a slow pace, as a way of stripping the imagery of shock value and helping students develop visual analysis skills.

It is also important for teachers to emphasize that although the political differences between feminists over the nature of pornography, the question of its harm and the appropriate activist response to the proliferation of pornography have been characterized as bipolar, there are actually many more than two views, and most people have doubts, questions and confusions that they should be encouraged to express in the classroom. We will start by characterizing our own mixture of views, as a way of encouraging users of this book similarly to examine their own beliefs, experiences and feelings, including perhaps ambivalent ones, as part of the process of discussing this difficult topic.

We have both been involved over many years in reading and teaching about the problem of pornography from a feminist perspective. One of us, Gail Dines, is an antipornography lecturer and activist as well as a teacher. Dines agrees with the radical feminist view that pornography is a form of violence against women, both in its production and consumption, and that pornography should be defined as a violation of women's civil rights. She believes that pornographic modes of representation have come to inform all of mass media imagery and have a profound impact on the way men perceive women, women perceive women, women perceive men and men perceive men. She also believes that the radical feminist position on pornography tends to be caricatured in the "anti-antipornography"[1] writings. She hopes that in this chapter the major arguments of the radical feminist position will be clearly heard.

Humez is a feminist teacher and parent. She believes that the quantity and kind of pornographic imagery currently produced and consumed in industrial cultures suggests profound (and potentially dangerous) feelings of psychosexual alienation, primarily of heterosexual men from women. She believes that pornography (defined as **sexist** erotica), as well as other media imagery that associates sexual arousal with male domination and violence in less sexually explicit ways, must help perpetuate sexist ideology and behavior, even if it cannot be shown directly to "cause" sexist violence. But she does not agree that pornographic imagery is indistinguishable from acts of violence against women. She also worries about the impact (on younger women in particular) of an excessive rhetorical stress by feminists on female sexual victimization. Humez has been attracted to the idea of defining sexist images of specific kinds as a violation of women's civil rights, as the Dworkin-MacKinnon Ordinance (from which we quoted earlier, in our definitions of pornography) does, but she is not persuaded that this legal mechanism would actually help remedy the problem, and she fears its misuse.

We agree in seeing pornography as a form of sexual representation that can also be a documentation of real events that once happened in the lives of sexually exploited women, children and men. Although on the level of representation, there are certain similarities between pornography and imagery in other media forms, such as MTV rock videos and fashion advertising, it is our argument that in terms of production and consumption, pornography is quite distinctive. On the level of production, pornography requires interlinked systems of domination, such as **racism, sexism** and **classism,** to provide the cultural and economic space by which most pornography can be made. On the level of consumption, pornography shares with "hate speech" the potential for being used to intimidate, harass and even terrorize women.

We have purposefully avoided entering here into the acrimonious and complex debate about the Dworkin-MacKinnon Ordinance (which aims to define pornography as a violation of women's civil rights rather than a criminal offense). This debate has dominated most discussions of the topic in recent years. We think that the public policy issues surrounding pornography are important ones, but the topic of pornography's legal control is complex enough to require a book in itself. (Indeed, many books have been written during the 10-year-plus period in which the ordinance has been contested in the United States and similar legal efforts made in Canada and Great Britain. We include in the bibliography for Part IV a selection of these books for students and teachers who want to explore this aspect of the subject in the depth it deserves.)

We have also decided to limit our focus in this chapter to heterosexual pornography, recognizing that although related to some degree, the debates over gay and lesbian pornography are distinct and, to be fairly represented, would require extensive contextualizing within gay and lesbian politics—a task that is beyond the scope of a reader like this one. We think it would be a mistake to assume that the conditions of production and consumption in gay and lesbian pornography mirror those in the heterosexual market, given that the gay and lesbian market is smaller and has some independent owners and producers. Moreover, in terms of consumption, gay and lesbian pornography necessarily has different meaning in the context of a heterosexist and homophobic society (Dyer, 1985; Greyson, 1985, Kipnis, 1993; Meyers, 1982; Rich, 1981; Watney, 1987; Waugh, 1985; also see bibliography for Part III).

Our primary intent in this chapter is to present a number of different critical viewpoints on what (heterosexual) pornography is, how it is produced and consumed, how it relates to male supremacy and other systems of domination and how the actual texts of pornography may be understood and analyzed within a variety of cultural contexts.

Because of space limitations and the complexity of the arguments, it is impossible to represent adequately all the voices that have been raised in the activist debate. We decided to select characteristic pieces by Andrea Dworkin and Gayle Rubin, to represent the major polarized positions (the radical feminist and anti-antipornography, respectively).

Dworkin's "Pornography and Male Supremacy" (Chapter 27) starts from the belief that the production and consumption of pornography needs to be understood within the context of a male supremacist society: "Pornography can only develop in a society that is viciously male-supremacist . . . ; and pornography depends for its continued existence on the rape and prostitution of women." She argues that pornography is a documentation of real events of sexual and economic exploitation, and that in its production and consumption, it condones, legitimizes and eroticizes real-world violence against women.

In striking contrast, in her essay "Misguided, Dangerous and Wrong," (Chapter 28) Gayle Rubin questions the usefulness of employing the concept of male supremacy in understanding both production and consumption of pornography. She calls for an analysis of pornography that foregounds female agency, arguing that coercion does not adequately explain why many women work in the "sex industries." Moreover, she critiques the radical feminist position on consumption, arguing that women can derive pleasure as consumers of all types of pornography, including sadomasochistic varieties (S & M). She seriously questions the degree to which pornography is documentation, arguing "It is ludicrous to assume that the level of coercion in an image is a reliable guide to the treatment of the actors involved."

These activist-oriented debates around the question of pornography have had a profound influence on academic theorizing and research on the issue, which has been plentiful and various in the last decade. It includes social science laboratory research on the short-term effects of pornography exposure on male and female consumers (Malamuth & Donnerstein, 1984; Weaver, 1992; Zillman & Weaver, 1989); sophisticated examination of the evolution of one of contemporary pornography's **genres,** the legal "hardcore" film, out of its ancestor form, the illegal stag film (Williams, 1989); and theorizing about pornography as a mode of representation (Coward, 1987; Kipnis, 1990; Kuhn, 1989; Modleski, 1991; Myers, 1987; Williams, 1989; Zita, 1988). There has as yet been relatively little work, however, that details the workings of the pornography industry within the wider **capitalistic** economy.

No discussion of the development of the industry would be complete without a consideration of the role of *Playboy Magazine* in mainstreaming the pornographic mode of representation. Gail Dines's chapter, "I Only Buy It for the Articles" (Chapter 29), examines how Hugh Hefner set out to bring pornography out of the closet, by producing a glossy, airbrushed, upscale magazine that not only commodified sex but also sexualized **commodities,** at a time when advertisers were looking to expand markets. One key to Hefner's success, according to Dines's analysis, was the centerfold, a complexly coded "soft-core" pornographic *text* that both Myers and Kuhn help us **decode** in their essays on **textual analysis.**

Kathy Myers, in "Towards a Feminist Erotica" (Chapter 30), and Annette Kuhn, in "Lawless Seeing" (Chapter 31), help us identify what sets apart "pornographic" visual images from the other more mainstream photographic images of women, which they to some degree resemble. Both of these scholars show the importance of close examination of the "codes" or symbolic conventions of actual photographic texts. These include aspects of the pose that specifically assume (and some would say create) a masculine **subject position**—that is, cause a viewer of either sex to take a "masculine" perspective toward the sexual object depicted. Kuhn and Myers are interested as well in how women consume images of themselves that are informed to varying degrees by pornographic modes of representation.

Until relatively recently, gender has been the primary concern in the discussion of pornography as a mode of sexual representation. However, as the analysis has deepened, it has become apparent that other systems of domination influence the construction of gender ideology in pornography, as Patricia Hill Collins argues in "Pornography and Black Women's Bodies" (Chapter 32). Drawing on a classic essay by Alice Walker (1980) about the problematics of pornography's use within the African American community, Patricia Hill Collins points out intersections between racist and sexist ideologies, as evident in consistent differences in pornographic imagery of African American women, Asian women and White women. Hill Collins suggests that "contemporary portrayals of black women in pornography represent the continuation of the historical treatment of their bodies," using, for example, symbols of slavery in such portrayals. A **content analysis** by Diana Russell and Alice Mayall of racist imagery in pornographic magazines, videos and books, based on research done in 1985 by Alice Mayall (Chapter 33), suggests the extent to which this sexualizing of historical periods of racist abuse, including the slave era and the Holocaust, is widespread.

Another important new direction in the academic discussion of pornography is the movement away from overreliance on the social-scientific (social psychological) experimental research model. This model has aimed to explore in the laboratory the link between exposure to pornography and real-world attitudes and behaviors. The problem with this model, as Robert Jensen argues in "Pornography and the Limits of Experimental Research" (Chapter 34), is that it fails to take into account the possible effects of the real-world contexts in which pornography is actually used, and it cannot tell us what **ideological** impact long-term use of pornography has. Jensen calls for a more **ethnographic** (anthropological) type of research on pornography's effects, one that would include analysis of women's and men's testimony about its place in their lives.

Taking Jensen's arguments seriously, we end the section with two pieces of first-person testimony, from people who stand in very different relationships to the pornography industry. Scott MacDonald's testimonial essay, "Confessions of a Feminist Porn Watcher" (Chapter 35), contextualizes the use of pornography, by describing one (White) man's experience of pornography consumption and exploring his ambivalent feelings as a "feminist male consumer." Antipornography activist and former prostituted woman Evelina Giobbe, in "Surviving Commercial Sexual Exploitation" (Chapter 36), provides an experiential basis for the argument that pornography is not simply a form of representation like other media imagery but is anchored within a wider system of power relations (familial, economic and physical) that subordinate women and girls.

NOTE

1. This includes those who designate themselves "prosex" and "anticensorship" as well as others who may not be affiliated with any specific activist organizations. After much discussion over the issue of naming the various factions in the debate, and in recognition that naming is political, we have decided to use the most inclusive and broadest possible term for the feminist critics of the radical feminist "antipornography" position.

REFERENCES

Coward, R. (1987). What is pornography? Two opposing feminist viewpoints. In R. Betterton (Ed.), *Looking on.* London: Pandora.

Dyer, R. (1985, March). Male gay porn: Coming to terms. *Jump Cut, 30,* 27-29.

Dyer, R. (1990). Towards lesbian erotica, or pornography. In R. Dyer, *Now you see it: Studies on lesbian and gay film* (pp. 206-210). London: Routledge.

Greyson, J. (1985, March). Gay video: The present context. *Jump Cut, 30,* 36-38.

Kipnis, L. (1990). (Male) desire and (female) disgust: Reading *Hustler.* In L. Grossberg, C. Nelson, & P. Treichler (Eds.), *Cultural studies.* New York: Routledge.

Kipnis, L. (1993). She-male fantasies and the aesthetics of pornography. In P. C. Gibson & R. Gibson (Eds.), *Dirty looks: Women, pornography, power.* London: British Film Institute.

Kuhn, A. (1989). Lawless seeing. In A. Kuhn, *The power of the image: Essays on representation and sexuality.* Boston: Routledge and Kegan Paul.

Longino, H. E. (1980). Pornography, oppression and freedom: A closer look. In L. Lederer et al. (Eds.), *Take back the night* (pp. 40-54). New York: William Morrow.

MacKinnon, C. A. (1993). *Only words.* Cambridge, MA: Harvard University Press.

Malamuth, N. M., & Donnerstein, E. (Eds.). (1984). *Pornography and sexual aggression.* New York: Academic Press.

Modleski, T. (1991). Lethal bodies: Thoughts on sex, gender and representation, from the main stream to the margins. In T. Modleski, *Feminism without women: Culture and criticism in a "postfeminist" age* (pp. 135-163). New York: Routledge.

Myers, K. (1982). Fashion'n'passion. *Screen, 23*(3-4).

Myers, K. (1987). Towards a feminist erotica. In R. Betterton, *Looking on: Images of femininity in the visual arts and media* (pp. 189-202). London: Pandora.

Rich, B. R. (1981, March). From repressive tolerance to erotic liberation. *Jump Cut, 24/25,* 44-50.

Soble, A. (1986). *Pornography, Marxism, feminism, and the future of sexuality.* New Haven, CT: Yale.

Steinem, G. (1978). Erotica and pornography: A clear and present difference. Reprinted in L. Lederer et al. (Eds.), *Take back the night.* New York: William Morrow.

Walker, A. (1980). Coming apart. In L. Lederer et al. (Eds.), *Take back the night.* New York: William Morrow.

Watney, S. (1987). *Policing desire: Pornography, AIDS and the media.* Minneapolis: University of Minnesota Press.

Waugh, T. (1985). Men's pornography: Gay versus straight. *Jump Cut, 30,* 30-35.

Weaver, J. (1992). The social science and psychological research evidence: Perceptual and behavioral consequences of exposure to pornography. In C. Itzin (Ed.), *Pornography: Women, violence and civil liberties*. Oxford: Oxford University Press.

Williams, L. (1989). *Hard core: Power, pleasure and the "frenzy of the visible."* Berkeley: University of California.

Zillman, D., & Weaver, J. (1989). Pornography and men's sexual callousness toward women. In D. Zillman & J. Bryant (Eds.), *Pornography: Research advances and policy consideration* (pp. 95-125). Hillsdale, NJ: Lawrence Erlbaum.

Zita, J. (1988). Pornography and the male imaginary. *Enclitic, 17/18*, 28-44.

.27

Pornography and Male Supremacy

ANDREA DWORKIN

We live in a system of power that is male-supremacist. This means that society is organized on the assumption that men are superior to women and that women are inferior to men. Male supremacy is regarded as being either divine or natural, depending on the proclivities of the apologist for it. Theologically, God is the supreme male, the Father, and the men of flesh and blood one might meet on the streets or in the corridors of universities are created in His image. There is also a divine though human though divine Son, and a phallic Holy Ghost who penetrates women as light penetrates a window. In both Jewish and Christian tradition, women are dirty, inclined to evil, not fit for the responsibilities of religious or civil citizenship, should be seen and not heard, are destined, or predestined as it were, for sexual use and reproduction and have no other value. Also, in both traditions (which are Father and Son respectively), the sexuality of women is seen as intrinsically seductive and sluttish, by its nature a provocation to which men respond. In theological terms, men are superior and women are inferior because God/He made it so, giving women a nature appropriate to their animal functions and men a nature with capacities that raise them above all other creatures.

The biological argument is even sillier, but because it is secular and university-sponsored, it has more credibility among intellectuals. Throughout patriarchal history, not just now, biological determinists have made two essential claims: first, that male superiority to women resides in an organ or a fluid or a secretion or a not-yet-discovered but urgently anticipated speck on a gene; and second, that we should study primates, fish, and insects to see how they manage, especially with their women. Sociobiologists and ethologists, the latest kinds of biological determinists, are selective in the species they study and the conclusions they draw because their argument is political, not scientific. The male, they say, regardless of what bug they are observing, is naturally superior because he is naturally dominant because he is naturally aggressive and so are his sperm; the female is naturally compliant and naturally submissive and exists in order to be fucked and bear babies. Now, fish do not reproduce through fucking; but that did not stop Konrad Lorenz's followers from holding up the cichlid as an example to the human woman. The cichlid is a prehistoric fish, and according to Lorenz the male cichlids could not mate unless the female cichlids demonstrated awe. Kate Millett wonders in *Sexual Politics* how one measures awe in a fish. But biological determinists do not wait around to answer such silly questions: they jump from species to species as suits their political purposes. And of course there are species they do avoid: spiders, praying mantises, and camels, for instance, since the females of these species kill or maim the male after intercourse. Biological determinists do not find such behaviors instructive. They love the gall wasp, which they have affectionately nicknamed the "killer wasp"—so one gets an idea of its character—and they do not pay much attention to the bee, what with its queen. There are also relatively egalitarian primates who never get a mention, and male penguins that care for the young, and so forth. And of course, no biological determinist has yet found the bug, fish, fowl, or even baboon who had managed to write *Middlemarch*. Humans create culture; even women create culture. "Sociobiology" or "ethology" may be new words, but biological arguments for the superiority of one group over another are not new. They are as old as genocide and slave labor. If women are held to be a natural class that exists to be fucked and to bear babies, then any method used to get women to do what they exist to do is also natural. And—to add insult to injury—they dare to call it Mother Nature.

The biological determinists believe precisely what the theologians believe: that women exist to be sexually used by men, to reproduce, to keep the cave clean, and to obey; failing which both men of religion and men of nature hypothesize that hitting the female might solve her problem. In theological terms, God raised man above all other creatures; in biological terms, man raised himself. In both systems of thought, man is at the top, where he belongs; woman is under him, literally and figuratively, where she belongs.

Every area of conflict regarding the rights of women ultimately boils down to the same issue: what are women for; to what use should women be put—sexually and reproductively. A society will be concerned that the birth rate is not high enough, but not that there is a paucity of books produced by women. For women as a class, sex and reproduction are presumed to be the very essence of life, which means that our fate unfolds in the opening of our thighs and the phallic penetration of our bodies and the introjection of sperm into our vaginas and the appropriation of our uteruses. In *The Dialectic of Sex*, Shulamith Firestone wrote: "Sex class is so deep as to be invisible." That is because sex class is seen as the work of God or nature, not men; and so the possession of women's bodies by men is considered to be the correct and proper use of women.

In male-supremacist terms, sex is phallic sex; it is often called possession or conquest or taking. A woman's body is taken or conquered or possessed or—to use another supposedly sexy synonym—violated; and the means of the taking or possessing or violating is penile penetration.

The sexual colonialization of women's bodies is a material reality: men control the sexual and reproductive uses of women's bodies. In this system of male power, rape is the paradigmatic sexual act. The word "rape" comes from the Latin *rapere*, which means to steal, seize, or carry away. The first dictionary definition of rape is still "the act of seizing and carrying off by force." A second meaning of rape is "the act of physically forcing a woman to have sexual intercourse." Rape is first abduction, kidnapping, the taking of a woman by force. Kidnapping, or rape, is also the first known form of marriage—called "marriage by capture." The second known form of marriage is basically prostitution: a father, rather than allow the theft of his daughter, sells her. Most social arrangements for the exchange of women operate on one ancient model or the other: stealing, which is rape; or buying and selling, which is prostitution.

The relationship of prostitution to rape is simple and direct: whatever can be stolen can be sold. This means that women were both stolen and sold and in both cases were sexual commodities; and when practices were codified into laws, women were defined as sexual chattel. Women are still basically viewed as sexual chattel—socially, legally, culturally, and in practice. Rape and prostitution are central contemporary female experiences; women as a class are seen as belonging to men as a class and are systematically kept subservient to men; married women in most instances have lost sexual and reproductive control of their own bodies, which is what it means to be sexual chattel.

The principle that whatever can be stolen can be sold applies not only to women as such, but also to the sexuality of women. The sexuality of women has been stolen outright, appropriated by men—conquered, possessed, taken, violated; women have been systematically and absolutely denied the right to sexual self-determination and to sexual integrity; and because the sexuality of women has been stolen, this sexuality itself, *it*—as distinguished from an individual woman as a sentient being—*it* can be sold. It can be represented pictorially and sold; the idea or suggestion of it can be sold; representations of it in words can be sold; signs and gestures that denote it can be sold. Men can take this sexuality—steal it, rape it—and men can pimp it.

We do not know when in history pornography as such first appeared. We do know that it is a product of culture, specifically male-supremacist culture, and that it comes after both rape and prostitution. Pornography can only develop in a society that is viciously male-supremacist, one in which rape and prostitution are not only well-established but systematically practiced and ideologically endorsed. Feminists are often asked whether pornography causes rape. The fact is that rape and prostitution caused and continue to cause pornography. Politically, culturally, socially, sexually, and economically, rape and prostitution generated pornography; and pornography depends for its continued existence on the rape and prostitution of women.

The word *pornography* comes from the ancient Greek *porné and graphos:* it means "the graphic depiction of whores." *Porné* means "whore," specifically the lowest class of whore, which in ancient Greece was the brothel slut available to all male citizens. There were distinct classes of prostitutes in ancient Greece: the *porné* was the sexual cow. She was, simply and clearly and absolutely, a sexual slave. *Graphos* means "writing, etching, or drawing."

The whores called *porneia* were captive in brothels, which were designated as such by huge phalluses painted on or constructed near the door. They were not allowed out, were never educated, were barely dressed, and in general were miserably treated; they were the sexual garbage of Greek society. Wives were kept in nearly absolute isolation, allowed the company of slaves and young children only. High-class prostitutes, a class distinct from the *porneia* and from wives both, had the only freedom of movement accorded women, and were the only educated women.

Two very significant words originated in the ancient Greece many of us revere: *democracy* and *pornography.* Democracy from its beginnings excluded all women and some men. Pornography from its beginnings justified and promoted this exclusion of all women by presenting the sexuality of all women as the sexuality of the brothel slut. The brothel slut and the sexuality of the brothel slut had been stolen and sold—raped and prostituted; and the rape and prostitution of that captive and degraded being with her captive and degraded sexuality is precisely the sexual content of pornography. In pornography, the will of the chattel whore is synonymous with her function: she is purely for sex and her function is defined as her nature and her will. The isolation of wives was based on the conviction that women were so sexually voracious on male terms that wives could not be let out—or they would naturally turn whorish. The chattel whore was the natural woman, the woman without the civilizing discipline of marriage. The chattel whore, of course, as we know, was the product of the civilizing discipline of slavery, but men did not then and do not now see it that way.

Pornography illustrated and expressed this valuation of women and women's sexuality, and that is why it was named *pornography*—"the graphic depiction of whores." Depicting women as whores and the sexuality of women as sluttish is what pornography does. Its job in the politically coercive and cruel system of male supremacy is to justify and perpetuate the rape and prostitution from which it springs. This is its function, which makes it incompatible with any notion of freedom, unless one sees freedom as the right of men to rape and to prostitute women. Pornography as a genre says that the stealing and buying and selling of women are not acts of force or abuse because women want to be raped and prostituted because that is the nature of women and the nature of female sexuality. Gloria Steinem has said that culture is successful politics. As a cultural phenomenon, pornography *is* the political triumph of rape and prostitution over all female rebellion and resistance.

A piece of Greek pornography may have been a drawing on a vase or an etching. No live model was required to make it; no specific sexual act had to be committed in order for it to exist. Rape, prostitution, battery, pornography, and other sex-based abuse could be conceptualized as separate phenomena. In real life, of course, they were all mixed together: a woman was beaten, then raped; raped, then beaten, then prostituted; prostituted, then beaten, then raped; and so on. As far back as we know, whorehouses have provided live sex shows in which, necessarily, pornography and prostitution were one and the same thing. We know that the world's foremost pornographer, the Marquis de Sade, tortured, raped, imprisoned, beat, and bought women and girls. We know that influential male thinkers and artists who enthused about rape or prostitution or battery had, in many cases, raped or bought or battered women or girls and were also users and often devotees of pornography. We know that when the technical means of graphic depiction were limited to writing, etching and drawing, pornography was mostly an indulgence of upper-class men, who were literate and who had money to spend on the almost always expensive etchings, drawings, and writings. We know that pornography flourished as an upper-class male pleasure when the power of upper-class men knew virtually no limitation, certainly with regard to women: in feudal societies, for instance. But in societies that did not find much to oppose in the rape and prostitution of women, there were certainly no inquiries, no investigations, no political or philosophical or scientific searches, into the role pornography played in acts of forced sex or battery. When pornography was in fact writing, etching, or drawing, it was possible to consider it something exclusively cultural, something on paper not in life, and even partly esthetic or intellectual. Such a view was not accurate, but it was possible. Since the invention of the camera, any such view of pornography is completely despicable and corrupt. Those are real women being tied and hung, gutted and trounced on, whipped and pissed on, gang-banged and hit, penetrated by dangerous objects and by animals. It is important to note that men have not found it necessary—not legally, not morally, not sexually—to make distinctions between drawing and writing on the one hand and the use of live women on the other. Where is the visceral outcry, the famous *humanist* outcry, against the tying and hanging and chaining and bruising and beating of women? Where is the visceral recognition, the *humanist* recognition, that it is impossible and inconceivable to tolerate—let alone to sanction or to apologize for—the tying and hanging and chaining and bruising and beating of women? I am saying what no one should have to say, which is simply that one does not do to human beings what is done to women in pornography. And why are these things done to women in pornography? The reasons men give are these: entertainment, fun, expression, sex, sexual pleasure, and because the women want it.

Instead of any so-called humanist outcry against the inhumanity of the use of women in pornography—an outcry that we might expect if dogs or cats were being treated the same way—there has been the pervasive, self-

congratulatory, indolent, male-supremacist assumption that the use of women in pornography is the sexual will of the woman, expresses her sexuality,
her character, her nature, and appropriately demonstrates a legitimate sexual function of hers. This is the same assumption about the nature of women
and the nature of female sexuality that men have always used to justify the
raping and prostituting of women. It is no less believed today than when
Greek men imprisoned chattel whores in the fifth century BC. Almost
without exception, the main premise of pornography is that women want
to be forced, hurt, and cruelly used. The main proof of the power of this
belief is when the female victim of rape, battery, or incest is blamed for the
crime. But the proof is also in the size and growth of the pornography
industry; the ever-increasing viciousness of the material itself; the greater
acceptance of pornography as part of the social and the domestic environment; the ever-expanding alliances between pornographers and lawyers,
pornographers and journalists, pornographers and politicians. Pornography is now used in increasing numbers of medical schools and other institutions of higher learning that teach "human sexuality." The pornography
is everywhere, and its apologists are everywhere, and its users are everywhere, and its pimps are rich, and surely if we assumed that the women in
the photographs and films were really human beings and not by nature
chattel whores we would not have been able to stand it, to acquiesce, to
collaborate through silence or cowardice or, as some in this room have done,
to collaborate actively. If we assumed that these women were human, not
chattel whores by nature, we would destroy that industry—with our bare
hands if we could—because it steals and buys and sells women; it rapes and
prostitutes women. In 1978, *Forbes* magazine reported that the pornography
industry was a $4-billion-a-year business, larger than the conventional film
and record industries combined. A big part of the pornography business is
cash-and-carry: for instance, the film loops, where one deposits quarters for
a minute or so of a woman being fucked by Nazis or the like. A huge part of
the pornography business is mail-order. Here one finds the especially scur-
rilous material, including both magazines and films of women being tortured, tied, hung, and fucked by large animals, especially dogs. Child
pornography—still photographs and films—is obtained under the counter
or through mail-order. Books of child pornography that are printed with
drawings and some magazines with photographs can be obtained in drug
stores as well as sex shops in urban areas. The above-ground slick so-called
men's entertainment magazines are flourishing, and every indication is that
the *Forbes* figure of a $4-billion industry was low to begin with and is now
completely outdated. *Playboy, Penthouse,* and *Hustler* together sell fifteen
million copies a month. According to *Folio,* a magazine for professionals in
magazine management, United States magazines with the greatest overseas
newsstand dollar sales were (1) *Playboy* with well over ten million dollars in
foreign newsstand sales; (2) *Penthouse* with well over nine million dollars in
foreign newsstand sales; (3) *Oui;* (4) *Gallery,* owned by F. Lee Bailey who
surprisingly could not convince a jury that Patricia Hearst had been raped;
(5) *Scientific American;* and (6) *Hustler.* Also in the top ten are *Vogue,* which
consistently publishes the work of S and M photographer Helmut Newton,

and *Easy Riders*, a motorcycle, gang-bang, fuck-the-bitch-with-your-Iron-Cross kind of magazine. This was as of October 1980. According to *Mother Jones* magazine, also in 1980, there are three to four times as many adult bookstores in the United States as there are MacDonald's Restaurants. And the live exhibition of women displaying genitals or being used in sex of various descriptions or being tied and whipped is increasing. And there is cable television and the home video market, both potentially huge and currently expanding markets for pornographers who use live women. Women. Real women. Live women. Chattel whores.

Now, some people are afraid that the world will be turned into a nuclear charnel house; and so they fight the nuclear industries and lobbies; and they do not spend significant amounts of their time debating whether the nuclear industries have the right to threaten human life or not. Some people fear that the world is turning, place by place, into a concentration camp; and so they fight for those who are hounded, persecuted, tortured, and they do not suggest that the rights of those who persecute supersede the rights of the persecuted in importance—unless, of course, the persecuted are only women and the torture is called "sex." Some feminists see the world turning into a whorehouse—how frivolous we always are—a whorehouse, in French *maison d'abattage*, which literally means "house of slaughter." Whorehouses have been concentration camps for women. Women have been kept in them like caged animals to do slave labor, sex labor, labor appropriate to the nature, function, and sexuality of the chattel whore and her kind. The spread of pornography that uses live women, real women, is the spread of the whorehouse, the concentration camp for women, the house of sexual slaughter. Now I ask you: what are we going to do?

.28

Misguided, Dangerous and Wrong

An Analysis of Anti-Pornography Politics[1]

GAYLE RUBIN

. . . Many feminists have accepted the notions that pornography is an especially odious expression of male supremacy, that pornography is violent, or that pornography is synonymous with violent media. They disagree merely about what should be done about it. For example, there are many feminists who think of porn as disgusting sexist propaganda, but who nevertheless are concerned about defending the First Amendment and who are cautious about invoking censorship. I certainly agree that concerns over censorship and freedom of expression are valid and vital. However, my purpose here is not to argue that pornography is anti-woman speech which unfortunately deserves constitutional protection. My goal is to challenge the assumptions that pornography is, *per se*, particularly sexist, especially violent or implicated in violence, or intrinsically antithetical to the interests of women.

The "pornography problem" is a false problem, at least as it is generally posed. There are legitimate feminist concerns with regard to sexually explicit media and the conditions under which it is produced. However, these are not the concerns that have dominated the feminist anti-porn politics. Instead, pornography has become an easy, convenient, pliant and overdetermined scapegoat for problems for which it is not responsible. To support

NOTE: Excerpts reprinted from *Bad Girls and Dirty Pictures: The Challenge to Reclaim Feminism*, edited by Alison Assiter & Avedon Carol (London: Pluto, 1993), by permission.

this contention I will examine the fundamental propositions and structure of the anti-porn argument.

PREMISES, PRESUPPOSITIONS AND DEFINITIONS

The Conflation of Pornography and Violence

One of the most basic claims of the anti-porn position is that pornography is violent and promotes violence against women.[2] Two assertions are implicit or explicit to this claim. One is that pornography is characteristically violent and/or sexist in what it depicts, and the other is that pornography is more violent and/or sexist in content than other media. Both of these propositions are false.

Very little pornography actually depicts violent acts. Pornography does depict some form of sexual activity, and these sexual activities vary widely. The most common behaviour featured in porn is ordinary heterosexual intercourse (although it is a convention of porn movies that male orgasm must be visible to the viewer, so ejaculation in porn films generally takes place outside the body). Nudity, genital close-ups and oral sex are also prevalent. Anal sex is far less common, but some magazines and films specialize in depicting it. While some films and magazines attempt to have "something for everyone," a lot of porn is fairly specialized and many porn shops group their material according to the primary activity it contains. Thus, there are often separate sections featuring oral sex, anal sex or gay male sex.

There is also "lesbian" material designed to appeal to heterosexual men rather than to lesbians. Until the last decade there was very little porn produced by or actually intended for lesbian viewers. This has been changing with the advent of some small circulation, low-budget sex magazines produced by and for lesbians. Ironically, this nascent lesbian porn is endangered by both right-wing and feminist anti-porn activity.[3]

There are several sub-genres of porn designed to cater to minority sexual populations. The most successful example of this is gay male porn. There are many specialized shops serving the gay male market. Much male homosexual pornography is produced by and for gay men, and its quality is relatively high. Transsexual porn is more rare and found in fewer shops. It is designed to appeal to transsexuals and those who find them erotic. Many of the models seem to be transsexuals who are working in the sex industry either because discrimination against them makes employment elsewhere difficult, or in order to raise money for sex change treatment.

Another specialized subgenre is SM [sadomasochistic] porn. SM materials have been used as the primary "evidence" for the alleged violence of porn as a whole. SM materials are only a small percentage of commercial porn and they are hardly representative. They appeal primarily to a distinct minority and they are not as readily available as other materials. For example, in San Francisco only two of the dozen or so adult theatres of the late

1970s and early 1980s regularly showed bondage or SM movies. These two theatres, however, have always been prominently featured in local anti-porn invective.[4]

Many of the local porn shops have small sections of bondage material, but only a couple have extensive collections and are therefore favoured by connoisseurs. Mainstream porn magazines such as *Playboy* and *Penthouse* rarely contain bondage or SM photographs. When they do, however, these again are emphasized in anti-porn arguments. Some bondage photos in the December 1984 *Penthouse* are a case in point. They have often been used as examples in slide shows and displays by anti-porn activists, who invariably neglect to mention that the occurrence of such spreads in *Penthouse* is exceedingly unusual and quite unrepresentative.[5]

SM materials are aimed at an audience that understands a set of conventions for interpreting them. Sadomasochism is not a form of violence, but is rather a type of ritual and contractual sex play whose aficionados go to great lengths in order to do it and to ensure the safety and enjoyment of one another. SM fantasy does involve images of coercion and sexual activities that may appear violent to outsiders. SM erotic materials can be shocking to those unfamiliar with the highly negotiated nature of most SM encounters. This is compounded by the unfortunate fact that most commercial SM porn is produced by people who are not practising sadomasochists and whose understanding of SM is not unlike that of the anti-porn feminists. Thus commercial SM porn often reflects the prejudices of its producers rather than common SM practice.[6]

Torn out of context, SM material is upsetting to unprepared audiences and this shock value has been mercilessly exploited in anti-porn presentations. SM porn is itself misrepresented, its relationship to SM activity is distorted, and it is treated as though it is representative of porn as a whole.

Pioneered by WAVPM [Women Against Violence in Pornography and Media] and adopted by WAP [Women Against Pornography], slide shows have been a basic organizing tool of anti-porn groups. Slides of images are used to persuade audiences of the alleged violence of pornography. The anti-porn movie *Not a Love Story* follows a format similar to the slide shows and utilizes many of the same techniques.[7] The slide shows and the movie always display a completely unrepresentative sample of pornography in order to "demonstrate" its ostensible violence. SM imagery occupies a much greater space in the slide shows and in *Not a Love Story* than it does in actual adult bookstores or theatres.

In addition to SM materials, the presentations utilize images from porn that are violent or distasteful, but that are again unrepresentative. An example of this is the notorious *Hustler* cover showing a woman being fed into a meat grinder. This image is upsetting and distasteful, but it is not even legally obscene. It is also unusual. *Hustler* is a magazine that strives to be in bad taste. It is as different from other comparable mass-circulation sex magazines as the *National Lampoon* is from *Esquire* or *Harpers*.

Arguing from bad examples is effective but irresponsible. It is the classic method for promulgating negative stereotypes and is one of the favoured rhetorical tactics for selling various forms of racism, bigotry, hatred and xenophobia. It is always possible to find bad examples—of, for example, women, gay people, transsexuals, blacks, Jews, Italians, Irish, immigrants, the poor—and to use them to construct malicious descriptions to attack or delegitimize an entire group of people or an area of activity. . . .

A great deal of anti-porn analysis is argued in a similar format. It jumps from examples of undeniably loathsome porn to unwarranted assertions about pornography as a whole. It is politically reprehensible and intellectually embarrassing to target pornography on the basis of inflammatory examples and manipulative rhetoric.

Is pornography any more violent than other mass media? While there are no reliable comparative studies on this point, I would argue that there are fewer images or descriptions of violence in pornography, taken as a whole, than in mainstream movies, television or fiction. Our media are all extremely violent, and it is also true that their depictions of violence against women are often both sexualized and gender specific. An evening in front of the television is likely to result in viewing multiple fatal automobile accidents, shootings, fistfights, rapes and situations in which women are threatened by a variety of creepy villains. Prostitutes and sex workers are invariably victims of violence in police and detective shows where they are killed off with relentless abandon. There are dozens of slasher movies characterized by hideous and graphic violence, disproportionately directed at women.

While much of this media is sexualized, very little is sexually explicit and consequently all of it would be completely unaffected by any new legal measures against pornography. If the problem is violence, why single out sexually explicit media? What is the justification for creating social movements and legal tools aimed at media that are sexually explicit rather than at media that are explicitly violent? . . .

Is Porn a "Documentary of Abuse"?

Catharine MacKinnon has argued that pornography is a literal photographic record of women being abused. She has listed various images found in porn, such as women being bound, tortured, humiliated, battered, urinated upon, forced to eat excrement, killed, or "merely taken and used." She has then concluded that a woman had to have had these things done to her in order for the pornography to have been made; thus for each such image some woman had been bound, tortured, humiliated, battered, urinated upon, forced to eat excrement, murdered, or "merely taken and used."[8] Or as Andrea Dworkin puts it, "Real women are tied up, stretched, hanged, fucked, gang-banged, whipped, beaten, and begging for more. In the photographs and films, real women are used . . . "[9] In this view, pornography is a photographic record of horrible abuse perpetrated upon the models and actors who appear in it. Several points may be made about this theory of pornographic harm.

The items on such lists are not all equivalent nor are they equally prevalent. I would guess that the "merely taken and used" is in reference to ordinary, non-kinky sexual activities, while the items bound, tortured, humiliated, urinated upon and forced to eat excrement may refer to kinky porn.

Porn featuring the eating of excrement is extraordinarily rare. Images of bondage, pain, humiliation and urination are found in porn but, again, are absent from the majority of pornography. I have heard references to porn showing women mutilated or murdered but have never seen any except some rare drawings—*not* photographs—in European materials not available in the United States. I hate to belabour the point, but there are more women battered and murdered on prime-time television and Hollywood films than in pornographic materials.

Perhaps more significantly, in this model of porn there is no concept of the role of artifice in the production of images. We do not assume that the occupants of the vehicles routinely destroyed in police chases on television are actually burning along with their cars, or that actors in fight scenes are actually being beaten to a pulp, or that western movies result in actual fatalities to cowboys and native Americans. It is ludicrous to assume that the level of coercion in an image is a reliable guide to the treatment of the actors involved. Yet this is precisely what is being asserted with regard to pornographic images.

In their characterizations of pornography as a documentary of abuse, both Dworkin and MacKinnon appear to think that certain sexual activities are so inherently distasteful that no one would do them willingly, and therefore the models are "victims" who must have been forced to participate against their will. Since SM often involves an appearance of coercion, it is especially easy to presume that the people doing it are victims. However, as I noted above, this is a false stereotype and does not reflect social and sexual reality. Sadomasochism is part of the erotic repertoire, and many people are not only willing but eager participants in SM activity.[10]

However, sadomasochism is not the only behaviour subjected to condescending and insulting judgements. For example, MacKinnon has also described porn in which someone was "raped in the throat where a penis cannot go."[11] There are plenty of gay men, and even a good number of heterosexual women, who enjoy cock-sucking. There are even lesbians who relish going down on dildos. Obviously, oral penetration is not an activity for everyone, but it is presumptuous to assume that it is physically impossible or necessarily coercive in all circumstances. Embedded in the idea of porn as a documentary of abuse is a very narrow conception of human sexuality, one lacking even elementary notions of sexual diversity.

The notion of harm embodied in the MacKinnon/Dworkin approach is based on a fundamental confusion between the content of an image and the conditions of its production. The fact that an image does not appeal to a viewer does not mean that the actors or models experienced revulsion while making it. The fact that an image depicts coercion does not mean that the actors or models were forced into making it.

One can infer nothing from the content of an image about the conditions of its production. Any discussion of greater protections for actors and models should focus on whether or not they have been coerced and on the conditions under which their work is performed *regardless of the nature of the image involved.* Any standards considered for the health, safety or cleanliness of working conditions in the sex industry should conform to those pertaining to similar occupations such as fashion modelling, film making, stage acting, or professional dancing. The content of the image produced, whether or not it is sexual, and whether or not it is violent or distasteful to a viewer, is irrelevant.

While anti-porn activists often claim to want to protect women in (and from) the sex industry, much of their analysis is based on condescension and contempt towards sex workers. The notion that pornography is a documentary of sexual abuse assumes that the women who work in the sex industry (as strippers, porn models or prostitutes) are invariably forced to do so and that such women are merely victims of "pornographers." This is a malignant stereotype and one that is especially inappropriate for feminists to reinforce.

There are, of course, incidents of abuse and exploitation in the sex industry, as there are in all work situations. I am not claiming that no one has ever been coerced into appearing in a porn movie or that in such cases the perpetrators should not be prosecuted. I am saying that such coercion is not the industry norm. Furthermore, I am not promoting a simple "free choice" model of employment, in which structural forces and limited choices have no influence on what decisions individuals make about how to earn a living. But those who choose sex work do so for complex reasons, and their choices should be accorded the respect granted to those who work in less stigmatized occupations.

Indeed, the degree to which sex workers are exposed to more exploitation and hazardous working conditions is a function of the stigma, illegality or marginal legality of sex work. People in stigmatized or illegal occupations find it difficult to obtain the protections, privileges and opportunities available for other jobs. Prostitutes, porn models and erotic dancers have less recourse to police, courts, medical treatment, legal redress or sympathy when they are subjected to criminal, violent or unscrupulous behaviour. It is more difficult for them to unionize or mobilize for protection as workers.

We need to support women wherever they work. We need to realize that more stigma and more legal regulation of the sex industry will merely increase the vulnerability of the women in it. Feminists who want to support sex workers should strive to decriminalize and legitimize sex work. Sex workers relieved of the threat of scandal or incarceration are in a better position to gain more control over their work and working conditions.[12]

Contempt towards sex workers, especially prostitutes, is one of the most disturbing aspects of the anti-porn invective. Throughout her book, *Pornography*, Dworkin uses the stigma of prostitution to convey her opprobrium and make her argument against pornography. She says, "Contemporary pornography strictly and literally conforms to the word's root meaning: the graphic depiction of *vile whores,* or in our language, *sluts, cows* (as in: *sexual cattle, sexual chattel*), *cunts* [italics added]."[13] This is a degrading and insulting description of prostitutes. Feminists should be working to remove stigma from prostitution, not exploiting it for rhetorical gain.

Is Porn at the Core of Women's Subordination?

Porn is often described as "at the centre" or "at the core" of women's subordination. Andrea Dworkin makes the following statement in *Right-Wing Women:*

> At the heart of the female condition is pornography: *it is the ideology that is the source of all the rest* [italics added]; it truly defines what women are in this system—and how women are treated issues from what women are. Pornography is not a metaphor for what women are; it is what women are in theory and in practice.[14]

This rather extraordinary statement is accompanied by several diagrams in which pornography is first placed literally "at the centre" of women's condition, then diagrammed as the underlying ideology of women's condition, and finally depicted as the surface phenomenon with prostitution the underlying system.[15] These are breathtaking claims, and they are made with little supporting evidence and not a single citation.

Since the 1960s, feminist theorists and academics have explored a multitude of explanations for female subordination and the oppression of women. There are hundreds of articles, essays and books debating the merits of various factors in the creation and maintenance of female subordination. These have included, for example, private property, the formation of state societies, the sexual division of labour, the emergence of economic classes, religion, educational arrangements, cultural structures, family and kinship systems, psychological factors and control over reproduction, among others. I cannot think of a single attempt prior to the porn debates to derive women's subordination from either pornography or prostitution. There is no credible historical, anthropological or sociological argument for such a position.

It would be difficult to argue that pornography or prostitution had played such critical roles in women's subordination since women are quite dramatically oppressed in societies that have neither (for example, sedentary horticulturalists in Melanesia and South America). Furthermore, pornography and prostitution as they now exist in the West are modern phenomena. The institutional structures of prostitution in, for example, ancient Greece, were entirely different from those that obtain today.

Pornography in the contemporary sense did not exist before the late nineteenth century. Other cultures have certainly produced visual art and crafts depicting genitalia and sexual activity (e.g., the ancient Greeks, the Egyptians and the Moche Indians from pre-Columbian coastal Peru). But there is no systematic correlation between low status for women and cultures in which sexually explicit visual imagery exists, or high status for women and societies in which it does not. Moreover, such images are not pornography unless porn is to be defined as all sexually explicit imagery, in which case anti-porn ideology would posit the impossibility of any acceptable explicit depictions of sex, and few feminists would support it.

Pornography could be thought of as being at the heart of women's condition if it is conceptualized as a trans-historical category existing throughout human history and culture. In *Pornography*, Dworkin states that the word "pornography" comes from Greek words meaning "writing about whores." She goes on to discuss the place of the "whores" in Greek society and concludes that, "The word pornography does not have any other meaning than the one cited here, the graphic depiction of the lowest whores." From this discussion, and similar accounts by others, it has often been inferred that the term "pornography" was used by the Greeks and that it refers to categories of Greek experience.[16]

However, the term "pornography" was not used by the ancient Greeks, did not refer to their painted vases, and should not be treated as evidence that the Greeks felt about porn the way Dworkin does. The term was coined *from Greek roots* in the nineteenth century, when many of the sex terms still in use (such as homosexuality) were assembled from Greek and Latin root words. It embodies not the prejudices of the Greeks, but those of the Victorians.[17]

There is one further sense in which it might be argued that pornography is "the ideology that is the source of all the rest" of women's oppression, and that is if pornography is conceived of as the quintessence of all ideologies of female inferiority. What, then, are we to make of all the religious and moral and philosophical versions of male superiority? Is the Koran pornography? The Bible? Psychiatry? And what has any of this to do with modern, contemporary commercial porn? What has it to do with adult bookstores or *Playboy?* . . .

COSTS AND DANGERS OF ANTI-PORN POLITICS

The focus on pornography trivializes real violence and ignores its gravity. Experiences of being raped, assaulted, battered or harassed are dramatic, devastating and qualitatively different from the ordinary insults of everyday oppression. Violence should never be conflated with experiences that are merely upsetting, unpleasant, irritating, distasteful or even enraging.

Anti-porn activity distracts attention and drains activism from more fundamental issues for women. Porn is a sexier topic than the more intractable problems of unequal pay, job discrimination, sexual violence and harassment, the unequal burdens of child-care and housework, increasing right-wing infringements on hard-won feminist gains and several millennia of unrelenting male privilege vis-à-vis the labour, love, personal service and possession of women. Anti-porn campaigns are pitifully misdirected and ineffective. They cannot solve the problems they purport to address. . . .

NOTES

1. This essay is a revision of an essay based on remarks that were originally submitted as testimony to hearings on pornography held by the National Organization for Women (NOW) in San Francisco, California, on March 26, 1986. Shortly after the hearings, I sent a written version to NOW for inclusion in a collection of bound photocopies of statements on pornography which were made available from the national NOW office. I have kept revisions for this 1992 publication as minimal as possible, but I have made changes to render the piece more intelligible to a contemporary audience and to readers who may be unfamiliar with many details of U.S. politics. I have also added references; some are more recent than the text and consequently induce unavoidable but vertiginous moments of anachronism.

Much has occurred since 1986 and it is impossible to update and recontextualize the article completely without major surgery. So I leave it as something out of time, a period piece unfortunately more prophetic than I knew.

2. In addition to the Lederer (Lederer et al., 1980) collection, other major anti-porn texts include Dworkin (1977, 1983); Griffin (1981); Dworkin and MacKinnon (1988); MacKinnon (1987, 1989); Brownmiller (1976); Barry (1979).

3. San Francisco's *On Our Backs*, Boston's *Bad Attitude* and *Outrageous Women*, Britain's *Quinn* and Australia's *Wicked Women* are a few of these lesbian oriented sexual publications. All have encountered governmental or community censorship.

4. Russell and Lederer (1980, p. 24). The Kearny and the North Beach were the two theatres that catered to the bondage crowd. When asked "what kinds of images are you talking about when you say you are opposed to 'violence in pornography and media'?" the response was, "We are talking about films like the ones shown in the Kearny Cinema in San Francisco."

5. Dworkin (Dworkin & MacKinnon, 1988, p. 63) is referring to this spread when she complains that "*Penthouse* hangs Asian women from trees."

6. There was a movement in the early 1980s to produce commercial SM erotica made by and for SM practitioners, which resulted in successful and now classic films such as *Story of K.* (The Film Company, 1980) and *Journey Into Pain* (Loving SM Productions, 1983). Ironically, none of these films are currently available due to the increasingly harsh legal climate for sexual materials in the United States.

7. For the slide shows, see Webster (1981) and D'Emilio (1980). *Not a Love Story: A Film About Pornography* purports to be a documentary of pornography. It was directed by Bonnie Sherr Klein and produced by Dorothy Todd Henaut, Studio D., National Film Board of Canada, 1981.

8. Hearings on Pornography, National Organization of Women, San Francisco, March 26, 1986.

9. Dworkin (1977, p. 201).

10. Samois (1987); Weinberg and Kamel (1993); Mains (1984); Stoller (1991); Thompson (1991); Grumley and Gallucci (1977); Rosen (1986, 1990).

11. Hearings on Pornography, National Organization for Women, San Francisco, March 26, 1986.

12. Delacoste and Alexander (1987); Jaget (1980); Pheterson (1989); Jennifer et al. (1977).

13. Dworkin (1977, p. 200).

14. Dworkin (1983, p. 223).

15. Dworkin (1983, pp. 222, 228, 229).

16. Dworkin (1977, pp. 199-200). This dubious history and phony etymology appears repeatedly throughout the anti-porn literature where it is often used as a key argument against pornography. In *Pornography and Civil Rights* (Dworkin & MacKinnon, 1988, p. 74), MacKinnon and Dworkin state that "we can trace pornography without any difficulty back as far as ancient Greece in the West. Pornography is a Greek word . . . It refers to writing, etching, or drawing of women who, in real life, were kept in female sexual slavery in ancient Greece. Pornography has always, as far back as we can go, had to do with exploiting, debasing and violating women in forced sex." Gloria Steinem (1978) employs it as the basis of her erotica/pornography distinction.

17. Actually, as Kendrick (1987, p. 11) points out, the term did exist in ancient Greece. But it appears so rarely in the surviving Greek texts that it could not have been indicative of a significant category of ancient experience, let alone one that so closely approximates the opinions of sexual materials held by Dworkin or nineteenth-century scholars (John J. Winkler, personal communication, 1986).

REFERENCES

Barry, K. (1979). *Female sexual slavery.* Englewood Cliffs, NJ: Prentice Hall.
Brownmiller, S. (1976). *Against our will: Men, women and rape.* New York: Bantam.

Delacoste, F., & Alexander, P. (1987). *SexWork: Writings by women in the sex industry.* San Francisco: Cleis Press.

D'Emilio, J. (1980, May). Women against pornography. *Christopher Street,* pp. 19-26.

Dworkin, A. (1977). *Pornography: Men possessing women.* New York: Perigree.

Dworkin, A. (1983). *Right-wing women.* New York: Perigree.

Dworkin, A., & MacKinnon, C. (1988). *Pornography and civil rights: A new day for women's equality.* Minneapolis: Organizing Against Pornography.

Griffin, S. (1981). *Pornography and silence: Culture's revenge against nature.* New York: Harper Colophon.

Grumley, M., & Gallucci, E. (1977). *Hard corps: Studies in leather and sadomasochism.* New York: Dutton.

Jaget, C. (1980). *Prostitutes: Our life.* Bristol: Falling Wall Press.

Jennifer, J., et al. (1977). *The politics of prostitution.* Seattle, WA: Social Research Associates.

Kendrick, W. (1987). *The secret museum: Pornography in modern culture.* New York: Viking.

Lederer, L. et al. (1980). *Take back the night: Women on pornography.* New York: William Morrow.

MacKinnon, C. (1987). *Feminism unmodified: Discourses on life and law.* Cambridge, MA: Harvard University Press.

MacKinnon, C. (1989). *Toward a feminist theory of the state.* Cambridge, MA: Harvard University Press.

Mains, G. (1984). *Urban aboriginals* San Francisco: Gay Sunshine.

Pheterson, G. (1989). *A vindication of the rights of whores.* Seattle, WA: Seal Press.

Rosen, M. (1986). *Sexual magic: The S&M photographs.* San Francisco: Shaynew.

Rosen, M. (1990). *Sexual portraits: Photographs of radical sexuality.* San Francisco: Shaynew.

Russell, D. E., & Lederer, L. (1980). What is pornography: Questions we get asked most often. In L. Lederer (Ed.), *Take back the night: Women on pornography* (pp. 23-29). New York: William Morrow.

SAMOIS (1987). *Coming to power.* Boston: Alyson.

Steinem, G. (1978, November). Erotica and pornography: A clear and present danger. *Ms.,* pp. 53-54, 75, 78.

Stoller, R. (1991). *Pain and passion: A psychoanalyst explores the world of S&M.* New York: Plenum.

Thompson, M. (1991). *Leatherfolk: Radical sex, people, politics and practice.* Boston: Alyson.

Webster, P. (1981). Pornography and pleasure. Sex issue. *Heresies, 12,* 48-51.

Weinberg, T., & Kamel, G.W.L. (1983). *S and M: Studies in sadomasochism.* Buffalo, NY: Prometheus.

29

"I Buy It for the Articles": *Playboy* Magazine and the Sexualization of Consumerism

GAIL DINES

Although pornography has been the focus of intense debate within the field of media studies (see for example, Kappeler, 1986; Kipnis, 1992; Ross, 1989; Williams, 1989; Zita, 1988), few scholars have actually conducted research on the workings of the pornography industry within the world of publishing and advertising. Any such study would need to take, as its starting point, *Playboy* magazine because it is the premier publication of a now much imitated genre, variously known as the "soft porn" or "men's entertainment" magazines. Moreover, *Playboy* played a major role in bringing pornography out of the closet and onto the coffee table, and in the process it helped to pave the way for the now $10 billion-a-year pornography industry (MacKinnon, 1993). In popular terminology, *Playboy* (and *Penthouse*) are often referred to as "soft-core" pornography whereas magazines such as *Hustler* and *Tit Torture* are referred to as "hard-core." It seems to me that one of the distinctions being drawn is that the latter advertise the woman (via the codes and conventions of pornographic representation) as *the* commodity on offer, whereas the former offer a "lifestyle" that involves the consumption of numerous upmarket commodities as a way of capturing the ultimate prized commodity: lots and

AUTHOR'S NOTE: I would like to thank Jean Humez, Rhea Becker and David Levy for their comments and assistance in developing the arguments in this chapter.

lots of attractive, young, big-breasted women, just like the ones masturbated to in the centerfold.

Although all those materials loosely classed as pornography are similar in that they address a mainly male subject position and aim to facilitate male masturbation, the lifestyle magazines occupy a very different place in the economics of the publishing industry. The two oldest and most successful lifestyle pornography magazines, *Playboy* and *Penthouse,* are not simply composed of photographs of women but also include "service" features on the latest upmarket consumer products, advice columns, short stories by notable authors, interviews with celebrities, movie reviews, readers' letters and cartoons.

Whereas most corporations avoid advertising their wares in magazines such as *Hustler* or *Tit Torture,* the pages of *Playboy* and *Penthouse* are filled with advertisements from companies such as Seagrams, Benson and Hedges, Mercedes, Sony and Bugle Boy—a sign of both their upscale readership and mainstream status. The so-called hard-core magazines could not entice President Jimmy Carter to talk about his erotic fantasies (as *Playboy* did) or get Princess Anne of the English Royal Family to officially open their English headquarters (as *Penthouse* did). This kind of public acceptance of *Playboy* and *Penthouse* tends to be taken for granted and is often explained away by phrases such as "They are tasteful," or "They are not real pornography." Implicit in these kinds of statements is a class bias. The "real" pornography is the poorly produced, low-budget type, that uses women who look like real women (whose life is very often inscribed on their bodies and faces) as opposed to the more upscale, airbrushed high-quality type that can afford to pay aspiring young fashion models to pose. Moreover, the former often present a working-class ambience where the women are photographed on fading sofas situated in cheaply decorated living rooms, bedrooms or motel rooms. *Playboy* and *Penthouse,* on the other hand, depict a world where wealth and (White) privilege are taken for granted, as evidenced in the settings for the centerfolds, which include luxurious rooms, beautiful beaches and expensive furniture. This is no accident. Hugh Hefner, founder and publisher of *Playboy* (and, later, Bob Guccione, founder and publisher of *Penthouse*), set out to produce a magazine whose center—the airbrushed, soft-focus, pinup-style pictorials of women—would be packaged in the trappings of upper-middle-class life. The thinking behind this packaging concept, according to John Mastro, the product manager of *Playboy,* was that "quality takes some of the shock off nudity" (Weyr, 1978, p. 33). All the products offered were to be of the highest "quality": the short stories, the interviews with famous people, the cars, the alcohol, the clothes, the food and, of course, the women. This is how Hefner marketed his magazine and he was extremely successful.[1]

SELLING CONSUMPTION, SELLING WOMEN

From the very start, Hefner was clear about his targeted audience. He wrote in the first issue of *Playboy* published in October of 1953:

If you are a man between 18 and 80, *Playboy* is meant for you . . . We want to make it clear from the start, we aren't a family magazine. If you are somebody's sister, wife or mother-in-law and picked us up by mistake, please pass us along to the man in your life and get back to the *Ladies Home Companion*.

Within the pages of *Playboy* you will find articles, fiction, pictures, stories, cartoons, humor and special features . . . to form a pleasure-primer styled to the masculine taste.

Hefner, however, was not interested in just any man but specifically the more affluent upwardly mobile male, those whose disposable income would attract high-paying advertisers. He wrote the following in the April 1956 issue, which provides a thumbnail sketch of what he saw as the "ideal reader":

What is a playboy? Is he simply a wastrel, a ne'er-do-well, a fashion-able bum? Far from it. He can be a sharp minded young business executive, a worker in the arts, a university professor, an architect or an engineer. He can be many things, provided he possesses a certain kind of view. He must see life not as a vale of tears, but as a happy time, he must take joy in his work, without regarding it as the end of all living; he must be an alert man, a man of taste, a man sensitive to pleasure, a man who—without acquiring the stigma of voluptuary or dilettante—can live life to the hilt. This is the sort of man we mean when we use the word playboy.

A close reading of the early issues of *Playboy* reveals the degree to which living "life to the hilt" was really about consuming. Articles abound on what to buy for the office, what to wear, where to eat, what gadgets to play with and how to decorate an apartment (the service side of the magazine). As with all advertising, the actual product on offer was not the commodity being advertised but rather the fantasy of transformation that this product promised to bring to the consumer's life. Within *Playboy*, the high-quality products would transform the reader into a "playboy" who could then have the real prize: all the high-quality women he wanted—just like the ones who populated the magazine. The women in the *Playboy* pictorials were designed to be "teasers" in that they demonstrated to the reader what he could have if he adopted the *Playboy* lifestyle of high-level consumption. In an inter-view, Hefner reveals this strategy of sexualizing consumption when he explains: "*Playboy* is a combination of sex . . . and status . . . the sex actually includes not only the Playmate and the cartoons and the jokes which describe boy-girl situations, but goes right down in all the service features" (Brady, 1974, p. 95).

Nowhere is the combination of sex and status more clear than in the *Playboy* cartoons. The male cartoon characters that populate this world are overwhelmingly rich, White and in the prime of life. They live in expensive homes outfitted with numerous gadgets, drive fast cars and take vacations on private yachts. They are nearly always accompanied by a younger, glamorous big-breasted female who is willing and ready to have sex at any time. The female character is regularly shown to be seduced by the gifts and overall wealth of her male companion. This image of the playboy depicted in the cartoons is one developed mainly by Hefner in that he ran the cartoon department for many years (Hefner himself was an aspiring cartoonist). When he eventually handed it over to his assistant, Michelle Urry, he made it clear that he wanted to remain involved in the selection of cartoons (personal interview, April 23, 1990).

In a recent interview, Urry (April 23, 1990) discussed the procedure the editors use for choosing the 20 or so cartoons a month from among the thousands that are submitted by amateur and professional cartoonists. One of the main criteria discussed by Urry was that "the cartoons speak in the same voice as the rest of the magazine" and that this requires above all "an ambience of good taste." This ambience, according to Urry, is created by locating the characters in high-status surroundings, which signals a lifestyle that "*Playboy* readers can identify with if not actually live." Thus the cartoon offers to the viewer an image of what his life could be like if he consumed products to the same degree as his cartoon counterpart, the very same products that are advertised in the surrounding pages of the magazine.

Hefner's strategy of offering a lifestyle, rather than just an ejaculation, quickly paid off, attracting both the readers and the advertisers to whom they would be delivered. The first issue sold 53,991 copies, and by its first anniversary *Playboy* had a monthly circulation of 175,000 copies. By 1959 circulation had reached 1,000,000, and by 1972 *Playboy* was selling 7,012,000 copies a month. One of the major factors behind this success was lack of any real competition. Hefner himself said in an interview for *Playboy* in the 20th anniversary issue that "the field was wide open for the sort of magazine I had in mind." During this time the most popular men's magazines were "full of blood, guts and fighting. They didn't pay much attention to women" (Weyr, 1978, p. 4). The pornographic magazines that did exist were the low-budget, under-the-counter type that consisted only of low-quality pictorials. When *Playboy* reached the stands in October 1953 it was the only publication that, according to Weyr, told readers "what to wear, eat, drink, read and drive, how to furnish their homes, and listen to music, which nightclubs, restaurants, plays and films to attend" (p. 55) as well as about "bringing nubile women to bed" (p. 55). Rather than just commodifying sex, *Playboy* also sexualized commodities, a combination that few advertisers could resist when looking for a hospitable location for their ads.

DEVELOPING THE SOFT-CORE MARKET

The founders of *Playboy* were very clear about the importance of the centerfolds in the marketing of the magazine. Even before the first issue hit the newsstands, Hefner marketed his magazine to the newsstand wholesalers by stressing, not the literary content or service features, but the pictorials. For the magazine (originally called *Stag Party*) Hefner promised major sales:

Dear Friend,

> STAG PARTY—a brand new magazine for men—will be out this fall—and it will be one of the best sellers you have ever handled . . . it will include male pleasing figure studies, making it a sure hit from the very start. But here's the really BIG news! The first issue of STAG PARTY will include the famous calendar picture of Marilyn Monroe—in full color! In fact every issue of STAG PARTY will have a beautiful full page, male pleasing nude study—in full natural color. Now you know what I mean when I say that this is going to be one of the best sellers you have ever handled . . . fill out the postage paid Air Mail reply card enclosed and get it back to me as quickly as possible. (Miller, 1984, p. 39)

Because *Playboy* did indeed become a "best seller," Hefner was forced to delegate responsibility, a task not easily accomplished because he had a dictatorial and controlling style (Brady, 1974). Toward the end of 1956, Hefner started looking around for a managing editor to help run the magazine. His eventual choice was Auguste Comte Spectorsky, who had been an editor for the *New Yorker* and was an aspiring author. On taking the job, Spectorsky claimed that he would devote his efforts to the literary side of the magazine and indeed within a few years *Playboy* became a magazine that attracted the most respected of American writers. Accounts of the early years at the magazine all point to a conflict brewing in the editorial offices on the central issue of content. Hefner and many of the founding editors stood firm in their belief that the selling point of the magazine was the centerfold and the pictorials, whereas the newer editors, especially the influential Spectorsky, were more interested in developing the literary and service features and felt that the magazine was being pulled down by its emphasis on sex. This ongoing battle split the editors into two camps with Hefner's side arguing that

> We could have all the Nabokovs in the world and the best articles on correct attire without attracting readers. They bought the magazine for the girls. We couldn't take the sex out. The magazine would die like a dog. (Weyr, 1978, p. 35)

An eventual compromise was worked out in which the pictorials would stay but the art and literary side would be developed also. This seemed to work for a number of years because *Playboy* continued to increase the number of pictorials while also becoming a literary force, publishing original pieces by writers such as John Steinbeck, Alex Haley, Allen Ginsberg and John Kenneth Galbraith. However, this unique positioning of *Playboy* in the publishing world—straddling the mainstream market and the pornography market—was really a balancing act and one that had to be constantly renegotiated.

Built into the magazine was a conflict between the need to attract advertising revenue and the need to keep the subscribers interested in the centerfolds. Although advertisers limited the degree of sexual explicitness, readers always had the potential to become bored with the same old conventions. When there was no competition, keeping the readers was relatively easy because the readers' only other option was the poorly produced, down-market variety of pornography, which certainly did not offer the reader a playboy image of himself. However, as the pornography market began to develop, other magazines adopted the *Playboy* formula, while pushing for more explicit imagery in the pictorials. Chief among these competitors was *Penthouse*.

FIGHTING THE COMPETITION

In the summer of 1969, *The New York Times*, the *Chicago Tribune* and the *Los Angeles Times* all carried full page advertisements showing the *Playboy* bunny caught in the crosshairs of a rifle. The caption read, "We're going rabbit hunting." This was an advertisement for *Penthouse* magazine, which would be on the newsstands in September of that year. According to Miller (1984), the news, at first, was greeted with some amusement on the part of the *Playboy* staff. *Playboy* in 1969 had a circulation of 4,500,000 monthly, a figure totally unmatched by competitors. Sicilian-born Robert Guccione, the editor-publisher of *Penthouse* magazine, aimed to topple *Playboy* from the number-one slot by following its literary and service format while making the pictorials more sexually explicit. Guccione was willing to forego the advertising revenue in the short term, planning to draw in the advertisers after he had put *Playboy* out of business.

Penthouse started with a circulation of 350,000. By February 1970 this figure had grown to 500,000. Miller (1984) argues that one major reason for the increase was that *Penthouse* photos included pubic hair. *Playboy* meanwhile continued to resist showing pubic hair and instead focused on what they called the "girl next door look," which largely consisted of a photographic convention Kuhn (1985) calls "caught unawares."[2]

By the end of 1970, *Penthouse*'s circulation had reached 1,500,000. Hefner decided that he could no longer ignore Guccione and there "began a contest between Hefner and Guccione to see who could produce the raunchier magazine" (Miller, 1984, p. 194). When *Penthouse* came out with the first full frontal centerfold in August 1971, *Playboy* followed suit, in January 1972. This change in policy must be seen as having some success for, by September 1972, *Playboy* broke all previous circulation records by selling 7,012,000 copies. By 1973, however, *Playboy*'s circulation began to decline while *Penthouse*'s was increasing past the 4 million mark. Miller (1984) argues that what followed could only be defined as an all-out circulation war fought over who could produce the most "daring" pictures.

To make matters worse for *Playboy,* their advertisers were beginning to complain about the explicit nature of the pictorials. A number of high-level *Playboy* executives flew to New York to meet with the advertising agents who were concerned over what they saw as the increasingly pornographic content of the magazine. Hefner had been one of the original proponents of keeping up with *Penthouse*, but due to the outside pressure of advertisers, internal battles with editors and the appearance of other competitors such as *Gallery* and *Hustler*, who captured the more hard-core market, Hefner capitulated, sending a memo to all the department editors informing them that *Playboy* would cease to cater to those readers interested in looking at "gynaecologically detailed pictures of girls" (Miller, 1984, p. 204) and would instead return to its previous standards.

Current circulation figures suggest that Hefner made the right decision. In 1993, *Playboy* had a monthly circulation of nearly 3.5 million whereas *Penthouse* reported just over 1 million. One possible explanation for this is that *Playboy*, by staking out its terrain as the "respectable soft-core" magazine, still has no real competitor. With its airbrushed shots of women's bodies sandwiched between the interviews, the political articles and the service features that presume a privileged male reader, *Playboy* is now seen as a kind of *New Yorker* for the playboy. The centerfold in the magazine barely warrants a comment in most articles in the mainstream press on *Playboy*. The pornography side of the magazine has been rendered invisible in the public debate on pornography.

Penthouse, on the other hand, because it does tend to be more explicit in its focus on women's genitals, simulated sexual intercourse, sexual violence and group sex, has only one foot in the acceptable soft-core market and the other in the more hard core market. This is probably the worst situation to be in because the magazine can compete with neither; it cannot attract the writers or interview subjects that provide *Playboy* with its markers of respectability and thus its advertising revenue, nor can it attract the readers away from the hard-core magazines by being even more explicit, for fear of offending the advertisers it already has. *Hustler* magazine, understanding Guccione's dilemma, owes much of its success to its decision to forego mainstream advertisers in order to have no advertising limits imposed on what it can and cannot show. This has allowed *Hustler* to do pictorials on electrocuting women, gang rape of women and women having their genitals licked by bears, as well as cartoons that trivialize and legitimize child sexual abuse, battery and murder.

PUTTING THE PORNOGRAPHY
BACK IN *PLAYBOY*

There is no doubt that *Playboy* occupies a remarkable place in the publishing history of the English-speaking world. Similarly, Hugh Hefner is probably the only pornographer in America who has achieved mainstream celebrity status. Like the magazine itself, Hugh Hefner was marketed as an upscale, high-quality commodity, to reduce the sleaze factor normally associated with pornographers. Regularly photographed by the press, in the fall of 1993 he made guest appearances on two network television shows: *Fresh Prince* and *The Simpsons*. In both of these shows, he was located in luxurious surroundings, presumed to be the "Playboy mansion," mixing with well-dressed celebrities and, of course, lots of young women. Rarely is Hefner shown outside of the context of his extremely wealthy lifestyle. It appears that much of the interest in Hefner is generated by his playboy image.

Part of this playboy image also involved his being a patron of liberal organizations such as the American Civil Liberties Union (ACLU) and National Organization for the Reform of Marijuana Laws (NORML). *Playboy* magazine has often run stories on Hefner's attendance at parties held in honor of his financial contributions to different causes. During the early years of the magazine, Hefner frequently wrote about his political beliefs in the "*Playboy* Philosophy" section of the magazine. Among the most controversial were those financial contributions made to women's organizations such as the National Organization for Woman (NOW) Legal Defense and Education Fund, the ACLU's Women's Rights Project, *Ms.* magazine and the National Institute for Working Women. Many in the feminist movement felt that *Playboy*'s money was made through the exploitation of women. For feminists to accept donations was to legitimize *Playboy* as a supporter of women's rights (MacKinnon, 1987). This debate became more heated in the early 1970s when a secretary leaked a memo written by Hefner concerning an article commissioned by the magazine on the growing feminist movement. Hefner wrote:

> It sounds as if we are off in our upcoming feminism piece . . . Jack indicates that what we have is a well balanced "objective" article but . . . What I am interested in is the highly irrational, emotional, kookie trend that feminism has taken . . . these chicks are our natural enemy . . . it is time to do battle with them and I think that we can do it in a devastating way. That's the kind of piece I want. (Weyr, 1978, p. 231)

The eventual article (it went through a number of writers) did indeed "do battle" with the feminist movement. Although the leaked memo was published in a number of Chicago newspapers, Hefner was never asked, in the numerous interviews he gave, to explain the contradiction between his claim that he supported women's rights and the portrayal of feminists in the memo.

This is no surprise. The mainstream media have played a major role in sanitizing both *Playboy* and Hefner by stressing their elite status while simultaneously demonizing the more explicit, low-budget pornography that is often associated with White, working-class males. In reality, all materials that have as their (overt or covert) selling point, the facilitation of male masturbation through the visual representation of women's bodies, dehumanize and subordinate woman as a class. Although the term for women may differ in the magazines—"Playmate" in *Playboy*, "Pet" in *Penthouse*, "Beaver" in *Hustler*, "Whore" in *Whores On Parade*—the relations of domination remain the same. In *Playboy*, as in all other pornographic magazines, women exist for male use. The "brilliance" of *Playboy* was that it combined the commodification of sex with the sexualization of commodities, with women being the prized commodity. However prized, though, a commodity is just a commodity—to be used and discarded when finished with.

NOTES

1. Clearly, the best indicator of success for any business is the bottom line, and by this standard, *Playboy* stands apart from all other "men's entertainment magazines." Besides the magazine, *Playboy* bought into clubs, hotels resorts, films, records, movie theaters, real estate and a modeling agency. By the 1970s, the *Playboy* company was a giant corporation, publishing in several countries, with 5,000 employees, magazine sales of almost $200 million and net earnings that exceeded $10,000,000 annually (Weyr, 1978, p. 70).

2. Here the woman appears not to know that she is being photographed because her head is turned away from the camera and she is lost in her own thoughts. Her partially naked body is positioned, however, to give maximum viewing ability to the spectator.

REFERENCES

Brady, F. (1974). *Hefner.* New York: Macmillan.

Kappeler, S. (1986). *The pornography of representation.* Cambridge, UK: Polity.

Kipnis, L. (1992). (Male) desire and (female) disgust: Reading *Hustler.* In L. Grossberg, C. Nelson, & P. Treichler (Eds.), *Cultural studies.* New York: Routledge.

Kuhn, A. (1985). *The power of the image: Essays on representation and sexuality.* London: Routledge.

MacKinnon, C. (1987). *Feminism unmodified: Discourses on life and law.* Cambridge, MA: Harvard University Press.

MacKinnon, C. (1993). *Only words.* Cambridge, MA: Harvard University Press.

Miller, R. (1984). *Bunny: The real story of* Playboy. London: Michael Joseph.

Ross, A. (1989). *No respect: Intellectuals and popular culture.* London: Routledge.

Weyr, T. (1978). *Reaching for paradise: The* Playboy *vision of America.* New York: Times Books.

Williams, L. (1989). *Hard core: Power, pleasure and the "frenzy of the visible".* Berkeley: University of California.

Zita, J. (1988). Pornography and the male imaginary. *Enclitic, 17/18,* 28-44.

30

Towards a Feminist Erotica

KATHY MYERS

. . . Many feminist critiques of the representation of women hinge on the assumption that it is the act of representation or objectification itself which degrades women, reducing them to the status of objects to be "visually" or "literally" consumed.

I want to argue that this assumption can lead feminism into deep water. On the one hand, it works to deny women the right to represent their own sexuality, and on the other it side-steps the whole issue of female sexual pleasure. I want to suggest that questions of representation and of pleasure cannot be separated, and that a feminist erotica could examine the nature of this relationship. . . .

. . . This article holds that images themselves cannot be characterised as either pornographic or erotic. The pornographic/erotic distinction can only be applied by looking at how the image is contextualised through its mode of address and the conditions of its production and consumption. . . .

. . . An analysis of pornography which focuses purely on its content is in danger of falling into a kind of "reductive essentialism," e.g., the notion that exploitation resides in the representation of female sexuality *per se*, rather than in its contextualisation: the conditions of its production and consumption; the ways in which meanings are created, etc. Unless we can shift the

NOTE: Excerpts reprinted from *Looking On: Images of Femininity in the Visual Arts and Media*, edited by Rosemary Betterton (London: Pandora, 1987), by permission of HarperCollins Publishers Limited.

Figure 30.1 Slix New Waves advertisement.
SOURCE: Unknown

debate on representation away from the image, there is very little "positive" work which can be done.

Whilst it is true that we designate certain images as pornographic, pornography also refers to a particular mode of productive relations which market and sell sexuality: e.g., the choice of model/subject matter, the photographer-model relationship and the conditions under which they work, the choice of medium and distribution, all affect our reception and interpretation of what constitutes pornography. This economy of pornography works to structure not only to whom the material is made available, but also the kinds of pleasures and responses which are elicited.

. . . We have to understand the ways in which images work to construct our own experience of our sexuality. Rather than running away from the powers of the imagination and fantasy, we have to reappraise the role of representations in structuring our needs and desires as a step towards constructing new meanings for the experience and representation of our sexuality.

I want to illustrate this point with one image taken from a softcore porn magazine and one from a woman's journal (Figures 30.1 and 30.2). By comparing them, I want to suggest that woman's sexuality is deployed in a variety of ways. This deployment is dependent upon the context in which the image appears, its mode of production as well as consumption.

On first impression, the two images seem remarkably similar: the model's pose and attitude, the seaside setting, etc. The main difference appears to be that the Slix model sports a bikini whilst the porn model is naked. It could be argued that women's exploitation is only a matter of degree along a scantily clad continuum. However, the surface similarities

Figure 30.2 Pornographic advertisement.
SOURCE: Unknown

belie fundamental differences in the representation of female sexuality and in the kinds of pleasures offered to audiences.

Many of these differences are hidden from the viewer. For example, the production of pornography differs in most respects from the production of a fashion advert. This affects their economic foundation, the choice of studio, photographer, model, etc. They are specialist discourses which retain their autonomy. For example, the "photographic life" of models is extremely limited. Few nude models ever make the transition to become fashion models, partly because of the stigma which certain forms of nude modelling carry, and partly due to the fact that different selection criteria operate. Fashion models have become increasingly slender, younger and taller. Most nude models are considered too "curvy" for fashion work: different "aesthetics" operate. In turn this visual aesthetic cannot be divorced from the respective audiences for fashion and pornographic imagery. To put it simply, there is an overall tendency to market "fleshier" women to men and thinner, sometimes sexually androgynous, images of women to female audiences. This micro-politics of body style speaks of the aesthetic and pleasurable segregation of sexuality across a range of visual discourses, which cannot be simply explained away in terms of "taste" nor patriarchal oppression but require further examination.

Selling female sexuality to a woman is not the same as selling it to a man. The anticipated gender of the audience is crucial in structuring the image. For example, look at the angle of the women's heads in the two images. The pornographic model's face is angled towards the viewer. Her mouth is open, a classic signifier of sexual receptiveness and anticipation. In the small inset photo the same model faces and acknowledges the camera. Behind the camera, we, the audience, are located.

By comparison the Slix model, sweeping back her hair, looks across the scope of the camera. She does not face us, her mouth is closed. Not so much a sulky pout as an expression of relaxed langour. Like the pornographic image, she is aware of being on display. But the tenor of her demeanour is proud and inaccessible. She sweeps back her hair from the heat of the sun, not from passion.

By comparison, her legs are together. The Slix model's mouth and legs offer no point of entrance. The body of the Slix model is a matt sandy tone, she is relaxed. The skin of the nude model is oiled to give the effect of a sheen of perspiration which can signify sexual activity and tension.

The girls in the background of the Slix image look at each other not at the camera. Self-absorbed, they reiterate the confident, self-engrossed narcissism of the foregrounded model. She takes pleasure in her sunbathing, not in the presence of her audience. Only the small inset model in the beach jacket to the right of the image pays the camera a cursory glance.

What differentiates the pornographic image from the fashion shot is the mode of address. The Slix mode of address is characterised by the tension which it establishes between the model's desirability in conventional terms, and her inaccessibility. The advert works to secure a distancing effect between image and audience.

By comparison, the nude model's sexuality is posed as invitational. The pleasure of looking at her merges with the pleasure of being with her. Her sexuality stretches out to embrace the viewer. The nude model "asks" the audience to possess her. It is a form of sexual consumption which implicitly genders the audience as male. The model's apparent expression of pleasure is not for herself. She is not autonomous, her pleasure is always for the consumption of another, and herein lies one of the fundamental alienations of pornographic imagery.

By comparison, the Slix advert positions the audience as spectator, to keep a safe distance and to observe, not to touch. Sexual inaccessibility is conveyed through the structure of the image. For example, the self-absorbed pose of the model, the cropping, editing and retouching of the photograph, work together to reinforce the displayedness of the model, and in doing so, distance the audience.

The impact of the Slix advert is based on the strength of the photograph. Its scale and use of full colour works to dominate the page. The seaside location, the pattern on the bikini, the sense of displayed style are all anchored in the copy line "New Waves." These associations are cemented by reference to the brand name of Slix which is in bold type. Image and copy line work together. "New Waves" links the image to the body of the text.

Whilst the image celebrates the tension between desirability and inaccessibility, the body of the text suggests sexual provocation. Unlike the provocative pose of the pornographic image, the Slix advert suggests sexual power as opposed to sexual availability and perhaps vulnerability. The wearer of the Slix bikini is promised power over others, the power of sexual display: "Slip into Slix and make a few ripples."

The target audience for this advert is women. The advert is designed to appeal to women. One of the pleasures which the advertising system offers women is the promise of a kind of power and self-determination. Images of women marketed to women rarely present female sexuality purely in terms of vulnerability, accessibility or availability. But the power which the advertising of beauty and personal products offers women is always of a limited kind, located in terms of sexual display, appearance and attractiveness. What the advert may offer for consumption is an ideal version of self. It also plays on women's pleasure in looking at attractive women. This kind of visual pleasure is inscribed in the image.

We may find many images of women unacceptable, glamourised, exploitative or whatever; but we cannot simply interpret women's pleasure in reading them as evidence for the extent to which the female consciousness has been colonised by patriarchy. We have to account for women's pleasure in looking at images of women.

The advertising image and the pornographic image offer different kinds of pleasure to their respective audiences. If audiences did not find them in some way pleasurable they wouldn't work; magazines and products wouldn't sell. It is their pleasurable associations which perpetuate them. But pleasure as a concept cannot be tackled in isolation, we need to understand how pleasure is produced through the structuring of power and sexuality.

TOWARDS A FEMINIST EROTICA

One of the central objections put forward by feminists in their critique of pornography and other modes of representation is that it "objectifies" women. Objectification has become a much abused term. There is a sense in which the process of sight and perception necessarily entail objectification in order to conceptualise and give meaning to the object of our gaze. Within feminism, objectification has a quite specific meaning: through the process of representation, women are reduced to the status of objects. This is partly derived from a commonsense use of the Marxist idea of commodity fetishism; images of women have become commodities from which women are alienated. Their status as commodity works to deny their individuality and humanity. The second sense of objectification which has informed its current usage is derived from Freud's concept of sexual fetishism: the idea that objects or parts of the anatomy are used as symbols for and replacements of the socially valued phallus. Hence, the argument goes, men have difficulty in coping with women's sexuality because of its castrating potential, and because of its lack of a phallus. In order to cope with this anxiety, men fetishise aspects of female sexuality—for example, the legs or breasts—as symbols of acceptable sexual power.

The use of the term "objectification" is coupled with a tendency to interpret all forms of sexual symbolisation as evidence of sexual fetishisation. In the analysis of female imagery two processes of symbolisation are brought under closer scrutiny: that of sexual fragmentation and sexual substitution. Frequently these processes of metonym (where the part stands for the whole) and metaphor (where one object or aspect of the anatomy stands for another) operate together. For example, the depiction of female sexuality through the representation of a stiletto-shod foot isolates and fragments the sexual by focusing on a part of the anatomy and fetishises the foot by over-valuing it as a phallic symbol. Psychoanalytic interpretations of this kind of imagery have suggested that the stiletto as phallic symbol serves to "give" the woman her missing phallus, thus circumnavigating the castration threat which she poses for male sexuality and rendering her safe.

Whilst this kind of analysis may provide an adequate interpretation of the dominant associations of stilettos in our culture, can we say that all forms of sexualised imagery can be interpreted in terms of phallic substitution? There exists a repertoire of conventionalised symbols which have become imbued with fetishistic associations of which the stiletto is only one example; but symbolisation is not a closed system of limited or fixed meaning. Symbolism is polysemic (has no one, fixed meaning); there always exists the possibility of powerful symbolism which works to activate forms of sexual expression which are not recognised by phallocentric interpretation.

Because fetishisation usually employs a fragmented image, there is a danger of assuming that all fragmentary images are necessarily fetishistic. The process of sexual fetishisation (specific phallic associations) is always complicated by that of commodity fetishisation, whereby the image of a woman's legs, for example, becomes isolated and estranged. They become a commodity, an object of display to be visually consumed by an audience.

What is at issue is not so much the perceptual processes of objectification and fragmentation which are a necessary part of rendering a complex world meaningful but rather the specific forms of objectification entailed in commodity and sexual fetishism. It therefore seems important to create a working distinction between the process of fragmentation, which implies a breaking up or disabling of the physical form, and what could be termed "a pleasure in the part"—the pleasure derived from looking at a picture which depicts the curve of an arm or the sweep of the neckline. Such images could be interpreted not as a butchering of the female form but as a celebration of its constituent elements, giving a sense of the scope and complexity of sensual pleasure which breaks with specific genital sexual associations and with the necessity of overdetermining phallic substitution in the representation of the female form.

It seems that we have to clarify whether it is the process of necessary objectification entailed in perception which we object to (used, for example, whenever we look at the world, at art, at a book, etc.) or the meaning which it carries for women under specific patriarchal formations. These are two separate issues which tend to be collapsed into each other when feminists talk about the representation of women in art, photography, etc. To refuse to differentiate between the two modes of objectification is to endorse a kind of perceptual essentialism—that objectification is inherently exploitative and demeaning.

To see objectification in essentialist terms is to deny the possibility of any alternative practice within the representation of women. Feminists would be denied the possibility of visual communication and new forms of perception. . . .

It is in terms of the pleasure derived from representational systems that we need to reintroduce a notion of the erotic. Within sexual politics we have to find a way of accounting for women's sexual attraction to each other; the visual pleasure of leafing through a glossy women's magazine; the appeal of the heroine star systems, etc. Such pleasure cannot be simply dismissed as more evidence of patriarchal oppression, that women are continually gulled into a search for the ideal type simply to appeal to "their man." We cannot dismiss sexual attraction as further evidence of patriarchal mystification.

. . . Ultimately the distinction between pornography and other modes of sexual representation cannot rest on the characteristics of the image. The differences between pornographic vaginal imagery and medical vaginal imagery are learned through contextualisation: they are not innate.

In the reappraisal of our sexuality, there may appear to be an overlap between the kind of images designated as pornographic as opposed to erotic. This means that the exploration of female sexual pleasure through imagery will remain politically controversial.

Some suggestions for the kind of questions which need to be asked when producing or appraising potentially progressive images of women:

- How is the image produced?
- Whose fantasy is being recorded?
- What power relationship exists in the photographer-model relationship?
- How are models selected; what is their relationship to the overall production process?

How will the image be distributed and where will it be circulated?

- The politics of distribution cannot be separated from those of production, nor of consumption. Where an image is distributed will affect who will see it, in what context, etc. It is obviously important to sort out whether an image is for private or public consumption, whether it will be seen in a gallery or a magazine, etc. It needs to be asked whether an image's validity or "usefulness" depends on how an audience will use or interpret an image. For example, does the risk of appropriation by men invalidate producing erotic imagery for women? This risk could be countered by showing these images in, for example, *Camerawork.*

Visual conventions of the image.

- How do we classify an image as erotic? What conventions and genres of representation does an image trade on?
- To what extent does an oppositional system need to reuse and question familiar styles in order to go forward and create new meanings?

- What are the signifiers of sexuality?
- How do we recognise the gender of the subject?
- In fact how important is the thwarting of easy gender assignment for erotic pleasure?

The audience and pleasure.
- What kind of pleasures does an image offer its audience?
- How is the sexuality and subject position of the audience constructed—are they sexed as male or female?
- What kind of emotional responses does the image demand?
- Does it demand any kind of audience interaction to interpret the meaning of the image? To what extent does the image challenge assumptions already held?

.31

Lawless Seeing

ANNETTE KUHN

. . . What I want to consider here are some of the ways in which pornography, as a regime of representation, addresses a particular audience in a particular context, producing meanings pivoting on gender difference: and how in this process it constructs a social discourse on the nature of human sexuality.

. . . Despite the fact that pornography has existed under that name since about the mid-nineteenth century, and depictions of erotic and sexual activity have been around—even if not called pornography—from time immemorial, such representations are by no means homogeneous in terms either of their textual operations or of the cultural meanings they carried in the societies in which they were produced. The nature of, and readings available from, representations of sexual activity will vary according to their social-historical conditions of production and consumption. . . .

When the term pornography first came into use, virtually the only medium in which representations could be reproduced in very large numbers was print. The printed word demands literacy, and not everyone was able to read. As a written medium, pornography was consequently limited as to the audience it could reach, and seems to have been something of a gentleman's pastime. Porn did of course exist in visual media as well: but paintings

NOTE: Excerpts reprinted from *The Power of the Image: Essays on Representation and Sexuality*, by Annette Kuhn (London: Routledge, 1985), by permission of the publisher.

and drawings also found a numerically small and socially exclusive market. Engravings and broadsheets, which did not call for literacy, were rather more widely circulated, but were still by no means a mass medium. Developments in techniques of mechanical reproduction of photographic images and consequently in the capacity to produce large quantities cheaply[1] opened up limitless horizons for pornographers. The apparent realism of the photographic image undoubtedly proved an added attraction for consumers, too. Mechanical reproduction of still photographic images, then, offered a breakthrough in the public availability of pornography. The advent of cheap, mass-produced visual pornography opened the market to the less well-off, foreign immigrants, the illiterate, the working classes.

. . . Present-day pornography is produced across a range of media, from the printed word through to television, though the market is dominated by visual forms drawing on various conventions of photographic realism. . . .

. . . Photography draws on an ideology of the visible as evidence. The eye of the camera is neutral, it sees the world as it is: we look at a photograph and see a slice of the world. To complete the circuit of recording visibility and truth set up by the photograph, there has to be someone looking at it. The spectator looks at the photograph, and the look of the camera is completed by the look of the spectator: the photograph says that these two looks are one and the same. Meaning is produced, finally, in the spectator's look: looking is crucial in reading photographs.

. . . The spectator can choose to gaze at length, to return again and again, to a favourite photograph. Looking may turn into contemplation, even into voyeurism. The voyeur's pleasure depends on the object of this look being unable to see him: to this extent, it is a pleasure of power, and the look a controlling one. Photographs are well equipped to produce this kind of pleasure: the apparent authenticity of what is in the image combines with the fact that it is of course actually not there—and so can be looked at for as long as desired, because the circuit of pleasure will never be broken by a returned look. . . . But how does all this tie in with pornography's ideological project of constructing sexual difference by, in, representation? How is this project realised in pornographic photographs?

Any sustained examination of photographic pornography will show that it draws consistently on a circumscribed set of conventions of photographic representation. These conventions relate both to the formal organisation of the pictures and also to the kinds of contents and narrative themes that repeatedly come up in them. They do, however, vary somewhat between different pornographic genres: while softcore, for example, consistently uses images of women on their own, in most forms of hardcore women are not portrayed on their own and are usually less central to what is represented. In some instances—notably gay male porn—women do not appear at all. But pornography's ideological project of constructing sexual difference usually, though by no means inevitably, demands that women be represented in some way or other. How does this work in particular images, in different types of pornographic photography? . . .

CAUGHT UNAWARES

... Her eyes are closed, she faces away from camera, but her body is wide open. The photograph pretends to be a candid shot, pretends she is unaware that the camera is there. An attractive woman takes a solitary bath and is carried away by the sensuousness of it all. The spectator sneaks a look at her enjoyment of an apparently unselfconscious moment of pleasure in herself: the Peeping Tom's favourite fantasy. Since she does not know he is there, he can take a good look at what a woman gets up to when she is on her own. He might even find out what women are really like, what their pleasure really is.

The voyeur's conviction is that the riddle of femininity will ultimately yield its solution if he looks long enough and hard enough. Since his desire is pinned to the actual process of investigation/scrutiny, though, the maintenance of desire depends upon the riddle's solution remaining just out of sight. Fortunately, the picture obliges. As a photograph, it starts out by exploiting the codes of authenticity attaching to the medium: the photo says that this woman, and so perhaps all women, do really pleasure themselves in this way. The spectator can indulge in the "lawless seeing" permitted by the photo's reassurance that the woman is unaware of his look: her eyes are closed, her face averted. He can gaze as long as he likes at her body, with its signs of difference on display. ...

... The photograph speaks to a masculine subject, constructing woman as object, femininity as otherness. This does not mean that female spectators cannot, or do not, engage in a "masculine" way with photographs like this, nor does it mean that women cannot adopt a position of voyeurism. Masculinity is not the same as maleness, even if it may be conventional in our society to construct it so. Women can and do derive pleasure from images of women, a fact which betokens the unifixity of sexual identity and the fluidity of our engagement with certain types of image. If women enjoy this picture, it is possible that they are adopting a masculine subject position in doing so. There is another possibility, however. A spectator (male or female) has the option of identifying with, rather than objectifying, the woman in the picture. The photo might evoke memories or fantasies of similar pleasures enjoyed by the spectator. In this case, the pleasure of looking is not completely voyeuristic. Indeed, an important attribute of this kind of softcore image is its openness: it may be read in a variety of ways. Its original context (a series of narratively-organised still photographs published in a men's pinup magazine) certainly proposes a masculine subject position for a male spectator. But other positions are possible, too.

... Lesbian scenes are a staple of the kind of pornography that bridges softcore and hardcore. Such scenes deploy some of the conventions of the stolen look at a woman alone, caught up in her own pleasure, while at the same time constructing codes for the representation, within a certain context, of more sociable sex. Lesbian scenes also neatly sidestep a cultural embargo on representing male genitalia. ...

For a regime of representation that constantly proclaims itself on the side of sexual liberation, pornography hedges itself about with an extraordinary array of limits. At present, for example, it draws very firm lines around representations of male sexuality and heterosexual activity. While censorship of representations of sexual activities conventionally regarded as socially unacceptable is perhaps to be expected, it appears hard to fathom why it is that both the sexual subjectivity which sets itself up as the cultural norm (masculinity) and the sexual practice we are all meant to strive for (heterosexuality) are both in certain respects unrepresentable. Photographs of erect penises, for example, are usually confined to hardcore and to gay male pornography, while representations of acts of heterosexual intercourse are also limited in availability. Such censorships, however, far from marginalising certain sexual practices, precisely construct them as the really important ones. The paradox of the unrepresentability of heterosexual intercourse turns out to be no paradox at all: the embargo confirms the cultural ascendancy of heterosexuality and the primacy within heterosexual sex of the act of coition, the reduction within ideology of all sexual activity to conjunction of penis and vagina. . . .

BITS AND PIECES

. . . In pornography, photographs are often composed in such a way that a particular bodily part is greatly emphasised. Or it may even fill the whole of the picture, in which case the body is fragmented, cut up, by the frame. In our society, only one convention of partial framing in visual images is generally regarded as an adequate substitute of bodily part for whole: this is the portrait. In the portrait, attention is directed at the subject's face. The face stands in for the person's whole being: the subject's essential humanity is seen as inhabiting his or her face, the "window of the soul." Within this perspective, an abstracted bodily part other than the face may be regarded as an expropriation of the subject's individuality. In consequence, the tendency of some pornographic photographs to isolate bits of bodies may be read as a gesture of dehumanisation.

But porn's attention to bits of bodies is never random. Pornography is preoccupied with what it regards as the signifiers of sexual difference and sexuality: genitals, breasts, buttocks. To the extent that pornography circulates such images, it also constructs human beings as sexual bodies. However, the process of fragmentation is by no means disinterested as regards gender. Although it is not difficult to find examples of fetishised representations of the male body, it is much more often the female body and its representation which receives this kind of treatment. Mass-circulation "girlie" magazines routinely go in for mild forms of fetishisation, with their emphasis on women's breasts and buttocks, while many of the more explicit, but still widely-circulated, "adult" magazines go a good deal further, in particular with close-ups of female genitals. . . .

. . . Pinup and softcore photography's interest in the female body is confined to a small repertoire of parts—those which mark the woman as feminine, not-male, different. This preoccupation is evident not only in the way particular images are composed—lighting, accessories, posture, gesture, framing—but also by virtue of the very repetitiveness of certain poses across a range of photos: the bosom thrust forward, the raised buttocks and, in recent years, the open legs and crotch shot. Softcore draws on and transforms conventions through which the female nude is represented in high art, placing them within a mass-market context.[2] There is a circumscribed, almost a rigid, set of codes or conventions of representation of the body in this type of photography, conventions with which even the most naive spectator is likely to be familiar.

For example, the woman's body is angled towards the camera to offer maximum display of whatever part of the body is at the moment being emphasised; breasts are accentuated by the placement of arms and elbows in certain ways, and so on. These poses are so commonplace—pinups of this kind appear every day in some popular newspapers[3]—that their cultural meanings acquire a degree of naturalisation. The woman in the picture, and so perhaps woman in general, is constructed as interesting because of her body, or certain parts of it. The photograph says: look at this, this body is there for you to look at, and you will enjoy looking at it. The formal arrangement of the body, the way it is displayed, solicits the spectator's gaze. The conventions of pinup photography work to construct the body, usually the female body, as a spectacle: and the female body is a spectacle because parts of it—the parts that say "this is a woman"—are pleasurable to look at. . . .

With the move away from pinups and softcore towards hardcore pornography, the fetishisation of body parts by their accentuation within the image gives way to a more literal fragmentation. The spectator's attention is directed to certain parts of the body in isolation, and interest is likely to be centred more exclusively on genitals as signifiers of sexual difference. . . .

. . . Pornography conflates femininity with femaleness, femaleness with female sexuality, and female sexuality with a particular part of the female anatomy. At the same time, it attempts to render these qualities visible, and thus fit objects of observation. The subject-object split proposed by positivist science puts in an unexpected appearance in pornography, then: porn places the masculine on the side of the subject, the feminine on the side of the object, of enquiry. . . .

THE INVITATION

Pornographic images participate in photography's more general project of privileging the visible, of equating visibility with truth. But porn inflects this concern with its own ruling obsessions—sexuality and sexual difference—which are made visible, become a spectacle which reveals itself to the spectator. The spectator is invited to look—with the promise that he will derive both pleasure and knowledge from his looking. His quest is mapped out for him in pornographic photographs—which always speak to his desire for pleasurable looking.

The desire for pleasurable looking—scopophilia—manifests itself in a variety of ways, voyeurism being only one. In voyeurism, the subject of the look, the Peeping Tom, separates himself in the act of looking from the object, which cannot look back at him. But although the power inherent in the voyeur's look, the power of catching its object unawares, may be pleasurable in itself, the object's unfathomable desire remains. What if she is not interested in him after all? Pornography promises to circumvent such a threat to the voyeur's pleasure by saying he can have it both ways. While in various respects the photograph proposes that the woman in the picture is unaware of the spectator's look, the risk of her indifference is mitigated by the fact that her body may at the same time be arranged as if on display for him. This implies an unspoken exhibitionism on the part of the object of the look, thus permitting the spectator a twofold pleasure. This combination of visual pleasures is taken one step further in what is probably the most common-place of all the conventions of pornography, of softcore in particular, the "come-on."

The woman in the picture, far from being caught unawares in her own pleasure, now seems openly to acknowledge the spectator by her direct look at the camera. This is a particular kind of look—the head is tilted so that her glance is slightly angled rather than face-on. The indirect look signifies sexual invitation or teasing, a reading underscored by the cultural connotations of the slightly parted lips. This facial expression, particularly in combination with the conventionalised display of the rest of the woman's body, may be read as an invitation. . . .

. . . The spectator's fantasy is given free rein: in one sense, there is no risk of disappointment—he is quite safe because it is only a picture and the woman in it will never, in real life, turn him down or make demands which he cannot satisfy. By the same token, of course, he can never "really" possess her. But the come-on in the photograph works—and to judge by the frequency with which we see it, keeps on working—precisely because it is such a tease. Desire is fueled because in the final instance its object is unattainable—and unthreatening. . . .

Facial expression, the come-on look in particular, is a key moment in the pinup's construction of a masculine subject position for the spectator. In offering itself as both spectacle and truth, the photograph suggests that the woman in the picture, rather than the image itself, is responsible for soliciting the spectator's gaze. In doing this, the photograph constructs her body as an object of scrutiny, suggesting at the same time that female sexuality is active, that women may invite sex. The pinup's singular preoccupation with the female body is tied in with the project of defining the "true" nature of female sexuality. Femaleness and femininity are constructed as a set of bodily attributes reducible to a sexuality which puts itself on display for a masculine spectator. In these ways the pinup invites the spectator to participate in a masculine definition of femininity.

IDENTIFYING POWER

... In general, the harder the porn, the more people, and—significantly—the more men in it. The tendency for men to feature more often in hardcore than in softcore pornography may be explained to some extent in terms of the relatively strong cultural taboo on representations of male sexual organs and of sexual activities involving men—though this of course begs the question of why the taboo exists in the first place. However, the presence of men also allows for a new variant of address "in the masculine": the male spectator may identify with a male protagonist. Although he is obviously not obliged to do so, pornography may nevertheless invite such an identification in various ways.

If men's participation as protagonists in the action becomes significant in hardcore pornography in general, the invitation to the spectator to identify is particularly strong in particular subgenres of hardcore. As voyeurism gives way to identification, the spectator sheds much of the responsibility for producing his own sexual fantasy, if only because the fantasy is more likely to be actually there in the picture. If hardcore porn is quite specific in its representation of sexual activities, it constructs a relatively limited range of possibilities for sexual fantasy. Identification may be said to go hand-in-hand with closure, with fixation of meaning. In instances where pornography evokes hostile and aggressive aspects of sexuality, the spectator may welcome the relief from guilt offered by identification and closure.

Sadomasochistic pornography—especially of the kind which details violence done to women by men—has been the subject of a good deal of concern of late, not only because for many women it is so disturbing in itself, but also because—or so it has been argued—more of it is being produced now than ever before.[4] Because of its capacity to disgust, it may be difficult for anyone who does not share the fantasies constructed by sexually violent pornography even to begin to understand the nature of the pleasure it gives to those who do enjoy it.[5] However, consumers who bring to their reading of this pornography a preoccupation with domination and sexuality-as-power may construct their pleasure around identification with its protagonists. Sadomasochistic pornography re-enacts a master-slave scenario of sex-as-power: so that, for example where women are subjected to sexual violence, mastery is constructed as operating on the side of the masculine. To this extent, it participates in pornography's more routine insistence on sexual difference, except that in this case sexual difference is reduced to relations of power rather than, or as well as, to bodily attributes.

But as with more commonplace variants of pornography, here too the female body frequently becomes the object of scrutiny and investigation: though not in this case as a relation between spectator and image, but within the image and the story themselves. This betokens an obsession with the otherness of femininity, which in common with many forms of otherness seems to contain a threat to the onlooker. Curiosity turns to terror, investigation to torture, the final affirmation of the objecthood of the other. The feminine here represents a threat to the masculine, a threat which demands containment. Sexually violent pornography of this kind concretises this wish for containment in representations which address the spectator as masculine, and place the masculine on the side of container of the threat. It insists that sexuality and power are inseparable.

NOTES

1. On social, cultural and political consequences of these developments, see Walter Benjamin (1973).

2. Berger (1972).

3. For a consideration of how pinups work in one popular newspaper, see Holland (1983).

4. Recent feminist commentaries emphasising violent aspects of pornography include Diamond (1980), Dworkin (1981), Lederer et al. (1980) and Russell and Griffin (1977).

5. The existence of pornography (directed at male consumers) in which women dominate men also calls for explanation. Jessica Benjamin (1984) begins such a project by discussing the psychic functions of sadomasochistic fantasy for both sexes in "Master and Slave: The Fantasy of Erotic Domination." The relationship between sexual fantasy and pornography cannot be assumed to be either simple or direct, however. In the case of sadomasochistic pornography, certainly, further investigation of this relationship is called for.

REFERENCES

Benjamin, J. (1984). Master and slave: The fantasy of erotic domination. In A. Snitow et al. (Eds.), *Desire: The politics of sexuality* (pp. 292-311). London: Virago.

Benjamin, W. (1973). The work of art in the age of mechanical reproduction. In *Illuminations* (pp. 219-253). London: Fontana.

Berger, J. (1972). *Ways of seeing.* Hammondworth: Penguin.

Diamond, I. (1980). Pornography and repression: A reconsideration. *Signs, 5*(4), 686-701.

Dworkin, A. (1977). *Pornography: Men possessing women.* New York: Peregree.

Holland, P. (1983). The page three girl speaks to women, too. *Screen, 23*(3), 84-102.

Lederer, L., et al. (1980). *Take back the night: Women on pornography.* New York: William Morrow.

Russell, D., & Griffin, S. (1977). On pornography. *Chrysalis, 4,* 11-17.

.32

Pornography and Black Women's Bodies

PATRICIA HILL COLLINS

BLACK WOMEN AND THE SEX/GENDER HIERARCHY

... Pornography, prostitution, and rape as a specific tool of sexual violence have been key to the sexual politics of Black womanhood. Together they form three essential and interrelated components of the sex/gender hierarchy framing Black women's sexuality.

PORNOGRAPHY AND BLACK WOMEN'S BODIES

For centuries the black woman has served as the primary pornographic "outlet" for white men in Europe and America. We need only think of the black women used as breeders, raped for the pleasure and profit of their owners. We need only think of the license the "master" of the slave women enjoyed. But, most telling of all, we need only study the old slave societies of the South to note the sadistic treat-

---

NOTE: Excerpt reprinted from *Black Feminist Thought* (1990), by Patricia Hill Collins, by permission of the publisher, Routledge, Chapman and Hall, Inc., and Dr. Patricia Hill Collins.

ment—at the hands of white "gentlemen"—of "beautiful young quadroons and octoroons" who became increasingly (and were deliberately bred to become) indistinguishable from white women, and were the more highly prized as slave mistresses because of this. (Walker, 1981, p. 42)

Alice Walker's description of the rape of enslaved African women for the "pleasure and profit of their owners" encapsulates several elements of contemporary pornography. First, Black women were used as sex objects for the pleasure of white men. This objectification of African-American women parallels the portrayal of women in pornography as sex objects whose sexuality is available for men (McNall, 1983). Exploiting Black women as breeders objectified them as less than human because only animals can be bred against their will. In contemporary pornography women are objectified through being portrayed as pieces of meat, as sexual animals awaiting conquest. Second, African-American women were raped, a form of sexual violence. Violence is typically an implicit or explicit theme in pornography. Moreover, the rape of Black women linked sexuality and violence, another characteristic feature of pornography (Eisenstein, 1983). Third, rape and other forms of sexual violence act to strip victims of their will to resist and make them passive and submissive to the will of the rapist. Female passivity, the fact that women have things done to them, is a theme repeated over and over in contemporary pornography (McNall, 1983). Fourth, the profitability of Black women's sexual exploitation for white "gentlemen" parallels pornography's financially lucrative benefits for pornographers (Eisenstein, 1983). Finally, the actual breeding of "quadroons and octoroons" not only reinforces the themes of Black women's passivity, objectification, and malleability to male control but reveals pornography's grounding in racism and sexism. The fates of both Black and white women were intertwined in this breeding process. The ideal African-American woman as a pornographic object was indistinguishable from white women and thus approximated the images of beauty, asexuality, and chastity forced on white women. But inside was a highly sexual whore, a "slave mistress" ready to cater to her owner's pleasure.[1]

Contemporary pornography consists of a series of icons or representations that focus the viewer's attention on the relationship between the portrayed individual and the general qualities ascribed to that class of individuals. Pornographic images are iconographic in that they represent realities in a manner determined by the historical position of the observers, their relationship to their own time, and to the history of the conventions which they employ (Gilman, 1985). The treatment of Black women's bodies in nineteenth-century Europe and the United States may be the foundation upon which contemporary pornography as the representation of women's objectification, domination, and control is based. Icons about the sexuality of Black women's bodies emerged in these contexts. Moreover, as race/gender-specific representations, these icons have implications for the treatment of both African-American and white women in contemporary pornography.

I suggest that African-American women were not included in pornography as an afterthought but instead form a key pillar on which contemporary pornography itself rests. As Alice Walker points out, "the more ancient roots of modern pornography are to be found in the almost always pornographic treatment of black women who, from the moment they entered slavery . . . were subjected to rape as the 'logical' convergence of sex and violence. Conquest, in short" (1981, p. 42).

One key feature about the treatment of Black women in the nineteenth century was how their bodies were objects of display. In the antebellum American South white men did not have to look at pornographic pictures of women because they could become voyeurs of Black women on the auction block. A chilling example of this objectification of the Black female body is provided by the exhibition, in early nineteenth-century Europe, of Sarah Bartmann, the so-called Hottentot Venus. Her display formed one of the original icons for Black female sexuality. An African woman, Sarah Bartmann was often exhibited at fashionable parties in Paris, generally wearing little clothing, to provide entertainment. To her audience she represented deviant sexuality. At the time European audiences thought that Africans had deviant sexual practices and searched for physiological differences, such as enlarged penises and malformed female genitalia, as indications of this deviant sexuality. Sarah Bartmann's exhibition stimulated these racist and sexist beliefs. After her death in 1815, she was dissected. Her genitalia and buttocks remain on display in Paris (Gilman, 1985).

Sander Gilman explains the impact that Sarah Bartmann's exhibition had on Victorian audiences:

> It is important to note that Sarah Bartmann was exhibited not to show her genitalia—but rather to present another anomaly which the European audience . . . found riveting. This was the steatopygia, or protruding buttocks, the other physical characteristic of the Hottentot female which captured the eye of early European travelers. . . . The figure of Sarah Bartmann was reduced to her sexual parts. The audience which had paid to see her buttocks and had fantasized about the uniqueness of her genitalia when she was alive could, after her death and dissection, examine both. (1985, p. 213)

In this passage, Gilman unwittingly describes how Bartmann was used as a pornographic object similar to how women are represented in contemporary pornography. She was reduced to her sexual parts, and these parts came to represent a dominant icon applied to Black women throughout the nineteenth century. Moreover, the fact that Sarah Bartmann was both African and a woman underscores the importance of gender in maintaining notions of racial purity. In this case Bartmann symbolized Blacks as a "race." Thus the creation of the icon applied to Black women demonstrates that notions of gender, race, and sexuality were linked in overarching structures of political domination and economic exploitation.

The process illustrated by the pornographic treatment of the bodies of enslaved African women and of women like Sarah Bartmann has developed into a full-scale industry encompassing all women objectified differently by racial/ethnic category. Contemporary portrayals of Black women in pornography represent the continuation of the historical treatment of their actual bodies. African-American women are usually depicted in a situation of bondage and slavery, typically in a submissive posture, and often with two white men. As Bell observes, "this setting reminds us of all the trappings of slavery: chains, whips, neck braces, wrist clasps" (1987, p. 59). White women and women of color have different pornographic images applied to them. The image of Black women in pornography is almost consistently one featuring them breaking from chains. The image of Asian women in pornography is almost consistently one of being tortured (Bell, 1987, p. 161).

The pornographic treatment of Black women's bodies challenges the prevailing feminist assumption that since pornography primarily affects white women, racism has been grafted onto pornography. African-American women's experiences suggest that Black women were not added into a preexisting pornography, but rather that pornography itself must be reconceptualized as an example of the interlocking nature of race, gender, and class oppression. At the heart of both racism and sexism are notions of biological determinism claiming that people of African descent and women possess immutable biological characteristics marking their inferiority to elite white men (Fausto-Sterling, 1989; Gould, 1981; Halpin, 1989). In pornography these racist and sexist beliefs are sexualized. Moreover, for African-American women pornography has not been timeless and universal but was tied to Black women's experiences with the European colonization of Africa and with American slavery. Pornography emerged within a specific system of social class relationships.

This linking of views of the body, social constructions of race and gender, and conceptualizations of sexuality that informs Black women's treatment as pornographic objects promises to have significant implications for how we assess contemporary pornography. Moreover, examining how pornography has been central to the race, gender, and class oppression of African-American women offers new routes for understanding the dynamics of power as domination.

Investigating racial patterns in pornography offers one route for such an analysis. Black women have often claimed that images of white women's sexuality were intertwined with the controlling image of the sexually denigrated Black woman: "In the United States, the fear and fascination of female sexuality was projected onto black women; the passionless lady arose in symbiosis with the primitively sexual slave" (Hall, 1983, p. 333). Comparable linkages exist in pornography (Gardner, 1980). Alice Walker provides a fictional account of a Black man's growing awareness of the different ways that African-American and white women are objectified in pornography: "What he has refused to see—because to see it would reveal yet another area in which he is unable to protect or defend black women—is that where white women are depicted in pornography as 'objects,' black women are depicted as animals. Where white women are depicted as human bodies if not beings, black women are depicted as shit" (Walker, 1981, p. 52).

Walker's distinction between "objects" and "animals" is crucial in untangling gender, race, and class dynamics in pornography. Within the mind/body, culture/nature, male/female oppositional dichotomies in Western social thought, objects occupy an uncertain interim position. As objects white women become creations of culture—in this case, the mind of white men—using the materials of nature—in this case, uncontrolled female sexuality. In contrast, as animals Black women receive no such redeeming dose of culture and remain open to the type of exploitation visited on nature overall. Race becomes the distinguishing feature in determining the type of objectification women will encounter. Whiteness as symbolic of both civilization and culture is used to separate objects from animals.

The alleged superiority of men to women is not the only hierarchical relationship that has been linked to the putative superiority of the mind to the body. Certain "races" of people have been defined as being more body-like, more animallike, and less godlike than others (Spelman, 1982, p. 52). Race and gender oppression may both revolve around the same axis of distain for the body; both portray the sexuality of subordinate groups as animalistic and therefore deviant. Biological notions of race and gender prevalent in the early nineteenth century which fostered the animalistic icon of Black female sexuality were joined by the appearance of a racist biology incorporating the concept of degeneracy (Foucault, 1980). Africans and women were both perceived as embodied entities, and Blacks were seen as degenerate. Fear of and distain for the body thus formed a key element in both sexist and racist thinking (Spelman, 1982).

While the sexual and racial dimensions of being treated like an animal are important, the economic foundation underlying this treatment is critical. Animals can be economically exploited, worked, sold, killed, and consumed. As "mules," African-American women become susceptible to such treatment. The political economy of pornography also merits careful attention. Pornography is pivotal in mediating contradictions in changing societies (McNall, 1983). It is no accident that racist biology, religious justifications for slavery and women's subordination, and other explanations for nineteenth-century racism and sexism arose during a period of profound political and economic change. Symbolic means of domination become particularly important in mediating contradictions in changing political economies. The exhibitions of Sarah Bartmann and Black women on the auction block were not benign intellectual exercises—these practices defended real material and political interests. Current transformations in international capitalism require similar ideological justifications. Where does pornography fit in these current transformations? This question awaits a comprehensive Afrocentric feminist analysis.

Publicly exhibiting Black women may have been central to objectifying Black women as animals and to creating the icon of Black women as animals. Yi-Fu Tuan (1984) offers an innovative argument about similarities in efforts to control nature—especially plant life—the domestication of animals, and the domination of certain groups of humans. Tuan suggests that displaying humans alongside animals implies that such humans are more like monkeys and bears than they are like "normal" people. This same juxtaposition leads spectators to view the captive animals in a special way. Animals acquire definitions of being like humans, only more openly carnal and sexual, an aspect of animals that forms a major source of attraction for visitors to modern zoos. In discussing the popularity of monkeys in zoos, Tuan notes: "some visitors are especially attracted by the easy sexual behavior of the monkeys. Voyeurism is forbidden except when applied to subhumans" (1984, p. 82). Tuan's analysis suggests that the public display of Sarah Bartmann and of the countless enslaved African women on the auction blocks of the antebellum American South—especially in proximity to animals—fostered their image as animalistic.

This linking of Black women and animals is evident in nineteenth-century scientific literature. The equality of women, Blacks, and animals is revealed in the following description of an African woman published in an 1878 anthropology text:

> She had a way of pouting her lips exactly like what we have observed in the orangutan. Her movements had something abrupt and fantastical about them, reminding one of those of the ape. Her ear was like that of many apes. . . . These are animal characters. I have never seen a human head more like an ape than that of this woman. (Halpin, 1989, p. 287)

In a climate such as this, it is not surprising that one prominent European physician even stated that Black women's "animallike sexual appetite went so far as to lead black women to copulate with apes" (Gilman, 1985, p. 212).

The treatment of all women in contemporary pornography has strong ties to the portrayal of Black women as animals. In pornography women become nonpeople and are often represented as the sum of their fragmented body parts. Scott McNall observes:

> This fragmentation of women relates to the predominance of rear-entry position photographs. . . . All of these kinds of photographs reduce the woman to her reproductive system, and, furthermore, make her open, willing, and available—not in control. . . . The other thing rear-entry position photographs tell us about women is that they are animals. They are animals because they are the same as dogs—bitches in heat who can't control themselves. (McNall, 1983, 197-198)

This linking of animals and white women within pornography becomes feasible when grounded in the earlier denigration of Black women as animals.

Developing a comprehensive analysis of the race, gender, and class dynamics of pornography offers possibilities for change. Those Black feminist intellectuals investigating sexual politics imply that the situation is much more complicated than that advanced by some prominent white feminists (see, e.g., Dworkin, 1981) in which "men oppress women" because they are men. Such approaches implicitly assume biologically deterministic views of sex, gender, and sexuality and offer few possibilities for change. In contrast, Afrocentric feminist analyses routinely provide for human agency and its corresponding empowerment and for the responsiveness of social structures to human action. In the short story "Coming Apart," Alice Walker describes one Black man's growing realization that his enjoyment of pornography, whether of white women as "objects" or Black women as "animals," degraded him:

> He begins to feel sick. For he realizes that he has bought some of the advertisements about women, black and white. And further, inevitably, he has bought the advertisements about himself. In pornography the black man is portrayed as being capable of fucking anything . . . even a piece of shit. He is defined solely by the size, readiness and unselectivity of his cock. (Walker, 1981, p. 52)

Walker conceptualizes pornography as a race/gender system that entraps everyone. But by exploring an African-American *man's* struggle for a self-defined standpoint on pornography, Walker suggests that a changed consciousness is essential to social change. If a Black man can understand how pornography affects him, then other groups emeshed in the same system are equally capable of similar shifts in consciousness and action. . . .

NOTE

1. Offering a similar argument about the relationship between race and masculinity, Paul Hoch (1979) suggests that the ideal white man is a hero who upholds honor. But inside lurks a "Black beast" of violence and sexuality, traits that the white hero deflects onto men of color.

REFERENCES

Bell, L. (Ed.). (1987). *Good girls/bad girls: Feminists and sex trade workers face to face.* Toronto: Seal Press.

Dworkin, A. (1981). *Pornography: Men possessing women.* New York: Perigree.

Eisenstein, H. (1983). *Contemporary feminist thought.* Boston: G. K. Hall.

Fausto-Sterling, A. (1989). Life in the XY corral. *Women's Studies International Forum, 12*(3), 319-331.

Foucault, M. (1980). *Power/knowledge: Selected interviews and other writings 1972-77* (C. Gordon, Ed.). New York: Pantheon.

Gilman, S. L. (1985). Black bodies, White bodies: Toward an iconography of female sexuality in late nineteenth-century art, medicine, and literature. *Critical Inquiry, 12*(1), 205-243.

Gould, S. J. (1981). *The mismeasure of man.* New York: Norton.

Gardner, T. A. (1990). Racism and pornography in the women's movement. In L. Lederer et al. (Eds.), *Take back the night: Women on pornography.* New York: William Morrow.

Hall, J. D. (1983). The mind that burns in each body: Women, rape, and racial violence. In A. Snitow, C. Stansell, & S. Thompson (Eds.), *Powers of desire: The politics of sexuality.* New York: Monthly Review Press.

Halpin, Z. T. (1989). Scientific objectivity and the concept of "the Other." *Women's Studies International Forum, 12*(3), 285-294.

Hoch, P. (1979). *White hero, Black beast: Racism, sexism and the mask of masculinity.* London: Pluto.

McNall, S. G. (1983). Pornography: The structure of domination and the mode of reproduction. In S. McNall (Ed.), *Current perspectives in social theory* (Vol. 4, pp. 181-203). Greenwich, CT: JAI.

Spelman, E. V. (1982). Theories of race and gender: The erasure of Black women. *Quest, 5*(4), 36-62.

Tuan, Y-F. (1984). *Dominance and affection: The making of pets.* New Haven, CT: Yale University Press.

Walker, A. (1981). Coming apart. In A. Walker, *You can't keep a good woman down* (pp. 41-53). New York: Harcourt Brace Jovanovich.

Racism in Pornography

ALICE MAYALL

DIANA E. H. RUSSELL

I visited seven largely heterosexual pornography stores in the San Francisco Bay area to investigate the kinds of racist pornography being sold. I also wanted to find out which ethnic groups are most often portrayed in pornography, and in what manner. Once in the store I looked at every accessible piece of pornography on every shelf. I noted all the titles and covers that displayed people of color.

I divided the pornography into the following categories: magazines, books, films, videos, and for one store, games and cards. I recorded the total number of items found in each category as well as the number containing people of color in each category.

Once I had identified the pornography as containing a person of color, I listed the title, a description of the cover picture, as well as the type of pornography it represented. My observations of magazines were limited to

NOTE: The original research for this chapter was conducted by Alice Mayall in 1985 when she was an undergraduate at Mills College in Oakland, California. Diana Russell, a professor of sociology at Mills College at that time, supervised Mayall's research. Russell excerpted a section of Mayall's much longer unpublished report on racism in pornography, and radically revised it for this anthology. The "I" in the rest of the chapter refers to Mayall, the "we" refers to both authors. Reprinted from *Making Violence Sexy*, edited by Diana E. H. Russell (New York: Teachers College Press, 1990), by permission of the authors.

their covers because most of them were encased in plastic. I also selected eight pornography books about people of color and Jews in order to make more detailed analyses of their contents.

The salience of skin color is evident in most of the materials displayed in pornography stores. White women were featured in most pornography (92% of total) presumably because they fulfill the prevailing racist equality of beauty with whiteness and Caucasian features. People of color fall into the special interest category, other examples of which are rape, bondage and sado-masochism, anal sex, sex with children, large breasted women, and sex between women. Some pornographic covers also focus on particular body parts or different methods of penetrating bodies.

A large majority of the magazine covers that portrayed people of color in sexual poses ($N = 109$), but not engaged in sexual contact, used African-American women: 73 covers exhibited African-American women, 18 Asian or Asian-American women, and 4 Hispanic women. Of the covers displaying men of color, 9 were African-American transvestites or transsexuals, while 2 others were portrayed as "normal," 3 were Asian transvestites, and only 1 was Hispanic.

My analysis of book titles revealed the same disproportionate numbers of portrayals of African-Americans compared with other people of color. Anti-Semitic pornography is another special interest evident in the book titles examined, along with a smaller amount of anti-Arab pornography. We can think of no explanation for the relatively small amount of pornography using Hispanics, nor why African-Americans are so overrepresented among people of color.

The breakdown of the ethnicity of the 131 cover pictures in which a person of color was displayed in a state of sexual contact is too complex to describe completely as there are so many possible interethnic and intraethnic permutations. The largest number of these covers portrayed African-American women with white men (28), followed by white women with African-American men (20), Asian women with white men (17), and Asian women with men of unknown ethnicity (12).

Significantly, as judged by these covers, interest in intraethnic heterosexual relations was minimal. For example, there were only six covers portraying sex between African-American women and men, and two portraying intra-Asian sex. Homosexual themes were also uncommon: There were six covers depicting sex between African-American and white men, four depicting African-American and white women, three depicting Asian women together, two African-American women together, and two African-American and Asian women together. Obviously there are some porn stores that cater specifically to the gay male community. The representation of gay men engaged in interethnic sex may well be very different in such stores.

When people of color are used in books, magazines, or videos, the titles usually conveyed this information for consumers. For example, an average of 77% of the magazines on display in six different stores identified the ethnicity of the person in the title. This presumably means that skin color is very salient to most consumers. It comes as no surprise in a racist culture like the United States, that people of color are a specialty item in pornography.

It was sometimes difficult to determine the ethnicity of the people on magazine covers portraying explicit sexual contact, especially in some of the bondage photographs. For example, I compiled a long list of "Asian Woman and Unknown Man" for which it was impossible to determine the ethnic identity of the penis photographed. With regard to magazines that portrayed explicit sexual-genital contact, there were *very* few in which African-Americans were present without whites. By and large, African-American men who consume pornography have a choice of buying magazines in which only whites are portrayed, or in which white men use African-American women or African-American men use white women. Whether these disproportionate portrayals of the ethnicity of pornographic covers reflect the interest of the consumers or the makers of pornography, we do not know. However, these findings are consistent with Alice Walker's (1981) observation that pornography serves to drive African-American men and women away from each other.

A majority of the men depicted in pornography as transvestites and transsexuals are people of color. Perhaps it is more acceptable to portray people of color as "social deviants." Some of the pornography titles listed in Figure 33.1 provide examples of blatant racist stereotypes, for example, "Animal Sex Among Black Women," "Black Bitch," "Black Girl's Animal Love," "Bitch's Black Stud," "Gang Banged by Blacks," "Geisha's Girls," "Oriental Sadist's Pet," "Raped by Arab Terrorists," "Bound Harem Girl."

Note that the term "bitch" is exclusively used for African-American women in the list of titles recorded in Figure 33.1. The word bitch means female dog. In contrast with other women of color, several titles in Figure 33.1 associate animals with African-American women. As Alice Walker has pointed out, "where white women are depicted in pornography as 'objects,' Black women are depicted as animals. Where white women are at least depicted as human bodies if not beings, Black women are depicted as shit" (Walker, 1981, p. 103). Luisah Teish (1980, p. 117) makes a similar point in her chapter "A Quiet Subversion."

Tracey Gardner makes an interesting observation about male preferences: "I have noticed that while white men like black women 'looking baaad' in leather with whips, Black men like Black women in bondage, helpless and submissive" (1980, p. 113).

Asian women tend to be depicted either as sweet young lotus blossoms or objects of bondage. The notorious December 1984 issue of *Penthouse* contained a nine-picture spread of Asian women, some of whom were

> bound tightly with ropes cutting into their ankles, wrists, labias and buttocks. Two of the images showed women bound and hanging from trees, heads lolling forward, apparently dead. . . . Throughout these murderous images are sprinkled "artsy" haiku quotes which exude dominance and subordination. (Farley, 1992)

African-Americans	*Nazi-Jewish*
Animal Sex Among Black Women	Gestapo Bondage Brothel
Animals and Black Women	Gestapo Lust Slave
Bisexual Teacher	Gestapo Sex Crimes
Bitch's Black Stud	Gestapo Stud Farm
Black Beauty	Gestapo Training School
Black Bitch	Nazi Dungeon Slave
Black Fashion Model	Nazi Sex Captives
Black Ghetto Teens	Nazi Whip Mistress
Black Girl's Animal Love	Sadist's Prisoner
Black Head Nurse	Sluts of the S.S.
Black Lady's Lust for Girls	Swastika She Devil
Black Leather Doll	
Black Passion	*Asian*
Black Stepfather	
Black Teacher	Bawdy Tales of Wu Wu Wang
Black Woman's Hunger	Bloody Encounters
Boy for Black Mama	Geisha's Girls
By Sex Possessed	Geisha's Torment
Candy's Black Lover	Japanese Sadist's Dungeon
Dark Detective	May Ling's Master
Diner Doll	Oriental Sadist's Pet
Demon Dictator	Samurai Slave Girl
Gang Banged by Blacks	Teen Slaves of Saigon
Garment Center Black Sex	Vietcong Rape Compound
The Heiress' Black Slave Boy	Whips of Chinatown
Her New White Master	
Hot for Black Studs	*Asian/Indian*
Man-Hungry Black Bitch	
Mother's Black Lovers	The Talking Pussy
Seductive Black Bitch	
Spread Black Thighs	*Arab*
Teacher's Black Passion	
Young Intern's Surprise	Bound Harem Girl
	Harem Hell
	Raped by Arab Terroists
	Sheik's Hand Maiden

This is a complete list of the pornography book titles that portrayed people of color on their covers from six stores.

Figure 33.1 Pornographic Book Titles Using People of Color

These femicidal photographs eroticizing the murder of Asian women prompted Nikki Craft and Melissa Farley to organize a 2-year feminist rampage against *Penthouse* in nine states. More than 100 women participants in the rampage were arrested for their civil disobedience activities (Farley, 1992).

Some of the book titles presented historical periods of abuse as if they were sexually stimulating, for example, the enslavement of African-Americans—"The Heiress' Black Slave Boy," "Her Non-White Master"—and the genocide of Jews—"Gestapo Lust Slave," "Nazi Sex Captives."

The magazine titles are much the same as those used on books. A few examples of particularly racist titles include "Jungle Babies," "Wet, Wild and Black," "Black Mother Fucker," "Geisha Twat," "Hot Asian Asses," "Oriental Pussy," and "Oriental Bondage."

Dorchen Leidholdt points out that "pornography contains a racial hierarchy in which women are rated as prized objects or despised objects according to their color" (1981, p. 20). Nevertheless, Hugh Hefner ignorantly boasted "that portraying women of color as sex objects to a predominantly white male readership is a radical development that shows *Playboy*'s social conscience" (Leidholdt, 1981, p. 20). Gardner perceives *Playboy*'s inclusion of African-American women as follows:

> So, Black women have been elevated from the status of whore to "Playmate." Now white boys can put them in *Playboy* without damaging the magazine's respectability too much (though after the first appearance of Black women in *Playboy*, there were some angry letters to the editor saying "get them niggers out." (1980, p. 113)

The following section presents a content analysis of eight books that exemplify the racism and violence against women prevalent in such "literature." These eight books represent literally thousands of books that are presumably read regularly by thousands of men in the United States, and of course, by men in other countries as well.

Soul Slave (Anonymous, 1981b) is one of a series of "Punishment Books" that presents violent sexual attacks as pleasurable for the women. A 16-year-old African-American woman is portrayed in *Soul Slave* as the willing victim of her white master. The following passages are typical examples of the contents of this book.

> Rance Godwin leaned over and drove his fist right into my lower stomach. I jerked and sighed when he gave me that blow, and I listened to the words that he had to say to me. "I told you to get naked, you nigger slut," he said. And I knew then that, no matter how much I loved the pain, I would have to get naked. (p. 22)

Soul Slave is filled with examples of this kind of masochism. The "hero" commands his "soul slave":

> "Say that you like it. I know that you do. There is nothing that a nigger girl likes more than being hit by a white man." And I did not know if the feelings that I had would be like the feelings that all nigger girls had, but I did know that I did like it. (p. 71)

The author implies that the woman's pain is special because it is inflicted on an African-American woman by a white man. The derogatory term "nigger" is used approximately 245 times in the 180-page book. This word is frequently put in the mouth of the young woman to describe herself and other African-Americans, and she is always depicted as enjoying it. For example, "Rance looked down at me and said, 'Get naked, Nigger!' And these words were like the greatest poetry in the world to me" (1981, p. 20).

A second book entitled *Black Head Nurse* (Dakin, 1977), is a compilation of sexual encounters between patients, nurses, and doctors in a Harlem hospital. Interracial sex is presumed to constitute evidence that racial or sexual discrimination is not a problem. "In this hospital there is no discrimination. . . . Black nurses, white doctors, black doctors, white patients. It's all the same when the great equalizer Sex comes into play" (p. 34). Absurd as this statement is, it is widely believed that sexual unions nullify sexism and racism.

For example, "It just blew their minds to see this white chick on her knees begging that black dude to give her a little" (p. 142). One of the messages here is that it is extraordinary for a white woman to beg an African-American man for sex. On the other hand, African-American women are frequently portrayed in pornographic literature as begging white men for sex. For example, "Sucking on this fancy white doctor's cock was certainly living the good life. No one could talk her out of that" (p. 178).

The stereotypically tough, powerful, African-American woman is played out in *Black Head Nurse*: "Up in the Harlem hospitals black nurses rule" (p. 34). The most powerful African-American women are portrayed as physically aggressive dykes. For example, the sadistic head nurse is depicted as whipping her nurses and as seducing another young woman.

Black Head Nurse presents other stereotypes about African-American life. For example, this is how the author describes the success story of an African-American doctor:

> He had worked his way through one of the toughest medical schools in the East and his mother hadn't even scrubbed floors! Of course, she had to push a lot of drugs and fuck a lot, but even Scott knew that some sacrifice was in order. After all, he had forfeited a lot of good times himself by studying.

The author also normalizes notions of sexually promiscuous African-American children. For example, a 13-year-old African-American female patient, the leader of a gang of girls who thrive on sex, is portrayed as propositioning an African-American doctor for a blow job. He eventually satisfies her wishes. In another case an African-American madam recalls her childhood: "She remembered her first sexual experiences as a small child in a crowded bedroom where all her brothers and sisters slept together. Already at the age of ten she was an expert at blowing her brothers off and eating out her sisters" (p. 175).

Abuse: Black and Battered (Anonymous, 1981a) is described as a collection of "true" case studies based on "Dr. Lamb's" interviews with eight African-

American women. Violent sexual attacks are vividly described in coarse and racist language in all of these stories. They begin with a description of the woman's skin color, so important in this racist country. For example, one woman is depicted as a mulatto, whose "skin is an incredible light cream color." And, "Ellie is a short, attractive black woman, whose skin is a lovely cream shade" (p. 5). "Shari is a very dark-skinned black girl . . ." (p. 22). Some descriptions focus on other ethnicity-related features of physical appearance. For example, "Her nose is flat and her nostrils are large, yet her lips are thin and sleek looking."

The first woman portrayed in these fake case studies observed after her alcoholic African-American husband raped her, "I thought he was letting me go, but you can bet no drunk nigger was gonna do that." In the second case, the woman gives a lengthy, gory description of watching her African-American father raping her mother. He and his friends later rape her when she is 16 years old. Four other cases also depict young girls observing their fathers raping their mothers.

In one particularly racist story, a young girl watches her white father having a positive sexual encounter with her mother. After his death, her mother remarries an African-American man who forces her into violent sexual acts. The mulatto daughter is later gang raped in school by a group of African-American girls and, at another time, by a gang of African-American boys, because she is a "half-nigger." When she gets out of the ghetto by going to college, she has a wonderful sexual relationship with a blonde college man.

The fourth story portrays a girl who is repeatedly raped and gang raped by her father and three brothers. In three other stories, the women have been raped as children or as young teenagers by their African-American fathers, other African American male family members, or male friends of their fathers. In one case a man is described as watching his father rape his mother. His mother then rapes him after his father dies.

The last interview depicts a woman who becomes a prostitute after she was raped by her father and by a gang of African-American men. She blames the ghetto, not the racist social structure, for all this violence: "So blow it up. . . . Just get it off the fucking face of the earth and save other ghetto girls from the shit we're put through" (Anonymous, 1981, p. 177). As is typical in pornography, all the perpetrators of sexual violence in these "case studies" escape punishment.

In *Black Ghetto Teens* (Marr, 1977), teenage African-American girls are depicted as thriving on "stealing, lying, and fucking those rich white dudes who come to the city looking for some nice Black meat" (p. 4). An African-American woman in *Soul Food* is raped by three white men. "He got to his feet and grabbed the black girl by her hair. He forced his thick, white cock into her mouth" (Berry, 1978, p. 21). As the pornography industry keeps broadcasting to the world, the victim ends up enjoying the rape: "She had gained some confidence from having sex [sic] with the three men." The woman tells her rapists, " 'You really have taught me something,' Pearl laughed. . . . "It can be fun. My ex asked me to do things like this and I always told Bruce 'no way' " Rape as a liberating experience for women is a popular male fantasy in pornography.

Another common racist and sexist myth about African-American women is articulated in *Soul Food*. One of the white rapists explains:

"I was curious to know what it would be like to screw a black girl," he told her. "I've heard some black women are more lewd and animalistic." "Were they right?" Pearl asked anxiously. Throwing his arms around her, Mike assured her that she was all he had hoped for and more.

After another man's first "screw" with an African-American woman, he compliments her on her "animal lustiness." In several other encounters with white men, African-American women's "animalistic lust," sexual prowess, and desire for pain are stressed.

In *Animal Sex Among Black Women* (Washington, 1983), the case study fabrication is used again, even including a bibliography listing other pornography books about sex with animals. This particular book presents five stories of African-American women having voluntary or coerced sexual encounters with animals. In one fantasy, a go-go dancer is coerced by two African-American men into having sex with a dog. In another, an African-American woman finds comfort in sex with a German shepherd after being dumped by a white man. "All of a sudden I felt a sense of belonging. I had found someone who needed me," she said of her new pet (p. 74). Later, she sees her need for the dog as punishment: "I guess it serves me right for fucking around with a white guy. . . . If I was going to fuck with a guy, it should have been a black guy, not some white stud like Gary" (pp. 80-81).

In a third fantasy, a 31-year-old twice-divorced dental assistant has sex with an African-American ex-fighter, and then has sex with her male cat. Another go-go dancer is paid by an African-American man to have sex with him and his Doberman. And finally, after a 34-year-old divorcee meets a white woman at a bar, she goes home to have sex with her and her Dalmatian.

In the 160-page *Black Fashion Model* (Wilson, 1978), the word "black" is used 155 times to describe people, "white" 50 times, and "Negress" eight times. As usual, the African-American rape victims end up loving the abuse. One victim's thoughts as she is forced to have oral sex with a man are described as follows: "I must be the worst little nigger girl in the entire city. . . . Here I am sucking this man's cock like a tramp . . . and worst of all, I'm enjoying it."

And again, the fact that the woman was African-American is portrayed as rendering the rape all the more gratifying for her white rapist: "It was twice as exciting to him because she was black and he was white." As consumers of pornography often do not know what is true and what is false about female sexuality, particularly the sexuality of women of color, myths like this one probably encourage some white men to rape African-American women in search of the heightened gratification described (for example, see Russell, 1975, pp. 129-140).

One blatantly anti-Semitic book, *Sluts of the S.S.* (Anonymous, 1979), uses the torture of Jewish women as its source of excitement. This book starts with a description of Rachel's first experience of intercourse with her Jewish boyfriend. The author emphasizes the relationship between sex and ethnicity: "Fuck me," Rachel whispered. "Fuck me, Aaron. I want to feel your hard Jewish cock inside me. Take me. Take me now." (p. 8).

Throughout the book there are rapes, killings, as well as non-violent sex. In the rapes by Nazis, Jewish women are referred to as "Jewish dog," "Jewish whore," "Yiddish swine," "Jewish slut," and so forth, while the Nazis refer to themselves as members of the master race. " 'Whore,' he yelled. 'You will love the cock of your master.' "

There are especially violent scenes of Jewish women being kicked to death, raped anally, forced to eat human excrement, and being killed by dogs. "Filthy Jewish slut," he barked. "Drink my Nazi piss, you little pig" (p. 106). And:

> She sucked off the cum and blood and shit from his dick as he pounded it into her throat. She gagged at the taste and at the force with which he was fucking her face. He let go with a stream of hot piss and nearly drowned her as he filled her mouth with his hot yellow piss stream choking her as she tried to swallow it. "Human toilet," he sneered. . . . (p. 107)

A relationship between a Nazi man and a Jewish woman is portrayed in the midst of all this violence. It begins when she is imprisoned as a prostitute for Nazis and he pays to have sex with her. She likes him and becomes the classic willing victim, no longer "enslaved." But their relationship turns violent when he sees her being forced to eat shit by another Nazi. In reaction to her "inherent dirtiness," he sets out to kill and rape Jews: "Hans could not wait to turn his dogs loose on a pack of helpless, cowering, filthy Jews" (p. 123). For her part, she goes out at night to lure Nazi men into dark corners for sex—then slits their throats instead.

Sluts of the S.S. is a series of explicit descriptions of sexual interactions—warped, violent, and sometimes "loving." It is written to excite the reader with the violence, which is portrayed as being highly pleasurable. The Jewish woman ends up needing and wanting the Nazi man despite the fact that he treated her perversely and physically assaulted her. According to this tale, she was as much at "fault" as he was, and in the end they were *both* able to forgive and forget.

CONCLUSION

This study's main purpose was to document the way different ethnic groups are portrayed in pornography. No comparable studies have been undertaken, to our knowledge.

The content analysis of seven pornography books about African-Americans shows that they were depicted in a variety of derogatory and stereotypic ways—as animalistic, incapable of self-control, sexually depraved, impulsive, unclean, and so forth. This kind of pornography is likely to foster racist-sexist stereotypes as well as racist-sexist behavior, including sexual abuse and sexual violence against African-American girls and women. Similarly, anti-Semitic pornography is likely to foster anti-Semitic sexism as well as sexual violence against Jewish girls and women. Future studies should include books portraying a greater variety of people of color, as well as whites.

An important unanswered question is why the liberal and radical community, as well as people of color who are not part of this community, appear to be totally unconcerned about the racism in pornographic materials in contrast to their concern about other manifestations of racism, such as those in ads, literature, media, verbal statements, and so on. If it is due to ignorance, then bringing the virulent racism in pornography to people's attention, as we have done in this chapter, will hopefully shock them into action.

Unfortunately, we think there is a more consequential explanation for this apathy about racist pornography. The combination of sex and racism appears to blunt people's response to pornographic racism just as the combination of sex and violence appears to dull concern about the consequences of violent pornography.

Teish explains the lack of reaction by African-American women as follows: "Pornography is a branch of the media that Black-activist feminists have considered a 'white market' " (1980, p. 117). Many others have shared the perception that pornography has little relevance for people of color ever since the President's Commission on Obscenity and Pornography reported that the buyers of pornography were "predominantly white, middle-class, middle-aged males" (1970). While not necessarily contradicting this view, Gardner nevertheless maintains that:

> The Black man, like the white man, is buying pornography. He is beating, raping, and murdering all kinds of women. Black women are going to have to deal with him on this. But when we do, we must deal with the Black man as a Black man, not as a white man. In this country it is the *white* man who is producing pornography, and it is the *white* man who is profiting from it. (1980, p. 113).

Dorchen Leidholdt offers two other reasons why the liberal left has been, and continues to be, indifferent to racism in pornography.

> First, in liberal ideology there is an invisible boundary separating the public and political from the personal and sexual. Whereas liberals readily deplore inequality and injustice in the public sector, the private sphere—and sexual relationships in particular—are sacrosanct. Radical feminists' insistence that the personal is political and that public life grows out of private, sexual interactions has been ignored or denied. Second, some "progressive" men have not simply ignored pornography's racism, they have incorporated it into their personal sexual repertoires. (1981, p. 20)

Whatever the best explanations turn out to be, it is vital that people start to question their old assumptions about pornography, including racist pornography. Addressing African-American activists in particular, Teish recommended in 1980 that the "clearly ignored" area of pornography deserves further investigation (p. 117). The liberal, radical, and feminist communities must recognize the glaring contradiction in being concerned about the destructive effects of racism and outraged by all manifestations of it—except when it appears in pornography.

REFERENCES

Anonymous. (1979). *Sluts of the S.S.* New York: Star.

Anonymous. (1981a). *Abuse: Black and battered.* New York: Star.

Anonymous. (1981b). *Soul slave.* New York: Star.

Berry, B. (1978). *Soul food.* Los Angeles: Sutton House.

Dakin, C. (1977). *Black head nurse.* New York: Star.

Farley, M. (1992). The rampage against *Penthouse.* In J. Radford & D. Russell (Eds.), *Femicide: The politics of woman killing* (pp. 334-445). New York: Twayne.

Gardner, T. (1980). Racism in pornography and the women's movement. In L. Lederer et al. (Eds.), *Take back the night: Women on pornography.* New York: William Morrow.

Leidholdt, D. (1981, March 15). Where pornography meets fascism. *WIN Magazine,* pp. 18-22.

Marr, M. (1977). *Black ghetto teens.* New York: Star.

President's Commission on Obscenity and Pornography. (1970). *The report of the Commission on Obscenity and Pornography.* New York: Bantam.

Russell, D. (1975). *The politics of rape.* New York: Stein & Day.

Teish, L. (1980). A quiet subversion. In L. Lederer et al. (Eds.), *Take back the night* (pp. 115-118). New York: William Morrow.

Walker, A. (1981). Coming apart. In A. Walker, *You can't keep a good woman down* (pp. 41-53). New York: Harcourt Brace Jovanovich.

Washington, S. (1983). *Animal sex among Black women.* North Hollywood, CA: American Art Enterprises.

Wilson, J. (1978). *Black fashion model.* South Laguna, CA: Publishers Consultants.

.34

Pornography and the Limits of Experimental Research

ROBERT JENSEN

We live in a culture that likes "science" answers provided by "experts," even when the questions are primarily about human values. Not surprisingly, experimental laboratory research has played an important role in the debate over pornography in the past three decades.[1] Advocates of regulation, both feminist and conservative, cite studies showing links between pornography and violence, whereas opponents of regulation point to other studies that show no link or that are inconclusive. One government commission read the evidence to support increased regulation (Attorney General's Commission, 1986); an earlier commission used the evidence available at that time to support lifting most regulation (Commission on Obscenity and Pornography, 1970).

Experimental research on pornography's effects looks at the perceptual and behavioral effects of viewing or reading sexually explicit material. A typical study might expose groups of subjects to different types or levels of sexually explicit material for comparison to a control group that views non-sexual material. Researchers look for significant differences between the groups on a measure of, for example, male attitudes toward rape. One such measure could be subjects' assessments of the suffering experienced by sexual assault victims or subjects' judgments of the appropriate prison sentence for a rapist. From such controlled testing—measuring the effect of an experimental stimulus (exposure to pornography) on a dependent variable (attitudes toward women or sex) in randomly selected groups—researchers make claims, usually tentative, about causal relationships.

Although there is disagreement among researchers about what has been "proved" by these studies (Linz, 1989; Zillmann, 1989), some themes emerge. I will be questioning the value of these studies, but I follow Weaver's (1992) assessment. He reads the evidence to support the sexual callousness model, which suggests that exposure to pornography activates sexually callous perceptions of women and promotes sexually aggressive behavior by men (Zillmann & Bryant, 1982; Zillmann & Weaver, 1989). This appears to be the result of both pornography's promotion of a loss of respect for female sexual autonomy and the disinhibition of men's expression of aggression against women (Weaver, 1992, p. 307).

After reviewing the experimental research, Russell (1988, 1993a) outlined four factors that link pornography to sexual violence. Pornography (a) predisposes some males to desire rape or intensifies this desire, (b) undermines some males' internal inhibitions against acting out rape desires, (c) undermines some males' social inhibitions against acting out rape desires and (d) undermines some potential victims' abilities to avoid or resist rape.

Taking a different approach, Donnerstein, Linz and Penrod (1987) argue that only pornography that combines violence and sex has been shown to be harmful, and then only in the sense of immediate effects; they hesitate to speculate on the long term. They conclude that there is not enough evidence to show that exposure to nonviolent pornography leads to increases in aggression against women under most circumstances, suggesting that "some forms of pornography, under some conditions, promote certain antisocial attitudes and behavior" (p. 171).

My work on pornography is grounded in a radical feminist critique that focuses on how male dominance and female submission is sexualized. Pornography is an expression and reinforcement of a male sexuality rooted in the subordination of women that endorses the sexual objectification of, and that can promote sexual violence against, women (Dworkin, 1981; Itzin, 1992; MacKinnon, 1987; Russell, 1993b). Although much of the experimental work supports that position, I argue that we need to be skeptical of the value of such studies, no matter what the results; the limits of the experimental approach should lead us to look elsewhere for answers.

THE LIMITS OF EXPERIMENTAL RESEARCH

In addition to a number of specific technical complaints over methodology and research design (summarized and rejected by Donnerstein et al., 1987, pp. 12-22), most of the critics of these studies suggest that any connection between pornography and sexual violence found in the lab is probably overstated; they warn of overgeneralizing from experimental studies because the effects found might evaporate outside the lab:

It is a considerable leap from the laboratory to the corner store where men rifle the pages of magazines kept on the top shelf. It is a long step from the laboratory exposure to such stimuli and subsequent aggression to real world sexual and physical abuse. (Brannigan & Goldenberg, 1987, p. 277)

Although it is possible that the research overreaches, we should be at least as concerned that lab studies underestimate pornography's role in promoting misogynistic attitudes and behavior (see also, Dines-Levy, 1988).

First, these studies may be incapable of measuring subtle effects that develop over time. If pornography works to develop attitudes and shape behavior after repeated exposure, there is no guarantee that studies exposing people to a small amount of pornography over a short time can accurately measure anything. For example, in one study, the group exposed to what the researchers called the "massive" category of pornography viewed six explicitly sexual 8-minute films per session for six sessions, or a total of 4 hours and 48 minutes of material (Zillmann & Bryant, 1982). The "intermediate" group saw half the number of sexual films. These categories are constructed, obviously, for comparative purposes, not to suggest that such an amount of viewing is massive. But even within the confines of a laboratory study, these amounts may be inadequate to test anything.

In addition, as Brannigan and Goldenberg (1987) suggest, no lab can reproduce the natural setting of the behavior being studied. They paint a rather harmless picture of men paging through magazines in the corner store, but what about the other common settings for the consumption of pornography. How is watching a pornographic movie in a university video lab (the experience of experimental subjects) different from being one of a dozen men in a dark movie theater, frightened but excited by the illicit nature of the setting? How is the lab different from the living room of a fraternity house where a group of young men might watch a pornographic videotape, drinking beer and urging each other to enjoy the tape? And how does the act of masturbating to pornography, a common male experience, influence the way in which men interpret and are affected by pornography?

The lab experience is unreal in terms of both the physical and the psychological environments. If experimental data seem to suggest, for example, that exposure to depictions in which women appear to enjoy being raped can increase men's acceptance of sexual violence against women and increase men's endorsement of that rape myth (Malamuth & Check, 1981), can we assume that those effects will be even more pronounced on a man who views that same sexual material in a real-world environment in which male aggression is often encouraged and sanctioned? Because it would be impossible, not to mention ethically unacceptable, to recreate such a situation in a lab, we must question the value of lab data. Instead of assuming that the lab overstates the potential for aggression, we should consider how it could understate the effect.

These problems are compounded if one acknowledges that such studies can never be impartial and objective and always are value-laden. Researchers generally accept a mainstream definition of what is to be considered "normal" sexuality. Although the existence of sexual drive and interests is in some ways "natural," or biologically based, the form our sexual practices take is socially constructed, and that construction in this culture is rooted in the politics of gender. Relying on the majority view to determine what is erotic implicitly endorses the sexual status quo, which means accepting patriarchal definitions.

This point about values often is used by sexual libertarians, who contend that by labeling practices such as sadomasochism "deviant," research is biased. But the critique also has to come from a different angle; in patriarchal society, what has been considered normal sex generally has been what serves to enhance men's pleasure; the line between "normal" intercourse and "deviant" rape is a fine one. As Catharine MacKinnon (1989) puts it, "Compare victims' reports of rape with women's reports of sex. They look a lot alike" (p. 146).[2] Researchers must make value judgments about what is erotic, nonviolent and normal, and those decisions define what is a deviant, unhealthy, callous or socially undesirable response to the material. It is not that any specific researcher has blundered by letting value judgments in, but that such research always makes normative judgments about sexuality.

LISTENING TO STORIES

> He held up a porn magazine with a picture of a beaten woman and said, "I want you to look like that. I want you to hurt." He then began beating me. (*Public Hearings*, 1983, p. 48)

It would be simplistic and misleading to suggest that the magazine was the sole cause of the beating, and the vast majority of activists and scholars in the feminist antipornography movement do not make such a claim (Russell, 1988, 1993a). Still, for many people that lack of deterministic causality means that society cannot give the woman who was beaten any legal recourse against the creators and peddlers of the pornography. That simplistic view of causation is of little value in examining human behavior, which is always the product of complex factors and unpredictable contingencies. The important research question is not, What kind of experiment will tell us about causation? but, rather, If we listen to people's accounts of the world, what do we learn?

Positivist social science considers the evidence that comes from such testimony to be merely "anecdotal" and warns that generalizing from personal experience is problematic. From that view, the fact that a woman was sexually assaulted by a man who modeled his attack on a pornographic work tells us nothing about how pornography generally influences male sexual behavior toward women. For proof of causation, social scientists look to the laboratory, not experience:

> Even if we were to observe a nearly one-to-one relationship between viewing violent pornography and committing a sexual assault or rape

in the real world, this finding is not as compelling in a causal sense as is an experiment. (Donnerstein et al., 1987, p. 10)

Donnerstein et al. have faith in the possibilities of lab research to answer these questions, although other researchers who share their loyalty to experimental methods are far less optimistic about proving causation. Zillmann (1989), for example, warns that "research on pornography cannot be definitive. It cannot satisfy the demands for rigor and compellingness that have been placed on it" (p. 398). He believes that social science can, however, be of value in guiding policy and making final decisions. Although not definitive, this research is "far superior to hearsay, guessing, and unchecked common sense" (p. 399). But is guessing the only alternative to experimental research?

The work of feminist scholars who have challenged Western science's claims of objectivity and neutrality (e.g., Harding, 1991) and proposed alternatives to traditional methods of social science research (Reinharz, 1992) makes it clear that human behavior and social patterns can be understood through research that takes seriously the stories people tell about their lives. This kind of research, as Marilyn Frye (1990) points out, rests "on a most empirical base: staking your life on the trustworthiness of your own body as a source of knowledge" (p. 177). Instead of looking to science for answers to questions it cannot answer, we can look to each other.

What we learn from the testimony of women and men whose lives have been touched by pornography is how the material is *implicated* in violence against women and how it can perpetuate, reinforce and be part of a wider system of woman hating. Rather than discussing simple causation, we think of how various factors "make something inviting."[3] In those terms, pornography does not cause rape but, rather, helps make rape inviting. Research should examine people's stories about their experiences with pornography and sexual violence to help us determine how close is the relationship between the material and the actions, which can inform personal and collective decisions. This kind of examination will not produce certainty. The work of judging narratives can be difficult and sometimes messy; the process doesn't claim clear, objective standards that experimental research appears to offer. There are no experts to ask for authoritative answers; we all are responsible for building responsible and honest communal practices.

Although often drowned out in the policy debate, the stories that people tell about pornography have begun to be collected, both in public hearings and through research. Sources for the experiences of women include the following:

1. Silbert and Pines's study (1984) of prostitutes, in which 73% of the 200 women interviewed reported being raped, and 24% of those women mentioned that their assailants made reference to pornography.

2. Russell's survey (1980) of more than 900 women about experiences with sexual violence, which includes women's responses to the question, "Have you ever been upset by anyone trying to get you to do

what they'd seen in pornographic pictures, movies, or books?" Of the women, 10% reported at least one such experience.

3. Kelly's (1988) detailed interviews with 60 British women about how they experience sexual violence, during which women reported that pornography often is a part of the continuum of violence.

4. The Minneapolis hearings (*Public Hearings*, 1983) on a proposed antipornography civil rights ordinance, which included the testimony of a number of women about how pornography was used in acts of sexual violence against them.

5. The hearings of the Attorney General's Commission (1986), which gave women a forum to tell about their experiences with pornography.

There also is a small but growing body of work on men's experiences with pornography through autobiography and research (e.g., Kimmel, 1990; Marshall, 1988). I have conducted in-depth interviews with male pornography consumers and convicted sex offenders that illustrate the different ways in which pornography is an important factor in the sexually abusive acts of some men (Jensen, 1992). Those interviews provide specific examples of how pornography can (a) be an important factor in shaping a male-dominant view of sexuality, (b) contribute to a user's difficulty in separating sexual fantasy and reality, (c) be used to initiate victims and break down resistance to sexual activity and (d) provide a training manual for abuse. A quick tour through some of those stories follows.

Although some of the pornography consumers I interviewed reported positive effects in their lives from pornography consumption, some of the consumers and all of the sex offenders identified pornography as an unhealthy influence on their sexuality, hurting their intimate relationships with women. One sex offender, echoing a common experience, reported that heavy use of pornography beginning as a child contributed to his belief that women "were made for sex and that's all." The men's narratives make it clear that pornography was not the only source of such messages in their lives but was important in shaping their sexuality.

Another theme that emerged in some men's accounts was pornography's role in blurring the line between fantasy and reality. One man, who was convicted of molesting two 6-year-old girls and said he also had raped teenage girls, explained how he would masturbate at home to pornography while thinking of the young girls who rode the bus he drove and then watch the girls on the bus while fantasizing about the pornography.

Another man convicted of sexually abusing his teenage stepdaughter explained that he watched pornographic videotapes with her before and during sex. The tapes served both to break down the girl's initial resistance to his sexual overtures, showing her that such sex was "normal," and provide him with fantasy material that allowed him to pretend that he was having sex with the women on the screen, not with his stepdaughter.

Finally, although pornography may not independently create desire for a specific sexual act, pornographic scenarios shaped some men's sexual practices. One man—who detailed an extensive history of pornography use, visits to prostitutes and rape and sexual abuse of women and girls—said he believed his obsession of having women perform oral sex on him was connected to the pornography he used. He explained how he would use "ways that would entice it in the movies" on his girlfriend, whose resistance often led to beatings. "I used a lot of force, a lot of direct demands, that in the movies women would just cooperate," he said. When women in his life didn't cooperate, he said he usually became violent.

None of the sex offenders avoided personal responsibility by contending that pornography caused them to rape; those who described themselves as heavy pornography users saw pornography as one of a number of factors that contributed to their abusive behavior.

CONCLUSION

Three decades of experimental research on pornography's effects have not answered questions about sexually explicit material and sexual violence. Should we hold out hope that more experimental studies will provide answers? Should we privilege that research in the public policy debate over pornography? To do so marginalizes a type of knowledge that holds out much more promise for helping us understand pornography, sexuality, sexism and violence.

Not taking steps to eliminate misogynist pornography is a political act that has consequences. Vulnerable individuals, mostly women and children, will continue to be hurt in the making and use of pornography, and the lack of definitive scientific proof of the connection between pornography and harm does not change that brutal reality. To postpone action until science gives us that definitive answer—which even scientists agree isn't possible— is simply a cover for unwillingness to confront the political and moral questions. We know enough to act, and we should.

NOTES

1. In the courts, however, such studies are not necessary to defend obscenity laws. Chief Justice Warren Burger's decision in *Paris Adult Theatre v. Slaton*, 413 U.S. 49, (1973), stated that conclusive empirical evidence was not needed for states to exercise their "legitimate interest" in regulating obscenity in local commerce and public accommodations to safeguard the quality of life, protect the total community environment and enhance public safety. The more recent attempts to confront pornography legally have focused on women's civil rights, not criminal obscenity law, but the courts have generally been unwilling to consider this new approach. For more on the differences between obscenity and the feminist antipornography critique, see MacKinnon (1987, 1989).

2. MacKinnon's assertion perhaps should be modified to say that *some* women's reports of sex look a lot like reports of rape. MacKinnon is often criticized for her "totalizing" theory that paves over the complexity of individual women's lives, and in this case that is a valid complaint. However, the essence of her point is well taken.

3. I borrow the phrase from feminist philosopher Marilyn Frye's remarks in an informal seminar at the University of Minnesota in 1991.

REFERENCES

Attorney General's Commission on Pornography. (1986). *Final report.* Washington, DC: U.S. Department of Justice.

Brannigan, A., & Goldenberg, S. (1987). The study of aggressive pornography: The vicissitudes of relevance. *Critical Studies in Mass Communication, 4*(3), 262-283.

Commission on Obscenity and Pornography. (1970). *Report.* New York: Bantam.

Dines-Levy, G. (1988). An analysis of pornography research. In A. W. Burgess (Ed.), *Rape and sexual assault II* (pp. 317-323). New York: Garland.

Donnerstein, E., Linz, D., & Penrod, S. (1987). *The question of pornography.* New York: Free Press.

Dworkin, A. (1981). *Pornography: Men possessing women.* New York: Perigee.

Frye, M. (1990). The possibility of feminist theory. In D. Rhode (Ed.), *Theoretical perspectives on sexual difference* (pp. 174-184). New Haven, CT: Yale University Press.

Harding, S. (1991). *Whose science? Whose knowledge?* Ithaca, NY: Cornell University Press.

Itzin, C. (Ed.). (1992). *Pornography: Women, violence and civil liberties.* Oxford, UK: Oxford University Press.

Jensen, R. (1992). *Knowing pornography.* Unpublished doctoral dissertation, University of Minnesota.

Kelly, L. (1988). *Surviving sexual violence.* Minneapolis: University of Minnesota Press.

Kimmel, M. S. (Ed.). (1990). *Men confront pornography.* New York: Crown.

Linz, D. (1989). Exposure to sexually explicit materials and attitudes toward rape: A comparison of study results. *Journal of Sex Research, 26*(1), 50-84.

MacKinnon, C. A. (1987). *Feminism unmodified: Discourses on life and law.* Cambridge, MA: Harvard University Press.

MacKinnon, C. A. (1989). *Toward a feminist theory of the state.* Cambridge, MA: Harvard University Press.

Malamuth, N., & Check, J. V. P. (1981). The effects of mass media exposure on acceptance of violence against women: A field experiment. *Journal of Research in Personality, 15,* 436-446.

Marshall, W. L. (1988). The use of sexually explicit stimuli by rapists, child molesters, and nonoffenders. *Journal of Sex Research, 25*(2), 267-288.

Public hearings on the proposed Minneapolis civil rights anti-pornography ordinance. (1983). Minneapolis: Organizing Against Pornography.

Reinharz, S. (1992). *Feminist methods in social research.* New York: Oxford University Press.

Russell, D. E. H. (1980). Pornography and violence: What does the new research say? In L. Lederer (Ed.), *Take back the night: Women on pornography* (pp. 218-238). New York: William Morrow.

Russell, D. E. H. (1988). Pornography and rape: A causal model. *Political Psychology, 9*(1), 41-73.

Russell, D. E. H. (1993a). *Against pornography: Evidence of harm.* Berkeley, CA: Russell.

Russell, D. E. H. (Ed.). (1993b). *Making violence sexy: Feminist views on pornography.* New York: Teachers College Press.

Silbert, M. H., & Pines, A. M. (1984). Pornography and sexual abuse of women. *Sex Roles, 10*(11/12), 857-869.

Weaver, J. (1992). The social science and psychological research evidence: Perceptual and behavioural consequences of exposure to pornography. In C. Itzin (Ed.),

Pornography: Women, violence and civil liberties (pp. 284-309). Oxford, UK: Oxford University Press.

Zillmann, D. (1989). Pornography research and public policy. In D. Zillmann & J. Bryant (Eds.), *Pornography: Research advances and policy considerations* (pp. 387-403). Hillsdale, NJ: Lawrence Erlbaum.

Zillmann, D., & Bryant, J. (1982). Pornography, sexual callousness, and the trivialization of rape. *Journal of Communication, 32*(4), 10-21.

Zillmann, D., & Weaver, J. B. (1989). Pornography and men's sexual callousness toward women. In D. Zillmann & J. Bryant (Eds.), *Pornography: Research advances and policy considerations* (pp. 95-125). Hillsdale, NJ: Lawrence Erlbaum.

35

Confessions of a Feminist Porn Watcher

SCOTT MacDONALD

For a long time I've been ambivalent about pornography. Off and on since early adolescence I've visited porn shops and theaters, grateful—albeit a little sheepishly—for their existence; and like many men, I would guess, I've often felt protective of pornography, at least in the more standard varieties.[1] . . . On the other hand, I've long felt and, in a small way, been supportive of the struggle for equality and self-determination for women; as a result, the consistent concern of feminist women about the exploitation and brutalization of the female in pornography has gnawed at my conscience. The frequent contempt of intelligent people for those who "need" pornographic materials has always functioned to keep me quiet about my real feelings, but a screening of *Not a Love Story* and a series of responses to it have emboldened me to assess my experiences and attitudes.

. . . From the instant my car is carrying me toward pornography, I feel painfully visible, as if everyone who sees me knows from my expression, my body language, whatever, precisely where I'm going. The walk from the car to the door—and later, from the door to the car—is especially difficult: will someone drive by and see me? This fear of being seen has, in my case at least (as far as I can tell), less to do with guilt than with a fear of being

NOTE: Excerpts reprinted from *Film Quarterly*, Vol. 36, No. 3 (1983), by permission of the University of California and the author. Copyright © the Regents of the University of California.

misunderstood. Even though the frequency of my experiences with pornography has nothing at all to do with the success of my sex life—I'm at least as likely to visit a porn arcade when I'm sexually active as when I'm lonely and horny—I always feel the power of the social stigma against such experiences. Unless the people who see me have been in my situation, I'm sure they'll deduce that my visit to the arcade reflects my inadequacy or some inadequacy in the person I'm living with, that either I "can't get any" or I'm not satisfied with what I can get. As a result, I try to look at ease during the walk to the door: any evident discomfiture on my part, I warn myself, will only fuel whatever laughter my presence has provoked.

Once inside an arcade or a theater, this anxiety about being seen continues, though with a different slant: will I run smack into someone I know? Of course, anyone I would run into would be unlikely to misunderstand the meaning of my presence; but such a meeting would interfere with what seems to me the most fundamental dimension of going to a porn arcade or movie house: the desire for privacy and anonymity. Meeting someone I know would, I assume (this has never happened to me), force us to join together in the phony macho pose of pretending that our interest in the pornographic materials around us is largely a matter of detached humor, that we've come for a few laughs. . . .

. . . When eye contact with one of the strangers present is unavoidable, I put my mind on erase. When I walk out of a porn arcade, I take with me no functional memory at all of the particular faces I saw there, though each visit has confirmed my feeling that in general the faces are those of quiet middle-class men pretty much like me.

I've always assumed that, essentially, those of us who co-exist with each other for a few minutes in porn theaters or arcades share the embarrassing awareness that we're there for the same thing: to look for awhile at forbidden sexual imagery which excites us and finally, to masturbate. In my experience, the masturbation itself seems less important as an experience than as a way of releasing the excitement created by the imagery. Even though most men seem to look rigorously frontward in porn theaters and even though porn arcade booths are designed so as to provide enough security for masturbation, the idea of being seen masturbating has always seemed so frightening to me (and, I assume, to others: I've never seen or heard anyone masturbate in an arcade) that I've never felt free to get deeply involved in the act the way I can when I have real privacy. Usually at a porn arcade I keep myself from masturbating for ten or twenty minutes, until I'm ready to leave; the act itself rarely takes more than fifteen or thirty seconds, and as soon as it's over, I'm on my way to my car. I move quickly because, often, despite my confidence that the other men I see have much the same experience I do, I leave terrified that someone will enter the booth I've just left, see the semen on the floor—impossible in the dimly lit booths—and yell after me. I've never masturbated in a theater (though on rare occasions I've seen others do so), but only later, outside the theater, in the privacy of a car or a men's room.

Since the reason for braving the kinesic complexity of the porn environment is exposure to the pornographic materials themselves, it's important to consider what these materials are. . . . The films seem centered (both in terms of the time allocated to specific imagery and in terms of the viewing gaze) on specific configurations, "acts." Even though there's always a skeletal narrative, this is so obviously a function of the need to create a context for the motifs, that one doesn't need to pay particular attention to it—except insofar as it raises the adrenalin by slightly withholding the awaited imagery.[2] The empty nature of the porn narratives is confirmed by the booths, which, in my experience, have all presented Super-8 films in loops, usually two or three films to a loop. Since each quarter, or whatever the fee is, buys only 30 seconds or so of film (then the film stops until another quarter is deposited), one doesn't automatically see a film from start to finish. The motif structure is also reconfirmed by the announcements on booth doors of the particular acts which are featured in particular booths.[3] . . .

The motifs themselves have generally involved a relatively limited number of sexual interactions. Sexual intercourse in a variety of poses is nearly inevitable, of course, but it's rarely the clincher in a film. Judging from my limited experience, blow jobs (especially ending in ejaculation into the woman's mouth or on her face) and anal intercourse seem the present-day favorites. Sometimes they involve more than a pair of partners (two men have intercourse—one vaginally, one anally—with one woman; two women provide a blow job to one man; a woman gives a blow job to one man while another has intercourse with her) and/or a mixture of ethnic backgrounds. While the women involved seem to mirror conventional notions of attractiveness, the men are frequently quite average-looking: nearly any man will do, apparently, so long as he has a large erection.

No doubt the psychology of wanting to view sexual performances on a movie screen is complex, but over the years I've been aware of two general functions of the experience: one of these involves its "educational" value, the other its value as psychic release. When I was younger, my interest was in seeing just what the female body looked like and how it moved. Sexuality, as I experienced it as an adolescent, was something that usually occurred in the dark, in enclosed spaces, and under the pressure of time. Often I was more engrossed in the issue of "how far I was going to be able to go" than with really seeing and understanding what I was doing. In those days (the fifties) there were no porn films or arcades, but newsstands were beginning to stock *Playboy, Nugget,* and a variety of other girlie magazines; and my hunger to see women's bodies—and to be able to examine them without the embarrassment of being observed by the women—resulted in periodic thefts of magazines. These thefts were serious extralegal transgressions to me; I was terrified of being caught, arrested, and made an example of, until I developed the courage to try buying magazines from drugstore owners. These early magazines seemed a godsend to me, and they provided the stimulation for countless hours of masturbation. But they were also carefully censored: the focus was on breasts, though there were frequent side views of demurely posed buttocks; and all vestiges of pubic hair were, for some reason, erased from the photographs. (I didn't realize this until I was 17 and had the shock of my life during a heavy petting session.) . . . Looking at girlie magazines may seem (and be) a callous manipulation of female bodies, but its function was never callous for me. I was powerfully drawn to women, but my complete ignorance of them frightened me; the magazines were like a nightlight: they allowed me to know a little more than I otherwise would have and they allowed me the fantasy (I always knew it was an illusion) that I'd "know what to do" the next time I got to see and touch a flesh-and-blood woman. . . .

I've become conscious of a second aspect of this first function of pornographic materials, the "educational" function, during the past few years. Feminists have made us aware of the politics of staring at women, but the culture at large—particularly the culture as evident in the commercial sphere—tells us constantly that looking at women is what men are supposed to do. Looking at other men continues to be another matter entirely. Of course, spectator sports, and other forms of physical performance, allow for almost unlimited examination of how bodies function, but knowledge of the naked male body continues to be a tricky matter for heterosexual men. In conventional American life men are probably naked together more often than women: in shower rooms, most obviously. And yet, as is true in porn arcades, the kinesics of the interaction between men in such places are very precisely controlled. Men certainly don't feel free to look at other men; our lives are full of stories about how one guy catches another looking at him and punches him out. Never mind that I've never witnessed such an incident: a taboo is at stake, and potential embarrassment, if not danger, seems to hover on the edge of it. This situation is complicated further by the fact that even if men felt free to look carefully at each other in shower rooms, or wherever, a crucial element of the male body—how it functions during sexual activity—would remain a mystery. Of course, I know what my own erection looks like, but so much stress is placed on the nature of erections that it's difficult not to wonder what the erections of other men look like (and how mine looks in comparison).

One of the things that distinguishes the pornographic materials available in porn movies and arcades from what is available on local newsstands—and thus, implicitly, one of the things that accounts for the size of the hardcore porn market—is the pervasive presence of erections. In fact, to a considerable extent theater and arcade porn films are about erections. The standard anti-porn response to this is to see the porn film phallus as a combined battering ram/totem which encapsulates the male drive for power. And given the characterizations of the vain strutting men on the other ends of these frequently awesome shafts, such an interpretation seems almost inevitable. And yet, for me the pervasiveness of erect penises in porn has at least as much to do with simple curiosity. The darkness of porn houses and the privacy of arcade booths allow one to see erections close-up. The presence of women has its own power, but in this particular context one of the primary functions of the female presence is to serve as a sign—to others and to oneself—that looking at erections, even finding them sexy, does not mean that the viewer defines himself as a homosexual.

A second function of the pornographic experience involves the exact converse of a number of cultural attitudes which feminists have often seen as subtly detrimental to women. . . . the same cultural history which has defined women as Beautiful has had, and to some extent continues to have, as its inevitable corollary, the Ugliness of men; women have been defined as beautiful precisely in contrast to men. Now, even if these definitions are seen as primarily beneficial to men, in the sense that not having to be concerned with appearances allows them more energy and time for attaining their goals and maintaining their access to power, I sense that the definition also creates significant problems for men, and especially in the areas of love and sex, where physical attractiveness seems of the essence. In recent years we've seen a growing acceptance of the idea that men, too, can be beautiful. . . . And yet, just as the pressure to see women as "the weaker sex" continues to be felt in a culture where millions of women dramatize the intrinsic bankruptcy of that notion, many men—I'd guess most men—continue to feel insecure about the attractiveness of their bodies.

Perhaps the most obvious aspect of male sexual functioning which has been conditioned by negative assumptions about male attractiveness is ejaculation. Even among people who are comfortable with the idea that men can be beautiful, semen is often (if not usually) seen as disgusting. Is it an accident that many of the substances that our culture considers particularly revolting—raw egg, snot . . . —share with semen a general texture and look? Accidental or not, I've heard and read such comparisons all my life. . . .

To me, the nature and function of pornography have always seemed understandable as a way for men to periodically deal with the cultural context which mitigates against their full acceptance of themselves as sexual beings. The fantasies men pay to experience in porn arcade booths and movie houses may ostensibly appear to be predicated on the brutalization of women. But from a male point of view, the desire is not to see women harmed, but to momentarily identify with men who—despite their personal unattractiveness by conventional cultural definitions, despite the unwieldy size of their erections, and despite their aggressiveness with their semen—are adored by the women they encounter sexually. Only in pornography will the fantasy woman demonstrate aggressive acceptance when a man ejaculates on her face. As embarrassingly abhorrent as it always strikes me, the hostility toward women which usually seems to hover around the edges of conventional film pornography (in the frequently arrogant, presumptive manner the male characters exhibit, for example), and which is a primary subject matter in some films, seems to be a more aggressive way of dealing with the same issues. In these instances the fantasy is in punishing resistant women for their revulsion. Of course, the punishments—usually one form of rape or another—often end with the fantasy woman's discovery of an insatiable hunger for whatever has been done to her. This frequent turnabout appears to be nothing more than a reconfirmation of the stupid, brutal myth that women ask to be raped or enjoy being raped, but—as sadly ironic as this seems—it could also be seen as evidence that, in the final analysis, men don't mean harm to women, or don't wish to mean harm to women: their fantasy is the acceptance of their own biological nature by women.[4] I've always assumed that porn and rape *are* part of the same general problem, though I've always felt it more likely that porn offers an outlet for some of the anger engendered by men's feelings of sensual aesthetic inferiority, than that it serves as a fuel for further anger. But I'm only speaking from my own experience. I've rarely spoken frankly about such matters with men who use porn.

To try to understand the reasons for the huge business of making and marketing pornographic movies is not necessarily to justify the practice. One can only hope for increasingly definitive studies of how porn functions and what its effects are.[5] But, however one describes the complex historical factors which have brought us to our present situation, the fact remains that in our culture men and women frequently feel alienated from their own bodies and from each other. Pornography is a function of this alienation, and I can't imagine it disappearing until we have come to see ourselves and each other differently. We don't choose the bodies we are born with; natural selection, or God—or whatever—takes care of that for us. And though we can't change the fact of our difference (and regardless of whether we choose to accept and enjoy this difference by being passionate about our own or the opposite sex, or both), surely we can learn to be mutually supportive about our bodies. My guess is that porn is a symptom not so much of a sexual need, but of a need for self-acceptance and respect. If we can come to terms with that need, as it relates to both sexes, my guess is that porn will disappear.

NOTES

1. During my twenties and early thirties I would guess I went to porn films and/or arcades half a dozen times a year. In the past few years (I'm 40) I've gone less frequently; it probably works out to two or three times a year at most. I assume that some men frequent such places, while others go once or twice in a lifetime. I have no information on how often or seldom an "average" man pays to see pornography. I've not been conscious of specific changes in the situation presented in the films or the attitudes which are evident in them. I assume there has been some evolution in this regard, but my experiences have been too sporadic (and too surrounded by personal anxieties) for me to be able to formulate useful conclusions about this evolution.

2. In this sense, the porn narratives seem rather similar to those of George Méliès's films (the acting is roughly comparable, too!).

3. Once I've decided to go to a porn theater, I go immediately, without checking to see when the movies begin or end; as often as not, I arrive in the middle of a film. (This is true only when the theater in question runs shows continuously; when a theater runs only one or two shows a day, I usually postpone a decision about going until just long enough before the beginning of the show so that the decision can be followed by immediate action.) With very rare exceptions, I've always left before a show is over; after one film had led up to and past its most stimulating motifs, I've waited only long enough to calm down and not leave the theater with a visible erection. I've never sat all the way through a double feature of porn films.

4. The frequency of anal sex in porn films seems to confute this, at least if one assumes that anal sex is annoying and painful for most, or many, women. Yet, a decision not to press for fulfillment of such a desire because its fulfillment will cause pain doesn't necessarily eliminate the desire. I would guess that for many men the anal sex in porn films functions as a way of giving harmless vent to a desire they've decided not to pressure the real women in their lives about (harmless, that is, unless one assumes the women in the films feel they are being harmed, something I have no information about).

5. One recent attempt to assess porn's effects is Dolf Zillmann and Jennings Bryant's "Pornography, Sexual Callousness, and the Trivialization of Rape," *Journal of Communication* (Autumn 1982). Unfortunately, this study's central finding—"our investigation focused on sexual callousness toward women, demonstrating that massive exposure to standard porno-

graphic materials devoid of coercion and aggression seem to promote . . . callousness (in particular, the trivialization of rape) . . ."—is based on testing procedures and supported by assumptions which raise nagging questions. The study's conclusions are based on a test of the impact of pornography on students exposed in groups, in a college setting, to "massive," "intermediate," and "no" amounts of conventional, nonviolent pornographic film. But in real life, porn films are seen in a very particular environment, at least in most instances I know of: in a public/private context.

36

Surviving Commercial Sexual Exploitation

EVELINA GIOBBE

To understand the harm of pornography, one must understand its connection to prostitution. Prostitution is the foundation on which pornography is built. Pornography cannot exist without prostitution. It is impossible to separate the two. The acts are identical, as is the population acted upon, except that in pornography there is a permanent record of the abuse that is later marketed and sold as "adult entertainment."

Pornography constructs the specific sexuality of prostitution. It is a direct causal factor in the sexual abuse of prostituted women. It simultaneously scripts the sex imposed on prostitutes and uses them as the raw material for its production. Pornography is both cause and effect. Stripped of all pretense, pornography is nothing less than the technological recycling bin of prostitution.

We can learn most about the connections between prostitution and pornography from the women who are used interchangeably between these two industries. The lives of women used in pornography bear a (not so) remarkable similarity to those used in prostitution. Like women in prostitution, most women used in pornography have grown up in circumstances of parental deprivation, abuse or both. They are typically young. Most were recruited into the porn industry as teenagers and are driven primarily by financial need.

In my case, I was forced into prostitution at the age of 13. I was one of many girls who ran away from home in the 1960s. The first night after I ran away, I was raped. The second night I was gang raped. The third night I was

314

wandering around the streets in a daze when I was befriended by an adult man. I confided my problems to him and he offered to take me in. He was kind to me, fed me and feigned concern. He also kept me drugged, spoke glowingly about prostitution and took nude photographs of me.

After a few weeks, he sold me to a pimp. I didn't understand what was happening at the time. He introduced me to a man who attempted to seduce me. When I resisted he raped me and told me that I would work for him as a prostitute. When I refused, he repeatedly battered and sexually assaulted me. He threatened my life and the lives of my family. He threatened to contact my mother and tell her I was a prostitute. He also threatened to turn me over to the authorities, whom he said would lock me up until my 21st birthday. The scandal, he said, would destroy my family. I believed him.

I tried several times to escape my first pimp. As a teenager without any resources, isolated from friends and family and believing that I was a criminal, I was an easy mark. Each time I ran away, he would track me down and force me back. He would drag me down streets, out of restaurants, even into taxis, all the while beating me while I protested, crying and begging for help from anyone passing by. No one wanted to get involved.

The men who bought me—the tricks—knew I was an adolescent. Most of them were in their 50s and 60s. They had daughters and granddaughters my age. They knew a child's face when they looked into it. Evidently I was not acting of my own free will. I was always covered with welts and bruises. They found this very distasteful and admonished me. It was even clearer that I was sexually inexperienced. So they showed me pornography to teach me and ignored my tears as they positioned my body like the women in the pictures and used me. Raised in New York City brothels by pimps and johns, pornography became my family photo album.

One of my regular customers had a vast collection of both adult and child pornography, including photographs of prepubescent children in bondage. He was a theater producer and had video equipment in his home long before it was mass produced. He made many pornographic videotapes of myself and another young woman. Once, two of us were taken to an apartment in New Jersey to meet some man. We were told that they were "gangsters"; that we "should be nice to them." When we arrived, we were taken into a room containing a large bed surrounded by lighting and film equipment. We were told to act out a lesbian scene. After about 15 minutes we were told to get dressed, that they couldn't use us. We returned to New York unpaid. Looking back, I realized that I'd been used in a commercial porn loop. I was often sent to an apartment on the West Side. There were usually two or three men there. After I had sex with them, they'd take pictures of me in various pornographic poses. I didn't have the vocabulary to call them pornographers. I used to think photography was their hobby. Today, I realize that the studio apartment, furnished with a bed and professional camera equipment, was in fact a commercial pornography mill.

My pimp sent me to "stag parties" attended by as many as 20 men. They took place in catering halls, bars and union halls. Initially, the men watched porn films. Afterward another girl and I would have to have sex with them. I was also sent to business conventions held at major hotels in New York.

The series of events was always the same. The films most often set the tone for the kinds of acts we were expected to perform.

When I was 16, I was picked up as a runaway. The courts labeled me as incorrigible and remanded me to a juvenile detention center. My incarceration was a nightmare of sexual abuse at the hands of the males employed to "guard" us. When I was transferred to a less secure facility, I escaped. There was no place left for me to go except back to prostitution. Many people assume that by returning to the sex industry I made a "choice" to "engage" in prostitution and "pose" for pornography. The ability to choose, however, minimally requires that one recognize that she has a choice, has a full range of comparable options to choose from and be free of coercive influences. Others wonder why I didn't turn to the police. In fact, I didn't have to walk to our local precinct to speak to the police. They were at our apartment every week for their payoff—me.

My last pimp was a pornographer and the most brutal of all. He owned about three women or girls at any given time. Every night, he'd run porn films after which he'd choose one of us for sex. The sex always duplicated the pornography. He used it to teach us to service him. He made pornography of all of us. He also made tape recordings of us having sex with him and of our screams and pleas when he battered us. Later he would humiliate us by playing the tapes for his friends in our presence, for his own sexual arousal and to terrorize us or other women he brought home.

This man recruited adult women into prostitution by advertising for models. When a woman answered his ad, he'd offer to put her portfolio together free, be her agent and make her a "star." He'd then use magazines such as *Playboy* to convince her to pose for "soft-core" porn. Eventually he'd engage her in a love affair and smooth talk her into prostitution. "Just long enough," he would say, "to get enough money to finance your career as a model." If sweet talk didn't work, violence and blackmail did. She became one of us.

I escaped prostitution by chance. Like most women, I took drugs while I was in prostitution to numb the physical and emotional pain of turning tricks. As I destroyed myself with heroin, my marketability declined. Eventually I was no longer usable by pimps or tricks, so I was freed. After 5 years of being used in prostitution and pornography, I was penniless, homeless and addicted to heroin.

I am an uncommon survivor. Most women who have shared my experiences are not as fortunate. It took close to 20 years to undo the physical and emotional trauma of being used in the sex industry. I escaped the pimps and outlived many of the johns, but the pornography made of me still exists. I know the men who made it. I know where some of them are. But there is nothing I can do about it. I live knowing that any time it could surface and be used to humiliate me. Because pornography is a profitable multimillion-dollar-a-year industry, I also know that what happened to me will continue to happen to other young women. They will continue to be used and hurt in the same way that I was. And if they should be fortunate enough to escape, they will live under the same threat of exposure and blackmail that I have in the past.

In the early 1980s I began to work with other feminists in the antipornography movement. It was only a matter of time before many of us became well-known to major pornographers: Bob Guccione of *Penthouse*, Al Goldstein of *Screw* and Larry Flynt of *Hustler*, to name but a few. In retaliation for our outspoken public criticism of their videos, magazines and newspapers, some began to publish pornographic articles, drawings, cartoons or, sometimes, actual or "doctored" pornographic photographs of us. We often heard that some pornographer was spreading a little money around in an attempt to sniff out an old lover or an estranged friend who might have a compromising photograph or bit of information that could discredit our work. Still we continued our struggle despite the knowledge that any one of us could be targeted next.

In 1985, I came out as a survivor of prostitution and pornography at a national women and law conference. Although over a decade had passed, I was still held hostage to my abuse. This time it wasn't an individual pimp profiting by prostituting me. It was the pornographers who had the power to continue to exploit me by publishing the product of my abuse: the pornography made of me by pimps and johns. To avoid the inevitable, I organized under the name Sarah Wynter. As I went on to speak out about my life at feminist conferences, I began to receive letters from women all over the country. They, too, described their experiences in the sex industry as violent, degrading and dehumanizing. From those letters, WHISPER (Women Hurt in Systems of Prostitution Engaged in Revolt) was born. By 1989, I gave up the illusion of safety that a pseudonym gave me and reclaimed my birth name. By then, I realized that no woman was "safe" as long as the pornography industry continued to flourish.

Since its inception, WHISPER has grown from a small grassroots response to the myths about prostitution to a nationally respected organization. We educate the public about prostitution as a form of violence against women and advocate for services to be made available to women trapped in the sex industry. Based on our advocacy and organizing efforts, we have developed an analysis of prostitution and pornography as systems of oppression that differentially harm women and children. By listening to survivors describe the tactics of control that kept them trapped in the sex industry and comparing this to our knowledge of battering, we've come to understand that prostitution is a form of violence against women. By documenting the brutality and manipulation used to recruit and trap women in the sex industry, we've educated the public that prostitution is not a "career choice" or a "victimless crime" but, rather, that prostitution creates an environment in which crimes against women and children are defined as a commercial enterprise.

Information provided by 19 women who participated in our Oral History Project has been consistently replicated by the hundreds of women who contact WHISPER for assistance every year. Women from each of these groups have revealed the ways in which pornography was a part of the abuse that they suffered at the hands of pimps and johns. Over half the women interviewed for the WHISPER Oral History Project reported that pornography played a significant role in teaching them what was expected of them as prostitutes. Fifty-three percent reported that their customers took pornographic pictures of them in addition to the sex that took place between them. Sometimes, the making of the pornography itself was the sex act for the john. Thirty percent of the women reported that their pimps regularly exposed them to pornography as a seasoning technique. Furthermore they told us that pimps also made pornography of them as a form of extortion, punishment or a sadistic combination of both.

The bridge connecting prostitution and pornography is a well-worn road suspended above an endless river of women's bodies. Pimps use pornography to recruit and keep women trapped in prostitution. Johns use pornography to show women how to do prostitution. Pornographers sell pictures of women doing prostitution. Existing law is blind to the connections between woman abuse—including prostitution—and pornography. First Amendment arguments used to defend pornography based on constitutional guarantees to "free speech" ignore the fact that this "speech" is literally manufactured from the bodies and blood of living women. Obscenity laws—which are designed to address public offensiveness instead of criminal offenses against women—offer no relief for the harm of pornography—the harm to young women who must endure sexual abuse to produce pornography; the harm to women who must endure sexual harassment, sexual abuse and outright rape at the hands of men who use pornography; the harm to our youths who have been socialized in a pornographic culture that, by definition, excludes the possibility of their engaging in mutually gratifying, egalitarian sexual encounters. WHISPER exists to be a constant and verbal witness to this harm.

PART V

TV BY DAY

Television is the most pervasive and some would say most influential conveyor of contemporary media culture in the United States. Despite its visuality, television's immediate ancestor is not film but radio. Like radio and unlike film, television technology had a "domestic" location and was sold to American consumers as a home technology, right from the beginning.

Karen Altman (1989) has shown that although two-way radio technology was originally associated with the masculine realm, with peripheral spaces of the home, such as the attic or basement, where men and boys could indulge in mechanical and electronic tinkering, radio was regendered by marketing practices in the 1920s that assumed women or the family as the target audience for the new, reception-only sets. When television technology was commercialized in the late 1940s, it was also marketed through advertising imagery that linked it primarily with the home, women and "femininity."

Early TV commercials developed in the postwar period, when women war workers ("Rosie the Riveter") were targeted with messages urging their "return to the home" to manage not only family life but also the consumption of newly available consumer goods. Thus the industry developed scheduling and programming practices that reflected (and even magnified) the gendered division of labor and the ideology of separation between domestic/"feminine" and public/"masculine" spheres of competence. Women were assumed to be the daytime audience, whereas families, at least nominally dominated by fathers, were assumed to be the audience at night. These assumptions were key to the gendering of daytime and prime-time television programming.

As entertainment **genres** developed and evolved on TV, variety shows giving way to comic and dramatic series, many of the new genres and

319

subgenres were clearly "gendered"—such as Westerns, police and spy adventures, which featured male protagonists and addressed a (presumed) masculine viewer. Others, such as the situation comedy (sitcom), were less overtly gendered (see Part VI) because they assumed a "family" viewing as a group. Very few genres, however, were targeted exclusively at women— and those that were developed in the low-budgeted daytime slots that helped pay (in larger quantities of advertising time) for the more expensive productions of the more prestigious nighttime TV genres (Williams, 1992, p. 4).

One of the most intensively explored genres of daytime TV is the soap opera—a despised but resilient serialized, multiplotted story form centering on female characters that began as a 15-minute daily offering on radio in the 1930s, made the transition to television in the 1950s and early 1960s and by the 1970s was drawing audiences of about 20 million (Williams, 1992, p. 3). Historically aimed at women at home, the soap opera form first drew the attention of social science researchers concerned about its negative social impact on wives and mothers (Allen, 1985).

In more recent years, it has generated enormous interest among **feminist** cultural critics who agree that although the audience base has broadened and overall viewing figures are down from the 1970s, the soap opera is still a major part of many women's cultural lives. Feminist critics of soap opera disagree, however, on the extent to which the text itself has subversive properties and on the way real audiences read the text.

Feminist critiques of soap opera from the 1970s and 1980s included (a) those that contrasted the images of working women on these serials with the actual situations of women workers (Robinson, 1978); (b) analyses of the conservative underlying messages about home, family and sexuality that were built into the stories for the housewife (Lopate, 1976); and (c) more recent analyses that see their feminist potential as limited, despite their enormous appeal to many women viewers (Jhirad, 1987; Rosen, 1986).

Deborah Rogers, in "Daze of Our Lives" (Chapter 37), updates the classic feminist critique of the **patriarchal ideology** in soap texts by reminding us of continuing tenets of their characterizations and plots. She argues that although sophisticated textual critics of daytime (and prime-time) soaps (e.g., Ien Ang, Robert C. Allen, Mary Ellen Brown, Charlotte Brunsdon, Jane Feuer, Christine Geraghty, Dorothy Hobson, E. Ann Kaplan, Tania Modleski and Carol Traynor Williams) may be able to take advantage of the form's "openness" to construct subversive readings, actual viewers (including a group she studied through interviews) may "simply fail to recognize latent discourses."

Karen Lindsey extends the feminist critique of the sexism in daytime soap texts into a discussion of the other ways in which a socially conservative message is the dominant or **preferred reading** (Chapter 38). Lindsey reminds us of the limits of soap opera's efforts to incorporate real social issues of difference (abortion, racism, AIDS and homophobia) into its plotlines. She critiques its inability to acknowledge and deal honestly with cultural differences in particular.

Drawing on Tania Modleski and other more recent feminist students of soap opera form, John Fiske argues in "Gendered Television: Femininity" (Chapter 39) that the endless storyline itself embodies "feminine values" that are potentially subversive of patriarchal ideology: "The emphasis on the process rather than the product, on pleasure as ongoing and cyclical rather than climactic and final, is constitutive of a feminine subjectivity in so far as it opposes masculine pleasures and rewards."

Similarly, he argues, by employing multiple plots woven together so that each storyline is constantly interrupted by another, "soap operas offer their subordinated women viewers the pleasure of seeing [the] status quo in a constant state of disruption." Thus the narrative form itself may be read as subverting the overt messages about marriage as the be-all and end-all for women. A related view of soap opera texts as offering their viewers complex and conflicting kinds of satisfaction is couched in **psychoanalytic** terms in Tania Modleski's classic "The Search for Tomorrow in Today's Soap Operas" (Chapter 40). She advances the influential theory that because of its multiple characters and constantly shifting perspectives, by which we are offered no single central character or protagonist to identify with, "the **subject/spectator** [italics added] of soap operas . . . is constituted as a sort of ideal mother: a person who possesses greater wisdom than all her children, whose sympathy is large enough to encompass the conflicting claims of her family (she identifies with them all)."

On the other hand, Modleski points to the "extreme delight viewers apparently take in despising the villainess," seeing this as testimony to "the enormous amount of energy involved in the spectator's repression and to her (albeit unconscious) resentment at being constituted as an egoless receptacle for the suffering of others."

However, more **ethnographic** studies of soap audiences show a mixed picture of the reading situation. One good example of this work is a 1986 study by Ellen Seiter and associations of 64 White Oregon soap watchers (15 of them men; 11 of them unemployed workers). The researchers focused on their informants' acquisition of "generic competence"—"their thorough and sophisticated knowledge of the genre" as soap readers. In addition, they reported that

> female anger was far less repressed than . . . Modleski's textual position allows for. In their interaction with the fictional world of the soap opera, women openly and enthusiastically admitted their delight in following soap operas as stories of female transgressions which destroy the ideological nucleus of the text—the sacredness of the family. (Seiter et al., 1989, p. 240)

In one of the few ethnographic studies so far to go beyond White viewership, Lee and Cho (Chapter 41) studied a Korean community in the United States, in which the wives braved their student husbands' displeasure with their choice of "trash" entertainment (in this case, videotaped Korean soap operas rented for replay on the VCR). The wives used the

Korean soap's antipatriarchal stories about a husband's marital infidelity to raise questions among themselves and with their husbands about the sexual double standard legitimated by Confucianism. Lee and Cho found that the viewers "challenge[d] the traditional patriarchy within limits," by forming a video club that functioned "as a kind of forum to evaluate and criticize the husband's behavior." This study suggests that the social situation of women viewing such TV material entertainment together can lead to a kind of feminist consciousness-raising under the right circumstances.

Studies such as Lee and Cho's that attempt to analyze the social situation of viewing and how it affects the decoding process are part of a growing body of work on family TV viewing, begun by David Morley and associates, many of which are summarized in "Home, Home on the Remote" (Chapter 42). These include assessments of the impact of new technologies such as the VCR and the remote control channel changer on the power dynamics between husbands and wives, parents and children while engaged in television watching as a social activity based in the home. Such work emphasizes the different meanings of the home as a viewing context for employed spouses and spouses working at home in the traditional "housewife" role, as well as the "guilty pleasure" women viewers continue to take in the less respected female-targeted forms such as the soap opera.

Another denigrated daytime TV form aimed primarily at women is the morning/afternoon talk show, originally pioneered by Phil Donahue in the 1970s. Looking closely at the actual structure and codes of a talk show text—an episode of the Geraldo Rivera show—Wayne Munson (Chapter 43) helps us see that "the show . . . shifts back and forth between expert analysis and individual emotional experience to demonstrate the limits of both in conversational performance." Although real women's testimonial in such a context appears to "build a resistant community of 'normal,' passionate, and honest people," against which "objectified knowledge looks increasingly absurd," Munson's analysis makes us aware of its performative aspects. Similarly, although we might applaud the fact that in the talk show, "spectatorship has been redefined as participatory," Munson points out that by encouraging the spectator's "perception of the media's efficacy and 'friendliness,' " the talk show form "encourages a greater dependence on the media."

Nevertheless, as Elayne Rapping argues in "Daytime Inquiries" (Chapter 44), "in structure, in process, and in subject matter," daytime talk shows such as Oprah Winfrey's "take their cues from an important political institution of the 1960s: the women's consciousness-raising movement." Although she warns that "the primary goal of talk shows as a television form is to lure curious audiences and sell them products, not revolution," she also asks us to look again at the implications of their "nonhierarchical structure," which permits "open discourse on serious issues," which she claims is "only possible because the issues discussed are not taken seriously by those in power."

Because women and other culturally marginalized groups do not have significant ownership of media outlets, such as television stations, they are in large measure in the position of having to appropriate whatever they can from what is available, as we see happening in Rapping's discussion of how women in the talk show audience and in their roles as guests can sometimes "take over" the discussion from the host. This is a kind of "raiding" of mainstream media culture for potentially subversive or **counterhegemonic** (against the ruling ideology) meanings.

One of the most interesting examples of this kind of raiding is given in Gloria Abernathy-Lear's chapter (Chapter 45), analyzing a **secondary text** of soap opera—namely, the soap opera "updates" or plot summaries broadcast on a Black-oriented radio station in Chicago by an African American male viewer/critic/performance artist. As Abernathy-Lear argues, through "selective appropriation, Ti-Rone generates laughter, which, in turn, helps to strengthen group cohesion." Here **resistance** consists of the irreverent public use of hegemonic texts, rather than in private individual **negotiated** or **oppositional readings** of them.

Although such strategies are meaningful ways that culturally marginalized groups have developed to resist total cultural colonization, we need to remind ourselves that a very different order of culture creation and transmission would be possible if such groups began to acquire real control over the production and transmission industries.

REFERENCES

Allen, R. C. (1985). *Speaking of soap operas.* Chapel Hill: University of North Carolina Press.

Altman, K. (1989, Summer). Television as gendered technology: Advertising the American television set. *Journal of Popular Film and Television, 17,* 46-56.

Jhirad, S. (1987, February). As the soaps turn. *Sojourner.*

Lopate, C. (1976). Day-time television: You'll never want to leave home. *Feminist Studies, 4*(6), 70-82.

Robinson, L. (1978). What's my line: Telefiction and women's work. In L. Robinson, *Sex, class and culture* (pp. 310-342). Bloomington: Indiana University Press.

Rosen, R. (1986). Search for yesterday. In T. Gitlin (Ed.), *Watching television* (pp. 41-67). New York: Pantheon.

Seiter, E., et al. (1989). "Don't treat us like we're so stupid and naive": Toward an ethnography of soap opera viewers. In E. Seiter et al. (Eds.), *Remote control: Televison audiences and cultural power* (pp. 233-247). New York: Routledge.

Williams, C. T. (1992). *It's time for my story: Soap opera sources, structure, and response.* Westport, CT: Praeger.

∎37

Daze of Our Lives

The Soap Opera as Feminine Text

DEBORAH D. ROGERS

Soap operas are the only fiction on television, that most popular of mass cultural media, specifically created for women. This genre can therefore provide us with a valuable opportunity to examine the complexities of feminine cultural codes the more easily as they are writ large in feminine popular culture. . . . I argue that the fragmentation of soap narrative form reinforces the status quo with respect to the nature of sex roles and of interpersonal relationships in a patriarchal culture. Although the mixed messages of soap operas may allow scholars to construct subversive readings, actual viewers fail to respond in this manner. . . .

Since they appeal to so many women, soap operas have naturally attracted the attention of feminists. . . . One major problem in dealing with soap operas is the historical denigration not only of television, but also of forms of feminine popular culture. Indeed, the very term "soap opera" has become so pejorative that it is applied condescendingly to a variety of genres and situations to indicate bathetic superficiality and kitsch. This is so much the case that one of the respondents to a recent survey I conducted attempted to justify her enthusiasm for *Days of Our Lives* by denial, insisting, "I really don't consider this show a soap opera."[1] Many feminists are similarly ambivalent about the genre: We desperately *want* to like a form that is

NOTE: Excerpts reprinted from *Journal of American Culture*, Vol. 14 (Winter 1991), by permission of the editor, *Journal of American Culture*, Bowling Green University Popular Press.

popular with so many women but are repulsed by the conservative ideology. This ambivalence manifests itself when the same scholars who criticize soaps for promoting patriarchal stereotypes praise them for being "in the vanguard . . . of all popular narrative art" (Modleski, 1984, p. 13). In countering the denigration of feminine forms, however, we must be wary of going in the opposite direction, celebrating them just because they are female genres—especially when they might be potentially harmful. . . .

The cumulative effect of introducing in a fragmented text messages that reconcile women to traditional feminine roles and relationships is to reinforce patriarchal cultural behavior in a way that is difficult to identify during a typical—that is, casual—viewing experience. Perhaps the easiest way to demonstrate this process is by isolating soap tenets, abstracting them from the disjointed context in which they are embedded.

If soaps are featuring more career women, their romances and families take precedence over jobs, which may simply provide sites for gossip and personal relationships. The same could, of course, be said of the portrayal of male professionals. (Victor Newman, CEO of the multi-million dollar Newman business empire, recently announced, "Generally I don't discuss business matters over the phone"—and generally he does not, and neither does anyone else.) Although soap jobs are hardly portrayed realistically, male professionals are depicted as superior beings who often transcend specialties. The same male doctor who handles AIDS patients, trauma victims and neonatal care also delivers babies. Male corporate lawyers handle homicides. When we do see women engaged in professional activities, they are usually subordinate to men. For example, on one soap a young female lawyer is solely responsible for a murder case until shortly before it goes to trial, when she feels compelled to hire a more seasoned (male) co-counsel.

Women who devote too much time to jobs at the expense of their relationships and families are usually punished. For example, the son of one career woman who spent little time with him turns out to be a rapist. Another strong, aggressive, competent and well meaning career woman, *All My Children*'s Barbara Montgomery, glanced away while she was babysitting for a friend whose child was consequently hit by a car and killed. Is it pure coincidence that this accident occurred even as Barbara was composing an updated resume? Here we can ask of the soaps what Rosenblum (1986) asks concerning the "careerless career women" of other media who make a mess of their personal lives: "Is there a hidden message here, namely that women had better stay out of the corner office or they'll get what's coming to them?"[2]

All this should not be surprising since in the soap world pregnancy within a marriage has always been the supreme state and children the ultimate "achievement" for women (Rogers, 1988). . . .

Mother Moran, a character in a radio soap, early elaborated the soaps' endorsement of patriarchal marriage and parenting ideas: "A cake ta bake, and a floor ta sweep. And a tired little babe ta sing ta sleep. What does a woman want more than this—A home, a man, and a child ta kiss" (quoted in Allen, 1985, p. 194). Similarly, on contemporary soaps, if childbearing is necessary for completeness, having both a child (or children) and a "good marriage" constitutes true bliss. (This sentiment may present some problems for women in the audience who, while they have their husbands and their babies, are still miserable.) For example, on *The Young and the Restless* Nikki tells her husband, Victor, "I am so lucky. I have everything a woman could want. . . . I have a beautiful daughter and a loving husband, and a wonderful marriage. . . ."

. . . In the fictionalized representation of motherhood on daytime soap operas, the myth of maternal omnipotence conceals the subordination and marginalization of women.

Employing the rhetoric of female apotheosis, soaps define having a baby as "the single most important thing in a woman's life." As one soap character remarked on the day she discovered she was pregnant: "This is what I've wanted all of my life, and now it's all coming true. . . . This is the most important day of my life." Male dominance is ideologically reinforced by the belief that women are gloriously suited for child care because they are by nature cheerfully domestic, nurturing and self-sacrificing. This "innate" selflessness, essential to fulfilling their roles as wives and mothers, allows for the happiness of women to reside in being constantly attentive to the needs of other family members. For example, after being told sarcastically "Lucky you—you get to listen to everybody's problems," one soap mother responded in all seriousness, "That's part of being a mother. You'll find out about it some day." Other soap mothers have recently made statements like "I'm here whenever you want to talk" and "I only want what's best for him" and have been asked such rhetorical questions as "what kind of mother are you, to put your feelings before the feelings of your child?" . . .

Without offspring, women are incomplete. Take, for example, the case of *General Hospital*'s Bobbie Meyer, who acknowledges the terrible emptiness of her barren state: "I'm thinking about the babies that I'm never going to have. . . . I just feel empty. . . . [My husband] is a man who *deserves* to have a child." Since failure to comply with moral norms is usually punished on soaps, and Bobbie is a former prostitute, her sterility may be no accident.

On another soap a new father extends this baby ethic to men:

[H]aving a child of my own was one dream I just could never turn loose of. And when [my wife] became pregnant, I thought . . . the gods are smiling on me. And there was nothing left for me to ask for because there was nothing else I wanted. Ya know, I was—complete.

If such sentiments of completeness imply more male sensitivity, they never seem to extend to beliefs about shared parenting. It is therefore likely that these expressions may simply be a variation of the traditional male fantasy of procreation as immortality. This myth is stressed repeatedly on the soaps, where men "deserve" to have children and, as one character puts it, "any man . . . would just go crazy to have a son that would carry on your name and follow in your footsteps."

. . . Although women are overtly respected for bearing children and for being mothers, ironically, men treat them like children. For example, one soap husband tells his wife she should go "sleepy-bye," while another calls his baby daughter his "other little good girl," equating his wife and his infant. On *One Life to Live*, at the very moment she tells her husband, Cord, the results of her pregnancy test, Tina is infantilized:

> **Tina:** Well, aren't you the least bit interested in whether you and I made a baby?—we didn't. What are you smiling for?
>
> **Cord:** Well, to tell you the truth, I kinda' didn't think we did, but I tell ya—I think it's real cute you being so excited about it.

Another soap wife gets worked up because she has tried to serve "the most important dinner of my life—and I blow it. . . . I spill the appetizers. . . . I burn the dinner. . . . " Her husband predictably responds, "I think you're cute."

Although it is difficult to see how women can be taken seriously as long as they are being treated like children, their subordination may be obfuscated, as they collude in this pattern, decoding it in terms of "cuteness" and male protection. Soap women are repeatedly imaged as children: like children, they frequently "flood out," losing control in gales of laughter or in tears. They are playfully fed by men and are the objects of mock-assault games (of the food- or pillow-fight variety) that are usually reserved for children. Although on the soaps these "attacks" usually collapse into love-making, sociologist Erving Goffman (1979) has pointed out in another context that such "games" suggest what men could potentially do, should they ever get serious about it.

Unsurprisingly, on the soaps men give more orders and advice than women. This often extends to female topics (Turow, 1974). Women have no relief from this ubiquitous male instructor—a de facto role of authority that demands subordination—even during commercial "breaks," when they are subject to predominantly male voice-overs.[3] Not only do male voice-overs dominate the commercials themselves, in what Robert Allen (1985, pp. 154-170) considers to be a vestige of the omnipotent male announcers of radio soaps, today's announcers—all of whom are male—seem to control the networks' programming. They point to commercials, promise that the soap will resume after interruptions, signal the end of the commercial segments and urge us to continue watching or to tune in tomorrow. While all these little expressions of male dominance and female submission may seem insignificant in and of themselves, they add up to create an effect that is overwhelming. Unfortunately, typical viewers do not seem to regard this behavior as suspect. . . .

Applying reader-response theories specifically to soaps, Jane Feuer (1984) finds *Dallas* and *Dynasty* "potentially progressive" because their serial form with its multiplicity of plot lines admits to unchallenged ideological stances: "Since no action is irreversible, every ideological position may be countered by its opposite" (p. 15). John Fiske (1987, pp. 179-197) argues that such a variety of reading positions allows for an interrogation of patriarchy. Ellen Seiter (1982) is hopeful about the progressive potential of the soaps for similar reasons:

> The importance of small discontinuous narrative units which are never
> organized by a single patriarchal discourse or main narrative line,
> which do not build towards an ending or closure of meaning, which in
> their very complexity cannot give a final ideological word on any-
> thing, makes soap opera uniquely "open" to feminist readings. (p. 4)

Although I find that the dominant ideology of the soap is patriarchal and
that any challenges implicit in contradictory readings are regularly trounced
on as patriarchy continually rears its ugly head, the potential that Feuer,
Fiske and Seiter posit for constructing feminist interpretations of soaps from
their inconsistencies certainly exists. But let me raise a crucial question:
What if viewers fail to identify the subtext? . . . For example, most of the
respondents to my survey are partially attentive viewers likely to gossip
about soap characters for fun but unlikely to read or analyze soap operas as
texts, watching with the rapt attention of the critic. . . .

When asked whether soaps contain messages, most of my respondents
said yes and pointed to blatant messages about issues like sex and alcoholism. Many remarked that soaps teach about relationships and practical
matters. One respondent, who credits the soaps with helping her get pregnant, first heard of ovulation prediction kits on *All My Children*, where they
were mentioned obliquely—"It's blue. Let's get into bed"—when Brooke
was trying to conceive. Some even mentioned world view and distinguished
between the obvious and the subtle. For example, an especially thoughtful
respondent wrote:

> A "say no to sex before you are ready" (married was the suggested
> time to be "ready") campaign was written into one story line in hopes
> of preventing teenage pregnancies and the spread of sexually trans-
> mitted diseases. I also see the message that being rich and powerful is
> not synonymous with happiness. There are both obvious and sublimi-
> nal messages. The subliminal messages are male dominated and fam-
> ily oriented, but the blatant messages may have in some cases redeem-
> ing social value.

Now consider one of the messages widely praised in the press and by
respondents as having this "redeeming social value." An astonishing number of respondents mentioned the rape story on *Santa Barbara*, recognizing
the obvious moral: report rapes to the authorities. They were totally oblivious to the subtext which undercut this message, insidiously destroying the
social value of this plot. On the soap Eden Castillo is raped. While this story
line is developed, daily after the program we see the constructedness of the
fiction, which is rare in the soap world (usually reserved for occasions like
the death of an actor). At the end of each episode, Marcy Walker steps out
of the frame, announcing that she is the actress who plays Eden and advising
victims to report rapes. Perhaps part of the reason for this strategy is that
the rape sequences are so gripping the audience needs to be reassured that
this is a fiction. The ostensible reason—to promote the message—is, however, vitiated. In the story Eden does indeed report the rape and undergoes

a pelvic examination. Our perspective is of her raised knees covered with a sheet. In the end we discover that the rapist is the very same gynecologist who performed the examination.

Unfortunately, the subtext here—the authorities we should report rapes to are equivalent to the rapists themselves—went unnoticed, even as it subverted the blatant message. This could create considerable anxiety for viewers who may find themselves unwilling to report male violence and brutality. The whole misogynistic plot may speak to women's fear of trusting male authority. . . .

Another familiar soap plot with a subtext that often goes unrecognized concerns the reformed rake. In perhaps the most famous example, *General Hospital*'s Luke raped—and later married—Laura, who subsequently referred to the event as "the first time we made love," perpetuating the fiction that women really want to be raped. (*General Hospital* producer Gloria Monty described the rape as "choreographed seduction"; Dullea, 1986). Luke and Laura became a romantic super-couple, as Luke underwent a transformation, eventually becoming not only mayor of Port Charles, but heartthrob to countless teenage girls. As Janice Radway (1984) found in her study of romances, in a society where male violence against women is a constant, women may deal with their fears by decoding male brutality as love. Such a strategy, however, fails to remedy the problem. In a recent cartoon in *Soap Opera Digest*, a woman tells a man, as they watch a male image on the screen, "For your information, he's now a sweet, sensitive person. You're not supposed to remember he used a chain saw on his sixth wife in 1982" (July 11, 1989, p. 59). Such transformations of soap villains are obviously recognized. Unfortunately, however, most viewers are oblivious of the fact that reinterpreting soap rapes and brutality as romance denies—if not legitimates and glorifies—male violence by reading it as love. Instead of constructing subversive readings of soaps, many viewers simply fail to recognize latent discourses. . . .

NOTES

1. This ongoing survey, which is composed of seventy-one multiple-choice questions and eleven additional questions requiring a written response, has been completed by over 100 viewers.

2. Rosenblum (1986) argues that if movies, theatre and prime time are now featuring women professionals, their careers are like "touches of trendy window dressing to spruce them up for the late 80s." From Glenn Close's Alex in *Fatal Attraction* to Heidi in Wendy Wasserstein's *Heidi Chronicles*, the portrayal of professional women of the eighties with their "toy careers" is far removed from the depiction of 1940s career women like Katharine Hepburn in *Woman of the Year* and Rosalind Russell in *His Girl Friday*. Although the message of such movies is that what a woman really needs is a good man, the women were consummate professionals.

3. According to Butler and Paisley, 90% of voice-overs in television commercials are male (cited in Cantor & Pingree, 1983, p. 202).

REFERENCES

Allen, R. C. (1985). *Speaking of soap operas.* Chapel Hill: University of North Carolina Press.

Cantor, M., & Pingree, S. (1983). *The soap opera.* Beverly Hills, CA: Sage.

Dullea, G. (1986, July 11). As Gloria Monty's world turns. *The New York Times,* p. Y19.

Feuer, J. (1984). Melodrama, serial form, and television today. *Screen, 25*(1), 4-16.

Fiske, J. (1987). *Television culture.* New York: Methuen.

Goffman, E. (1979). *Gender advertisements.* New York: Harper.

Modleski, T. (1984). *Loving with a vengeance: Mass-produced fantasies for women.* New York: Methuen.

Radway, J. (1984). *Reading the romance.* Chapel Hill: University of North Carolina Press.

Rogers, D. D. (1988, September 23). The soaps: Do they support or undermine the family? *Christian Science Monitor,* p. 21.

Rosenblum, C. (1986, February 26). Drop-dead clothes make the working woman. *The New York Times,* p. 1H.

Seiter, E. (1982). Eco's TV guide—the soaps. *Tabloid, 5.*

Turow, J. (1974). Advising and ordering: Daytime, prime time. *Journal of Communication, 24,* 138-141.

Race, Sexuality and Class in Soapland

KAREN LINDSEY

Writing negatively about soap opera can be problematic, since it is a form historically despised because of its primary audience—housewives. Sexism has created an unwillingness to perceive soap opera as an art form or even to take it seriously as a cultural phenomenon. Thus to critique it seriously is to risk collaborating with that dismissive mentality. For many people, however, the soap opera *is* an art form and deserves to be regarded as such.

Such a regard, however, does not preclude—indeed, demands—a serious look at its drawbacks. And among the drawbacks of soap opera is, not surprisingly, a failure to adequately depict racial, social and sexual minorities. (I am confining my discussion here to the true soap opera, the five-day-a-week afternoon serial, not the nighttime serials that adopted soap opera's continuous-story form but that are fundamentally different in many ways.)

When soap opera began in radio in the 1930s, and through its earliest TV days, people of color were nonexistent, as they were in most broadcast fiction, except for minstrel show comedies such as *Amos and Andy*. In the late 1960s, TV had made enough of a concession to the civil rights movement to offer a handful of token Black characters and, again, the soaps were no exception. Almost every soap had its Black couple, who were occasionally given storylines that mirrored, palely, those of the White stars. *General Hospital*'s Brian and Claudia were typical: They fell in love, quarreled, got married, quarreled, had kids, quarreled and, when a new Black character temporarily moved to town, suffered anxieties about possible infidelity. But these storylines were brief and infrequent. Brian and Claudia, like Angie and

Jesse on *All My Children*, Ed and Carla on *One Life to Live* and their counterparts on the other soaps, were chiefly sympathetic best buddies to the White heroes.

Occasionally, the shows addressed issues of race. *One Life to Live* borrowed from the film *Imitation of Life* and significantly advanced on its predecessor, showing a light-skinned African American who, scarred by racism, had succeeded in a White world by passing. Even her name had been Whitened: Carla was once Clara, and, as author Martha Nochimson (1992) notes in *No End to Her*, there was a powerful scene in which she countered her servant-mother's anger with a reminder that it was the mother herself who unconsciously convinced Carla that passing was the key to survival in a White world.

However, once that issue was resolved—and it was resolved with the ease typical of all wrenching soap dilemmas—Carla and her husband went back to being aracial, comfortable Black tokens. When handsome Doctor Jack Scott showed up in Llanview, we knew their marriage was in trouble: Why else would the show bring on another Black character?

There were also, as there still are, a handful of background Blacks, usually police officers and doctors. Often, to show that they don't indulge in racial stereotypes, soaps have used Black judges to preside over one of the frequent murder or custody trials. Indeed, if you got your knowledge of American culture from soaps alone, you would be fairly convinced that the large majority of judges were Black women.

And so it went until the late 1980s, when the numbers of Black characters began to increase in virtually every soap. A *Soap Opera Digest* ("Minorities on the Soaps" 1989) article rated the soaps in terms of their depiction of racial and ethnic minorities, and although their grades were perhaps overgenerous, it is significant that such an article even ran in the major soap-fanzine. That was also the year that *Generations* debuted—the first soap to begin with a cast of characters equally divided between Black and White. *Generations* lasted just over a year. It's hard to judge whether racism played a large part in its demise, simply because it was never a good soap opera. The writing was poor, the acting largely stilted. It was an exciting premise, drearily executed. Even when the marvelous Debbi Morgan, who had been Angie on *All My Children* since 1982, defected to *Generations*, she could not save the show.

But the show's existence and the controversy over its cancellation may have triggered a slight improvement in Soapland. More Black characters began to appear in the other soaps. Today African Americans are far more visible than even 5 years ago. Gerard Waggett, a writer for *Soap Opera Weekly*, has studied the casts of all the soaps for an article he is working on and discovered that, on average, the hour-long soaps have between 40 and 50 characters, between 4 and 7 of whom are Black (G. Waggett, personal communication, November 1993). This remains tokenism, to be sure, but it does represent a significant increase in Black characters.

More important than numbers, however, are the ways the characters function on the shows. The numbers don't necessarily correlate with the quality of the depiction. Although it's still refreshing to see Black faces, often, the characters are simply imitations of White characters, and there is no awareness of racial oppression or cultural difference. Indeed, a Black character's angry response to racism can at times be seen as negative, a rebellious "phase" to be "gotten over" before true, and desirable, assimilation into the White community is achieved. For an illustration, let's look at one of the best situations involving Black characters and the one that, in my view, is clearly the worst.

As the World Turns has (in 1993) only one Black character of primary importance and two of secondary importance. But more than most soaps, it allows its characters to *be* Black and to explore their lives in the context of their race as well as in the context of their place in the overall White fictional community in which they live. Jessica is a light-skinned African American, whom we met in 1987 as a typical soap opera Black: a glamorous, successful attorney, seemingly removed from any Black cultural context. She told her friends that she had come out of a bad relationship with a White man, but we didn't see them as a couple, and for the most part, the interracial relationship was ignored.

But in the 1990s, we have begun to see a new side to Jesse. She is from the South Bronx and her parents, brother, sister and the sister's children still live in the ghetto apartment in which she grew up. They resent her for what they see as her abandonment of them and of her Blackness. We learn that by putting herself through law school, she moved into a White world in which she became highly successful but at the price of loss of family and of identity. For the previous year or so, there were several segments in which she and her family confronted each other, grappling with the thorny issue of her new identity. Jessica realizes that she is both the girl from the ghetto and the successful professional who works in a White world, and she struggles to maintain the integrity of both identities. When she falls in love with another White man, the heroic Duncan (a character the audience has known and loved for years), she must deal with her family's fury, various expressions of White racism from the most crass to the relatively subtle and Duncan's smug naivete. He has never experienced racism and can afford to natter about love conquering all. She has been victimized by racism and knows the struggles they'll face.

Whereas *General Hospital*'s earlier interracial couple, Tom and Simone, faced racism only from "nigger"-shouting bigots brought on to show the nastiness of racism and the goodness of the Whites of Port Charles, *As the World Turns* has taken a more honest and disturbing route. Duncan's adult, likable daughter Beatrice rejects the couple, severing her relationship with her father. Lisa, one of the major characters on the show since the 1950s, opposes the marriage, in spite of her friendship for both Duncan and Jessica and has to work through her rationalizations about concern for their future children, coming to grips with a bigotry she has never before known was part of her makeup. Coming from a character the viewers have long known and have some identification with, her struggle shows the way well-intentioned Whites have inherited the culture's racist attitudes and need to take responsibility for struggling against their racism. Lisa is not condemned so much as she is shown a flaw in her character that she must, and does, confront and work to change.

Equally important, Jess is clearly here to stay, and so far her storylines involve her both in stories that deal with race and with nonracial stories that mirror the situations of the other characters. Thus we see her dealing with the same nonracial problem two of her friends, Tom and Barbara, are facing. Duncan, although not a detective, is an adventurer constantly getting caught up in dangerous confrontations with violent evildoers. Tom's wife Margo and Barbara's husband Hal are detectives in love with their work. Tom, Barbara and Jesse are all, at different times, confronted with situations that create frustrated anxiety over the safety of their spouses.

At the same time, Jessica is dealing with the anger of her brother Lamar, who now lives in Oakdale. He has done badly at the executive job that Duncan, in an excess of White-liberal zeal, gave him before he was experienced enough to handle it and has been fired. Both storylines are building up, which means that Jessica is unlikely to be relegated either to honorary Whiteness or occasional Blackness. This is different from almost any other soap to date. Other soaps sometimes have their Black characters confront racism, but it tends to be a one storyline deal, and they rarely show any sense of struggle over identity within Black families or Black communities. *Days of Our Lives*, for example, did a remarkably strong storyline in early 1990 in which a prominent Black character relived the horror of the murder of a group of Black schoolchildren by a racist hate group that he had witnessed and repressed years before. But when that story was resolved, Doctor Hunter returned to his back burner status, eventually drifting out of the show. (Nochimson's [1992] book does an excellent analysis of this storyline and its aftermath.)

Before overpraising *As the World Turns*, it's important to note that the absence of other Black characters makes Jessica's sense of herself as a Black woman difficult to sustain, outside of the clashes with her brother. She has a casual friendship with the only other regular Black character, police officer Joel, but her closest friends are all White, so Black culture and Black bonding are never seen. We see her only in conflict situations, not in pleasurable ones, when her race is part of the story.

It's also worth noting that the Jessie-Duncan relationship, as in the few other interracial relationships on soaps, involves a White man with a Black woman. It's true that on *One Life to Live* Hank Gannon is a Black man divorced from a White woman, but as actor Nathan Purdee noted in a recent *Soap Opera Digest*, we see them only as ex-spouses and never in any intimate moments. It makes sense. Because in the classical order of things, men own women and Whites own Black, a Black wife-White husband combination is far less threatening than a Black husband-White wife combination would be.

Still, *As the World Turns* has done a fairly decent job of acknowledging racism and the conflicts of Black characters in a White world. By contrast, *The Young and the Restless*, although it has more Black characters, has for the most part erased their Blackness. Worse, when it has allowed one character to actually *be* Black, it depicted her anger at racism as the petty whining of a troubled delinquent, thus dismissing the real anger of Black viewers and encouraging smug disregard of racism in White viewers.

For years, the show's only regular Black character was the appropriately named Mamie, longtime live-in housekeeper to the rich Abbot family. In the early 1990s, two of her nieces came to town. One, Olivia, a doctor, was the classic assimilated Black dear to Soapland's heart. She fell in love with the equally assimilated Nathan, best-buddy partner to blond private eye Paul Williams. Then her sister Drusilla showed up at the Abbot home—a street-wise, angry teenager who challenged Mamie's position in the household. Why was Mamie so grateful to be a servant to White people? Drusilla demanded. If, as she said, she was part of their family, why did she cook their dinner, serve it in the dining room and eat her own in the kitchen? Why did she call her employer "Mr. Abbot" when he called her "Mamie"?

Incredibly, we were clearly expected to see all these questions as Drusilla's immature, wrongheaded rebelliousness, a symptom of her juvenile delin-quency. She was sulky and rude, whereas Mr. Abbot, a figure viewers had known and loved for several years, was patient and fatherly to the "con-fused" young girl. There could be no doubt in viewers' minds that she *was* confused, because she was up against long-beloved characters such as Abbot and Mamie. Further, we had contrasts and comparisons for both her age and her race. Nathan and Olivia were "good" Blacks. Cricket, another young (White) character, was the "good" teen. Nina, Cricket's one-time enemy and now good friend, had been a "troubled" teen, like Drusilla was now, and, as we knew Drusilla was about to be, she had been saved by the help of various virtuous characters. There was no way any viewer could misinterpret the meaning of her defiance of Mamie's position in the Abbot household—and thus, by extension, the position of African Americans in White society.

In an interesting conjunction of racism and sexism, Drusilla was saved from reform school by a kindly judge who sent her to live with the strict, White-identified Nathan. Aside from the ludicrousness of having a judge send a teenage girl to live with a single man in his mid-20s, the plot clearly served to show the proper place for a Black female. Nathan used his "tough love" techniques to force the illiterate girl to learn both to read and to cook. As a result, she not only ended her resistance, but fell in love with Nathan. Her love was unreciprocated, but Nathan had succeeded in curing her of her rebelliousness—and with it, it seems, her racial awareness.

Moreover, Drusilla later fell in love with and married another assimilated Black character, her sister's former suitor, Neal. By 1993, we learned the real source of her suffering—not the racism she had once rebelled against, but her cold, dominating mother.

Nathan and Olivia (his real love), as the "good" Black characters, seem wholly oblivious to their race. A year or so after Drusilla's conversion into a still feisty but no longer angry good girl, Olivia and Nathan's baby was born. Nathan wanted his partner Paul to be the godfather; Olivia held out for her old friend Neal. The argument was lengthy, bringing in overtones of Nathan's jealousy of Olivia's past relationship. Olivia fought long and hard for Neal. Yet never once did she suggest that Neal might be a better godfather for their son because he was Black and would thus be part of the child's racial heritage. Whereas Jessica struggles, at least intermittently, with what it means to be a Black professional in a largely White world, Olivia is comfortable and oblivious.

Thus in the Drusilla story, we have had two "bad" Black women—a Black matriarch figure (Drusilla's cold mother) and a teenager who challenges racism. And we have had two "good" Black women—a happy servant and a pallid, White-identified doctor. We've also had two "good" Black men, who appear equally oblivious to racism.

If Soapland has improved somewhat in its depiction of African Americans, it has done nothing for other people of color and little for other minorities. *General Hospital* used Asian Americans in a highly offensive story in the late 1980s in which there suddenly appeared in Port Charles an Asian Quarter, full of Fu Manchu-type criminals. Woven into the story was a good, "colorful character" Asian housekeeper and a pair of good, bland Asian Americans (one cutely named Yank). But when the crime story was resolved, all but the cute housekeeper vanished, and she followed soon afterward. Around the same time, two soaps had storylines in which a Eurasian teenager appeared on a hero's doorstep, claiming to be his daughter, conceived during his stint in Vietnam. The character on *As the World Turns* remained for several years, even facing racist attacks at one point, but the actress eventually left the show and there have been no more Asians since.

Hispanics too are rare. Cord, a longtime *One Life to Live* hunk hero is half Hispanic (his mother was a psychotic lunatic, who showed up, caused trouble and got killed). Occasionally, Hispanics from fictional, war-torn South American countries appear on a show, but they rarely stay long. (One, Tonio Reyes, was the resident archvillain on *As the World Turns* for several years). Even in environments where the absence of minorities is wholly unrealistic, they are rare. For example, *Ryan's Hope*, which ended in the late 1980s, was set in New York—a city, it would appear, inhabited almost exclusively by Irish and Italian Catholics. There was one Jew who ran a deli—New York's only Jewish establishment, evidently—for a few years, a Hispanic nurse and her sick little brother, a Black doctor and, later, a Black paralegal. Even California's *Santa Barbara* was a town where only a handful of Hispanics lived, and the most central Hispanic character was passionately and permanently in love with a blond WASP.

And none of Soapland's towns have gay communities. Once in a great while a lesbian or gay man wanders into one of the more liberal Soapland venues, but soon disappears. In the late 1980s, there was a spate of AIDS stories, each featuring a pale, wispy blonde woman—a virgin who got AIDS from her hooker-mother's blood transfusion, a virginal wife who got it from her drug-addicted husband and a virginal ex-hooker who got it from a john. There were a few support group scenes where we briefly met nice gay men and a few well-intentioned stabs at homophobia and AIDs-phobic behavior. But these scenes took as much time as a public service announcement—the right things were said, the right attitudes expressed by the good guys, and then gays faded back into the woodwork from which they had emerged only in faint bas-relief.

In a sense, the AIDS stories illustrated the way that soaps become victims of their own tokenism. Had there been a reasonable number of gay characters, they could have easily brought in homosexuals with AIDS and made them the focus, or a focus, of AIDS storylines. In the absence of a tradition of gay characters, it would have been oppressive, suggesting that AIDS is a gay disease and that gay men are, by definition, people who get AIDS, rather than complex individuals with differing personalities who are more at risk for AIDS than most other Americans.

Three times in Soapland's history there have been significant exceptions to the invisibility of homosexuality. In 1983, there was a lesbian character on *All My Children.* She was good and unpredatory and celibate and she left town within a few months. In the early 1990s, *As the World Turns* introduced Hank Eliot, a gay fashion designer involved in a marriagelike relationship— with a lover who lived in New York. The storyline was good, showing the difficulties his teenage friend Paul and Paul's stepfather had dealing with his sexuality and depicting varying levels of homophobia, clearly presented as an evil that forced the good folk of Oakdale into some serious soul-searching. When he learned his lover had AIDS, we got to see him briefly in his own story, before he left Oakdale to care for the dying man. He has never returned. Challenged on why he wrote out Hank, the late headwriter, Doug Marland, insisted that it was because the actor did not want to return—a lame excuse for a show that has recast several key characters numerous times over the years. Hank had served his purpose: The residents of Oakdale and the viewers who identify with them got to pat themselves on the back for their tolerance and then go on ignoring homosexuality. In 1993, *One Life to Live* ran a story about a gay teenager and the straight White minister who defended him against gay bashing—even refusing to deny "accusations" that he himself was gay. Yet when the story was finished and the forces of tolerance had won out, the boy left town and there are no more homosexuals on the Llanview scene.

Finally, how does Soapland deal with the poor and the working class? Again, not too well. In fact, here is the one area where its social consciousness has actually worsened. Not that soaps were ever good about depicting non-middle-class life, but at least in the old days it *was* middle-class life. Few people in Soapland were poor, but even fewer were rich. It was a world of comfortable middle-class professionals. It still is, but now, in the wake of *Dallas* and *Dynasty* and the other nighttime "soaps," there are far more rich characters in virtually every soap. And unlike the truly wealthy in real life, they spend most of their time with their middle-class friends. This creates an aura of wealth even for the nonwealthy characters, who can always, in a pinch, borrow their friends' private jets when an emergency calls for quick traveling.

Poor characters sometimes appear, but they are either brief objects of charity for the gracious middle- and upper-class folks, or they quickly acquire jobs that make them indistinguishable from their new friends. Working-class characters also demonstrate a wonderful economic mobility. (Witness Lamar's rise from busboy to business exec, discussed earlier. Losing his new job, he promptly got hired as public relations man for a gambling boat.) There are a few "colorful" working-class jobs available in Soapland—tending a friendly bar, chasing criminals as a uniformed cop, for example. But as likely as not, the bartender will soon own the bar and the uniformed cop will soon be a plainclothes detective. No one ever has to decide between going to the movies or eating out with their little extra money; certainly no one has to decide whether to eat or pay the rent.

Soapland is at heart a country composed of middle Americans. Whether or not the mythical town is actually in the Midwest, as in *As the World Turns'* Oakdale, Illinois, the spirit is that popular American midwestern small-town image. All the accents are the carefully trained, Midwest nonaccent, with an occasional sprinkle of Irish, Scottish or Australian. (There are sporadic Greeks and Italians, but they're usually crafty criminals.) Even in the New York of *Ryan's Hope*, there were lots of Irish accents but no Brooklyn accents.

It's an image that has an enormous appeal. As Ruth Rosen (1986) notes, soap opera maintains the "ideal replica" of the vanishing small town—"the image of a community in which everyone knows or is related to everyone else, where continuity counts more than transience, where right and wrong are unambiguous, where good triumphs over evil" (p. 49). It's a compelling vision and one not without merit. But soaps rarely stretch the parameters of that vision, confining it to a comfortable and usually unchallenging picture of a world that middle America is at peace with.

And in that world, "we" are all White, we are all straight, we are all Christian, and, although we are kind to the outsiders, they are really always outsiders unless they manage to become believable imitations of the mythical "us." Sadly, in a genre much of whose power rests in the fact that it shows us life through the subjective view of a gender traditionally defined by its "otherness," no other otherness gets much validation.

REFERENCES

Nochimson, M. (1992). *No end to her: Soap opera and the female subject.* Berkeley: University of California Press.

Rosen, R. (1986). Search for yesterday. In T. Gitlin (Ed.), *Watching television.* New York: Pantheon.

Minorities on the soaps. (1989, March 21). *Soap Opera Digest,* pp. 92-99.

■ 39

Gendered Television

Femininity

JOHN FISKE

... I wish to explore some of the strategies by which television copes with, and helps to produce, a crucial categorization of its viewers into masculine and feminine subjects. Mellencamp (1985) traces this back to the 1950s, where she finds the origin of "the 'gender base' of television, with sport and news shows for men, cooking and fashion shows for women, and 'kidvid' for children" (p. 31). Television's techniques for gendering its audience have grown more sophisticated, and nowhere more so than in its development of gender-specific narrative forms. I propose to look at soap opera as a feminine narrative. . . .

SOAP OPERA FORM

Brown (1987) lists eight generic characteristics of soap operas:

1. serial form which resists narrative closure
2. multiple characters and plots
3. use of time which parallels actual time and implies that the action continues to take place whether we watch it or not
4. abrupt segmentation between parts

NOTE: Excerpts reprinted from *Television Culture*, by John Fiske (London: Routledge, 1987), by permission of the publisher.

5. emphasis on dialogue, problem solving, and intimate conversation
6. male characters who are "sensitive men"
7. female characters who are often professional and otherwise powerful in the world outside the home
8. the home, or some other place which functions as a home, as the setting for the show. (p. 4)

Each of these characteristics merits considerable discussion, particularly if and why they constitute a feminine aesthetic. I wish to concentrate on the first two characteristics, that is, soap opera's ongoing, serial form with its consequent lack of narrative closure, and the multiplicity of its plots. . . . Traditional realist narratives are constructed to have a beginning, a middle, and an end, but soap opera realism works through an infinitely extended middle. Traditional narrative begins with a state of equilibrium which is disturbed: the plot traces the effects of this disturbance through to the final resolution, which restores a new and possibly different equilibrium. Comparing the states of equilibrium with which it begins and ends and specifying the nature of the threat of disturbance is a good way of identifying the ideological thrust of a story. The end of such a narrative is the point of both narrative closure and ideological closure. The narrative resolves the questions it posed, makes good its lacks and deficiencies, and defuses its threats. The resolutions of these disturbances prefer a particular ideological reading of its events, settings, and characters. For the aim of realist narrative is to make sense of the world, and the pleasure it offers derives from the apparent comprehensiveness of this sense. This comprehensiveness is evaluated according to relation to the ideologies of the reader, and through them, to the dominant ideology of the culture. So a narrative with no ending lacks one of the formal points at which ideological closure is most powerfully exerted. Of course, individual plotlines can end, often with the departure or death of the characters central to them, but such endings have none of the sense of finality of novel or film endings. Departed characters can, and do, return, and even apparently dead characters can return to life and the program— four did so within two years on *Days of Our Lives*! But even without physical presence, the departed characters live on in the memory and gossip both of those that remain, and of their viewers.

DISRUPTION

This infinitely extended middle means that soap operas are never in a state of equilibrium, but their world is one of perpetual disturbance and threat. The equilibrium of a happy, stable family is constantly there in the background, but is never achieved. Even a soap opera marriage, and marriages are ritual high points to be greatly savored, is not the same as a marriage in a traditional romance in which the couple are expected to live happily ever after. All soap opera marriages have within them the seeds of their own destruction. On one level the fans know that this is because a happy, unthreatened marriage is boring and incapable of producing good plotlines. But these generic conventions have not grown from some formalist ideal world of "good plotlines"; they have a social base. Marriage is not a point of narrative and ideological closure because soap operas interrogate it as they celebrate it. Building the threat into the celebration opens marriage up to readings other than those preferred by patriarchy. This double evaluation is generic to soap opera, and is part of the reason for its openness. A wife's extra-marital sex, for instance is evaluated both patriarchally as unfaithfulness, but also, more resistingly, as a woman's independence and right to her own sexuality. Such affairs often spring from the man's, or the marriage's, inability to satisfy her. A wife's "unfaithfulness," then, is capable of being read by both masculine and feminine value systems simultaneously.

As Seiter et al. (1987) found in their study of soap opera fans,

> women openly and enthusiastically admitted their delight in following soap operas as stories of female transgressions which destroy the ideological nucleus of the text: the priority and sacredness of the family. (p. 27)

Two of the women to whom they talked expressed their pleasure in seeing marriage disrupted and one went so far as to use this in a playful, but actual challenge to the power of her husband as it is inscribed in the conventions of marriage:

> **SW:** But there's lots of times when you want the person to dump the husband and go on with this. . . .
>
> **JS:** Oh Bruce [her husband] gets so angry with me when I'm watching the show and they're married and I'm all for the affair. (*Laughter.*) It's like it's like (*voice changed*) "I don't like this. I don't know about you." (*Laughter.*) Dump him. (p. 27)

The dominant ideology is inscribed in the status quo, and soap operas offer their subordinated women viewers the pleasure of seeing this status quo in a constant state of disruption. Disruption without resolution produces openness in the text. It can be read dominantly (patriarchally): such readings would produce fans who return to their more "normal" marriages with a sense of relief. But disruption can also serve to interrogate the status quo. As we shall see in our discussion of soap opera characters, the powerful women who disrupt men's power are both loved and hated, their actions praised and condemned.

The marital relationship is not the only one being simultaneously affirmed and questioned. One of the commonest plot themes is that of family ties and relationships. This concern to clarify relationships within the disrupted and unstable family may be seen as "women's matters," that is, as a domain where patriarchy grants women a position of some power. But if it is, its representation and the pleasure it offers overspill these ideological constraints. The ability to understand, facilitate, and control relationships is often shown as a source of women's power, used disruptively by the bitches and more constructively by the matriarchs. Men are often shown as deficient in these abilities and knowledges, and cause many problems by this masculine lack. This set of abilities and knowledges, normally devalued by patriarchy, is given a high valuation and legitimation in soap operas, and can serve as a source of self-esteem for the fans and as an assertion of women's values against the place assigned to them in patriarchy. . . .

DEFERMENT AND PROCESS

Disruption is not the only effect of the infinitely extended "middle"; deferment is an equally important characteristic. As Modleski (1982, p. 88) puts it, a soap opera "by placing ever more complex obstacles between desire and fulfillment, makes anticipation of an end an end in itself." A soap opera narrative strand has no climax to close it off, no point at which it is seen to have finished: indeed, the outcome of most plotlines is relatively unimportant, and often not really in doubt. What matters is the process that people have to go through to achieve it. As Brunsdon (1984) argues, the pleasure in soap opera lies in seeing how the events occur rather than in the events themselves. Indeed, the soap opera press often summarizes future plotlines: the reader knows the events before they occur, her interest lies in how the characters behave and feel as they react to the events. Each event always has consequences, final outcomes are indefinitely deferred, and narrative climax is rarely reached. Instead there is a succession of obstacles and problems to be overcome and the narrative interest centers on people's feelings and reactions as they live through a constant series of disruptions and difficulties. No solutions are final, smooth patches are never free from the sense of impending disasters. The triumphs are small-scale and temporary, but frequent. . . . These minor pleasures "buy" the viewers, and win their apparently willing consent to the system that subordinates them. Women, this argument runs, harm themselves as a class by their pleasure as individuals.

But this endless deferment need not be seen simply as a textual transformation of women's powerlessness in patriarchy. It can be seen more positively as an articulation of a specific feminine definition of desire and pleasure that is contrasted with the masculine pleasure of the final success. . . . The emphasis on the process rather than the product, on pleasure as ongoing and cyclical rather than climactic and final, is constitutive of a feminine subjectivity in so far as it opposes masculine pleasures and rewards. This feminine subjectivity and the pleasures which reward and legitimate it are not bound to be understood according to their dominant construction as inferior to their masculine counterparts. Indeed, soap opera narratives consistently validate these feminine principles as a source of legitimate pleasure within and against patriarchy.

Deferment and process are enacted in talk and facial expression. The sound track of soap operas is full of words, and the screen is full of close-ups of faces. The camera lingers on the telling expression, giving the viewers time not just to experience the emotion of the character, but to imagine what constitutes that emotion. Porter (1977, p. 786) suggests that "a face in close-up is what before the age of film only a lover or a mother saw."

Close-ups are, according to Modleski (1982, pp. 99-100), an important mode of representation in feminine culture for a number of reasons. They provide training in the feminine skills of "reading people," and are the means of exercising the feminine ability to understand the gap between what is meant and what is said. Language is used by men to exert control over the meanings of the world but women question its effectivity in this, and find pleasure in the knowledges that escape it. Close-ups also encourage women's desire to be implicated with the lives of the characters on the screen, a desire that is also satisfied by the comparatively slow movement of soap opera plots which allow reactions and feelings to be savored and dwelt on. As Brown (1987) says, "soaps allow us to linger, like the pleasure of a long conversation with an old friend." Feuer (1984) suggests that the acting style of soaps is excessive and exaggerates the hyperintensity of each emotional confrontation. Editing conventions work in the same way:

> Following and exaggerating a convention of daytime soaps, *Dallas* and *Dynasty* typically hold a shot on screen for at least a "beat" after the dialogue has ended. . . . [This] leaves a residue of emotional intensity just prior to a scene change or commercial break. (pp. 10-11)

An event, however momentous or climactic, is never significant for itself, but rather for the reactions it will cause and the effects it will have. Events originate or reactivate plots instead of closing them.

SEXUALITY AND EMPOWERMENT

As Davies (1984) argues, soap opera sexuality is concerned with seduction and emotion rather than, as masculine sexuality is, with achievement and climax. If a woman's body and sexuality are all that patriarchy allows her, then, according to Davies, soaps show her how to use them as a weapon against men. It has been pointed out (e.g., by Geraghty, 1981) that soaps show and celebrate the sexuality of the middle-aged woman, and thus articulate what is repressed elsewhere on television as in the culture generally. In the prime-time soaps the sexual power of the middle-aged woman goes hand in hand with her economic power in a significant reversal of conventional gender ascription. . . . The powerful women in soap opera never achieve a settled state of power, but are in a continual process of struggle to exercise control over themselves and others. . . .

. . . The "good" male in the daytime soaps is caring, nurturing, and verbal. He is prone to making comments like "I don't care about material wealth or professional success, all I care about is us and our relationship." He will talk about feelings and people and rarely expresses his masculinity in direct action. Of course he is still decisive, he still has masculine power, but that power is given a "feminine" inflection. This produces different gender roles and relationships:

Women and men in the soap operas are probably more equal than in any other form of art or drama or in any area of real life. By playing down men's domination over women (and children) the soaps and the game shows make the family palatable. On daytime TV the family is not a hierarchy, starting with the father and ending with the youngest girl, but an intimate group of people, connected to each other intimately through ties of love and kinship. (Lopate, 1977, pp. 50-51, in Hartley, 1985, p. 23)

The "macho" characteristics of goal centeredness, assertiveness, and the morality of the strongest that identify the hero in masculine television, tend here to be characteristics of the villain. It is not surprising that, in women's culture, feminized men should be seen positively while the masculine men are more associated with villainy, but the reversal is not a simple one. The villains are typically very good-looking, and are often featured in the press as desirable "hunks"; they are loved and hated, admired and despised. Similarly, the good, feminized men, particularly the younger ones, typically have the strong good looks associated with conventional heterosexual masculinity. It is rare to find sensitive, feminized looks (with their possible threat of homosexuality) going with the sensitivity of the character. . . .

Brown (1987), on the other hand, argues that soaps are positive and empowering in the way they handle sexuality and sexual pleasure:

Thus the image of the body as sexual currency is absent, but the spoken discourse of the power of the female body to create is given crucial importance. There is no need to reiterate here the number of pregnancies, the importance attached to paternity and sometimes to maternity or the large number of sexual liaisons between characters in soap operas. However, contrary to the discourse which places the pregnant woman as powerless over natural events, often women in soaps use pregnancy as power over the father of the unborn child. The father will usually marry the mother of his child, whether or not he loves her (or whether or not the pregnancy is real), thereby achieving the woman's felt need to be taken care of in the only way that is available to her in the dominant system. Women characters, then, use their bodies to achieve their own ends. (pp. 19-20)

A woman's sexuality does not, in soap opera, result in her objectification for the male. Rather it is a positive source of pleasure in a relationship, or a means of her empowerment in a patriarchal world. The woman's power to influence and control the male can never be finally achieved but is constantly in process. It is a form of power not legitimated by the dominant ideology, and can thus exist only in the continuous struggle to exercise it. . . .

Modleski's (1982) account of the soap opera villainess reveals . . . contradictions. She argues that the villainess is a negative image of the viewer's ideal self, which is constructed by the soaps as the ideal mother, able to sympathize with and understand all the members of her (and the soap opera's) extended family. Such a mother role is, of course, specific to the patriarchal family, for it denies the mother any claims on herself, and requires her to find her satisfaction in helping her children to come to terms with and resolve their multiple difficulties. She is other-directed and decentered. . . .

. . . Seiter et al. (1987), found that many of their subjects explicitly rejected this textually constructed role:

> While this position [the Ideal Mother] was partially taken up by some of our middle-class, educated informants, it was also consciously resisted and vehemently rejected by most of the women we interviewed, especially by working-class women. (p. 24)

The villainess turns traditional feminine characteristics (which are often seen as weaknesses ensuring her subordination) into a source of strength. She uses pregnancy (real or alleged) as a weapon, she uses her insight into people to manipulate them, and she uses her sexuality for her own ends, not for masculine pleasure. She reverses male and female roles (which probably explains why Alexis in *Dynasty* is popular with the gay community) and, above all, she embodies the female desire for power which is both produced and frustrated by the social relations of patriarchy. The final control that the villainess strives for is, Modleski argues (1982, p. 97), control not over men, but over feminine passivity.

Seiter et al. (1987) found clear evidence of the appeal of the strong villainess for women chafing against their subjection in patriarchy:

> All of these women commented on their preference of strong villainesses: the younger respondents expressed their pleasure in and admiration for the powerful female characters which were also discussed in terms of transgressing the boundaries of a traditional pattern of resistance for women within patriarchy:

> | | |
> |---|---|
> | **LD:** | Yeah, they can be very vicious (*laughs*) the females can be very vicious. |
> | **JS:** | Seems like females have more of an impact than the males and they have such a mm . . . conniving . . . |
> | **SW:** | brain! Yeah! (*Laughter.*) |
> | **LD:** | They're sneaky!!! Yeah! |
> | **SW:** | They use their brain more (*laughter*) instead of their body! They manipulate, you know! (pp. 25-26) |

But there was little evidence of any hatred for the villainess, rather the respondents despised the woman who suffered despite her middle-class privileges, a character type they called the "whiner," or "the wimpy woman" (pp. 24-25).

But, in the portrayal of the villainess, soap operas set these "positive" feminine characteristics in a framework of moral disapproval, and follow them at work through a repeated narrative structure that denies their ultimate success. The woman viewer loves and hates the villainess, sides with her, and desires her downfall. The contradictions in the text and its reading position reflect the contradictions inherent in the attempt to assert feminine values within and against a patriarchal society. . . .

REFERENCES

Brown, M. E. (1987). The politics of soaps: Pleasure and feminine empowerment. *Australian Journal of Cultural Studies, 4*(2), 1-25.

Brunsdon, C. (1984). Writing about soap opera. In L. Masterman (Ed.), *Television mythologies: Stars, shows, and signs* (pp. 82-87). London: Comedia/MK Media Press.

Davies, J. (1984). Soap and other operas. *Metro, 65,* 31-33.

Feuer, J. (1984). Melodrama, serial form and television today. *Screen, 25*(1), 4-16.

Geraghty, C. (1981). The continuous serial—A definition. In R. Dyer, C. Geraghty, M. Jordan, T. Lovell, R. Paterson, & J. Stewart (Eds.), *Coronation street* (pp. 9-26). London: British Film Institute.

Hartley, J. (1985). *Invisible fictions, television audiences and regimes of pleasure.* Unpublished manuscript, Murdoch University, Perth, WA.

Lopate, C. (1977). Daytime television: You'll never want to leave home. *Radical America, 2,* 3-51.

Mellencamp, P. (1985). Situation and simulation: An introduction to "I Love Lucy." *Screen, 26*(2), 30-40.

Modleski, T. (1982). *Loving with a vengeance: Mass produced fantasies for women.* London: Methuen.

Porter, D. (1977). Soap time: Thoughts on a commodity art form. *College English, 38,* 783.

Seiter, E., Kreutzner, G., Warth, E. M., & Borchers, H. (1987, February). *"Don't treat us like we're so stupid and naive": Towards an ethnography of soap opera viewers.* Paper presented at the seminar on *Rethinking the Audience,* University of Tübingen, Germany.

40

The Search for Tomorrow in Today's Soap Operas

TANIA MODLESKI

. . . John Cawelti defines melodrama as having

> at its center the moral fantasy of showing forth the essential "right-ness" of the world order. . . . Because of this, melodramas are usually rather complicated in plot and character; instead of identifying with a single protagonist through his line of action, the melodrama typically makes us intersect imaginatively with many lives. Subplots multiply, and the point of view continually shifts in order to involve us in a complex of destinies. Through this complex of characters and plots we see not so much the working of individual fates but the underlying moral process of the world.[1]

It is scarcely an accident that this essentially nineteenth-century form continues to appeal strongly to women, whereas the classic (male) narrative film is, as Laura Mulvey points out, structured "around a main controlling figure with whom the spectator can identify."[2] Soap operas continually insist on the insignificance of the individual life. A viewer might at one moment be asked to identify with a woman finally reunited with her lover, only to have

NOTE: Excerpts reprinted from *Loving With a Vengeance: Mass-Produced Fantasies for Women,* by Tania Modleski (Hamden, CT: Shoestring Press, 1982), by permission of the publisher.

that identification broken in a moment of intensity and attention focused on the sufferings of the woman's rival.

If, as Mulvey claims, the identification of the spectator with "a main male protagonist" results in the spectator's becoming "the representative of power,"[3] the multiple identification which occurs in soap opera results in the spectator's being divested of power. For the spectator is never permitted to identify with a character completing an entire action. Instead of giving us one "powerful ideal ego . . . who can make things happen and control events better than the subject/spectator can,"[4] soap operas present us with numerous limited egos, each in conflict with the others, and continually thwarted in its attempts to control events because of inadequate knowledge of other peoples' plans, motivations, and schemes. Sometimes, indeed, the spectator, frustrated by the sense of powerlessness induced by soap operas, will, like an interfering mother, try to control events directly:

> Thousands and thousands of letters [from soap fans to actors] give advice, warn the heroine of impending doom, caution the innocent to beware of the nasties ("Can't you see that your brother-in-law is up to no good?"), inform one character of another's doings, or reprimand a character for unseemly behavior.[5]

Presumably, this intervention is ineffectual, and feminine powerlessness is reinforced on yet another level.

The subject/spectator of soap operas, it could be said, is constituted as a sort of ideal mother: a person who possesses greater wisdom than all her children, whose sympathy is large enough to encompass the conflicting claims of her family (she identifies with them all), and who has no demands or claims of her own (she identifies with no one character exclusively). The connection between melodrama and mothers is an old one. Harriet Beecher Stowe, of course, made it explicit in *Uncle Tom's Cabin*, believing that if her book could bring its female readers to see the world as one extended family, the world would be vastly improved. But in Stowe's novel, the frequent shifting of perspective identifies the reader with a variety of characters in order ultimately to ally her with the mother/author and with God who, in their higher wisdom and understanding, can make all the hurts of the world go away, thus insuring the "essential 'rightness' of the world order." Soap opera, however, denies the "mother" this extremely flattering illusion of her power. On the one hand, it plays upon the spectator's expectations of the melodramatic form, continually stimulating (by means of the hermeneutic code) the desire for a just conclusion to the story, and, on the other hand, it constantly presents the desire as unrealizable, by showing that conclusions only lead to further tension and suffering. Thus soap operas convince women that their highest goal is to see their families united and happy, while consoling them for their inability to realize this ideal and bring about familial harmony.

This is reinforced by the character of the good mother on soap operas. In contrast to the manipulating mother who tries to interfere with her children's lives, the good mother must sit helplessly by as her children's lives disintegrate; her advice, which she gives only when asked, is temporarily soothing, but usually ineffectual. Her primary function is to be sympathetic, to tolerate the foibles and errors of others. Maeve Ryan, the mother on "Ryan's Hope," is a perfect example. "Ryan's Hope," a soap opera centered around an Irish-Catholic, bar-owning family which, unlike the majority of soap families, lives in a large city, was originally intended to be more "realistic," more socially oriented than the majority of soap operas.[6] Nevertheless, the function of the mother is unchanged: she is there to console her children and try to understand them as they have illegitimate babies, separate from their spouses (miraculously obtaining annulments instead of divorces), and dispense birth control information in the poor neighborhoods.

It is important to recognize that soap operas serve to affirm the primacy of the family not by presenting an ideal family, but by portraying a family in constant turmoil and appealing to the spectator to be understanding and tolerant of the many evils which go on within that family. The spectator/ mother, identifying with each character in turn, is made to see "the larger picture" and extend her sympathy to both the sinner and the victim. She is thus in a position to forgive all. As a rule, only those issues which can be tolerated and ultimately pardoned are introduced on soap operas. The list includes careers for women, abortions, premarital and extramarital sex, alcoholism, divorce, mental and even physical cruelty. An issue like homosexuality, which could explode the family structure rather than temporarily disrupt it, is simply ignored. Soap operas, contrary to many people's conception of them, are not conservative but liberal, and the mother is the liberal par excellence. By constantly presenting her with the many-sidedness of any question, by never reaching a permanent conclusion, soap operas undermine her capacity to form unambiguous judgments.

. . . To take one example, Trish, on "Days of Our Lives," takes her small son and runs away from her husband David in order to advance her singing career. When she gets an opportunity to go to London to star in a show, she leaves the child with her mother. When the show folds, she becomes desperate to get back home to see her child, but since she has no money, she has to prostitute herself. Finally she is able to return, and after experiencing a series of difficulties, she locates her son, who is now staying with his father. Once she is in town, a number of people, angry at the suffering she has caused David, are hostile and cruel towards her. Thus far, the story seems to bear out the contention of the critics who claim that soap opera characters who leave the protection of the family are unequivocally punished. But the matter is not so simple. For the unforgiving people are shown to have limited perspectives. The larger view is summed up by Margo, a woman who has a mysterious and perhaps fatal disease and who, moreover, has every reason to be jealous of Trish since Trish was the first love of Margo's husband. Margo claims that no one can ever fully know what private motives drove Trish to abandon her family; besides, she says, life is too short to bear grudges and inflict pain. The spectator, who sees the extremity of Trish's sorrow, assents. And at the same time, the spectator is made to forgive and understand the unforgiving characters, for she is intimately drawn into their anguish and suffering as well.

These remarks must be qualified. If soap operas keep us caring about everyone; if they refuse to allow us to condemn most characters and actions until all the evidence is in (and, of course, it never is), there is one character whom we are allowed to hate unreservedly: the villainess, the negative image of the spectator's ideal self.[7] Although much of the suffering on soap opera is presented as unavoidable, the surplus suffering is often the fault of the villainess who tries to "make things happen and control events better than the subject/spectator can." The villainess might very possibly be a mother trying to manipulate her children's lives or ruin their marriages. Or perhaps she is a woman avenging herself on her husband's family because it has never fully accepted her.

This character cannot be dismissed as easily as many critics seem to think.[8] The extreme delight viewers apparently take in despising the villainess testifies to the enormous amount of energy involved in the spectator's repression and to her (albeit unconscious) resentment at being constituted as an egoless receptacle for the suffering of others.[9] The villainess embodies the "split-off fury" which, in the words of Dorothy Dinnerstein, is "the underside of the 'truly feminine' woman's monstrously overdeveloped talent for unreciprocated empathy."[10] This aspect of melodrama can be traced back to the middle of the nineteenth century when *Lady Audley's Secret*, a drama based on Mary Elizabeth Braddon's novel about a governess turned bigamist and murderess, became one of the most popular stage melodramas of all time.[11] In her discussion of the novel, Elaine Showalter shows how the author, while paying lipservice to conventional notions about the feminine role, managed to appeal to "thwarted female energy":

> The brilliance of *Lady Audley's Secret* is that Braddon makes her would-be murderess the fragile blond angel of domestic realism. . . . The dangerous woman is not the rebel or the bluestocking, but the "pretty little girl" whose indoctrination in the female role has taught her secrecy and deceitfulness, almost as secondary sex characteristics.[12]

Thus the villainess is able to transform traditional feminine weaknesses into the sources of her strength.

Similarly, on soap operas, the villainess seizes those aspects of a woman's life which normally render her most helpless and tries to turn them into weapons for manipulating other characters. She is, for instance, especially good at manipulating pregnancy. . . .

. . . In contrast to the numerous women on soap operas who are either trying unsuccessfully to become pregnant or who have become pregnant as a consequence of a single unguarded moment in their lives, the villainess manages, for a time at least, to make pregnancy work for her. She gives it the "style of enterprise." If she decides she wants to marry a man, she will take advantage of him one night when he is feeling especially vulnerable and seduce him. And if she doesn't achieve the hoped-for pregnancy, undaunted, she simply lies to her lover about being pregnant. The villainess thus reverses male/female roles: anxiety about conception is transferred to the male. He is the one who had better watch his step and curb his promiscuous desires or he will find himself burdened with an unwanted child. . . .

Furthermore, the villainess, far from allowing her children to rule her life, often uses them in order to further her own selfish ambitions. One of her typical ploys is to threaten the father or the woman possessing custody of the child with the deprivation of that child. She is the opposite of the woman at home, who at first is forced to have her children constantly with her, and later is forced to let them go—for a time on a daily recurring basis and then permanently. . . . Into the bargain, she also tries to manipulate the man's disappearance and return by keeping the fate of his child always hanging in the balance. And again, male and female roles tend to get reversed: the male suffers the typically feminine anxiety over the threatened absence of his children. On "Ryan's Hope," for example, Delia continually uses her son to control her husband and his family. At one point she clashes with another villainess, Raye Woodward, over the child and the child's father, Frank Ryan, from whom Delia is divorced. Raye realizes that the best way to get Frank interested in her is by taking a maternal interest in his child. When Delia uncovers Raye's scheme, she becomes determined to foil it by regaining custody of the boy. On "The Young and the Restless," to take another example, Derek is on his way out of the house to try to intercept Jill Foster on her way to the altar and persuade her to marry him instead of Stuart Brooks. Derek's ex-wife Suzanne thwarts the attempt by choosing that moment to inform him that their son is in a mental hospital.

The villainess thus continually works to make the most out of events which render other characters totally helpless. Literal paralysis turns out, for one villainess, to be an active blessing, since it prevents her husband from carrying out his plans to leave her; when she gets back the use of her legs, therefore, she doesn't tell anyone. And even death doesn't stop another villainess from wreaking havoc; she returns to haunt her husband and convince him to try to kill his new wife.

The popularity of the villainess would seem to be explained in part by the theory of repetition compulsion, which Freud saw as resulting from the individual's attempt to become an active manipulator of her/his own powerlessness.[13] The spectator, it might be thought, continually tunes into soap operas to watch the villainess as she tries to gain control over her feminine passivity, thereby acting out the spectator's fantasies of power. Of course, most formula stories (like the Western) appeal to the spectator/reader's compulsion to repeat; the spectator constantly returns to the same story in order to identify with the main character and achieve, temporarily, the illusion of mastery denied him or her in real life. But soap operas refuse the spectator even this temporary illusion of mastery. The villainess's painstaking attempts to turn her powerlessness to her own advantage are always thwarted just when victory seems most assured, and she must begin her machinations all over again. Moreover, the spectator does not comfortably identify with the villainess. Since the spectator despises the villainess as the negative image of her ideal self, she not only watches the villainess act out her own hidden wishes, but simultaneously sides with the forces conspiring against fulfillment of those wishes. As a result of this "internal contestation,"[14] the spectator comes to enjoy repetition for its own sake and takes her adequate pleasure in the building up and tearing down of the plot. In this way, perhaps, soap operas help reconcile her to the meaningless, repetitive nature of much of her life and work within the home.

Soap operas, then, while constituting the spectator as a "good mother," provide in the person of the villainess an outlet for feminine anger: in particular, as we have seen, the spectator has the satisfaction of seeing men suffer the same anxieties and guilt that women usually experience and seeing them receive similar kinds of punishment for their transgressions. But that anger is neutralized at every moment in that it is the special object of the spectator's hatred. The spectator, encouraged to sympathize with almost everyone, can vent her frustration on the one character who refuses to accept her own powerlessness, who is unashamedly self-seeking. Woman's anger is directed at woman's anger, and an eternal cycle is created.

And yet, if the villainess never succeeds, if, in accordance with the spectator's conflicting desires, she is doomed to eternal repetition, then she obviously never permanently fails either. When, as occasionally happens, a villainess reforms, a new one immediately supplants her. Generally, however, a popular villainess will remain true to her character for most or all of the soap opera's duration. And if the villainess constantly suffers because she is always foiled, we should remember that she suffers no more than the good characters, who don't even try to interfere with their fates. Again, this may be contrasted to the usual imperatives of melodrama, which demand an ending to justify the suffering of the good and punish the wicked. While soap operas thrive they present a continual reminder that women's anger is alive, if not exactly well. . . .

NOTES

1. Cawelti (1976, pp. 45-46).
2. Mulvey (1977, p. 420).
3. Mulvey (1977, p. 420).
4. Mulvey (1977, p. 420).
5. Edmondson and Rounds (1976, p. 193).
6. See Mayer (1977).
7. There are still villains on soap operas, but their numbers have declined considerably since radio days—to the point where they are no longer indispensable to the formula. "The Young and the Restless," for example, does without them.
8. According to Weibel (1977), we quite simply "deplore" the victimizers and totally identify with the victim (p. 62).
9. "A soap opera without a bitch is a soap opera that doesn't get watched. The more hateful the bitch the better. Erica of 'All My Children' is a classic. If you want to hear some hairy rap, just listen to a bunch of women discussing Erica. 'Girl, that Erica needs her tail whipped.' 'I wish she'd try to steal my man and plant some marijuana in my purse. I'd be mopping up the street with her new hairdo' " (Campbell, 1978, p. 103).
10. Dinnerstein (1976, p. 236).
11. "The author, Mary Elizabeth Braddon, belonged to that class of writers called by Charles Reade 'obstacles to domestic industry' " (Rahill, 1967, p. 204).

12. Showalter (1977, p. 204).

13. Speaking of the child's *fort-da* game, Freud (1961) notes, "At the outset he was in a passive situation—he was overpowered by experience; but by repeating it, unpleasurable though it was, as a game, he took on an *active* part. These efforts might be put down to an instinct for mastery that was acting independently of whether the memory was in itself pleasurable or not" (p. 10).

14. Jean-Paul Sartre's (1966, p. 133n) phrase for the tension surrealism's created object sets up in the spectator is remarkably appropriate here.

REFERENCES

Campbell, B. M. (1978, November). Hooked on soaps. *Essence*, pp. 100-103.

Cawelti, J. C. (1976). *Adventure, mystery and romance.* Chicago: University of Chicago Press.

Dinnerstein, D. (1976). *The mermaid and the minotaur: Sexual arrangements and human malaise.* New York: Harper & Row.

Edmondson, M., & Rounds, D. (1976). *From Mary Noble to Mary Hartman: The complete soap opera book.* New York: Stein & Day.

Freud, S. (1961). *Beyond the pleasure principle* (J. Strachey, Trans.). New York: Norton.

Mayer, P. (1977). Creating *Ryan's Hope.* In J. Fireman (Ed.), *T.V. book.* New York: Workman.

Mulvey, L. (1977). Visual pleasure and narrative cinema. In K. Kay & G. Peary (Eds.), *Women and the cinema.* New York: E. P. Dutton.

Rahill, F. (1967). *The world of melodrama.* University Park: Pennsylvania State University Press.

Sartre, J-P. (1966). *What is literature?* (B. Frechtman, Trans.). New York: Washington Square Press.

Showalter, E. (1977). *A literature of their own.* Princeton, NJ: Princeton University Press.

Weibel, K. (1977). *Mirror, mirror: Images of women reflected in popular culture.* New York: Anchor.

41

Women Watching Together

An Ethnographic Study of
Korean Soap Opera Fans in the United States

MINU LEE

CHONG HEUP CHO

Understanding the audience watching programs on video tape is never a simple task. It becomes a more complicated matter and requires new theorization and empirical support if the audience is from another country, but consumes rather its own cultural products in a foreign country where more program choices are seemingly available. More specifically, this paper concerns a question of "why is it that some Korean housewives in America prefer Korean soap operas to American ones?" The Korean programs were rented on tape from a local store, and watched by women in a group.

. . . In order to collect the audience responses, twelve in-depth interviews were conducted with Korean student families residing in Madison, Wisconsin, in November 1988. Subjects were all college graduates and they were middle or upper-middle class.

Ann Gray's study on the VCR in the home is one of the few examples of researches in which the use of VCRs is addressed in the context of gender relations within the family. She found in her study that, for many women, viewing choices are often negotiated and the programs which "women enjoy are rarely, if ever, hired by their male partners for viewing together because

---

NOTE: Excerpts reprinted from *Cultural Studies*, Vol. 4, No. 1 (1990), by permission of the publisher, Routledge, Chapman and Hall Ltd.

they consider such films to be 'trivial' and 'silly' and women are laughed at for enjoying them" (Gray, 1987, pp. 49-50). This observation is confirmed in the statements of most of the women we talked to:

> **S1:** Fridays are my favorite day of the week. That's when we go to supermarkets together and rent some videos for the weekend. I usually let him choose his tape first and select mine later to avoid any nasty comments on my selection. If he is still sarcastic about my tape, he has to wait one more week to have his favorite dish on the dinner table.

> **S2:** I think men consider whatever involves infidelities, incests, and complicated love stories as trash. But I don't see much quality in the martial art films either. Just as they need them to be excited, I need soap operas.

While some women insist on their own cultural tastes or viewing choices, most women feel shame when they enjoy soap operas. This underlying sense of denigration has influenced their viewing habit in such a way that they either watch alone late in the evening after the husband and children have gone to bed or together with friends during the day. But both viewing habits are not mutually exclusive as women often watch the same program twice.

> **S3:** I know it's disappointing to indulge myself in the "low quality" soap operas, but I have nothing else to do to release my stress. I like to watch the tapes together with my friends when the big kid (husband) has gone to school. But when we get together, we just turn on the video and talk about something else such as cooking recipes, big sales, scandals. . . . So, I watch the program again late in the evening.

> **S4:** My husband just hates to see me watch the video. Once I stopped renting the video tapes for a while and read novels instead. But he complained again and asked me to do more constructive things. And that really hurt my feelings and pride, but I still asked him nicely "What's more constructive than reading a book?" His answer was just incredible; "Do you call that a book? You are reading trashes!". . . . After that incident, I watch the tape late in the evening when I am all alone.

The common strategy for the husband to discourage his wife from watching soap operas is to compare her viewing choice to that of a housemaid. The usual comment (that's something the housemaid watches) makes the women feel shame as they violate the natural law of the Confucian notion of family which specifies the role and the status of each family member based on gender and age. The Confucian code of behavior prescribes what constitutes appropriate women's behavior and what does not. The woman must not only respect her husband and elders but also must not damage the family image and honor. She must not begrudge her subjection, but must learn to be obedient to her husband. The superior status of the husband within the family is more than common sense. Woman's everyday life and her pleasures exist only within the realm of the Confucian world view. While she is subjected to the family structure, however, her status may be ranked as superior to that of housemaid according to this "natural law." By equating the act of viewing with that of those who are at the bottom of the social order and thus generating the feeling of shame, something undesirable for family image, men try to regulate wife's viewing choice. It is not surprising then that many women tend to denigrate their cultural taste as in the statement of the above subjects.

The testimonies also show that women often negotiate their program choices. Many women rarely do what they want to do for themselves and this is most evident in television watching. It is because the home is not considered as a sphere of leisure, but rather a work place, which constantly interrupts their television viewing. In other words, they have to negotiate the pleasures of television watching with their domestic responsibilities. Within this context, it would be difficult for them to concentrate on and enjoy television. As for men, however, home is the place for their leisure activities. What complicates the matter is the persistent social demand for the traditional work ethics in Asian societies where leisure is considered largely as "evil conduct" or "a waste of time." This social norm is so prevalent that women may feel shame when they watch television. These conflicting situations may also make women rearrange their viewing time and prefer to watch the video when they are alone.

It should be noted, however, that the very same women consciously challenge the traditional patriarchy within limits, using the skills they know best. It took various forms in the case of women we talked to: using her husband's favorite dish as a weapon against him (S1), enjoying gossip and thus releasing emotional strains (S3), or just women's refusal to view the video in company (S4): all seem to indicate women's continuous struggle to expand their own social space although the power this cultural struggle gives is limited. The seemingly rigid patriarchal control then never guarantees its dominant ideology as it is faced with various cultural forms of resistive power possessed only by women. Social practice is the site on which the dominant ideology is constructed, but, at the same time, it is also the site of resistance to that ideology. The fact that men have to work hard to determine women's viewing taste indicates the difficulty of ideological control: "control," as Fiske (1987, p. 184) argues, "is a process that needs constant struggle to exercise it, it is ongoing, never finally achievable."

The difficulty of ideological control is most evident in the example of the video club operated by the women. In order to share the video rental fees, they have formed a video club. It is the secondary function, however, that is far more significant in terms of its potential as a means of resistance. As in the statement of S3, the program is sometimes not so important as the opportunities the video club creates to talk about scandals or problems common to their everyday lives. The topics range from a bargain sale at a local department store to the love life of famous television stars. But the social gathering usually ends up with talking about husbands' behavior in the family. Women are curious about other people's lives and compare them with their own. As such the video club operates as a kind of forum to evaluate and criticize the husband's behavior.

> **S1:** Time passes really fast when we get together. What I hate most is that I have to prepare dinner before my husband gets home. This is especially true when I hear from my friend that her husband has just bought her a nice birthday present— My husband always forgets my birthday.
>
> **S3:** I always promise to myself I would never talk about my husband. But if somebody starts talking about last night's fight with her husband, I cannot help joining her and complaining about my husband—and it makes me feel a hundred times better.
>
> **S7:** If you talked to other people, you will be amazed how similar problems we all have. You learn a lot of things how to get your husbands by just chatting with more experienced wives.

It is clear from these examples that oral culture plays an important role in making meanings and pleasures from the routines of everyday life. More importantly, oral culture can be resistant and television is made into oral culture by gossip. And its meanings are recirculated in everyday life. Thus, the pleasure women find comes not from absorbing the dominant ideology but from their conscious resistance to the political power their husbands exercise. As we saw, this politics of family between husband's power and wife's resistance has little to do with the program itself. This struggle for meanings and pleasures already exists even before women watch the program. As Fiske (1987, p. 77) notes, "television, with its already politicized pictures of the world, enters a context that is formed by, and subjected to, similar political lines of power and resistance. The intersection of its textual politics and the politics of its reception is a crucial point in its effectiveness and functions in our culture." For this reason, we now turn to the text and the process of viewing.

. . . Television entertainment programs have, then, played an important role, in developing countries, by providing a forum for the most progressive ideas to bear witness to the grim realities of everyday life.

A good example of the point is the Korean television mini-series *The Sand Castle*, which consists of eight episodes and depicts the family crisis of a middle-aged couple. The story is a typical love triangle story of a husband's extramarital affair. The wife's preoccupation with her feeling of rejection by the husband and his irresolute attitude toward both his wife and lover make the marriage unsuccessful and eventually lead the wife to decide to divorce him. The traumatic state of her emotions is much emphasized, if not exaggerated, as compared to the rational approach the husband takes to cope with the problem. Much of the subplot deals with the mistress who is also depicted as a victim. What is unusual about this story is its feminist approach in representing sympathetically the female characters' points of view in a country where the Confucian notion of family prevails and a husband's extramarital affairs are considered as a norm rather than an exception. . . .

The controversy surrounding the program was enormous in Korea. Male audiences complained about the way the program dealt with the extramarital affair and were furious about the station's decision to broadcast such a feminist program. The complaints centered on female audiences' supposed inability to distinguish between reality and fiction. . . .

. . . The program had different appeals to different people. Women mobilized the meanings and pleasures differently from the same program, and the popularity of it depended in part on the way the text was recognized by the audience. One subject, for example, citing the case of her sister, told us how remarkably similar the program was to her sister's case. Thus her pleasure of reading the program was increased as she brought her own intertexual experience and attitudes. For her, the pleasure she found lay in the way the wife was portrayed. She was depicted as strong and resolute as contrasted to her real sister who forgave her husband after an affair.

> S9: When my friend recommended it to me, she was trying to tell me the plot. At first, I thought it was just another typical story about a husband's affair. But as it was revealed, I was stunned. It was about my sister! So, I told her to stop telling me the story. I wanted to know exactly how it would end and how it would be different from my sister's real life story. . . . I loved the way she treated her husband at the end.

In many cases, subjects rejected the dominant ideology and expressed sympathy for the wife and dislike for the mistress and the husband. The husband was most criticized for his arrogance and ambivalent attitude toward both women. It is interesting to note that many expressed dislike for the mistress although they agreed that "she was a victim of the system.." . .

. . . The operation of the video club made it possible for [the women] to feel comfortable to talk about the program and share their experiences together. Moreover, the inevitable consequence of this mode of watching was that the program became an important social issue and women took advantage of the occasion to evaluate their husbands' behavior at home by positing the topic as a real problem they faced. After watching the program together with their friends, two subjects rented it again and tried to show it to their husbands. One had a similar experience to the woman reported in the magazine:

> S7: After we watched the program together, no, he did not actually pay attention to the program much. I asked him a question anyway. I first asked him whether or not he would have an affair if he returned to Korea and I was shocked and disappointed to hear him saying "Men can have an affair." I was upset because he took it as a matter of truth. I thought it was other men, not my husband who can actually say that! I felt cheated and asked myself "Is this the man I dedicate myself to?" But I was still curious to know how he would handle the situation if he had the same problem. He then refused to an-

swer the question because he knew I was upset by then. I did
not talk to him for two days after that.

The other, too, aroused male resistance:

> **S3:** We talked about the program until one o'clock in the morn-
> ing. I did not understand why he sympathized with the
> husband. . . . We then changed the topic and ended up with
> talking about my career when we returned to Korea. I said to
> him, "Women too should have a career to avoid that prob-
> lem." He said no and I said yes . . . we had a terrible fight
> that night.

. . . The operation of the video club can be seen as a form of oral culture
and it has been an important forum for women to participate in the discussion of their social experiences. . . .

. . . Our research leads us to . . . argue that Third World audiences are not
simply exposed to the television texts, but are active meaning-producers
themselves, selecting, rejecting and transforming the text based on their
cultures and experiences.

The following remarks are based on some of the descriptions by our
subjects on the generic conventions of indigenous soap opera text as compared to those of American programs. In most cases, "realness" was the
reason for selecting the Korean programs instead of American alternatives.

> **S1:** I don't think any Korean audience understands one hundred
> per cent of American programs. It's not the problem of lan-
> guage but the problem of culture. No matter how fluently
> you speak English, you never get the feeling of their culture.
> They don't look real as compared to the Korean programs.

While this subject describes the differences broadly, one woman explained the cultural differences in more concrete terms.

> **S2:** I like to watch American programs. Actors and actresses are
> glamorous and the pictures are sleek. But the ideas are still
> American. How many Korean women are that independent?
> And how many men commit incest? I think American pro-
> grams are about American people. They are not the same as
> watching the Korean programs. But I watch them for fun. And
> I learn the American way of living by watching them. I like the
> Korean programs because I get the sense of what's going on
> in my country. That helps me to catch up with the changes in
> my country I have forgotten while I am in America.

There is an obvious contradiction in this subject between the subject
position produced by the consumption of American programs and her social
subject position offered by the norms of Confucian morality. . . .

Despite cultural imperialism arguments, Third World audiences like to
watch their own cultural products. Even when they are exposed to foreign

programs, they don't necessarily soak up the dominant ideology transparently. . . . If the television text becomes meaningful to the audiences, it becomes meaningful in the sense that the text is transformed into the existing cultural context of the audiences. . . .

REFERENCES

Fiske, J. (1987). *Television culture.* London: Methuen.
Gray, A. (1987). Behind closed doors. In H. Baehr & G. Dyer (Eds.), *Boxed in: Women and television.* London: Methuen.

42

Home, Home on the Remote

Does Fascination With TV Technology Create Male-Dominated Family Entertainment?

On a recent segment of a popular television news magazine program, the television anchors joked about a new cultural phenomenon: men's almost anatomical affinity for television remote-control devices. The segment ended when the female member of the team noted that in view of men's tendencies not only to control situations but also to maintain some distance from their activities, their liking for zapping the channel flicker from afar made perfect sense.

Referring to the new world of communications media as "a masculine domain," Germany's Jan-Uwe Rogge and Klaus Jensen are one of several research teams around the world beginning to examine how family members interact with each other in the presence of sophisticated home entertainment media: remote-control-driven televisions, VCRs, video games, stereo systems and even computers. The findings are providing significant new insight into the influence of today's mass media on relationships between husbands and wives, parents and children, male and female siblings.

NOTE: This article originally appeared in "Men, Myth and Media," *Media&Values*, No. 48 (Fall 1989). Some material in this article is reprinted by permission from *World Families Watch Television*, edited by James Lull, 1988, Sage Publications, Inc. Portions were contributed by Los Angeles writer/editor Marybeth Crain. Excerpt reprinted with permission from *Media&Values* (Fall 1992), published by the Center for Media and Values, Los Angeles, CA.

Indeed, some families seem to be experiencing a thorough "rearrangement" of the moral economy of the household, particularly in regard to traditional child-rearing practices, family communication rituals and, especially, power relationships between the spouses.

These cultural trends are being watched and documented by researchers such as David Morley and his colleagues Roger Silverstone and Eric Hirsch at the Centre for Research into Innovation, Culture and Technology at Brunel University near London. Although still a new area of investigation, their initial studies, along with those from six other countries, make fascinating reading in *World Families Watch Television* [Sage Publications, 1988], edited by James Lull of San Jose State University. The following vignettes reveal some of the more interesting findings from the book and related research.

"We discuss what we all want to watch, and the biggest wins. That's me, I'm the biggest."

Masculine power is evident in a number of the families as the ultimate determinant on occasions of conflict over viewing choices. It is even more apparent in the case of those families that have a remote-control device. None of the women in any of the families use the remote regularly, and a number of them complain that their husbands use the device obsessively, channel-flicking across programs even when the wives are trying to watch something else.

Characteristically, the remote-control device is the symbolic possession of the father (or the son, in the father's absence) that sits "on the arm of Daddy's chair" and is used almost exclusively by him. It is a highly visible symbol of condensed power relations, the descendant of the medieval mace, perhaps?

Interestingly, the main exceptions to this overall pattern are those families in which the husband is unemployed while his wife is working. In these cases it is slightly more common for the man to be expected to let other family members watch what they want to when it is broadcast while he videotapes what he would like to see in order to watch later at night or the following day. His timetable of commitments is more flexible than those of the working members of the family.

Thus, the man's position of power is based not simply on the biological fact of being male but rather on a social definition of masculinity of which employment (that is, a "breadwinner") is a necessary and constituent part. When the condition is not met, the pattern of power relations within the home changes noticeably.

It is noteworthy that a number of the men interviewed show some anxiety to demonstrate that they are "the boss" of the household, and their very anxiety around this issue perhaps betokens a sense that their domestic power is ultimately a fragile and somewhat insecure thing, rather than a fixed and secure possession which they can always guarantee to hold with confidence. Hence perhaps the symbolic importance to them of physical possession of the channel-control device.

A man accustomed to this dominance feels he has the power to change channels whenever he wants—even in the midst of his wife's favorite show or events the children are watching. "The television's flickering all the time while he's flickering the timer," noted one wife.

Interestingly, male dominance of viewing choices is almost entirely absent in Venezuela, where researcher Leoncio Barrios found that the traditional matrilineal Venezuelan family structure reversed the pattern found elsewhere. Thus, in Venezuelan families it is often the grandmother of the household who walks around with the remote tucked in her apron, to the distress of her grandchildren.

"I knit because I think I am wasting my time just watching.
I know what's going on, so I only have to glance up.
I always knit when I watch."

One major finding is the consistency with which both men and women describe their viewing activity. Essentially, men state a clear preference for viewing attentively, in silence, without interruption "in order not to miss anything."

Moreover, they display puzzlement at the way their wives and daughters watch television. For the women, viewing is fundamentally a social activity, involving ongoing conversation and usually the performance of at least one other domestic activity (ironing, etc.) at the same time. Indeed, many women feel that to just watch television without doing anything else would be an indefensible waste of time, given their sense of domestic obligations. The women note that their husbands are always "on them" to shut up, and the men can't really understand how their wives can follow the programs if they are doing something else.

A number of women explain that their greatest pleasure is to be able to watch a "nice weepie" or their favorite soap opera when the rest of the family isn't there. Only then do they feel free enough of their domestic responsibilities to "indulge" themselves in the same kind of attentive viewing in which their husbands routinely engage.

What is at issue here is the guilt that these women feel about their own pleasures. They are, on the whole, prepared to concede that the dramas and soap operas they like are "silly" or inconsequential, yet they accept the masculine worldview that defines their preferences as having low status. Having accepted these terms, they then find it hard to argue for their preferences because, by definition, what their husbands want to watch is more prestigious.

They then deal with this by watching their programs, when possible, on their own or only with their women friends and fit their viewing arrangements into the crevices of their domestic timetables.

Lull observes that home is the site of leisure for employed men, a place they can relax when the work day is done. For women, however, home is a site of work; they can never fully relax and enjoy viewing in the same way that men can.

> "I can't use the video. I tried to tape something for him
> and I done it wrong. He went barmy. I always ask him
> to do it for me because I can't. I always do it wrong."

Although women routinely operate extremely sophisticated pieces of domestic technology (such as microwave ovens, washing and sewing machines), British researcher Ann Gray has discovered that many women feel alienated from operating the family's VCR.

"The reasons for this are manifold and have been brought about by positioning within the family, the educational system and the institutionalized sexism which divides appropriate activities and knowledge in terms of gender. But there is also, as I discovered, something I call 'calculated ignorance': 'If I learnt how to do the video, it would become my job just like everything else,' said one woman."

In a novel experiment reported in *Boxed In: Women and Television*, Gray asked women to "color code" pieces of home technology. "When a new piece of technology is purchased," observes Gray, "it is often already inscribed with gender expectations. By asking the women to imagine pieces of equipment colored either pink or blue, I've been able to throw the gender of domestic technology into high relief."

Within this visual classification, irons become pink and electric drills blue; the washing machine is pink on the outside, but the motor is almost always blue.

Gray noticed, however, that the color coding of the VCR was more complex. "The record, rewind and play modes are usually lilac (a genderless color), but the timer switch is nearly always blue, with women having to depend on their male partners or their children to set the timer for them." And, corroborating Morley, Lull and others, Gray found that "the blueness of the timer is exceeded only by the deep indigo of the remote control switch, which in all cases is held by the man."

Interestingly, the major exception to this by-and-large universally accepted allocation of technological power involves the soap opera. Across cultures, women are fiercely attached to the "telenovella," the "Oshin," the "daily weepie"—so much so that when their viewing of these extended romantic sagas is at stake, they will often rise to the occasion and learn how to operate the VCR.

In one Kentucky family observed by Thomas Lindlof, Milton Schatzer and Daniel Wilkinson at the University of Kentucky, the wife, Patty D., "had the most interest in purchasing the new family VCR so that she could time-shift her favorite soap operas." Then, reversing the traditional role, she "remained in control of almost all the taping events." Nonetheless, the researchers found that in the other families, "most female family members generally disavowed interest in operating the VCR and regarded it as a technical matter," and that even Patty D. was "wary" of the pre-program function "until the exigency of archiving material for her children motivated her to learn to program the machine."

Lull adds another insight: males are usually more involved in making the VCR purchase decision and, as a consequence, are initially more competent in its features and functions when the machine arrives in the household. With more initial expertise, and perhaps having more time to devote to taping and other more advanced applications, the male dominates in using the VCR.

.43

Constellations of Voices

How Talkshows Work

WAYNE MUNSON

. . . The inevitability of the talkshow's growth stems to a degree from the recent economics of broadcast production. At a cost of $25,000 to $50,000 per half-hour, the syndicated audience participation talkshow and tabloid news show are among the cheapest to produce. Young, low-paid, yet enthusiastic staffers—including bookers who locate the many guests—work in a highly charged, "can do" atmosphere.[1] Usually, a program is taped for airing in national syndication within a day or two. In markets of origin, however, shows are often broadcast live to permit phone-in participation, as is the Chicago-based *Oprah Winfrey Show* when in Chicago, although many *Oprah* shows are taped on the road in cities throughout the country.[2] These shows are timely, appear live even if on tape, and are readily changeable with respect to topics, guests, audience participants, and locales—uniquely able to take advantage of instability.

The kind, numbers, and organization of production staff make possible that capacity. Most shows have several of two particular kinds of personnel: bookers and producers. Bookers—also called talent executives, talent coordinators, or sometimes producers—spend endless hours on the phone seeking guests. Predominantly women, they juggle a stream of guest and topic possibilities in an effort to put together the right mix of personality and

---

NOTE: Excerpts reprinted from *All Talk: The Talkshow in Media Culture*, by Wayne Munson (Philadelphia: Temple University Press, 1992), by permission of the publisher.

experts. Bookers must "be creative" and show "moxie" in their persuasive efforts. The daily unpredictability of the outcome of their efforts is evident in the frequent difficulty of finding guests—due, in part, to the sheer proliferation of talkshows. . . .

The bookers for political talkshows have earned the label "powertots": the "underpaid, overworked 25-year-olds" who are "among the most powerful people in Washington: they get to decide who goes on TV."[3] As "lowly" as they may seem, they assert power over the powerful—lobbyists, think-tank experts, investment bankers, and so forth—whose media appearances can prove crucial to the success of their businesses. Like the talkshow's audience participant, the booker exemplifies boundary-violating inversion and an empowerment of women. The booker, who is likely to burn out by age thirty, has assumed a position of power in a time and context when decisionmakers from "inside the Beltway" rely heavily on the media. The booker thus becomes an institutional embodiment of what the interactive talkshow itself is: a localized inversion of the relationships between the powerful and the common, between the mass media communicator and the "feminized," supposedly passive spectator.

Working hand in hand with the booker is the producer. He or she—again, usually "she"—is one of several producers on the show who put together programs in rotation, since most participatory talkshows are five-day-a-week "strip" syndications or live local broadcasts. The "hub of creative ideas *before* the show" (whereas host and director "carry" the show as it is taped),[4] the producer develops an episode largely from a content standpoint (the show's format and host remaining more or less "fixed") and is responsible for all research, guest, and logistical arrangements. The *executive* producer oversees the program's "look," budget, and distribution. Complementing these producers are the director, who "calls" the show during taping; publicity and promotion people responsible for generating media attention for a particular show's topic (which is not usually known more than a few days in advance, creating a special challenge for a genre that is itself highly promotional and success oriented); and an occasional field producer for taped inserts recorded and edited in advance.[5]

Along with an institutional structure built to handle the participatory talkshow's fundamental resource—a chaos driven by the news, personalities, and the interactive "liveness" of the form—guest practices demonstrate the same ad hoc, contingent structure adapted to the unpredictable. Besides celebrities, who can be interviewed either as stars or as "private people," the participatory talkshow focuses on guests who are issue motivated, "average" people culled from either the headlines, support groups, or a list of stand-by experts. Especially valuable are "crossover guests," persons expert and articulate on several issues; they are the most efficient, adaptable, and often available on short notice. Agents and publicists pushing their clients for appearances are often unsuccessful in part because a client fails to fit the crossover profile. Richard Mincer, *Donahue*'s executive producer, encourages prospective guests who cannot qualify as crossovers to be *especially* unique or different, to take advantage of rather than repress difference.[6]

By the same token, the audience participation talkshow has taken advantage of the power instabilities in the contemporary media environment, particularly the Big Three networks' loss of audience share and the uncertainties of programming in an era of deregulation and corporate consolidation.[7] Network audience erosion, which has received substantial coverage in the trade and mainstream press, is one result of the proliferation of channels and choices created by cable and the rise of independent broadcasters, "superstations" carried by cable systems as distant signals, and the Fox "fourth network" offering original programs to affiliates comprising formerly independent (largely UHF) stations.[8] Such stations have long relied heavily on syndications, of which the talkshow is a significant part.

Interestingly, talk hosts have practiced an anti-network discourse for years, an "anti-big guy" line rife with populist overtones and consistent with a participatory form purporting to give its audience unique media access. Ironically, Phil Donahue talked this line even when NBC, in the late 1970s, began running short segments of his upcoming shows on *Today* each morning.[9] Geraldo Rivera more recently espoused a similar line when, in light of his syndicated talkshow's success, he pronounced, "The network monopoly on real life [programming] has been broken forever."[10] . . .

. . . If "uncanned"-looking programming is the grazer-resistant fare of the 1990s, the audience participation talkshow is among the best at generating or exploiting the productive instability that has become vital to gaining and keeping spectatorial attention. Long-time media consultant Paul Bortz best summed up these developments: "It's definitely no longer business as usual. . . . The old formulas don't hold any more."[11]

"I DON'T SING ONE SONG":
GERALDO

The title sequence *Geraldo* used in early 1990 (since replaced) began with dozens of postage-stamp-like, digitized video still-frames.[12] They seemed to be floating on a blue-purple background—some facing the viewer, others at an angle—accompanied by a synthesized rock-fusion score. Each floating "snapshot" illustrated a potential topic. One, for example, pictured an elderly yet healthy-looking couple smiling at each other, apparently enjoying their "golden years." Another suggested a naked teenage couple in sexual embrace. The snapshots reflected the diversity of topics that *Geraldo* discusses and their "extraparliamentary" politics of interpersonal and "self" issues, intentional communities, and affective alliances.[13] That such topics shift daily demonstrates the talkshow's unique power to respond to the moment.

Although the show occasionally features celebrities, its guests and participants are usually "average" citizens with particular problems, stories, experiences, or expertise. The individuals represented in the floating snapshots signified this everydayness as well as a wide experiential, intonational, and affective range. With the further connotation of high-tech sophistication conveyed by its digitized design, the opening linked urgent topics with both common people and the in-the-know, in ways expressive of the show's intention to offer the spectator-participant identification with all three. The dozens of floating frames appeared in no particular order. A sense of randomness, multiplicity, and diversity prevailed. This is part of the audience-interactive talkshow's premise, since its guests, topics, participants, and even locales shift daily. Such instability is here linked with a whole set of positive connotations: democratic inclusion, dynamic change, "pumped up" energy and affect, and constant novelty. Chaos becomes productive. Anything that can happen or has happened to anyone is fair game for the show, as is the individual to which it happens. He or she is eligible to be a participant.

Geraldo Rivera has explained that his success is a product of his performative diversity as investigative journalist *and* emotional man: "If the audience rejects the host, then the talkshow has no chance of making it . . . what the audience knew that the critics didn't know was that, just like most people, I have the full range of human emotions. I don't go through life crashing through doors."[14] A stated or implied "and" marks Geraldo's discourse and is indicative of his postmodern journalism. He describes his journalistic style as "responsible . . . passionate . . . involved." He also sees himself *in* and *as* his audience: "There's a populist aspect to what I do that's important . . . a feeling of almost surrogacy. . . . I represent them" in such a way that there is "a kind of feeling of being looked in the eye."[15] He also finds his audience "tremendously helpful" to what he describes as his "spontaneous . . . improvisational . . . rock-and-roll" show "because they come up with the questions that either you knew too much to ask, or just didn't think of." The chance aspects of audience participation are, for Geraldo, eminently productive.[16]

The last element of the 1990 opener was the appearance of the show's title: *Geraldo*. Like the title logos for two other talkshows—*Oprah* and *Sally Jesse Raphäel*—it materialized signaturelike over the floating images, as if written by an invisible hand. Along with oral and interpersonal communication, a signature confers a sense of nonmediation. The high-tech computer graphic simulates a low-tech *look*; it resembles a handwritten signature at the bottom of a note from a friend. . . .

The *Geraldo* episode I want to discuss aired on February 14, 1990—Valentine's Day. The host makes his way down to an area between the stage, where his guests are seated, and the audience gallery. Here, as in most audience participation talkshows, the steeply pitched audience area is an integral part of the set, lit and arranged with respect to sightlines and camera coverage—almost as well as the guests seated on the stage. This is obviously important for visually representing audience members, who are initially integrated into the discourse through their applause, the visual backdrop they provide, and their appearance in tight reaction-shot close-ups. Eventually, some of them take the opportunity to speak when Geraldo acknowledges them: he moves toward and stands next to them, microphone in hand. A moment of interpersonal contact with what is initially the discourse's dominant subjectivity—Geraldo—becomes the condition for participation: an equality-connoting, side-by-side, face-to-face contact in which the spectator-performer simultaneously addresses Geraldo, the guests and studio audience, and a nation of television spectators. It is a moment, however brief, when a huge institution becomes accessible.

Geraldo hosts the show on his feet and often in his shirt sleeves, moving—sometimes bounding—around the full space of the set. Spatially, he spends most of his on-air time "with" the audience, in the aisles. His mobility between stage and audience space denotes dynamism, labor, and border-crossing. His mobile, responsive presence and microphone transform the spectators into performers, a parallel set of available guests, experts, experiences, and intonations. But Geraldo retains a special enunciative status. His intros, transitions, questions, comments, tape segments, conversational turn-taking prompts and cues, and his affect all orchestrate the conversation, the shift between story and discourse spaces, the audio track and the televisual picturization that follows it, and especially *him*, fish-in-a-barrel style.[17]

The camera locations around the set both represent and enable the inclusion-through-host. Two cameras are back with the audience and to the sides for shooting the on-stage guests; the television spectator can observe the guests from the same general position as do Geraldo and the studio audience. At least another two are located at either edge of the area separating audience gallery and stage, thereby offering visual access to Geraldo (one camera is always on him, assuring his primary enunciative position with the audience) and prospective audience participants. Often, one of these cameras is hand-held for greater flexibility. Such a use of setting and apparatus obviously blurs typical boundaries between audience, performer, and performance space, giving the show—somewhat like environmental theater and performance art—an interactive, liminal dimension.

The focus of this Valentine's Day program, which Geraldo announces to the camera with the audience behind him, is "Romeo ripoff artists": men who charm, then "con, fleece," and abandon the women they said they loved. Before and after each commercial break, Geraldo repeats this focus in catchy "tabloid" headline terms: "Our subject today is Romeo ripoffs," or "We're discussing when Cupid is a crook" (his address uses "we" copiously, extending the sense of inclusion). Such phraseology efficiently emphasizes what his program is doing: exposing the everyday emotional and financial victimization of women. In other ("tabloidese") words, the program looks behind the "Cupid" to the "crook." The discursive strategy plays with an appearance/reality opposition; it frames the show as an epistemological inquiry beneath "normal" but often deceptive appearances. Like the modernist detective-journalist story, Geraldo also inquires into the integrity of the sign: how does a woman "see" a possible con artist, the "ripoff" behind the "Romeo"? Geraldo's subjectivity provides a springboard, a guide to this inquiry.[18] . . .

After Geraldo directly addresses the camera to introduce the topic he introduces his guests, each of whom has been swindled by a Romeo rip-off artist: Sylvia, Linda, Karen, Kate, and Joan. As he makes each brief introduction in voiceover, the camera pans to the woman he is describing. She is visually rendered in point-blank chest shot, accompanied by a bottom-of-frame superimposition of her first name and a brief description of her experience—for example, "Linda: swindled for money." None of the women is smiling; their affects suggest the painful experience of victimization each is about to relate under Geraldo's sympathetic questioning. While they are all reasonably well dressed and attractive, their silent, close-up countenances become, at this point, metonymic of suffering as well as every-womanness. They tap an existential commonality; their stories will suggest how things can go awry and how hard it is to "read the signs" of a swindle when one is in love.

After the first commercial break, Geraldo introduces today's experts: the persons invited to appear by virtue of their extraexperiential credentials or a special knowledge from the position of helper rather than victim. Such credentials give the experts the modernist aura of objectified knowledge, a residual holdover from the culture of expertise. They have the "right" (socially sanctioned) degrees, the "right" positions of authority, judgment, and counsel; they are therefore recognized as legitimately able (they have "the right") to help the guests, whose knowledge is solely experiential and presumably more tentative. If the expert is an author, his or her book appears in a close-up, limbo shot as the host makes the introduction. The talkshow's promotional aspect resurfaces here in its link with expertise and commodified knowledge. Yet, like Geraldo, the experts do not hold a monopoly on knowledge. Instead, knowledge ends up dispersed among guests, experts, and host (himself a knowledgeable journalist and lawyer). As part of a single conversation inquiring into a particular question, each of the three parties represents a voice speaking from within its particular situation. . . .

The experts on this Valentine's Day *Geraldo* are a social worker who counsels swindled women, a detective from the Washington, D.C., police department who specializes in investigating con artists, and a New Jersey private detective who has helped "conned" clients. The detective and social worker are African American, as are two of the guests, Linda and Karen. The social worker presents a list of four telltale signs warning that a lover may actually be a charming con: he is often unavailable for phone calls, asks frequently about money, disappears for days on end, and fails to repay borrowed money. As she speaks, the four signs are also listed graphically on the screen. An expert thus contributes an objectified knowledge, semiotically separated from her as performer to underline its objectivity and distinguish it from the rest of the show's performed knowledges. Momentarily, such knowledge seems to be privileged.

Geraldo next turns our attention to Linda, who, under his questioning, relates her particular experience as a kind of "case study" illustrating the expert's points. Geraldo guides her narrative with such questions as "How did the subject of money come up?" and "When did you start to lose confidence in him?" She reveals that she fell "totally in love" with a man whom she thought sincere, only to find him behaving in accordance with the social worker's four telltale symptoms.

As the other women's stories unfold, the experts' prescriptions seem more and more qualified, even inadequate. The typical "ripoff Romeo" ultimately plays on a woman's emotions to a point where those feelings "blind" the victim to any objectified knowledge. Next to the far more complex reality of the guests' knowledge, which is primarily emotional experience, objectified knowledge looks increasingly absurd. The Washington detective's advice for preventing these financial "crimes of the heart" (Geraldo's words) is incongruously reductive: "Get a receipt." When Geraldo asks why two of the women continued to date the "ripoff Romeo," they tell him that they were not yet reading him as particularly suspicious. Geraldo's reaction is one of incredulity: "C'mon!" But the detective comes to Karen's defense by acknowledging the dominance of the contingent and the affective in a complex situation. The unfortunate truth is that the vulnerable victim becomes aware only ex post facto: that is, as a result of altered contingencies and affects. "They're looking for romance, he's looking for finance" is the detective's catchy tabloidese for the difference in intent and perception of the two parties to a "Romeo ripoff."

Under Geraldo's conversational direction and affect, the show dialogically shifts back and forth between expert analysis and individual emotional experience to demonstrate the limits of both in conversational performance. The postmodern "collapse of critical distance and the crisis of authority," in Lawrence Grossberg's words, are both evident here.[19] The women victimized by the "Romeo ripoffs" achieve an affective alliance more than they constitute clinical case studies or a legalistic preponderance of evidence, although both those modernist intertexts echo here, as do the confessional and the revival meeting. The women's redemptive "confessions" build a resistant community of "normal," passionate, and honest people—qualities also reflected in the host and the audience participants.

This sense of alliance is reinforced by the show's close, which gives addresses and phone numbers for the use of viewers who may be able to help track down one of the con artists. *Geraldo* and other talkshows frequently end with viewer-activating, self-empowering information. *Geraldo* may commodify such alliances and resistances, but knowledge, community, and interlocution in postmodern culture can, in Dick Hebdige's words, circulate "on the other side of the established institutional circuits" through affective alliances: support groups, issue-based organizations, and intentional communities.[20] Spectatorship has been redefined as participatory: the viewer is encouraged to connect interpersonally, via telephone, in a collective self-help narrative. Participatory talk offers the possibility of the spectator's physical and communicative involvement in narrative and spectacle, thereby encouraging his or her perception of the media's efficacy and "friendliness." This, in turn, encourages a greater dependence upon the media; beyond offering distraction, pleasure, or information, the media project themselves as somehow "deinstitutionalized" through their seeming accessibility. *Geraldo*'s participatory cues and openings for spectators challenge their heretofore "safe" distance while giving them a sense of mastery, despite interactivity's "deeper" intrusion.

The episode continues with Kate, whose own "flip side of the chocolate candy box" (another of Geraldo's transitional tags) involved a man who ended up with half of her inheritance. The source of her own "blind spot to his machinations (besides his charm), she confesses, lay in two closely occurring events: her father's death, and her start at a new job. She was unsettled, insecure, and especially vulnerable. Geraldo asks, "If he is watching, what do you want to say to him?" Her answer: "What goes around, comes around." The discussion returns to a concern for justice and the empowerment of "everywoman"—a concern here realized through a spectacle of performative conversation.

After commercials for a denture adhesive and life insurance for seniors (pitched by Ed McMahon),[21] the remaining guests tell their stories. Like Kate before her, Joan was swindled when she purchased a condo, in *his* name, with $30,000 *she* inherited; again, trust and affection were violated. Like the others, Joan became suspicious only after it was too late. Geraldo turns to the experts: "Are we blinded by pride? Shouldn't she have known?" The experts' response, paradoxically, is to deny the utility of expertise in the very midst of such affective situations. The detective says, "It's a con game, pure and simple. It crosses all socioeconomic and intelligence lines."

Geraldo's closing gesture is to give each of his guests a bundle of roses and a kiss, his Valentine's Day "thank you" for sharing their stories. As he does this we hear the detective, in live voiceover, enumerate the things one can do to build a criminal case against a "Cupid con artist." The orientation of expertise has shifted from detection and prevention to therapeutic restoration and justice, from epistemology to ontology. Since the expert enunciates only in voiceover, he does not have the "last word"; rather we watch the emotional exchange of roses and kisses and hear sporadic audience "ohs" and applause. . . .

NOTES

1. See Carter (1989). An hour of slick network entertainment programming costs an average of $900,000 to $1,000,000. Also see Robins (1988) and Keale (1988).

2. Cohen (1988).

3. Carlson (1988). Carlson, a regular contributor to *Time,* overstates the bookers' power in a way that divorces them from their institutional constraints, but she validly points out that by the late 1980s bookers had become increasingly important to the more cost-conscious broadcast industry. She characterizes political talk as a "producer's dream" because it is "cheap and highminded at the same time." The demand for good political talkers is such that some shows now have regulars under contract.

4. Mincer and Mincer (1982).

5. Mincer and Mincer (1982). Richard Mincer has been executive producer of *Donahue* since its beginning in 1967. The Mincers' book is a "how-to" for prospective guests who see talkshow appearances as critical to the success of their causes or careers. Part of the authors' agenda, however, is to meet the endless need for well-spoken guests who have the "ordinariness" crucial to the talkshow's populist, town-meeting dynamic of identification.

6. Mincer and Mincer (1982, pp. 23-37, 39-70).

7. For a look at the consolidation and diversification of the broadcast-involved media industries, see "Concentrating on Concentration" (1989). For a critical overview of broadcast deregulation in the 1980s, see Ferrall (1989).

8. See Jaffee (1989). According to Arbitron's analyses of the top fifty ADIs during sweeps periods from May 1984 through May 1989, the share drop in household viewing of broadcast television overall was 5 percentage points, averaging a 1 percent drop per year. Breaking out

the between percentages by network affiliate versus independent stations, however, reveals a significant contrast: "indie" shares have risen slightly, while the erosion in the top fifty markets has been "confined basically to affiliates" (p. 36). The drop in commercial television station shares, caused by the network affiliates' losses, was from 81.9 percent in May 1984 to 76.9 percent in May 1989. During the same period, indie shares increased from 14.6 to 15.76 percent. By November 1989, Fox had 128 affiliates (17 VHF, 111 UHF), giving the network a reach of 90 percent of U.S. television homes. National advertisers require 70 percent of national coverage from networks. See Block (1990). Also see "Three-Network Viewing Falls below 70%" (1989).

9. "The Talk of Television" (1979, p. 76).

10. Quoted in Robins (1988, p. 40).

11. Quoted in Ainslie (1988, p. 61).

12. The replacement opener centers on Geraldo's broad range of affects through a rapid, pixillated, MTV-style montage of the host in different talkshow situations.

13. For more on postmodern politics, see Aronowitz (1988) and Grossberg (1988).

14. Quoted in "Pushing the Limits of Talk-show TV" (1988, p. 94).

15. Quoted in "Geraldo Rivera: Bloodied But Unbowed" (1988, pp. 43-48).

16. Quoted in "Pushing the Limits of Talk-show TV" (1988, p. 94).

17. This analysis is generally applicable to *Donahue* as well: Both hosts become the channel most acknowledged by the apparatus: their mikes are always on, a camera is always on them, and they cue most of the conversational turn-taking.

18. *The Oprah Winfrey Show* and *Donahue* tend to approach the occasional celebrities they interview as having "hidden lives," however mundane, which are revealed in the course of questioning. At the same time, the *host* as celebrity reveals more of his or her own personality during the interaction, which thus becomes a conversation between celebrities as well as between celebrities and fans.

19. Grossberg (1989, p. 67).

20. Hebdige (1988).

21. See Budd, Craig, and Steinman (1985) and Browne (1987). In this view, American commercial television is an indisputable ideological practice wedding plenitude with capitalist consumption; any gaps such programming opens up are closed accordingly. The advertised product becomes, for Browne, the "ultimate referent." Disputing this totalizing view, John Fiske (1987, p. 101) sees the programs and practices of television as replete with fissures that offer a myriad possibilities for negotiated or oppositional readings and even resistant spectatorial practices, such as the gay and camp audiences' use of the *Dynasty* series.

Many of the commercials inserted in *Geraldo* and the other daytime talkshows echo the problems taken up in the shows, offering commodified solutions; e.g., obesity and insurance needs are "solved" by weight-loss programs and no-one-will-be-refused policies for senior citizens. But, to posit a direct relationship between program and product is simplistic.

REFERENCES

Ainslie, P. (1988, September). The new TV viewer. *Channels*, pp. 52-62.

Aronowitz, S. (1988). Postmodernism and politics. In A. Ross (Ed.), *Universal abandon? The politics of postmodernism* (pp. 46-62). Minneapolis: University of Minnesota Press.

Block, A. B. (1990, January). Twenty-first century Fox. *Channels*, pp. 36-40.

Browne, N. (1987). The political economy of the television (super)text. In H. Newcomb (Ed.), *Television: The critical view* (4th ed., pp. 585-599). New York: Oxford University Press.

Budd, M., Craig, S., & Steinman, C. (1985). Fantasy island: Marketplace of desire. In M. Gurevitch & M. Levy (Eds.), *Mass communications review yearbook* (Vol. 5, pp. 27-40). Beverly Hills, CA: Sage.

Carlson, M. B. (1988, May 9). Powertots: The media kids who run Washington. *New Republic*, pp. 13-14.

Carter, B. (1989, September 13). News is a hit on TV's bottom line. *New York Times*, p. D1.

Cohen, J. (1988, October). Oprah, it's for you. *Emmy*, pp. 14-18.

Concentrating on concentration. (1989, June 5). *Broadcasting*, pp. 50-52.

Ferrall, V. (1989, Winter). The impact of television deregulation on private and public interests. *Journal of Communication, 39*, 8-38.

Fiske, J. (1987). *Television culture*. New York: Methuen.

Geraldo Rivera: Bloodied but unbowed. (1988, December 19). *Broadcasting*, pp. 43-48.

Grossberg, L. (1988). Putting the pop back into postmodernism. In A. Ross (Ed.), *Universal abandon? The politics of postmodernism* (pp. 167-190). Minneapolis: University of Minnesota Press.

Grossberg, L. (1989). It's a sin: Politics, postmodernity and the popular. In L. Grossberg, A. Curthoys, P. Patton, & T. Fry (Eds.), *It's a sin: Essays on postmodernism, politics and culture*. Sydney: Power.

Hebdige, D. (1988). *Hiding in the light: On images and things*. London: Routledge/Comedia.

Jaffee, A. J. (1989, August 21). Major market TV erosion analysis shows continuation. *Television/Radio Age*, pp. 36-39.

Keale, D. (1988, May 18). Titillating channels: TV is going tabloid as shows seek sleaze and find profits, too. *Wall Street Journal*, pp. 1, 25.

Mincer, R., & Mincer, D. *The talkshow book: An engaging primer on how to talk your way to success*. New York: Facts on File Publication.

Pushing the limits of talk-show TV. (1988, May). *Channels*, pp. 94-95.

Robins, J. M. (1979, September). Here come the news punks. *Channels*.

The talk of television. (1979, October 29). *Newsweek*.

Three-network viewing falls below 70%. (1989, April 17). *Broadcasting*.

.44

Daytime Inquiries

ELAYNE RAPPING

"On *Oprah* today: Women who sleep with their sisters' husbands!"

"Donahue talks to women married to bisexuals!"

"Today—Sally Jessy Raphäel talks with black women who have bleached their hair blond!"

These are only three of my personal favorites of the past television season. Everyone's seen these promos and laughed at them. "What next?" we wonder to each other with raised eyebrows. And yet, these daytime talk shows are enormously popular and—more often than we like to admit— hard to stop watching once you start.

As with so much else about today's media, the knee-jerk response to this state of affairs is to hold one's nose, distance oneself from those who actually watch this stuff, and moan about the degradation and sleaze with which we're bombarded. But this doesn't tell us much about what's really going on in America—and television's role in it. Worse, it blinds us to what's actually interesting about these shows, what they tell us about the way television maneuvers discussions of controversial and contested topics.

It's no secret that television has *become* the public sphere for Americans, the one central source of information and public debate on matters of national import. Ninety-eight per cent of us live in homes in which the TV set is on, and therefore in one way or another being experienced and

NOTE: Reprinted by permission from *The Progressive* (October 1991), 409 East Main Street, Madison, WI 53703.

absorbed, an average of seven-and-a-half hours a day; 67 per cent of us get *all* our information from TV. This is not a matter of laziness, stupidity, or even the seductive power of the tube. It is a tragic fact that illiteracy—actual and functional—is rampant. It is difficult if not impossible for more and more of us to read, even when we try. Television, in such cases, is a necessity, even a godsend.

In the early 1950s, when TV emerged as the dominant cultural form, it presented to us a middle-aged, middle-class, white-male image of authority. Network prime time *was* TV, and what it gave us, from dusk to bedtime, was a series of white middle-class fathers—Walter Cronkites and Ward Cleavers—assuring us night after night that they knew best, that all was in good hands, that we needn't worry about the many scary, confusing changes wrought by postwar capitalism.

Network prime time still plays that role, or tries to. The fathers sometimes are black now, the authority occasionally shared with mothers, a voice from the ideological fringes invited from time to time to be a "guest" (and behave appropriately or not get asked back). But prime time is still the home of Official, Authoritative Truth as presented by experts and institutional power brokers. Whatever oppositional voices are heard are always controlled by the Great White Fathers in charge, who get paid six- and seven-figure salaries for their trouble.

The money value of these guys to the media—the Koppels, the Jenningses—is so high because their jobs are increasingly difficult. TV, in a sense, was developed to put a reassuring, controlling façade over the structural fault lines of American life.

Ever since the 1960s, however, this has been harder and harder to manage. The breakdown of the family, the crises in education, religion, and the credibility of the state, the growing visibility and vocality of minority groups and ideas—all these took the country and media by storm. The most recent dramatic proof of the impact of social crises and the progressive movements they spawned is the amazing media hullabaloo over "multiculturalism" and "political correctness" on campuses. The Left, people of color, women, gays, and lesbians are apparently making the old white men extremely nervous.

At night, all of this tumult is being handled more or less as it has always been handled. Things seem to be under control. *MacNeil/Lehrer* and *Nightline* have their panels of experts, which now often include women, blacks, and—on rare occasions—"leftists" who really are leftists. But the structure of these shows makes it impossible seriously to challenge the host and, therefore, seriously to challenge TV hegemony.

A much juicier and, in many ways, more encouraging kind of ideological battle rages before 5 P.M., however. Daytime, women's time, has always been delegated to "domestic matters." If Father Knew Best in the evening, on the soaps the women always ruled the roost and what mattered were family and relationship issues—sex, adultery, childbirth, marriage, and the negotiating of the social and domestic end of life in a class- and race-divided society.

This is still true on daytime. In fact, the soaps are more likely to treat such social issues as rape, incest, aging, and interracial relationships with depth and seriousness than any prime-time series. In the sexual division of labor, these matters of emotional and relational caretaking and socialization have always been seen as "women's domain." And so it goes in TV Land. Daytime equals women equals "soft" issues. Prime time equals men and the "hard" stuff.

Except that what used to be soft isn't so soft anymore. The social movements of the 1960s—especially feminism, with its insistence that "the personal is political"—changed all that. Everyone who isn't brain-dead knows—and feels with great intensity—that all the old rules for living one's life are up for grabs. Relations between the sexes, the generations, the races, among co-workers, neighbors, family members—all of these are matters of confusion and anxiety.

What is the line, in the workplace, between being friendly and sexual harassment? How do we deal with our children, who are increasingly media-savvy and street-savvy and whose social environments are radically different from ours? What about sex education? Drugs? Condoms? Interracial dating? How do we handle social interactions with gay men and lesbians, now that more and more people are out and proud?

These are just the obvious issues. But they grow out of changes in the larger political and economic environments and they resonate into every crevice of our lives in far stranger, more confusing ways. In the breakdown of accepted views about things, and of the ties that kept us on the straight and narrow in spite of ourselves, unconventional behavior is both more common and more visible.

Women do, in fact, sleep with their sisters' husbands or find themselves married to bisexuals. Or perhaps they always did these things but never dreamed of discussing it, never saw it as a social topic, a matter for debate and disagreement about right and wrong. The same is true of something as seemingly trivial as one's choice of hair color. For black women, such tensions are rife, reflecting divisions brought on by political and cultural issues raised by black liberation movements.

The personal is ever more political, and inquiring minds not only want to know, they need to know. Or at least they need to talk and listen about these things. And so the coming of daytime talk shows, a financial gold mine for the media and a sensationalized, trivialized "political" event for confused and frightened people everywhere.

The political roots of this form are apparent. In structure, in process, and in subject matter, they take their cues from an important political institution of the 1960s: the women's consciousness-raising movement. In those small groups, through which hundreds of thousands of women passed during a brief, highly charged four- or five-year period starting in about 1968, we invented a democratic, emotionally safe way of bringing out in the open things we never before spoke of. We found we were not alone in our experiences and analyzed their meanings.

Of course, the purpose of these consciousness-raising groups was empowerment, political empowerment. The idea that the personal was political led to a strategy for social change. We hoped that when previously isolated and privatized women recognized common sources of our unhappiness in the larger political world, we could organize to change things.

The words "political" and "organize" do not, of course, occur on daytime TV. The primary goal of talk shows as a television form is to lure curious audiences and sell them products, not revolution. Thus the circus-like atmosphere and the need for bizarre and giggle-inducing topics and participants.

Still, the influence of feminism (and other social and cultural movements) is there, and the result is more interesting and contradictory because of it. Donahue, Oprah, and pals have reproduced, in a plasticized format, the experience of being in a group and sharing deeply personal and significant matters with others in the same boat. Consciousness-raising, unfortunately, is long gone. But from 9 to 11 A.M. and from 3 to 5 P.M. on weekdays, there is a reasonable facsimile thereof.

One reason these shows appeal is because, in line with the democratic thrust of 1960s feminism, their structure approaches the nonhierarchical. The host is still the star, of course. But in terms of authority, she or he is far from central. The physical set enforces this fact. Audiences and participants sit in a circular form and—this is the only TV format in which this happens—speak out, sometimes without being called on. They yell at each other and at the host, disagree with experts, and come to no authoritative conclusions. There is something exhilarating about watching people who are usually invisible—because of class, race, gender, status—having their say and, often, being wholly disrespectful to their "betters."

The discussion of black women with blond hair, for example, ignited a shouting match between those for whom such behavior meant a disavowal of one's "blackness," a desire to "be white," and those who insisted it was simply a matter of choosing how one wished to look, no different from the behavior of white women who dye their hair or tan their bodies. The audience, selected from the black community, took issue with everything that was said. Both participants and audience members attacked the "expert," a black writer committed to the natural—to BLACK IS BEAUTIFUL.

This is as close as television gets to open discourse on serious issues. But it is only possible because the issues discussed are not taken seriously by those in power. And that is why the sensationalism of these shows is double-edged. If they were more respectable in their style and choice of issues, they'd be reined in more. By allowing themselves to seem frivolous and trashy, they manage to carry on often-serious discussions without being cut off the air or cleaned up.

This may seem contradictory, but it's not. The truth is that the fringy, emotional matters brought up on Oprah, Donahue, Sally, and the others are almost always related in some way to deep cultural and structural problems in our society. Most of us, obviously, wouldn't go on these shows and spill our guts or open ourselves to others' judgments. But the people on these shows are an emotional vanguard, blowing the lid off the idea that America is anything like the place Ronald Reagan pretended to live in.

A typical recent program, for instance, featured a predictably weird ratings lure as topic: FAMILIES WHO DATE PRISONERS. It featured a family of sisters, and some other women, who sought out relationships with convicts. The chance for humor at guests' expense was not spared; Procter

& Gamble doesn't care if people watch just to feel superior, as long as they watch. But in the course of the program, important political points came out.

Two issues were of particular interest. The "expert," a psychologist, pushed the proto-feminist line that these women had low self-esteem— "women who love too much." Some admitted to it. Others, however, refused to accept that analysis, at least in their own cases. They stressed the prejudice against prisoners in society and went on to discuss the injustices of the criminal-justice system and to insist that their men were good people who had either made a mistake or were treated unfairly by the courts.

Our discomfort on watching what seems to be gross exhibitionism is understandable. We are taught, as children, that we don't air our dirty laundry in public. We learn to be hypocritical and evasive, to keep secret our own tragedies and sorrows, to feign shock when a public official is exposed for his or hers. It is not easy, even today, for most of us to reveal difficulties to neighbors. We are rightly self-protective. But the result of this sense of decorum is to isolate us, to keep us frightened and alone, unwilling to seek out help or share problems.

And so we sit at home, from Omaha to Orlando, and watch Oprah in order to get some sense of what it all means and how we might begin to handle it, whatever it is. These talk shows are safe. They let it all hang out. They don't judge anyone. They don't get shocked by anything. They admit they don't know what's right or wrong for anyone else. They are, for many people, a great relief.

Let me give one final example of how these shows operate as forums for opposing views. A recent segment of *Donahue* concerned women and eating disorders. This show was a gem. It seems Phil had not yet gotten the word, or understood it, that eating disorders are serious matters from which women suffer and die. Nor had he grasped that this is a feminist issue, the result of highly sexist stereotypes imposed upon women who want to succeed at work or love.

Donahue's approach was to make light of the topic. His guests were actresses from Henry Jaglom's film *Eating*, which concerns women, food, and body image, and he teased them about their own bouts with food compulsions. After all, they were all beautiful and thin; how bad could it be?

First the call-in audience, then the studio audience, and finally the actresses themselves, rebelled. Women called in to describe tearfully how they had been suicidal because of their weight. Others rebuked the host's frivolous attitude. Still others offered information about feminist counseling services and support groups. And finally, one by one, those downstage and then those on stage—the celebrities— rose to tell their stories of bulimia, anorexia, self-loathing, many with tears streaming down their faces.

Donahue was chastened and, I think, a bit scared. Ted Koppel would never have allowed such a thing to happen. He would have several doctors, sociologists, or whatever, almost all of them white and male, answer *his* questions about what medical and academic professionals know about eating disorders. There would be no audience participation and very little dialogue among guests. Certainly none would yell or cry or show any other "excessive" emotional involvement in the matter. If they did, Koppel, the smoothest of network journalists, would easily take control and redirect the show. For that matter, only when such a subject as eating disorders is deemed nationally important by the media gatekeepers will it ever get on *Nightline* anyway. Daytime is less cautious.

I have been stressing the positive side of these shows primarily because of their differences from their highbrow, primetime counterparts, which are far more reactionary in form and content. It is, in the grand scheme of things as they are, a good thing to have these arenas of ideological interaction and open-endedness.

But, finally, these shows are a dead end, and they're meant to be. They lead nowhere but to the drug store for more Excedrin. In fact, what's most infuriating about them is not that they are sleazy or in bad taste. It is that they work to co-opt and contain real political change. What talk shows have done is take the best insights and traditions of a more politicized time and declaw them. They are all talk and no action. Unless someone yells something from the floor (as a feminist did during the eating discussion), there will be no hint that there is a world of political action, or of politics at all.

This makes perfect sense. It is the nature of the mass media in a contradictory social environment to take progressive ideas, once they gain strength, and contain them in the large, immobilizing structure of the political status quo.

We are allowed to voice our woes. We are allowed to argue, cry, shout, whatever. We are even allowed to hear about approved services and institutions that might help with this or that specific bruise or wound. But we are not allowed to rock the political or economic boat of television by suggesting that things could be different. That would rightly upset the sponsors and network heads. Who would buy their Excedrin if the headaches of American life went away?

.45

"His Name Was Not on the List": The Soap Opera Updates of Ti-Rone as Resistance to Symbolic Annihilation

GLORIA ABERNATHY-LEAR

Those viewers who watch CBS daytime serials may have seen promos featuring an African American male named Cla'ence. On a "Black-oriented, urban contemporary FM radio station in Chicago, many African Americans hear this same male as Ti-rone providing the *The Young and the Restless Update*.[1] General contemporary radio listeners in other markets[2] hear him as Cla'ence giving *The Young and the Restless Updates* in a hip although ostensibly assimilated persona. Cla'ence is the negotiated persona—that which suppresses African American language idiosyncrasies to have access to mainstream opportunities. Ti-rone is the African American grassroots persona—that which accentuates African American vernacular. This man's reward for assimilation as Cla'ence is a contract with CBS to appear in its television promos. Additionally, CBS daytime serial executives permit his presentation of *The Young and the Restless Updates*—as straight plot summaries—on 200 other radio stations. His contribution to the African American community is applying color (pun intended) to *The Young and the Restless* in an update on a Chicago Black-oriented radio station Monday through Friday.

That a negotiated persona is necessary is evidence of cultural incongruity or a societal power relationship wherein African American cultural particularities are not accepted as part of "mainstream" popular culture. This man's performance as dual personalities for two different audiences is characteristic of African Americans' survival and cultural resistance modes. Accord-

383

ing to Dormon and Jones (1974), "ethnic duality has been part of [their] experience from the beginning" (p. 100). There are those African Americans who effect bilingual, or negotiated, personae as an investment for survival—using the English language as it is taught in school when in the corporate world (Weber, 1991),[3] then returning to their "communities" and conversing in tropes learned through African American cultural osmosis (Smitherman, 1986, p. 12). Smitherman (1986) notes, "Black semantics crosses generations, sexual, education and occupation lines" (p. 72). While in their communities, African Americans are able to partake of the collective rituals that affirm the self and/or those that, as Cornel West would say, "keep absurdities at bay"[4]—for example, church, Black-oriented radio stations/music, friends.[5] The roles shift, but their performance is affected by their own communities' agreed-upon needs. Ti-rone's performance also exemplifies the case of African Americans' selective appropriation of a dominant culture's television product, daytime serials—a genre that has denied the incorporation of those symbols of culture, such as language and behavior, that are widespread in the African American community.

Originally Ti-rone/Cla'ence gave *All My Children Updates* on ABC, but in 1986 ABC expressed dissatisfaction with his invention and sued him for copyright infringement (Caploe, 1990). CBS, however, viewed his presentation as an opportunity. For CBS, the benefits are several: Ti-rone/Cla'ence's radio updates are radio promos to valuable demographics; Cla'ence's television presence gives the appearance of CBS as an equal opportunity employer without actually increasing the soap's cast to include African American families;[6] and Ti-rone's update on a major market, Black-oriented, urban contemporary radio station retains and possibly gains African American viewers for the *The Young and the Restless.*[7]

AFRICAN AMERICANS AND DAYTIME SERIALS

Nielsen and several African American media representatives estimate that during the last decade African Americans have been 17% to 37% of the total daytime serial audience.[8] Although African Americans consistently have constituted a significant portion of the soap audience and proportionately view soaps more than do the general audience, historically, the soap opera genre has not depicted the diverse aspects of the African American community. Generally, when African Americans have been included in storylines, they have been, or evolve into, what Clark (1969) calls "regulatory" roles—doctor, attorney, policeman, among others—wherein fictional assimilation has been realized without the benefit of the African American community (MacDonald, 1983; Schemering, 1985). For example, in Pine Valley there is no African American community; it is as though the African American community is not a necessary ingredient in those African American characters' everyday lives; as though color, or ethnicity, does not matter.

If African Americans are included in the soap community, they are required to have the visage of assimilation (or sanction) and employ the dominant culture's behavior styles. The result is whitewashed African

American roles sans African American viewpoints, language or behaviors. The result of this assimilation implies that certain African American cultural behaviors are not valued in American society. Gerbner (1972) calls such cultural exclusion "symbolic annihilation" and suggests that a response to such cultural exclusion would be for the underrepresented to create their own cultural products for their own community's use and pleasure.

African Americans have always created their own amusements for pleasure for their intracommunity use. Salaam (1985) wrote regarding the nature of African American culture:

> African-American culture is the culture of resistance and alternative. That is, we not only defend ourselves, our way of life; we also build alternatives to what exists in order to . . . develop our own lives and lifestyles.

Ti-rone's radio soap opera update is an example of an African American alternative. This update, based on creative intertextuality—the crossbreeding of texts from other genres and/or media—does more than function as prosaic entertainment. It generates and reproduces meanings for the African America community. This update is one answer to Fiske's (1989) query about how it is that "the people can turn the products of the mainstream industry into their popular culture and can make them serve their interests" (p. 75).

Ti-rone's use of TV-generated soap text on radio exemplifies Fiske's (1989) view of "culture as a web of intertextual meanings [which] recognizes no boundaries of genre or medium" (p. 75). Black-oriented radio has a special relationship with the African American community; it is able to target its messages in the context of music, public affairs and other programs.[9] Managers of Black-oriented radio stations value their stations as "the one place to go for information about" African Americans. African American Marv Dyson, Chicago's WGCI-FM manager, in Chicago, stated: "We have to entertain and inform the black community . . . in terms of the music we play, the news we cover and the promotional and community affairs things we get involved in" (Heim, 1989, p. 10). Presenting a soap opera update along with music and public affairs to generate meanings and pleasures in the African American community is in line with the general aesthetics of Black-oriented radio. Moreover, soaps are very popular with the African American audience, and a need exists for working persons without VCRs to keep up with the storyline.

Ti-rone has stated that he decides what to include in the text of the update according "to whatever advances the storyline."[10] However, as we shall see, explication of these update excerpts suggests several possible interpretations of their functions for this audience. In general, the updates

1. establish that it is acceptable for African American men to watch and gossip about storylines, validating that African American men view daytime serials, as well as discuss them[11]

2. provide an African American male viewpoint from which men and women can launch a discussion about values, gender roles, relationships and other cultural issues

3. reproduce dialogue and decode storylines into culturally relevant vernacular, which calls on the cultural resource bank and "social realities" of the African American community in Chicago (Such vernacular also may include value-laden spinoffs.)

4. illustrate some standard verbal aspects of African American culture.

All of the preceding interpretations serve to generate and circulate meanings and pleasures among Ti-rone's audience in the African American community.

READING THE TEXT
OF A TI-RONE SOAP OPERA UPDATE

The following excerpt from an *All My Children Update* illustrates many of these points.

The update radio format presents Ti-rone on the telephone with the time period's African American disc jockey discussing the day's events on their "favorite soap opera." This excerpt focuses on an interracial romantic triangle with Angie, an African American doctor, being pursued by both Cliff, a White doctor, and Remi, an African American businessman.

Introduction—*All My Children* theme music:

Ti-rone:	Well, Remi asked Angie out for dinner. She hesitated [mimicking Angie:] "Oh, well uh . . ." [mimicking Remi, suavely:] "What's the matter? Do I bore you?" [Angie:] "Of course not; with your quick mind you make me think." [Remi:] "Well tonight I don't wanna make you think; I wanna make you feeelll."
DJ:	Uh oh!
Ti-rone:	[Interjecting] Fine, I'll feel you at 7.
DJ:	Ha, ha, ha,. . .
Ti-rone:	Then Cliff came and asked her out to dinner.
[Angie:]	"I'm sorry I made plans with Frankie [her son] and Mom."
Ti-rone:	That's when Richard Dawson stuck his head out de camera and said [in a melodic voice mimicking *The Family Feud* exhost], "The survey said . . ." [then making a sound like the wrong answer buzzer on that game show] "No, White boy!"
DJ:	Ha, ha, ha . . . [extended laughter . . .]
Ti-rone:	No, White boy! . . . [chuckling] . . .
DJ:	Ha, ha, ha, . . . We counted the mail . . . ha, ha . . .
Ti-rone:	Zap, zap . . . No, White boy! . . . sor-r-r-y. . . .
DJ:	[mimicking Richard Dawson:] Survey said, it's Remi!

Ti-rone:	[in a chant] Remi, Remi, Remi, Remi . . . hee, hee, hee, hee . . . [extended laughter] I don't know how he got Richard Dawson there; I didn't know he was available.
DJ:	Ha, ha, ha [extended laughter]
Ti-rone:	But they had him.
DJ:	[mimicking Richard Dawson:] Survey said . . .
Ti-rone:	Zap, not there . . . heh, heh, heh; no his name was not on the list.
DJ:	Ha, ha, ha, [extended laughter] . . .
Ti-rone:	[proceeding to discuss another storyline:] Now Brooke was with the . . .

The preceding update is an illustration of many African American cultural continuities offered to counteract the symbolic annihilation of this ethnic group in the soap opera genre on television. The two men's exchange, in the gossip-call-response configuration, provides an example of the use of gossip as generator of meanings and pleasures. The content of the gossip and the manner in which it is exchanged are both bases of the meanings and pleasures obtained.

The purpose of the update is pleasure. Initially, pleasure is derived from asserting Ti-rone and the DJ's prerogative to discuss one television popular culture artifact on another broadcast medium. Although, as previously mentioned, radio—in contrast to the medium of television—tolerates cultural particularities, Ti-rone and the DJ play with the rules of the soap opera genre and the media to generate pleasure. Often, pleasure in the African American communities functions as antihegemonic in that it generates alternative meanings and emphasizes cultural particularities. The hegemonic nature of the soap text, as presented by the dominant culture and viewed by a people whose strong diverse culture has been devalued in that genre, provides the copy for the antihegemonic discourse as the basis of the gossip in the update. In the preceding update, in the phrase "No, white boy" and the simultaneous chant of "Remi, Remi, . . ." Ti-rone and the DJ play with the rules as to what can be said on radio as well as resist the forced assimilation rules of the soap opera genre.

Fiske (1987) has written, "Pleasure for the subordinate is produced by the assertion of one's social identification in resistance to, in independence of, or in negotiation with the structure of domination" (p. 19). According to Salaam (1985), for African Americans, as perpetual subordinates, resistance has been perpetual.

> The only culture that we can claim as actually ours, totally ours, is the culture of resistance—those acts, ideas, attitudes along with the necessary materials systems, that equip and sustain our resistance to external domination and our assimilation into the larger society which enslaved us and within which we presently struggle to live. (p. 82)

Scholars have observed how humor can be used as modes of resistance. In *Jokes and Their Relation to the Unconscious*, Freud analyzed the joke as a vehicle for meanings and pleasure. He theorized that " 'tendentious jokes make aggressiveness or criticism possible against persons who claim to exercise authority. The joke then represents a rebellion against that authority, a liberation from its pressure' " (quoted in Levine, 1977, pp. 320-321). In his chapter entitled "Black Laughter," Levine (1977) recognized that Freud's assertions are applicable to the tradition of African American humor regarding Whites, as evidenced in the trickster tales of the slaves. Ja A. Jahannes ("Africa - America," 1988, p. 697) asserts that resistance to "psychological warfare" is a continuing theme throughout African American literary products.[12] Finally, Levine (1977) also asserts that "black humor presupposed a common experience between the joke teller and audience . . . to foster a sense of particularity and group identity by widening the gap of those within and those outside the circle of laughter" (p. 359). The use of the pejorative term "White boy" by African American males—a verbal inversion of societal power relations—has a long history, and the term's use continues to be prevalent in the community. Ti-rone's use of that term on a broadcast medium tests the rules in a way that generates pleasure for the targeted audience. In playing with the rules of the soap opera text and media, Ti-rone, as African American producer, has knowledge of the diverse cultural assumptions and attitudes of his audience. For this audience, use of non-European form of English for emphasis is further evidence of cultural resistance—hence the phrases "wanna make you . . ." and "out of de camera. . . ." As Weber (1991) has declared

> The use of black language is the black man's defiance of white America's total indoctrination. The use of black language by choice is a reflection not of a lack of intelligence, but of a desire to retain and preserve black life styles. (p. 282)

Mitchell-Kernan (1971) also has stated that when "Black English" is used "it appears that language is functioning to underline shared cultural identity or, alternately, it is serving separatist functions" (p. 9).

Criticism of the soap opera's interracial storyline is evidenced in the use of the game show extended metaphor, as well. The choice of *Family Feud* as the particular game show from which to appropriate an aesthetic is ingeniously apropos. Each family contestant group on *Feud* usually has an homogeneous racial/ethnic identity as does each family in soap operas; and, participants' actions in each genre usually are based on contest for personal reward.[13] In the excerpt, the juxtaposition of the "White boy" comment within the context of a game show metaphor makes Angie the prize and devalues the White male, Cliff, as the unsuitable solution to the rivalry.

This discourse of resistance divulges Ti-rone and the DJ's indignation about the homogenizing efforts of the soap opera writers. Ti-rone and DJ oppose the kind of "racial integration" of the cast, which takes place at the expense of the African American male, and find humor in Cliff's defeat. Their discourse also exemplifies some African American male perceptions regarding their proprietary position vis-à-vis African American women;

they do not desire competition from White men in either their personal *or* professional arenas. Here, Ti-rone, an African American male has played with the rules of an original television text and provided a cheerleading experience for the African American male on a broadcast medium. The excerpt chant of "Remi, Remi . . ." exemplifies their pleasure. Also, values have been recirculated in that this discourse will probably generate discussions among listeners of attitudes regarding African American men in general and/or African American romantic liaisons.

As shown earlier, the verbal language manipulations or "qualities of expression" are the infrastructure of Ti-rone's presentation. Smitherman (1986) has written that "qualities of expression," some of which are difficult to depict in print, are common in verbal presentations in the African American community. The presentation includes tonal semantics—voice rhythm/inflection, mimicry—used for authenticity and/or ridicule—and punning. Ti-rone's mimicry of Angie and Remi in the preceding excerpt could be considered either as criticism of their whitewashed roles or as mimicry used for authenticity. Tonal semantics, the emphasis on the words "sorry" and "feel," were used for accentuation.

The play on words, "I'll feel you at 7," manipulates the narrative and was used to generate humor/pleasure. In another update, Ti-rone manipulates the narrative when he mimics Adam, a middle-aged man, discussing his desire for an offspring: "As long as I know I can father a child, I want the fruit of my loins . . . and I don't mean underwear!" Whereas comprehension of that play on words relies on general knowledge about advertising, on other occasions he has used puns that rely heavily on audience knowledge about community language and objects in Chicago, Illinois. In a reference to the White character Barbara getting angry at a restaurant he states, "Don't be trying to give me no chitlins when I want filet mignon! I can't eat everybody's chitlins . . . everybody's chitlins don't be clean!" Embellishing the narrative, he mocks her ungracious behavior and uses a phrase that has circulated in the African American community for years. By calling on soap opera as well as ethnic cultural capital, such a maneuver generates humor.[14]

Smitherman (1986) has written that verbal performance in the African American community "becomes both a way of establishing 'yo rep' as well as a teaching and socializing force" (p. 79). She further reports that included in such tradition might be the "semi-serious tradition of 'lying' "—as exemplified in the embellishment of the narrative during storytelling. Moreover, scholars also acknowledge the pervasive use of "signifying"—which, using Mitchell-Kernan's (1972) definition, is "an artistic and clever way of encoding multileveled meanings which involve, in most cases, an element of indirection" (p. 325)—and other verbal arts in the African American community.

When Ti-rone recaps soap opera storylines, his rewrites operate through narrative sequencing both to produce humor and to depict values. For example, the following excerpt suggests value inferences about drugs. He is recapping a plotline involving Tad and Barbara, platonic friends, wherein Tad suspects Barbara is using drugs:

Ti-rone: Now while Barbara's over there illing at the restaurant, Tad was at her house rumbling through the drawers an' everything, so by the time she come thru the door, Tad don laid down on de couch waiting for her.

[mimicking Barbara:] "Tad, what you doing here? I'm mo call the police!" Tad say "yeah, but before you do call the police, tell me what you doing with these bops in here . . . why you trying to throw your life down the toilet?" [interjecting:] That's right Tad! Get her off them drugs!

DJ: That's right! Tad to the rescue!

Ti-rone: Yeah! You know Nancy Reagan would be upset if she knew that Barbara was on DOPE! and she didn't just say NO!! . . . Ha, ha, ha.

DJ: Thank you, Ti-rone. Boy you sure get dramatic sometimes . . . ha, ha, . . .

Ti-rone: Aw yeah man, I have to whenever I think about Nancy Reagan; I have to get dramatic . . . heh, heh, heh

[Music up]

The preceding exchange provides social commentary on societal ills and the current drug policy "solution" and uses language appropriate with a "Black" accent. By signifying, Ti-rone also obliquely has expressed his displeasure with the Reagan administration, which was perceived by many to be unfriendly to the African American communities (Douglas, 1989; Hatchett, 1989). He underscores the elite's failure to recognize the complexities of drug usage and challenges the blame-the-victim thesis implied by the slogan. Why can't Barbara "just say no" and take responsibility for her own problems? Additionally, mentioning the word "dramatic" he is signifying about President and Mrs. Reagan's past employment as movie actors, at the same time noting how African Americans' psychological survival often depends on creative live performance.

SUMMARY

Ti-rone's soap opera updates give evidence of African American cultural continuities—using verbal arts to resist, teach, entertain and cope. Bilingualism,[15] humor, invocation of group cohesion and identity are examples of resistance to (and coping with) the hegemonic content of mass mediated cultural products. Through selective appropriation, Ti-rone generates laughter, which, in turn, helps to strengthen group cohesion.

This analysis provides support for the necessity for framing inquiries about African American television viewing practices within the context of African Americans' everyday lives.[16] Distinct social, cultural and historical experience(s) have shaped African Americans' worldviews. African Americans, as Patricia Hill Collins (1990) notes, have "special angles of vision," and any assessment(s) about their engagement with mass-mediated products must be interpreted within a distinctive cultural context.

NOTES

1. Brad Sanders, a Los Angeles actor/comedian, is the originator of these roles.

2. Notes Premiere Radio Network. Also mentions "Ti-rone, described as 'an urban Dear Abby,' also broadcasts on contemporary radio stations."

3. See also Signithia Fordman (1988): "Black English reinforces the indigenous culture from which they are separated through the process of schooling" (p. 57).

4. Seminar at Northwestern University, February 15, 1990.

5. Karen Grigsby Bates (1990) includes comments regarding people in a predominantly African American neighborhood not desiring to interact with Whites in the evening after having done so at work.

6. Recently, the African American maid's "family" has been included in "The Young and the Restless cast. Cla'ence has not appeared as frequently since those additions.

7. Per Nielsen ratings, as of November 1990, *All My Children* was the top-rated program in Chicago's African American households.

8. *Black American Study* (1982), *Black American Study* (1990), "Black Soap" (1982), Mason (1988), Carter (1992).

9. In the medium of television, Black entertainment television's goal is to provide diverse programming to the African American audiences.

10. Personal telephone interview with Brad Sanders aka "Ti-rone" (November 1988).

11. Bebe Moore Campbell (1978), in an article entitled "Hooked on soaps: 'A show is a show, but a soap is a slice of life.' " mentions her grandfather and other men who watch soaps.

12. Jahannes asserts that evidence of resistance to psychological warfare is exhibited in self-generated African American literature—for example Claude McKay, "If We Must Die" and Ja A. Jahannes, "Survivors Creed."

13. African American daytime serial roles could be considered analogous to the essence of the *Family Feud* game show. In *Family Feud*, the winning answers are those that are the same as "the top one hundred people surveyed." The winners obtain a monetary reward for supplying "the most popular answers." Thus the show implies that to be successful, you must think like others. The whitewashing of African American characters in soaps carries the same implication.

14. See also Cecil Brown (1981), regarding Richard Pryor's use of language of the average person on the street in the African American community to effect comedic humor.

15. See also Asante (1987, pp. 114-115) in regard to using another language to equalize the power relationship.

16. Abernathy-Lear is completing a book on African Americans engagement with daytime serials.

REFERENCES

Africa–America: Perspectives from Brazil and the U.S.A. (transcript of Ja A. Jahannes address delivered at the Center for Philosophy and Human Sciences, Federal University of Pernambuco, Recife, Brazil). (1988, May 4). *Vital Speeches, 54,* 695-699.

Asante, M. K. (1987). *The Afrocentric idea.* Philadelphia: Temple University Press

Bates, K. G. (1989, September 18). View Park: A case study in racial ironies. *Los Angeles Times,* Section V, pp. 1-2.

Black American study: October 1981-February 1982. (1982). New York: A. C. Nielsen.

Black American study: October 1981-November 1990. (1990). New York: A. C. Nielsen.

Black soap. (1982). *Tony Brown's journal* (Transcript of Show No. 525, November 18, 1982). New York: Journal Graphics.

Brown, C. (1981, January). Blues for Blacks in Hollywood. *Mother Jones,* p. 22.

Campbell, B. M. (1978, November). Hooked on soaps: "A show is a show, but a soap is a slice of life." *Essence,* pp. 100-103.

Caploe, R. (1990, May 29). Hipper than hip: Cla'ence raps to a soap beat. *Soap Opera Digest*, p. 97.

Carter, A. (1992, August). All my sistuhs. *Essence*, p. 70.

Clark, C. (1969). Television and social control: Some observations of the portrayal of ethnic minorities. *Television Quarterly, 8*, 18.

Collins, Patricia Hill. (1990). *Black feminist thought: Knowledge, consciousness, and the politics of empowerment*. New York: Routledge.

Dormon, J. H., & Jones, R. R. (1974). *The Afro-American experience: A cultural history through emancipation*. New York: John Wiley.

Douglas, C. (1989, November). The chilling effect of the Reagan legacy. *Emerge*, pp. 24-28.

DuBois, W.E.B. (1978). Black culture and creativity. The problem of amusement. In D. S. Green & E. D. Driver (Eds.), *W.E.B. DuBois: On sociology and the Black community*. Chicago: University of Chicago Press. (Original work published 1897)

Electronic media. (1990, July 16). p. S17.

Fiske, J. (1987). *Television culture*. London: Methuen.

Fiske, J. (1989). Moments of television: Neither the text nor the audience. In E. Seiter et al. (Eds.), *Remote control: Television, audiences, and cultural power* (pp. 56-78). London: Routledge.

Fordman, S. (1988). Racelessness as a factor in Black students' school success: Pragmatic strategy or pyrrhic victory. *Harvard Educational Review, 58*(1), 54-84.

Gay, G., & Baber, W. L. (Eds.). (1987). *Expressively Black: The cultural basis of ethnic identity*. New York: Praeger.

Gerbner, G. (1972). Violence in television drama: Trends and symbolic functions. In G. A. Comstock & E. A. Rubinstein (Eds.), *Media content and control: Television and social behavior* (Vol. 1, pp. 28-187). Washington, DC: U.S. Government Printing Office.

Hatchett, D. (1989, November). The state of race relations. *The Crisis, 96*(9), 15.

Heim, C. (1989, February 12). Radio roots: From blackface "Amos 'n Andy" to white-hot Tom Joyner; Black radio in Chicago has come a long way. *Chicago Tribune Magazine*, p. 10.

Levine, L. (1977). *Black culture and Black consciousness: Afro-American folk thought from slavery to freedom*. New York: Oxford University Press.

MacDonald, J. F. (1983). *Blacks and White TV: Afro-Americans in television since 1948*. Chicago: Nelson-Hall.

Mason, J. (1988, August). I wrote for the soaps. *Essence*, pp. 115-116.

Mitchell-Kernan, C. (1971). *Language behavior in a Black urban community* (Monographs of the Language-Behavior Research Laboratory, No. 2). Berkeley: University of California Press.

Mitchell-Kernan, C. (1972). Signifying, loud-talking and marking. In T. Kochman (Ed.), *Rappin' and styling out: Communication in urban Black America* (pp. 325-355). Urbana: University of Illinois Press.

Salaam, K. Y. (1985). Naming and claiming our own. In B. J. Reagon (Ed.), *Black American culture and scholarship: Contemporary issues* (pp. 77-85). Washington, DC: Smithsonian Institute.

Schemering, C. (1985). *The soap opera encyclopedia*. New York: Ballantine.

Smitherman, G. (1986). *Talkin and testifyin: The language of Black America*. Detroit, OH: Wayne State University Press.

Special report: Black American market (Nielsen station index). (1990, November). Chicago.

Weber, S. N. (1991). The need to be: The socio-cultural significance of Black language. In L. A. Samovar & R. E. Porter (Eds.), *Intercultural communication: A reader* (6th ed., pp. 277-282). Belmont, CA: Wadsworth.

PART VI

TV BY NIGHT

Entertainment programming on nighttime TV includes a wide variety of standardized types or **genres,** including situation comedies set in homes or homelike workplaces; action and adventure dramas, such as police shows; hybrids, such as prime-time soaps, soap-influenced dramatic series or "reality-based" dramatic reenactments; telefeatures (made-for-TV movies); late night talk and comedy shows; sports events; game shows; and "specials," such as award shows.

Many TV critics have used a genre-based analysis to help them sort out the **televisual codes** and conventions governing the sheer quantity of entertainment material appearing on TV at night. As John Fiske (1987) points out, "Genre is part of the textual strategies by which television attempts to control its polysemic [multiple meaning] potential" (p. 114). We all draw on a kind of "cultural capital" that we accumulate, as long-time consumers of a wide variety of TV entertainment genres. Depending on whether the generic context is narrative or nonnarrative, comic, melodramatic or "realist," experienced viewers—and this can include relatively young children— make very different judgments about what characters, actions and speech mean. As another TV critic puts it,

> Audiences' different potential pleasures are channeled and disciplined by genres, which operate by producing recognition of the already known set of responses and rules of engagement. Audiences aren't supposed to judge a western for not being musical enough, a musical for not being very horrific, or a sitcom for not being sufficiently erotic. (Hartley, 1985, quoted in Fiske, 1987, 114)

But just as people do not generally attempt to understand single episodes in isolation from the series context or one series in isolation from others like it, so we do not watch comic genres in isolation from commercials or news. Rather, we "watch TV" and derive meaning from one segment of it in relation to the entire "flow," the integrated experience rather than the isolated genre. As Herman Gray says in Chapter 49, "Although fictional and nonfictional representations . . . emanate from separate generic quarters of television, they activate meanings for viewers across these boundaries. . . . The representations make sense in terms of their **intertextuality** between and within programs."

Some recent audience reception studies have also suggested that although we know at a relatively young age how to differentiate TV fiction from "reality," we still at some level "read" entertainment TV as containing reliable nonfictional information about the world. For example, a recent study of Black and White viewing groups' responses to *The Cosby Show* "found that many viewers were so engaged with the situation and the characters on television that they naturally read beyond the scene or program they were discussing and speculated about them as real events and characters" (Jhally & Lewis, 1992, p. 19). Similarly, Andrea Press (1989) identified significant differences in middle-class and working-class women's view of the "realism" in several family sitcoms: Her working-class viewers seemed "more susceptible to the class-specific features of the liberal, middle-class ideology characterizing the television entertainment medium," whereas "middle-class women are more responsive to its gender-specific features" (pp. 229-230).

In addition to looking at its intertextuality, it is also vital to place genre analysis in the context of the **political economy** of television. For example, we need to recognize the role of entertainment genres of all kinds in luring advertisers in the risk-aversive industrial context of network TV. As Jane Feuer (1987) puts it, historically, "Television takes to an extreme the film industry's reliance upon formulas in order to predict audience popularity" (p. 119).

Yet televisual entertainment formulas today have become increasingly unstable, shifting, evolving and merging rapidly in response both to new economic realities and to perceived and projected demographic trends. Hybrids emerge as producers attempt in an increasingly competitive industry to blend the successes of originally distinct forms to capture larger audiences. It is also important to be aware of how dramatic changes in the organization of the mass entertainment industries have altered the TV programming picture in the last several years.

One significant factor has been the Fox network's challenge to the virtual three-way monopoly of the major networks. The so-called fourth network has shaken up industry conventions by creating series that target younger viewers and push the limits of what was formerly considered acceptable on the conservative medium of TV (*Married . . . With Children, The Simpsons, In Living Color* and others).

Second, cable television's technology has made possible the proliferation of dozens of new specialized channels offering a wide selection of specialized fare to the pool of consumers who could afford to pay their monthly fees. The coming of cable TV originally promised a growth in "narrowcast" programming—programming designed specifically for viewers that the three networks had traditionally treated as "marginal." This has happened, although to a much more limited extent than originally envisioned by advocates of community-based programming. Community-based public access channels required as part of cable operators' licenses still tend to be woefully underfunded and underwatched. Nevertheless, adolescents are now served by such relatively new outlets as MTV, VH1 and other music video stations; and African American viewers can now see a much greater variety of material targeted for them on Black Entertainment Television (BET).

A less noticed effect of this increasingly fractionalized and competitive distribution environment has been the trend toward what might be considered a television "economic ghetto." Although the network audience shares overall are dramatically decreasing, a disproportionately large proportion of less affluent African American households are among those still watching "free TV" because of the prohibitive cost of subscribing to a cable service (MacDonald, 1992, p. 267). This has meant that the broadcasting networks are under more pressure than before to come to terms with a "minority" audience that is an increasingly large proportion of the total network viewership—both in terms of number of hours watched and in terms of its lesser likelihood to "flee" to high-cost (and sometimes unavailable) cable.

Although evening TV entertainment is increasingly varied as a result of the competitive and fractionated distribution environment, it is still very largely dominated by situation comedies, drama series and TV movies. The chapters in this part have been chosen to illustrate how **representations** of **race, class** and **gender** in entertainment television at night resonate both within and across these genres, in terms of production, **text** and **audience reception.**

Going behind the texts we see on the screen to investigate the production conditions of the network dramatic series, Richard Butsch demonstrates (Chapter 46) that the creative personnel (television producers and writers) unwittingly reproduce their own class privilege in the network situation comedy, in part because of assumptions they (and advertisers) make about who audiences are and what they want, and in part because of the way the industry is set up to avoid financial risk. Although he focuses on the representation of the White working-class male in situation comedy, his analysis can be applied equally well to the history of racial representation on nighttime TV.

One particularly good example of this is "Is This What You Mean by Color TV?" (Chapter 47). Aniko Bodroghkozy has studied both producer assumptions about and audience responses to *Julia*, "the first situation comedy to feature an African American in the starring role since *Amos 'n' Andy* and *Beulah* went off the air in the early 1950s." *Julia* did represent a significant break from the traditional **stereotyped** "mammy" and shrew roles for African American women in the 1950s. (Jane Rhodes reviews these roles and brings the critique of representations of African American women up through the 1980s by examining "new stereotypes" in Chapter 48, "Television's Realist Portrayal of African-American Women and the Case of *L.A. Law*.") However, appearing as it did in the historical context of the civil rights and Black liberation social movements of the late 1960s (running from 1968-1971), *Julia's* racial, class and gender representations were highly contested, as the producers' file of letters from Black and White viewers of that era demonstrates. White viewers clearly "read" *Julia* in the context of the racial strife of the time, as communicated to them largely through TV news:

> Being a white person I hope this program helps all of us to understand each other. Maybe if my children watch this program they will also see the good side of Negro people [rather] than all the bad side they see on the news programs such as riots, sit-ins, etc. I know this program will help my two sons so when they grow up they won't be so prejudice [sic].

That racial representation emerges out of multiple genres resonating with and against each other on TV (including the news genres) is Herman Gray's main point in Chapter 49, "Television, Black Americans and the American Dream." He analyzes the ways in which representations of the "underclass" Black male have been constructed in apparently nonfictional programs such as Bill Moyers's award-winning public television documentary essay, *The Vanishing Family*, as well as nightly TV news shows. Although this imagery seems at first worlds apart from the depiction of the successful and attractive bourgeois Black family created by Bill Cosby for situation comedy in the 1980s, Gray argues that they are read side by side **(intertextually)**, each providing context for the other. Together, they help support the dangerous and pervasive social myth that economic success is purely a result of individual energy and effort. In both the Moyers documentary and the Cosby sitcom, Gray argues that

> the personal side of social life is privileged over, and in many cases displaces, broader social and structural factors. . . . The assumptions and framework that structure these representations often displace representations that would enable viewers to see that many individuals trapped in the under class have the very same qualities [as the Cosby family] but lack the options and opportunities to realize them.

Herman Gray's piece was written in the late 1980s, before the recent explosion of new comedy series, such as *Roc, Martin, Sinbad, Fresh Prince* and *Living Single*, which feature African American casts (including some hip-hop entertainers "crossing over" into mainstream popular culture). These shows are highly popular with young Black audiences, and in some cases are even produced by African American creative personnel. Such a proliferation of African American imagery on nighttime entertainment TV was in part due to the overwhelming ratings success of Bill Cosby's adaptation of the 1950s' White suburban "Father Knows Best" sitcom formula to an African American middle-class context in the 1980s. *The Cosby Show* (still playing in reruns) has been immensely popular with White and Black viewers alike. Although some critics argued that its text made it possible for White viewers to read the Huxtable's social and economic success as "absolving" White America in the Reagan era of racial guilt (e.g., Downing, 1989; Dyson, 1989; Entman, 1990; Gates, 1989; Jhally & Lewis, 1992; Real, 1991), it has undeniably been an important source of affirmation, enjoyment and pride for large numbers of African American viewers (MacDonald, 1992; Washington, 1986), and its popular formula helped convince the networks that situation comedies with African American casts could be profitable.

The same issues raised by the possibility of multiple readings of racial representations in nighttime entertainment TV texts as were identified in *Julia* and *The Cosby Show* also obtain in the case of the Black-controlled production by Keenan Ivory Wayans, *In Living Color,* a weekly satirical comedy show discussed in Chapter 50, "Laughing Across the Color Barrier." Schulman points out the **polysemic** (having multiple potential meanings) nature of the show's racial humor, seeing it as "an interesting example of how difficult it is to attack racism in a comedic format without giving the appearance of reinforcing those very stereotypes whose absurdity is being ridiculed." Shulman contrasts the "in-group" skits that are modeled on self-deprecating racial humor told in an all-Black setting (but are susceptible of racist readings by White viewers) with other, less problematic "table-turning" skits about racial roles that "seem to take the 'white eye' of the non-minority audience into account."

Just as the civil rights movement and the subsequent greater entry of Black professionals into the television industry, as well as the growth in the financial leverage of Black audiences, have all affected the nature of **racial representation,** so the women's movement and its attendant social and economic changes have opened up some cultural space for **counterhegemonic gender representation.** Commenting on the birth and growth of the made-for-TV movie in the 1970s, Elayne Rapping (Chapter 51) notes that "Feminists, gays, and other more progressive groups have obviously had a significant impact on programming." Rapping argues that "the TV movie has, in less than twenty years, become the dominant mass form for the dramatic portrayal of major social issues," including rape, abortion, incest, battering and homosexuality.

The telefeature was cheap and easy to produce, compared with the series, and represented less of a commitment on the part of network executives. These factors made it a relatively hospitable environment when liberal feminist ideas began to influence creative personnel in the TV industry. As Julie D'Acci shows (Chapter 52), the original idea for the groundbreaking female detective show *Cagney and Lacey* was rejected as a series, but after its success as a TV movie, it was easier to sell to the network. In this 1980s workplace police drama, both gender and class representational traditions were challenged, by its two female protagonists, one of whom was clearly working class. (Mary Beth Lacey's unemployed and family-oriented husband Harvey was also portrayed in a dignified manner, in contrast to the prevailing pattern identified by Butsch in Chapter 46 of the working-class husband as buffoon.) D'Acci shows that the original idea for the plot came

from the impact on its producer and writer of an early feminist book on
sexist patterns in Hollywood film history; and she traces the role of organized feminist protest in the show's rebirth after a first cancellation. Her study
of the show's evolution from its origins through its 6-year run illustrates
how the representation of "new woman" in this show was contested among
many groups—"the network, the individual production company and production team, the television audience, the press, and various interest and
pressure groups." Although the replacement of one actress with another
who was perceived by the network as "more feminine" was the price the
show paid in the early years for renewal by the network, the effort to cleanse
the text of a possible lesbian subtext was ironically unsuccessful among
lesbian viewers, as D'Acci points out.

The current sitcom hit *Roseanne* owes much to the legacy of the progressive TV movie and liberal feminist "female buddy" and "working woman"
series such as *Cagney and Lacey* and *Kate and Allie.* But the show's successful
effort to create a respectful (yet unsentimental) portrait of working-class
family life is also due to the power and commitment of two of its creators,
writer Matt Williams (a *Cosby* writer who came from a blue-collar background himself) and Roseanne Barr, a feminist stand-up comedienne whose
persona was based on her own life as working-class wife and mother
(Mayerle, 1991). In Chapter 53, Janet Lee argues that the *Roseanne* show's
text "might also offer the possibilities for a resistance away from a rigidly
defined and controlled patriarchal definition of feminine subjectivity." She
sees it as a "conscious fracturing of the myth of the happy suburban family
of TV land," but at the same time "woman-centered entertainment" that
allows for "outward show of affection alongside the rough-edged portrayal."

Even when the entertainment text does not itself seem "progressive" in
the ways *Roseanne* may be, audiences of family sitcoms may not be taking
away a simple confirmation of the "myth of the happy suburban family."
Sarah Schuyler's "Confessions of a Sitcom Junkie" (Chapter 54) provides a
fascinating glimpse of how the sitcom form, with its reassurance of the
restoration of order and harmony in the "family" after the disturbance of
the "situation," can be both a source of satisfaction and an occasion for
"subversive jokes" for a lesbian couple/family. Giving us greater insight
into the complications of our viewing positions, Schuyler's picture of lesbian viewing reminds us of Jaqueline Bobo's negotiating viewers of *The Color
Purple* (Chapter 8).

REFERENCES

Downing, J. (1988). *The Cosby Show* and American racial discourse. In G. Smither-
    man-Donaldson & T. A. van Dijk (Eds.), *Discourse and discrimination* (pp. 46-74).
    Detroit, MI: Wayne State University Press.
Dyson, M. (1989, September). Bill Cosby and the politics of race. *Zeta.*
Entman, R. (1990). Modern racism and the images of Blacks in local television news.
    Critical Studies in Mass Communication, 7(4).

Feuer, J. (1987). Genre study and television. In R. C. Allen (Ed.), *Channels of discourse: Television and contemporary criticism* (pp. 113-133). Chapel Hill: University of North Carolina Press.

Fiske, J. (1987). *Television culture.* New York: Methuen.

Gates, H. L. Jr. (1989, November 12). TV's Black world turns—But stays unreal. *The New York Times.*

Jhally, S., & Lewis, J. (1992). *Enlightened racism:* The Cosby Show. *Audiences and the myth of the American dream.* Boulder, CO: Westview.

MacDonald, J. F. (1992). *Blacks and White TV: Afro-Americans in TV since 1948* (2nd ed.). Chicago: Nelson-Hall.

Mayerle, J. (1991). *Roseanne*—How did you get inside my house?—A case study of a hit blue-collar situation comedy. *Journal of Popular Culture, 24*(4), 71-88.

Press, A. L. (1989). Class and gender in the hegemonic process: Class differences in women's perceptions of realism and identification with television characters. *Media Culture and Society, 11*(2), 229-252.

Real, M. (1991). Bill Cosby and recoding ethnicity. In L. R. Vande Berg & L. A. Wenner (Eds.), *Television criticism.* New York: Longman.

Washington, M. H. (1986, March 22). Please, Mr. Cosby, Build on Your Success. *TV Guide.*

Ralph, Fred, Archie and Homer

Why Television Keeps Recreating the White Male Working-Class Buffoon

RICHARD BUTSCH

Strewn across our mass media are portrayals of class that justify class relations of modern capitalism. Studies of 50 years of comic strips, radio serials, television drama, movies and popular fiction reveal a very persistent pattern, an underrepresentation of working-class occupations and an overrepresentation of professional and managerial occupations among characters.[1]

My own studies of class in prime-time network television family series from 1946 to 1990 (Butsch, 1992; Butsch & Glennon, 1983; Glennon & Butsch, 1982) indicate that this pattern is persistent over four decades of television, in 262 domestic situation comedies, such as *I Love Lucy, The Brady Bunch, All in the Family* and *The Simpsons*. In only 11% of the series were heads of house portrayed as working-class, that is, holding occupations as blue-collar, clerical or unskilled or semiskilled service workers. Blue-collar families were most underrepresented: only 4% (11 series) compared with 45% of American families in 1970.

Widespread affluence was exaggerated as well. More lucrative, glamorous or prestigious professions predominated over more mundane ones: 9 doctors to one nurse, 19 lawyers to 2 accountants, 7 college professors to 2 school teachers. Working wives were almost exclusively middle-class and in pursuit of a career. Working-class wives, such as in *Roseanne*, who have to work to help support the family, were very rare. Particularly notable was the prevalence of servants: one of every five series had a maid or butler.

The working class is not only underrepresented; the few men who are portrayed are buffoons. They are dumb, immature, irresponsible or lacking in common sense. This is the character of the husbands in almost every sitcom depicting a blue-collar (white) male head of house, *The Honeymooners*, *The Flintstones*, *All in the Family* and *The Simpsons* being the most famous examples. He is typically well-intentioned, even lovable, but no one to respect or emulate. These men are played against more mature, sensible wives, such as Ralph against Alice in the *Honeymooners*.

In most middle-class series, there is no buffoon. More typically, both parents are wise and work cooperatively to raise their children in practically perfect families, as in *Father Knows Best*, *The Brady Bunch* and the *Bill Cosby Show*. In the few middle-class series featuring a buffoon, it is the dizzy wife, such as Lucy. The professional/managerial husband is the sensible, mature partner. Inverting gender status in working-class but not middle-class sitcoms is a statement about class.

HOW DOES IT HAPPEN?

The prevalence of such views of working-class men well illustrates ideological hegemony, the dominance of values in mainstream culture that justify and help to maintain the status quo. Blue-collar workers are portrayed as requiring supervision, and managers and professionals as intelligent and mature enough to provide it. But do viewers, and particularly the working class, accept these views? Only a handful of scattered, incidental observations (Blum, 1969; Gans, 1962; Jhally & Lewis, 1992; Vidmar & Rokeach, 1974) consider how people have responded to portrayals of class.

And why does television keep reproducing these caricatures? How does it happen? Seldom have studies of television industries pinpointed how specific content arises. Studies of production have not been linked to studies of content any more than audience studies have. What follows is an effort to make that link between existing production studies and persistent images of working-class men in domestic sitcoms. In the words of Connell (1977), "No evil-minded capitalistic plotters need be assumed because the production of ideology is seen as the more or less automatic outcome of the normal, regular processes by which commercial mass communications work in a capitalist system" (p. 195). The simple need to make a profit is a structural constraint that affects content (see also Ryan, 1992).

Let us then examine how the organization of the industry and television drama production may explain class content in television series. I will look at three levels of organization: (a) network domination of the industry, (b) the organization of decisions within the networks and on the production line, and (c) the work community and culture of the creative personnel. I will trace how these may explain the consistency and persistence of the portrayals, the underrepresentation of the working class and the choice of the particular stereotypes of working-class men in prime-time domestic sitcoms.

Network Domination and Persistent Images

For four decades ABC, CBS and NBC dominated the television industry. Of television audiences, 90% watched network programs. The networks accounted for over half of all television advertising revenues in the 1960s and 1970s and just under half by the late 1980s (Owen & Wildman, 1992). They therefore had the money and the audience to dominate as almost the sole buyers of drama programming from Hollywood producers and studios.[2]

During the 1980s, the three-network share of the audience dropped from about 90% to 60%; network share of television ad revenues declined from 60% to 47% (Owen & Wildman, 1992). These dramatic changes have generated many news stories of the demise of the big three. Cable networks and multistation owners (companies that own several local broadcast stations) began to challenge the dominance of the big three. They became alternative markets for producers as they began purchasing their own programs.

But program development is costly; even major Hollywood studios are unwilling to produce drama programs without subsidies from buyers. Nine networks have sufficient funds in the 1990s to qualify as buyers of drama programming: the four broadcast networks (ABC, CBS, Fox and NBC) and five cable networks (Disney, HBO, Showtime, TNT and USA Network) (Blumler & Spicer, 1990). But ABC, CBS and NBC still account for the development of the overwhelming majority of new drama series, the programming that presents the same characters week after week—and year after year in reruns.

This is the case in part because the broadcast networks still deliver by far the largest audiences. Even in 1993, the combined ratings for the 20 largest cable audiences would still only rank 48th in ratings for broadcast network shows. The highest rated cable network, USA Network, reached only 1.5% of the audience, compared to an average of 20% for ABC, NBC and CBS. The larger audiences translate into more dollars for program development.

And producers still prefer to work for the broadcast networks. When sold to broadcast networks, their work receives much broader exposure, which enhances their subsequent profits from syndication after the network run and increases the likelihood for future purchases and employment.

Moreover, whether or not dominance by the big three has slipped, many of the same factors that shaped their programming decisions shape the decisions of their competitors as well. The increased number of outlets has not resulted in the innovation and diversity in program development once expected. Jay Blumler and Carolyn Spicer (1990) interviewed over 150 industry personnel concerned with program decision making and found that the promise of more openness to innovation and creativity was short-lived. The cost of drama programming limits buyers to only a handful of large corporations and dictates that programs attract a large audience and avoid risk. How has this affected content?

Using their market power, the networks have maintained sweeping control over production decisions of even highly successful producers from initial idea for a new program to final film or tape (Bryant, 1969, pp. 624-626;

Gitlin, 1983; Pekurny, 1977, 1982; Winick, 1961). Their first concern affecting program decisions is risk avoidance. Popular culture success is notoriously unpredictable, making decisions risky. The music recording industry spreads investment over many records so that any single decision is less significant (Peterson & Berger, 1971). Spreading risk is not a strategy available to networks (neither broadcast nor cable), because only a few programming decisions fill the prime-time hours that account for most income. Networks are constrained further from expanding the number of their decisions by their use of the series as the basic unit of programming. The series format increases ratings predictability from week to week. Each decision, then, represents a considerable financial risk, not simply in production costs but in advertising income. For example, ABC increased profits from $35 million in 1975 to $185 million in 1978 by raising its average prime-time ratings from 16.6 to 20.7 (personal communication, W. Behanna, A. C. Nielsen Company, June 1980).

Because programming decisions are risky and costly and network executives' careers rest on their ability to make the right decisions, they are constrained, in their own interest, to avoid innovation and novelty. They stick to tried-and-true formulas and to producers with a track record of success (Brown, 1971; Wakshlag & Adams, 1985). The result is a small, closed community of proven creative personnel (about 500 producers, writers, directors) closely tied to and dependent on the networks (Gitlin, 1983, pp. 115, 135; Pekurny, 1982; Tunstall & Walker, 1981, pp. 77-79). This proven talent then self-censor their work on the basis of a product image their previous experience tells them the networks will tolerate (Cantor, 1971; Pekurny, 1982; Ravage, 1978) creating an "imaginary feedback loop" (DiMaggio & Hirsch, 1976) between producers and network executives.

These same conditions continue to characterize program development in the late 1980s (Blumler & Spicer, 1990), as the new buyers of programming, cable networks, operate under the same constraints as broadcast networks.

To avoid risk, network executives have chosen programs that repeat the same images of class decade after decade. More diverse programming has appeared only in the early days of an industry when there were no past successes to copy—broadcast television in the early 1950s and cable in the early 1980s—or when declining ratings made it clear that past successes no longer worked (Blumler & Spicer, 1990; Turow, 1982b, p. 124). Dominick (1976) found that the lower the profits of the networks, the more variation in program types could be discerned from season to season and the less network schedules resembled each other. For example, in the late 1950s, ABC introduced hour-long western series to prime time to become competitive with NBC and CBS (Federal Communications Commission [FCC], Office of Network Study, 1965, pp. 373, 742). Again, in 1970, CBS purchased Norman Lear's then controversial *All in the Family* (other networks turned it down) to counteract a drift to an audience of undesirable demographics (rural and over 50). Acceptance by networks of innovative programs takes much longer than conventional programs and requires backing by the most successful producers (Turow, 1982b, p. 126). *Roseanne* was introduced by Carsey-Werner, producers of the top-rated *Cosby Show*, when ABC was trying to counter ratings losses (Reeves, 1990, 153-154). Hugh Wilson, the creator of *WKRP* and *Frank's Place*, described CBS in 1987 as desperate about slipping ratings; "Consequently they were the best people to work for from a creative standpoint" (Campbell & Reeves, 1990, p. 8).

Network Decision Making—Program Development

The second factor affecting network decisions on content is the need to produce programming suited to advertising. What the audience wants—or what network executives imagine they want—is secondary to ad revenue. (Subscriber-supported, pay cable networks, which do not sell advertising, also do not program weekly drama series.) In matters of content, networks avoid that which will offend or dissatisfy advertisers (Bryant, 1969). For example, ABC contracts with producers in 1977 stipulated that

> no program or pilot shall contain . . . anything . . . which does not conform with the then current business or advertising policies of any such sponsor; or which is detrimental to the good will or the products or services of . . . any such sponsor. (FCC, Network Inquiry, 1980, Appendix C, p. A-2)

Gary Marshall, producer of several highly successful series, stated that ABC rejected a story line for *Mork & Mindy*, the top rated show for 1978, in which Mork takes TV ads literally, buys everything and creates havoc. Despite the series' and Marshall's proven success, the network feared advertisers' reactions to such a story line.

An advertiser's preferred program is one that allows full use of the products being advertised. The program should be a complimentary context for the ad. In the 1950s, an ad agency, rejecting a play about working-class life, stated, "It is the general policy of advertisers to glamourize their products, the people who buy them, and the whole American social and economic scene" (Barnouw, 1970, p. 32). Advertisers in 1961 considered it "of key importance" to avoid, "irritating, controversial, depressive, or downbeat material" (FCC, Office of Network Study, 1965, p. 373). This requires dramas built around affluent characters for whom consuming is not problematic. Thus affluent characters predominate, and occupational groups with higher levels of consumer expenditure are overrepresented.

A third factor in program decisions is whether it will attract the right audience. Network executives construct a product image of what they *imagine* the audience wants, which surprisingly is not based on actual research of audiences in their homes (Blumler & Spicer, 1990; Pekurny, 1982). For example, Michael Dann, a CBS executive was "concerned the public might not accept a program about a blue collar worker" when offered the pilot script for *Arnie* in 1969 (before *All in the Family* proved that wrong and after a decade in which the only working-class family appearing in prime time was *The Flintstones*). On the other hand, in 1979 an NBC executive expressed the concern that a couple in a pilot was too wealthy to appeal to most viewers (Turow, 1982b, p. 123).

With the exception of the few anecdotes I have mentioned, almost no research has examined program development or production decisions about class content of programs. My research found no significant differences between characters in sitcom pilots and series from 1973 to 1982, indicating that class biases in content begin very early in the decision-making process, when the first pilot episode is being developed (Butsch, 1984). I therefore conducted a mail survey of the producers, writers or directors of the pilots from 1973 to 1982. I specifically asked how the decisions were made about the occupation of the characters in their pilot. I was able to contact 40 persons concerning 50 pilots. I received responses from 6 persons concerning 12 pilots.

Although this represents only a small portion of the original sample, their responses are strikingly similar. Decisions on occupations of main characters were made by the creators and made early in program development, as part of the program idea. In no case did the occupation become a matter of debate or disagreement with the networks. Moreover, the choice of occupation was incidental to the situation or other aspect of the program idea; thus it was embedded in the creator's conception of the situation. For example, according to one writer, a character was conceived of as an architect "to take advantage of the Century City" location for shooting the series; the father in another pilot was cast as owner of a bakery after the decision was made to do a series about an extended Italian family; in another pilot, the creator thought the actor "looked like your average businessman." The particular occupations and even the classes are not necessitated by the situations that creators offered as explanations. But they do not seem to be hiding the truth; their responses were open and unguarded. It appears they did not think through themselves why this *particular* class or occupation; rather, the occupations seem to them an obvious derivative of the situation or location or actors they choose. The choice of class is thus diffuse, embedded in their culture.

This absence of any awareness of decisions about class is confirmed by Gitlin's (1983) interviews with industry personnel about social issues. Thus the process of class construction seems difficult to document given the unspoken guidelines, the indirect manner in which they suggest class and the absence of overt decisions about class. Class or occupation is not typically an issue for discussion, as are obscenity or race. To examine it further, we need to look at the organization of the production process and the culture of creative personnel.

The Hollywood Input—Program Production

Within the production process in Hollywood studios and associated organizations, and in the work culture of creative personnel, we find factors that contribute to the use of simple and repetitious stereotypes of working-class men.

An important factor in television drama production is the severe time constraints (Lynch, 1973; Ravage, 1978; Reeves, 1990, p. 150). The production schedule for series requires that a finished program be delivered to the networks each week. Even if the production company had the entire year over which to complete the season's 22 to 24 episodes, an episode would have to be produced on the average every 2 weeks, including script writing, casting, staging, filming and editing. This is achieved through an assembly line process in which several episodes are in various stages of production and being worked on by the same team of producer, writers, director and actors, simultaneously (Lynch, 1973; Ravage, 1978; Reeves, 1990).

Such a schedule puts great pressure on the production team to simplify the amount of work and decisions to be made as much as possible. The series format is advantageous for this reason: When the general story line and main characters are set, the script can be written following a simple formula. For situation comedy, even the sets and the cast do not change from episode to episode.

The time pressures contribute in several ways to the dependence on stereotypes for characterization. First, if ideas for new series are to be noticed, they cannot be "subtle ideas and feelings of depth" but, rather, "have to be attention getters—loud farts," in the words of a successful director (Ravage, 1978, p. 92).

Also, time pressure encourages type-casting to obtain casts quickly. The script is sent to a "breakdown" agency, which reads the script and extracts the description of characters that need to be cast. One such agency, employing six persons, provided this service for the majority of series (Turow, 1978). These brief character descriptions, not the script, are used by the casting agency to recommend actors, particularly for minor characters. Not surprisingly, the descriptions are highly stereotyped (Turow, 1980). Occupation—and by inference, class—was an important part of these descriptions, being identified for 84% of male characters.

Producers, casting directors and casting agencies freely admit the stereotyping but argue its necessity on the basis of time and dramatic constraints. Type-casting is much quicker. They also argue that to diverge from stereotypes would draw attention away from the action, the story line or other characters and destroy dramatic effect. Thus, unless the contradiction of the stereotype is the basic story idea—as in *Arnie,* a blue-collar worker suddenly appointed corporate executive—there is a very strong pressure, for purposes of dramatic effect, to reproduce existing stereotypes.

The time pressures also make it more likely that the creators will stick to what is familiar to them whenever possible. Two of the most frequent occupations of main characters in family series were in entertainment and writing, that is, modeled on the creators' own lives (Butsch & Glennon, 1983). The vast majority of producers grew up in middle-class homes, with little direct experience of working-class life (Cantor, 1971; Gitlin, 1983; Stein, 1979; Thompson & Burns, 1990). Moreover, the tight schedules and deadlines of series production leave no time for becoming familiar enough with a working-class lifestyle to be able to capture it realistically. Those who have done so—for example, Jackie Gleason, Norman Lear—had childhood memories of working-class neighborhoods to draw on.

Thus the time pressure encourages creative personnel to rely heavily on a shared and consistent product image—including diffuse and undifferentiated images of class—embedded in what Elliott (1972) called "the media culture." The small, closed community of those engaged in television production, including Hollywood creators and network executives (Blumler & Spicer, 1990; Gitlin, 1983; Stein, 1979; Tunstall & Walker, 1981; Turow, 1982a) shares a culture that includes certain conceptions of what life is like and what the audience finds interesting. According to Norman Lear, the production community draws its ideas from what filters into it from the mass media (Gitlin, 1983, p. 204). From this, they try to guess what "the public" would like and formulate images of class they think are compatible (Gitlin, 1983, pp. 225-226).

Although the consistency of image, the underrepresentation of the working class and the use of stereotypes can be explained by structural constraints, the particular stereotypes grow from a rather diffuse set of cultural images, constrained and framed by the structure of the industry. Any further specification will require a close examination of the construction of the consciousness of the program creators and network executives from, among other things, their exposure to the same media they create—a closed circle of cultural reproduction. Whether one can indeed extract the process of class image making from the totality of this occupational culture remains a challenge to researchers.

NOTES

1. Subordinate statuses, generally, race and gender as well as class, are underrepresented and/or presented negatively.

2. The sellers, the production companies, on the other hand, are not an oligopoly. Market concentration is low compared to the buyers (broadcast and cable networks); there was high turnover in the ranks of suppliers and great year-to-year fluctuation in market share; and collusion between suppliers is very difficult (FCC Network Inquiry Special Staff, 1980; Owen & Wildman, 1990).

REFERENCES

Barnouw, E. (1970). *The image empire: A history of broadcasting in the U.S. from 1953.* New York: Oxford University Press.

Blum, A. (1969). Lower class Negro television spectators. In A. Shostak (Ed.), *Blue collar world* (pp. 429-435). New York: Random House.

Blumler, J., & Spicer, C. (1990). Prospects for creativity in the new television marketplace. *Journal of Communication, 40*(4), 78-101.

Brown, L. (1971). *Television: The business behind the box.* New York: Harcourt, Brace Jovanovich.

Bryant, A. (1969). Historical and social aspects of concentration of program control in television. *Law and Contemporary Problems, 34,* 610-635.

Butsch, R. (1984, August). *Minorities from pilot to series: Network selection of character statuses and traits.* Paper presented at the annual meeting of Society for the Study of Social Problems, Washington, DC.

Butsch, R. (1992). Class and gender in four decades of television situation comedy. *Critical Studies in Mass Communication, 9,* 387-399.

Butsch, R., & Glennon, L. M. (1983). Social class: Frequency trends in domestic situation comedy, 1946-1978. *Journal of Broadcasting, 27*(1), 77-81.

Campbell, R., & Reeves, J. (1990). Television authors: The case of Hugh Wilson. In R. Thompson & G. Burns (Eds.), *Making television: Authorship and the production process* (pp. 3-18). New York: Praeger.

Cantor, M. (1971). *The Hollywood TV producer.* New York: Basic Books.

Connell, B. (1978). *Ruling class, ruling culture.* London: Cambridge University Press.

DiMaggio, P., & Hirsch, P. (1976). Production organization in the arts. *American Behavioral Scientist, 19,* 735-752.

Dominick, J. (1976, Winter). Trends in network prime time, 1953-1974. *Journal of Broadcasting, 26,* 70-80.

Elliott, P. (1972). *The making of a television series: A case study in the sociology of culture.* New York: Hastings.

Federal Communications Commission, Network Inquiry Special Staff. (1980). *Preliminary reports.* Washington, DC: Government Printing Office.

Federal Communications Commission, Office of Network Study. (1965). *Second interim report: Television network program procurement* (Part 2). Washington, DC: Government Printing Office.

Gans, H. (1962). *The urban villagers.* New York: Free Press.

Gitlin, T. (1983). *Inside prime time.* New York: Pantheon.

Glennon, L. M., & Butsch, R. (1982). The family as portrayed on television, 1946-78. In National Institute of Mental Health, *Television and social behavior: Ten Years of scientific progress and implications for the eighties* (Vol. 2, Technical Review, 264-271). Washington, DC: Government Printing Office.

Jhally, S., & Lewis, J. (1992). *Enlightened racism: The* Cosby Show, *Audiences and the myth of the American dream.* Boulder, CO: Westview.

Lynch, J. (1973). Seven days with *All in the Family:* A case study of the taped TV drama. *Journal of Broadcasting, 17*(3), 259-274.

Owen, B., & Wildman, S. (1992). *Video economics.* Cambridge, MA: Harvard University Press.

Pekurny, R. (1977). *Broadcast self-regulation: A participant observation study of NBC's broadcast standards department.* Unpublished doctoral dissertation, University of Minnesota.

Pekurny, R. (1982). Coping with television production. In J. S. Ettema & D. C. Whitney (Eds.), *Individuals in mass media organizations.* Beverly Hills, CA: Sage.

Peterson, R. A., & Berger, D. (1971). Entrepreneurship in organizations: Evidence from the popular music industry. *Administrative Science Quarterly, 16,* 97-107.

Ravage, J. (1978). *Television: The director's viewpoint.* New York: Praeger.

Reeves, J. (1990). Rewriting culture: A dialogic view of television authorship. In R. Thompson & G. Burns (Eds.), *Making television: Authorship and the production process* (pp. 147-160). New York: Praeger.

Ryan, B. (1992). *Making capital from culture: The corporate form of capitalist cultural production.* New York: Walter de Gruyter.

Stein, B. (1979). *The view from Sunset Boulevard.* New York: Basic Books.

Thompson, R., & Burns, G. (Eds.). (1990). *Making television: Authorship and the production process.* New York: Praeger.

Tunstall, J., & Walker, D. (1981). *Media made in California.* New York: Oxford University Press.

Turow, J. (1978). Casting for TV parts: The anatomy of social typing. *Journal of Communication, 28*(4), 18-24.

Turow, J. (1980). Occupation and personality in television dramas. *Communication Research, 7*(3), 295-318.

Turow, J. (1982a). Producing TV's world: How important is community? *Journal of Communication, 32*(2), 186-193.

Turow, J. (1982b). Unconventional programs on commercial television. In J. S. Ettema & D. C. Whitney (Eds.), *Individuals in mass media organizations*. Beverly Hills, CA: Sage.

Vidmar, N., & Rokeach, M. (1974). Archie Bunker's bigotry: A study in selective perception and exposure. *Journal of Communication, 24,* 36-47.

Wakshlag, J., & Adams, W. J. (1985). Trends in program variety and prime time access rules. *Journal of Broadcasting and Electronic Media, 29*(1), 23-34.

Winick, C. (1961). Censor and sensibility: A content analysis of the television censor's comments. *Journal of Broadcasting, 5*(2), 117-135.

.47

"Is This What You Mean by Color TV?"

Race, Gender, and
Contested Meanings in NBC's Julia

ANIKO BODROGHKOZY

America in 1968: Police clash with the militant Black Panthers while one of the group's leaders, Huey Newton, is sentenced for murder; civil rights leader Martin Luther King is assassinated in Tennessee, sparking violent uprisings and riots in the nation's black ghettos; the massive Poor People's Campaign, a mobilization of indigent blacks and whites, sets up a tent city on the Mall in Washington, DC; at Cornell University, armed black students sporting bandoliers take over the administration building and demand a black studies program.[1] In the midst of all these events—events that many Americans saw as a revolutionary or at least an insurrectionary situation among the black population—NBC introduced the first situation comedy to feature an African-American in the starring role since *Amos 'n' Andy* and *Beulah* went off the air in the early 1950s.[2] *Julia*, created by writer-producer Hal Kanter, a Hollywood liberal Democrat who campaigned actively for Eugene McCarthy, starred Diahann Carroll as a middle-class, widowed nurse trying to bring up her six-year-old-son, Corey. After the death of her husband in a helicopter crash in Vietnam, Julia and Corey move to an integrated apartment complex, and she finds work in an aerospace industry clinic.

NOTE: Excerpts reprinted from *Private Screenings: Television and the Female Consumer*, by permission of Lynn Spigel and Denise Mann, editors (Minneapolis: University of Minnesota Press, 1992).

413

NBC executives did not expect the show to succeed.[3] They scheduled it opposite the hugely successful *Red Skelton Show* where it was expected to die a noble, dignified death, having demonstrated the network's desire to break the prime-time color bar. Unexpectedly, the show garnered high ratings and lasted a respectable three years.

Despite its success, or perhaps because of it, *Julia* was a very controversial program. Beginning in popular magazine articles written before the first episode even aired and continuing more recently in historical surveys of the portrayals of blacks on American television, critics have castigated *Julia* for being extraordinarily out of touch with and silent on the realities of African-American life in the late 1960s. While large numbers of blacks lived in exploding ghettos, Julia and Corey Baker lived a luxury lifestyle impossible on a nurse's salary. While hostility and racial tensions brewed, and the Kerner Commission Report on Civil Disorders described an America fast becoming two nations separate and unequal, tolerance and colorblindness prevailed on *Julia*.

The show came in for heavy criticism most recently in J. Fred Mac-Donald's (1983) *Blacks and White TV: Afro-Americans in Television Since 1948*. MacDonald describes *Julia* as a "comfortable image of black success . . . in stark juxtaposition to the images seen on local and national newscasts."[4] The show, according to MacDonald, refused to be topical; when dealing with racial issues at all, it did so only in oneliners. He also describes black and white discomfort with the show, claiming that the series was a sell-out intended to assuage white consciences and a "saccharine projection of the 'good life' to be achieved by those blacks who did not riot, who acted properly, and worked within the system."[5]

MacDonald's text-based criticism of *Julia* would appear to be quite justified. However, there was a whole range of politically charged meanings attributed to the program during its network run that critics like MacDonald haven't discussed. What critics of the program have ignored are the diverse and often conflicted ways in which both the producers and viewers of *Julia* struggled to make sense of the show in the context of the racial unrest and rebellions erupting throughout American society. Historically situated in a period of civil dislocations when massive numbers of black Americans were attempting, both peacefully and not so peacefully, to redefine their place within the socio-political landscape, *Julia* functioned as a symptomatic text—symptomatic of the racial tensions and reconfigurations of its time.

The extent to which *Julia* functioned as a site of social tension is particularly evident in the viewer response mail and script revisions in the files of producer Hal Kanter, and it is also apparent in critical articles written for the popular press at the time.[6] These documents allow us to begin to reconstruct the contentious dialogue that took place among audiences, magazine critics, and the show's producer and writers. They also provide clues to how such conflicts materialized in the program narrative itself. A key feature of this dialogue was a discursive struggle over what it meant to be black and what it meant to be white at the close of the 1960s. Black viewers, white viewers, and critics all made sense of the program in notably different ways. . . .

. . . The viewer mail (some 151 letters and postcards) filed in the Hal Kanter papers provides a particularly rich case study of how *Julia*'s audiences attempted to make sense of the program and how they grappled with racial difference and social change through their engagement with the show. At times, the statements in the letters echo those in the popular press; more frequently, both the reading strategies and the debates are different. Many of the letters have carbon copy responses from Kanter attached, setting up a fascinating, often contentious dialogue. But what is most compelling about the letters is the way they reveal the remarkably conflicted, diverse, and contradictory responses among audience members.

These letters, the majority of which came from married women, should not be seen as representative of the larger audience's responses to the program.[7] Letter writers tend to be a particularly motivated group of television viewers. There is no way to determine whether the sentiments that crop up over and over again in the letters were widespread among viewers who did not write to the producers. Thus my analysis of these letters is not an attempt to quantify the *Julia* audience or to use the documents as a representative sample. While neither the letter writers nor the critics in the popular press were representative of the audience as a whole, their readings were symptomatic of struggles over racial definition. . . .

One trend that became evident almost immediately among the favorable letters written by white viewers was a marked self-consciousness about racial self-identification: "I am white, but I enjoy watching 'Julia.'"[8] "Our whole family from great grandmother down to my five year old, loved it. We just happen to be Caucasian." "As a 'white middle class Jewish' teacher, may I say that it is finally a pleasure to turn on the T.V. and see contemporary issues treated with honesty, humor, and sensitivity."[9]

One way in which to account for the self-consciousness of many letter writers identifying themselves as whites was that the novelty of a black-centered program raised questions about traditional and previously unexamined definitions of racial identity and difference. One mother of two boys in Ohio struggled with this very issue in her letter:

> Being a white person I hope this program helps all of us to understand each other. Maybe if my children watch this program they will also see the good side of Negro people [rather] than all the bad side they see on the news programs such as riots, sit-ins, etc. I know this program will help my two sons so when they grow up they won't be so prejudice[*sic*].

While the woman made some problematic distinctions between good black people and bad black people, there was an attempt to grapple with racial difference. Definitions of what it meant to be white had suddenly become an uncertain terrain. The crisis in race relations signified by "riots, sit-ins, etc." made the black population visible, and the depiction of African-Americans had ceased to be a stable field. As representations of black people had become an arena of contested meanings, so too had self-representations of whites become uncertain. One manifestation of that uncertainty was self-consciousness. In the aftermath of the civil rights movement and in the midst of black power sentiment, the question of what it now meant to be white in America was an issue that needed working through.

Another way to think about race was, perhaps, paradoxically, to deny difference. A letter from a rather idealistic fifteen-year-old girl in Annandale, Virginia, affirmed, "Your new series has told me that at least SOME people have an idea of a peaceful and loving existence. So what if their skin pigmentation is different and their philosophies are a bit different than ours *they are still people.*" Another woman from Manhattan Beach, California, who described her race as Caucasian and her ancestry as Mexican, wrote, "I love the show. Keep up the good work. This way the world will realize that the Negro is just like everyone else, with feelings and habits as the Whites have." A mother of twins in Highland Park, New Jersey, observed, "And it's immensely valuable to the many non-Negroes who just don't know any Negroes, or don't know that all people mostly behave like people."

Perhaps these viewers engaged in a denial of the "otherness" of black people in an attempt to reduce white anxiety about racial difference. By affirming that blacks were "just people" and just like everyone else, these viewers defined "everyone else" as white. White was the norm from which the Other deviated. In their sincere attempts to negotiate changing representations of race, these viewers denied that blacks historically had not fit the constructed norm of the white middle-class social formation. In this move, the viewers were, of course, assisted by the program itself. The show's theme music was a generic sit-com jingle lacking any nod to the rich traditions of African-American musical forms. Julia's apartment, while nicely appointed, and with a framed photo of her dead hero husband prominently displayed, was also completely generic. Unlike a comparable but more recent black family sit-com, *The Cosby Show,* with its lavish townhouse decorated with African-American artworks, Julia's home contained no culturally specific touches. Diahann Carroll's speech was also completely uninflected, on the one hand differentiating her from her prime-time predecessors such as *Amos 'n' Andy* and *Beulah,* but on the other hand evacuating as much ethnic and cultural difference as possible. For viewers picking up on the interpretive clues provided by the show, black people were "just people" to the extent that they conformed to an unexamined white norm of representation.

While this denial of difference may have been typical, it was by no means the dominant interpretive strategy employed by viewers who wrote letters. In fact, many viewers were clearly struggling with the problem of representation, both of blacks and of whites. The criticism leveled by many viewers—that the show was unrealistic and was not "telling it like it is"—reveals a struggle over how reality should be defined.

The refrain "tell it like it is" became a recurring theme in debates about *Julia,* both in the popular press and among the viewer letters. In a rather scathing review, *Time* magazine criticized the show for not portraying how black people really lived: "She [Julia] would not recognize a ghetto if she stumbled into it, and she is, in every respect save color, a figure in a white milieu." [10] Robert Lewis Shayon, the TV-radio critic for *Saturday Review,* was also particularly concerned with *Julia*'s deficiencies in representing this notion of a black reality. In the first of three articles on the series, he, like the *Time* reviewer, castigated the program for turning a blind eye to the realities of black life in the ghettos. For Shayon, the reality of the black experience was what was documented in the Kerner Commission report: "Negro youth, 'hustling in the jungle' of their 'crime-ridden, violence-prone, and poverty-stricken world'—that's the real problem, according to the commission report." [11] The world of *Julia,* on the other hand, was a fantasy because it did not focus on the problems of black youth (which for Shayon meant young black males) and because it did not take place in a ghetto environment. The unconsciously racist notion that the black experience was essentially a ghetto experience remained unexamined in these popular press accounts. . . .

Unlike the critics, viewers generally did not want to relocate Julia and Corey to a ghetto. Instead, viewers who criticized the show for not "telling it like it is" were more concerned with the presentation of black characters than they were with the upscale setting. A male viewer in Chicago wrote:

> On another point which bears remarks is the unwillingness to allow the program to be "black." I do not object to white people being in the cast. What I do object to is selecting the black cast from people (black people) who are so white oriented that everyone has a white mentality, that is, their expressions are all that of white people. Choose some people whose expressions and manners are unquestionably black. The baby-sitter was, for example, so white cultured that you would have thought she was caucasian except for the color of her skin.

Hal Kanter's reply to this letter indicated how contested this issue was: "We all make mistakes, don't we, Mr. Banks? Please try to forgive me for mine in the spirit of universality and brotherhood we are attempting to foster." . . .

Other viewers, also uncomfortable with the unrealistic quality of the program, pointed out more problems in the representation of blacks. A woman in Berkeley, California, observed:

> Your show is in a position to dispell [*sic*] so *many* misconceptions about Black people & their relationships to whites. I am just one of many who are so *very* disappointed in the outcome of such a promising show.
> *Please,* help to destroy the misconceptions—not reinforce them! Stop making Miss Carroll super-Negro and stop having blacks call themselves "colored" and make your characters less self-conscious and tell that "babysitter" to quit overacting.

This concern with representing blacks as "Super Negro" was also voiced in the popular press. In a *TV Guide* article in December 1968, Diahann Carroll was quoted as saying:

With black people right now, we are all terribly bigger than life and more wonderful than life and smarter and better—because we're still proving. . . . For a hundred years we have been prevented from seeing accurate images of ourselves and we're all overconcerned and overreacting. The needs of the white writer go to the superhuman being. At the moment, we're presenting the white Negro. And he has very little Negro-ness.[12] . . .

This problem of racial definition was raised by other viewers who objected to blacks being differentiated and defined at the expense of white characters. Many viewers, particularly white housewives, took exception to the juxtaposing of Julia to her white neighbor, Mrs. Waggedorn. One mother of a four-year-old in Philadelphia said she would not watch the program anymore "as I believe you are portraying [sic] the white mother to be some kind of stupid idiot.—The colored boy & mother are sharp as tacks which is fine but why must the other family be portrayed as being dumb, dumb, dumb." Another "white suburban mother of four" in Fort Worthington, Pennsylvania, complained that Mrs. Waggedorn was a "dumb bunny" while Julia was a "candidate for 'Mother of the Year.' " A third letter from a "quite typical New England housewife and mother of three" in Hyde Park, Massachusetts, stated:

> If Diahann Carroll were to play the roll [sic] of the neighborly housewife, and vice verser [sic], the black people of this country would be screaming "Prejudice." Why must Julia be pictured so glamorously dressed, living in such a luxurious apartment, dining off of the finest china while her white neighbor is made to appear sloppy, has rollers in her hair. . . .
> If your show is to improve the image of the negro woman, great! But—please don't accomplish this at the expense of the white housewife.

The reading strategy these viewers brought to the text was one of polarization. They saw a form of reverse discrimination. Explicit in their letters was an anxiety over the representation of race, black versus white. Implicit, however, was a nascent critique of the representation of gender. All three of these letter writers self-consciously defined themselves by occupation: white housewives and mothers. In the depiction of Mrs. Waggedorn, they saw a stereotypical representation of themselves and were quite aware that they were being demeaned as women. . . .

The viewer response letters examined so far attempted, either by denying difference or by trying to grapple with it, to engage with the program in order to think through ways in which to rework race relations. While many of the letters exhibited unexamined racist discourses, the racism seemed unintended and unconscious, a manifestation of the shifting ground. *Julia*, as a text that worked hard to evacuate politically charged representations and potentially disturbing discourses of racial oppression, would appear to be an unlikely candidate for overtly racist attacks. However, a surprisingly large number of the letters in the Hal Kanter papers reveal an enormous amount of unmediated anxiety felt by some viewers about changes being wrought in the wake of the civil rights and black oppositional movements.

Concerns that reappeared in these letters tended to focus on a discomfort with seeing increasing numbers of African-Americans on television, fears that traditional racial hierarchies were being eradicated, and anxieties about interracial sexuality. While *Julia* never dealt with issues of miscegenation or intermarriage, many of these viewers read them into the program anyway. Some of these viewers may have done so because, unlike the black mammy figures traditionally predominant in the mass media, Julia conformed to white ideals of beauty. That her white male bosses were shown recognizing her sexuality may have provided the cues some viewers needed to construct scenarios such as the one provided by an anonymous viewer from Los Angeles:

> What are you trying to do by making "Julia." No racial problems—she is playing opposite a white, she is suppose [*sic*] to live in an all white apt house. It's racial because you will have it so Nolan [Dr. Chegley, Julia's boss] will fall in love with her and have to make her over—re-pulsive—You had better write a part for a big black boy so he can mess with a white girl or they will get mad.

Anxiety over social change and transformations in race relations erupted here in a full-blown fear of interracial sexuality. For this viewer, integration created a moral panic whereby the sudden visibility of blacks in "white society" could only mean that "big black boys" wanted to mess with white girls.

Other viewers, less obsessed with questions of miscegenation, exhibited fears about integration by expressing anger at television as an institution. They blamed television for creating social strife and causing blacks to forget their proper place. One anonymous viewer from Houston, Texas, who signed her or his comments "the silent majority," wrote:

> Living in Texas all my life I have always lived around the negroes and they used to be really fine people until the T.V. set came out & ruined the whole world! Not only have you poor white trash taken advantage of them & ruined their chances now you have ruined the college set. You are good at getting people when they are most vulnerable and changing their entire thinking!

. . . Such letters show the ideological extremes viewers could go to in their meaning-making endeavors. *Julia* as a text certainly did not encourage these interpretations. But since meanings are neither entirely determined nor controlled by the text and since viewers are active agents in the process of constructing their own meanings, we can see how disturbing the process can be. Cultural studies theorists analyzing oppositional reading strategies have

generally focused on how such viewers position themselves against dominant ideology. By implication such reading positions are often seen as positive evidence of cultural struggle against the constraining policies, perspectives, and practices of the ruling social order or "power bloc."[13] However,
as these letters show, an oppositional reading strategy need not be a liberatory or progressive strategy.

Another issue that seemed to bother the hostile viewers was the mere
presence of blacks on television. Blacks were slowly becoming more visible
as supporting players in such popular programs as *I Spy, The Mod Squad,
Hogan's Heroes,* and *Daktari.* Blacks were also occasionally being featured in
commercial advertisements by 1967. But in the summer of 1968, the networks, at the urging of the Kerner Commission, outdid themselves offering
an unprecedented number of news documentaries on the state of black
America, including CBS's acclaimed *Of Black America,* a seven-part series
hosted by Bill Cosby.[14] For some viewers this was clearly too much: "We
have had so much color shoved down our throats on special programs this
summer its [*sic*] enough to make a person sick," wrote one viewer from
Toronto. An anonymous viewer from Eufaula, Oklahoma, wrote, "After the
riots and [the] network filled 'Black American' shows all summer, white
people aren't feeling to [*sic*] kindly toward colored people shows. You are
ahead of the time on this one." Yet another anonymous viewer from Red
Bluff, California, asserted, "I will not buy the product sponsoring this show
or any show with a nigger in it. I believe I can speak for millions of real
Americans [*sic*]. I will write the sponsors of these shows. I am tired of niggers
in my living room." A third anonymous viewer from Bethpage, Long Island,
asked, "Is this what you mean by color T. V. ugh. *Click*!!" Moreover, many
of these people made no distinction between documentary representations
of civil strife and the fictional world of *Julia.* Since both in some way
concerned black people, *Julia* was really no different from the news specials
about ghetto riots.

In the end, the reason it is useful to consider these disturbing and
offensive letters is because of what they can tell us about the polysemic
nature of reception. *Julia* was heavily criticized for constructing a "white
Negro," for playing it safe in order not to scare off white viewers, for
sugar-coating its racial messages. While all of that may be true, the show's
"whiteness," middle-classness, and inoffensiveness did not defuse its threat
to entrenched racist positions. This threat was also made evident by the fact
that many of the hostile letters carried no return address. Unlike other
viewers who wrote letters, both favorable and unfavorable, these letter
writers were not interested in opening up a dialogue with the show's
producers. The anonymity both shielded their besieged positions and revealed that such positions were no longer easily defensible.

While the majority of letters in the Hal Kanter papers appear to be from
white viewers, there are a significant number of letters from viewers who
identified themselves as black.[15] . . .

One crucial distinction between black and white viewers was that many
of the black viewers displayed a participatory quality in their engagement

with the program. They tended to erase boundaries between themselves and the text. Many letter writers asked if they could write episodes or play parts on the show. An eleven-year-old boy from the Bronx wrote:

> I am a Negro and I am almost in the same position as Corey. . . . Your show really tells how an average black or Negro person lives. I like your show so much that if you ever have a part to fill I would be glad to fill it for you.[16]

A teenage girl from Buffalo wanted to create a new character for the show: Julia's teenage sister. She proceeded to describe what the sister's characteristics would be and how she would like to play the part. A female teacher from Los Angeles wrote:

> The thought occurred to me that *Julia* may be in need of a close friend on your television show—and/or Corey Baker may need a *good* first grade teacher (me). . . . I am not a militant but a *very proud Negro*.[17]

The viewers who wanted to write episodes generally made their offer at the end of the letter after having detailed what they considered wrong with the show. Other viewers wanted to get together with Kanter personally to discuss the matter. One young woman from Detroit, studying mass media at college, suggested a meeting with Kanter: "Perhaps I can give you a better idea of what the Black people really want to see and what the white person really *needs* to see." [18]

While white viewers offered criticisms of the program, only the black viewers took it upon themselves to offer their assistance in improving the show. Their participatory relationship to the text indicated a far more active attempt at making the show meaningful. For the black viewers the struggle over representation was between the actual program as created by the white producers and a potential, but more authentic, program to be created by the black viewers. By acting in and writing for the show, they became producers of meaning, rather than mere recipients of meaning constructed by whites. Asserting the values of their cultural codes, they attempted to bring their own knowledge to the text. The positive engagement evidenced by these viewers arose from an articulation of self-affirming representation.

Ebony, a mass-circulation magazine targeted at a primarily middle-class black readership, also tried to find racially-affirming representations in the program. Unlike other popular press accounts, *Ebony* took pains to emphasize the show's positive aspects while acknowledging its shortcomings. Pointing to *Julia*'s four black scriptwriters, the article indicated that the show would provide new opportunities for African-Americans in the television industry.[19] *Ebony* appeared to support the program specifically because the magazine saw that blacks were assisting (even if in a limited way) in its production.

One of the main areas of concern for many black viewers was whether the representation of blacks was realistic or whether the program portrayed a white world for white viewers. The denial of difference that numerous white viewers applauded was challenged by many, although not all, black viewers. A black woman from Los Angeles wrote:

> Your show is geared to the white audience with no knowledge of the realness of normal Negro people.
>
> Your work is good for an all white program—but something is much missing from your character—Julia is unreal.
>
> To repeat again—Julia is no Negro woman. I know & I'm Negro with many friends in situations such as hers.

Kanter replied somewhat sarcastically: "I'm glad you think our work is 'good for an all white program.' I'll pass your praise along to our black writer and black actors."

. . . The woman with many friends in Julia's situation searched the text in vain looking for confirmation of her identity as a black woman. Unlike the black women Jacqueline Bobo studied who found positive, progressive, and affirming meanings about black womanhood in *The Color Purple*, this particular woman found nothing in *Julia*. The text did not speak to her experiences. It did not construct a reading position from which she could use her cultural codes and find useful meanings. On the contrary, her experience as a black woman, along with those of her friends, blocked any possibility of finding a place for herself within the text. The strategy of breaking down textual boundaries and inserting oneself into the program by offering to write episodes or play a role may have functioned to avert this problem. It may have given some black viewers a mechanism by which to place themselves within the program and assert their own identities as African-Americans. . . .

NOTES

1. Caute (1988).

2. *Amos 'n' Andy* remained in syndication until 1966. NBC attempted a short-lived variety show with Nat King Cole in 1957.

3. Brown (1971).

4. MacDonald (1983, p. 116).

5. MacDonald (1983, p. 117). *Julia* was also criticized by the U.S. Commission on Civil Rights (1977) in its influential publication *Window Dressing on the Set: Women and Minorities in Television.*

6. The Hal Kanter papers are located at the Wisconsin Center Historical Archives, State Historical Society, Madison, Wisconsin. The Kanter papers contain primarily final draft scripts for all the *Julia* episodes; Kanter's personal correspondence, production materials for the series, and ratings information; and a large selection of viewer letters. Most of the letters to which I will be referring later . . . are filed in folders labeled "fan letters, favorable" and "fan letters, unfavorable." Some viewer letters are also scattered among Kanter's correspondence folders.

7. Sixty-one of the letters came from married women and twenty-three from single women or those whose marital status was unidentifiable. Thirty-three letters came from men. The rest were either unidentifiable by gender or from children and young people. The preponderance of women viewers is mirrored in ratings materials located in a ratings folder in Hal Kanter papers, Box 18. A breakdown of the *Julia* audience for a two-week period ending

Sept. 28, 1969, showed that women between the ages of 18 and 49 formed the largest bulk of the audience, followed by female teens. Men between the ages of 18 and 49 formed the smallest share of the audience.

8. All of the following viewer letters, unless marked otherwise, are in the Hal Kanter papers, Box 18.

9. The writers of these letters are, respectively, a male viewer from DuBois, Pennsylvania; a female viewer from Colton, California; and a female viewer from New York City.

10. "Wonderful World of Color" (1968, p. 70).

11. Shayon (1968, p. 49).

12. Lewis (1968, p. 26).

13. See, for instance, Fiske (1987, 1989).

14. MacDonald (1983, pp. 138-139).

15. Thirteen women, one man, and three children or young people identified themselves as black. There was also a group of thirteen letters from an inner-city grade school writing class. From the tone of the letters, I suspect the class was predominantly made up of black children.

16. This letter is located in the Hal Kanter papers, Box 1, among Kanter's general correspondence. A significant number of letters from self-identifying black viewers can be found in this general correspondence rather than in the fan letter files.

17. Hal Kanter papers, Box 1.

18. Hal Kanter papers, Box 1.

19. *Ebony* (November 1968), pp. 56-58.

REFERENCES

Brown, L. (1971). *Television: The business behind the box.* New York: Harcourt Brace Jovanovich.

Caute, D. (1988). *The year of the barricades: A journey through 1968.* New York: Harper & Row.

Fiske, J. (1987). *Television culture.* New York: Methuen.

Fiske, J. (1989). *Understanding popular culture.* Boston: Unwin Hyman.

Lewis, R. W. (1968, December 14). The importance of being Julia. *TV Guide.*

MacDonald, J. F. (1983). *Blacks and White TV: Afro-Americans in television since 1948.* Chicago: Nelson-Hall.

Shayon, R. L. (1968, April 20). Julia—Breakthrough or letdown. *Saturday Review.*

U.S. Commission on Civil Rights. (1977). *Window dressing on the set: Women and minorities in television.* Washington DC: Government Printing Office.

Wonderful world of color. (1968, December 13). *Time.*

■ 48

Television's Realist Portrayal of African-American Women and the Case of *L.A. Law*

JANE RHODES

. . . Realist drama has been marketed by the television industry as containing "real life" representations of diverse social groups and issues. Thus viewers might expect more accurate or progressive portrayals of African-American women in this genre as compared with soap operas or situation comedies. Some scholars have suggested instead that realism is a reactionary mode of television representation which seeks to maintain the status quo. My paper provides support for the latter argument.

THE LEGACY OF BLACK FEMALE TV CHARACTERS

The history of black women on television reflects what MacDonald (1983) terms the medium's unfulfilled promise; instead of using its potential to reverse ridicule and misinformation, it has perpetuated the worst stereotypes of blacks found in American popular culture. During the 1950s, they were portrayed as mammy figures to various white employers in both

NOTE: Excerpts reprinted from *Women and Language*, Vol. 15, No. 1 (1991), by permission of the publisher and the author.

dramatic and comedy programming. For example, actress Lillian Randolph spent nine years beginning in 1953 in the role of Louise the maid on "Make Room for Daddy"; Ethel Waters and Louise Beavers played the role of "Beulah" between 1950-1953 while Butterfly McQueen portrayed her dim-witted friend Oriole; and Ernestine Wade was the shrieking, manipulating Sapphire on the "Amos 'n Andy Show" from 1951-1954.[1] In addition to being in unimaginative and restrictive roles, these images of black women "brought comfort to white television viewers" because they were non-threatening, unappealing and did not question their social position.[2] These images persisted because television adopted many of its early story lines and stereotypes from successful radio programs, and program sponsors who worried about public acceptance of realistic portrayals of blacks, had heavy control over program content.[3]

With the exception of occasional appearances on variety shows as singers and dancers, more substantial roles for black women were scant. Claudia McNeil won acclaim for her appearance in "A Member of the Wedding" in 1958, and Ethel Waters appeared on "The General Electric Theater." But even on these occasions, their dramatic portrayals were of the "faithful servant, beloved darkie or suffering mother"[4], and little would change until the following decade when some attempts were made to break the stereotypes.

In the 1960s the networks gradually acquired greater control over program production and scheduling, and coupled with the growing influence of the civil rights movement, began to create new—although minor—roles for blacks. Diahann Carroll won an Emmy as best actress in a single performance in a 1962 episode of "Naked City" and Diana Sands was nominated for an Emmy in 1963 for an episode of "The Nurse." The first black woman to get a leading role in a series was Cicely Tyson, who played a secretary in the inner-city drama "Eastside/Westside" which lasted just one year (1963-1964).[5] The temporary nature of these programs would be a harbinger of future trends affecting black women on television.

Perhaps the most controversial program of the sixties involving a black woman was "Julia," starring Diahann Carroll, which was broadcast from 1968-1971. The show was clearly a "first": the first time a black woman was the bone fide star of a television program and one of the first roles—a nurse and single parent—that avoided the servant-mammy stereotypes. Although this would have been a breakthrough ten years earlier, in the late 1960s Julia's totally assimilated "white Negro" character drew harsh criticism, even from the program's star. MacDonald noted that "Julia Baker was the most assimilated black character ever to appear in the American mass media. Julia made no pretense at dealing with contemporary social issues. Indeed, it studiously avoided them."[6]

Ironically, there would not be another black woman in a leading role for a decade. With the exception of Denise Nicholas as a teacher on "Room 222" (1969-1974), the new trend for both male and female blacks would be comedic portrayals. In the early 1970s Norman Lear and Tandem productions created several series with black characters, including "All in the Family," "Sanford and Son," "Good Times," and "The Jeffersons." Producer Bud Yorkin added "What's Happening" to the growing ghetto of black comedies. While these comedies enjoyed considerable success, with many going into syndication and still broadcast today, they also returned black characters to some of the grossest stereotypes. Black women found themselves in the midst of a "resurrection of the loud-but-loveable mammy,"[7] while black men played Stepin' Fetchit, both in a surge of what critics called self-deprecating racial humor.

One deviation from this trend was the short-lived "Get Christie Love" (1974-1975), the first weekly detective show starring a black actor, male or female. However, the show's plots were considered improbable for a black woman, and actress Theresa Graves was said to have too much sex appeal and too little talent.[8] Ironically, similar programs of the period which flaunted the sexuality of white actresses such as "Charlie's Angels" and "Police Woman" went on to considerable success.

As television moved into the 1980s there were few changes in the roles played by black women. With a few important exceptions, notably the success of "Roots," "The Autobiography of Miss Jane Pittman" and "Fame" in the late seventies, network television seemed incapable of stretching beyond the comfortable, comedic roles to fully developed dramatic characters. At the same time that Mary Tyler Moore and Valerie Harper were stretching the limits of women's roles in comedy to situate themselves as prototype feminists, black women were still projecting the "Mammy" image. Perhaps the strongest criticism was heaped on Nell Carter for her character on "Gimme a Break," beginning in 1981, termed a "return to the proud but servile, cocky but nurturing, loyal mammy."[9] Carter acknowledged the negative images generated by her ill-tempered servant's role but countered that other roles for black women were too scarce. Thus, she like many black performers was forced to choose between a demeaning role, or none at all. . . .

BLACK WOMEN IN REALIST TV DRAMA

In recent years "The Cosby Show," "227," "Amen," and "A Different World" have provided more interesting and diverse vehicles for black women, yet they continue within the context of comedic, and often slapstick, portrayals. In Diahann Carroll's return to prime time on "Dynasty" she plays a role that resembles her "Julia" character in its avoidance of racial issues and total assimilation into a white environment. The realist genre made popular by writer/producer by Stephen Bochco on "Hill Street Blues," and carried over into "L. A. Law" and other programs, has been acclaimed for tackling serious social issues, and for portraying women and minorities in a more accurate light. But the question remains whether this form has been more progressive in depicting black women as characters.

When NBC aired the pilot for "Hill Street Blues" in January 1981, the network introduced a genre that mixed the serial soap opera and the cop show with generous doses of realism. The program, created by Stephen Bochco, was unique in its claim to realism through its practice of borrowing heavily from fact to supplement fiction.[10] It also sold itself to upscale audiences with the claim of presenting accurate, and frequently graphic and harsh depictions of social realities. According to Gitlin "Race issues perfectly illustrated the show's approach to the real world. 'Hill Street' conveyed the ambivalence of white middle-class feelings about the black and brown underclass . . . The show's split image of ethnics matches both a split in the mind of the white middle class and a real divide in the black community between respectable, upwardly mobile ethnics and the underclass." [11] Bochco and Terry Louise Fisher later used this formula to create "L. A. Law" which premiered on NBC in 1986.

While the appeal of these dramas is distinctive, they have generally denied black women ongoing, fully developed characters, thus failing to live up to their promise of realism. On "Hill Street Blues" black women formed the backdrop of poverty, crime and hopelessness upon which the plots were built. They were hookers and drug addicts, abused wives and rape victims, but rarely cops or public defenders or upstanding members of the community. Black women were invariably cast as romantic interests for the two black male police officers in the cast. The one critically acclaimed performance by a black actress was from Alfre Woodard, who won an Emmy for her two-episode appearance as a single parent whose child is accidentally killed by a police officer. Woodard's impact on the show was brilliant but short-lived. Gitlin acknowledged that "Hill Street's" promise of racial realism fell short, noting that Hispanics and blacks on the show were underdeveloped, stereotyped characters.[12]

Less has been written about "L.A. Law," but my analysis of 11 episodes broadcast in 1986-1987 and 1987-1988 shows a similar trend. One of the program's creators, a former deputy district attorney, said that she drew from actual cases and her own experience in developing the show's story lines.[13] This program has been particularly ambitious in building the concerns of numerous minority groups into its plots, i.e. gay men and lesbians, the mentally retarded, the physically disabled and obese women. Two central characters among the program's stable of attorneys are an Hispanic man and an African-American man. Yet women of color are conspicuously absent from even the most menial roles. As in "Hill Street," they form the background of society—silent, nearly invisible characters found in the black rows of the courtroom, on the street, or in the jury box.

One gripping but brief role for a black woman was the show's pilot which starred Alfre Woodard as a terminal cancer patient who was a rape victim. Her character paralleled the Emmy-winning role on "Hill Street," eliciting sympathy from the audience and action from the powerful white authority figures who came to her rescue. Once again the black woman was a tragic figure, tormented by the rapists because of her gender and by the defense attorney because of her race. Casting Woodard was a shrewd marketing device—she enjoyed fame as an award-winning actress, and she had appeared regularly on another NBC drama, "St. Elsewhere."

Less predictable than this opening episode is the occasional twist "L.A. Law" offers in casting black women in nominal roles as judges and attorneys. Clearly these depictions also lack realism because black women comprise less than 2 percent of the nation's judges. The black women judges on

"L.A. Law" seem clearly to be positioned for symbolic purposes. They have few, if any, lines, and are frequently seen for less than two minutes as the camera pans across the courtroom amid one of the show's numerous sub-plots. In one 1988 episode, a mature black woman presided as judge over a humorous and trivial case of a man being sued for "killing" another's car. The judge uttered no words, and her character was reduced to gestures and expressions. In another episode in which the law firm's mentally retarded clerk Benny faced rape charges, the judge was a young black woman who controlled the court proceedings and the two combative white male attor-neys with a stern look and the words "overruled" and "let them proceed." Both women represent a unique status for black women on television: power, authority, control and considerable success. . . .

Among the programs surveyed in this analysis, there was a single episode in which a black woman had a significant speaking part as an attor-ney. The role played by Wanda DeJesus, a district attorney who opposed the star female lawyer played by Jill Eikenberry, appeared capable, confident and tough even as she lost a controversial case. But ultimately, she was positioned as foil for the program's star, and there was nothing about the role that was developed into a legitimate character. During her three minutes on screen, the viewer learned little of her life, experiences or perspective, and it was assumed that she would disappear from the plot once the scene shifted.

. . . In some respects, "L.A. Law" has managed to create new stereotypes of black women similar to those found in Gray's[14] analysis of black male television characters. These women, when apparent, are either impover-ished victims or successful, middleclass and thoroughly assimilated. Black women may be central to the story lines, but are dispensable to the program as a whole. They are neither major nor minor stars. They do not reappear as part of the serial structure which enables the viewer to engage and form relationships with the characters. . . .

In the case of "L.A. Law" new stereotypes of black women have simply replaced the old ones. Some may herald these images as positive role models that counter the negative comedic ones. A structuralist argument may insist that placing black women in powerful roles is a subversive act that will prompt a new range of readings of the character by the audience. Indeed, the presence of a black woman judge in a courtroom scene is likely to elicit tensions in the text that make the readings more interesting or more pleas-urable. But if that role lasts a mere two minutes, that potential has been severely reduced.

I would suggest that these constructions of black women both reflect and functionally perpetuate their powerlessness by denying them a greater presence in television. Not only are black women stereotyped, as are all television characters, they are depicted in a manner that reinforces their position as having no voice. In this way, such characterizations can be seen as maintaining the status quo of American social stratification, rather than offering an agenda for social change. Clearly some of the characters of the realist genre have introduced television viewers to more progressive read-ings of urban life in America. And "L.A. Law" has gone further than some programs in developing new, although limited, roles for black women. But overall, television writers, directors and producers have made little progress in freeing black women from their underclass status in the television ghetto.

NOTES

1. Primary sources of this historical data include MacDonald (1983); Wilson and Gutiérrez (1985); and Woll and Miller (1987).
2. Dates (1987, p. 451).
3. Woll and Miller (1987, pp. 70, 73).
4. MacDonald (1983, p. 40).
5. MacDonald (1983, p. 103).
6. MacDonald (1983, p. 115).
7. MacDonald (1983, p. 176).
8. Woll and Miller (1987, p. 87).
9. Dates (1987, p. 457).
10. Gitlin (1985, pp. 287-288).
11. Gitlin (1985, p. 313).
12. Gitlin (1985, p. 313).
13. Johnson (1987).
14. Gray (1986).

REFERENCES

Dates, J. L. (1987). Gimme a break: African-American women on prime time television. In A. Wells (Ed.), *Mass media and society.* Lexington, MA: D. C. Heath.

Gitlin, T. (1985). *Inside prime time.* New York: Pantheon.

Gray, H. (1986). Television and the new Black man: Black male images in prime time situation comedy. *Culture, Media and Society, 8,* 223-242.

Johnson, B. D. (1987, February 23). Legal eagles and the law of the jungle. *Maclean's,* p. 53.

MacDonald, J. F. (1983). *Blacks and White TV.* Chicago: Nelson-Hall.

Wilson, C. J., & Gutiérrez, F. (1985). *Minorities and media.* Beverly Hills, CA: Sage.

Woll, A. L., & Miller, R. (1987). *Ethnic and racial images in American film and television.* New York: Garland.

■ 49

Television, Black Americans, and the American Dream

HERMAN GRAY

This essay examines fictional television representations of black middle class success and nonfictional representations of black urban poverty. It suggests that these representations operate intertextually to produce an ideology which explains black middle class success and urban poverty by privileging individual attributes and middle class values and by displacing social and structural factors. Jameson's (1979) notion of reification and utopia in popular culture are used in support of this ideological reading.

. . . My interest here is in the relationship between representations of black life in fictional and nonfictional television and the ideological meanings of these representations when television is viewed as a complete ideological field (Fiske, 1987). In the following section, I theoretically situate the problem. I then turn to a discussion of black failure as represented in the CBS News documentary *The Crisis of Black America: The Vanishing Family* and the representation of upper middle class black affluence in *The Cosby Show*.

THEORETICAL CONTEXT

. . . Media representations of black success and failure and the processes that produce them are ideological to the extent that the assumptions that organize the media discourses shift our understanding of racial inequality away from structured social processes to matters of individual choice. Such ideological representations appear natural and universal rather than as the result of social and political struggles over power.

The process of media selection and appropriation, however, is only one part of the play of hegemony. Mass media and popular culture are, according to Stuart Hall (1980), sites where struggles over meaning and the power to represent it are waged. Thus, even as the media and popular cultural forms present representations of race and racial (in)equality, the power of these meanings to register with the experiences (common sense) of different segments of the population remains problematic. Meanings constantly shift and are available for negotiation. It is in this process of negotiation that different, alternative, even oppositional readings are possible (Fiske, 1987; Hall, 1980). Because of this constantly shifting terrain of meaning and struggle, the representations of race and racial interaction in fictional and nonfictional television reveal both the elements of the dominant racial ideology as well as the limits to that ideology.

. . . In television representations of blacks, the historical realities of slavery, discrimination, and racism or the persistent struggles against domination are displaced and translated into celebrations of black middle class visibility and achievement. In this context, successful and highly visible stars like Bill Cosby and Michael Jackson confirm the openness and pluralism of American society.

. . . The black underclass appears as menace and a source of social disorganization in news accounts of black urban crime, gang violence, drug use, teenage pregnancy, riots, homelessness, and general aimlessness. In news accounts (and in Hollywood films such as *Colors*), poor blacks (and Hispanics) signify a social menace that must be contained. Poor urban blacks help to mark the boundaries of appropriate middle class behavior as well as the acceptable routes to success. As a unity, these representations of black middle class success and underclass failure are ideological because they are mutually reinforcing and their fractured and selective status allows them to be continuously renewed and secured. Furthermore, the meanings operate within a frame that privileges representations of middle class racial pluralism while marginalizing those of racial inequality. This constant quest for legitimacy and the need to quell and displace fears at the same time as it calls them forth are part of the complex ideological work that takes place in television representations of race. . . .

Although fictional and nonfictional representations of blacks emanate from separate generic quarters of television, they activate meanings for viewers across these boundaries. That is, the representations make sense in terms of their intertextuality between and within programs (Fiske, 1987; Fiske & Hartley, 1978; Williams, 1974). Television representations of black life in the late 1980s cannot be read in isolation but rather should be read in terms of their relationship to other television texts. . . .

. . . I begin with a discussion of the CBS News report about the black urban under class. The special report which aired in January 1985 is titled *The Vanishing Family: Crisis In Black America.* CBS senior correspondent Bill Moyers hosted the 90-minute documentary which was filmed in Newark, New Jersey. Through interviews and narration by Moyers, the report examines the lives of unwed mothers and fathers, detailing their education, employment, welfare history (especially across generations), hopes, frustrations, and disappointments.

The appearance of the terms "vanishing family" and "crisis" in the title of the program implicitly suggests the normalcy of everyday life when defined by stable nuclear families (Feuer, 1986; Fiske, 1987). Missing is recognition that families and communities throughout the country are in the midst of significant transformation. Instead, the program title suggests an abnormal condition that must be recognized and addressed.

In the report's opening segment, visual representations also help frame the ideological terms of the report. Medium and long camera shots are used to establish perspective on the daily life in the community. Mothers are shown shopping for food and caring for children; groups of boys and young men appear standing on street corners, playing basketball, listening to music, and working out at the gym. Welfare lines, couples arguing, the police, housing projects, and the streets are also common images.

These shots tie the specific issues addressed in the story into a broader discourse about race in America. Shots of black men and youth standing on corners or blacks arrested for crime are conventionally used in newscasts to signify abnormalities and social problems. These images operate at multiple levels, so even though they explicitly work to frame the documentary, they also draw on and evoke images of crime, drugs, riots, menace, and social problems. People and communities who appear in these representations are labeled as problematic and undesirable.

The documentary's four segments are organized around three major themes, with each segment profiling unmarried couples. By the end of the four segments, the dominant message of the report is evident: self-help, individual responsibility, and community accountability are required to survive the crisis. This conclusion is anticipated early in the report with a promotional tease from a black social worker. In a 30-second sound bite, the social worker notes that the problem in the black community is not racism or unemployment but the corruption of values, the absence of moral authority, and the lack of individual motivation. This dominant message is also reinforced in the introduction to the report by correspondent Moyers:

> A lot of white families are in trouble too. Single parent families are twice as common in America today as they were 20 years ago. But for the majority of white children, family still means a mother and a father. This is not true for most black children. For them things are getting worse. Today black teenagers have the highest pregnancy rate in the industrialized world and in the black inner city, practically no

teenage mother gets married. That's no racist comment. What's happening goes far beyond race.

Since blacks dominate the visual representations that evoke images of crime, drugs, and social problems, little in the internal logic and organization of the documentary supports this contention. Even when voice-over data is used to address these issues among whites, it competes with rather than complements the dominance of the visual representations. Moyers' comment is also muted because the issues are examined primarily at the dramatic and personal level.

For example, the first segment considers the experiences of urban single parent families from the viewpoint of women. The opening piece profiles Clarinda and Darren, both young and poorly prepared emotionally or financially to care for an infant. Clarinda supports the baby with welfare and is also the baby's primary source of emotional nurturance. Darren occasionally sees his baby but takes little economic or emotional responsibility for her. On camera he appears distant and frustrated.

The second segment focuses on Alice, 23, and Timothy, 26. They are older but financially no more prepared to raise a family than Clarinda and Darren. Unlike Darren, Timothy is emotionally available to Alice. (On camera they confess their love for each other, and Timothy is present at a birthday party for one child and the delivery of another.) In the interview Alice freely shows her frustration with Timothy, especially his lack of work and unwillingness to take responsibility for his family.

Timothy on the other hand lives in a world of male sexual myths and a code that celebrates male sexual conquest and virility (Glasgow, 1981). Although he confesses love for Alice and his kids, he avoids economic and parental responsibility for them, especially when his own pleasures and sexual conquests are concerned.

The mothers in these segments are caring, responsible, and conscientious; they raise the children and provide for them. They are the social, economic, and emotional centers of their children's lives. As suggested in the interviews and visual footage, the fathers are absent, immature, selfish, irresponsible, and exploitive. Where women are shown at home with the children, the men are shown on street corners with other men. Where women talk of their children's futures, men speak in individual terms about their present frustrations and unrealistic aspirations.

The dramatic and personal tone of these representations makes them compelling and helps draw in the viewer. These strategies of organization and presentation also help personalize the story and, to a limited extent, give the people texture and dimension. Nevertheless, these representations are also mediated by a broader set of racial and class codes that continue to construct the people in the documentary as deviant and criminal, hence marginal. The members of the community are contained by these broader codes. They remain curious but distant "others."

The third segment features Bernard, a 15-year-old single male who still lives at home with Brenda, his 30-year-old single mother of three. This segment tells the story of life in this community from the young male point of view. The male voice takes on resonance and, in contrast to Darren and Timothy, we learn that the men in this community have feelings and hopes too. The segment shows Bernard's struggle to avoid the obstacles (drugs, educational failure, unemployment, homicide, jail) to his future. From Brenda's boyfriend (and role model for Bernard) we learn about the generational persistence of these obstacles to young male futures.

In each of these segments the dramatic dominates the analytic, the personal dominates the public, and the individual dominates the social. Individual mobility, character, and responsibility provide powerful explanations for the failures presented in the story. Indeed, by the final segment of the report the theme of moral irresponsibility and individual behavior as explanations for the crisis of the underclass is fully developed. Moyers introduces the segment this way:

> There are successful strong black families in America. Families that affirm parental authority and the values of discipline, work, and achievement. But you won't find many who live around here. Still, not every girl in the inner city ends up a teenage mother, not every young man goes into crime. There are people who have stayed here. They're outnumbered by the con artists and pushers. It's not an even match, but they stand for morality and authority and give some of these kids a dose of unsentimental love.

As a major "actor" in the structure of this report, Moyers is central to the way that the preferred meanings of the report are conveyed. As an economically and professionally successful white male, Moyers' political and moral authority establishes the framework for identifying the conditions as trouble, for articulating the interests of the dominant society, and for demonstrating that in the continued openness of the social order there is hope. Through Moyers' position as a journalist, this report confirms the American dream even as it identifies casualties of the dream.

Moyers' authority in this story stems also from his position as an adult. During his interviews and stand-ups Moyers represents adult common sense, disbelief, and concern. This adult authority remains throughout the report and is reinforced (and activated) later in the story when we hear from caring (and successful) black adults of the community who claim that the problems facing the community stem from poor motivation, unclear and unsound values, and the lack of personal discipline. Like Moyers, these adults—two social workers, a psychologist, and a police officer—do not identify complex social forces like racism, social organization, economic dislocation, unemployment, the changing economy, or the welfare states as the causes of the crisis in their community. They blame members of the black community for the erosion of values, morality, and authority. This is how Mrs. Wallace, the social worker, puts it:

> We are destroying ourselves. Now it [the crisis] might have been motivated and plotted and seeded with racism, but we are content to be in this well now. We're just content to be in this mud and we need to get

out of it. There are not any great white people running around this block tearing up stuff. It's us. We've got to stop doing that.

When combined with the personal tone of the documentary and Moyers' professional (and adult) authority, this comment, coming as it does from an adult member of the community, legitimates the emphasis on personal attributes and benign social structure.

At the ideological level of what Stuart Hall (1980) calls preferred readings, each segment of the documentary emphasizes individual personalities, aspirations, and struggles for improvement. These assumptions and analytic strategies are consistently privileged over social explanations, and they provide a compelling vantage point from which to read the documentary. This displacement of the social by the personal and the complex by the dramatic both draws viewers into the report and takes them away from explanations that criticize the social system. Viewers question individual coping mechanisms rather than the structural and political circumstances that create and sustain racial inequalities.

MIDDLE CLASS UTOPIA

. . . In contrast to the blacks in the CBS documentary, successful blacks who populate prime time television are charming, unique, and attractive individuals who, we assume, reached their stations in life through hard work, skill, talent, discipline, and determination. Their very presence in formats from talk shows (Bryant Gumbel, Arsenio Hall, Oprah Winfrey) to situation comedy (Bill Cosby) confirms the American value of individual success and mobility.

In the genre of situation comedy, programs like *The Cosby Show, 227, Frank's Place,* and *Amen* all show successful middle class black Americans who have effectively negotiated their way through benign social institutions and environments (Gray, 1986). Their family-centered lives take place in attractive homes and offices. Rarely if ever do these characters venture into settings or interact with people like those in the CBS documentary. As doctors, lawyers, restaurateurs, ministers, contractors, and housewives, these are representations of black Americans who have surely realized the American dream. They are pleasant and competent social actors whose racial and cultural experiences are, for the most part, insignificant. Although black, their class position (signified by their occupations, tastes, language, and setting) distances them from the codes of crime, drugs, and social problems activated by the urban underclass. With the exception of the short-lived *Frank's Place,* the characters are never presented in situations where their racial identity matters. This representation of racial encounters further appeals to the utopian desire in blacks and whites for racial oneness and equality while displacing the persistent reality of racism and racial inequality or the kinds of social struggles and cooperation required to eliminate them. At the level of the show's dominant meanings, this strategy accounts in part for the success of *The Cosby Show* among blacks and whites.

In virtually any episode of *The Cosby Show*, the Huxtable children—Sandra, Denise, Vanessa, Theo, and Rudi—are given appropriate lessons in what appear to be universal values such as individual responsibility, parental trust, honesty, the value of money, the importance of family and tradition, peer group pressure, the value of education, the need for independence, and other important guides to successful living in America.

In contrast to the experience of the young men in the CBS documentary, *Cosby's* Theo learns and accepts lessons of responsibility, maintaining a household, the dangers of drugs, the value of money, and respect for women through the guidance of supportive parents. In Theo's relationship to his family, especially his father Cliff, the lessons of fatherhood and manhood are made explicit. Theo and his male peers talk about their aspirations and fears. They even exchange exaggerated tales of adolescent male conquest. Because similar discussions among the young men in the documentary are embedded within a larger set of codes about the urban black male menace, this kind of talk from Timothy, Darren, and Bernard signals their incompetence and irresponsibility at male roles. In the middle class setting of *The Cosby Show*, for Theo and his peers this same talk represents the ritual of adolescent male maturation. Together, these very opposite representations suggest a contemporary version of the culture of poverty thesis which attributes black male incompetence and irresponsibility to the absence of male role models, weak personal values, and a deficient cultural environment.

The strategy of imparting explicit lessons of responsibility to Theo (and to young black male viewers) is deliberate on the part of *Cosby*. This is not surprising since the show has enjoyed its greatest commercial success in the midst of increasing gang violence and epidemic teen pregnancy in urban black communities. The show's strategy illustrates its attempt to speak to a number of different audiences at a number of different levels (Fiske, 1987a; Hall, 1980).

Shows about middle class black Americans revolve around specific characters, settings, and situations (Gitlin, 1983; Gray, 1986). The personal dimension of social life is privileged over, and in many cases displaces, broader social and structural factors. In singling out *The Cosby Show*, my aim is not to diminish the unique qualities, hard work, and sacrifices that these personal representations stress. Nevertheless, I do want to insist that the assumptions and framework that structure these representations often displace representations that would enable viewers to see that many individuals trapped in the underclass have the very same qualities but lack the options and opportunities to realize them. And in the world of television news and entertainment, where production conventions, ratings wars, and cautious political sensibilities guide the aesthetic and journalistic decisions of networks, the hegemony of the personal and personable rules. Whether it is Bill Cosby, Alicia Rashad, Darren, Alice, or Bill Moyers, the representation is of either deficient or gifted individuals.

Against fictional television representations of gifted and successful individuals, members of the urban underclass are deficient. They are unemployed, unskilled, menacing, unmotivated, ruthless, and irresponsible.

They live differently and operate with different attitudes and moral codes from everyone else; they are set apart. Again, at television's preferred level of meaning, these assumptions—like the images they organize and legitimate—occupy our common sense understandings of American racial inequality. . . .

REFERENCES

Feuer, J. (1986). Narrative form in American television. In C. MacCabe (Ed.), *High theory/low culture: Analyzing popular television and film* (pp. 101-115). New York: St. Martin's.

Fiske, J. (1987). *Television culture.* London: Methuen.

Fiske, J., & Hartley, J. (1978). *Reading television.* London: Methuen.

Gitlin, T. (1983). *Inside prime time.* New York: Pantheon.

Glasgow, D. (1981). *The black underclass.* New York: Vintage.

Gray, H. (1986). Television and the new black man: Black male images in prime-time situation comedy. *Media, culture, and society, 8,* 223-242.

Hall, S. (1980). Encoding/decoding. In S. Hall, A. Lowe, & P. Willis (Eds.), *Culture, media, language* (pp. 128-139). London: Hutchinson.

Jameson, F. (1979). Reification and utopia in mass culture. *Social Text, 1,* 130-148.

Williams, R. (1974). *Television: Technology and cultural form.* New York: Oxford University Press.

.50

Laughing Across the Color Barrier

In Living Color

NORMA MIRIAM SCHULMAN

Keenan Ivory Wayans' program *In Living Color*, one of only a handful of prime-time television shows that is both written and produced by African Americans, presents an interesting example of how difficult it is to attack racism in a comedic format without giving the appearance of reinforcing those very stereotypes whose absurdity is being ridiculed. Its often hard-hitting satire, which seems to appeal to white as well as black audiences, is double edged enough to allow viewers with different orientations to tailor its message to their own particular perceptions of the racial climate of America of the 1990s.

Its ambiguity gives it bimodal appeal—a quality deemed all important in a commercial medium for whom the aggregate minority viewing audience is insufficient in itself to garner the kind of ratings that yield substantial revenue.[1] As Dates and Barlow (1990) have pointed out, a "tolerance for ambiguity" can appeal to "urbane black audiences who have learned to live with ambiguity, as well as white audiences for whom, too, racial matters have grown less starkly black and white" (p. 166).

In Living Color's satire depends on the evocation of age-old stereotypes, used to caricature African Americans since the Reconstruction, and, conse-

NOTE: Reprinted from the *Journal of Popular Film and Television*, Vol. 20, No. 1 (1992, May). Reprinted with permission of the Helen Dwight Reid Educational Foundation. Published by Heldref Publications, 1319 Eighteenth St., N.W., Washington, DC 20036-1802. Copyright © 1992.

quently, its impact is at least potentially destructive. Particularly within the minority community, it is feared that it might have the harmful effect of *reinforcing* bigotry—instead of exposing it for the ridiculously illogical phenomenon that it is.

Such a fear is not ill founded. After all, empirical studies of *All in the Family*, conducted in the mid-1970s by Vidmar and Rokeach and later by Brigham and Giesbrecht, concluded, rather surprisingly, that the long-running Norman Lear sitcom allowed both viewers high in prejudice and viewers low in prejudice to perceive confirmation of their existing attitudes. Although *All in the Family* won an award from the Los Angeles chapter of the NAACP in 1972 for contributing to the establishment of positive racial relations, it invited selective perception with its heavy reliance on essentially derogatory stereotypes, insisted on by an often jovial, potentially likeable bigot.

At a time when one might claim with at least some degree of assurance that overt displays of racial prejudice are considered socially unacceptable on television, white and black audiences alike are apt to wince at Fox's updated version of the old disreputable pantheon of demeaning images of African Americans, remarkably unchanged in substance from their historical antecedents: the nurturing Mammy figure, the sultry temptress, the deferential Uncle Tom, the flashy con-artist operating just outside the law, the happy-go-lucky Negro whose banjo has been replaced by a "boom box." Along with these stereotypes are the accompanying marks of the underclass: mispronunciations, dialect, malapropisms, social backwardness, and extreme naivete—all things that have historically helped to rationalize keeping blacks in subordinate roles. (As the white director of a segregated golf club states, in an *In Living Color* sketch about discrimination at a country club staffed by black waiters, "there has always been a place for blacks at our club as long as they are not holding one.")

Appropriating a language of blatant stereotypes in order to undermine the perceptions of the dominant order is an age-old device employed by persecuted groups to subvert the status quo. But it carries an impact that can all too easily appear on the surface to be accommodating instead of resisting racism, sexism, or classism, especially on television where, as Winston (1982) has noted, the medium tends to buoy up the use of stereotypes because it generates a visual "sense of authenticity" (p. 173).

The implicit claim of each episode of *In Living Color* is, however, that the viewer is engaging in a bit of "black talk" among brothers—a claim underscored by the rap that is its theme song. Although the cast is racially mixed, the viewer is reminded at the opening of each show (when Keenan Ivory Wayans or one of the many talented members of his black production team is introduced to the audience and appears on camera) that this is to be a half-hour of jokes about African Americans that has been written and produced by African Americans.[2] This fact makes a difference in the way the humor is to be interpreted. As Omi (1989) explains it, "the setting in which 'racist' jokes are told determines the function of humor. Jokes about blacks where the teller and audience are black constitute a form of self-awareness;

they allow blacks to cope and 'take the edge off' of oppressive aspects of the social order which they commonly confront" (p. 121).

The problem comes, of course, in the fact that the circuit of all-black discourse assumed by *In Living Color* is merely an illusion. There is no question that a significant portion of the viewing audience for commercial television programs with a black focus is white, perhaps in part because viewing a program about blacks can provide white audiences with a sense that they are not prejudiced (Entman, 1990, p. 342) while, at the same time, serving as an outlet for satisfying a certain amount of curiosity about African Americans. In light of its multiracial audience, the meaning of the sketches in the show changes. As Omi (1989) has noted, "the meaning of [the] same jokes . . . is dramatically transformed when told across the 'color line.' If a white, or even black, person tells these jokes to a white audience, it will, despite its 'purely' humorous intent, serve to reinforce stereotypes and rationalize the existing relations of racial inequality" (p. 121).

RECTIFYING RACIAL IMBALANCE: COMEDY
AS A VISION OF THE BEST OF ALL POSSIBLE WORLDS

Other stylistic devices used by Keenan Ivory Wayans, however, do seem to take the "white eye" of the non-minority audience into account, parading in front of it a vision of a new, idealized social order in which African Americans achieve parity and doing so with an easy, unself-conscious confidence that this is the way things ought to be. The show displays its genuinely innovative character by routinely reversing the conventional roles of blacks and whites in skits where mixed race pairs of characters are featured. These portions of the television program are anti-stereotypical. If anything, they tend to tip the scales in favor of African Americans to make the tacit point that it should not seem surprising for a black policeman to ticket a white motorist, for a black corrections officer to oversee a white prisoner, for a black preacher to prove more intelligent and articulate than his white counterpart, or for a black child to play the part of the princess in a school play while her white classmate is cast in the role of the farm animal.

In contrast to the stereotypical antics of the "homeboys," Ice and Wiz, unashamedly out to make "mo' money, mo' money" by fair means or foul, or the jive-talking salesmen for "funky finger products," with their "see you later, when your hair gets straighter," these anti-stereotypical characters consistently invert the hierarchies of power that are symptomatic of a racist social order. The vignettes in which they are featured avoid any explicit reference to racism, offering instead an idealized view of human relations that transforms conventional racial demarcations—demarcations that even in America of the 1990s would, for example, make it unlikely that a black obstetrician like Cliff Huxtable would have so many white patients.

Such fictional portrayals of a fully integrated society in which racism has been completely eradicated do two different things simultaneously. For black audiences, they offer a vision of a perfect equilibrium—that dream that Martin Luther King, Jr., saw on the horizon—a dream that is still as unreal as it is inspiring. On the other hand, for white audiences, they help to naturalize the assumption of positions of power by members of the minority community, who are given all the hallmarks of middle-class membership and, in their dramatic context, display the virtue of being color blind in their dealings with other racial groups as well.

Color blindness is essential in such depictions of situations where social and/or personal power reverts to minorities in order to dispel any suggestion that the replication of racial inequalities by black oppressors is being advocated as a means of redress. In such scenarios, indeed racial elements are played down severely. Characters appear to have risen to positions of power—either in their personal or professional lives—purely because of their individual abilities. Whether the scene is a prison or a schoolyard, black characters seem appropriately cast in choice roles in the comedy of human relationships that *In Living Color* depicts, simply because they have demonstrated qualities like fairness, self-discipline, and restraint.

But if some viewers are tempted to conclude from these vignettes that the ideological thrust of these skits is that racial impediments can be overcome simply by the acquisition of positive personal qualities, the anti-realism of the production techniques employed in them argues against such a facile view. For example, the sketch in which a black policeman tickets a white motorist—part of the program's ironic "tribute" to a Hollywood film industry historically inhospitable to blacks—depicts the policeman in color footage and the motorist in vintage black and white. The policeman speaks in a contemporary conversational idiom; the motorist delivers the melodramatic, overblown lines of a movie script. He plays it straight; she hams it up. Ideally, such a black authority figure will be a common character in future more egalitarian Hollywood films; she is a static, stock character from the cinematic past. Their interaction cannot be mistaken for a representation of things as they might be: They are segmented by an aesthetic and historical distance even more insurmountable than their racial distance.

These stylistic discordances act to insure that such interpersonal exchanges are not used to mask the fact that "in our society power is distributed along axes of gender, class, and race" (Fiske, 1987, p. 214). This is an important point since mainstream media programming is repeatedly accused of trying to "shift our understanding of racial inequality away from structured social processes to matters of individual choice" (Gray, 1989, p. 377).

On the contrary, at every juncture, we are reminded by the producers of *In Living Color* that we are being given an artificially constructed scenario, not a realistic object lesson in how to be socially mobile in a fundamentally white society, as *The Cosby Show* is sometimes accused of being.[3] *In Living Color* does not offer a plausible picture of American society as open and pluralistic. Nor does it, taken as a whole, suggest that the American Dream is accessible to people of color. Ironically, its subtext seems to be that whether individual African Americans are "deficient" or "gifted" has mattered little to white society, which has historically viewed them as "all alike."

In the spirit of turning the tables, many of the skits in *In Living Color* parody the great leveling effect of racism by stereotyping characters of other races, by making them "all alike" as well. In a paradigmatic contrast, white characters are depicted as tense and joyless against a background of the unrestrained antics of stereotypical "black buffoonery." They dramatize the discontents of an over-refined (white) world that tends to look askance at the pleasures of black life—pleasures often rendered in this program (as they are often rendered in the world of mainstream media as a whole) in terms of easy, unfettered movement or fluent self-expression in a musical vein.

All such polarized contrasts between black and white—as conventional minority stereotypes are juxtaposed against stereotypes of socially dominant groups—are, however, carefully contained in the show by the framing device of its song and dance numbers, which involve a multiracial (though predominantly black) cast engaged in mutual and harmonious creative interaction. Thus, each show concludes with a suggestion of multiracial harmony as the entire cast of the show comes on stage to join the "Fly Girls" and "S.W. 1" in saying goodbye to the audience. There are plenty of interracial hugs and the mood is decidedly upbeat: a classic comedic ending that works to reconcile the tensions and conflicts that have preceded it.

However biting the satire, the viewing audience (in true commercial network fashion) must be left with an affirmation, a sense that there are signs that someday (as the opening rap would have it) there will be a time when "prejudice [will be] obsolete," a time when "at night it [will be] safe to walk down the street."

THE LOWEST COMMON DENOMINATOR: SEXISM AS A CORRELATE FOR RACISM

In Living Color seems to want to be a show about race, yet a look at the comedy sketches in any given month is apt to reveal a somewhat peculiar fact: There seem to be almost as many overt parodies of sexism (including homophobia) as racism, though racism and sexism are often tightly intertwined. For example, on a semiregular basis a "Men on Movies" skit appears in which two obviously homosexual men assess the content of recent movies "from a male point of view." Their denial of their sexual positioning, as well as their hostility toward things blatantly heterosexual, is presented with very little coyness. Clearly, they are on the fringes of mainstream American culture in their personal lives: Their assumed roles as movie critics allow them to vent their spleen in the guise of disinterested commentary. All the jibes they utter refer back to their own sexuality and their own needs as members of a disempowered group to at least symbolically assert power.

The two men are black, yet it is sexual disempowerment that is the focal point here, not racial prejudice. There is diffusion and displacement of hostility toward a larger, less confrontational base: the heterosexual community as a whole. Certainly, rage is more safely directed against it on commercial television than against the white race. Indeed providing a commonality that transcends race, heterosexual orientation can be seen to serve as the great unifier in a television program whose operative and disruptive meta-phor is color.

Sometimes *In Living Color* sexism appears to act as a stand-in for racial prejudice as a generalized source of hatred and frustration—especially when the satirical thrust of the show might threaten to fan the flames of genuine racial antagonism. This process of substitution is not as farfetched as it might at first seem. After all, these two forms of subjection have many similarities, as nineteenth-century American feminists understood with their predilection for using a "slave-woman analogy" to dramatize what they saw to be a common type of domination.

Fiske (1987) has noted that, even in this day and age, there are aspects of the discourse of race that are still "socially taboo" and apt to be replaced by discourses of nationality (p. 52) when mixed audiences are involved. By the same token, as "African Americans attempt to negotiate [images] past the industry's gatekeepers" (Dates & Barlow, 1990, p. 253), class or occupation or sexuality can be used to mask potentially bitter racial antagonisms that might alienate large segments of the viewing audience.

"Categorizing race-relevant issues as purely non-racial" has long functioned as a way outsiders have tried to discredit minority demands for redress and compensation. In an era in which the attitude toward outright expressions of discrimination in the mainstream mass media can best be characterized as "social disapproval," it can be argued that it comprises a covert form of racism (Entman, 1990, p. 342). However, it can also be a way that African Americans themselves can deflect potentially searing, racially induced insecurities and self-hatreds—devising fictional portrayals of minorities that implicitly ascribe their individual predicaments to isolated personal traits, rather than acknowledging that racial identity has a formative role to play in how each person sees himself or herself.

Certainly, an obsession with race can be unhealthy, but perhaps equally destructive can be a failure to acknowledge the effects of what W.E.B. DuBois in *The Souls of Black Folk* termed the "double consciousness" of the American negro in a "world which yields him no true self-consciousness," where, like all oppressed groups, the need to survive has forced him to constantly envision how he must appear to those who wield ultimate power in his society. As DuBois so eloquently put it, "it is a peculiar sensation this double consciousness, this sense of always looking at one's self through the eyes of others, of measuring one's soul by the tape of a world that looks on in amused contempt and pity" (cited from Dates & Barlow, 1990. p. 1).

In the final analysis, a great deal of this double consciousness is exhibited in *In Living Color*. Perhaps no where is it as poignant as in a sketch where the insecurities of a young woman drive away both her blind date and the man seated next to her in the movie theater. She has an unshakable conviction that she is repulsive. Suffering from a terrible case of self-hatred, she sees herself as black but not beautiful; and the sketch makes everything but her racial identity appear to be a possible source of her anxiety: her weight, the size of her breasts, the image of Meryl Streep on the screen.

So does it seem at times that *In Living Color* sends mixed messages to both black and white viewers. Using laughter to exorcise the demons of racism, it appears at the same time to have internalized something of the very despicable images that oppressors of the black community have harbored for centuries, however blatantly it parodies their absurdity and illogic. The result is dark comedy with a truly disquieting twist.

NOTES

1. The show, which was first aired on the Fox network in April 1990 and has received an Emmy in the Best Variety Show category, has been in the top 20 Nielsen ratings.

2. This certainly does *not* go without saying in the American mass media today. Indeed, what Stuart Hall has referred to as the "white eye" is assumed to give perspective to the viewing experience: "lurking outside the frame and yet seeing and positioning everything within . . . the unmarked position from which . . . 'observations' are made and from which, alone, they make sense" (Omi, 1989, p. 116). Certainly, it is true that since the 1960s, television has had "more to say *about* blacks in American society, but very seldom was any of this said *by* blacks. Even when the messenger was black, the message was usually from a white point of view" (Winston, 1982, p. 180).

3. See Dyson (1991).

WORKS CONSULTED

Corea, A. (1990). Racism and the American way of media. In J. Downing (Ed.), *Questioning the media* (pp. 255-266). Newbury Park, CA: Sage.

Dates, J. L., & Barlow, W. (1990). *Split image: African Americans in the mass media.* Washington, DC: Howard University Press.

Donovan, J. (1986). *Feminist theory.* New York: Ungar.

Downing, J.D.H. (1991). *The Cosby Show* and American racial discourse. In J. Hanson & A. Alexander (Eds.), *Taking sides* (pp. 30-33). Guilford, CT: Dushkin.

Dyson, M. (1991). Bill Cosby and the politics of race. In J. Hanson & A. Alexander (Eds.), *Taking sides* (pp. 34-40). Guilford, CT: Dushkin.

Entman, R. M. (1990). Modern racism and the images of Blacks in local television news. *Critical Studies in Mass Communication, 7,* 332-345.

Fiske, J. (1987). *Television culture.* London: Methuen.

Geist, C. D. (1983). From the plantation to the police station: A brief history of Black stereotypes. In C. Geist & J. Nachbar (Eds.), *The popular culture reader* (pp. 157-170). Bowling Green, OH: Bowling Green University Press.

Gray, H. (1989). Television, Black Americans, and the American dream. *Critical Studies in Mass Communication, 6,* 376-386.

Martindale, C. (1986). *The White press and Black America.* New York: Greenwood.

Omi, M. (1989). In Living Color: *Race and American culture.* In I. Angus & S. Jhally (Eds.), *Cultural politics in contemporary America* (pp. 111-122). London: Routledge, Chapman and Hall.

Real, M. R. (1991). Bill Cosby and reading ethnicity. In L. R. Vande Berg & L. A. Wenner (Eds.), *Television criticism* (pp. 58-84). London: Longman.

Winston, M. R. (1982). Racial consciousness and the evolution of mass communications in the U.S. *Daedalus, 13,* 171-182.

51

The Movie of the Week

ELAYNE RAPPING

SOCIAL ISSUE DRAMA:
FROM MGM TO NBC

... Theatrical films, which during the 1930s and 1940s were the major source of social issue dramas—many of which influenced the direction of public discourse on matters like race, religious prejudice, and war—increasingly, since the advent of television, have been geared toward blockbuster extravaganzas and youth-oriented films. It is, after all, kids—the dating crowd—who always want to get out of the house and socialize, particularly at the new suburban malls that have become the social centers of middle America (Rapping, 1988, p. 14). Their parents, on the other hand, prefer to stay in, avoiding babysitter costs and parking problems, and watch current movies on their home TV screens, via cable or videocassette recorder. The need and desire for more meaty, challenging narratives that dramatically pose and resolve the central concerns of the nation at large remains.

If movies increasingly renounced this task, in part perhaps out of fear of competing unsuccessfully with the small, home-centered screen, it remained for television—which in news, talk shows, and magazine formats already played the role of arbiter of social issues, concerns, and values—with an open field to develop an adult movie form of its own, the made-for-TV movie. The telefeature, or movie of the week, came, most interestingly, to replace the Hollywood social issue film. Coming on the scene in 1964 and rapidly becoming established as an important economic and dramatic form

NOTE: Excerpts reprinted from chapters 1 and 3 of *The Movie of the Week: Private Stories, Public Events*, by Elayne Rapping (Minneapolis: University of Minnesota Press, 1992), by permission of the publisher.

by 1972, with the airing of *Brian's Song,* its first ratings blockbuster, the TV movie has, in less than twenty years, become the dominant mass form for the dramatic portrayal of major social issues. . . .

TV MOVIES FROM THE BUSINESS ANGLE

. . . While much has changed about television and its production of telefeatures, some things have remained more or less the same. The economic reasons for producing TV movies, the dramatic, thematic, and narrative forms they take, and their place in the overall social/cultural role played by home television remain largely the same as in 1964, if some of the figures and techniques are radically different.

First, let us consider the FCC and its role in structuring and overseeing networks and affiliates. A station's FCC license requires that it air a certain amount of "public service" programming, which generally means news, documentaries, and other such socially informative and educational matter. Since television is a public trust that uses a national resource, the airwaves, to communicate, it is clearly responsible to government and taxpayers. Indeed, the FCC in some sense codifies what media scholar Raymond Williams suggests has always been government's intention as far as the development of home TV was concerned: it insists that community and national concerns be given time for the greater public good.

While TV movies were not originally seen as a part of this commitment to FCC mandates, but only as money makers, over the years the networks began to see them differently. Social issue movies quickly garnered popular approval. With money as a bottom line, the executives could readily see how their own interest as capitalists would dovetail neatly with their need to serve the people.

There is yet another twist to this grand scheme. The FCC also requires that local stations be free to run material that has direct bearing on local concerns. If this mandate were taken seriously we would have much less national programming of all kinds—including telefeatures about current national concerns—and much more locally produced and oriented fare, but this Jeffersonian ideal of decentralized communities with distinct cultures and structures rarely is realized. Except for the highly lucrative local news, affiliates rarely produce their own programs. It is more profitable for them to accept network programs, for which they are given "station compensation." The only time affiliates actually balk at network fare is when programming is deemed potentially controversial and likely to turn away viewers.

While this kind of caution has traditionally been seen primarily in highly religious, conservative, or rural areas, in recent years it is far more common everywhere. This is because of the growing power (or what appears to executives as the probable power) of conservative lobbyists like the "moral majority" with their threatened boycotts of morally or politically "liberal" programs.

So now, added to the networks, sponsors, and FCC, we have public interest groups joining the battle over what will be seen on television. In fact, it is not only the right that brings pressure to bear on networks. Feminists, gays, and other more progressive groups have obviously had a significant impact on programming. Networks usually do not cancel controversial shows, and sometimes they run them at a loss when sponsors bolt. This has happened in such cases as *The Women's Room, Roe v. Wade,* and *The Day After* (which was not controversial politically but nonetheless made sponsors nervous about being associated with a film that portrayed the nuclear destruction of the world).

If networks do not automatically cancel controversial programs, even when affiliates are queasy or rebellious, they do analyze the costs and benefits of airing those programs. Matters of image and public opinion vie against dollars, for even a controversial show—in fact, very often a controversial show—may gain huge ratings in the vast majority of markets that air them. Losses in immediate sponsor revenues are then weighed against future earnings based on the higher advertising rates high ratings will earn later. . . .

Actually, it is the producer rather than the director who gives form and life to the TV movie. The networks today do not produce their own feature films but contract to have them done by independent producers. These producers must pitch ideas to executives in competition for a limited number of slots during any season, and they must keep money and ideology very much in the foreground at this crucial stage: they depend on network financing because they cannot afford to produce films alone. The networks, for their part, insist on various certainties. They require specific writers, directors, and, especially, stars before they sign a contract. And they demand control of money—which determines schedule, production values, and quality of the other technical and artistic crew members (who, though invisible to the public, are as important technically to the final product as anyone else and who, in sheer numbers, actually dominate the process).

The networks themselves of course are funded by sponsors who pay for the right to run commercials on specific shows or at specific times. The affiliates accept this national advertising for a fee paid and the right to run local ads at certain times during the slot. In the early days it was common for sponsors to own shows outright and so to exert direct control over content. In the 1960s, the networks began to exert more and more control, and most shows were then licensed to networks, which sold time slots to sponsors. At that time there was also a shift to "spot advertising": sponsors bought advertising slots on specific shows rather than sponsoring an entire program. The higher the ratings for that show, the more the networks could charge for advertising time.

By 1970, when the telefeature was coming into its own, the ratings system had undergone massive changes. Before that, ratings had measured only gross numbers of viewers for given shows. In the late 1960s, however, marketing research came to television. NBC researcher Paul Klein, who later became vice president in charge of "audience measurement," was responsible for two innovations. First, he noticed that rather than watching particular programs, people simply watch television as a flow of fragments over a time span. From this observation he developed the idea of least objectionable programming: since people simply watch what they have on, it is more profitable to discover what the most people find unobjectionable enough not to turn off than to try to provide what they actually want to watch.

His other innovation was demographic, the study of which segments of the population viewed particular programming. If it turned out (as it did) that, say, affluent, heavy-spending segments of the country watched a show that, in the aggregate, had relatively few viewers, the show would stand a better chance of being retained because the sponsors of appropriate products stood to earn substantial profits. In this way, subtle judgments made on the basis of such factors as age, race, sex, geographic region, and so on came to inform the previously heavy-handed ratings business.

While Klein's two ideas are in some ways contradictory, they share a common focus: they rationalize decisions about money for the profit-oriented TV business. Entire network departments were formed to find formulas to make money by these methods. . . .

THE MOVIE OF THE WEEK IN EMBRYO

Television, at its birth, owed little to cinema. Its direct precursor was obviously radio: thirty- and sixty-minute time slots for news and series programs, with time for commercial breaks. TV news followed its radio model at least until the 1960s. Before the minicam came on the scene, there was little film footage; newscasters read from scripts while still shots appeared behind them.

TV drama also imitated radio, not film. Many sitcoms and other series came directly from radio. Sponsors' needs were felt, and since in these shows visuals were the major feature, the fit between ads and programs was unquestioned. Sets, clothing, and other details had to reflect the values and tastes portrayed in commercial messages selling commodities (Barnouw, 1978, p. 106). The view of family life, of good and evil, right and wrong, by and large reflected the views of consumer capitalism.

Theatrical films obviously operate differently. For one thing, the "sponsor" is not visible, and the ties between funders and programs is less direct. Aesthetically, there are obvious and major differences. Movies are capable of pulling viewers into their imaginative universes by virtue of setting and technological sophistication and power. One sits in a darkened theater and watches larger-than-life figures and settings in images that are strong, bright, and detailed (Ellis, 1982, pp. 21-91).

TV, by contrast, is seen in a usually bright living room in which people move about, speak, and allow their attention to wander. The image is small and aesthetically inferior to film. Most importantly for this chapter, television, unlike film, must be written around commercial breaks in a series of brief scenes. The narrative must be clear and easy to follow in order to attract the largest number of viewers and hold their attention through commercial breaks, varying viewing times and patterns, and the competition of other channels (Ellis, 1982, pp. 173-194). For these reasons, television writers follow fairly specific writing formulas. Action is circumscribed, physically and intellectually, to fit the limits of video technology and the realities of home viewing.

We must consider all of this when we examine the actual mechanics of producing telefeatures. Obviously, when the networks began this venture, they were taking an old form, the "movie," and translating it to a medium for which it was not suited. Theatrical films had been shown on the small screen, and the problems were clear: the annoyance of commercials, the poor visual image, and the difficulty of following complex or subtle narratives, not to mention those that moved more slowly than the action series on the next channel. It was already obvious that the most positively received films were the simplest, in every way.

When they began to produce their own movies, the networks successfully rationalized the process in the interests of time, costs, and viewer acceptance. Writers learned to fit material to the medium's aesthetic and commercial needs. TV movies are generally broken into segments. The earliest segments are the longest, to capture viewer interest. Once viewers are hooked, commercial breaks are more frequent. Each segment is tightly constructed of actions and dialogue that further plot and do not confuse the viewer.

While the form of the genre has changed some over the years, as have the style and presentational devices, there is much more that has stayed the same. Even the political vicissitudes that accompany changing times are less apparent, or at least more ambiguous and varied, on the long form than in series television. This is clear from recent seasons. The Reagan/Bush years undoubtedly changed the slant of series TV. Even the most "liberal" family sitcoms—"Family Ties," for instance—are woefully lacking in substance or challenge to the right-wing vision of a stable nuclear family. There is far less difference between that show, spawned out of the experiences of 1960s activists raising children, and "The Cosby Show," which unblushingly mimics the self-satisfied conservatism of the 1950s models all these programs must to some extent follow.

Not so telefeatures. In 1989, along with heavily ideological films like *Adam*, about a father's brave efforts to find his missing son (among a list of some ten or eleven telefeatures of that season that focus on missing or otherwise endangered small children and feature strong male figures as patriarchal heroes keeping the traditional family intact and secure), such clearly antipatriarchal, feminist films as *Roe v. Wade* and *Brewster Place* also figured prominently. This may be what is most interesting about the form. Because the TV movie is shown only once (except for possible reruns) it takes more risks. It is not a staple of weekly scheduling, so it can be a bit adventurous. In fact, in many ways, that is its role on network television. It offers the spice (to use Gitlin's term) in a repetitive, static schedule, and that spice can be anything unusual or notable—including dissent from the network's political norm. Indeed, the reason the networks began to produce these features was, according to Gitlin, to "spice up the weekly schedule" (Gitlin, 1984, p. 157). "The three networks now underwrite more original movies than all the studios combined," and TV movies take up a full 25 percent of prime time slots (Gitlin, 1984, p. 168).

One of the most interesting ways in which TV movies have most obviously taken over the role of movies in the old studio system is in their mode of production. The network movies and miniseries departments have taken over where the studios left off at the end of the war, mass producing large numbers of feature films each year based on clear, simple guidelines and budget constraints, and using a more or less constant crew of workers from within the networks or in the crews brought together by the independent producers out of a stable list of preferred artists and technicians. Theatricals are now geared to packaged superstar blockbusters, but telefeatures, like the old studio films, are low-budget, formula narratives with brief lifespans. The average telefeature may cost $3 million or $4 million, the theatrical at least $25 million and usually more.

The money these films make, and the chance they offer to develop more complex stories and themes than series, make them attractive to the independent producers. About fifty producers, mostly in Los Angeles, pitch to networks regularly. They have a certain amount of artistic leeway: because a TV movie is shown only once, it can be more downbeat, even ending on a tragic note as a series cannot. Principals can be killed off without killing the entire season. The blacker sides of human nature can be explored without worrying sponsors or audiences too much.

As Lawrence Schiller, who produced the TV version of Norman Mailer's *The Executioner's Song* (a film so artistically excellent it played in first-run theaters in Europe) about Gary Gilmore, the convicted murderer who insisted on being executed, put it, "TV isn't afraid of downbeat stories because it doesn't depend on word of mouth" (Farber, 1983, p. 46). In fact, TV movies are promoted entirely through promotional clips aired on the network itself. Like commercials, they demand attention by intruding within the regularly programmed fare. Also like commercials, they tend to be visually intense; in a few ten-second scenes, they play to the audience's love of sensation and drama. High concept is the word in the production of these teasers. "If you can't put the idea into a sexy sentence when pitching it," says Robert Greenwald, producer of *The Burning Bed, The Cheryl Pierson Story, Lois Gibbs and the Love Canal* and other serious social dramas, "you can't sell it" (Rapping, 1985, p. 6).

Greenwald, always concerned with serious drama but also savvy about the system, found that one way to produce grim themes is to use top stars. His idea of casting Farrah Fawcett as the battered wife in *The Burning Bed* when she was known only for the jiggly "Charlie's Angels," while at first fought by the studios, turned out to be box office magic. The movie's success made Greenwald one of the hottest producers in town. Such are the contradictions of the form: feminism and seriousness are sold through sex and violence. . . .

THE FEMALE GAZE

One of the most profound insights of feminist film theory has been the realization that film traditionally assumes a "male gaze," that the implied audience is the male moviegoer who is assumed to identify with the male hero and to view the female protagonist as object, not subject. The importance of this realization cannot be overstated. It means that women viewers have been placed in a compromising position. They are seduced into identifying with the male point of view, the male protagonist. And yet, being women, they also identify, in obviously complicated ways, with the woman-as-object. Much of feminist film discourse has been taken up with this issue and how to resolve it. Should women opt out of the mainstream and produce independent films by and for women about their own experiences? Should they work within these conventions and try to subvert them? Or should they look more closely at the experience of the woman viewer and find, perhaps, ways that women have already and always "negotiated" their readings of male-oriented films in feminist ways? . . .

These theories and debates have been inestimably valuable in helping us to see the complex and ambiguous issues involved in interpreting a film's meaning or effect. Whether negative in their view of the effects of family melodrama on women viewers or positive in their arguments for an ultimately "progressive" effect, these studies all have one thing in common: they understand that Hollywood, as an institution, produced films that at least on one important level reproduced the ideology that kept women trapped in patriarchal roles and self-images. Even those theories based on the belief—a belief I share—that the spectator has at least a limited ability to read films according to her own agenda acknowledge that this reading against the grain, as it were, implicitly assumes a level of sophistication and autonomy on the part of female spectators in the 1940s and 1950s that is complex and difficult to generalize.

I introduce this discussion of reader response theory and its various uses in interpreting the classic woman's film because it raises the question of a target audience, a matter that is key to any realistic reading of the movies we are analyzing and of the effect of movies targeted toward women on their chosen audience. It allows for a reading of the TV movies we have been discussing as, in certain important ways, more progressive and less ambiguous than the Hollywood melodramas now receiving so much critical attention. Artistically, they may be less interesting, but there is no denying their woman-focused approach to the very issues addressed in films like *Stella Dallas*. Certainly, as in the earlier films, we have to contend with institutionally programmed contradictions. But, it seems to me, it is easier to make a case for the (limited) progressive impact of these movies than for the Hollywood melodrama simply because they are so much less complex and convoluted in their presentations. They are so very simple and obvious, as their critics endlessly claim, that what is progressive about them is unmistakable to everyone watching.

To understand why a commercial, government-regulated form like television would present so many more or less progressive women's features, we need to look, once more, at television as institution. The fact is that television, far more than Hollywood, has always geared a hefty percentage of its product to an assumed female audience. If theatrical films almost universally assume a male gaze, and in rare cases where a female gaze is assumed provide narratives that are at best ambiguous, television as often as not assumes a female gaze and provides it with far more upbeat dramatic treatments of women's issues. The reasons in both cases are economic. Couples attend movies and—even today—men buy most of the tickets. Decisions about what to see are also assumed to be made primarily by the male. Television is different. Women, after all, are the primary shoppers. Sponsors, selling commodities, not movies, tend to play to that paying audience. Even though, as David Morley's fascinating studies of British family viewing habits show (Morley, 1987), the man of the house tends to control the program selection process, women do watch television alone far more often than they go to movie houses. Most family homes today have more than one TV, and the rise of the VCR has made solo viewing even easier. The very fact that at least half of the made-for-TV movies are about women's issues is, after all, surprising and significant enough to have led me to write this book. In terms of feminist film and media theory, the fact that these movies assume a female gaze is a particularly important and overlooked fact.

. . . Rape and woman battering are—it is fair to say—almost never treated as political or even social issues in theatrical films. On the contrary, they are typically, and endlessly, presented as "normal" occurrences in films that deal with violence and crime.

When, in *The Godfather*, Michael Corleone punches his wife, upon learning she has had an abortion, there is no hint that this act constitutes wife abuse, a widespread, socially pathological crime. And from there the examples get worse and worse. How many films have you seen in which women are brutalized, raped, sexually demeaned? Hundreds. How many have in any way presented this sordid material from the victim's point of view? It is hard to name one. These actions always seem to play, in the more serious films like *Godfather,* as just one more symbol of the corruption and decadence of the hero and the social world he inhabits. In nonserious films, of course, they are simply part of the sleazy world of exploitation movies generally.

Seen in this perspective, movies like *Burning Bed* and *Silent Witness* seem all the more politically remarkable. From start to finish, no matter what their other flaws, they put the viewer solidly in the heroine's shoes and show her experiences as she lives and understands them. All other characters are secondary. . . . It may be contradictory and problematic that these women are vindicated and triumph over their enemies; that they go on to live "better" lives; that the rest of the characters are made to come around to the woman's view or go down to defeat, humiliation, and worse. Nonetheless, from the perspective of the female audience, these movies provide something most mass media—or high art for that matter—deny them: a view of women as important, commendable, even remarkable people. These movies care about women's problems and treat them with dignity and respect. . .

Movies such as *The Burning Bed* do not have the kind of nightmare power that comes from art that treats unresolvable contradictions in the context of a world that will not allow difference or change. They tie things up in a neat, oversimplified bow. They exaggerate the amount of change that is actually possible through sheer individual effort. Nonetheless, as women's drama, they deserve recognition for the positive and powerful message they provide the millions of women who see them.

REFERENCES

Barnouw, E. (1978). *The sponsor: Notes on a modern potentate.* New York: Routledge.

Ellis, J. (1982). *Visible fictions.* London: Routledge & Kegan Paul.

Farber, S. (1983, November). Making books on television. *Film Comment,* pp. 46-49.

Gitlin, T. (1984). *Inside prime time.* New York: Pantheon.

Morley, D. (1987). *Family television: Cultural power and domestic leisure.* London: Comedia.

Rapping, E. (1985). *Interview with Robert Greenwald.* Unpublished manuscript.

Rapping, E. (1988). Teen cult films. *Cineaste, 19*(3), 14-21.

52

Defining Women

The Case of Cagney and Lacey

JULIE D'ACCI

... Because of its six-year run, its departure from traditional norms of the "TV woman," and its embattled history, *Cagney and Lacey* provides a rich case study of the struggles over competing definitions of what it means to be a woman. ...

Cagney and Lacey was the first dramatic program in television history to star two women. It appeared on CBS between 1982 and 1988 and dealt with two white middle-class and upper middle-class female detectives in the New York City Police Department. Created by Barbara Avedon and Barbara Corday, its executive producer was Barney Rosenzweig and its production company was Orion Television. The characters—Cagney (played by Meg Foster and Sharon Gless, respectively) and Lacey (played by Tyne Daly)—were represented as active heroines who solved their own cases (both mentally and physically), were rarely shown as "women in distress" and were virtually never rescued by their male colleagues.[1] In addition to their roles as active protagonists in the narrative, they were also active subjects, rarely objects, of sexual desire. Christine Cagney, a single woman, had an ongoing sexual life in which she often pursued men who interested her. Similarly, Mary Beth Lacey, a married woman, was a sexual initiator with

NOTE: Excerpts reprinted from *Private Screenings: Television and the Female Consumer*, edited by Lynn Spigel and Denise Mann (Minneapolis: University of Minnesota Press, 1992), by permission of the publisher and of *Camera Obscura*, Indiana University Press, and the author.

her husband, Harvey. Lacey was also the primary breadwinner of the family, while Harvey, an often unemployed construction worker, cooked and took care of the house and their two children. Cagney and Lacey were depicted as close friends who took a lot of pleasure in one another's company and spent a lot of screen time talking to each other.

When the program first appeared, the actresses and characters were in their mid-thirties, and there was a distinct minimization of glamour in their clothing, hairstyles, and makeup. The characters were originally from working-class backgrounds and were both "working women." Much of the initial script material was modeled on the concerns of the early liberal women's movement in America, especially equal pay and sexual harassment at work. The first scripts dealt with male discrimination on the job and contained such material as a riff between Cagney and Lacey about the various ways in which Lt. Samuels, their commanding officer, was a "pig."

During its creation, and for the whole of its production, *Cagney and Lacey* became the site of intense public debates over various definitions of femininity. Many of the key players involved in the series' production and reception continuously battled over what women on television should and should not be. Among these players were those we would expect to be part of any negotiation of television content—the network, the individual production company and production team, the television audience, the press, and various interest and pressure groups.

These players, of course, were invested in definitions of women that suited their particular interests, whether those were political, economic, social, personal, or some combination thereof. The television industry, for instance, was looking for relevance and topicality while simultaneously hoping to preserve many of its conventional ways of depicting female characters. These conventions included the depiction of women as young, white, middle class, stereotypically "beautiful," and demure. They also included the presentation of female characters who were wives, mothers, heterosexual sex objects, subsidiaries to men, "vulnerable," and "sympathetic."[2] Within such conventions women were destined to be cast in situation comedies rather than in prime-time dramas. *Cagney and Lacey's* production company, Orion Television (formerly Filmways), was at least somewhat committed to generating more innovative representations of women. Richard Rosenbloom, Orion Television's president, was, in fact, known in Hollywood at the time for producing the highest percentage of properties written by women.[3] The individual production team was, for its part, directly influenced by the liberal women's movement, and quite explicitly fashioned *Cagney and Lacey* according to early feminist terms. A significant segment of the women's audience for *Cagney and Lacey,* and for other programs aimed at working women, was actively seeking progressive, interesting, and, in an often-cited viewer term, "real" representations of women in television fiction. As can be imagined, the mainstream press was extremely varied in its interests. One sector, very much influenced by feminism, agitated for a wider range of women characters, and specifically for roles shaped by the concerns of the women's movements. Other segments called for a return to "tried and true" femininity. Similarly, a number of interest and pressure groups had stakes in greatly divergent depictions of women. The National Gay Task Force, for example, vehemently protested the network's effort to ward off connotations of lesbianism in *Cagney and Lacey* by replacing one Cagney actress (Meg Foster) with another "more feminine" one (Sharon Gless). The National Right to Life Committee fiercely opposed *Cagney and Lacey's* support of a woman character who chose to have an abortion. Planned Parenthood and the National Abortion Rights League applauded the series' embrace of reproductive rights. And spokespeople for the liberal women's movement generally and consistently championed the series for depicting "independent" working women and women's friendship.[4]

GETTING NEW REPRESENTATIONS OF
WOMEN TO THE SCREEN

. . . *Cagney and Lacey's* first script was conceived in 1974 squarely within the conceptual terms of the liberal women's movement: it featured role reversals, that is, women in a traditionally male profession, and women in a standard male public-sphere genre. Historically and industrially speaking, its creators considered it an idea whose time had come.[5] According to Barbara Avedon, Barbara Corday, and Barney Rosenzweig, *Cagney and Lacey* was specifically conceived as a response to an early and influential book from the women's movement, Molly Haskell's *From Reverence to Rape: The Treatment of Women in the Movies.* Avedon and Corday were engaged in the literature and politics of the early women's movement, and both were in women's groups. Rosenzweig was "setting out to have his consciousness raised."[6] They read Haskell's book and were intrigued by the fact that there had never been a Hollywood movie about two women "buddies" comparable to *M*A*S*H* or *Butch Cassidy and the Sundance Kid.*[7] According to Rosenzweig:

> The Hollywood establishment had totally refused women those friendships, the closest thing being perhaps Joan Crawford and Eve Arden in *Mildred Pierce,* the tough lady boss and her wise-cracking sidekick. So I went to my friend Ed Feldman, who was then head of Filmways (now Orion), and I said "I want to do a picture where we turn around a conventional genre piece like *Freebie and The Bean* with its traditional male situations and make it into the first real hit feminist film."[8] . . .

Avedon and Corday prepared for writing the script by spending ten days with New York policewomen. Avedon recalled "The women cops we met were first and foremost cops. Unlike Angie Dickinson in *Police Woman* who'd powder her nose before she went out to make a bust, these women took themselves seriously as police officers."[9] Both Corday and Avedon were convinced that the only way for *Cagney and Lacey* to work was if they cast "strong, mature" women, with "senses of humor." . . .

After getting the script financed by Filmways, Rosenzweig needed a major motion picture studio to pick it up and do the actual production. He took the original property to every studio in Hollywood and got predictably "Hollywood" responses, such as "these women aren't soft enough, aren't feminine enough."[10] At MGM, Sherry Lansing (who was later to become the first woman head of a major motion picture studio, Twentieth Century Fox) persuaded her boss, Dan Melnik, to make the movie. MGM said it would but only if well-known "sex symbols" Raquel Welch and Ann-Margret starred. (Welch and Ann-Margret had not yet demonstrated their true versatility as actresses at this point in Hollywood history.) The other stipulation was a 1.6-million-dollar budget which, in a kind of Catch-22 fashion, prohibited the hiring of such high-priced actresses.[11] The property, therefore, lay dormant for the next five years.

In 1980, Rosenzweig decided to have another go at it. This time, he took it to the television networks as a pilot for a weekly series. Corday and Avedon reconceived the script to update it and make it less of a spoof and more of a "realistic" crime drama.[12] Although CBS would not pick up *Cagney and Lacey* as a series, it decided it would take it as a less costly, less risky, made-for-TV movie, and it also suggested that Rosenzweig cast "two sexy young actresses."[13] According to Rosenzweig, he told CBS:

> You don't understand, these policewomen must be mature women. One has a family and kids, the other is a committed career officer. What separates this project from *Charlie's Angels* is that Cagney and Lacey are women; they're not girls and they're certainly not objects.[14] . . .

The pre-production publicity represented Cagney and Lacey as important for the causes of the women's movement. Gloria Steinem at *Ms.* magazine had been sent a script by the creators and was so enthusiastic that she appeared with Loretta Swit on the *Phil Donahue Show* to plug the movie. According to one media critic, they were so "reverential" it "sounded as though they were promoting the first woman president."[15] Steinem also featured Loretta Swit and Tyne Daly, in police uniforms as Cagney and Lacey, on the cover of the October issue of *Ms.*[16] . . .

The movie aired at 8:00 PM on Thursday, October 8, 1981, and captured an astonishing 42 share of the television audience (CBS had been getting a 28 or 29 share in this time period).[17] Within 36 hours, CBS was on the telephone to Barney Rosenzweig asking him to get a weekly program together.[18] Gloria Steinem and *Ms.* magazine staff members had already lobbied members of the CBS board, urging them to make a series out of the movie.[19]

CONTROVERSIAL REPRESENTATIONS OF WOMEN

The second phase of *Cagney and Lacey*'s history, the television series starring Tyne Daly and Meg Foster (as Swit's replacement for Cagney), was aired from March 25, 1982, to August 1982 (including summer reruns). This period coincides with that during which the network was most ardently courting an audience of working women. The massive entry of women into the labor force in the 1970s and 1980s produced what advertisers in the mid-1970s began to call the "new working women's market," a demographic group made up of American women in control of and spending their own disposable income. Other culture industries including magazines, movies, radio, and cable TV channels had pursued such women well before prime-time network television did, but in the late 1970s the three major networks began casting about for programs to attract them. The prime-time soaps (beginning with *Dallas* in 1978) and a series of made-for-TV movie melodramas were the first forms successful at capturing this new target audience. By the early 1980s, the television industry, having cloned and spun off a crop of prime-time soaps, was looking for other vehicles with which to do the same. The huge ratings success of the *Cagney and Lacey* made-for-TV movie seemed to indicate that women-oriented programming that drew on feminist discourses and subject matter was a good bet. Such a hunch, in the midst of the Reagan years' backlash against the women's movements, only intensified the contestatory nature of the negotiations surrounding the production and reception of female television characters at the time. . . .

The very night and hour *Cagney and Lacey* premiered, the series *9 to 5*, based on the hit movie of the same name (and dealing with secretaries agitating for better working conditions) premiered on the competing ABC network.[20] The fact that *Cagney and Lacey* and *9 to 5* were scheduled opposite one another would prove costly for both series in terms of ratings. Gloria Steinem, speaking at a Hollywood Radio and Television Society luncheon a month before the premieres, had protested this scheduling, saying it might "split the audience and hurt each other's [the two series'] chances."[21] . . .

Despite favorable press, and without much consideration for the fact that it was scheduled in competition with *9 to 5*, the network wanted to cancel *Cagney and Lacey* after two episodes.[22] In fact, CBS did not allocate advertising money to promote the series' third episode in *TV Guide* (*9 to 5* had a half-page ad).[23] There is no doubt that the first episodes of *Cagney and Lacey* were a ratings disappointment to the network and were responsible for losing the large lead-in audience attracted by *Magnum P.I.*, the program that immediately preceded it.[24]

The show would have been canceled abruptly had not Rosenzweig persuaded Harvey Shephard, vice president in charge of programming for CBS, to give *Cagney and Lacey* a *Trapper John* rerun spot on Sunday, April 25, at 10.00 p.m. Rosenzweig argued that *Cagney and Lacey* was an adult program that required a time slot later than 9:00 p.m.[25] Shephard reluctantly agreed, but once again voiced CBS's ambivalence by telling Rosenzweig to "save his money" when Rosenzweig told him that Filmways planned to spend $25,000 on new publicity.[26] However, Filmways did take the financial risk, sending Foster and Daly on a cross-country tour. In a one-week campaign, organized by the Brocato and Kelman public relations company, Daly and Foster traveled to major urban areas and gave approximately fifty radio, television, and print interviews, including a Washington, DC, television talk show interview with Tyne Daly and Betty Friedan "on the topic of women's rights."[27]

The Sunday, April 25, episode of *Cagney and Lacey* pulled in an impressive 34 share and ranked 7 in the overall ratings. Despite the success, Harvey Shephard told Rosenzweig that many members of the CBS board (responsible for the final renewal decisions) would consider the 34 share "a fluke."[28] He said he would fight for the series' renewal only if Rosenzweig made a significant change in the program. The change was to replace Meg Foster.[29]

. . . In a *Daily Variety* article on May 25, 1982, and a *Hollywood Reporter* article on May 28, Harvey Shephard spoke publicly about Foster's replacement. Shephard was quoted in both articles as saying that "several mistakes were made with the show in that the stories were too gritty, the characterizations of both Cagney and Lacey were too tough and there was not enough contrast between these two partners."[30] Several weeks after the statements appeared, an article in *TV Guide* revealed yet other factors behind CBS's ambivalence and its decision to replace Foster. According to critic Frank Swertlow, *Cagney and Lacey* was to be "softened" because CBS believed the main characters were "too tough, too hard and not feminine." The article quoted an unnamed CBS programmer who said the show was being revised to make the characters "less aggressive." "They were too harshly women's lib," he continued. "These women on 'Cagney and Lacey' seemed more intent on fighting the system than doing police work. We perceived them as dykes."[31]

It would appear that the association of *Cagney and Lacey* with the "masculine woman" and with lesbianism gave CBS a way in which to think about and cast its objections to the unconventional and apparently threatening representations of women on the series. This would explain why CBS rushed to cancel the program and remove Foster. It would also explain why the network gave such importance to the comments it may have picked up in the audience research rather than, for instance, to the positive comments in the press reviews.

New and expanded representations of women could not, apparently, include even a hint of lesbianism. This, of course, must be situated within the history of lesbianism's representation on prime time, but space permits only a few comments. During the 1970s quest for "relevance" and socially "hip" subject matter, several programs featured episodes about lesbians, including *All in the Family*. Likewise, into the 1980s, prime-time programs such as *Kate and Allie, Hotel, Hill Street Blues, St. Elsewhere,* and *The Golden Girls* included lesbianism as a single-episode storyline, and the daytime serial *All My Children* had an ongoing lesbian character for several weeks in 1983. By the late 1980s, *Heartbeat* featured an ongoing lesbian character whose inclusion was instrumental in the show's cancellation by ABC after protests from religious groups. The main point to be made here is that each of these "liberal" representations of lesbianism, in one way or other and to varying degrees (*Heartbeat* and *All My Children* trying to downplay this facet), underscore the "social problem" aspect of lesbianism and play off the notion that lesbianism is an "aberration."[32] That viewers would interpret the relationship between Cagney and Lacey as having lesbian overtones, or that two strong women characters would be perceived as "dykey" without the accompanying suggestion that "dykeyness" was considered a deviation from the norm, was something the television industry simply could not permit. Indeed, this stretched the limits of difference regarding the representation of women well beyond the boundaries of television's permissible zone. . . .

The differential treatment given to the characters and the actresses during this incident demonstrates some of the specific dimensions of the network's anxiety. The *TV Guide* article says the *married* character played by Tyne Daly was being kept because CBS considered her "less threatening." Conversely, CBS thought that the original Chris Cagney's non-glamorous, feminist, sexually active image and her working-class and single status manifested too many "non-feminine" traits. She also had no acceptable class, family, or marriage context that could contain, domesticate, or "make safe" those threatening differences. . . .

BRINGING WOMEN BACK IN LINE

CBS's ultimate decision on *Cagney and Lacey* was that the series should be revised to "combine competency with an element of sensuality."[33] Its solution was twofold: to replace Meg Foster with someone more "feminine" (Sharon Gless) and to change Chris Cagney's socioeconomic background.[34] The Gay Media Task Force, in light of the allegations that the original characters were "too masculine," protested the replacement, saying that Gless's acting was "very kittenish and feminine."[35]

Instead of being from the working class, Cagney would now have been raised by a wealthy Westchester mother and grandmother. Her father, a retired New York policeman who had already been featured in the series, would be the divorced husband of that mother, and the marriage a cross-class mistake. A new CBS press kit was issued to publicize the series in a different way. "Cagney and Lacey," it read, "are two cops who have earned the respect of their male counterparts and at no expense to their femininity."[36]

Furthermore, after the Meg Foster episodes, Cagney underwent a radical fashion change to accompany her class transformation. A network memo stated that "the new budget will include an additional $15,000 for wardrobe costs, the revised concept for character calls for Cagney to wear less middle-class, classier clothes so that her upward mobility is evidenced."[37] This revision must also be seen in relation to the history of television's skewed representations of class and to the advertising industry's decision, at this time, to target the upscale professional segment of the working women's market.[38]

The new Chris Cagney was more of a rugged individualist than a feminist and was actually conservative on many social issues. Lacey espoused most of the feminism and liberal politics. A CBS promo for the 1982-1983 season made these new differences between the characters explicit and also foregrounded Cagney's heterosexuality. The promo ran like this:

Mary Beth:	Ya know Chris, there've been some great women in the 20th century.
Chris:	Yeah! And some great men (dreamily).
Mary Beth:	Susan B. Anthony
Chris:	Jim Palmer!
Mary Beth:	Madame Curie . . .
Chris:	Joe Montana . . . ooo can he make a pass!
Mary Beth:	(lightly annoyed with Chris) Amelia Airhart! [sic]
Chris:	The New York Yankees!
Mary Beth:	Chris, can't you think about anything else than men?[39]

STRUGGLING OVER FEMININITY:
THE PRESS AND THE VIEWERS

The new and revised *Cagney and Lacey* with Sharon Gless and Tyne Daly began in the fall of 1982 and generated a good deal of attention and enthusiasm in the press. This revised program makes the most sense when seen in the context of the overall changes in the new television programs directed toward working women and drawing on feminism, and in the context of a backlash against the women's movements. During this same period, the program *9 to 5*, with Jane Fonda as executive co-producer, endured revisions that led to an episode in which the once-politicized secretaries spent much of the program dressed in negligées. *Remington Steele*, about a woman running her own detective agency, underwent changes in which the lead female character became considerably less aggressive and much more traditionally feminine in her relationship with the male character.[40]

The mainstream press, in commenting on the first season of the Gless/ Daly *Cagney and Lacey*, focused on the "changes" from the previous run. Many wrote of the general "softening" and "feminization" of the program. For example, one critic noticed that "the entire show this season appears less gritty than last year's style," while another remarked, "some of the rougher, tougher edges are gone."[41] . . .

Some articles that commented on the "feminization" also wrote of the changes in the relationship between the characters and the innuendos of lesbianism:

> Miss Daly's tomboy quality was balanced by the introduction of a partner with more feminine characteristics than her original costar. . . . This second-season rematch [is] perhaps more compatible with the network's definition of a conventional female relationship . . . [but] who cares if a cop is gay or not as long as he or she shoots straight.[42]

Judging from audience letters, viewers were at first reluctant to accept Gless, but within two months a large and avid following began to develop. An exemplary letter from a woman who had been angered by Meg Foster's removal reads:

> I thought Meg Foster and Tyne Daly were a great combination, but
> apparently some "genius" of the male persuasion, obviously, decided
> that Meg Foster wasn't "feminine" enough. My Gawd, should cops
> wear aprons and be pregnant? Gimme a break! However, *Lady* Luck
> was with you when you found Sharon Gless. I must admit that you
> did something right by putting her in the Cagney role. . . . She's ex-
> tremely feminine with just the right amount of "butch" to strike a very
> appealing balance.[43]

An irony in the history of the series, and a strong testament to the
operation of multiple and contradictory viewer interpretations, is that
Sharon Gless (according to published articles and viewer letters) had a large
lesbian following at the time of the series' first run and now in reruns.[44] And
this audience interpreted the Cagney character according to a variety of
unpredictable and unconventional viewing strategies. When seen in relation
to the viewer response letters surrounding the removal of Meg Foster and
the press comments on the appeal of the friendship between Cagney and
Lacey, this development demonstrates the ways in which the television
industry's investments in particular notions of "femininity" and at least
certain viewer investments can be at odds. The potential homoerotic overtones in the representation of the two women that formed the basis for the
network's discomfort were, in fact, the bases of certain viewers' pleasure.
There was, of course, a continuum of response ranging from viewers who
responded pleasurably to the fictional representation of a close friendship
between Cagney and Lacey to those whose viewing strategies purposely
highlighted the homoerotic overtones in the relationship.

After the initial run of articles on the "feminization" of the characters and
the series, a wide array of feminist-oriented pieces highlighting the importance of *Cagney and Lacey* to women appeared in mainstream newspapers.
The series was hailed as "pioneering the serious role of women on TV" and
"helping to break new TV ground."[45] Many of these articles emphasized the
notion that Cagney and Lacey, unlike previous television characters, portrayed "real women." Despite this critical acclaim the first season of the
Gless/Daly *Cagney and Lacey* did not do well in the overall ratings and did
only marginally well with a women-only target audience. Its competition
during much of the season was female-oriented prime-time movies. Consequently, CBS put *Cagney and Lacey* on its cancellation list. In an effort to save
the series, Barney Rosenzweig coordinated a large letter-writing campaign
in which CBS and major newspapers throughout the country were deluged
with thousands of viewer letters protesting the impending cancellation.[46]
The Los Angeles chapter of the National Organization for Women and
National NOW publicized the campaign and urged their members to write.
According to state delegate Jerilyn Stapleton, the Los Angeles chapter had
only two goals for the period: to get Ronald Reagan out of office and to keep
Cagney and Lacey on the prime-time schedule.[47] . . .

Repeatedly, writers said such things as "It's good to see smart, functioning, strong women"; "It's a pleasure to see women in such active roles"; "It's

one of the few programs that neither glamorizes nor degrades women"; and "At last women are being portrayed as three-dimensional human beings." There were numerous long letters describing the particular significance of the series to the writer. One viewer wrote:

> My office alone contains six technical editors, RABID fans of "Cagney and Lacey." We're all highly paid, well-educated women in our forties with very different life-styles. Since we are "specialists" and work very closely with each other, each of us regards the others as "extended family," and we nurture and support each other in the best ways possible. We enjoy "Cagney and Lacey" because it contains so many moments that ring familiar in a woman's daily life. We see ourselves in it so often, even though OUR jobs are unbelievably unexciting. It's gotten so that Tuesday mornings are spent hashing over Monday night's episode. We're really addicted.

Another said:

> It's such an exciting show from a woman's point of view. Watching those two women makes one realize how much more attractive we are as women when we dare to be all our possible dimensions rather than the stereotypical images we have been taught to be and continually see on the screen. You have affected some of us profoundly. . . .

Despite the volume of viewer mail, and despite the fact that it primarily came from the desired target audience (upscale working women between the ages of 18 and 54), the series was canceled in the spring of 1983. However, several factors combined to cause CBS to reverse its decision and bring it back on the air. First, people continued to send letters. Second, after cancellation, *Cagney and Lacey* received four Emmy nominations, and Tyne Daly won an Emmy for best dramatic actress. Third, *Cagney and Lacey* scored number one in the ratings for the first week of summer reruns and remained in the top ten throughout the period. Nonetheless, CBS hedged its bets by reinstating the series with a very limited seven-episode trial run.

THE STRUGGLE CONTINUES: THE PRODUCTION TEAM, THE NETWORK, AND INTEREST GROUPS

The period of *Cagney and Lacey*'s history that begins with the reinstated Gless/Daly series in the spring of 1984 reveals several industry trends occurring at the time. With regard to television's portrayal of feminism, the period was characterized by "mainstreaming." Hence, the radical edge of feminist issues was tempered and channeled into character traits and behaviors. In addition, the meaning of feminism itself was becoming increasingly ambiguous so that programs offered "something for everyone" to fulfill many different viewers' political positions and interpretations. Terry Louise

Fisher, a producer/writer for *Cagney and Lacey*, described this as a move from political issues to "entertainment value." [48] During this period, some of the key players on *Cagney and Lacey*'s production team, particularly Barney Rosenzweig, began to think more in industry terms and less in women's movement terms when it came to portraying the characters. This resulted in disputes among the production team members over the representations of Cagney's and Lacey's hairstyles, makeup, and clothing. Determined to get the series renewed beyond the limited seven episodes, Rosenzweig called for a general upgrading of the style and "looks" of the two characters. [49] He wanted a renovation of the Cagney "look" to include more "stylish," "glamorous" outfits, and a new hairstyle that would "move" and "bounce."

For several months, Rosenzweig had wanted to change Lacey's wardrobe and hairstyle. Tyne Daly, who had designed the Mary Beth Lacey "look" by shopping with wardrobe designer Judy Sabel in the sale and basement sections of New York department stores, continually refused to change the character's plain, eccentric style. [50] Battles over Lacey's hair were also frequent occurrences on the set. Rosenzweig would ask Daly's hairdresser to get to her between takes and tease and spray her hair. [51] During one such incident, Daly shouted to the crew and staff, "Can anyone tell me why my producer wants me to look like Pat Nixon?" [52] . . .

During this period, the producers and writers also talked about where, in general, to go with the Cagney character. [53] The discussions revolved around making Cagney a more "sympathetic" character. They decided they would do this by making her more "committed" as a character, and this would be done by having her become seriously involved with one man. According to Terry Louise Fisher and Barbara Avedon the word "sympathetic" is industry jargon directed almost exclusively toward female characters and used to describe female roles that evoke "feminine" behavior and situations. [54] But the decision to make Cagney sympathetic by having her in a committed relationship with her boyfriend, Dory, was unpopular with viewers. One of the reporters on *60 Minutes* during the "letters-from-viewers" segment read a viewer letter that called for the removal of Dory from the *Cagney and Lacey* series.

During the 1984-1985 season, the Cagney character was once again associated with some conventionally feminist actions. In the episode in which she brings an end to her relationship with Dory, she overtly rejects (in a long conversation with Lacey) the institution of marriage. In other episodes, she files sexual harassment charges against a captain in the police department, urges Lacey to get a second opinion on a mastectomy, and consequently introduces the option of a lumpectomy. The season concludes with Cagney being the only one in her precinct to make the rank of sergeant, thereby emphasizing the importance of her career and her goal to become the first woman chief of detectives. With critical and industry acclaim, a more secure place in the ratings (at least with the target female audience), and the requisite changes in class and glamour, the network, it appears, became less skittish about the less conventional representations of women. . . .

CLOSING THOUGHTS

. . . Just as the 1970s' quest for young, urban audiences led to a spate of "socially relevant" television programs and to the increased representation of black women, working-class women, and single mothers, the quest for the working women's market in the late 1970s and 1980s led to women-oriented programs and feminist subject matter in prime time. But as we have seen, when these representations deviated too much from the acceptable conventions of the industry, they were quickly brought back in line. Given the outpouring of letters about *Cagney and Lacey* from women viewers who were desperate for new representations, and the fact that *Cagney and Lacey* attracted so many working women to the prime-time screen, we might have expected the networks to be more adventurous in future programs, more eager to please female audiences. Although they have featured some female leads in dramatic programs since the mid-1980s (*Kay O'Brien*, *The Days and Nights of Molly Dodd*, *China Beach*, *Heartbeat*, *Nightingales*, and *The Trials of Rosie O'Neill*), many of which met with cancellation or controversy, the networks continued to channel women, and especially "transgressive" women (such as Roseanne and Murphy Brown) into situation comedies.

The case of *Cagney and Lacey* ultimately illuminates, I think, two major facets of a complex phenomenon: the specific ways television texts tend to "shut down" and limit the meanings of "woman," and the ways in which large numbers of viewers, voracious for innovative representations, continued throughout the history of the series and its changes to read the text for meanings that echoed and shored up their conceptions of themselves as "non-traditional" women. The fact, moreover, that many lesbian viewers continued to find homoerotic overtones in the program and continued to generate pleasure from active "misreadings" confirms that textual limits do not shut down audience interpretations. But, from my point of view, the production of oppositional or alternative readings is not, finally, enough. I am confident that those of us who spend time in front of television sets will always interpret programming in creative ways, always produce meanings that escape the confines of the text. I hope, however, we will also continue to analyze television texts and industry practices for the ways they contribute to constraining the representations of gender, sexuality, race, class, and ethnicity. And finally, I hope we continue to agitate for a greater representation of *difference* in all the mass media. . . .

NOTES

1. At the conclusion of the *Cagney and Lacey* made-for-TV movie, Swit's Cagney appears as a "woman in distress" and is rescued by the squad (most of whom, with the exception of Lacey, are men). The representation of the protagonists as classic "women in distress," however, is absent from the Foster/Daly series. The Gless/Daly series does have a few sequences that feature "women in distress" figures. Lacey, for instance, is rescued from a high beam by Harvey, and Lacey is taken hostage. Mimi White (1987) cites two instances in which Cagney is shown as "trapped" or "caged" by the framing and the *mise en scène*. White finds this problematic for

the series' representation of women. By and large, however, the characters are not, I would maintain, regularly produced as the classic "women in distress" or in need of help from male colleagues.

2. These are the two terms used most often by the television networks to describe what they want in women characters. From Terry Louise Fisher and Barbara Avedon, personal interviews, February 1984, Los Angeles.

3. Leahy and Annenberg (1984). According to Leahy and Annenberg, Orion TV hired women to write 37% of its projects.

4. The liberal women's movement had such an enormous effect on *Cagney and Lacey's* production and reception that I want to clarify my conception of it here. In America, the movement is generally associated with *Ms.* magazine, with Gloria Steinem and with the National Organization for Women. Its primary emphasis, especially in the 1970s and early 1980s, was on equality in the labor force, with a focus on white middle-class women, and its programs for social change were oriented toward reform rather than radical structural reorganization of American social and cultural life. Nonetheless, the movement was vigilant in keeping public attention on the material conditions of women's everyday lives, on women's solidarity, and on the importance of mass media to social change.

5. Barbara Corday, personal interview, February 1984, Los Angeles; Barney Rosenzweig, personal interview, October 1983, Los Angeles.

6. Barney Rosenzweig, personal interview.

7. Barbara Corday, personal interview; Barney Rosenzweig, personal interview.

8. Rosen (1981).

9. Avedon quoted in Rosen (1981, p. 49).

10. Rosen (1981, p. 49).

11. Rosen (1981, p. 49).

12. Rosen (1981, p. 50).

13. Barney Rosenzweig, personal interview.

14. Rosen (1981, p. 50).

15. Rosenthal (1983).

16. Barney Rosenzweig, personal interview; *Ms.* 4 (October 1981), cover.

17. Turner (1983).

18. Turner (1983, p. 52).

19. *Soho News* (March 9, 1982), page unknown, from clipping file of Barney Rosenzweig, Los Angeles.

20. Six months later, in the fall of 1982, three other working-women-oriented and women's movement-influenced programs, *Gloria, Remington Steele,* and *It Takes Two,* also joined the schedule.

21. Bierbaum (1982, p. 25).

22. Turner (1983, p. 53); Barney Rosenzweig, personal interview.

23. *TV Guide* (April 3-10, 1982), pp. A-116-117.

24. *Magnum PI* was getting an average share of 38. When *Cagney and Lacey* aired it pulled in a 25 share the first week and 24 the second week. According to Rosenzweig, "At 9 o'clock all over America, 12 million people were getting up out of their seats *en masse* and walking away, or leaving the network" (cited in Turner, 1983, p. 53).

25. Turner (1983, p. 53).

26. Turner (1983, p. 53).

27. Brocato and Kelman, Inc., Public Relations, "Itinerary for Tyne Daly and Meg Foster" (April 27, 1982), Barney Rosenzweig files.

28. Turner (1983, p. 54).

29. Turner (1983, p. 54); Barney Rosenzweig, personal interview. After Meg Foster was released from her contract she had initial difficulty getting other work. According to a United Feature syndicate article (Dick Kleiner, "TV Scout Sketch #1: Cagney and Lacey Situation, The Story Behind Meg's Ouster," week of August 23, 1982), prior to that she "was an in-demand actress. But there was no official announcement of why she was fired, so people jumped to some pretty wild conclusions. . . . They want no part of a troublemaker." The article continues, "Later an official story came out and from then on Meg's offers picked up again." Rosenzweig says he tried to save Foster's job by suggesting to CBS that they dye her hair blonde (as a way

of achieving character contrast with the brunette Daly). He admits, however, to giving in to the network rather quickly and making Foster the "scapegoat" in order to save the series (Rosenzweig, personal interview). As of this writing, Foster appears as a district attorney on *The Trials of Rosie O'Neill,* starring Sharon Gless and produced by Barney Rosenzweig.

30. Hack (1982, p. 6); Kaufman (1982).

31. Swertlow (1982, p. A1).

32. My point here is that even though the programs were presenting "positive" representations of lesbians, they highlighted the fact that lesbianism is considered socially "deviant" as the organizing principle of the story—the point of the humor or drama.

33. Arnold Becker, quoted in Rosenberg (1982, p. 7).

34. O'Connor (1984, p. 42) in speaking of the "new" Cagney, described Gless as "blond, single, [and] gorgeous in the imposing manner of Linda Evans on *Dynasty.*"

35. Brooks and Marsh (1985, p. 136).

36. Du Brow (1983).

37. *Cagney and Lacey* offices, "Analysis of Costs for CBS for 'Cagney and Lacey,' " 1982, Rosenzweig files.

38. Since the mid-1950s advertisers made it clear that they did not want their products associated with lower-class characters and settings. See Barnouw (1970, pp. 5-8).

39. CBS Entertainment, Advertising and Promotion, "Program Promotion," 1982, Rosenzweig files.

40. Warren (1983).

41. "Review" (1982, p. 9).

42. O'Flaherty (1983).

43. Viewer letters from Barney Rosenzweig files, Los Angeles.

44. Harrison (1986).

45. Caption for cover photo of Tyne Daly and Sharon Gless, *Los Angeles Herald Examiner* (January 25, 1983).

46. I am quoting from a sample of 500 letters from this period which I arbitrarily pulled and duplicated from Barney Rosenzweig's files. The letters are written to Bud Grant (president of CBS entertainment), Barney Rosenzweig, Tyne Daly, Sharon Gless, and Orion Television. Since each letter was written to save the series from the network's ax, the sample is thoroughly biased in favor of the series and its representations. No critical letters or letters of complaint are present.

47. Jerilyn Stapleton, personal interview, February 1984, Los Angeles.

48. Terry Louise Fisher, personal interview, February 1984, Los Angeles.

49. Barney Rosenzweig, personal interview, January 1984, Los Angeles.

50. Judy Sabel, personal interview, February 1984, Los Angeles.

51. Personal observation on the set of *Cagney and Lacey* and conversation with Eddie Barron, hairdresser for Tyne Daly, February 1984, Los Angeles.

52. Personal observation on the set of *Cagney and Lacey,* February 1984.

53. Personal notes, writer-producer meetings, January-March, 1984, Los Angeles.

54. Terry Louise Fisher, personal interview, January 1984, Los Angeles; Barbara Avedon, personal interview.

REFERENCES

Barnouw, E. (1970). *The image empire.* New York: Oxford University Press.

Bierbaum, T. (1982, February 2). Steinem takes right turn on TV violence. *Daily Variety,* p. 25.

Brooks, T., & Marsh, E. (1985). *The complete directory to prime time network TV shows: 1946—The present.* New York: Ballantine.

Du Brow, R. (1983, January 25). Cagney and Lacey hang tough. *Los Angeles Herald Examiner,* pp. C-1, C-4.

Hack, R. (1982, May 28). TeleVisions. *Hollywood Reporter,* p. 6.

Harrison, B. G. (1986, February 23). I didn't think I was pretty: An interview with Sharon Gless. *Parade Magazine*, pp. 4-5.

Kaufman, D. (1982, May 25). CBS Ent Prez Grant asks crix for fair chance. *Daily Variety*, p. 19.

Leahy, M., & Annenberg, W. (1984, October 13-19). Discrimination in Hollywood: How bad is it? *TV Guide*, p. 14.

O'Connor, J. J. (1984, July 5). Cagney and Lacey—Indisputably a class act. *The New York Times* News Service to *The Patriot Ledger*.

O'Flaherty, T. (1983, October 11). Women in the line of fire. *San Francisco Chronicle*, p. B9.

Review. (1982, October 28). *Daily Variety*, p. 9.

Rosen, M. (1981, October). Cagney and Lacey. *Ms. Magazine*, pp. 47-50, 109.

Rosenberg, H. (1982, June 23). "Cagney and (Uh) Lacey," A question of a pink slip. *Los Angeles Times*, Calendar Section, p. 7.

Rosenthal, S. (1983, June 3). Cancellation of Cagney and Lacey to mean loss of rare TV series. *New York Daily News*, pp. 31, 35.

Swertlow, F. (1982, June 12-18). CBS alters "Cagney," calling it "too women's lib." *TV Guide*.

Turner, R. (1983, October 8-14). The curious case of the lady cops and the shots that blew them away. *TV Guide*, p. 41.

Warren, E. (1983, October 31). Where are the real women on TV? *Los Angeles Herald Examiner*, sec. 1, p. 10.

White, M. (1987). Ideological analysis and television. In R. C. Allen (Ed.), *Channels of discourse*. Chapel Hill: University of North Carolina Press.

53

Subversive Sitcoms

Roseanne *as Inspiration for Feminist Resistance*

JANET LEE

INTRODUCTION

The television's show begins with a large woman in curlers standing in her kitchen. It is Thanksgiving morning and she is stuffing a turkey surrounded by the realities of everyday life as a blue collar working wife and mother facing this "holiday." With the perfect timing and satirical wit that viewers have come to expect, we hear her thoughts:

> Here I am, 5 o'clock in the morning stuffing bread crumbs up a dead bird's butt.

The show is the popular *Roseanne* series, watched by millions of American viewers every Tuesday evening on ABC. My interest in this situation comedy arises out of my research on feminist resistance in popular culture and the possibilities for "disturbances" within the traditional formats of the conventional media.[1] While we have known for a long time how popular culture seems to secure the dominant interests of the ruling elites and facilitates consent and control among people,[2] it is only recently that we have started to ponder how popular media forms might also offer the possibilities

NOTE: Excerpts reprinted from *Women's Studies*, Vol. 21 (1992), by permission of the publisher, Gordon and Breach Science Publishers, Switzerland.

for a resistance away from a rigidly defined and controlled patriarchal definition of feminine subjectivity.[3]

My purpose in this paper is to explore the messages of the situation comedy *Roseanne* and its creator Roseanne Barr[4] through a textual analysis of this television show as a source of feminist resistance. . . .

ROSEANNE:
GODDESS OF RETRIBUTION

I went down to the comedy club to absolve all womenkind from smutty little jokes. I became Nemesis, the goddess of retribution. (*Ladies Home Journal*, September 1989, p. 218)

The sitcom *Roseanne* which premiered in the Fall of 1988 has become a number one success in the television ratings, and has propelled the witty, original, "domestic goddess" Roseanne Barr, its co-producer, writer and actor into a "cover queen" who appeared on the fronts of more than 30 separate magazines in 1989, and was crowned "TV's Funniest Lady" by *US* Magazine (*Advertising Age*, January 8, 1990, p. 45). Her autobiography *Roseanne: My Life as a Woman* also became a best-seller that same year. While Roseanne Barr who was known before her most recent fame as an outrageously abrasive and radical stand-up comedian has certainly softened her image and restricted the range of issues she deals with in order to achieve a mass appeal, she has retained her women-identified wit. Roseanne Barr is a woman with radical politics around gender and class. In the preface to her autobiography she writes how this book is about the Women's Movement and about the Left; how she discovered her feminism in a woman's bookstore in Denver and how she felt the need to critique the white middle class politics of much of traditional feminist writings.

Roseanne is fat, is in her late 30s and is Jewish. The character she plays is Roseanne Connor, a smart working class, apparently non-Jewish housewife and mother who holds a series of pink-collar jobs outside the home. She is employed at different times in a plastic factory, a fast-food restaurant, as a receptionist, a bar-tender, a telephone salesperson and in a beauty parlour. She is glaringly heterosexual, comfortable with her large body and her sexuality and is portrayed as actively engaging the latter. In the series she has three children, an equally large construction worker husband and a house that is rarely clean. In defence of her messy home, one of Roseanne's famous quotes is that she's waiting for Sears to come out with a riding vacuum.

The plot of this sitcom revolves around real "slice of life" situations of living and surviving in a blue-collar community in the midwest of the United States. As *Ladies Home Journal* (September 1989, p. 137) has described her—"She's the champion of sass-warfare, a true-blue collar heroine who takes no lip from her boss, her spouse or her kids." The series demonstrates in its narrative and plot the constant tension of working class existence, and, through humour, the absurdities and pain of living and participating in the American Dream. In the description and problematisation of class issues Roseanne does a wonderful job of modeling class-conscious, assertive behaviour, and on the interpersonal level she comes across as a woman who knows her own mind and has a strong sense of her power as a working class woman. In the series we see her refusing to be intimidated by middle class authority; she has the last outrageous word with her bosses, she refuses to be intimidated by the principal at her daughter's school, or the IRS or anyone else for that matter.

In this sense the series revolves around the realities of most of their viewers' lives, but seldom does it explicitly challenge the class system except in an individual-interpersonal way through a character's problematisation of classism in a narrative. Rarely do we see the series suggesting systematic strategies for change even though in many episodes Roseanne portrays and describes the class and gender hierarchies inherent in different occupations. Exceptions occur where strategies are introduced, such as in episodes where Roseanne stands up to her employer and leads the walk-out in the factory where she works, and where she leads the debate over safety and occupational health. In the context of commercial television she is probably pushing about as far as she can go against these class boundaries, and this movement is nonetheless considerable. If this is correct, it is interesting to speculate on the acceptability and integration of these ideas which relate specifically to class and gender hierarchies which must not be perceived as too contrary to sponsors' success.

On the issue of racism and anti-Semitism there is a troubling silence. While during her stand-up routine, in interviews in the tabloids and in her autobiography, Roseanne Barr has referred consistently to her background as a Jew living in Utah, passing as a Mormon and experiencing anti-Semitism, the Roseanne series has not politicised this or dealt with issues of racism. One wonders why this is the case. . . .

What distinguishes this mostly conventional family sitcom from ones that have come before is its more honest representation of family life which "would drive the Brady Bunch right out of the neighborhood" (*Ladies Home Journal*, February 1989, p. 102). There is a conscious fracturing of the myth of the happy suburban family of TV land, something which is in direct contrast to, and creates a parody of, the affluence and perfection of other family sitcoms such as the popular *Cosby Show*. . . .

Another distinguishing feature of this series which sets it apart as a vehicle of resistance is that it is woman-centred entertainment. Roseanne as scriptwriter and co-creator of the series has been its pioneer and has complained publicly about efforts to tone down the feminist message of the show. She delivers all the one-liners we always wanted to say in navigating the waters of street harassment. For example when a young male co-worker accuses her of wanting to be a man she replies "That makes two of us, huh?" "I want to be a voice for working women, to get the same kind of roar from them that Lenny Bruce and Richard Pryor did for their subgroups," she told an interviewer for *Time* magazine (May 8, 1989, p. 83).

Roseanne, her will, feelings and perspective come through as central narrator and protagonist. Importantly she is situated, and thus gender is located, within a social totality. We see her balancing the demands of home, work and society in an authentic way as a strong and assertive woman. Yet she also comes across as a woman who has contradictions like all of us. Importantly, Roseanne excels at taking stereotypes about women and turning them around. It has been said that this is her mission, her rebellion (*Redbook*, February 1989, p. 38). In one session she asks her family who are unable to find something and expect her to know where it is, whether they think a uterus is a tracking device. This is a very clever focus on the stereotypes associated with biological determinism. As Roseanne said in a *Good Housekeeping* interview (July 1989, p. 63)

> I just try to say stuff that I think not everybody thinks about . . . I go back to things that have stuck in my head from when I was growing up, and look at them honestly. Almost invariably, they are things that men have said, and then I turn them around to what I feel, and what I think a lot of other women feel.

The powerful representation of autonomous womanhood is made more salient because Roseanne is a fat woman. We live in a society where thin is the norm, fat is seen as disgusting and a multi-million dollar industry exists to perpetuate these norms. For Roseanne Barr, her weight is a feminist issue. As she has said "If someone asks me how my diet is going, I say, 'Fine. How was your lobotomy?' " (Dworkin, 1987, p. 108). On talking about how people respond to her size she says: "They totally erase my sexuality because they think fat erases sexuality . . . The truth is I have always had men whether I was 200 lbs. or 100 lbs. Maybe I had more when I was skinnier, but there ain't enough hours in the day anyhow" (*People Weekly*, October 9, 1988, p. 98).

Roseanne's swift one-liners on and off the screen provide a humorous come-back to a misogynist society that tries to mould women into the pornographic image. Roseanne provides a role model for women in that she defines herself and her sexuality for herself, and offers a feminist critique of fat oppression at the same time. Her words are in *Glamour*, *Ladies Home Journal*, *Redbook* and other such women's magazines, easily accessible for women to read, even though they may often be interspersed with magazine advertisements for diet aids and shape-up programmes. She feels women "should take up more space . . ." (*Redbook*, February 1989, p. 40). At the same time however, she often comes across as feeding the stereotype of the fat jolly person and this tends to render her feminism less threatening as well as maintaining fat-oppressive values.

Motherhood is a frequent topic for Roseanne's wit and parody. This is one institution that has certainly been overrepresented for women in the media, and it is the target for Roseanne's humour and thus a site for cultural interference. She is quoted as saying about motherhood: "This is why some animals eat their young" (*People Weekly*, October 17, 1988, p. 175). These messages are conscious and intentional: "I wanted to be the first mom ever to be on TV. I wanted to send a message about mothers and how much we do." This performance makes her even more "real" or at least someone with whom women can identify. As Roseanne says "I see myself as a role model for people . . . not a token, not a supermom. I'm trying to show that there is a lot more to being a woman than being a mother, but that there's a hell of a lot more to being a mother than most people suspect" (*Time,* May 8, 1989, p. 83).

Especially central in the series' plot is the focus on motherly guilt—an emotion which is difficult for mothers not to have in a society that equates mothering with self sacrifice and primary parenting. She is quoted in *Redbook* (February 1989, p. 34) as saying "I love my husband and I love my kids, but I need something more. Like maybe a life! . . . the worst time in my life was when I lived in a trailer with three children and a husband who wanted Jell-o every night." She follows this assertion with the comment: "I breed well in captivity." These comments certainly ring of Betty Freidan's "problem that has no name." In this way Roseanne acts as an accessible role model for millions of mothers and wives. What always comes through in the midst of all the put-downs and one-liners (such as "What did I tell you about killing your brother in the living room?") is a deep affection that Roseanne has for her children and for husband Dan. There is an outward show of affection alongside the rough-edged portrayal of working class family life.

Messages of female friendship and solidarity come through as she interacts with her workmates and her sister, modeling a close and caring, yet honest relationship. We see Roseanne coming to trust and enjoy the friendship of women in the beauty parlour where she is "the shampoo girl." This is a degrading job according to society and her family, yet one she comes to appreciate, because, as she says to Dan and the kids: "Nobody there makes me feel like it is (degrading). That's your job." Powerful words. These most recent episodes, as of this writing, demonstrate the woman-space of the beauty parlour and the important sense of female community that is present. Roseanne toys with her irritating friend Crystal and gets overinvolved in sister Jackie's lovelife. They argue and bellow at each other, they make up and they show the feelings and contradictions that viewers can share. Importantly we see plots centering on female friendship and relationships that can start to subvert the messages that we must give up the love of women in order to gain the approval of men.

The few adult male characters in the sitcom sometimes become intentional narrative devices to represent sexism and macho behaviour. For example when Dan is discussing how many of his male buddies will come over for poker, Roseanne responds that she was asking who was coming, not about their IQs; and when he offers to cook dinner she replies "Oh, but honey, you just cooked dinner three years ago." . . . Yet Dan as Roseanne's husband also models some progressive male domestic behaviour in his tuned-in relationship with Roseanne and his work in the household.

The men also function to frame the series in a heterosexual format. Roseanne, despite her jovial "male-bashing" is overwhelmingly heterosexual and all feminist messages are made more acceptable by this explicit framing. While in the series there is no critique of heterosexism as a system of power that privileges and oppresses, there are messages supporting women's community and solidarity. Heterosexism seems to be reinforced at the same time that issues are raised that chip away at its power. . . .

Roseanne, of course has not gone without popular criticism by both women and men. She has been found to be "forceful and abrasive" and some have criticised the show as emitting "a crassness . . . a belligerance and a sneering sense of unhappiness that are often hard to take" (*Variety*, September 20, 1989, p. 134). One man writing for *Esquire* magazine (August 1989, p. 99) described her as "not nearly daring, original, or honest enough." These reactions tend to underline her subversive potential as a source of resistance and inspiration for feminist change. Here is a woman breaking a lot of rules and gaining mass popularity for it—scary![5] Also among feminist circles she may not always represent the ideal subversive. On this issue Ehrenreich (1990, p. 31) comments: "If middle-class feminism can't claim Roseanne, maybe it's gotten a little too dainty for its own good." . . .

NOTES

1. With respect to the terms popular culture and mass culture, I use them to mean everyday cultural forms as represented in society and especially in the mass media: television, magazines, newspapers and journalism, cinema, music videos, popular music, fashion, art and literature. These are signifiers which compose systems that are involved in all forms of everyday social activity. For a discussion of definitions of popular culture see Ray Browne (1972, pp. 1-12).

2. See Althusser (1986) for a pertinent discussion of the powers of ideology and the role of culture as a constant site of struggle between those with and those without power; and Gramsci's (1981) theory of hegemony. Gramsci discusses the process by which a dominant class wins the willing consent of subordinate groups of people.

While Tuchman et al. (1978) offered a pioneering book on the portrayal of women in the media, a text which I have found useful in discussing the "cultivation effects" hypothesis or the way in which television particularly affects viewers attitudes and behaviour is Wober and Gunter (1988). Judith Williamson's (1985) book *Consuming Passions* is an important text also. Especially interesting in writings on the power of television is the notion, as discussed by Gerbner and Gross (1976, pp. 197-199), that television acts as a religion and has become our culture's most powerful myth-maker. However Modleski (1986, p. xii) offers a warning about invoking analogies based upon older cultural forms.

3. For texts which focus on cultural production through popular culture see Chambers (1986); Fiske (1987); Grossberg (1984). For specifically feminist analyses refer to Coward (1985); Gamman and Marshment (1989); Kuhn (1982); Lewis (1987); Modleski (1986); McRobbie (1984, undated); Roberts (1990).

4. Since the writing of this essay, the *Roseanne* series has continued and its popularity (and Roseanne's wit and parody) has been upheld. A couple of interesting events have occurred— one being that Roseanne Barr has changed her last name to Arnold upon her marriage, and another that she spoke publicly about being a survivor of incest and the need for women to understand their victimisation and come together for change. Contradictions abound—on the one hand a symbol of patriarchy in the family, and on the other a critique.

5. Roseanne Barr's recent rendition of the national anthem at a baseball game, complete with crotch scratching in parody of male athletes, caused considerable public uproar.

REFERENCES

Althusser, L. (1986). *Essays on ideology.* London: Verso.

Browne, R. B. (1972). Popular culture: Notes toward a definition. In R. B. Browne & R. J. Ambrosetti (Eds.), *Popular culture and curriculum.* Bowling Green, OH: Bowling Green University Popular Press.

Chambers, I. (1986). *Popular culture: The metropolitan experience.* New York: Methuen.

Coward, R. (1985). *Female desires: How they are bought and packaged.* New York: Grove.

Dworkin, S. (1987, July/August). Roseanne Barr: The disgruntled housewife as stand-up comedian. *Ms. Magazine,* p. 106.

Ehrenreich, B. (1990, April 2). The wretched of the hearth. *The New Republic,* pp. 23-31.

Fiske, J. (1987). British cultural studies and television. In R. C. Allen (Ed.), *Channels of discourse* (pp. 254-290). Chapel Hill: University of North Carolina Press.

Gamman, L., & Marshment, M. (Eds.). (1989). *The female gaze: Women as viewers of popular culture.* Seattle, WA: Real Comet Press.

Gerbner, G., & Gross, L. (1976). Living with television: The violence profile. *Journal of Communication, 26,* 173-199.

Gramsci, A. (1981). *Selections from the prison notebooks* (Hoare, Quintin, & Smith, Eds. and Trans.). New York: International Publishers.

Grossberg, L. (1984). "I'd rather feel bad than feel nothing at all": Rock and roll, pleasure and power. *Enclitic, 8,* 94-110.

Kuhn, A. (1982). *Women's pictures: Feminism and cinema.* New York: Routledge & Kegan Paul.

Lewis, L. A. (1987, Winter). Female address in music video. *Journal of Communication Inquiry, 11,* 73-84.

McRobbie, A. (1984). Dance and social fantasy. In A. McRobbie & M. Nava (Eds.), *Gender and generation* (pp. 130-161). London: Macmillan.

McRobbie, A. (undated). Post-modernism and popular culture. In Institute of Contemporary Arts (Ed.), *Postmodernism documents* (Vol. 4, pp. 54-58). London: ICA.

Modleski, T. (1986). *Studies in entertainment: Critical approaches to mass culture.* Bloomington: Indiana University Press.

Roberts, R. (1990). "Sex as a weapon," Feminist rock music videos. *National Women's Studies Association Journal, 2*(1), 1-15.

Tuchman, G., Kaplan Daniels, A., & Benet, J. (1978). *Hearth and home: Images of women in the mass media.* New York: Oxford University Press.

Williamson, J. (1985). *Consuming passions: The dynamics of popular culture.* London: Marion Boyers.

Wober, M., & Gunter, B. (1988). *Television and social control.* New York: St. Martin's.

54

Confessions of a Sitcom Junkie

SARAH SCHUYLER

. . . I'm long past the graham crackers and milk phase, but even so when I want to space out today one of my first choices remains a tv sitcom re-run. Lately I've even got my lover hooked on this vice. A local station shows re-runs of *The Dick Van Dyke Show* and *The Honeymooners* every evening at seven and seven-thirty, and she and I tune in regularly over dinner. What's it like for lesbians to watch these shows? As Jill puts it: "I like *the Honeymooners* because it's fun to watch heterosexuals fighting." We also have a standing joke about Alice Cramden leaving Ralph and running off with her best friend, Trixie. But two things we can be sure about are that the Cramdens will always make up at the end of a half hour, and that Trixie and Alice will not run off together. The "diff'rent strokes" just don't get that different in sitcomland—a land where "normality" is a nowhere in perpetual motion.

I suspect that the regularity of the shows is as much an appeal for us as our subversive jokes, however. Another game we play is predicting what's going to happen next—and it's not difficult to get it right. It's a lot less easy to predict what's going to happen next in our own lives—maybe that's why it's satisfying to do it for Alice and Ralph.

Sitcoms are easy to predict because their form makes them perpetual motion machines. A perpetual motion machine does not deplete its energy and will continue to perform the same tasks indefinitely. The formula for sitcoms is as follows: set up a family of characters, which may be a work family, as on *Cheers, Taxi,* or *The Mary Tyler Moore Show;* or an at-home family of friends, relatives, servants, or some combination of these (on *Family Affair,* for example, the family consists of an uncle, a butler and three kids). It's important to the perpetual motion that each member of the family have a certain set of personality traits and recognizable habits that do not and cannot change during the series. The shows are comic because on each show, a "sit"—or situation—threatens to throw the family into some degree of havoc. But by the end of the show things work out and the family returns to whatever position it had at the beginning of the episode. This is where the perpetual motion comes in; the same characters can go on to make the same kinds of mistakes or fall into the same kinds of situations in the future because no energy has been lost and the machine is perpetually renewing itself. Lucy Ricardo on *I Love Lucy* will always be coming up with schemes for doing kinds of work she fails at (as a singer at Ricky's nightclub, or as a candy factory assembly-line worker, as a door-to-door salesperson, et cetera). The show may teach that Lucy is best off accepting the 1950s middle-class rule that happy wives are housewives, but it never teaches Lucy to remember that lesson for more than the last ten minutes of any one episode.

"Forgetting" on one show what happened on the last is one sitcom law; keeping the characters' relationships to one another the same is another law. What this means is that in the sitcom, the nuclear family is always being shaken up by the sit, but always returns to its traditional structure at the end of the show. One question a feminist may ask is whether these shows are popular because they always produce disruptions to the nuclear family or because of the stable and traditional solution that ends each show. I tend to think it's both of these that give viewers pleasure—even at my house, where "watching heterosexuals fight" has a special sort of humor, we usually let out a happy "Awww" at the end of *The Honeymooners* when Ralph and Alice kiss and make up. Lesbian couples know their sexuality places them outside traditional definitions of the nuclear family; nevertheless, I also think that lesbians have a desire to understand their difference partly according to the terms available in the popular culture we grew up part of. Ralph and Alice can fight and make up and go on from there; so do we. Alice accepts Ralph despite his regular lapses into infantile behavior; I hope Jill will allow me mine.

But it can be dangerous to fall into the assumption that everyone "reads" every show the same way. The source of pleasure is different depending on who is watching. The "we're all alike in the end" idea in fact is one of the more insidious messages sitcoms teach, because progressive politics always begins at the point of a recognition of differences. For example, when I told Jill about my interpretation of *I Love Lucy,* she agreed that "middle-class women will watch the show and learn that they're right if they make home and family their first priority, and feel good about that. But a working-class woman might watch the show and think 'I can do jobs that Lucy can't do,' and feel good about *that.*" Perhaps she is right—she and I come from different class backgrounds and it's possible that we have readings of the show different from each other's.

Even though the families return to stability at the end of each episode, as I have said, sitcoms need their disruption—their sit. More often than not the sit evolves from a conflict between different "classes" of characters. This may mean a conflict between children and adults (*Leave It to Beaver*, for example), between liberals and conservatives (*All in the Family, Family Ties*), between social classes (*The Beverly Hillbillies*), or between men and women (*I Love Lucy*). The constant crises become even more glaring when one watches re-runs which come on every day instead of once a week. If the traditional nuclear family forms the basic model for all sitcom families, then sitcoms put family ties in perpetual danger of crisis.

The recurring crises make sitcoms a popular cultural way audiences get to look at the mixture of equality and inequality that characterizes the "family." Families traditionally are built on hierarchies, even though everyone within a family is also "the same"—whether this means they all share the same last name or that they all work for the same tv station in Minneapolis. It's the "sameness" of the family members that the shows' conclusions emphasize in order to banish the threat of the sit in each episode. . . .

PART VII

MUSIC VIDEOS AND RAP MUSIC: CULTURAL CONFLICT AND CONTROL IN THE AGE OF THE IMAGE

Rap music and rock music videos (including "crossover rap" videos) are both contemporary youth-targeted cultural forms that have evoked panicked responses to their supposed antisocial messages in parents and audiences from mainstream or "middle-American" cultural locations. Both have been criticized as **sexist** and violent by much of the public outside their targeted audiences—although this has begun to change recently for rap music, as the form itself has come under the challenge of women musicians and as intellectuals and cultural critics have begun to look more closely at the variety in the form and at its relationship to African American cultural history. But there are crucial differences between rap music and music videos that will emerge sharply in the chapters in this part.

Rap music (and hip-hop culture more generally) is one of the most important U.S. cultural phenomena of the last decade by many measures, "a form of profound musical, cultural and social creativity," in the words of Michael Dyson (1993, p. 15). Or in the words of Alan Light (1991), it is "unarguably the most culturally significant style in pop, the genre that speaks most directly to and for its audience . . . the single most creative, revolutionary approach to music and to music making that this generation has constructed" (p. 857). Originating in African American urban street culture of New York in the late 1970s—which had already produced Black and Puerto Rican graffiti art and break dancing—rap also was fed through a wide variety of former musical and oral-culture roots, such as verbal insult games (Craddock-Willis, 1991; Dyson, 1993, chap. 1; Flores, 1993; Tate, 1992; Toop, 1991). From its beginnings as "rhythmic, repetitive speech" originally layered over "samples" of African American rhythm and blues music hits selected by DJs at dance parties, early rap music evolved into a multigeneric form that has significantly influenced the U.S. music, fashion and advertising industries. It has taken root in films by a generation of young independent African American filmmakers dealing with African American life in the 1980s and 1990s and crossed over into TV entertainment forms, such as talk shows and the new African American situation comedies, such as *Fresh Prince* or *Living Single.*

In its more political forms and its continuing association with African American nationalism on the one hand and street culture on the other, rap music continues to have a strong impact on Black-White social and cultural politics and on politics within the African American community (including **gender** politics). For this book, its major significance is in its ability to establish a cultural arena in which the worldview and experience of those socially marginalized by poverty **(class), race** and age can be publicly enacted and political strategies for organizing debated. Although it is now certainly in part a **capitalist** enterprise like other arms of the entertainment industries, it can still be understood as distinctive—as a manifestation of "economic nationalism" or community-based capitalism.[1]

In contrast, rock music videos are a "hybrid" form resulting from a "marriage" of televisual advertising style with rock music—a **genre** of (largely White male) popular musical culture generally considered to embody a rebellious, anti-establishment, even left-liberal or radical political ideology (Kaplan, 1987, pp. 14, 52). Four-minute promotional clips that consisted of a televisual component designed to accompany song excerpts selected from underadvertised record albums, rock videos came into being at a time when the recording industry was experiencing a serious sales slump and the failure of its traditional promotional methods to boost flagging sales (Henke, 1982, p. 51; Lewis, 1990, p. 23).

The first 24-hour music video station created for "basic" (nonpremium) cable TV service, MTV, was launched in 1981 when 29-year-old founder Robert Pittman (already running the Movie Channel for Warner Amex Satellite Entertainment Company) set out to capture "the 13 to 35 year olds of 'middle America' " (Pettegrew, Chapter 55), including in its upper range what advertisers considered "the most difficult to reach of all audiences," the 24- to 34-year-olds. As John Pettegrew points out (Chapter 55), "the station's format went further than anything else on television in breaking down the distinction between commercial and program."

The creators of MTV believed that a fusion of "album-oriented rock"—considered "progressive" and "avant-garde" by rock music afficianados (Lewis, 1990, p. 25)—with an advertising-styled televisual sequence of images that would "move very quickly with quick cuts, no transitions" would have maximum appeal for the target audience—in Pittman's phrases— "television babies who grew up on TV and rock and roll." Pittman persuaded the executives of the cable company (Warner-Amex), the recording industry and, ultimately, the corporate advertisers that the format of "an around-the-clock, circular flow of interchangeably artistic and commercial appeals to the viewer's senses" would attract and hold the attention of the desired audience. One result, as Lisa Lewis (1990) has pointed out, was that

> what had begun as a practical approach to securing cheap (free) pro-
> gramming within the parameters of MTV's concept ended up being
> a factor that determined MTV's program content. By getting record
> companies to supply videos, MTV ensured that the videos would look
> like advertisements for record company products. (p. 24)

Pettegrew calls the founding of the MTV channel in the 1980s a **"post-modernist** moment," invoking a term that many cultural critics have associated with both the stylistic, technical strategies of rock video texts and
with MTV's broader role in contemporary media culture (e.g., Fiske, 1986;
Kaplan, 1987). Although a detailed discussion of the multifaceted critical
concept of postmodernism is beyond the scope of our book, a brief note here
on its usefulness to critics of MTV is in order.

The term postmodernism is a recent coinage that has been used most
influentially by Marxist critic Frederic Jameson (and others, such as Lyotard
and Baudrillard) to describe what is seen as an alarming new consciousness
manifested in younger-generation cultural producers and consumers in the
contemporary period, a consciousness that is

> perhaps partly the result of the Cold War, nuclear technology, multina-
> tional corporate capitalisms, star wars, advanced computer and other
> high tech developments, as well as . . . highly sophisticated new mar-
> keting strategies, building upon ever-increasing knowledge of psycho-
> logical manipulation. (Kaplan, 1987, p. 7)

Such a postmodernist consciousness is conceptualized in contrast to the
critical and political consciousness seen expressed in "modernism," artistic
movements and styles in painting, literature and architecture in the earlier
20th century that are seen as rebellious, often politically engaged, anti-
bourgeois, avant-garde, manifestations of individual artists' creativity in
"high art." Critics who contrast a contemporary postmodernist culture to an
earlier modernist cultural past are often concerned by what they see as a
complete breakdown of old categories and aesthetic distinctions, such as
those between "high" (elite, serious, respected) and "low" (popular and
commercial) arts. They also see a lack of "the sense of history" and of a
politically based critical attitude toward late-capitalist industrial commercialism and consumerism, as well as a failure to distinguish "self" from
"image" (Kaplan, 1987, pp. 40-47). As one recent MTV analyst put it,

> Postmodern critics see in MTV a mirror-image of the ideal postmodern
> text: "Fragmentation, segmentation, superficiality, stylistic jumbling,
> the blurring of mediation and reality, the collapse of past and future
> into the moment of the present, the elevation of hedonism, the domi-
> nance of the visual over the verbal." (D. Tetzlaff, 1986, quoted in Good-
> win, 1993, p. 45)

Not all critics who think MTV expresses a postmodernist sensibility deplore this fact. Using approaches largely developed in film criticism, they attempt to look closely at the different types of rock videos that have emerged, analyzing the way the **televisual apparatus** underlies the **codes** of the rock video **text** (e.g., Kaplan, 1987). However, other critics and historians of MTV and music videos believe that the fit between a postmodernist analysis and MTV has never been a good one, because of the overemphasis on the supposedly postmodern stylistic characteristics of the televisual component and the underemphasis on the music (Goodwin, 1993; Walser, 1993). One critic argues that very different technical and *formal* elements in the music itself (such as musical repetition) and in MTV's scheduling practices (such as the anchoring function of the face and talk of the MTV "veejay") counteract televisual fragmentation within the clips and provide aural stability as well as a stable point of viewer identification (Goodwin, 1993). (Our selection of essays in this chapter admittedly shares in this tendency of much MTV criticism, in privileging the televisual over the musical, but we have tried to include a good selection of readings on rock and rap music in the bibliography.)

MTV originally "followed the music industry in defining 'rock' in essentially **racist** terms, as a form of music that excluded blacks," concentrating for its first 5 years on British New Pop (1981-1983) and then on (White) heavy metal (Goodwin, 1993, p. 49). One Black artist, Rick James, filed a suit charging racial discrimination (Peterson-Lewis & Chennault, 1986, p. 108); and White rock musician David Bowie publicly challenged the censorship of African American musicians in 1983. In response, MTV justified the exclusionary practice by an appeal to its demographics, which assumed White aversion to Black music as performed by Black musicians: "We have to play music we think an entire country is going to like" (Levy, 1983, p. 37). It took the economic lessons of Michael Jackson's "phenomenal cross-over success" (Lewis, 1990, p. 40) with the 1982 album *Thriller* to convince MTV executives that Black music and musicians would not alienate the White target audience, it seems.[2] The album was followed in 1983 with a highly innovative and influential video *Thriller*, which has been much discussed by postmodern MTV critics interested in its "playful parody of the stereotypes, codes and conventions of the 'horror' genre" (Mercer, 1993, p. 96; see also Dyson, 1993, chap. 4).[3] By 1989, rap music's commercial success and crossover appeal had made a special program segment on MTV, *Yo! MTV Raps*, not only possible but the most popular show in the now increasingly segmented schedule (Light, 1991).

One of the staples of the visual **image system** of rock videos in the early 1980s was the sexualized female form, used decoratively to enhance the emotional appeal of the video for the (presumed White male youthful) viewer/listener (Pelka, 1991). Undoubtedly, this use of sexualized sexist visual imagery in rock videos needs to be analyzed in the context of sexist representational traditions within rock lyrics and within the qualities of the sounds of rock music itself—particularly in the "heavy metal" rock style or subgenre, which dominated MTV's scheduling in the early years. As Robert Walser (1993) argues in an interesting recent analysis of gender imagery in heavy metal music videos of the 1980s, "Metal has developed discourses of male victimization, exscription [absence of women in male-bonding scenarios], and androgyny," some of which "embody challenges to or transformations of **hegemonic ideology**," whereas others "reproduce rather directly the hegemonic strategies of control and repression of women that pervade Western culture" (p. 161).

Because MTV was born into a world in which the feminist movement's perspectives were already active, from the founding moment it encountered criticism of its **representations** of women. **Content analysis** studies of MTV imagery explored its potentially damaging effects on adolescents (e.g., Brown & Campbell, 1986; Vincent, 1989). There was also a firestorm of public criticism of sexist and sexually violent imagery on MTV as well as in the rock music industry more generally, by parents' organizations concerned with the nature and effect of such images on young audiences, such as the Parents Music Resource Center and the Parents Choice Foundation. (Tipper Gore, wife of the current vice president, was one of the organizers of the effort to institute a rating system for records similar to that for Hollywood films.)

Feminist critics of MTV coming from film studies brought with them more complex questions about the representation of gender, both within the individual rock video text and throughout the 24-hour "flow" of MTV programming. One of the earliest and most influential of these, Ann Kaplan (1987), argued (employing a feminist **psychoanalytic** framework like that discussed in Part III) that in contrast to the situation that feminist film critics saw in extended Hollywood classic film narratives, MTV as a channel "constructs several different kinds of gender address and modes of representing sexuality, several different positions for the spectator to take up in relation to sexual difference" (p. 89).

Lisa Lewis, another prominent feminist critic of rock videos, points out (Chapter 56) that "exposure on MTV has and is contributing to an upsurge in female rock and roll musicianship" and suggests that "female musicians are actively participating in making the music video form work in their interest." Several conventional features of the rock video form, Lewis believes, including "the centrality of the musician's image in the video," have worked to the advantage of female rock artists, allowing them to create an "authorship" role out of a formerly secondary role as "vocalist." Lewis also points to the female fan's role in constructing an "authorial voice" for the singer, through an "attempt to reconcile the text" of the song "with the extratextual information about the singer's personal history," as in the case of reading Tina Turner's personal experience with Ike Turner into the song "What's Love Got to Do With It?" (lyrics not actually written by Tina Turner). Closely analyzing the texts of some of these female-authored rock videos, Lewis identifies "images that signal both the **appropriation** of male leisure forms and practices, and the celebration of specifically female ones" and examines the way these images could possibly disrupt hegemonic representations of femininity.

That music video texts are open to a surprisingly wide variety of interpretations by actual historical viewers is made evident in Brown and Schulze's study of how race and gender (and to a lesser extent, class) interact to produce distinct and often unanticipated interpretations of two contro-versial Madonna videos from the mid-1980s, as well as widely varying and unpredictable fandom patterns (Chapter 57). Black and White students expressed significantly different views of what both video plots were cen-trally "about," for example.

Gender differences were also significant in fairly predictable ways. For example, "While female viewers struggled against the patriarchal dis-courses in play in Madonna's videos, many of the male viewers and almost all of the male fans felt comfortably hailed as masculine subjects" and White males in particular "were quite clear about the desire the video stimulated;" moreover, in one video, "males of both races were more likely than females to see the primary theme as sexual love, while females were more likely to identify a platonic relationship between the dancer and the boy." Some female fans commented on "the pleasures of identification with a strong, successful woman," but a few "felt that Madonna's body problematized theirs."

Although the Brown and Schulze chapter reminds us that rock videos on MTV have often been controversial and have provoked strong feelings in viewers and the public, it seems clear that rap music has aroused far greater fear and loathing in (White) middle America than even the most apparently rebellious and "nihilistic" forms of White rock, such as punk and heavy metal—largely because of its association with the overtly expressed social anger of disenfranchised Black (predominantly male) street youth.

In "Fear of a Black Planet: Rap Music and Black Cultural Politics in the 1990s" (Chapter 60), Tricia Rose shows how White "media and institutional attacks on rap" are different in intensity from "attacks sustained by rock-and-roll artists." She focuses particularly on how media reports of violence at rap concerts have been used as justifications by venue owners "to contain Black mobility and rap music, not to diminish violence against Blacks." In her view, "Contestation over the meaning and significance of rap music, controversies regarding its ability to occupy public space, and struggles to retain its expressive freedom constitute critical aspects of contemporary Black cultural politics."

As Michael Eric Dyson (1993) has pointed out, in an essay first published in June 1989, "countless black parents, too, have had negative reactions to rap, and the black radio and music establishment . . . allocat[ed] much less airplay and print coverage to rap than is warranted by its impressive record sales" (p. 6). The class and generational differences within the African American community that help account for the variety of reactions to rap music are not new.

> The blues functioned for another generation of blacks much as rap functions for young blacks today: as a source of racial identity, permit-ting forms of boasting and asserting machismo for devalued black men suffering from social degradation, allowing commentary on so-cial and personal conditions in uncensored language, and fostering the ability to transform hurt and anguish into art and commerce. Even in its heydey, however, the blues existed as a secular musical genre over

against the religious traditions that saw the blues as "devil's music" and the conservative black cultural perspectives of the blues as barbaric. (Dyson, 1993, p. 9)

In "Reconstructions of Nationalist Thought in Black Music and Culture," (Chapter 58), Kristal Brent Zook further contextualizes rap music within African American cultural, social and economic history, and in a "cross-medial" present in which

the various media such as television, music, film, and video speak to and through one another and are intimately connected by a growing number of black men (for the most part) who insist on capturing full productive control over their artistic works.

She sees the invocation of Black nationalism in rap music, as a "necessary vision of safety, protection, and . . . an empowering 'home.' " As she argues, "nationalism is not just a metaphoric or aesthetic vision which appears in the creative product" but is also expressed in "the actual material mechanisms of cultural production itself (i.e., the marketing, promotion, and distribution of this product)." She points to the formation of the Stop the Violence movement as an example of what she terms "material nationalism"—by which she means a variety of forms of networking and mutual economic support among Black cultural producers, with the goal of nurturing "a heightened sense of racial collectivity, group solidarity, and even political responsibility."

Many critics have deplored the overt misogyny in some rappers' lyrics and public statements and have urged female rappers to "rap back," and male antisexists within the African American community to speak out as well (Dyson, 1993; Tate, 1992, pp. 127-128; Wallace, 1990). Zook's view of rap music as "part of a larger conduit of culturally specific, 'in-house' intercommunication among blacks" is very useful when we consider the way rap music is currently a place of intensive conflict and conversation among Black men and women over sex, sexism and gender.

Paula Ebron (1991) has characterized some 1980s nationalist rap as "gendered commentary" largely featuring Black men addressing White men "in their discussion of race and politics." Although African American women have been present in hip hop from the beginning, "a new generation" of female rappers who came into prominence in 1989 have become a much more significant part of the conversation (although they have not generated anything like a comparable level of coverage in mainstream media). In "It's My Thang and I'll Swing It the Way That I Feel! Sexuality and Black Women Rappers" (Chapter 59), Imani Perry considers the ways in which female rappers are producing a Black feminist voice within the context of hip hop, representing Black female sexuality as active, for example—a source of empowerment rather than vulnerability.

Rap music, like any African American cultural expression in the context of the contemporary U.S. media world, of necessity has multiple audiences with different social identities and relationships to the street culture from which hip hop came. The music's enormous commercial success has meant that the responses of White audiences (and other non-White audiences, as rap gains a global distribution) are an increasingly large factor in assessing and contesting the social and cultural meaning of rap. However, in the specific context of the well-known history of White appropriation of (and profit from) a myriad of originally Black musical forms—including jazz, blues, and rhythm and blues—White youths' admiration of rap music (as manifested in both White rap performers and fans) has come under close scrutiny. In "Imitation of Life" (Chapter 61), James Ledbetter points out that in the contemporary period, "there are a number of intersecting multi-billion-dollar American industries (music, advertising, television, sports) whose survival at current profit levels depends on the existence of a massive audience of White Negroes."

Ledbetter traces the **co-optation** of rap music by these industries, which has the effect of harnessing "black slang, music, and energy . . . for immense profits," while stripping the original cultural form of its political edge. He also asks us to consider what "the 1990s white suburbanite gets . . . from listening to Public Enemy." In his view, "By listening to rap and tapping into its extramusical expressions, . . . whites are attempting to bear witness to—even correct—their own often sterile, oppressive culture."

Ledbetter ends with a challenge to those White youths who identify with Black culture through the consumption of such cultural expressions as rap music, to stop "ignoring those political causes that seem to affect blacks almost exclusively."

NOTES

1. Michael Dyson, writing in 1989, pointed to the fact that "the rap industry has spawned a number of independent labels, providing young blacks (mostly men) with experience as heads of their own businesses. . . . Until recently, rap flourished, for the most part, outside of the tight artistic and economic constraints imposed by major music corporations" (Dyson, 1993, p. 12). He claimed that even in the distribution area, independent labels were still "teaching the major music corporations invaluable lessons about street sales" (p. 12).

2. By 1983, Black artists were already using the music video form to promote albums on BET (Black Entertainment Television), in "a form of cultural red-lining," as Lisa Lewis (1990, p. 40) points out.

3. Several of Michael Jackson's later videos, which apparently explore racial and sexual identity issues, such as *Bad* and *Man in the Mirror,* as well as what Dyson (1993) calls Jackson's "postmodern spirituality," have been intensively examined by African American cultural critics Michael Dyson (1993, chap. 4) and Michelle Wallace (1990).

REFERENCES

Brown, J. D., & Campbell, K. C. (1986). Race and gender in music videos: The same beat but a different drummer. *Journal of Communication, 36*(1), 94-106.

Craddock-Willis, A. (1991). Rap music and the Black musical tradition: A critical assessment. *Radical America, 23*(4), 29-38.

Dyson, M. E. (1993). *Reflecting Black: African-American cultural criticism.* Minneapolis: University of Minnesota Press.

Ebron, P. (1991). Rapping between men: Performing gender. *Radical America, 2*(4), 23-27.

Fiske, J. (1986). MTV: Post-structural post-modernism. *Journal of Communication Inquiry, 10*(1).

Fiske, J. (1987). *Television culture.* London: Routledge.

Flores, J. (1993). Puerto Rican and proud, Boyee! Rap, roots and America. *Centro de Estudios Puertorriquenos, 5*(1), 22-32.

Goodwin, A. (1993). Fatal distractions: MTV meets postmodern theory. In S. Frith, A. Goodwin, & L. Grossberg (Eds.), *Sound and vision.* New York: Routledge.

Henke, J. (1982, March 4). 1981: Another bad year for the record industry. *Rolling Stone,* p. 51.

Kaplan, E. A. (1987). *Rocking around the clock: Music television, postmodernism and consumer culture.* London: Methuen.

Lewis, L. (1990). *Gender politics and MTV: Voicing the difference.* Philadelphia: Temple University Press.

Levy, S. (1993, December 8). Ad nauseum: How MTV sells out rock and roll. *Rolling Stone,* pp. 30-37, 74-79.

Light, A. (1991). About a salary or reality?—Rap's recurrent conflict. *South Atlantic Quarterly, 90*(4), 855-870.

Mercer, K. (1993). Monster metaphors: Notes on Michael Jackson's *Thriller.* In S. Frith, A. Goodwin, & L. Grossberg (Eds.), *Sound and vision* (pp. 93-108). New York: Routledge.

Pelka, P. (1991, Winter). Dreamworlds: How the media abuses women: Interview with Sut Jhally. *On the Issues, 21.*

Peterson-Lewis, S., & Chennault, S. A. (1986, Winter). Black artists' music videos: Three success strategies. *Journal of Communication,* pp. 107-114.

Tate, G. (1992). *Flyboy in the buttermilk: Essays on contemporary America.* New York: Simon & Schuster.

Toop, D. (1991). *Rap attack 2: African rap to global hip hop* (rev. ed.). New York: Serpent's Tail.

Vincent, R. C. (1989). Clio's consciousness raised? Portrayal of women in rock videos reexamined. *Journalism Quarterly, 66,* 155-160.

Wallace, M. (1990, November). Women rap back. *Ms.,* 60-61.

Walser, R. (1993). Forging masculinity: Heavy metal sound and images of gender. In S. Frith, A. Goodwin, & L. Grossberg (Eds.), *Sound and vision* (pp. 153-181). New York: Routledge.

55

A Post-Modernist Moment

1980s Commercial Culture and the Founding of MTV

JOHN PETTEGREW

. . . As the sociologist Daniel Bell has shown in his valuable work on modernism, both twentieth-century secular culture and industrial capitalism have grown from the same ethic of self gratification and consumption. Advertising brought the two even closer together, using artistic innovation and experiment to catch the eye of the consumer. But while twentieth-century art has been continuously appropriated by advertising, many of the producers and distributers of that art tried to work apart from and oftentimes against the reach of commercialism—(along with political subversion) that is what has been meant by "cultural radicalism" or "counterculture." Post-modernism signifies the end of this ideal of autonomy from the dominant institutions of American business and commerce. More than anything else the concept marks the adjustment of art to the commercial interests of a mature capitalist society.[1]

SELLING AN AUDIENCE

MTV's success in commercial television depended on achieving three interrelated goals. First, to establish the content of its programming the

NOTE: Excerpts reprinted from *Journal of American Culture*, Vol. 15, No. 4 (1992), by permission of the editor.

station needed to make connections with the rock music industry. This was accomplished rather easily. The recording business had been experiencing a serious slump in the late-1970s, so many record companies welcomed the added exposure of their performers through a music television station. By the time telecasting began in August 1981, Arista, MCA, Polygram and other major companies had agreed to supply MTV with music videos at no cost. The investment paid off. Record sales increased dramatically and, in general, the added dimension of television stimulated greater attention to pop music. MTV not only advertised albums, but it also developed a new form of entertainment. MTV quickly rivaled FM radio as the leading medium for promoting new talent; mega-stars Michael Jackson and Madonna, among others, made their names on MTV. By the mid-1980s, record company executives would consider the station one of the most important links to America's youth culture.[2]

MTV's second challenge was convincing cable operators to distribute its programming to American viewers. The station began in only 1.5 million homes, as many local cable operators were reluctant to include a 24-hour music video channel in their package of cable stations. So MTV executives decided to skip over the operators and promote the station by contacting viewers through leaflets, television commercials and other advertising. Tom Freston, the station's vice president of marketing, has said that with this strategy he hoped "to show cable operators that people were willing to subscribe to basic cable in order to get MTV." The key phrase in the direct-response marketing campaign was "I Want My MTV," words that encouraged viewers to contact their cable companies and demand the latest in television programming. Most operators got the message and included music television in their service. Within a year the station increased its viewership ten-fold—10.7 million homes had MTV by 1982 and that number grew to 18.9 million homes after another year.[3]

The third and most important key to MTV's success was the sale of advertising time on the station. Even after record companies supplied music videos and cable operators agreed to distribute its programming, MTV's long-term success in commercial television depended on turning a profit for its corporate backers. This last goal was emphasized in January of 1981, when MTV founder and future president Robert Pittman met with the chairmen of Warner Amex Cable Communications, the station's parent company. As creator of MTV's programming, Pittman would have to develop a format that attracted corporate sponsors; and what they wanted, of course, was a steady national audience for their commercials. In other words, MTV needed to sell its audience: it had to be able to guarantee corporate advertisers both a certain section of the American viewing public and that group's attention to commercial messages while watching MTV.[4]

... Pittman felt that to draw viewers and advertisers away from network television he had to create a complete on-screen "environment" of which music videos would only be part. Pittman began building this environment by looking closely at the station's target market; before being sold to corporate advertisers, the audience became the subject of considerable attention and research. Pittman explained that he first liked "to go in and study the market and then build the creative elements once you've learned what is happening, as opposed to coming out with a wonderful creative idea and then trying to find a market." The audience he wanted for MTV was those most interested in pop music—the 13-to-35-year olds of "middle America." Accordingly, Pittman focused on trends in rock music, television, Hollywood and parts of New York's art and street scene and then pieced together MTV's format based on his findings.[5]

Pittman called his strategy "zero-based" programming and he turned out to be quite good at it. Or at least corporate advertisers thought so. By 1985, 23 of the top 25 network advertisers had bought time on MTV. Pepsi Cola and Ford Motor Company were the first major accounts in 1981, followed by others like Proctor and Gamble, General Foods, Dr. Pepper, Wendy's, Swatch, U.S. Navy, Doritos, Honda, Miller Beer, Quaker Oats, Nabisco and AMC. What advertisers liked most about MTV was the station's ability to deliver its target audience. MTV had connected with "the most difficult to reach of all audiences," as New York advertising executive Howard Nass said, "those elusive 24-to-34 year olds." Another New York advertising executive agreed: "MTV is the perfect medium for reaching teens and young adults, and that's the beauty of it all."[6]

The ability to deliver an audience also meant large profits for MTV and Warner Communications. After earning just $7 million in advertising revenue in its first eighteen months, MTV took in $25 million in 1983. That amount more than doubled to $54 million the next year and by 1985 MTV made $96 million in advertising. And, finally, with MTV's success came some security in commercial television and a lasting connection to its target market. "I think we are now institutionalized to a certain extent," Pittman concluded in 1985. "Today we're pretty much a fixture in the youth culture, pretty much the way rock radio was for 20-25 years."[7]

CORPORATE HEGEMONY

. . . In unraveling the implications of MTV's connection with corporate America, it is best to begin with the point that the station's format went further than anything else on television in breaking down the distinction between commercial and program. Advertisers looked at MTV and knew they were getting a viewing environment in which it made less and less sense to separate selling from entertainment and consumption from enjoyment. MTV's programming amounted to almost a complete context of selling. The music videos themselves were produced by the record companies as advertisements for performers' albums. Also, through the playing of its own logos and short videos and the announcement of its special programming, MTV spent a considerable amount of time selling itself. And, of course, MTV's format included a substantial number of corporate commercials: by 1985 the station spent 40% of its time advertising over 800 brand names.[8] . . .

But in considering how viewers watched MTV in the early-1980s, how do we know that advertisers got what they wanted? It is difficult to deny some element of autonomy from advertising, beginning with the viewer's ability to change channels during commercials. Some critics have even talked about a "post-modern hero" of the 1980s: an ad-wise child of television who gained autonomy through ironic disbelief of what appears on the screen. Such a person made creative use of the remote control, as historian Jackson Lears emphasizes, "flipping channels and creating a fluid sense of self that can slip through the boundaries of suburban convention."[9] Whether heroic or not, most people raised in the electronic age have developed a certain expertise in watching television. At the least they have learned to rely on a sense of knowing better, an attitude that offers some protection from the deluge of commercial messages one encounters each day.

It is also possible that viewers could have extracted subjective meaning from MTV's early programming despite its commercial content. As the station replaced FM radio as the newest source of pop music, viewers started to expect music videos to preserve the rebellious edge that had always been part of rock culture. MTV tried to develop this sense of subversion. The station aired special programs like "The Post-Modern MTV" and "120 Minutes" of "underground music," emphasizing its contact with "avant-garde culture." In 1983 Pittman hired a "talent and relations staff," which would "stay on the street all night, in every club, and hear every buzz."[10] And, for some, the station undoubtedly delivered important change through new music and performance. Madonna probably reached the greatest number of MTV viewers in the 1980s. Her multi-media persona encouraged others to explore the possibilities of self mastery, and many of her videos challenged women to press contemporary conventions of sexuality and feminine understanding. To be sure, Madonna's politics were not a matter of social protest. At best, she added an element of personal feminism to popular culture by offering a positive example of self fashioning—one of the higher ideals of art in the 1980s.[11]

. . . Corporate influence was not complete: the meaning an individual got from MTV was at the juncture of commercial purpose and viewer subjectivity. But while viewers disbelieved, advertisers knew that resistance was really only partial.[12] MTV's would-be rebels were also full-time consumers and corporate advertisers banked on the fact that patterns of consumption could be influenced through commercial programming.

The more subtle point of corporate hegemony was that MTV had become a perfectly integrated text for commercial appeals to consumers' senses. The station not only aired commercials that looked like the rest of its programming, but MTV had quickly developed into an important engine of 1980s' consumerism: its nexus to pop music and art put it into an ideal position to provide the styling changes necessary for a culture based on consumption. As video artist Rebecca Blake said in 1985, "The most valuable aspect of MTV is the acculturation process that brings together youth, culture, street and fashion."[13] By supporting MTV, advertising connected itself to cultural change, believing that a sense of newness or even rebellion would be associated with its product.

MODELLING THE VIEWER

In buying time on MTV, corporate advertisers were told that their audience was especially receptive to commercial messages because of the particular way the station made use of the aesthetics of television. Advertisements sunk in on MTV because its format exaggerated the fast pace, fluid look of television—an environment already suited for 15-30 second commercials of the early 1980s. Pittman discussed this point in a broad-ranging speech he gave to the American Association of Advertising Agencies in 1985. . . .

. . . Pittman focused on how corporations could take advantage of his audience of "TV generation" viewers. "You in the advertising industry understand the value of a non-narrative message. As a result, the ways in which you gain the viewer's attention and persuade him to buy have changed dramatically." For commercials to fit into MTV's format, they should "move very quickly with quick cuts, no transitions." Today's commercials, Pittman stated, should emphasize this non-narrative mode and "create a feeling for the product rather than a logical argument filled with facts and claims." Pittman assured the advertisers that "if you can get their emotions going, forget their logic, you've got 'em."[14] Of course Pittman was not really telling his audience anything they did not already know. Advertisers had been using the visual vocabulary of quick cuts and sense impressions since the early 1960s. The presentation is important, though, for illustrating Pittman's understanding of how MTV could create the perfect medium for advertising based on "mood and emotion." Pittman concluded his speech by stating how the station offered a "pure environment" for commercial messages—an around-the-clock, circular flow of interchangeably artistic and commercial appeals to the viewer's senses.[15] . . .

By the mid-1980s the people of MTV had learned to use the station's logos and other in-house produced clips to define the channel's intended contribution to American culture. As a central strategy of its programming, MTV tried to create a model viewer—a contemporary, in-tune individual who had the right attitude and sense of how the station affected his or her life. In a 1986 segment that worked as a testimonial for the station, MTV interviewed a young man, a "performance artist," and asked what the channel meant to him. "When I first saw music videos," the man answered, "I was mesmerized. I just watched it for hours and hours, because one thing was coming after the next." He explained, "I liked being taken to all these different places, all these different people, all this information being thrown at you." As the camera started to move quickly around his head and the background music picked up, the man spoke more excitedly: "I like to watch anything that is linked right into the culture and that is happening right now." He concluded, "this is really the wave of the future."

In another 30-second spot entitled "History Lesson," a group of three young people talk about pop music as they make dinner; the video is shot in black-and-white documentary style. After the oldest of the three complains that today's "music is all mindless," the youngest expresses MTV's message by asking "since when is mindless bad?" She continues, "You can be mindless and it's O.K. You don't have to be mindless all the time." The video ends with the words "Meaningful Mindlessness" super-imposed on the screen.

Many of MTV's spots assured viewers that a certain level of freedom and irresponsibility could be found in its programming. To be "mesmerized" by the station was to separate one's self from the more serious or the more mindful aspects of life. More specifically, MTV worked to create a split in the viewer's identity between the hard-working, rational individual of the day and the free, impulsive self of the night. This strategy was developed fully in 1985, with the introduction of Randy of the Redwoods, MTV's on-screen personality. Wearing frizzy, uncombed hair, a head band made of rag, over-sized sunglasses, MTV's Randy is a caricature of a 60s hippie and the apparent alter-ego of the station's model viewer. In one 30-second spot produced by MTV in early-1987, a man in pajamas looks into the bathroom mirror and sees Randy looking back with a smile on his face (the same actor plays both parts). "Get out of here," says the man gravely. Randy responds nonsensically, "You know Hawaiians don't shave." The next scene shows the business man getting ready for work and Randy hovering over him annoyingly. As the man starts to put on his tie, Randy warns jokingly, "That's the wrong color for a power tie." And finally, as the man—now dressed in his corporate best—opens his front door to leave for his job he warns Randy that, "When I come back I want you gone." Randy responds, "Oh right, where am I supposed to go, Mars?" After the corporate man is out the door the camera focuses closely on Randy's face. He says coyly of his other, "I like that guy a lot—not!" The spot ends with MTV's logo flashing in Randy's sunglasses.

This split in the personality of MTV's model viewer is a powerful illustration of Daniel Bell's conception of a "cultural contradiction of capitalism." The freedom and irresponsibility of MTV's post-modernist programming actually supported American corporatism and its ethic of consumption. "On the one hand," Bell writes, "the business corporation wants an individual to work hard, pursue a career, accept delayed gratification—to be in the crude sense an organization man. And yet," Bell continues, "in its products and advertisements, the corporation promotes pleasure, instant joy, relaxing and letting go." MTV strengthened consumer capitalism, then, by enacting this disjuncture of the self. The message for the viewer became clear, as Bell concludes about late-twentieth century culture, "One is to be 'straight' by day and a 'swinger' by night."[16] The corporation is served by both halves of the postmodernist self. And while MTV clearly sided with Randy the "anti-establishment" figure, the station still reinforced the corporate enterprise by leading the viewer back to its advertising. Randy was a burnt-out version of a once free self—the embodiment of 1980s' cultural stasis. Unable to leave the house, Randy finds meaning in his connection with MTV. The viewer—who identified with Randy's humor and irreverence towards the business executive—was reassured about MTV; corporate interests seemed subordinated by the station's critical view of big business. But that position only worked to legitimize further the station's vast commercial programming. With the viewer's confidence in MTV secure, more legitimacy was given to the hundreds of corporate messages the station played each day.[17]

FREE ASSOCIATION OF MEANING

The deep structure of commercial influence in post-modernist culture had a great impact on the potential meaning an individual could receive from art and entertainment in the 1980s. One of the most disturbing aspects of this was the growing ability of advertising to attach itself to other meanings in popular culture, as in the corporate music videos played on MTV. It should be emphasized that the original advertising strategy behind corporate videos was not so much to use the star's name as an endorsement of the product, but rather to have the music and imagery attract and hold the viewer's attention long enough for a connection to be made to the brand name. "Endorsements are old hat," Roger Enrico, former President of Pepsi USA and head of the company's 1986-1987 $50 million advertising campaign featuring Michael Jackson, said, "It's not that Pepsi is Michael Jackson's favorite soft drink," he continued, adding that the performer would not drink any beverage with caffeine. "We're trying to captivate people so they won't switch channels or zap the commercial." Enrico concludes, "our notion is entertainment."[18]

What was lost in corporate entertainment of the 1980s was the meaning that drove performers to create the music in the first place. Individual meaning was freely associated from the personal (and potentially political) to the commercial. Of course this association was not "free" in the monetary sense of the word—advertisers paid dearly for it; but, rather, free in how easily meaning could be transferred from one context to the next. In 1987, MTV aired a Seven-Up commercial that featured a young man enjoying its soft drink during a rain storm. As the man tilts his head into the rain with delight, the music of a South African tribal band plays joyously in the background. The effect for Seven-Up was perfect: young urban dweller consumes familiar product while recognizing the soothing voice and sound of a distant and exotic culture. The social and political realities of Apartheid were not eliminated as much as subordinated to the sensation the viewer received from the combination of imagery and new music. Seven-Up depended on some sort of viewer understanding of Black South Africans as being different from himself, as having a quality of otherness; but no chance existed for any rudimentary political consciousness to develop. It became enough to recognize simply the cultural difference and then disregard the implications of the song during the subsequent, unrelated commercial or music video. The potential meaning of the music was exchanged for its ability to capture the attention of consumers of the soft drink.

This process of free association of meaning is best seen in the Nike shoe company's 1986 television commercial featuring the Beatle's song "Revolution." The 30-second, black-and-white documentary style commercial shows young athletes intercut with sports heroes like Michael Jordan and John McEnroe, while John Lennon sings, "You say you want a revolution." Once again, one might have momentarily thought of the past significance of the song, but the viewer was then taken away by the fast-paced imagery of the athletes and their shoes. Some people were furious with the release of the commercial: "When 'Revolution' came out in 1968 I was getting tear-gassed in the streets of Madison," *L.A. Reader*'s rock critic Chris Morris said. "That song is part of the sound track of my political life. It bugs the hell out of me that it has been turned into a shoe ad." Others, however, subordinated the political and cultural aim of Lennon's song to different interests. While explaining why she allowed Nike to use her husband's music, Yoko Ono said that "John's songs should not be a part of glorified Martyrdom. They ought to be enjoyed by kids today." Ono added that the Nike "ad is a way to communicate John's songs to them [the young people], to make it part of their lives instead of the distant past." Meaning is transformed from the experience of the 1960s to encouraging the purchase of Nike's product. "Sports shoes are part of a fitness consciousness," Ono concluded, "that is actually better for your body than some of the things we were doing in the 1960s."[19]

As Ono's statements demonstrate, free association of meaning finally led to a practice of forgetting. Combinations of sound and image were valued more for their ability to titillate than to posit a connection to history or social experience. MTV, like many other texts of the 1980s, created a surface-like quality of culture—a "seamless web" of short and appealing impressions that cut across individual perception.[20] This sense of surface played itself out in Michael Jackson's 1987 music video "Man in the Mirror." As the video begins, the message seems clear enough: Jackson sings, "Gonna make a change for once in my life" as newsreel-footage flashes images of riots in South Africa and starving African children with bloated stomachs and flies crawling across their faces. Jackson responds to this sight by singing that he "sees the kids in the street without enough to eat, who am I to be blind pretending not to see their needs?" As the tempo of the song picks up the viewer sees shorter clips of Lech Welesa and Desmond Tutu crying. Jackson then sings the chorus of the song, "I'm stuck with the man in the mirror, I'm asking him to change his ways. . . ." And finally the pace of the film clips becomes so quick that the viewer loses perception of the words to the song in an effort to keep up with the flow of the disparate imagery of the Kent State shootings, a Ku Klux Klan rally . . . John Kennedy, John Lennon, the Robert Kennedy assassination . . . a mushroom cloud from a nuclear bomb . . . Mohatma Ghandi . . . an African child eating a Pop Tart and . . . an image of a Black child wearing a Live-Aid t-shirt.

MTV aired Jackson's "Man in the Mirror" video in the winter of 1987, the same time the station played a *Life* magazine commercial in which Ray Charles sings "America the Beautiful" in time with a series of the publication's well-known photographs of national events and figures. In both the Jackson video and the *Life* commercial, once important representations of recent history lost their referents in social and political thought; the fast-paced sequences of images offered the viewer no chance of finding any sort of depth of understanding. The attitude of "mindlessness" prompted by MTV's early programming is one of the most suggestive metaphors of post-modernism and of the 1980s American culture in general. It describes the random, arbitrary nature of an aesthetic based on sense impressions and also the inability of art to relate down to a personal, cognitive level of meaning. The condition was not all encompassing in the 1980s, but it became pervasive enough for many people to refer to a sense of disengagement or disenfranchisement from American culture. As the novelist Brett Easton Ellis said of his "Twenty Something" generation, "contemporary subversiveness" was all "on the surface" in the 1980s and therefore culture did not "play the same role in our lives that it did for previous generations."[21] To recognize this post-modernist crisis of art as something basic to the 1980s gives historians a way to distance themselves from the last decade and it should encourage all of us to move past its values of irresponsibility and forgetting.

NOTES

1. Bell (1976). . . .

2. Paskowski (1985). In addition to the general increase in record sales after the founding of MTV, there is other evidence that the station influenced music purchases. One study of MTV viewers in 1984 found that 46% said they buy more albums and 62% said they are more excited about music since they began receiving MTV. Another survey found 62% of the MTV viewers saying that MTV was an important influence on their record-buying decisions (Paskowski, 1985, p. 66). Today, it is not uncommon for record companies to forego FM radio initially and introduce a song through MTV. As Mark Di Dia, general manager of the record company Def American, says of marketing the new music: "MTV is the single most important factor on your side. You still need radio, but if MTV's on your side, it's the equivalent of 100 radio stations playing your song" (Browne, 1991).

3. Paskowski (1985, pp. 64-66); Silverman (1985, p. 87). MTV continued to grow in popularity throughout the early 1980s. By the end of 1985 MTV was available in 29 million American homes ("Salescall," 1985).

4. Paskowski (1985, p. 64). . . .

5. Pittman quote from Paskowski (1985, pp. 64, 66).

6. "Salescall" (1985, p. 100), Paskowski (1985, p. 67). The Madison Avenue trade papers repeatedly made this point about MTV and its unusual hold on teenagers and young adults. Knowing that they were among the freest-spending consumers, advertisers have always been after this group but unable to pin them down because of their irregular viewing habits and suspicion of commercial messages on television.

7. Motavalli (1986).

8. Aufderheide (1986, p. 5).

9. Lears (1989, p. 59). In keeping with the tenor of his article, Lears describes this "post-modernist hero" in only an ironic sense.

10. Pittman quoted in Paskowski (1985, p. 68).

11. While recognizing this potential of significant meaning in MTV it is important to keep in mind what was also missing from the station's early programming. MTV played a very limited range of music videos in the early 1980s. Rap was the most glaring omission along with other types of African-American music; Michael Jackson was one of the only black performers that MTV carried during its first years. Despite its self-conscious appeal to subversion, MTV's programming was circumscribed by the corporate interest of drawing a large audience of "middle American" consumers. MTV wanted to titillate but also make sure it did not take any risks and lose a chunk of its audience. As Pittman put it in adopting the creed of advertising, "We always program one step ahead of that crowd [of 'middle America'], but only one step ahead so we're still accessible" (Paskowski, 1985, p. 68).

12. The cartoonist Matt Groening offered a wonderful illustration of the knowing advertisers have in a 1990 episode of *The Simpsons*. In one scene Bart is reading the advertisements on the back page of a comic book with complete cynicism: "yeah right . . . give me a break . . . no way . . . you gotta be kidding." But then, finally: "Oh wow, a spy camera. Neat man!" The point is that despite self-conscious skepticism, people do make purchasing decisions based on advertising.

13. Blake cited in Heim (1988, p. 16). An important concept running throughout the discussion of MTV and American commercial culture is *hegemony,* which I define as the way that corporatism maintains its dominant position in society through a process of legitimation to the public.

14. Pittman (1985).

15. Pittman (1985).

16. Bell (1976, pp. 71-72).

17. This hegemonic process repeated itself throughout MTV's early programming. For example, in 1986 the station produced and aired parodies of Nissan automobile and Wang computer spots—commercials that were generally acknowledged as being particularly offensive. While it may have seemed as if the station was trying to establish a critical distance from commercialism in general, the parodies only worked to separate MTV from especially obtrusive advertising and thereby reassure the viewer that its programming offered something better and more sophisticated.

18. Enrico cited in Hornblower (1986).

19. Morris and Ono cited in Weiner (1987).

20. "Seamless web" is from Lears (1987, p. 138). Surface is one of the most accepted metaphors of post-modernist criticism. Frederic Jameson (1984) probably makes the best use of it in his description of the "emergence of a new kind of flatness or depthlessness" as the "supreme formal feature of all the postmodernisms" (p. 60).

21. Ellis (1990). . . .

REFERENCES

Aufderheide, P. (1986). Music videos: The look of the sound. *Journal of Communications,* pp. 57-58. Reprinted in Gitlin, T. (Ed.). (1986). *Watching television* (pp. 111-135). New York: Pantheon.

Bell, D. (1976). *The cultural contradictions of capitalism.* New York: Basic Books.

Browne, D. (1991, July 28). Pop radio suffers a midlife crisis. *The New York Times.*

Ellis, B. E. (1990, December 2). The twenty somethings: Adrift in a pop landscape. *The New York Times.*

Heim, C. (1988, September 4). Tuning up music videos. *Chicago Tribune.*

Hornblower, M. (1986, May 29). Madison Avenue adapts to generation of skeptics. *Washington Post.*

Jameson, F. (1984, July/August). Postmodernism, or the cultural logic of late capitalism. *New Left Review,* pp. 53-92.

Lears, J. (1987, Spring). Uneasy courtship: Modern art and modern advertising. *American Quarterly, 39,* 133-155.

Lears, J. (1989, January 9, 16). Deride and conquer. *The Nation*, pp. 59-62.

Motavalli, J. (1986, September 15). Growing up with rock. *Cablevision*, pp. 26-37.

Paskowski, P. (1985, Spring). Everybody wants their MTV. *Marketing and Media Decisions*, pp. 61-68.

Pittman, R. (1985, May 27). MTV's lesson: We want what we want immediately. *Cablevision*.

Salescall. (1985, December). *Madison Avenue*.

Silverman, F. (1985, April). Getting back to basic. *Madison Avenue*.

Weiner, J. (1987, May 11). Beatle's buy-out. *The New Republic*, p. 14.

56

Form and Female Authorship in Music Video

LISA A. LEWIS

"Sexist and violent against women." That's the reputation that MTV has acquired since its inception in 1981 as America's 24-hour music video channel.[1] What with parents buying lock boxes to prevent music video viewing, and senators' wives on the trail of pornographic rock lyrics,[2] it's small wonder that women critics have been reluctant to speak up in its defense. Austin, my adopted home, has a proud and progressive musical heritage traditionally supportive of female musicians, yet when the local magazine that covers the music scene asked writer Brenda Sommer if she'd like to do a regular column on music video, she turned it down. *The Austin Chronicle* printed her explanation (Sommer, 1985, p. 9):

> You asked me to tell you why I couldn't review music videos for you. And I told you that I realized I couldn't because I didn't have anything nice to say about them.

It's true music video does bring together two cultural forms that have notorious histories as promulgators of female objectification—rock music and television imagery. And specific examples of women in chains, in caged boxes, and strewn across sets in skimpy leather outfits can certainly be called upon to justify such claims. But focusing on the sexist representations

---

NOTE: Excerpts reprinted from *Communication*, Vol. 9 (1987), by permission.

boxes, and strewn across sets in skimpy leather outfits can certainly be called upon to justify such claims. But focusing on the sexist representations present in many male videos overshadows an aggregate of videos produced for songs sung by female musicians and their popularity with female fans. . . . Music video's role in popularizing female musicians and in serving as the newest terrain for the negotiation of gender politics has been largely ignored, particularly by the academic press.[3]

. . . Exposure on MTV has and is contributing to an upsurge in female rock and roll musicianship. Female musicians are actively participating in making the music video form work in their interest, to assert their authority as producers of culture and to air their views on female genderhood. The generic emphasis in music video on using the song as a soundtrack, together with the centrality of the musician's image in the video, formally support the construction of female authorship. The result is a body of video texts that refer to an explicitly female experience of life, addressing a gendered spectatorship even as they maintain a generic consistency that secures their broad appeal.

First, consider the importance of MTV in providing female rock musicians the opportunity to gain the audience recognition and industry backing that women interested in music have historically been denied.[4] In the years leading up to the start of music video programming, female rock musicians were struggling for recognition both as vocalists (the traditional female niche), and as instrumentalists and composers. The contemporary women's movement in the late 1960s and early 1970s provided momentum for change, but the early punk movement in Britain at the end of the 1970s was equally, if not more, important to female musicians. Although punk emerged essentially as a working-class male subculture, Hebdige (1983) makes the point that punk included a minority of female participants who aggressively tried to carve out a specifically female form of expression, a sharp contrast to the usual subsuming of women by subcultural phallocentrism:

> Punk propelled girls onto the stage and once there, as musicians and singers, they systematically transgressed the codes governing female performance. . . . These performers have opened up a new space for women as active participators in the production of popular music. (pp. 83-85)

Punk's advocacy of "defiant amateurism" (Swartley, 1982, p. 28) undermined the devalued status of the amateur musician, granting women unprecedented access to musical information and audiences.

Under the capitalist economic system that operates rock and roll as a commercial enterprise, commercial distribution commands the largest audiences and the financial backing to produce music. Indeed the aspirations of most rock musicians, women included, lie with commercial distribution. But in 1979, just when new female musicians were preparing to break into the music scene, the U.S. recording industry went into a tailspin as the combined effects of a sluggish economy, home-taping, and the diversification of the home entertainment market began to be felt. Any individual or group without a proven track record, and this especially applied to women musicians, was hard pressed to win a record company contract, an essential step in the quest for a large audience. That began to change, however, in the summer of 1981 with the introduction of music video programming.[5] . . .

MTV initiated an upward spiral for many new and unknown bands and vocalists, women musicians included. As album and singles sales began to rise to all time highs, in some cases even surpassing industry sales records, financing and promotion brought new female faces to MTV. A national audience rewarded their favorites by buying more records, thereby catapulting the new and unknowns to star status virtually overnight.

In 1982, the Go-Gos became the only all-female vocal and instrumental group ever to make the top 10. Their first album, *Beauty and the Beat*, was also the first album by an all-women rock band to hit number one on the charts. That same year, *Ms.* magazine ran an article entitled "At Last . . . Enough Women Rockers to Pick and Choose" (Brandt, 1982). Although many women gained recognition as instrumentalists, the real success story was in the musical category where women had traditionally excelled, that of vocalists. But seldom has success come so big and so fast as it did on MTV.

The 1985 winner of the top Grammy award, Tina Turner, was a woman without a record deal one year, and with a top hit single the next. Cyndi Lauper's debut album, *She's So Unusual*, remained in the top 30 for more than 60 weeks, having sold close to 4 million copies in the U.S. alone. Lauper's album produced four Top 5 hit singles, a new record for a female singer. In a February 1985 *Rolling Stone* Readers' Poll, Lauper was ranked first in the category for "New Artist," second to Tina Turner in the "Female Vocalist" category, and while a distant third to Bruce Springsteen and Prince as "Artist of the Year," she outranked Michael Jackson. Madonna, the newest female vocalist success story, sold 3.5 million copies of her album *Like a Virgin* in just 14 weeks. The album was "triple platinum" before its artist had even set foot on a touring stage, the principal promotion device before the age of music video. Female musicians such as Pat Benatar, Chaka Khan, and the Pointer Sisters have all reached a million in sales with recent albums.[6]

There is a dialectic operating with respect to female musicianship, MTV distribution of their videos, female fan viewing, and the creation of woman-identified videos. Music videos of female vocalists shown on MTV give those women the exposure they need to become popular music stars. The popularity of the musicians and their videos among fans provides clout to musicians looking to use woman-identified videos as vehicles of expression and breaks ground for fellow female musicians. The generic conventions of form and content that have developed to define the MTV product (and music video in general) structurally enable female musicians to promote a woman-identified image. Music video form and female authorship work hand in hand to make woman-identified videos possible.

Conventionally, music video is organized by the use of a pre-recorded popular music song (which usually contains lyrics) as the soundtrack of the video, and by the use of the musician in key on-screen roles. The use of a musical track as the video soundtrack involves two distinct modes of production, the production of the song and the subsequent production of the video. Female musician authorship of music videos, therefore, takes shape along these two axes.

The relations of production of the song tend to assign authorship to the vocalist, particularly the responsibility for the lyrical content, despite the fact that the division of labor in the production of pop songs often means the vocalist has neither written the song nor its instrumentation. Expanding on this tendency for vocalists to be handed authorship on a platter, female musicians have employed several tactics to insure that their authorship takes a woman-identified form, to counter-balance the fact that they must often work with male writers' lyrics. Neither Tina Turner nor Cyndi Lauper, for example, wrote the songs that have made them famous, yet each has won female authorship through their vocalization style, their rewriting of selected lyrical phrases, and their manipulation of their images in the promotional press.

In constructing her authorship of the song "What's Love Got to Do With It?," Tina Turner concentrated on vocalization style. She self-consciously describes in the fan magazine *Record* how she made the award winning song her own by reworking its musical rendition:

> The song was this sweet, little thing. Can you imagine me singing like Diana Ross or Barbra Streisand, trying to sound velvety and smooth? I really fought. Eventually, we roughened it out instrumentally and I added some (rock) phrasing, and we changed the song's attitude and got a hit. I have input, not just in song selection but in treatment too. I'll never be a musician, but I know what's right. (Mehler, 1984, p. 20)

Turner's self-deprecating assessment of herself as a non-musician at the end of the statement is in line with what Rieger (1985) suggests is a historically-constructed myth that positions performance outside of creative practice. The false distinction between performance and composition as it relates to creative contributions is in effect responsible for the disproportionately high number of female vocalists compared to female lyricists and composers: "Women have always only been allowed a first foothold in those areas where creativity was considered to be of secondary importance" (p. 136). In fact, the example provided by Turner reveals musical rendition to be not only a creative process but a politically empowered one.

A promotional blitz, timed to coincide with the release of Turner's album, *Private Dancer* (on which "What's Love Got to Do With It?" appears), publicized the previously hidden details of her years as a battered wife and personal slave to her ex-music partner and husband, Ike Turner. The biographical information functions to turn the lyrics of her songs into autobiographical statements. Stanzas of "What's Love Got to Do With It?" may not have been written by Turner, but her authorial voice is created as a consequence of the fan's attempt to reconcile the text with the extratextual information about the singer's personal history:

> *It may seem to you,*
> *that I'm acting confused*
> *when you're close to me.*
> *If I tend to look dazed,*
> *I read it someplace,*
> *I've got cause to be.*[7]

Quotes by Turner in the press saying things such as "I've never sung anything I couldn't relate to" (Mehler, 1984, p. 21) lend credibility to auto-biographical readings of the songs she sings. In fact, Turner's appeal to women seems largely based on the notion of experience. Her ability to survive and come out on top after many years of male harassment and lack of professional recognition makes her a fitting female hero. Her courageous image is only underscored for women by the rumble of reactionary male attraction to counter-statements by Ike Turner such as the feature article in the new music magazine, *Spin,* entitled "Ike's Story": "Yeah, I hit her, but I didn't hit her more than the average guy beats his wife" (Kiersh, 1985, p. 41). . . .

It is the conventional usage of the song as soundtrack in music video that formally extends female musician authorship to the video text. In videos that feature a narrative scenario, the soundtrack provided by a female vocalist can operate like a narrator's omnipotent voiceover guiding the visual action. Sometimes she manages to literally put words in the mouths of other characters (sometimes male) through the use of a common music video device whereby a selected lyrical phrase is lip-synched as if it were dialogue. In "Girls Just Want to Have Fun," the burly ex-wrestler Lou Albano, as Cyndi Lauper's father, lip-synchs Cyndi's lyric, "What you gonna do with your life?" as she is shown pinning his arm behind his back in a self-reflexive wrestling maneuver. The technique in this scene, by re-placing the father's scolding voice with the daughter's, parodies and under-mines the authority of the father, and by symbolic extension patriarchy itself. . . .

Vocalists are privileged actors in the videos because they play lead roles and lip-synch most of the lyrics. Feminist critics, in their desire for female musician parity with male musicians in the broad spectrum of divisions of labor in music, have sometimes pointed to and criticized the assignment of female musicians to the category of vocalist. In music video, however, the prerogative rests most squarely on the shoulders of the vocalist, making female musicians' traditional role into an asset. . . .

Many female musicians have proved to be quite adept at manipulating elements of visual performance in their video act, thereby utilizing music video as an additional authorship tool. In "What's Love Got to Do With It?," the gestures, eye contact with the camera and with other characters, and the walking style of Tina Turner add up to a powerful and aggressive on-screen presence. Her miniskirt, show of leg, and spike heels could operate to code her as a spectacle of male desire. Instead, the image she projects struggles for a different signification. It's easier to imagine the spikes as an offensive weapon than as a sexual lure or allusion to her vulnerability. Turner's control over her own body and interactions with others in the video, particularly with men, encourages a revaluation of her revealing clothes and high heels from indices of her objectification to signs of her own pleasure in herself.[8] Similarly, in "Girls Just Want to Have Fun," Cyndi Lauper's kinetic body movement mediates against the voyeur's gaze. Almost constantly in motion, Lauper's choreographed performance fills the frame, her gyrating arms and legs stealing space away from men on city streets in location footage. . . .

. . . Woman-identified videos rely heavily on images that signal both the appropriation of male leisure forms and practices, and the celebration of specifically female ones. In this way, motifs based on street symbolism and leisure themes can become powerful social commentaries for female audiences. This is the context in which feminists have made the refrain of "Girls Just Want to Have Fun" into a slogan. The song gets its hard edge from the audiences' reading of the music video's image content and the quality of Cyndi Lauper's look and performance.

Shots of a mother (played by Lauper's own mother) at her morning duties in the kitchen contrast with the Lauper character's role as her adolescent daughter who comes bounding into the kitchen after a wild night out. The mother, to express her distress over the daughter's disregard of appropriate feminine behavior, breaks an egg over her heart. A montage sequence of the daughter chattering on the phone with her many girlfriends celebrates a girl leisure practice which is usually ridiculed in the public media. The bouncing Lauper then leads her band of girlfriends through New York City streets in a frenzied snake dance, a carnivalesque display that turns women's experience of the street upsidedown. Their arms reaching out for more and more space, the women push through a group of male construction workers who function as symbols of female harassment on the street. The image of men cowering in the wake of the women's dance epitomizes female fantasies of streets without danger or fear, and women's desire for an unmitigated release from socially-imposed restrictions on female bodily expression. The men, their threatening status overturned, are brought back to the daughter's home to experience female fun: dancing with wild abandon in one's bedroom. . . .

The multiplicity of authorship opportunities for female musicians and the strong woman identified statements that MTV and the music video genre have made possible should by now be apparent. This is no small accomplishment in a mass medium largely closed to personal expressions from a female perspective and to portrayals of female fantasies of the overthrow of male domination and the forming of alliances among women, and where creative control over production by women is severely limited. Far from being the absolute bastion of male desire, as some critics argue, MTV is providing a unique space for the articulation of gender politics by female artists and audiences.

NOTES

1. MTV is an advertiser-supported cable television channel dedicated to the programming of record company-produced music video clips for a target audience aged 12 to 34. It premiered on August 1, 1981. Its owner/operator is the Warner Amex Satellite Entertainment Company, a joint venture between Warner Communications and American Express. In 1985, MTV was sold to Viacom, a television syndication company. Examples of popular criticism that describe music video as sexist and violent include Levy (1983) and Barol (1985).

2. The co-founders of the Parents Music Resource Center, organized in protest of "pornographic" rock music lyrics, includes Susan Baker, wife of Treasury Secretary James Baker; Tipper Gore, wife of Senator Albert Gore (D-Tenn); and Ethelynn Stuckey, wife of Williamson Stuckey, a former representative from Florida. Hoping eventually to see the enactment of a system for rating records similar to the one used for rating movies, the Center won a lesser concession in August 1985 when 19 top record companies agreed to start printing warnings of sexually explicit lyrics on album and music video packaging. Although male musicians, such as Prince and Twisted Sister, are most under fire, Cyndi Lauper's song "She Bop" has been targeted because of its reference to female autoeroticism. For more information see "The Women Behind the Movement" (1985).

3. Frith and McRobbie (1978/1979) provide an early exploration of gender and rock music. McRobbie's work on girl subcultures (1976, 1980) and dance (1984) is pertinent to the analysis of music video and female audiences although it has not been used as such. Steward and Garratt (1984) trace the history of female musician involvement in rock and roll and provocatively suggest ways that pop's success depends on female fan support. Brown and Campbell (1984) focus on gender in their content analysis of music video, but without attention to female musicians or woman-identified videos. Holdstein (1985) provides a textual reading of Donna Summer's "She Works Hard for the Money," arguing against a feminist interpretation. Kaplan has explored female representation in music video in several papers (1985a, 1985b, 1985c, 1985d).

4. Rieger (1985) dates the institutional exclusion of women from musical composition and performance back to the beginning of these institutions themselves. Churches in the middle ages made it an official practice to bar females from participation in liturgical rites, effectively creating a gender boundary to "high music" culture. Early educational institutions reserved musical training and opportunities primarily for their male students. Women's music-making was forced into popular culture forms, and, with respect to the formation of the bourgeoisie in the 18th century, into domestic space. Female piano playing and singing were designed as appropriate forms of musical expression for women and incorporated into the bourgeois woman's role in the family: "It was important to a man's prestige that his wife could entertain his guests with music, and of course a musical education for his daughter served as a good investment for an advantageous marriage" (p. 141). Music performed by women was conceived as a service provided for fathers, husbands, and children, not as a source of pleasure for themselves, or as a career direction, a means for making money. Prior to the influx of women, men were accustomed to performing music in the home. But as music in a domestic setting became associated with bourgeois female roles, men responded by establishing professional standards and devaluing the amateur status. The legacy of too little institutional support and the ideological attitude toward the suitability of musical expression for women form the basis for male-dominated musical forms today, including rock and roll.

5. The following sources enabled me to trace the decline of the record industry and to feel justified in crediting the start of music video cable distribution with its subsequent turnaround: Henke (1982), Hickling (1981), Kirkeby (1980), Loder and Pond (1982), Pond (1982), Sutherland (1980), and Wallace (1980).

6. Information about sales and rankings of female musicians were constructed from the following sources: Brandt (1982), Loder (1984), Miller et al. (1985), *Rolling Stone* (February 28, 1985), and Swartley (1982).

7. These are selected lyrics from "What's Love Got to Do With It?" Written by Terry Britten and G. Lyle, the song was recorded under the Capitol Records label. Copyright © 1984 by

Myaxe Music Ltd. & Good Single Music Ltd. Myaxe Music Ltd, published in U.S.A. by
Chappell & Co., Inc. International Copyright Secured. All rights reserved. Used by permission.

   8. The term "revaluation" is borrowed from the work of anthropologist Marshall Sahlins
(1981). In this regard, I have also found useful the discussions of "active" signs in Volosinov
(1973) and de Lauretis (1984). Another example of Tina Turner's attempt to revalue signs that
have acquired an association with male desire is her adoption of the song "Legs," popularized
by a ZZ Top video, for her concert stage act.

REFERENCES

Barol, B. (1985, March 4). Women in a video cage. *Newsweek,* p. 54.

Brandt, P. (1982, September). At last . . . Enough women rockers to pick and choose.
   Ms., pp. 110-116.

Brown, J. D., & Campbell, K. C. (1984, January). *The same beat but a different drummer:
   Race and gender in music videos.* Paper presented at the University Film and Video
   Association Conference, Harrisonburg, VA.

de Lauretis, T. (1984). *Alice doesn't: Feminism, semiotics, and cinema.* Bloomington:
   Indiana University Press.

Frith, S., & McRobbie, A. (1978/1979). Rock and sexuality. *Screen Education, 29,* 3-19.

Hebdige, D. (1983). Posing threats, striking poses: Youth, surveillance, and display.
   SubStance, 37/38, 66-68.

Henke, J. (1982, March 4). 1981: Another bad year for the record industry. *Rolling
   Stone,* p. 51.

Hickling, M. (1981, October 15). Record sales hold steady with last year's. *Rolling
   Stone,* p. 52.

Holdstein, D. H. (1985, February). Music video: Messages and structures. *Jump Cut,*
   pp. 13-14.

Kaplan, E. A. (1985a). A postmodern play of the signifier? Advertising, pastiche and
   schizophrenia in music television. In R. Collins et al. (Eds.), *Proceedings of the
   international television conference.* London: British Film Institute.

Kaplan, E. A. (1985b, March). *History, the historical spectator and gender address in music
   television.* Paper presented at the Yale Conference on History and Spectatorship.

Kaplan, E. A. (1985c, April). *The representation of women in rock videos.* Paper presented
   at Lafayette College, Easton, PA.

Kaplan, E. A. (1985d, July). *Sexual difference, visual pleasure and the construction of the
   spectator in rock videos on MTV.* Paper presented at the Conference on Sexual
   Difference, Southampton University.

Kiersh, E. (1985, August). Ike's story. *Spin,* pp. 39-43, 71.

Kirkeby, M. (1980, October). The pleasures of home taping. *Rolling Stone,* pp. 2, 62-64.

Levy, S. (1983, December 8). Ad nauseam: How MTV sells out rock and roll. *Rolling
   Stone,* pp. 30-37, 74-79.

Loder, K. (1984, October 11). Sole survivor. *Rolling Stone,* pp. 19-20, 57-60.

Loder, K., & Pond, S. (1982, September 30). Record industry nervous as sales drop
   fifty percent. *Rolling Stone,* pp. 69, 78-79.

McRobbie, A. (1976). Girls and subcultures. In S. Hall & T. Jefferson (Eds.), *Resistance
   through rituals: Youth subcultures in post war Britain.* London: Hutchinson.

McRobbie, A. (1980). Settling accounts with subcultures: A feminist critique. *Screen
   Education, 34,* 37-49.

McRobbie, A. (1984). Dance and social fantasy. In A. McRobbie & M. Nava (Eds.),
   Gender and generation. London: Macmillan.

Mehler, M. (1984, December). Tina Turner's still shaking that thing. *Record,* pp. 17-21.

Miller, J., et al. (1985, March 4). Rock's new women. *Newsweek*, pp. 48-57.

Pond, S. (1982, September 2). Record rental stores booming in U.S. *Rolling Stone*, pp. 37, 42-43.

Rieger, E. (1985). "Dolce semplice"? On the changing role of women in music. In G. Ecker (Ed.), *Feminist aesthetics*. London: Women's Press.

Sahlins, M. (1981). *Historical metaphors and mythical realities*. Ann Arbor: University of Michigan Press.

Sommer, B. (1985). At home with video. *The Austin Chronicle*, p. 9.

Steward, S., & Garratt, S. (1984). *Signed, sealed, and delivered: True life stories of women in pop*. London: Pluto.

Sutherland, S. (1980, May). Record business: The end of an era. *Hi Fidelity*, p. 96.

Swartley, A. (1982, June). Girls! Live! On stage! *Mother Jones*, pp. 25-31.

Volosinov, V. N. (1973). *Marxism and the philosophy of language*. New York: Seminar Press.

Wallace, R. (1980, May 29). Crisis? What crisis? *Rolling Stone*, pp. 17, 28, 30-31.

The women behind the movement. (1985, July 15). *Broadcasting*.

.57

The Effects of Race, Gender, and Fandom on Audience Interpretations of Madonna's Music Videos

JANE D. BROWN

LAURIE SCHULZE

. . . In this study we considered how the race, gender, and fandom of older adolescent audiences affect how they interpret music videos. Previous research has shown consistent differences in how blacks and whites, and males and females, use the mass media (Comstock & Cobbey, 1982). Regardless of social class, black adolescents are more frequent users of television (including music videos) and radio than their white counterparts. Female adolescents generally prefer family-oriented drama and comedy, while males are heavier viewers of action, adventure, and sports programming (Brown, Childers, Bauman, & Koch, 1990). Young black males and black and white females are more likely than white males to say they watch music videos to learn the latest dances and fashions. Blacks are more likely than whites to say they watch because they want to be like the people in the videos (Brown, Campbell, & Fisher, 1986). . . .

NOTE: Excerpts reprinted from the *Journal of Communication*, Vol. 40, No. 2 (1990), by permission.

We chose two videos featuring the rock star Madonna—"Papa Don't Preach" and "Open Your Heart"—as examples of the portrayal of sexuality in music videos. As an "intertextual conglomerate" (Fiske, 1987a, p. 285), Madonna provokes multiple and contradictory meanings. Madonna can be taken "straight," as conforming to patriarchy's positioning of women, or as resisting that subordination. She can be taken as pure commodity ("sex sells"), or as independent auteur evading the culture industry's commodification of female sexuality. So *Playboy* can write that "her onstage contortions and Boy Toy voice have put sopping sex where it belongs—front and center in the limelight" ("Madonna," 1985, p. 122) while *Spin* magazine maintains that "Madonna is not . . . selling sex, she is representing power" (Janowitz, 1987).

The most visible and most scrutinized Madonna fans are the "wanna-be's," adolescent white girls who came to Madonna's "Virgin Tour" concerts wearing fingerless gloves, crucifixes, and lace bras, and to the "Who's That Girl" concerts in black lingerie. Madonna's strong following among young girls most often is attributed to the way she challenges patriarchal definitions of feminine sexuality and to how her "look" can be appropriated by a "girl culture" that resists masculine privilege, parental authority, and institutional constraints (Lewis, 1987a).

To our knowledge, academic and mainstream popular discussions of Madonna have ignored black Madonna fans, though they have been there since the earliest stages of Madonna's career. At number 15, her first album, *Madonna*, was the only one by a white female artist in Billboard's 1984 year-end ranking of top black albums,[1] and her showing was equally strong on the black charts in 1985. This success with young black audiences may be in part due to her albums' production qualities. Black producer Reggie Lucas worked on the *Madonna* album, and Nile Rodgers, formerly of the popular black group Chic, produced her second album, *Like a Virgin*. While the third album, *True Blue* (which spun off the "Papa" and "Open" videos), was less popular on the black charts, we expected to find that Madonna had remained relevant among blacks, at least to some extent.

The possible "meanings" of Madonna's music videos occasionally have resulted in vehement controversy. The most prominent incident (which occurred after our study was completed) involved "Like a Prayer," released in March 1989. The Reverend Donald E. Wildmon, who heads a pressure group against "anti-Christian, anti-family" media representations, interpreted "Like a Prayer" as a video in which "Madonna . . . represents Christ" and "has sex with a priest, obviously to free him from sexual repression" ("Pepsi Refuses," 1989). When Wildmon's organization, the American Family Association, threatened a boycott, Pepsi-Cola cancelled a $5 million ad campaign featuring Madonna and the song "Like a Prayer."[2]

Academic critics see the Madonna presented in music videos as a model that counters "traditional feminine ideals of dependency and reserve" (Lewis, 1987b). In "Papa Don't Preach," according to Kaplan (1987, p. 130), Madonna evolves a kind of postmodern feminist image that builds on, or combines, elements of the "new" woman. . . . The heroine is a determined, self-asserting teenager who, having fallen in love and become pregnant, insists on keeping her baby. . . . It is precisely the blurring of the lines between the "virgin" and "whore" images that suggest a post-feminist stance; the heroine is neither, but rather a sexy young teenager, in love and pregnant, and refusing to conform to social codes and give up her baby (as her friends, she says, tell her to do). . . . The reconciliation only happens because the father decides to relent, the heroine simply refusing to be what he demands; she insists on being herself. . . . [Madonna] is at once strong and feminine, sexy and "innocent," offering an image that perhaps makes sense to young women growing up after the recent feminist movement.

Some social critics have disagreed. Shortly after the video was released in the summer of 1986, the Planned Parenthood affiliate in New York City condemned it for sending "a potent message to teenagers about the glamour of sex, pregnancy and childbearing" (Planned Parenthood of New York City, 1986). Characterizing the media as a "crucial shaper of teen values and attitudes," they argued that the video "provided only fantasy" and that "repetition of [Madonna's] messages by radio and television stations can encourage more teens to engage in sex prematurely and suggest that getting pregnant and having a baby is always good and carries no risk or danger." Syndicated newspaper columnist Ellen Goodman (1986) called the video "a commercial for teen-age pregnancy."

Groups opposed to abortion, in contrast, saw "Papa" as a positive, pro-life song. The California chapter of Feminists for Life in America played the video for girls living in a Los Angeles maternity home and reported, "These were young girls living through tough times, going against parents and boyfriends. Knowing someone like Madonna is in their corner, saying, 'All right! Go for it!' was so uplifting" (Dullea, 1986).

In an interview with the *New York Times* before the song was released, Madonna described it as a "message song that everyone is going to take the wrong way." She predicted that she would be accused of "advising every young girl to go out and get pregnant." She said that the song

tells of a girl who is making a major decision in her life. She has a very close relationship with her father and wants to maintain that closeness. To me it's a celebration of life. It says, "I love you, father, and I love this man and this child that is growing inside me." Of course, who knows how it will end? But at least it starts off positive. (Holden, 1986, p. H-22)

After the song was released, a spokesperson for Madonna said, "She's singing a song, not taking a stand. Her philosophy is people can think what they want to think" (Holden, 1986, p. H-22).

Despite its references to pornography, "Open Your Heart" engendered much less public controversy than the "Papa" or "Like a Prayer" videos, but it was also a prime site for debate. Kaplan (1987) called it a "daring critique of 'carousel' porn parlours, such as proliferate on 42nd Street." Madonna rescues "the innocent young boy who has wandered into the carousel and wants to 'play' Madonna" and in the end she "escapes from sexuality into innocent boyhood" (p. 157). Another critic, however, described Madonna's video role as "peepshow performer and runaway big sister" (Coates, 1988).

We showed the videos to students in undergraduate communication classes at three state universities. These students represent what industry spokesmen claim is the intended target audience for MTV music videos, 18- to 34-year-olds (Gardner, 1983). A majority of the students in this study reported watching music videos at least 15 minutes per day. The study was conducted in the spring of 1988, two years after the songs had first been popular. . . .

. . . Ultimately, 186 students (68 blacks and 118 whites) viewed "Papa," and 290 students (69 blacks and 221 whites) viewed "Open" and completed questionnaires. Because only 24 of the students who viewed either of the videos were Hispanic or Asian, we did not include them in these analyses.

The open-ended questions about reactions to the videos began with very broad questions, such as "How did this video make you feel?" We also asked "What images stick in your mind?" and "What do you think this video is about?"

A series of questions assessed how the students understood the video's narrative. For "Open Your Heart," for example, we asked, "Who is the woman and why is she dancing?" "Who are the people watching the dancer and why are they there?" Then we asked them to complete the story ("What would you say happens to the little boy and the woman?"). We asked if the video made them think "about anything in your own life or someone you know?" and if they thought the video was trying to tell them anything. We also asked them, "If you could give this video to someone you thought would like it, who would you give it to? Why?" . . .

Each viewer was asked, "How much do you like Madonna?" ("a whole lot, she's one of my favorites," "some," or "not at all"). Viewers who responded "a whole lot" after seeing either video were categorized as fans. Viewers who responded "not at all" after seeing either video were designated as "haters." . . .

Viewers differed dramatically in how they interpreted the two videos and did not all agree about even the most fundamental story elements. While almost all of the white females and nearly as many white males said that "Papa Don't Preach" is about teen pregnancy, a large proportion of the black students thought that the "baby" of which Madonna sings is her boyfriend, not an unborn infant.

As can be seen at the top of Table 57.1, almost all (97 percent) of the white females and 85 percent of the white males mentioned somewhere in their responses that they thought the girl in the video is pregnant. In contrast, only 73 percent of the black females and 43 percent of the black males mentioned or alluded to the girl's pregnancy. Coders also analyzed the

Table 57.1 Reactions to "Papa Don't Preach," by Race and Sex

	Black male (n = 28) %	Black female (n = 40) %	White male (n = 54) %	White female (n = 64) %
Mentioned pregnancy[a]	43	73	85	97
% of those also mentioning				
Abortion	8	21	28	29
Marriage in future	25	54	65	51
Primary theme				
Teenage pregnancy	21	40	56	63
Boy/girl relationship	21	5	15	5
Father/daughter relationship	43	50	22	25
Independent girl/decision making	14	5	7	8
Total	99[b]	100	100	101[b]

a. Not all coded categories are included.
b. Rounding error.

open-ended responses for a dominant theme and again found racial differences. Even when blacks "saw" a pregnancy, they were less likely than whites to focus on it as the central theme of the video, but instead focused on the relationship depicted between the father and daughter. As one black male wrote, "This video is about a father's desire not to let anything come between him and his daughter. They are arguing about her boyfriend." Another wrote that the video is about "two young people in love and wanting their parents to understand."

Both black and white males were more likely than females to discuss the video in terms of the teens' relationship; few viewers described Madonna's character in the video as the "independent girl" seen by Kaplan (1987). Black males were the most likely group to see Madonna's independence as the video's primary theme, but most viewers (including black males) saw the girl not as issuing an ultimatum but rather as turning to her father for love, support, and perhaps advice.

Our results also suggest that viewers were not as likely to see the video as "romanticizing" teen pregnancy as Planned Parenthood had predicted. Only about one-quarter of those viewers (and fewer than 10 percent of the black males) who discussed a pregnancy mentioned abortion as an alternative. But, when asked to project the couple's lives into the future, about 48 percent of those who saw the girl as pregnant predicted either no marriage or marriage and divorce; females (53 percent) were more likely than males (41 percent) to think the young couple ultimately would not be together. White males were most likely to imagine the couple married and living together outside their parents' homes; black males were the least likely to anticipate that outcome. Females, in contrast, frequently imagined a divorce (or no marriage) and the girl returning home to live with her father. In the words of one white female, "She has the baby, stays single and raises it the best way she can. The father is still against it but does accept his grandchild."

These analyses strongly support the notion that race and gender position media audiences in very different ways. The black cultural experience in the United States is very different from that of whites, particularly around issues of sexuality and family (Allen, 1981). Statistics show that early unmarried pregnancy and childbirth is a familiar pattern in black communities. Anthropologists suggest that these patterns are adaptive reactions to current economic and social situations (Connor, 1988). Black males may not see pregnancy among unmarried teens as the "trouble" most whites think it is. The black viewers' focus on the boy/girl and father/daughter relationship may reflect the currently more problematic nature of establishing lasting cross-sex relationships in black society (Braithwaite, 1981).

While Fiske (1987b) has suggested that Madonna's image tends to polarize her audiences into ardent haters and fans, most of our sample (62 percent) fell in the middle, saying they liked Madonna "some." Some may be indifferent, seeing Madonna as marginally relevant to their lives. Others may be ambivalent, liking some things about Madonna and disliking others. Here we concentrated on the fans and the haters—those in the audience who did find Madonna relevant and were relatively unambivalent.

As Fiske would predict, we found that those who liked Madonna liked her very much, and those who disliked her hated her. One female fan wrote, for example, "Madonna is God (besides Belinda Carlisle)." A male Madonna hater wrote that he liked Madonna "as much as slamming my fingers in the car door . . . as much as getting teeth drilled without novacane [sic]." The thing that he liked most about the videos was that they ended after "what seemed an eternity of Hell." Another wrote that he would show the videos to "someone on death row," presumably to add to the torment of the prisoner's last days on earth.

We did not expect the relatively high proportion of black male fans. Twenty-three percent of black males (8 out of 35) said they liked Madonna "a lot," as compared to 16 percent of black females (9 out of 55), 9 percent of white males (11 out of 120), and 6 percent of white females (7 out of 122). Both black males (17 percent) and black females (6 percent) were less likely than whites (33 percent) to be Madonna haters. Comments from black fans suggest that Madonna's appeal is not due solely to her "sound." When asked what they liked most about the "Papa" video, black male fans wrote: "Madonna is sexy and a good performer"; "Madonna's body. Because she's sexy"; "The part when Madonna started dancing, because I like her body movements."

We also were surprised by the few white female fans in this older adolescent sample. This may be because Madonna projects a "girlness" that works against young females' attempts to assert themselves in the adult world. Madonna herself describes her voice as a "girl's voice" and has remarked, "I do feel like an adult [now] and that's something I say grudgingly. I'd rather be a girl all my life" (McKenna, 1988, p. 70). Her most recent concert had asked, after all, "Who's That *Girl?*" not "Who's That *Woman?*"

. . . A few white and a few black females, however (7 and 9, respectively), could be classified as fans. And the male and female fans derived strikingly different meanings, pleasures, and displeasures from the videos. For the female fans, Madonna offers the pleasures of identification with a strong, successful woman. One black female fan wrote that what she liked best about "Papa" is Madonna, "because she is a female making her way to the top." The female fans also were more likely than the male fans to take pride in the ideological "stand" they saw Madonna making in her music videos. Another black female fan wrote that "Papa" made her feel "great. . . . I always like to see what Madonna's up to. Also it had a positive message." A white female fan said that in "Papa" Madonna "took a stand on an issue (not necessarily on abortion but on the right to have a choice)."

But viewers—even the fans—had trouble liking the "Open Your Heart" video. As can be seen in Table 57.2, many viewers expressed confusion when asked to describe what the video was about; many said they were "disgusted." Some of the confusion may have been due to the unfamiliar setting portrayed in the video. Only 15 percent of the Southern students identified the setting as a peep show, while 49 percent of Northeastern students recognized the setting. The sexual content of the video also contributed to the viewers' discomfort.

Viewers identified four primary themes in the "Open" video. About one-half of the white viewers saw the primary theme as pornography/sexual perversion and/or women as sex objects, while only a fifth of the blacks did; another 13 percent of the viewers saw the primary theme as sexual love. However, about one-fifth focused on the "platonic love" between the woman and the boy, and another tenth described Madonna's character primarily as a working woman. Males of both races were more likely than females to see the primary theme as sexual love, while females were more likely to identify a platonic relationship between the dancer and the boy. These results are consistent with studies showing that men are more likely than women "to perceive the world in sexual terms" (Abbey, 1982, p. 836). . . .

Female Madonna fans embraced the ending, reading it (like Kaplan, 1987) as an escape into innocence, an escape from a patriarchal construction of woman as something "to be looked at" by an objectifying male gaze. One fan wrote that "until the end . . . the scenes of her dancing in front of the sleazoids was, I think, degrading. The ending scene with the kid was uplifting—it was a switch back to innocence."

The ending may redeem, but it does not seem to recuperate or critique what a number of fans labeled the "pornographic" construction of woman in the first part of the video. Only one viewer (a white female fan) read "Open" as "a kind of mock on pornography. I do not think the video *is* pornographic." Madonna's black teddy bothered most of them. One white female called it "that horrid outfit," and a black female found the costume neither "pretty nor sexy." Another wrote that it made Madonna look "cheap."

Table 57.2 Reactions to "Open Your Heart," by Race and Sex

	Black male (n = 24) %	Black female (n = 45) %	White male (n = 116) %	White female (n = 105) %
Felt[a]				
Nothing, confusion	50	45	25	34
Disgust	8	24	23	36
Happy	21	13	15	14
Turned on	4	4	16	3
Primary theme				
Pornography/sexual perversion/ women as sexual objects	21	22	43	50
Platonic love	13	29	18	22
Sexual love	17	9	16	12
Working woman	—	11	10	9
No clear theme	50	29	14	8
Total	100	100	100	100

a. Not all coded categories are included.

Almost without exception, the female fans felt this video spoke to patriarchal pleasure, and the only people they would show it to were male—"a frustrated male friend," "a perverted old man," "any human male," "my friend Michael. He thinks she's hot." In sharp contrast, viewers were most likely to say they would give the "Papa" video to females so they might learn something ("a friend of mine who might be in a similar situation in the future").

The same female fans who felt anxious and angry about what they perceived to be Madonna's compliance with patriarchy's definition of female sexuality could, however, struggle through "Open" to the positive pleasures of dance. Many of them liked Madonna's dancing more than anything else in the video, especially the dance sequence with the boy. One fan wrote, "Madonna is using . . . her body to express her thoughts. . . . I like the way she dances. Since I am a female, I watch her to learn how to move like her, not to be turned on." . . .

While female fans struggled against the patriarchal discourses in play in Madonna's videos, many of the male viewers and almost all of the male fans felt comfortably hailed as masculine subjects. White males were the most likely to express an erotic reaction to the video. They also were the most likely to say they best liked Madonna's body and watching her dance. Some were quite clear about the desire the video stimulated. One 21-year-old male wrote that "Madonna's shapely and oh so tasty figure" was the image that stuck in his mind. He liked most "the cheerful upbeat tempo and the way her breasts shake." A white male fan wrote that "Open" made him feel like "going out, finding my girlfriend, and having some sex. Madonna's body is hot and I like the way she struts her stuff . . . but I thought [she] could've taken off the lingerie." Other white male fans wrote that "Open" made them feel "real pumped," "turned on," and "sexual excitement," and they wrote at length about the pleasures of watching "Madonna's body." Male fans used the term "Madonna's body" more often than "Madonna" in naming what they liked about the videos. No female fans wrote about "Madonna's body," although two white females who liked Madonna "some" wrote about their own bodies. Both, in response to the question of how "Open" made them feel, said, in a word, "fat." Not surprisingly, no male viewers felt that Madonna's body problematized theirs. . . .

Social allegiances other than gender, race, and fandom are reflected in the readings of these videos as well. Half of the Madonna fans in this study were from working-class backgrounds, and hostility toward Madonna was stronger among the upper-class respondents. One Madonna-hater, for example, wrote that Madonna "is a cheap, pseudo rock star whose image is nothing but sleazy [sic]. I pity the fact that she tries so hard to be Marilyn Monroe but has about $\frac{1}{123}$rd the class that Monroe had." We have more to learn about how the discourses of social class and cultural capital are used to validate pleasures and displeasures in popular media, and we have more to learn about how other rock stars are perceived and valued.

Larry Grossberg (1987) has argued that statistics generate "the data that critical theorists should be interpreting" (p. 98). The data generated by this study ask for further critical interpretation and point toward the need for deeper empirical investigation—perhaps ethnographic studies of fans and music video viewers—in an effort to learn more about how audiences use popular media to develop their own understandings of sexuality and sexual pleasure.

NOTES

1. Culture Club's *Colour by Numbers*, at number 31, was the only other album by white artists to make the top 50 that year.

2. In a *New York Times* interview, Madonna described the video's pivotal encounter as a "dream" in which a "saint becomes a man. . . . As the choir sings, she reaches an orgasmic crescendo of sexual fulfillment intertwined with her love of God. . . . She wakes up" (Holden, 1989, p. 12).

REFERENCES

Abbey, A. (1982). Sex differences in attributions for friendly behavior: Do males misperceive females' friendliness? *Journal of Personality and Social Psychology*, 42(5), 830-838.

Allen, W. R. (1981). Moms, dads, and boys: Race and sex differences in the socialization of male children. In L. E. Gary (Ed.), *Black men* (pp. 99-111). Beverly Hills, CA: Sage.

Braithwaite, R. L. (1981). Interpersonal relations between Black males and Black females. In L. E. Gary (Ed.), *Black men* (pp. 83-97). Beverly Hills, CA: Sage.

Brown, J. D., Campbell, K., & Fisher, L. (1986). American adolescents and music videos: Why do they watch? *Gazette, 37,* 19-32.

Brown, J. D., Childers, K. W., Bauman, K. E., & Koch, G. G. (1990). The influence of new media and family structure on young adolescents' television and radio use. *Communication Research, 17*(1), 65-82.

Coates, P. (1988, February). Desperately seeking Marilyn: Madonna, myth, and MTV. *The World & I,* pp. 250-254.

Comstock, G., & Cobbey, R. (1982). Television and the children of ethnic minorities: Perspectives from research. In G. L. Berry & C. Mitchell-Kernan (Eds.), *Television and the socialization of the minority child* (pp. 245-257). New York: Academic Press.

Connor, M. E. (1988). Teenage fatherhood: Issues confronting young Black males. In J. T. Gibbs (Ed.), *Young, Black, and male in America: An endangered species* (pp. 188-218). Dover, MA: Auburn House.

Dullea, G. (1986, September 18). Madonna's new beat is a hit, but song's message rankles. *New York Times,* pp. B1, B9.

Fiske, J. (1987a). British cultural studies and television. In R. C. Allen (Ed.), *Channels of discourse* (pp. 254-289). Chapel Hill: University of North Carolina Press.

Fiske, J. (1987b). *Television culture.* New York: Methuen.

Gardner, F. (1983, August). MTV rocks cable. *Marketing & Media Decisions,* pp. 66-68, 113.

Goodman, E. (1986, September 20). Commercial for teen-age pregnancy. *Washington Post,* p. A-23.

Grossberg, L. (1987). Critical theory and the politics of empirical research. In M. Gurevitch & M. R. Levy (Eds.), *Mass communication review yearbook* (Vol. 6, pp. 86-106). Newbury Park, CA: Sage.

Holden, S. (1986, June 29). Madonna goes heavy on heart. *New York Times,* p. H-22.

Holden, S. (1989, March 19). Madonna re-creates herself—Again. *New York Times,* sec. 2, p. 12.

Janowitz, T. (1987, April). Sex as a weapon. *Spin,* pp. 54-62.

Kaplan, E. A. (1987). *Rocking around the clock: Music television, postmodernism, and consumer culture.* New York: Methuen.

Lewis, L. A. (1987a). Female address in music video. *Journal of Communication Inquiry, 11*(1), 73-84.

Lewis, L. A. (1987b). Form and female authorship in music video. *Communication, 9,* 355-377.

Madonna: The Lee Friedlander sessions. (1985, September). *Playboy,* pp. 118-131.

McKenna, K. (1988, February). Madonna. *Spin,* pp. 45-48, 70.

Pepsi refuses to drop Madonna as role model for youth despite offensive video. (1989, April). *Journal of the American Family Association,* pp. 1, 23.

Planned Parenthood of New York City, Inc. (1986, September 26). *Memorandum re: The need for balanced messages in the media.* New York: Author.

■ 58

Reconstructions of Nationalist Thought in Black Music and Culture[1]

KRISTAL BRENT ZOOK

A Black Nationalist attitude is protection against a system that keeps us back.
                                                    —Chuck D (Public Enemy)

In March 1990, *Newsweek* published several articles on rap, which it described as a "crude," "offensive," and "loud" music produced by "angry young males." While the introduction in the table of contents recognized that other interpretations have viewed rap as a "bold call for 'Afrocentric' political consciousness," this latter reading was apparently not to be presented in any kind of equal proportion to the former. In fact, rap's liberatory potential is completely undermined, discredited, and silenced in these articles. For example, rap group NWA is simplistically equated with rockers, Guns 'n' Roses, for having an all around "bad attitude." This attitude is so belligerent, *Newsweek* scolds, that the rappers "even got into trouble with the FBI." Similarly, 2 Live Crew is narrowly presented as the controversial Miami rap group being prosecuted for "alleged violations of obscenity laws"; Ice-T is lambasted for his sexist and violent depictions of women and intimacy; and, of course, Public Enemy's Professor Griff is slammed for attempting "to make hatred 'hip.' " . . . Unconvincingly, *Newsweek* concludes that rap "is mostly empty of

NOTE: Excerpts reprinted from *Rockin' the Boat: Mass Music and Mass Movements,* edited by Reebee Garofalo (Boston: South End Press, 1992), by permission of the publisher.

political content" and, as we learned from the rock and roll of the 1960s, "has little power . . . to change the world."[2]

I want to make one point unequivocally clear here: I'm not about to argue that sexism, obscenity, homophobia, and even hatred haven't been present in both the musical arena of rap and in the dominant (until now) male lifestyle of its performers. They have. Rap is an expressive form which is inherently belligerent and confrontational as a result of the specific historical, socio-political, and economic context from which it comes. It is also much more than this. To say that rap is no more than a sad by-product of oppression is to take an explanatory, *defensive* stance when, in actuality, rap is a fundamental component of what may be the strongest political and cultural *offensive* gesture among African Americans today.

While I do not see myself as a missionary of rap, attempting to convert disbelievers who remain untouched by its power, I am concerned with the ways in which propaganda like the *Newsweek* article are formulated from specific social locations in order to uphold specific (usually unspoken) ideological and political agendas. My suspicion is that the need to repudiate rap's liberatory potential is in reaction to a deeply rooted fear of African-American empowerment. Because it is situated within a comprehensive, historical frame of reference (nationalism), which evokes radical traditions of racial solidarity and resistance, rap is quite capable of sensitizing people and of fostering a sense of political consciousness. This consciousness may then be used to subvert, and even, to dislodge hegemonic powers that be.

My main argument, then, is two-fold. First, I believe that there are persistent elements of Black Nationalist ideology which underlie and inform both rap music and a larger "hip hop" culture. These elements include a desire for cultural pride, economic self-sufficiency, racial solidarity, and collective survival. They are manifested in certain aesthetic moods and attitudes and are present in contemporary fashion, language, dance and overall lifestyles. I argue that nationalism has continued to manifest itself through cultural expressive forms, as well as through various political arenas, precisely because of the fact that complete racial equality has not yet been achieved in this country. Within this context, nationalism represents a necessary vision of safety, protection, and what I refer to as an empowering "home."

The second part of my argument is simply that nationalist elements are presented, not only within the creative content of rap and other expressive forms (in film, literature, and television), but they are also manifested through the modes of production and consumption which surround these forms. In other words, nationalism is not just a metaphoric or aesthetic vision which appears in the creative product, but it is also that which informs the actual material mechanisms of cultural production itself (i.e., the marketing, promotion, and distribution of this product). . . .

A BRIEF HISTORY OF RAP

Emerging in the mid- to late-1970s among black and Puerto Rican male youths of the South Bronx, rap music was clearly an extension of African expressive forms such as "signifying," "playing the dozens," and creating praisesongs in the tradition of the *griot*, or the African storyteller. Along with these earlier traditions, rap also traces its antecedents to the bebop singers, the funk of James Brown, and the rhythmic jazz of The Last Poets, to name but a few influences.[3] What was immediately clear about this cultural movement (which came to be called "hip hop" and included other activities such as graffiti-art and breakdancing) was that it expressed certain sentiments that genuinely reflected the lives of working-class Black and Puerto Rican male youths in a way that the more romanticized disco scene, popularized by middle-class whites, did not.

Part of rap's streetwise edge came, undoubtedly, from the fact that most of its participants were from the "hood," that is, the neighborhoods of New York which required this edge for day-to-day survival, such as the South Bronx. For example, Grandmaster Flash and the Furious Five's 1982 hit, "The Message," bitterly refers to living conditions of the ghetto.

> Don't push me cuz, I'm close to the edge,
> I'm trying not to lose my head.
> It's liked a jungle sometimes, it makes me wonder
> how I keep from going under . . .
> broken glass everywhere,
> people pissing on the stair,
> you know they just don't care.
> I can't take the smell, I can't take the noise.
> Got no money to move out,
> I guess I got no choice.[4]

While cuts such as "The Message" are part of a long tradition of politically conscious black music (Curtis Mayfield is another precursor to this kind of rap), such "conscious" raps are only a fragment of that which sells and gains widespread recognition among consumers. It is important to recognize that a great deal of commercially popular rap is little more than self-aggrandized boasting. Highly politicized rap is often overlooked by the average consumer since it doesn't receive the same radio airplay, and other such advantages. For instance, Brother D's (Daryl Asmaa Nubyah), "How We Gonna Make the Black Nation Rise?" (1980) was, in spite of its limited recognition, one of the first "message" raps to be recorded. And although the desire for some kind of safe home or "nation" is one which was rarely articulated explicitly in the early days of rap, the existence of this, and other, similar cuts indicates that many of the underlying assumptions behind rap were, in fact, profoundly nationalistic. . . .

CONTINUED EXPRESSIONS OF NATIONALISM

. . . Black articulations of the "nation" which were voiced in the political realm of the 1960s have not died in the popular memories of the people. Instead, they have been transferred to a cultural arena and reformulated in popular expressive forms such as film, television, rap music, clothing, literature, and language. I argue that there is evidence of a collective desire to identify a usable past among a large number of African-Americans of my generation (16 to 25 years old). This usable past is one which will aid in the regeneration of a nationalistically centered present. Most important, it is a past which must be imaginatively remembered and constantly re-visioned in order to remain valuable. . . .

. . . Rap music . . . forms part of a larger conduit of culturally specific, "in-house" intercommunication among blacks. It is also "cross-medial" in the sense that the various media such as television, music, film, and video speak to and through one another and are intimately connected by a growing number of black men (for the most part) who insist on capturing full productive control over their artistic works. . . .

. . . Both the form and content of rap express black autonomy, self-determination, and cultural pride. But what is perhaps most fascinating is not only the way that rap confirms a sense of imagined, metaphorical community, but rather, the fact that this fantasy of "home" is simultaneously constructed materially through the very modes of production, marketing, and the critical discourses which surround it. In other words, just as Anderson argues that literary forms such as the newspaper and the novel made European nationalisms possible, I would say that the forms of television, music videos, film, literary works, and the networks involved in producing these forms are also nurturing a heightened sense of racial collectivity, group solidarity, and even political responsibility—all of which are important elements of nationalist thought.

A clear example of such material nationalism is Nelson George and Ann Carlin's organization of the "Stop the Violence movement," a collective of noted rappers who participated, as a group, in the making of the recording and video, *Self-Destruction*. This album contained powerful messages about gang violence, education, racism, and resistance. Because of its production, over $200,000 was sent to the National Urban League in an effort to combat illiteracy and black-on-black crime."[5] Interestingly, Nelson George was also an early investor in Spike Lee's first film and consequently, Lee, with his "Forty Acres and an Empire," was in a position to help finance production of *Self-Destruction*, which he has done.[6] The recent production of *We're All in the Same Gang* is another good example of a black coalition of rappers working toward the collective "uplift of the race." With lyrics which repeatedly emphasize the idea that black genocide is being committed by black people themselves, "Same Gang" is, in fact, a powerful statement against self-destruction.

Another case in point: when rapper Ice Cube left the group NWA (Niggas With Attitude) as a result of pay inequities between him and his white manager (who made $23,000 and $130,000 in 1989, respectively), Public Enemy's Chuck D and Hank Shocklee agreed that they would produce his solo album. This is clearly an example of what some have traditionally referred to as "economic nationalism," or self-sufficiency. Placing rap music within a historical context rife with white appropriation and the theft of Black creativity, it becomes essential to look at the ways in which this theft is being resisted and subverted. The early productions of Spike Lee's "Forty

Acres" enterprise as well as his recent decision to found "Forty Acres and a Mule Music Works," his own record label, are further examples of a move away from exploitative commodification toward black productive control over black creativity. This developing trend is one which has undoubtedly created an atmosphere conducive to partnerships such as that between Ice Cube and Chuck D. It is a mood which has fostered and nourished a sense of racial solidarity and empowering economic autonomy.

Similarly, the recently released film, *Listen Up: The Lives of Quincy Jones*, emphasizes common ties between musical legends such as Miles Davis, Sara Vaughn, and contemporary rappers. This connection is further reinforced in *The Fresh Prince of Bel Air*, rap's initiation into prime-time commercial television. Being a Quincy Jones Production, this phenomenally successful experiment is in keeping with what seems to be Jones's political agenda: the bridging of gaps between generations, economic classes, and most importantly, between African-American individuals who seem to have acculturated themselves into mainstream U.S. culture and those who have not. . . .

Similarly, Keenan Ivory Wayans, part of a closely knit crew of young independent black film-makers, comedians, actors, and actresses is the only African American to produce, direct, and star in his own television series (*In Living Color*). This show, which has had guest appearances of rappers, Monie Love, Queen Latifah, and Flavor Flav, is grounded in a definitive hip hop aesthetic manifested in dress styles, graphic art, music, and language.[7]

Interestingly, Robert Townsend, who co-wrote the film, *I'm Gonna Git You Sucka* with Wayans, has released another film called *The Five Heartbeats*. Although it began as "pure comedy," it took a different turn after Townsend "travelled on the road for a few months with an actual group from the '60s (the Dells), and heard their stories of being ripped off and taken advantage of by people in the business." Also in the works for Townsend is a filmmaking workshop for inner-city children, since an important part of his agenda is "giving back to the community" some of what he has received.[8]

Finally, rappers Big Daddy Kane, Chuck D, Flavor Flav, and Ice Cube joined together (with Spike Lee, whose name is invoked but who does not appear in the actual video) in a recently released music video called *Burn Hollywood Burn*, a commentary on the racist control of representation and production in Hollywood's film industry. Not coincidentally, this video is strongly reminiscent of *Hollywood Shuffle*, one of Townsend's earlier films. While it is an example of what is positive and hopeful in the current resurgence of nationalist thought, its narrow demand for the "black man's" rights must, nevertheless, be recognized as a dangerous and disheartening mimicry of patriarchal Black Nationalism. . . .

I suspect that there are many more examples of quiet, behind-the-scenes-back-scratching which may not even be explicitly articulated as nationalistic moves but which are, nevertheless, implicated in these conversations. Whereas we do not yet have electoral power, there is more and more potential for economic leverage as the percentage of black-owned businesses continues to climb at a faster rate than the national average.[9] . . .

If my suspicions have foundation, then these cultural manifestations may, in fact, be the impetus for increasing awareness and insight in a way that is not clearly measurable at this historical moment. Just as Malcolm X eventually moved beyond bourgeois, economic nationalism and into the realm of a more fundamentally revolutionary socialist thought, my hope is that we, as a people, have both the desire and the imagination to move beyond the nationalistic trend that bell hooks call "a gesture of powerlessness." At the same time, I firmly believe that the nationalist vision of home is a necessary one which we need to offer us strength and relative safety in this endeavor.

NOTES

1. An earlier version of this chapter was first presented at the annual conference of the International Association for the Study of Popular Music (IASPM) in May 1990. I am grateful to the members of this organization who offered me very generous feedback (especially Herman Gray, who first encouraged me to present this paper, Reebee Garofalo, Portia Maultsby, Venise Berry, and Rosalinda Fregoso) and to the Feminist Research and Action Group at UC Santa Cruz (FRA) for their financial support.

2. This special section in "The Arts" is actually composed of two essays. The first, "The Rap Attitude" begins with the following subheading in bold print: "A new musical culture, filled with self-assertion and anger, has come boiling up from the streets. Some people think it should have stayed there." The essay which follows is called "Decoding Rap Music," and it begins with a clear indicator of who *Newsweek* believes its audience to be: "Feeling out of it 'cause you're not into it? . . . Sooner or later you're just going to have to deal with it. The guys with the names you don't understand—what is a Tone-Loc, anyway?" The collective title for both essays is "Rap's Mixed Message: Rage and Responsibility" (1990).

3. For a more detailed elaboration of these traditions, see Toop (1984).

4. "The Message." Sugarhill Records, 1982.

5. George (1990b, p. 19).

6. Nelson George (1990a) describes the nature of this empire and the decidedly nationalist stance of its owner in "Forty Acres and an Empire: Spike Lee Plants the New Motown in Brooklyn."

7. It is both ironic and distressing that members of the musical group, Living Colour (also co-founders of the Black Rock Coalition, a group with inherently nationalist assumptions) have recently been engaged in litigation with Wayans about his unauthorized use of their name. See *Jet Magazine* (May 28, 1990, p. 37).

8. Samuels (1990).

9. *Emerge* Magazine (February 1991, p. 31) reported that black-owned businesses increased by 38 percent between 1982 and 1987, while the total number of U.S. businesses grew by only 14 percent. *Emerge* also reported an increase in African-American consumer support for these businesses during that same period.

REFERENCES

George, N. (1990a, August 7). Forty acres and an empire: Spike Lee plants the new Motown in Brooklyn. *Village Voice.*

George, N. (Ed.). (1990b). *Stop the violence: Overcoming self-destruction: Rap speaks out.* New York: National Urban League.

The message. (1982). Sugarhill Records.

Rap's mixed message: Rage and responsibility. (1990, March 19). *Newsweek.*

Samuels, A. (1990, September). This time, it isn't about jokes. *Los Angeles Times,* Calendar section.

Toop, D. (1984). *The rap attack: African jive to New York hip hop.* London: Pluto.

59

It's My Thang and I'll Swing It the Way That I Feel![1]

Sexuality and Black Women Rappers

IMANI PERRY

As in all popular American music, sex talk flows through the veins of rap music and hip-hop culture. It is clear that the subject of sexuality has various meanings within the music. The treatment of sexuality in hip-hop is not limited to the recounting of sexual escapades but includes using sexuality as a metaphor for creativity, cunning and excellence. Euphemism, double entendre, layered speech and linguistic dexterity play a central role in the sexual speak of rap music. This chapter will address the specific ways in which women rappers use sexual "speak" as a means to liberation and subjectivity as women and empowerment as lyricists and artists.

Women rappers who articulate sexual desire or activity are also participating in a tradition of symbolic use of sexuality inherited through Black women's oral-musical history, specifically blues music. In the article "It Jus' Be's Dat Way Sometime: The Sexual Politics of Women's Blues," Hazel Carby (1992) expands the examination of Black feminist authorship by analyzing the explicit and powerful voices of Black women who sang the blues during the era of the great migration of Black Americans from the southern to the northern United States. She writes, "By analyzing the sexual and cultural politics of Black women who constructed themselves as sexual subjects through song, in particular the Blues, I want to assert an empowered presence" (p. 746).

Carby's essay provides a framework for understanding the Black feminism and femininity that we see in hip-hop as part of a tradition of Black female oral and self-liberatory culture. As well, it gives insight into some of the significances and objectives seen in the texts of women's rap. Black female blues music has many distinct textual parallels to women's hip-hop born out of their sharing a politicized female discourse articulated through music. Carby's article speaks to the tone, content and goals that the blues singers asserted in their music and particularly to the ways in which constructing oneself as a sexual subject was a liberating act for them. "The Blues singers had assertive and demanding voices; they had no respect for sexual taboos or for breaking through the boundaries of respectability and convention" (p. 754).

The ways in which this sexual subjectivity is used to empower self are remarkably similar between rap and blues music. A good example of this is available in comparing Ida Cox's (1980) "One Hour Mama," which Carby (1992) cites, and BWP's (Bytches With Problems) "Two Minute Brother" (1991). Cox sings about wanting a man that can "go the distance":

> *I'm a one hour mama so no one minute papa*
> *Ain't' the kind of man for me.*
>
> *I can't stand no greenhorn lover,*
> *Like a rookie goin' to war*
> *With a load of big artillery*
> *But don't know what it's for*
> *He's got to bring me reference*
> *With a great long pedigree*
> *And must prove he's got endurance*
> *Or he don't mean snap to me*

BWP raps:

> *But here's the type of man that we can't stand*
> *One who always holds his thing in his hand*
> *Lyin' and sayin' it's about size nine*
> *Always got his hands between his legs*
> *You know the kind that always begs*
> *The one who claims to be the real good lover*
> *Usually he's a two minute brother*

In addition to sharing the same subject matter, these two songs have similar functions. They both use comedy and sexual demands to voice their power and irreverence for decorum as defined through societal expectation of the behavior of "respectable" women and male expectations of female subordination and stroking of the male ego. As Carby (1992) writes, "The comic does not mellow the assertive voice but on the contrary undermines mythologies of phallic power and establishes a series of women-centered heterosexual demands" (p. 757). BWP (1991) dislocates the power of the myths with the humor of the situation of the man's sexual failure and his demands and exposes the myth that the man has created about his own phallus as false. The male voice says early in the rap: "I got the full nine stretchin' out to twelve/Like a burnt offering we're goin' straight to hell," but she finds out when they come to the moment of the sexual act, "When he said Buford is ready to enter thee/Lift 'em up spread 'em out, Hold up somethin's wrong/Buford was only three inches long." Such lyrics undermine the physical representation of phallic power and consequently undermine phallocentric sexuality, thus endowing the woman with power as she positions herself as the sexual subject. Sexual subjectivity does not merely come in the deconstruction of phallocentrism but in the inversion of the sexual gaze to make the male the object. In Salt 'n Pepa's (1993) "Shoop," they clearly situate themselves as the "gazers." Pepa raps:

> Here I go, Here I go, Here I go again,
> Girls what's my weakness (chorus) MEN! . . .
> Yo Salt I looked around and I couldn't believe this,
> I stared, I swear, my niece my witness,
> the brother had it goin' on with somethin' kinda wicked, wicked,
> had to kick it, I'm not shy so I asked for the digits,
> a Ho no that don't make me, see what I want slip slide to it quickly

At once she asserts her desire and her ability to fulfill it.

Frequently, in a fashion similar to women blues singers, women rappers are asserting their sexuality outside the limits of propriety in American music. Their lyrics function in strong contrast to the "sex innuendo" and objectification of the female body that is generally seen in popular music. Often the words and demands are jarring to the casual listener, accustomed to less direct statements of sexuality from women. A recent trend in this domain has been the discussion and demand of cunnilingus. In "Shoop," (Salt 'n Pepa, 1993), a man's voice says, "Yo Sandy I wanna like taste you," and the response is, "Get your lips wet 'cause it's time to have Pep." In the video for this song, such statements accompany scenes of her scissoring her legs open as if to suggest her readiness for the act. Another example of the presence of oral sex in women's rap is found in "Gimme Head" by Le Shaun (1993). She says,

> Yo I got a fuckin' plane to catch and Baby I'm feelin kinda tense
> So what's up, won't you loosen me up Baby no offense
> But your dick don't do the trick I mean the job for me
> Get on Your knees and just slob for me . . .

Although this song spirals into a hostile and competitive debate between Le Shaun and her male partner over the subject of oral sex as opposed to the amicable interaction between Pepa and her partner, both songs are a powerful metaphor for sexual power relationships between men and women.

Women rappers not only claim *their* sexual selves but also enter the male body, generally as a metaphor for their strength and power but also to expand self-definition. MC Lyte (1993a) raps:

> I got the intro along with the cash flow
> Make all the bad boys seem like nymphos,

Yeah I'm hard, I get sexy like Veronica,
Use sex as an instrument, like the philharmonica

In this stanza, she claims phallic imagery through the double meaning of being "hard" as being strong and street smart for both men and women and being sexually erect for men—and through the description for her sexuality as an "instrument." Yet she doesn't relinquish femininity because she claims Veronica, a hyperfeminized character from Archie comics, as a symbol for her sexiness. Consequently the boundaries of female gender and sexuality are not just equal to those of men in rap lyrics but more expansive.

The state of gender consciousness that this stanza reveals is succinctly stated by Helene Cixous (1992): "I don't want a penis to decorate my body with. But I do desire the other, whole and entire, male or female; because living means wanting everything that is, and wanting it alive" (p. 334). The desire is to enter all spaces while remaining inside oneself. There are various examples where women claim the phallus to describe giving pleasure to the hearer of the music, such as Salt 'n Pepa's (1989) "We do it to you in your ear hole," Monie Love's (1993) "I'm a giver of lyrical sex to your ear drum," or Ladybug's "To the virgin ears we give a kiss" (Digable Planets, 1992). They use the phallus as a metaphor describing their ability to give pleasure through oral skill, thus claiming for themselves the male obsession with performance and sexual braggadocio.

Both the consciousness that is articulated through desire and the claim to various sexual spaces seem to be a method of speaking that is very aware of the body, its function and its role in establishing identity. Trinh Minh-Ha (1989), a critical theorist, writes of "writing through the body," which seems to characterize the type of physical consciousness (which is constructed from a subjective rather than an objectified stance) that we find in hip-hop artists. Trinh Minh-Ha writes, "Women must write through their bodies, must not let themselves be driven away from their bodies . . . must thoroughly rethink the body to re-appropriate femininity (p. 36).

To write through the body, to own the body anew, allows for new avenues to conceptualize what it means to be a woman. MC Lyte's (1993b) song "Ruffneck" is an example of how writing through the body allows for a new construction of Black womanhood that negates wounding connotations that American society holds of both Blackness and womanhood. The song is dedicated to the "badboys" of the Black community—the ones who are hard-core and unruly. These are the men who throughout American history have been constructed in the popular imagination as the murderers, muggers and rapists in society—the most hostile and aggressive individuals in our culture—young "bad ass" Black men. Despite their irreverence for society, however, in her song these men pose no threat to her and pay ready attention to her sexual and emotional desires.

Pumpin in and out and out and in and here we go
He knows exactly how I want my flow and that's slow
Never questionin' can he get buck wild
He's got that smack it lick it swallow it up style.

Modifying the words of the Bell Biv Devoe song "Do Me!," which included the phrase "Smack it up flip it, rub it down, oh no!," MC Lyte changes the lyrics from an objectifying male description of what he will do with the female body to a statement of her "Ruffneck" partner's sexual ability in intercourse and in performing oral sex. This statement is made with a clear consciousness as to where her physical self exists and what its desires are; she is writing through her body. Audre Lorde (1990) wrote about how Black women must be able to distinguish between their own personal assertions of liberation from male dominance and being used as pawns to advance the demonization of the Black male. In this song, MC Lyte manages to at once defy negative representations of Black men as hostile and dangerous by stating the mutual affection between herself and roughnecks, and to state her sexual subjectivity and importance within the context of romantically interacting with the roughest men in her community.

The physical presentation of women as a sign of sexual self possession and power is another parallel that can be drawn between the symbols of the blues woman and those of the hip-hop female. Carby (1992) writes about blues singers:

> The women Blues singers occupied a privileged space; they had broken out of the boundaries of the home and taken their sensuality and sexuality out of the private to the public sphere . . . their physical presence was a crucial aspect of their power; the visual display of spangles, dresses, of furs, of gold teeth, of diamonds, of all the sumptuous and desirable aspects of their body reclaimed private sexuality from being an objectification of male desire to a representation of female desire. (p. 755)

The representation of female desire that one sees in the physical display of women rappers is complex. The sense of glamour and elegance that one saw among blues artists is not uniform among women rappers. There are women rappers who assert their sexuality through emphasizing their physical femininity and those that minimize the importance of a strong visual statement of femininity as related to sexiness or prettiness. However many of them seem to at once reclaim private sexuality from males and to construct a culture of female grooming and dress that is separate from popular notions of femininity that frequently have White women's looks or attributes as their template. Yo Yo, Latifah (at certain times), Harmony, Isis and Queen Mother Rage are women who are explicitly "feminine" and invested in a notion of femininity that is distinctly Afrocentric. They adorn themselves with braided or natural hairstyles or African headwear and fabrics, nose rings, African self-naming and so on. This meticulous attention to grooming and Afrocentric self-admiration announces a self-possessed sexuality and nationalism that is uniquely Black and female. There are also women rappers who have been accused of lacking any physical or verbal signs of femininity. MC Lyte and Boss are two women who have faced such accusations at various times. These are women who have usually presented themselves with very baggy clothing but always with stylish hair and wearing lipstick. Regardless, they are deemed unfeminine by some. Boss responds to such comments with the following statement:

> There's a lot of pressure on female rappers to dress up like hoes but me and Dee (her friend and rapping partner) won't be wearin' push-up bras and tight pants; female rappers who do that are tryin' to compensate for the fact that they don't have any good lyrics. (Boss, 1993)

That statement signifies the importance of voice for Boss. It is a statement that to be taken seriously as artists they must be subject instead of object (an object consumed for her body instead of talent). Their decision to avoid any possibility of objectifying themselves by wearing sexually provocative clothing is a sign of the pride they have in claiming their voice. Although Lyte and Boss may be on one end of the spectrum in terms of the non-explicitly sexual way they groom themselves (Lyte [1993a] says "Never ever have I said I was good-lookin' just one bad ass bitch from Brooklyn"), in general, women rappers who command respect are not the women who wear push-up bras and tight pants but are more often seen in baggy pants, boots, maybe a fitted top, with well-groomed hair and noticeable lipstick, or/and adherents of the Afrocentric aesthetic.

In conclusion, it is important to note that claiming of the body and its desires is one of various ways in which women are carving an empowered space in hip-hop. Included in this movement are the appropriation of male spaces, the discussion of traditionally feminist issues against male domination and the personification of folk heroes to characterize themselves. However, the sexuality present in women's voices in hip-hop is a clear example of a symbolic vehicle to the articulate power and self-possession these women possess in their lyrics and lives.

> *On stage we behave like sizzlin' flame*
> *And oh so cool when we rap you need a sweater*
> *The rhymes so tough you swear they're made of leather*
> *Get the best of your bunch and I'll bet that we're better*
> *Tell 'em why Pepa, tell 'em why, "Cause I desire"*
> —Salt 'n Pepa (1988)

NOTE

1. From Salt 'n Pepa (1988).

REFERENCES

Boss, Interview, *Art Forum Magazine*, June 1993.
BWP (Bytches with Problems), "Two Minute Brother," *The Bytches*, No Face Records, 1991.

Carby, H. (1992). It jus be's dat way sometime: The sexual politics of women's blues. In R. R. Warhol & D. P. Herndl (Eds.), *Feminisms: An anthology of literary theory and criticism.* New Brunswick, NJ: Rutgers University Press.

Cixous, H. (1992). The laugh of the Medusa. In R. R. Warhol & D. P. Herndl (Eds.), *Feminisms: An anthology of literary theory and criticism.* New Brunswick, NJ: Rutgers University Press.

Cox, I. (1980). One hour mama. *Mean mothers: Independent women's blues, Vol. I* (RR 1300). New York: Rosetta Records.

Digable Planets. (1992). It's good to be here. *A new refutation of time and space.* Burbank, CA: Warner Brothers Records.

Le Shaun featuring Cee W Da Blackmarket. (1993). Gimme head. *Roll wit da flava.* New York: Sony Music Entertainment.

Lorde, A. (1990). "Age, race, class and sex: Women redefining difference." In R. Ferguson, M. Gever, T. T. Minh-ha, & C. West (Eds.), *Out there: Marginalization and contemporary cultures* (pp. 281-287). Cambridge: MIT Press.

MC Lyte. (1993a). Brooklyn. *Ain't no other.* New York: First Priority Music.

MC Lyte. (1993b). Ruffneck. *Ain't no other.* New York: First Priority Records.

Minh-ha, T. (1989). *Woman, native, other: Writing post-coloniality and feminism.* Bloomington: Indiana University Press.

Monie Love. (1993). Mo Monie. *In a word or two.* Burbank, CA: Warner Brothers Records.

Salt 'n Pepa, "Get Up Everybody (Get Up)," *A Salt With a Deadly Pepa.* New York: London Records, 1988.

Salt 'n Pepa, "I Desire," *Hot, Cool and Vicious.* New York: London Records, 1988.

Salt 'n Pepa, "Shoop." *Very Necessary.* New York: London Records, 1993.

Salt 'n Pepa, "Shake Your Thang." *A Salt With a Deadly Pepa.* New York: London Records, 1988.

60

"Fear of a Black Planet"

Rap Music and Black Cultural Politics in the 1990s

TRICIA ROSE

SHOW-STOPPERS

Picture this: Thousands of young Black folks milled around waiting to get into the large arena. The big rap summer tour was in town, and it was a prime night for one to show one's stuff. The pre-show show was in full effect. Folks were dressed in the latest "fly gear": bicycle shorts, high-top sneakers, chunk jewelry, baggy pants, and polka-dotted tops. The hair styles were a fashion show in themselves: high-top fade designs, dreads, corkscrews, and braids. Crews of young women were checking out the brothers; posses of brothers were scoping out the sisters, each comparing styles among themselves. Some wide-eyed pre-teenyboppers were soaking in the teenage energy, thrilled to be out with the older kids.

As the lines for entering the arena began to form, dozens of mostly White private security guards dressed in red polyester v-neck sweaters and grey work pants began corralling the crowd through security checkpoints. The free-floating spirit started to sour, and a sense of hostility mixed with humiliation crystallized. Men and women were lined up separately in preparation for the weapons search. Coed groups dispersed and people moved toward their respective search lines. Each person had to submit to a full-

---

NOTE: Excerpts reprinted from the *Journal of Negro Education*, Vol. 60, No. 3 (1991), by permission of the publisher and the author.

body pat-down and a pocketbook, knapsack, and soul search. Generally, however, it appeared that the men were being treated with less respect and more hostility.

As I approached the female security guards, fear began to well up inside me. What if, I wondered to myself, they find something I was not allowed to bring inside? What is prohibited, anyway? I stopped to think: "All I have in my small purse is my wallet, eyeglasses, keys, and a notepad, nothing 'dangerous.' " The female security guard patted me down and scanned my body with an electronic scanner while anxiously keeping an eye on the other sisters in line to make sure no one slipped past her. She opened my purse and fumbled through it, pulling out a nail file. She stared at me as if to say, "Why did you bring this in here?" I did not answer her right away, hoping she would drop the file back into my purse and let me go through. She continued to stare at me, trying to size me up to see if I was there to cause trouble. By now, however, my attitude had turned foul; my childlike enthusiasm to see my favorite rappers had all but fizzled out. I did not know the file was in my purse, but the guard's accusatory posture rendered such innocent excuses moot. Finally, I replied tersely: "It's a nail file, what's the problem?" The guard handed it back to me, satisfied (I supposed) that I did not intend to use it as a weapon, and I proceeded into the arena. As I passed her, I thought bitterly to myself: "This arena is a public place and I am entitled to come here and bring a nail file if I want to." Yet, my words rang hollow in my head; the language of entitlement could not erase my sense of alienation. I felt harassed and unwanted: "This arena isn't mine, it is hostile, alien territory." An unspoken message hung in the air. "You're not wanted here, let's get this over with and then we'll just send you all back where you came from." By this point, I was glad I had brought the nail file. I mused: "At least if one of those guards harasses me I'll have something to fight back with."

I recount this incident for several reasons. First, incidents similar to it continue to take place when rap concerts are held. A hostile tenor, if not one of actual verbal abuse, is a regular part of the rap fan's contact with arena security and police. Second, I want to provide a depiction of the high-level anxiety and antagonism that confronts young Black rap fans who are often merely tolerated and regarded with heightened suspicion and hostility by concert security forces. Imagine now the level of frustration that might possibly well up in a young Black teenaged boy or girl faced with this kind of social antagonism on a consistent basis. Large arenas and other hostile institutions that treat young African Americans with suspicion and fear are themselves often the subject of rappers' lyrics. Indeed, Hip Hop artists articulate a range of counter-reactions to a variety of institutional policing efforts faced by many young African Americans.[1] . . .

This is not surprising since most young African Americans are positioned in fundamentally antagonistic relationships to the institutions that most prominently frame and constrain their lives. The public school system, the police, and the popular media perceive and construct them as a dangerous internal element in urban America—an element that if allowed to roam about freely will threaten the social order, an element that must be policed. The social construction of rap and rap-related violence is fundamentally linked to the social discourse on Black containment and fears of a Black planet. In this light, arena security forces are the metaphorical foot-soldiers in the war to contain African Americans' public presence and public pleasure. The paramilitary posture of concert guards is a surface manifestation of a complex network of ideological and economic processes that attempt to justify the policing of rap music, Black youth, and African Americans generally.

It is this ideological position regarding Black youth that frames media and institutional attacks on rap and separates resistance to rap from attacks sustained by rock-and-roll artists. Black expression is by no means the only expression under attack. Popular White expressions, especially heavy metal rock music has recently sustained increased sanction and assaults by politically and economically powerful organizations such as the Parent's Music Resource Center (PMRC), American Family Association (AFA), and Focus on the Family (FF). These organizations are not fringe groups; they are supported by major corporations, national school associations, and local police and municipal officials.[2] However, critical differences exist between the nature of the attacks made against Black youth expression and White youth expression. The terms of the assaults on rap music, for example, are part of a long-standing sociologically based discourse that positions Black influences as a cultural threat to American society.[3] Consequently, rappers, their fans, and Black youth in general are constructed as co-conspirators in the spread of Black aesthetic and discursive influence. Heavy metal rock music may be viewed as a threat to the fiber of American society by the anti-rock organizations but the fans (e.g., "our children") are depicted as *victims* of its influence. Unlike heavy metal's victims, the majority of rap's fans are the youngest representatives of a Black presence whose cultural difference is an ongoing internal threat to America's cultural development. These differences between the ideological nature of sanctions against rap and heavy metal are of critical importance because they articulate the ways in which racial discourses deeply inform social control efforts in the United States.

According to Haring (1989), "venue availability [for rap tours] is down 33% because buildings are limiting rap shows."[4] The apparent genesis of arena owners' "growing concern" is the September 10, 1988, Nassau (NY) Coliseum rap show when the stabbing death of 19-year-old Julio Fuentes focussed national attention on rap concert-related "violence." As Haring notes:

> In the wake of that incident, TransAmerica [a major insurance company] cancelled blanket insurance coverage for shows produced by G Street Express in Washington D.C., the show's promoter. Although G Street has since obtained coverage, the fallout of that cancellation has cast a pall over rap shows, resulting in many venues imposing stringent conditions or refusing to host the shows at all. (p. 80)

That the experience was frightening and dangerous for those involved is incontestable; however, the incident was not the first to result in an arena death, nor was it the largest or most threatening. During the same weekend of the Fuentes stabbing, 1,500 people were hurt when a "crowd without tickets tried to pull down fences" during singer Michael Jackson's performance in Liverpool, England (Associated Press, 1988). Yet, the Associated Press article made no mention of insurance company cancellations, no similar pall was cast over Jackson's music or musical genre, nor was any particular group held accountable for the incident. What sparked the venue owners' panic in the Nassau event was a preexisting anxiety regarding rap's core audience, namely Black working-class youth. The growing popularity of rap music and the media's interpretation of the incident fed directly into those anxieties. The Nassau incident and the social control discourse that frames it provides justification for a wide range of efforts to contain the Black teen presence while shielding these practices behind naturalized concerns over public safety.

The pall cast over rap shows was primarily facilitated by New York media coverage of the incident. The *New York Post* headline, "Rampaging Teen Gang Slays 'Rap' Fan" (Pelleck & Sussman, 1988) fed easily into White fears that Black teens need only a spark to start an uncontrollable urban forest fire. Fear of Black anger, lawlessness, and amorality were affirmed by the media's interpretation and description of this incident. . . . According to the *New York Times* coverage of the Nassau incident, the stabbing was a byproduct of a "robbery spree" conducted by a dozen or so young men (Marriott, 1988); Fuentes was apparently stabbed while attempting to retrieve his girlfriend's stolen jewelry. Marriott notes that of the 10,000 concertgoers, this dirty dozen was solely responsible for the incident. While the race of the perpetrator was not mentioned in the text, a photo of a handcuffed Black male (sporting a Beverly Hills Polo Club sweatshirt!) and mention of the assailants' Bedford-Stuyvesant residences stereotypically positioned them as members of the inner-city Black poor. This portrait of wanton Black male aggressiveness was framed by an enlarged inset quote which read: "A detective said the thieves 'were in a frenzy, like sharks feeding.' " By contrast, my own conversations with people who attended the event revealed that many concertgoers had no idea the incident even took place until they read the newspapers the next day.

. . . The event was framed exclusively by the perspective of the police; no quotes were included from other concert patrons or anyone other than Nassau County Police Commissioner Rozzi and a Detective Nolan. In the Nassau Coliseum case, police reports and media coverage form a solitary text binding racist depictions of Blacks as animals to ostensibly objective, statistically-based police documentation, thus rendering any other interpretation of the so-called night of rampage irrelevant. Ultimately, this reporting provides venue owners with perfect justification to significantly curtail or ban rap performances at their arenas. . . .

Venue owners may have the final word on booking decisions but they are not the only site of institutional gate keeping. Another major power broker, the insurance industry, can refuse to insure an act approved by venue management. By way of explanation, to gain access to a venue a touring band or group first hires a booking agent to negotiate the act's fee. The booking agent then hires a concert promoter who "purchases" the group's show and presents the show to both the insurance company and the venue managers. If an insurance company will not insure a show because they believe it represent an unprofitable risk, then the venue owner will not book the show. Moreover, the insurance company and the venue owner reserve the right to charge whatever insurance or permit fees they deem reasonable on a case-by-case basis. For example, Three Rivers Stadium in Pittsburgh (PA) recently tripled its normal $20,000 permit fee for the group The Grateful Dead. Those insurance companies that will insure rap concerts have raised their minimum coverage from about $500,000 to almost $5 million worth of coverage per show (Rose, personal interview with Richard Walters of Famous Talent Agency, 1990). Accordingly, several major arenas have made it almost impossible to book a rap show, and others have flatly refused to book rap acts at all.

During my interview with Richard Walters, a booking agent with the Famous Talent Agency (a major booking agency that books many prominent rap acts) I asked him if booking agents had responded to venue bans on rap music by leveling charges of racial discrimination against venue owners. His answer was stunning:

> These facilities are privately owned, [owners] can do anything they want. You say to them: "You won't let us in because you're discriminating against Black kids." They say to you, "Fuck you, who cares? Do whatever you got to do, but you're not coming in here. You, I don't need you. I don't want you. Don't come, don't bother me. I will book hockey, ice shows, basketball, country music and graduations. I still do all kinds of things 360 days out of the year. But I don't need you. I don't need fighting, shootings and stabbings." Why do they care? They have their image to maintain. (Rose, 1990)

Walters' imaginary conversation is a brutally candid description both of the scope of power venue owners have over access to large public urban spaces and the racially exclusionary silent code that governs booking policies. . . .

The rap community is aware that the "violence at rap concerts" label is being used to contain Black mobility and rap music, not to diminish violence against Blacks. Rappers have re-articulated a long-standing awareness among African Americans that crimes against Blacks (especially Black-on-Black crimes), do not carry equal moral weight or political imperative. Ice Cube's (1990) "Endangered Species" captures a familiar reading of state-sanctioned violence against young Black males. In it, Ice Cube graphically illustrates the sustained hostility many police officers exhibit toward young black men. At one striking point, Ice Cube rewrites the familiar police department slogan from "To serve and protect" to "to serve, protect and break a nigga's neck."

Since the Nassau Coliseum incident "violence" at rap concerts has continued to take place, and the media's assumed links between rap and disorder have grown more facile. The media's repetition of rap-related violence and the urban problematic that it conjures is not limited to the crime blotters: it also informs live performance critiques. In either circumstance the assumption made is that the significance of rap is its aesthetic and spatial disruptions, not its musical innovation and expressive capacity.[5] Consequently, the dominant media critiques of rap's aesthetic are conditioned by the omnipresent fears of Black influence—again, fears of a Black (aesthetic) planet.

In a particularly hostile *Los Angeles Times* review of Public Enemy's 1990 summer tour stop at the San Diego Sports Arena, newspaper critic John D'Agostino (1990) articulates a complex microcosm of social anxieties concerning Black youth, Black aesthetics, and rap music. D'Agostino's extensive next-day review column, entitled "Rap Concert Fails to Sizzle in San Diego," features a prominent caption: "Although it included a brawl, the Sports Arena concert seemed to lack steam and could not keep the under-sized capacity audience energized" (p. F-1). In the opening sentence D'Agostino confesses that "rap is not a critic's music; it is a disciple's music." This confession hints at its author's cultural illiteracy and is itself sufficient to render his subsequent critique irrelevant; yet D'Agostino continues, offering a description of the event which completely contradicts the article's title and caption. Despite the caption's suggestion of a slow and less than exciting event, the article's opening paragraph presents the audience as mindless and dangerous fanatics, mesmerized by rap's rhythms:

> For almost five hours, devotees of the Afros, Queen Latifah, Kid 'n Play, Digital Underground, Big Daddy Kane and headliners Public Enemy were jerked into spasmodic movement by what seemed little more than intermittent segments of a single rhythmic continuum. It was hypnotic in the way of sensory deprivation, a mind- and body-numbing marathon of monotony whose deafening, pre-recorded drum and bass tracks and roving klieg lights frequently turned the audience of 6,500 into a single-minded moveable beast. Funk meets Nuremberg Rally. (p. F-5)

Apparently, rap music is completely unintelligible to D'Agostino; moreover, his inability to interpret the sounds frightens him. This reading of the concert event, which makes explicit his fear and ignorance, condemns rap on precisely the grounds that make it compelling. For example, because the reviewer cannot explain why a series of bass or drum tracks moved the crowd, the audience seemed "jerked into spasmodic movement" suggestive of an "automatic" or "involuntary" response. The coded familiarity of the rhythms and "hooks" that rap samples from other Black music (especially funk and soul music) carries with it the power of Black collective memory. These sounds are cultural markers, and responses to them are in a sense "automatic" because they immediately conjure collective Black experience, past and present (Lipsitz, 1990). D'Agostino, while he senses the rhythmic continuum, interprets it as "monotonous" and "mind- and body-numbing." The very pulse that fortified the audience in San Diego, left him feeling sensorially deprived; the rhythms that empowered and stimulated the crowd numbed him, body and mind. D'Agostino's subsequent description of the music as capable of moving the crowd as a "single-minded, moveable beast" further amplifies his confusion and anxiety regarding the power and meaning of the drums in Black musical culture. What he perceives as monotonous percussive rhythms is frightening to him precisely because that same pulse energized and empowered the mostly Black, youthful audience. Unable to negotiate the relationship between his fear of the audience and of the wall of sound that supported their pleasure yet pushed him to the margins, D'Agostino interprets Black pleasure as dangerous and automatic.

. . . By linking funk (rap) music to a Nazi rally, D'Agostino ultimately depicts Black youth as an aggressive, dangerous, fascist element whose behavior is sick, inexplicable, and orchestrated by rappers (whom he likens to hatemongering rally organizers). Rap, he suggests, is thus not even a disciples' music but rather a soundtrack for the celebration of Black fascist domination. Once this construction of Black fascism is in place, D'Agostino devotes the bulk of his review to the performances, describing them as "juvenile," "puerile," and, in the case of Public Enemy, an act that "relies on the controversy to maintain interest." In mid-review he describes a brawl that followed Digital Underground's performance:

> After the house lights were brought up following DU's exit, a fight broke out in front of the stage. Security guards, members of various rappers' entourages, and fans joined in the fray that grew to mob size and then pushed into a corner of the floor at one side of the stage. People rushed the area from all parts of the arena, but the scrapers were so tightly balled together that few serious punches could be thrown, and, in a few minutes, a tussle that threatened to become a small scale riot instead lost stream. (p. F-5) . . .

D'Agostino concludes by suggesting that rap is fizzling out, that juvenile antics and staged controversy no longer hold audiences' attention and therefore signify the death of rap music. What happened to the "single-minded, moveable beast" that reared its ugly head in his introduction? How did Black fascism dissolve into harmless puerility in fewer than five hours? D'Agostino had to make that move; his distaste for rap music, coupled with his fear of Black youth, left him little alternative but to slay the single-minded beast by literally disconnecting its power source. Ultimately, his review sustains a fear of Black energy and passion while it simultaneously attempts to allay this fear by suggesting that rap is dying. The purported imminent death of rap music, however, is a myth that deliberately misconstrues Black rage as mere juvenile rebellion yet retains the necessary specter of Black violence to justify the social repression of rap music and Black youth alike. The concert that D'Agostino claims "failed to sizzle" was, in fact, too hot to handle. . . .

Rap music is fundamentally linked to larger social constructions of Black culture as an internal threat to dominant American culture and social order. According to hooks (1990), rap's capacity as a form of testimony and an articulation of the young, Black, urban critical voice has profound potential as a language of liberation and social protest. Contestation over the meaning and significance of rap music, controversies regarding its ability to occupy public space, and struggles to retain its expressive freedom constitute critical aspects of contemporary Black cultural politics.

During the centuries-long period of Western slavery, elaborate rules and laws were designed to control slave populations. Constraining the mobility of slaves, especially at night and in groups, was of special concern because slave owners reasoned that revolts could be organized by Blacks who moved too freely and without surveillance (Davis, 1966). Whites were rightfully confident that Blacks had good reason to escape, revolt, and retaliate. Contemporary laws and practices that curtail and constrain Black mobility in urban America function in much the same way and for similar reasons. Likewise large groups of today's African Americans, especially teenagers, represent a modern threat to the social order of oppression. Albeit more sophisticated and more difficult to trace, contemporary policing of African Americans resonates with the legacy of slavery.

Rap's poetic voice is deeply political in content and spirit, but its hidden struggle—that of access to public space and community resources and the interpretation of Black expression—constitutes rap's hidden politics. . . .

NOTES

1. For example, see Public Enemy, *Fear of a Black Planet* (Columbia Records, 1990); Salt n Pepa "Negro wit an Ego," *Blacks Magic* (Next Plateau Records, 1990); and NWA "**** The Police," *Straight Outta Compton* (Priority Records, 1988).

2. See *Rock and Roll Confidential* (RRC), especially their special pamphlet, "You've Got a Right to Rock: Don't Let Them Take It Away" (1990). This pamphlet is a detailed documentation of the censorship movements and their institutional bases and attacks. *RRC* is edited by David Marsh and can be subscribed to by writing to *RRC*, Dept. 7, Box 341305, Los Angeles, CA 90034.

3. Attacks on earlier popular Black expressions such as jazz and rock-and-roll were grounded in fears that White youth were deriving too much pleasure from Black expressions, and that these primitive, alien expressions were dangerous to young people's moral development (see Chapple & Garofalo, 1979; Erenberg, 1981; Jones, 1963; Lipsitz, 1990; Ogren, 1989).

4. Obviously, Haring (1989) is referring to building owners. In my research on venues, writers and venue representatives consistently refer to the buildings as the point of power and not their owners. This language serves to render invisible the powerful people who control public space access and make discriminatory bureaucratic decisions.

5. John Parales and Peter Watrous, two prominent popular music critics for the *New York Times*, have made noteworthy attempts to offer complex and interesting critiques of rap music. In many cases, however, a significant number of letters to the editor have appeared complaining about the appearance and content of their reviews and articles.

REFERENCES

Associated Press. (1988, September 12). 1500 hurt at Jackson concert. *New York Post*, p. 9.

Chapple, S., & Garofalo, R. (1979). *Rock 'n roll is here to pay*. Chicago: Nelson Hall.

D'Agostino, J. (1990, August 28). Concert fails to sizzle in San Diego. *Los Angeles Times* (San Diego edition), pp. F-1, F-5.

Davis, D. B. (1966). *The problem of slavery in Western culture.* Ithaca, NY: Cornell University Press.

Erenberg, L. A. (1981). *Steppin'out: New York night life and the transformation of American culture, 1890-1930.* Chicago: University of Chicago Press.

Haring, B. (1989, December 16). Many doors still closed to rap tours. *Billboard*, p. 1+.

hooks, b. (1990). *Yearning: Race, gender and cultural politics.* Boston: South End Press.

Ice Cube. (1990). *Amerikka's most wanted.* Priority Records.

Jones, L. (1963). *Blues people.* New York: Morrow Quill.

Lipsitz, G. (1990). *Time passages: Collective memory and American popular culture.* Minneapolis: University of Minnesota Press.

Marriott, M. (1988, September 19). 9 charged, 4 with murder, in robbery spree at L.I. rap concert. *New York Times*, p. B-3.

Ogren, K. J. (1989). *The jazz revolution: Twenties America and the meaning of jazz.* New York: Oxford University Press.

Pelleck, C. J., & Sussman, C. (1988, September 12). Rampaging teen gang slays "rap" fan. *New York Post*, p. 9.

Rose, T. (1990). Personal interview with Richard Walters, Famous Talent Agency.

.61

Imitation of Life

JAMES LEDBETTER

In 1989, Madonna gushed to an interviewer: "When I was a little girl, I wished I was black. . . . If being black is synonymous with having soul, then, yes, I feel that I am." In concert, the Beastie Boys strut around the stage in an exaggerated "black" walk and chant a street dialect somewhere between an imitation of black speech and a bad translation of it. Radio clown Howard Stern has said of his childhood: "I remember for the longest time wanting to be black." A 16-year-old white Pennsylvanian says his high school is full of "wiggers," whites so desperate to adopt black modes of dress and conduct that they end up being parodies. Call 'em wanna-be's, call 'em rip-offs, call 'em suckers, but they're everywhere—white folks who think they're black, or wish they were.

The arrival of hip-hop as a leading musico-cultural force has created an entire subclass of these wanna-be's. Following the Beasties' lead, there was 3rd Bass, white rappers who, until their recent breakup, expressed an almost painful identification with New York blacks. Then came House of Pain, an Irish-American rap group whose video cuts from black-styled hip-hop dancing to marching bagpipe players. Now there's A.D.O.R., a hard-core white rapper whose name means Against Discrimination of Race and a Definition of Real. Perhaps most extreme are Young Black Teenagers, an all-white and not very good rap group whose strut and postures are "blacker" than most of their fans, even more so than most blacks. What's more,

NOTE: Reprinted from *Vibe*, premiere issue (Fall 1992), by permission of the author.

millions of white fans of black rappers have adopted modes of dress, speech, and style that they consider black.

The phenomenon isn't new. American writers, sociologists, and armchair sociologists have long spotlighted black wanna-be's, arguing that their desire to be black has some tenuous connection to African-American social oppression. Norman Mailer, in his prescient, bizarre, and overwritten 1957 essay "The White Negro" asserted that "it is no accident that the source of Hip is the Negro for he has been living on the margin between totalitarianism and democracy for two centuries." Nor is it new that attempted race bending expresses itself musically, with earlier examples ranging from minstrel shows, a dominant Southern entertainment form through the mid-20th century, to Janis Joplin, who a generation ago told a reporter: "Being black for a while will make me a better white."

It's a curious spectacle, and one that pisses off a lot of people, both black and white. Americans take their segregation very seriously, and not just the de facto racial separation of housing, education, and income, but our cultural apartheid as well. America reacts dramatically, even violently, to cultural expressions that suggest racial admixture—the original 1952 rock 'n' roll riot in Cleveland was due not only to an oversold show, but also, some say, to the fact that inside the Cleveland Arena ballroom, blacks and whites were dancing together to the same music.

In part, the disgust with wanna-be's comes from the sheer vulgarity of the white who cavalierly adopts the black mantle without having to experience life-long racism, restricted economic opportunity, or any of the thousand insults that characterize black American life. (Similar ridicule was aimed at an earlier generation's purveyors of radical chic.) And, as depicted in Lou Reed's outrageous lyrics, whites' interpretation of what it means "to be black," even when they're attempting to "understand" or "empathize with" victims of racism, often results in a version that looks an awful lot like racism itself. Finally, whites have been riffing off—or ripping off—black cultural forms for more than a century and making a lot more money from them. Whether it's Al Jolson, Elvis, the Rolling Stones, Blues Brothers, Commitments, New Kids, or Beasties, it's impossible to deny that, as a rule, the market responds much better to a black sound with a white face.

There are two crucial factors separating the minstrel of past generations from today's racial flaneurs. The first is easily identified: the market. In Mailer's essay, for example, the white hipster was necessarily on the margins; Mailer even identified him with the psychopath. The white Negro, with his lust for jazz and grass, was a threat to the American way of life, a figure whose existential insight was contingent on his isolation from society. Today, the inverse is true: There are a number of intersecting multibillion-dollar American industries (music, advertising, television, sports) whose survival at current profit levels depends on the existence of a massive audience of white Negroes.

Take *Saturday Night Live*'s fall 1991 premiere, hosted by Michael Jordan, with musical guest Public Enemy and cameo appearances by Spike Lee and Jesse Jackson. It was punctuated by Gatorade ads featuring white and black kids singing "If I Could Be Like Mike." Coincidentally, it aired the night

Miles Davis died and thus the live program carried several allusions to the jazz legend. The resulting episode was the highest-rated *SNL* season opener ever. It wasn't just black viewers who made those Nielsens jump, but whites who, as fans of basketball, hip-hop, jazz, and Lee's movies, have become more or less integrated into a black ethos. Rap music may be, as Chuck D says, black people's CNN, but there are a lot of white folks tuning into that signal too.

And where such black-oriented whites do not exist, they must—through advertising, fashion, MTV, and magazines such as this one—be created. Somewhere in the mid-Black Power period, America's culture industry discovered that, instead of being polarizing and threatening, black slang, music, and energy could be harnessed for immense profits. (My earliest memory of this co-optation was the slogan "Write on, Bros., write on," used to sell 19-cent Write Bros. pens.) Just as on the record charts, hip-hop and its derivatives have taken over this promotional agenda; its beat and style are today used to hype not just hip-hop artists, but also television shows, children's clothing, bubble gum—even hair-care products for whites. This guarantees thousands, even millions more hipsters than Mailer could ever have imagined, but their value is accordingly debased. If a white can become "hip" simply by buying the right shampoo or CD, then the control of "hip" has been passed from society's rebels to its representatives.

The second factor differentiating the contemporary wanna-be is more obscure, and not as powerful as the market, though its rise also corresponds to the development, beginning in the mid-1960s, of a more militant black agenda. There exists today a limited (but nonetheless quasi-institutional-ized) school of music critics, artists, record industry honchos, intellectuals, and activists whose tolerance for the white Negro has more or less expired. This isn't to say that, in the past, white beatniks or hippies were universally embraced by the blacks they emulated. But there has been a shift in the balance of power: Whereas black jazz musicians in the 1940s had to shrug (or innovate further) when whites copied their musical styles, today the more exploitative wanna-be's—Vanilla Ice is the best example—are called out as the frauds they are. Armed with a body of criticism that extends from LeRoi Jones through Greg Tate, and with an ideology that draws strength from Afrocentrism (even while rejecting portions of it), rappers and writers today regularly dis wanna-be's in public as opportunists or racists or both. One of the more extraordinary developments is that even the contemporary white hipster must go through this ritual of denouncing a fellow wanna-be as somehow being less authentic. Both 3rd Bass albums, for example, seem almost obsessed with denouncing Vanilla Ice, as if his downfall would inflate their "genuine" attachment to blacks and to rap.

The authenticity argument gets even blurrier when rappers rank on Hammer, thus far their most commercially successful colleague. To say, as so many have, that Hammer can't rap or has sold out introduces the idea of the Oreo, the inauthentic black, cousin to the wanna-be (and a target of equally vehement criticism from many black artists and critics, notably Ice Cube in "True to the Game" on *Death Certificate*). It also breaks down the simple dichotomy under which both wanna-be's and some black artists and critics operate; it admits the possibility that blackness is a quality other than pigmentation, even other than a social condition, since Hammer's upbringing wasn't radically different from those considered true black rappers. This is the direction in which a number of intellectuals, notably Stuart Hall and Paul Giroy, have been heading, insisting that "blackness" is too complex, too amorphous a code to be reduced to a simple question of color or even class.

In a way, the very existence of the wanna-be implies this complexity. Because while the Vanilla Ices of the world can be explained as mere economic exploiters, the 1990s white suburbanite gets no money from listening to Public Enemy. And at least he or she gets out of it some exposure to a black urban reality—which is more than Beaver Cleaver ever got. Janis Joplin's comment, sincere as it was naïve, speaks to the multiple motivations behind youth's racial switcheroo—it's intended to resolve a racial gap that the white kid doesn't feel responsible for. Lou Reed's offensive, funny lyrics are a frank expression of the self-emptiness that makes some renegade whites want to be "black" (and, at the same time, a vicious parody of that desire). Later in the song, Reed sings of wanting to be shot like Martin Luther King and wanting to be like Malcolm X. Those lyrics, as nasty as they are, speak to a genuine yearning: There is, for young American whites, no white leader in recent memory who invokes such a powerful self-identity and moral force. The closest for them may be artists and rock stars (including Reed), but they never achieved anything approaching the status and power those men had. That both were gunned down only enhances, for black and whites, their embodiment of authenticity and unapologetic rebellion.

By listening to rap and tapping into it as extramusical expressions, then, whites are attempting to bear witness to—even correct—their own often sterile, oppressive culture. Cornel West has referred to this as the Afro-Americanization of American youth, a potent thought since this country is fast headed toward a non-white majority for the first time since its colonization. If current populations growth trends hold, with Asian, Latino, black, and other nonwhite segments growing at much higher rates than white, the U.S. will be a "minority majority" nation within the next century. Wanna-be's, in that sense, are harbingers of America's multicultural future.

Intentions, though, aren't enough, today or ever. The most difficult (and almost always unasked) question for wanna-be's, particularly those with access to airwaves and media, is: Does their identification with what they view as black culture extend to taking concrete steps to end America's political and cultural apartheid? Are they at the very least willing to renounce, up front, the systemic abuses of the white order, from which, regardless of their implicit dissent, they have doubtlessly benefited? It accomplishes nothing to play at being black and ignore the society that made you want to do it. Indeed, the wanna-be is at great risk of using black posturing solely as a way to assuage his or her conscience.

The challenge for the wanna-be is to make the critique of America more explicit. There are very clear analogies in politics. Whites would find themselves on the defensive a lot less if they stopped ignoring those political causes that seem to affect blacks almost exclusively. For example, where are the white political leaders willing to put themselves on the line to oppose the Bush Administration's unconscionable wholesale repatriation of Haitian refugees, announced not coincidentally in an election year? More shocking is that even after a willingly slumbering nation was awakened by the video-tape of white cops bashing Rodney King, no prominent white leader has announced that police brutality against people of color is an outrage that must be stopped. If America's wanna-be's wanna be taken seriously, they ought to be adopting such issues. For white hip-hop artists, this means using the music as a vehicle to discuss segregation and economic blight, rather than simply as a way to provide one more commercial distraction. For the far more numerous white fans, it means screaming out that you accept the criticism of the American system offered by the likes of Ice Cube and Public Enemy, and you want the society to do something more than buy and sell their records.

Afterword

Media Activism

One motivation for producing this book was our desire to see media studies become a multicultural field of inquiry. Toward this end, we have attempted to select articles that speak to the complex ways in which race, class and gender are central organizational features of Western society. We see our book as part of a much larger project taking place in education today that "excavates, affirms, and interrogates the histories, memories, and stories of the devalued others who have been marginalized from the official discourse of the canon" (Giroux, 1992, p. 101). Many text books in media studies tend to perpetuate the marginalization of people of color and White women by having separate chapters on race and gender where the "minority" group is the focus of interest (the working class almost never get mentioned, much less have their own chapter). This tends to problematicize "color" or "femininity," diverting attention from the ways in which Whiteness and masculinity are socially constructed. Our initial intention was to ensure a larger presence of articles that examined the privileged group, but it soon became apparent that, by and large, these still have to be written. Our more scaled-down aim is that this book will play a part in encouraging students to examine how race, class and gender inform the production, construction and consumption of media representation in this society.

Although we made every attempt to include articles that examine all the moments in the communication process, it is apparent that the majority of selections privilege textual analysis, reflecting an overall tendency in cultural studies in this country. There is no doubt that this focus on text is a much needed balance to the previous tendency in both the Marxist and the social scientific (positivist) schools of communication studies to see the text as the unproblematic bearer of meaning. However, one of the results of what we see as this overemphasis on text is the undertheorizing of how the politics of ownership "have traceable consequences for the range of discourses and representations in the public domain and for audiences' access to them" (Golding & Murdock, 1991, p. 15).

This discussion regarding the nature of scholarship and research on the media is not simply academic because, ultimately, it affects the realm of social activism. If, as some of the more text-orientated scholars suggest, audiences have the ultimate power over meaning, then it seems that there is little need to organize for collective ownership of the means of cultural production. If on the other hand, we examine the incredible inequalities that exist not only in ownership but also in access, then activists may decide that transformation of the present advertising-based funding system is indeed a major goal. Clearly, if cultural studies is to retain its potentially transformative and liberatory edge, then political economy needs to be given more space than it is presently allotted.

We end our book with a call for media activism from George Gerbner. Over the years, Gerbner, together with colleagues Larry Gross, Michael Morgan and Nancy Signorielli, has been involved in research on the long-term effects of media violence. The Cultural Indicators Study has been one of the most important long-term studies in this country of both the content of media and the effects of living in a society where the supreme storyteller is the television. In addition to his scholarship, Gerbner has been active in giving testimony before numerous government committees and in organizations that aim to provide public access to the media. In this chapter, he clearly analyzes patterns of "entertainment violence" using a political economy approach, illustrating the power of combining scholarly research with an activist agenda. Reframing the concept of censorship, Gerbner's work suggests that corporate control of the media within a capitalist economy needs as much of an activist's attention as does government censorship.

REFERENCES

Giroux, H. (1992). *Border crossings: Cultural workers and the politics of education*. New York: Routledge.

Golding, P., & Murdock, G. (1991). Culture, communications, and political economy. In J. Curran & M. Gurevitch (Eds.), *Mass media and society*. London: Edward Arnold.

Television Violence

The Power and the Peril

GEORGE GERBNER

Humankind may have had more bloodthirsty eras, but none as filled with *images* of violence as the present. We are awash in a tide of violent representations such as the world has never seen. Images of expertly choreographed brutality drench our homes. There is no escape from the mass-produced mayhem pervading the life space of ever larger areas of the world.

The television overkill has drifted out of democratic reach since it was first reported by the National Association of Educational Broadcasters in 1951. The first Congressional hearings were held by Senator Estes Kefauver's Subcommittee on Juvenile Delinquency in 1954. Through several more rounds of hearings in the 1960s and 1970s, despite the accumulation of critical research results, despite condemnation by government commissions and virtually all medical, law enforcement, parents', educational and other organizations, and in the face of international embarrassment, violence has saturated the airways for the nearly 30 years we have been tracking it in our ongoing Cultural Indicators project[1] (Gerbner, Gross, Morgan, & Signorielli, 1993).

Broadcasters are licensed to serve "the public interest, convenience, and necessity." They are also paid to deliver a receptive audience to their business sponsors. Few industries are as public relations conscious as television. What compels them to endure public humiliation, risk the threat of repressive legislation and invite charges of undermining health, security and the social order? The answer is not popularity.

The usual rationalization that television violence "gives the audience what it wants" is disingenuous. As the trade knows well, and as we shall see, violence is not highly rated. But there is no free market or box office for television programs through which audiences could express their wants.

Unlike other media use, viewing is a ritual; people watch by the clock and not by the program. Ratings are determined more by the time of the program, the lead-in (previous program) and what else is on at the same time than by their quality or other attractions. Therefore, ratings are important because they set the price the advertiser pays for "buying" viewers available to the set at a certain time, but they have limited use as indicators of popularity. And even to the limited extent that a few violent programs may have a larger share of a certain time slot and can, therefore, extract a higher price for commercials, the incremental profits are hardly worth the social, institutional and political damage they exact. Why would the business establishment subsidize its own undoing?

Therefore, it is clear that something is wrong with the way the problem has been posed and addressed. Either the damage is not what it is commonly assumed to be, or television violence must have some driving force and utility other than popularity, or both. Indeed it is both, and more.

The usual question—"Does television violence incite real-life violence?—is itself a symptom rather than diagnostic tool of the problem. It obscures and, despite its alarming implications and intent, trivializes the issues involved.

Television violence must be understood as a complex scenario and an indicator of social relationships. It has both utility and consequences other than those usually considered in media and public discussion. And it is driven by forces other than free expression and audience demand.

Whatever else it does, violence in drama and news demonstrates power. It portrays victims as well as victimizers. It intimidates more than it incites. It paralyzes more than it triggers action. It defines majority might and minority risk. It shows one's place in the "pecking order" that runs society.

Violence is but the tip of the iceberg of a massive underlying connection to television's role as universal storyteller and an industry dependent on global markets. These relationships have not yet been recognized and integrated into any theory or regulatory practice. Television has been seen as one medium among many rather than as the mainstream of the cultural environment in which most children grow up and learn. Traditional regulatory and public interest conceptions are based on the obsolete assumption that the number of media outlets determines freedom and diversity of content. Today, however, a handful of global conglomerates can own many outlets in all media, deny entry to new and alternative perspectives and homogenize content. The common carrier concept of access and protection applicable to a public utility like the telephone also falls short when the issue is not so much the number of channels and individual access to them but the centralized mass production of stories to grow on.

Let us, then, preview the task of broadening a discourse that has gone on too long in a narrow and shallow groove. Violence on television is an integral part of a system of global marketing. It dominates an increasing share of the world's screens despite its relative lack of popularity in any country. Its consequences go far beyond inciting aggression. The system inhibits the portrayal of diverse dramatic approaches to conflict, depresses independent television production, deprives viewers of more popular choices, victimizes some and emboldens others, heightens general intimidation and invites repressive postures by politicians that exploit the widespread insecurities it itself generates.

The First Amendment to the U.S. Constitution forbade the only censors its authors knew—government—from interfering with the freedom of their press. Since then large conglomerates, virtual private governments, have imposed their formulas of overkill on media they own. Therefore, raising the issue of overkill directs attention to the controls that in fact abridge creative freedom, dominate markets and constrain democratic cultural policy.

Behind the problem of television violence is the critical issue of who makes cultural policy on whose behalf in the electronic age. The debate about violence creates an opportunity to move the larger cultural policy issue to center stage, where it has been in other democracies for some time.

The convergence of communication technologies concentrates control over the most widely shared messages and images. Despite all the technocratic fantasies about hundreds of channels, and with antiviolence posturing filling the mass media, it is rare to encounter discussion of the basic issue of who makes cultural policy. In the absence of such discussion, cultural policy is made on private and limited grounds by an invisible corporate directorate whose members are unknown, unelected and accountable only to their clients.

We need to ask the kinds of questions that can place the discussion of television violence as a cultural policy issue in a useful perspective. For example, What creative sources and resources will provide what mix of content moving on the "electronic superhighway" into every home? Who will tell the stories and for what underlying purpose? How can we assure survival of alternative perspectives, regardless of profitability and selling power?

There are no clear answers to these questions because, for one thing, they have not yet been placed on the agenda of public discourse. It will take organization, deliberation and exploration to develop an approach to answering them. What follows, then, is an attempt to draw from our research answers to some questions that can help develop such an approach. We will be asking, What is unique about television and about violence on television? What systems of "casting" and "fate" dominate its representations of life? What conceptions of reality do these systems cultivate? Why does violence play such a prominent, pervasive and persistent role in them? And, finally, how can we as a society deal with the overkill while, at the same time, enhancing rather than further curtailing cultural freedom and diversity?

THE NEW CULTURAL ENVIRONMENT

Nielsen figures show that, today, an American child is born into a home in which television is on an average of over 7 hours a day. For the first time in human history, most of the stories about people, life and values are told not by parents, schools, churches or others in the community who have something to tell but by a group of distant conglomerates that have something to sell.

Television, the mainstream of the new cultural environment, has brought about a radical change in the way children grow up, learn and live in our society. Television is a relatively nonselectively used ritual; children are its captive audience. Most people watch by the clock and not by the program. The television audience depends on the time of the day and the day of the week more than on the program. Other media require literacy, growing up, going out and selection based on some previously acquired tastes, values and predispositions. Traditional media research assumed such selectivity. But there are no "previously acquired tastes, values and predispositions" with television. Viewing starts in infancy and continues throughout life.

Television helps to shape from the outset the predispositions and selections that govern the use of other media. Unlike other media, television requires little or no attention; its repetitive patterns are absorbed in the course of living. They become part and parcel of the family's style of life, but they neither stem from nor respond to its particular and selective needs and wants. It is television itself that cultivates the tastes, values and predisposition that guide future selection of other media. That is why television has a major impact on what movies, magazines, newspapers and books can be sold best in the new cultural environment.

The roles children grow into are no longer homemade, handcrafted, community inspired. They are products of a complex, integrated and globalized manufacturing and marketing system. Television violence, defined as overt physical action that hurts or kills (or threatens to do so), is an integral part of that system. A study of "The Limits of Selective Viewing" (Sun, 1989) found that, on the whole, prime-time television presents a relatively small set of common themes, and violence pervades most of them.

Now, representations of violence are not necessarily undesirable. There is blood in fairy tales, gore in mythology, murder in Shakespeare. Not all violence is alike. In some contexts, violence can be a legitimate and even necessary cultural expression. Individually crafted, historically inspired, sparingly and selectively used expressions of symbolic violence can indicate the tragic costs of deadly compulsions. However, such a tragic sense of violence has been swamped by "happy violence" produced on the dramatic assembly line. This happy violence is cool, swift, painless and often spectacular, even thrilling, but usually sanitized. It always leads to a happy ending. After all, it is designed to entertain and not to upset; it must deliver the audience to the next commercial in a receptive mood.

The majority of network viewers have little choice of thematic context or cast of character types and virtually no chance of avoiding violence. Nor has the proliferation of channels led to greater diversity of actual viewing (see, for example, Gerbner, 1993; Gerbner et al., 1993; Morgan & Shanahan, 1991). If anything, the dominant dramatic patterns penetrate more deeply into viewer choices through more outlets managed by fewer owners airing programs produced by fewer creative sources.

MESSAGE SYSTEM ANALYSIS

My conclusions are based on the findings of our Cultural Indicators project (CI) that began in 1967. CI is based at the University of Pennsylvania's Annenberg School for Communication. It is a cumulative database and an ongoing research project that relates recurrent features of the world of television to media policy and viewer conceptions of reality. By 1994 its computer archive contained observations on 2,816 programs and 34,882 characters coded according to many thematic, demographic and action categories. The study is directed by this author in collaboration with Michael Morgan at the University of Massachusetts at Amherst and Nancy Signorielli at the University of Delaware.

CI is a three-pronged research effort: "Message system analysis" is the annual monitoring of television program content; "institutional policy analysis" looks at the economic and political bases of media decision making; "cultivation analysis" is an assessment of the long-range consequences of exposure to television's systems of messages.

Message system analysis is the study of the content of television programs. It includes every dramatic (fictional) program in each annual sample. It provides an unusual view of familiar territory. It is not a view of individual programs but an aggregate picture of the world of television, a bird's-eye view of what large communities of viewers absorb over long periods of time.

The role of violence in that world can be seen in our analysis of prime-time network programs and characters. Casting and fate, the demography of that world, are the important building blocks of the storytelling process. They have presented a stable pattern over the almost 30 years of monitoring network television drama and coding every speaking character in each year's sample. Middle-class White male characters dominate in numbers and power. Women play one out of three characters. Young people and the elderly make up one third and one fifth, respectively, of their actual proportions of the population. Most other minorities are even more underrepresented. That cast sets the stage for stories of conflict, violence and the projection of White male prime-of-life power. Most of those who are underrepresented are also those who, when portrayed, suffer the worst fate.

The average viewer of prime-time television drama (serious as well as comedic) sees in a typical week an average of 21 criminals arrayed against an army of 41 public and private law enforcers. There are 14 doctors, 6 nurses, 6 lawyers and 2 judges to handle them. An average of 150 acts of violence and about 15 murders entertain them and their children every week, and that does not count cartoons and the news. Those who watch over 3 hours a day (more than half of all viewers) absorb much more.

About one of three (31%) of all characters and more than half (52%) of major characters are involved in violence either as victims or as victimizers (or both) in any given week. The ratio of violence to victimization defines the price to be paid for committing violence. When one group can commit violence with relative impunity, the price it pays for violence is relatively low. When another group suffers more violence than it commits, the price is high.

In the total cast of prime-time characters, defined as all speaking parts regardless of the importance of the role, the average "risk ratio" (number of victims per 10 violents) is 12. Violence is an effective victimizer—and characterizer. Its distribution is not random; the calculus of risk is not evenly distributed. Women, children, poorer and older people and some minorities pay a higher price for violence than do males in the prime of life. The price paid in victims for every 10 violents is 15 for boys, 16 for girls, 17 for young women, 18.5 for lower class characters and over 20 for elderly characters.

Violence takes on an even more defining role for major characters. It involves more than half of all major characters (58% of men and 41% of women). Most likely to be involved either as perpetrators or victims, or both, are characters portrayed as mentally ill (84%), characters with mental or other disability (70%), young adult males (69%) and Latino/Hispanic Americans (64%). Children, lower class and mentally ill or otherwise disabled characters, pay the highest price—13 to 16 victims for every 10 perpetrators.

Lethal victimization extends the pattern. About 5% of all characters and 10% of major characters are involved in killing (kill or get killed or both). Being Latino/Hispanic or lower class means bad trouble: They are the most likely to kill and be killed. Being poor, old, Hispanic or a woman of color means double trouble, a disproportionate chance of being killed; they pay the highest relative price for taking another's life.

Among major characters, for every 10 "good" (positively valued) men who kill, about 4 are killed. But for every 10 "good" women who kill, 6 are killed, and for every 10 women of color who kill, 17 are killed. Older women characters get involved in violence only to be killed.

We calculated a violence "pecking order" by ranking the risk ratios of the different groups. Women, children, young people, lower class, disabled and Asian Americans are at the bottom of the heap. When it comes to killing, older and Latino/Hispanic characters also pay a higher than average price. In other words, hurting and killing by most majority groups extracts a tooth for a tooth. But minority groups tend to pay a higher price for their show of force. That imbalance of power is, in fact, what makes them minorities even when, as is the case for women, they are a numerical majority.

CULTIVATION ANALYSIS: THE "LESSONS" OF TELEVISION

What are the consequences? These representations are not the sole or necessarily even the main determinants of what people think or do. But they are the most pervasive, inescapable and policy-directed common and stable cultural contributions to what large communities absorb over long periods of time. We use the term *cultivation* to distinguish the long-term cultivation of assumptions about life and values from short-term "effects" that are usually assessed by measuring change as a consequence of exposure to certain messages. With television, one cannot take a measure before exposure and only rarely without exposure. Television tends to cultivate and confirm stable conceptions about life. Cultivation analysis measures these "lessons" as it explores whether those who spend more time with television are more likely than comparable groups of lighter viewers to perceive the real world in ways that reflect the most common and repetitive features of the television world (see Morgan & Signorielli, 1990, for a detailed discussion of the theoretical assumptions and methodological procedures of cultivation analysis).

The systemic patterns in television content that we observe through message system analysis provide the basis for formulating survey questions about people's conceptions of social reality. These questions form the basis of surveys administered to large and representative national samples of respondents. The surveys include questions about fear of crime, trusting other people, walking at night in one's own neighborhood, chances of victimization, inclination to aggression and so on. Respondents in each sample are divided into those who watch the most television, those who watch a moderate amount and those who watch the least. Cultivation is assessed by comparing patterns of responses in the three viewing groups (light, medium and heavy) while controlling for important demographic and other characteristics, such as education, age, income, gender, newspaper reading, neighborhood and so on.

These surveys indicate that long-term regular exposure to violence-laden television tends to make an independent contribution (e.g., in addition to all other factors) to the feeling of living in a mean and gloomy world. The lessons range from aggression to desensitization and to a sense of vulnerability and dependence.

The symbolic overkill takes its toll on all viewers. However, heavier viewers in every subgroup express a greater sense of apprehension than do light viewers in the same groups. They are more likely than comparable groups of light viewers to overestimate their chances of involvement in violence; to believe that their neighborhoods are unsafe; to state that fear of crime is a very serious personal problem and to assume that crime is rising, regardless of the facts of the case. Heavy viewers are also more likely to buy new locks, watchdogs and guns "for protection." It makes no difference what they watch because only light viewers watch more selectively; heavy viewers watch more of everything that is on the air. Our studies show that they cannot escape watching violence (see, for example, Gerbner et al., 1993; Sun, 1989).

Moreover, viewers who see members of their own group underrepresented but overvictimized seem to develop a greater sense of apprehension, mistrust and alienation, what we call the "mean world syndrome." Insecure, angry people may be prone to violence but are even more likely to be dependent on authority and susceptible to deceptively simple, strong, hardline postures. They may accept and even welcome repressive measures such as more jails, capital punishment, harsher sentences—measures that have never reduced crime but never fail to get votes—if that promises to relieve their anxieties. That is the deeper dilemma of violence-laden television.

THE STRUCTURAL
BASIS OF TELEVISION VIOLENCE

Formula-driven violence in entertainment and news is not an expression of freedom, viewer preference or even crime statistics. The frequency of violence in the media seldom, if ever, reflects the actual occurrence of crime in a community. It is, rather, the product of a complex manufacturing and marketing machine.

Mergers, consolidation, conglomeratization and globalization speed the machine. "Studios are clipping productions and consolidating operations, closing off gateways for newcomers," notes the trade paper *Variety* on the front page of its August 2, 1993, issue. The number of major studios declines while their share of domestic and global markets rises. Channels proliferate while investment in new talent drops, gateways close and creative sources shrink.

Concentration brings denial of access to new entries and alternative perspectives. It places greater emphasis on dramatic ingredients most suitable for aggressive international promotion. Having fewer buyers for their products forces program producers into deficit financing. That means that most producers cannot break even on the license fees they receive for domestic airings. They are forced into syndication and foreign sales to make a profit. They need a dramatic ingredient that requires no translation, "speaks action" in any language and fits any culture. That ingredient is violence. (Sex is second but, ironically, it runs into more inhibitions and restrictions.)

Syndicators demand *action* (the code word for violence) because it "travels well around the world," said the producer of *Die Hard 2* (which killed 264 compared to 18 in *Die Hard 1*). "Everyone understands an action movie. If I tell a joke, you may not get it but if a bullet goes through the window, we all know how to hit the floor, no matter the language" (quoted in Auletta, 1993). Our analysis shows that violence dominates U.S. exports. We compared 250 U.S. programs exported to 10 countries with 111 programs shown in the United States during the same year. Violence was the main theme of 40% of home-shown and 49% of exported programs. Crime-action series composed 17% of home-shown and 46% of exported programs.

The rationalization for all that is that violence "sells." But what does it sell to whom and at what price? There is no evidence that, other factors being equal, violence per se is giving most viewers, countries and citizens "what they want." The most highly rated programs are usually not violent. The trade paper *Broadcasting & Cable* (Editorial, 1993) editorialized that "the most popular programming is hardly violent as anyone with a passing knowledge of Nielsen ratings will tell you." The editorial added that "Action hours and movies have been the most popular exports for years" (p. 66)—that is, with the exporters, not with audiences. In other words, violence may help sell programs cheaply to broadcasters in many countries despite the dislike of their audiences. But television audiences do not buy programs, and advertisers, who do, pay for reaching the available audience at the least cost.

We compared data from over 100 violent and the same number of nonviolent prime-time programs stored in the CI database. The average

Nielsen rating of the violent sample was 11.1; the same for the nonviolent sample was 13.8. The share of viewing households in the violent and nonviolent samples was 18.9 and 22.5, respectively. The amount and consistency of violence in a series further increased the gap. Furthermore, the nonviolent sample was more highly rated than the violent sample for each of the five seasons studied.

However, despite their low average popularity, what violent programs lose on general domestic audiences they more than make up by grabbing the younger viewers that advertisers want to reach and by extending their reach to the global market hungry for a cheap product. Even though, typically, these imports are also less popular abroad than quality shows produced at home, their extremely low cost, compared to local production, makes them attractive to the broadcasters who buy them.

Of course, some violent movies, videos, video games and other spectacles do attract sizable audiences. But those audiences are small compared to the home audience for television. They are the selective retail buyers of what television dispenses wholesale. If only a small proportion of television viewers growing up with the violent overkill become addicted to it, they can make many movies and games spectacularly successful.

PUBLIC RESPONSE AND ACTION

Most television viewers suffer the violence daily inflicted on them with diminishing tolerance. Organizations of creative workers in media, health professionals, law enforcement agencies and virtually all other media-oriented professional and citizen groups have come out against "gratuitous" television violence. A March 1985 Harris survey showed that 78% disapprove of violence they see on television. A Gallup poll of October 1990 found 79% in favor of "regulating" objectionable content in television. A Times-Mirror national poll in 1993 showed that Americans who said they were "personally bothered" by violence in entertainment shows jumped to 59% from 44% in 1983. Furthermore, 80% said entertainment violence was "harmful" to society, compared with 64% in 1983.

Local broadcasters, legally responsible for what goes on the air, also oppose the overkill and complain about loss of control. *Electronic Media* reported on August 2, 1993, the results of its own survey of 100 general managers across all regions and in all market sizes. Three of four said there is too much needless violence on television; 57% would like to have "more input on program content decisions."

The Hollywood Caucus of Producers, Writers and Directors, speaking for the creative community, said in a statement issued in August 1993:

> We stand today at a point in time when the country's dissatisfaction with the quality of television is at an all-time high, while our own feelings of helplessness and lack of power, in not only choosing material that seeks to enrich, but also in our ability to execute to the best of our ability, is at an all-time low.

Far from reflecting creative freedom, the marketing of formula violence restricts freedom and chills originality. The violence formula is, in fact, a de facto censorship extending the dynamics of domination, intimidation and repression domestically and globally. Much of the typical political and legislative response exploits the anxieties that violence itself generates and offers remedies ranging from labeling and advisories to even more censorship.

There is a liberating alternative. It exists in various forms in most other democratic countries. It is public participation in making decisions about cultural investment and cultural policy. Independent grassroots citizen organization and action can provide the broad support needed for loosening the global marketing noose around the necks of producers, writers, directors, actors and journalists.[2]

More freedom from violent and other inequitable and intimidating formulas, not more censorship, is the effective and acceptable way to increase diversity and reduce the dependence of program producers on the violence formula, and to reduce television violence to its legitimate role and proportion. The role of Congress, if any, is to turn its antitrust and civil rights oversight on the centralized and globalized industrial structures and marketing strategies that impose violence on creative people and foist it on the children and adults of the world. It is high time to develop a vision of the right of children to be born into a reasonable, free, fair, diverse and nonthreatening cultural environment. It is time for citizen involvement in cultural decisions that shape our lives and the lives of our children.

NOTES

1. Cultural Indicators is a database and a research project that relates recurrent features of the world of television to viewer conceptions of reality. Its cumulative computer archive contains observations on over 3,000 programs and 35,000 characters coded according to many thematic, demographic and action categories. These form the basis for the content analyses cited in the references. The study is conducted at the University of Pennsylvania's Annenberg School for Communication in collaboration with Michael Morgan at the University of Massachusetts at Amherst and Nancy Signorielli at the University of Delaware. Thanks for research assistance are due to Mariaeleana Bartezaghi, Cnythia Kandra, Robin Kim, Amy Nyman and Nejat Ozyegin.

2. One such alternative is the Cultural Environment Movement (CEM). CEM is a nonprofit educational corporation, an umbrella coalition of independent media, professional, labor, religious, health-related, women's and minority groups opposed to private corporate as well as government censorship. CEM is working for freedom from stereotyped formulas and for investing in a freer and more diverse cultural environment. It can be reached by writing to Cultural Environment Movement, P.O. Box 31847, Philadelphia, PA 19104.

REFERENCES

[Editorial]. (1993, September 20). *Broadcasting & Cable*, p. 66.
Auletta, K. (1993, May 17). What won't they do? *The New Yorker*, pp. 45-46.

Gerbner, G. (1993). "Miracles" of communication technology: Powerful audiences, diverse choices and other fairy tales. In J. Wasko (Ed.), *Illuminating the blind spots.* New York: Ablex.

Gerbner, G., Gross, L., Morgan, M., & Signorielli, N. (1993). Growing up with television: The cultivation perspective. In J. Bryant & D. Zillmann (Eds.), *Media effects: Advances in theory and research.* Hillsdale, NJ: Lawrence Erlbaum.

Morgan, M. & Shanahan, J. (1991). Do VCRs change the TV picture?: VCRs and the cultivation process. *American Behavioral Scientist, 35(2), 122-135.*

Morgan, M., & Signorielli, N. (1990). Cultivation analysis: Conceptualization and methodology. In N. Signorielli & M. Morgan (Eds.), *Cultivation analysis: New directions in media effects research* (pp. 13-33). Newbury Park, CA: Sage.

Sun, L. (1989). *Limits of selective viewing: An analysis of "diversity" in dramatic programming.* Unpublished master's thesis, the Annenberg School for Communication, University of Pennsylvania, Philadelphia.

Resources for Media Activism

Over the years, activists have come to realize that there is no one route to social change but, rather, a number of different roads that can be taken, all of which aim to see a more equal and just society. For this reason, we have provided lists of organizations that produce alternative media, monitor the mainstream media, organize boycotts and run media literacy workshops.

Media/Cultural Analysis Groups and Publications

Adbusters: A Magazine of Media and Environmental Strategies
    The Media Foundation
    1243 W. Seventh Avenue
    Vancouver, British Columbia
    V6H 1B7 Canada

Center for the Integration and Improvement of Journalism
    Journalism Department
    San Francisco State University
    1600 Holloway Avenue
    San Francisco, CA 94132

Challenging Media Images of Women
 P.O. Box 902
 Framingham, MA 01701

Columbia Journalism Review
 700 Journalism Building
 Columbia University
 New York, NY 10027

Extra! (Fairness and Accuracy In Reporting, FAIR)
 130 W. 25 Street
 New York, NY 10001

Gender and Mass Media Newsletter
 c/o Madeline Kleberg
 Department of Journalism, Media and Communication
 University of Stockholm
 Gjorwellsgaten 26
 S-112 60 Stockholm
 Sweden

GLAAD (Gay and Lesbian Alliance Against Defamation)
 80 Varick Street
 New York, NY 10013

Jump Cut
 Box 865
 Berkeley, CA 94701

Lies of Our Times
 Institute for Media Analysis
 145 W. 4th Street
 New York, NY 10012

Media&Values
 Media Action Research Center
 Center for Media and Values
 1962 South Shenandoah
 Los Angeles, CA 90034

Media Watch
 1803 Mission Street, #7
 Santa Cruz, CA 95060

National Asian American Telecommunications Association
 346 Ninth Street
 San Francisco, CA 94103

National Black Media Coalition
    38 New York Avenue, NE
    Washington, DC 20002

Project Censored
    Communications Studies Department
    1801 E. Cotati Avenue
    Sonoma State University
    Rohnert Park, CA 94928

The Viewer
    Newsletter of Viewers for Quality Television, Inc.
    P.O. Box 195
    Fairfax Station, VA 22039

Alternative Media

Advocate
    P.O. Box 4371
    Los Angeles, CA 90078

Alternet (Alternative news service)
    2025 Eye Street, NW, #1124
    Washington, DC 20006

Black Planet Productions
    P.O. Box 435
    Cooper Station
    New York, NY 10003-0435

Black Scholar
    485 65th Street
    Oakland, CA 94609

Disability Rag
    Box 145
    Louisville, KY 40201

Educational Video Center (Media arts center for inner city youth)
    60 E. 13th Street
    New York, NY 10003

Facets Video Images Series (Distributors of independent film and video)
    C/O Facets Multimedia
    1517 West Fullerton Avenue
    Chicago, IL 60614

Guardian
West 17th St.
New York, NY 10001

Insight Features
3411 W. Diversity, Suite 5
Chicago, IL 60647

In the Life (monthly gay/lesbian TV variety show)
c/o Media Network
39 West 14th Street, Suite 401
New York, NY 10011

In These Times
2040 N. Milwaukee
Chicago, IL 60647

Media Report to Women
10606 Mantz Road
Silver Spring, MD 20903-1228

Ms. Magazine
P.O. Box 50008
Boulder, CO 80321-0008

Mother Jones
731 Market Street, Suite 600
San Francisco, CA 94103

The Nation
72 Fifth Avenue
New York, NY 10011

National Boycott News
6506 28th Avenue, NE
Seattle, WA 98115

New Day Films (Alternative filmmakers)
121 W. 27th Street
New York, NY 10001

Off Our Backs
2423 18th Street
Washington, DC 20009

On The Issues
Women's Medical Center, Inc.
97-77 Queens Blvd.
Flushing, NY 11374-3317

Out/Look: National Lesbian and Gay Quarterly
P.O. Box 460430
San Francisco, CA 94146-0430

Pacifica Radio (Alternative radio broadcast)
3729 Cahuenga Blvd. West
North Hollywood, CA 91604

Paper Tiger/Deep Dish (Alternative television and video)
339 Lafayette Street
New York, NY 10012

The Progressive
409 E. Main Street
Madison, WI 53703

Radical America
1 Summer Street
Somerville, MA 02134

Third World Newsreel (Alternative video and film by people of color)
355 W. 38 Street, 5th Floor
New York, NY 10012

Tikkun Magazine
P.O. Box 1778
Cathedral Station
New York, NY 10025

Utne Reader
The Fawkes Building
1624 Harmon Place
Minneapolis, MN 55403

Video Project: Films and Videos for a Safe and Sustainable World
5332 College Avenue, Suite 101
Oakland, CA 94618

Women Make Movies
225 Lafayette Street, Suite 212
New York, NY 10012

Z Magazine
116 St. Botolph Street
Boston, MA 02115

Media Education
and Literacy Organizations

American Center for Children's Television
1400 Touhy, Suite 260
DesPlanes, IL 60018

Asian American Journalists Association
1765 Sutter Street
San Francisco, CA 94115

Assembly of Media Arts (National Council of Teachers of English)
Hempstead High School
3715 Pennsylvania Avenue
Dubuque, IA 52001

Association for Media Literacy
40 McArthur
Weston, Ontario
M9P 3M7 Canada

Center for Media and Values
1962 S. Shenandoah
Los Angeles, CA 90034

Center for Media Education
1012 Heather Avenue
Takoma Park, MD 20912

Center for the Study of Commercialism
1875 Connecticut Avenue NW, Suite 300
Washington, DC 20009

Center for Media Literacy
38½ Battery Park Avenue, Suite D
Asheville, NC 28001

Institute for Media Analysis
145 W 4th Street
New York, NY 10012

National Alliance for Media Education
Contact: Julian Low
1212 Broadway, Suite 816
Oakland, CA 94612

Not Channel Zero (African American and Latino video collection)
P.O. Box 435 Cooper Station
New York, NY 10003

Strategies for Media Literacy
Contact: Kathleen Tyler
1095 Market Street, #410
San Francisco, CA 94103

Z Media Institute
18 Millfield Street
Woods Hole, MA 02543

Films and
Videotapes on the Media

Buy Me That
Films Inc.
5547 N. Ravenswood Avenue
Chicago, IL 60640
(A film for elementary and middle school students on the
techniques advertisers use to sell to kids.)

Buy Me That Too!
Ambrose Video Publishing
1290 Avenue of the Americas
Suite 2245
New York, NY 10104
(Looks at more techniques of persuasion.)

Calling the Shots
A film by Jean Kilbourne
Cambridge Documentary Films
P.O. Box 385
Cambridge, MA 02139
(An analysis of the techniques used to sell alcohol in
advertisements.)

Commercial Free Zone
UNPLUG
360 Grand Avenue
P.O. Box 384
Oakland, CA 94610
(Introduction to issue of commercialism in schools.)

Dream Worlds: Desire/Sex/Power in Rock Videos
    Sut Jhally
    Foundation for Media Education
    P.O. Box 2008
    Amherst, MA 01004-2008
    (Analyzes the representations of women on MTV.)

Ethnic Notions
    California Newsreel
    149 Ninth Street
    San Francisco, CA 94103
    (Historical analysis of the mainstream media representations
    of African Americans.)

Color Adjustments
    California Newsreel
    See address above
    (Picks up where *Ethnic Notions* end by examining more contem-
    porary representations of African Americans.)

Killing Screens: Media and the Culture of Violence
    Mediated: Media Education Foundation
    26 Center Street
    Northampton, MΛ 01061
    (Examines the issue of violence in the media.)

Pack of Lies
    Mediated: Media Education Foundation
    26 Center Strcct
    Northampton, MA 01061
    (Examines the way advertisers sell smoking.)

Psycho Killers and Twisted Sisters
    Frameline
    346 9th Street
    San Francisco, CA 94103
    (Looks at mainstream cinema's stereotypes of lesbians and gays.)

Public Mind
    P.B.S.
    (A four-part series on the media by Bill Moyers.)

Still Killing Us Softly
    A film by Jean Kilbourne
    Cambridge Documentary Films
    P.O. Box 385
    Cambridge, MA 02139
    (An insightful analysis of the image of women in advertising.)

The World Is a Dangerous Place: Images of the Enemy in Children's Television
   Center for Psychological Studies in the Nuclear Age
   1493 Cambridge Street
   Cambridge, MA 02139
   (Looks at popular children's cartoons in terms of the images of
   the "bad guys" and the "good guys.")

War on Lesbians
   Women Make Movies
   462 Broadway, Suite 501
   New York, NY 10013
   (A humorous look at the invisibility of lesbians in mainstream
   media such as talk shows and radio self-help programs.)

Warning: The Media May Be Hazardous to Your Health
   Media Watch
   P.O. Box 618
   Santa Cruz, CA 95061
   (Media literacy video addressing sexism and racism in
   movies, cartoons and news media.)

Glossary

Antihegemonic. See **hegemony.**

Appropriation. This term is used two ways in this book. First, it refers in a neutral sense to how we make sense of the meanings encoded into cultural texts and incorporate these into our daily lives. Second, it is used in a way that highlights power relations in an unequal society. Thus *appropriation* can refer to the process whereby members of relatively privileged groups "raid" the culture of marginalized groups, abstracting cultural practices or artifacts from their historically specific contexts. Frequently, this involves **co-optation,** by which a cultural item's resistant or counterhegemonic potential is lost through its translation into the dominant cultural context. Adding insult to injury, appropriation frequently means profit for the appropriator. See James Ledbetter (Chapter 61) on how the African American cultural form of rap music is appropriated by White performers.

Artifact. Cultural Artifact. These terms are borrowed by cultural studies from anthropological usage, where it refers to any human-created object. Cultural studies scholars use the terms as a way of broadening the definition of what aspects of culture in modern societies are worthy of serious study. As used in relation to media culture, they refer not only to tangible objects such as photographs in magazines but also to intangible verbal, visual and auditory expressions, such as those in a rock music video.

Audience Decoding. See **encoding/decoding.**

Audience Reception. See **reception theory.**

Black Feminist Perspective. See **feminist studies.**

Capitalism. This is an economic system based on (a) private (rather than public or collective) ownership of the means of production, (b) the market exchange of goods and services and (c) wage labor. This book tends to adopt the Marxist critique of capitalism, which sees it as a system based on oppression and coercion, rather than on consensus.

Class. Social Class. These are much debated terms in both sociology and economics. They tend to be used by sociologists to refer to a social stratum whose members share certain social, economic and cultural characteristics. However, critical sociologists use a modified version of the classic Marxist usage, which defined class as a group of people occupying a similar position within the social relations of economic production. Whereas Marx argued that there are only two major classes under capitalism, the bourgeoisie (owner class) and the proletariat (worker class), critical sociologists distinguish five: the ruling class, the professional/managerial class, small-business owners, the working class and the poor.

Codes. Semiotic Codes, Media Codes. These terms are used in **semiotics**-influenced media studies to refer to rules and conventions that structure representations on a number of levels—some specific to certain media such as narrative film or advertising photographs, whereas others are shared with other modes of communication. Audiences learn to "read" the conventional verbal, visual and auditory features that make up the "languages" or "sign systems" of media and other cultural forms in much the same way children learn the complex, often arbitrary systems of meaning in natural languages. See **semiotics** and **encoding/decoding**.

Commidify. To *commidify* something is to turn into a commodity. See **commodity**.

Commodity. A *commodity* is any object or service that can be bought and sold in the marketplace. Marxists argue that capitalism reduces all aspects of life to commodities.

Content Analysis. This is a social-scientific method of describing and analyzing the "content" of a range of media texts, either in qualitative or quantitative terms. Quantitative content analysis (counting the number of times certain types of material appear) is especially useful for describing the broad contours of a large quantity of texts, but it tends to miss the more subtle and complex ways in which texts construct meaning.

Co-opt. Co-optation. See **appropriation**.

Counterhegemonic. Counterhegemonic Gender. Counterhegemony. See **hegemony**.

Cultural Studies. This is an approach to the study of communications in society that is drawn from a number of sources, including Marxism, semiotics, literary and film analysis, psychoanalysis, feminism and African American or Third World studies. As used in this book, it locates the production, textual construction and consumption of media texts in a society characterized by multiple systems of inequality. Of key importance is the study of the role that media forms play in the production and reproduction of these systems of inequality.

Culture. This term has many different meanings, depending on the school of thought in which it occurs. In anthropology, it refers to everything created by humans, including artifacts or objects, ideas, institutions and expressive practices. In traditional humanities fields, such as art history and literature, *culture* has tended to be conceptualized as the highest-status arts of the wealthy and socially dominant, such as oil paintings, opera or poetry. **Cultural studies** rejects this view of culture as elitist, replacing it with the more anthropological usage. In particular, cultural studies takes as its area of study all of the expressive, meaningful, interactive aspects of everyday life in an industrial society.

Decode. See **encoding/decoding.**

Encoding/Decoding (model for **audience reception**). "Encoding/Decoding" is the title of an influential article by British cultural studies writer Stuart Hall. It proposes that meaning does not simply reside in a *media text's codes* but is the result of a complex *negotiation* between specific audiences and texts. In contrast to former critical media theorists who assumed that audiences had very little control over meaning and were vulnerable to being "brainwashed" by the media, Hall proposed three possible audience responses to the dominant ideology contained in the media text's codes or three distinct reading positions, corresponding to audiences' different social situations: *dominant reading* (accepting the *preferred meaning*), *negotiated reading* (accepting aspects of the preferred meaning but rejecting others) and *oppositional reading* (rejecting the preferred meaning) (see Fiske, 1987a, p. 260).

Ethnographic Research. Ethnography (in media studies) is a social research method first used by anthropologists and now adopted by some cultural studies scholars for understanding the role of media audiences in the production of meaning. It can involve participant observation, which requires that the researcher becomes a part of the group studied for a specified period. For an example of an ethnographic media study, see Janice Radway (Chapter 24). Also see **reception theory.**

Feminist Criticism. Feminist Film Theory. This influential strand of cultural studies combines a feminist view of the centrality of gender in cultural analysis with a generally psychoanalytic orientation to the study of how audiences experience the "meanings" in classic Hollywood narrative film. Feminist film theorists working through textual analysis have explored such issues as *gendered spectatorship*, the ways in which the film text through its formal codes "addresses" the hypothetical or ideal viewer as either male or female. An early formulation asserted that any viewer of classic Hollywood narrative film was encouraged by both plot and camera work and editing to adopt a "masculine subject position" and share in the **male gaze** of both protagonist and camera at a female object of desire. Some feminist film theorists have questioned the universal applicability of a Freudian-based psychoanalytic account of the development of gender differences; others have worked to explore how real audiences actually (consciously) experience film spectatorship. See also the introduction to Part III.

Feminist Studies. This is a **multidisciplinary** approach to social analysis, rooted in the contemporary women's movement(s) and the gay/lesbian liberation movement. Emphasizing gender as a major organizing feature of power relations in society, feminists argue that the role of the media is crucial in the construction and dissemination of gender ideology and thus in gender socialization. In recent years, feminists of color have critiqued the tendency in feminism to privilege gender over other categories of experience. In particular, cultural analysts with a **Black feminist perspective** have brought to the foreground the ways in which gender is "inflected" or modified by race and class factors.

Formal Analysis. Formalism. These refer to studying the way in which the construction of a cultural artifact influences the range of meanings it may have.

Formalistic is sometimes used in a negative sense to refer to an analysis that is preoccupied with form and loses sight of other important considerations.

Gaze. Male Gaze. See **feminist film theory.**

Gender. Whereas sex differences (anatomical and hormonal) between genetic males and genetic females are biological in nature, *gender* is a social concept, by which a society defines as "masculine" or "feminine" one particular set of characteristics and behaviors and then socializes children accordingly. Just which characteristics belong to which gender can vary tremendously over time and between cultures and even between different social groups within cultures. Feminists do not necessarily agree with one another over the question of whether certain feminine values displayed disproportionately by women in our contemporary Western society are to some degree "natural" or biologically based, rather than entirely the result of "nurture." Those who would argue that women are *by nature* more nurturant than men, for example, are termed "essentialists"—believers in a feminine "essence"—by those who argue that gender is an entirely socially based construct.

Gendered Subjectivity. See **gender** and **subject position.**

Genre. Genre Analysis. Genre Criticism. Originally used by literary and art critics to refer to categories of works marked by distinctive styles, form or content, *genre* is also used to group together into categories related types of film, television shows and popular music forms. In cultural studies genre criticism, which is influenced by **semiotics,** genres "are not neutral categories, but rather, they are ideological constructs that provide and enforce a pre-reading," acting as a contract between producer and consumer that "serves to limit the free play of signification" (Feuer, 1987, p. 118). Feminist critics of popular literature and film have explored the distinctive aspects of **women's genres,** forms targeting female audiences, in an effort to bring the experiences and perspectives of women to the foreground in cultural studies. See introductions to Parts III and V.

Hegemonic. Hegemonic Gender. Hegemony. *Hegemony* is a term developed by Italian Marxist theorist Antonio Gramsci to refer to the process by which those in power secure the consent of the socially subordinated to the system that oppresses or subordinates them. Rather than requiring overt force (as represented by the military or police), the elite, through their control of religious, educational and media institutions, attempt to persuade the populace that the hierarchical social and economic system is fixed and "natural," and therefore unchangeable. According to Gramsci, however, such consent is never secured once and for all but must continually be sought, and there is always some room for **resistance** through subversive (**counterhegemonic**) cultural work.

Heterosexism. This term was coined by analogy with **sexism.** The dictionary defines it as "discrimination or prejudice against gay or homosexual people by heterosexual people." As with **racism** and **sexism,** this book takes the view that it is structural or institutional forces that underpin social inequalities rather than individual prejudiced attitudes. Thus heterosexism would refer to the heterosexual ideology that is encoded into and characteristic of the major social, cultural and economic institutions of our society. See **racism** and **sexism.**

Ideological Textual Analysis. See **ideology** and **text.**

Ideology. Traditionally, this term has been used by Marxists to refer to ideas imposed on the proletariat (working class) by the bourgeoisie (owners of the means of production) to get the subservient classes to consent to their own oppression. Today, critical theorists tend to use a broader concept of ideology. For example, "the complex of ideas in society and their expression in social institutions, whether the military or the arts or the courts, which in turn dominate the way we live and how we understand the world around us" (Downing et al., 1990, p. 366). For a definition of *ideology*, see the essay by Stuart Hall in this reader (Chapter 2).

Image. Media Image. *Image* has two distinct meanings for media critics: (a) any **representation** of social reality, as in "images of women in media." (This use of "image" suggests, as in "mirror image," a closer, less constructed relationship with "reality" than is now proposed for media representations, by those scholars working with more complex theoretical paradigms.) See **representation.** (b) A specifically **visual representation.** See Sut Jhally (Chapter 10).

Imagery. Image System. See **image.**

Intertextuality. John Fiske (1987b) has explicated a theory of *intertextuality* to help explain the way audiences experience a wide variety of media texts as interrelated, allowing their knowledge of one to influence their reading of another. "The theory of intertextuality proposes that any one text is necessarily read in relationship to others and that a range of textual knowledges is brought to bear upon it" (p. 108). Fiske also distinguishes "horizontal textuality"—relationships that exist among texts of a similar kind—from "vertical textuality"—the relations of one kind of texts with others "of a different type that refer explicitly to it." For example, if a *primary media text* is a specific book, film or television show, then a *secondary text* might be "studio publicity, journalistic features, or criticism" about the primary text, and *tertiary texts* might include viewers' letters, gossip and conversation about the primary text (pp. 108-109). Also see **text.**

Marxism. This is a general theory of historical change originally developed by 19th-century German philosopher Karl Marx. Marx argued for the centrality of economics in social history and developed a critique of capitalism that has had a major influence on political theory and on social revolutions in the 19th and 20th centuries. In the realm of cultural studies, classic Marxism argued that the economic structure of society (the "base") shapes major cultural institutions (the "superstructure"), including the military, legal system, educational system, arts and media. This is because, according to Marx, "the class which has the means of material production at its disposal has control over the means of mental production" (Marx & Engels, 1938, p. 39). For a modification of classic Marxist ideas of this relationship, see **hegemony.**

Multicultural. Multiculturalism. As used in this book, *multiculturalism* refers to a movement affecting curricula, teaching methods and scholarship in a variety of fields within universities and colleges in the United States. The broad objectives of activists in this educational movement include democratizing knowledge and education, by bringing to the foreground and validating the experiences and perspectives of all those groups formerly marginalized or culturally and socially dominated in our society.

Multidisciplinary. This is an approach that encourages students and teachers to cross the boundaries between traditional academic disciplines or areas of knowledge (such as history, sociology, philosophy, economics or political science), to be able better to capture the complexity of the subject studied.

Negotiated Reading. See **encoding/decoding.**

Oppositional Reading. See **encoding/decoding.**

Patriarchal. Patriarchy. These terms literally mean "rule by the father," and refer to family (and clan) systems in which one older man had absolute power over all members of the group, including women, children and younger male relatives and servants. As used by contemporary feminists, it is a concept developed to examine and critique continuing male domination of social institutions, such as the family, the state, the educational system and the media.

Political Economy. In critical theory, this is a perspective that "sets out to show how different ways of financing and organizing cultural production have traceable consequences for the range of discourses and representations in the public domain and for audiences' access to them" (Golding & Murdoch, 1991, p. 15). This often involves studying who owns the media industries and analyzing how ownership influences media content. See, in particular, Richard Butsch's article in this reader (Chapter 46).

Polysemic Text. A *polysemic text* is one that is "open" to various readings or that has multiple meanings. Cultural studies scholars currently disagree among themselves about how "open" texts are. See **encoding/decoding.**

Postmodernism. Originally, *postmodern* referred, in literary and art criticism, to "art, architecture or literature that reacts against earlier modernist principles." ("Modernism" was itself "the deliberate departure from tradition and the use of innovative forms of expression," in many styles of European art and literature in the early 20th century.) In the wake of many influential applications of the term postmodern to aspects of contemporary, media-formed sensibility that many observers find discouraging or even frightening, those who use the term acknowledge that it is used in so many different ways as to be virtually impossible to define. In the context of cultural studies as represented in this book, it refers primarily to a particular style of televisual aesthetics best displayed in music videos and the MTV Channel. In John Fiske's (1987b) formulation, "postmodernism emphasizes the fragmentary nature of images, their resistance to sense, the way that the images are more imperative than the real and have displaced it in our experience" (p. 254). Also see the introduction to Part VII, on music videos, MTV and rap music.

Preferred Reading. This is a concept developed by Stuart Hall to circumscribe the degree of "openness" ((*polysemy*)) of media texts. According to Hall, the structure of mainstream media texts always "prefers" or strongly suggests a single "correct" meaning that tends to promote the dominant ideology. Within cultural studies, there continues to be a lively debate over whether a preferred meaning can be said to be a property of the text; some would argue that the making of meaning ultimately resides with audiences. Also see **encoding/decoding.**

Psychoanalysis. Psychoanalytic. According to feminist film and TV analyst Sandy Flitterman-Lewis (1987), "Psychoanalysis, as a theory of human psychology, describes the ways in which the human being comes to develop a specific personality and sexual identity within the larger network of social relations called culture. It takes as its object the mechanisms of the unconscious—resistance, repression, sexuality, and the Oedipal complex—and seeks to analyze the fundamental structures of desire that underlie all human activity." The French psychoanalytic philosopher Lacan, "by reinterpreting Freud in linguistic terms," had a major impact on one strand of cultural studies—especially film studies. He built on the Freudian theory of how a sense of self as distinct from the mother, as well as a firm gender identity, is established in children through the Oedipal stage (which works differently for boys and girls). "Because of his emphasis on language, Lacan rereads the Oedipal complex," giving the childhood acquisition of language a central role in moving the child "out of the pre-Oedipal unity with the mother," but leaving aspects of our relationship to language unconscious. Later film theorists, such as Christian Metz and Laura Mulvey drew on the Lacanian theory of the unconscious in developing the idea of *gendered spectatorship* (1987, p. 173). See **feminist film theory.**

Race. Many people tend to think of "race" as a fixed entity linked to biological realities. However, in this book, as in critical theory generally, "the effort must be made to understand race as an unstable complex of social meanings constantly being transformed by political struggle" (Omi & Winant, 1987). See Pieterse (Chapter 3).

Racism. Racist. In everyday usage, *racism* can be used to mean holding or displaying prejudiced or bigoted attitudes or indulging in discriminatory behavior toward someone else (usually toward people of color but sometimes toward Whites as well) on the basis of that person's apparent race, ethnicity or color. However, in critical theory, and in this book, we use the term to refer to the White-supremacist ideology encoded into and characteristic of the major social, cultural and economic institutions of this society.

Reception Theory. According to Robert C. Allen (1987), "reader-response criticism," "reception theory," and "reader-oriented criticism" are all names given to the variety of recent works in literary [and media] studies that foreground the role of the reader in understanding and deriving pleasure from . . . texts." Those who take this approach believe "that . . . meaning should no longer be viewed as an immutable property of a text but must be considered as the result of the confrontation between reading act and textual structure" (p. 75).

Representation. Cultural Representation. Media Representation. Racial Representation. These terms refer to "The creation of a convincing illusion of reality," through such media as painting, drawing, graphic prints, still photographs, films, recorded sound, live acting on stage, television technology, computer graphics or the like. *Representations* include all kinds of media imagery that, no matter how convincing their likeness to everyday social reality, are always to be recognized as "constructions taken from a specific social and physical viewpoint, selecting one activity or instant out of vast choices to represent, and materially made out of and formed by the technical processes of the medium and its conventions" (King, 1992, p. 131).

Resistance. In critical cultural studies, this can refer to the refusal by a media text's reader, viewer or audience to take up or accept the **preferred reading** and/or the **subject position** encoded into the text. There is a general debate among cultural studies scholars on how much opportunity to resist is offered by the text (how "open" or **polysemic** it is). Some have criticized the tendency to "romanticize" the idea of the interpretive community's resistance (Scholle, 1990, p. 8). Others question the notion that *resistance* is in and by itself positive, citing the resistance of those with conservative social ideologies to texts whose preferred meaning is politically "progressive" (see Kellner, Chapter 1). Finally, many point out that "resistive readings" may or may not translate into political resistance to cultural **hegemony.**

Secondary Text. See **intertextuality.**

Semiotics. Semiology. *Semiotics* is the study of "signification," or the ways in which both languages and nonlinguistic symbolic systems operate to associate meanings with arbitrary "signs," such as words, visual images, colors or objects. Semiotics is a linguistics-based field of study that has had an important influence on the way cultural studies scholars discuss the "codes" in media texts. "Semiotics is the study of everything that can be used for communication. . . . Semiotics first asks how meaning is created, rather than what the meaning is" (Seiter, 1987, p. 17). See **encoding/decoding.**

Sexism. Coined by the women's movement in an analogy with **racism,** *sexism* is also used several ways. In common usage, it can refer to prejudicial or disrespectful attitudes or discriminatory behavior on the part of individuals toward others (usually toward women but sometimes toward men as well) on the basis of gender. In this book, we use it to refer to male-supremacist (**patriarchal**) ideology encoded into and characteristic of the major social, cultural and economic institutions of this society.

Sexist. See **sexism.**

Spectatorship. See **feminist film theory.**

Stereotype. This is a popular term used in 1970s media criticism and activism to describe and critique reductive, much repeated social imagery (as in "Uncle Tom and Aunt Jemima are racist stereotypes"; "Aunt Jemima and the Playboy Bunny are sexist stereotypes"). For a more nuanced concept of the relationship between cultural artifacts and social reality, see **representation.**

Subject Position. This concept was developed within psychoanalytically-oriented media theory, particularly literary and film criticism, which claims that narrative texts themselves produce through their codes an ideal "viewing position" or "subject position," from which the narrative is experienced by any viewer/reader. See **feminist film theory** as well as **reception theory.**

Subject/Spectator. See **feminist film theory.**

Symbolic Annihilation. This term was coined in the 1970s to describe and critique the way mass media either ignored or misrepresented certain marginalized social groups. See Larry Gross's article (Chapter 9).

Televisual Apparatus. By analogy with a similar concept in film studies, the *televisual apparatus* is everything distinctive about television as a business, cultural institution and a communications medium. This would include its distinctive complex of technological characteristics and text forms, its sites of consumption (the living room at home and other locations) and its system of production, distribution and finance.

Televisual Codes. See **codes.**

Text. Media Text. Originally referring to a verbal/written cultural artifact (such as a story, play, or song lyrics), *text* is now used much more broadly by cultural critics. It can refer to any communicative or expressive artifact produced by the media industries. **Textual analysis,** or a close examination of how particular media texts generate meaning, is one of the key activities of contemporary cultural studies. However, Kellner argues in his introductory essay (Chapter 1) that **audience reception** and **political economy** approaches are also needed to locate texts in their social and political contexts.

Textual Analysis. See **text.**

Textual Codes. See **text** and **codes.**

Textual Encoding. See **encoding/decoding.**

The Woman's Film. Women's Film. Women's Genres. See **genre.**

REFERENCES

Allen, R. C. (1987). Reader-oriented criticism and television. In R. C. Allen (Ed.), *Channels of discourse* (pp. 74-112). Chapel Hill: University of North Carolina Press.

Downing, J., Mohammadi, A., & Sreberny-Mohammadi, A. (1990). *Questioning the media.* Newbury Park, CA: Sage.

Feuer, J. (1987). Genre study and television. In R. C. Allen (Ed.), *Channels of discourse* (pp. 113-133). Chapel Hill: University of North Carolina Press.

Fiske, J. (1987a). British cultural studies and television. In R. C. Allen (Ed.), *Channels of discourse* (pp. 254-289). Chapel Hill: University of North Carolina Press.

Fiske, J. (1987b). *Television culture.* London: Methuen.

Flitterman-Lewis, S. (1987). Psychoanalysis, film and television. In R. C. Allen, (Ed.), *Channels of discourse* (pp. 172-210). Chapel Hill: University of North Carolina Press.

Golding, P., & Murdoch, G. (1991). Culture, communication and political economy. In J. Curran & M. Gurrevitch (Eds.), *Mass media and society.* London: Edward Arnold.

King, C. (1992). The politics of representation: A democracy of the gaze. In F. Bonner et al. (Eds.), *Imagining women* (pp. 131-139). Cambridge, UK: Open University Press.

Marx, K., & Engels, F. (1983). *German ideology* (R. Pascal, Trans.). London: Lawrence & Wishart.

Omi, M., & Winant, H. (1987). On the theoretical concept of race. In S. M. James & A. P. A. Busia (Eds.), *Theorizing Black feminisms: The visionary pragmatism of Black women.* New York: Routledge.

Seiter, E. (1987). Semiotics and television. In R. C. Allen (Ed.), *Channels of discourse* (pp. 17-41). Chapel Hill: University of North Carolina Press.

Scholle, D. (1990). Resistance: Pinning down a wandering concept in cultural studies discourse. *Journal of Urban and Cultural Studies, 1*(1), 87-105.

Bibliography

PART I: A CULTURAL STUDIES APPROACH
TO GENDER, RACE AND CLASS IN THE MEDIA

A. Critical Theory/Cultural Studies/General

Allen, R. C. (Ed.). (1987). *Channels of discourse: Television and contemporary criticism.* Chapel Hill: University of North Carolina Press.

Altman, K. E. (1989, Summer). Television as gendered technology: Advertising the American television set. *Journal of Popular Film and Television,* pp. 46-56.

Angus, I., & Jhally, S. (Eds.). (1989). *Cultural politics in contemporary America.* New York: Routledge, Chapman & Hall.

Aronowitz, S. (1989). Working class culture in an electronic age. In I. Angus & S. Jhally (Eds.), *Cultural politics in contemporary America.* New York: Routledge, Chapman & Hall.

Bagdikian, B. (1987). *The media monopoly* (2nd ed.). Boston: Beacon.

Bagdikian, B. (1989). The lords of the global village. *Nation, 248,* 805 820.

Barker, M., & Beezer, A. (1992). *Reading into cultural studies.* New York: Routledge.

Barnow, E. (1978). *The sponsor: Notes on a modern potentate.* New York: Oxford University Press.

Barry, A. (1987). *The rise of a gay and lesbian movement.* Boston: Twayne.

Berman, R. (1982). *How television sees its audience.* Beverly Hills, CA: Sage.

Brunt, R., & Rowan, C. (Eds.). (1982). *Feminism, culture and politics.* London: Lawrence and Wishart.

Budd, B., Entman, R., & Steinman, C. (1990). The affirmative character of American cultural studies. *Critical Studies in Mass Communication, 7*(2).

Burns, G., & Thompson, R. T. (1989). *Television studies: Textual analysis.* Westport, CT: Greenwood.

Butsch, R. (Ed.). (1990). *For fun and profit: The transformation of leisure into consumption.* Philadelphia: Temple University Press.

Caputi, J. (1991). Charting the flow: The construction of meaning through juxtaposition in media texts. *Journal of Communication Inquiry, 15*(2), 32-47.

Carey, J. W. (1983). The origins of radical discourse on cultural studies in the United States. *Journal of Communication, 33*(3), 311-313.

Cocks, J. (1989). *The oppositional imagination.* New York: Routledge.

Cohen, A. (1985). *The symbolic construction of community.* New York: Tavistock.

Condit, C. (1989). The rhetorical limits of polysemy. *Critical Studies in Mass Communication, 6*(2).

Connor, S. (1989). *Postmodernist culture: An introduction to theories of the contemporary.* Oxford, UK: Blackwell.

Curran, J., & Gurevitch, M. (Eds.). (1991). *Mass media and society.* London: Edward Arnold.

D'Emilio, J. (1983). *Sexual politics, sexual communities.* Chicago: University of Chicago Press.

Downing, J. (1984). *Radical media.* Boston: South End Press.

Downing, J., Mohammadi, A., & Sreberny-Mohammadi, A. (1990). *Questioning the media: A critical introduction.* Newbury Park, CA: Sage.

During, S. (Ed.). (1993). *The cultural studies reader.* New York: Routledge.

Dyer, R. (1984). *Gays and film.* New York: Zoetrope.

Dyer, R. (1986). *Heavenly bodies: Film stars and society.* London: British Film Institute/ Macmillan.

Dyer, R. (1990). Coming to terms. In R. Ferguson, M. Gever, T. T. Minh-ha, & C. West (Eds.), *Out there: Marginalization and contemporary cultures.* New York: New Museum of Contemporary Art.

Dyer, R. (1990). *Now you see it: Studies on lesbian and gay film.* New York: Routledge.

Ellis, J. (1982). *Visible fictions: Cinema, television, video.* London: Routledge & Kegan Paul.

Entman, R. M. (1988). *Democracy without citizens: Media & the decay of American politics.* New York: Oxford University Press.

Fiske, J. (1986). Television: Polysemy and popularity. *Critical Studies in Mass Communication, 3*(2), 391-408.

Fiske, J. (1987). *Television culture.* London: Routledge.

Fiske, J. (1989). *Reading the popular.* Boston: Unwin Hyman.

Fiske, J. (1991). Postmodernism and television. In J. Gurran & M. Gurevitch (Eds.), *Mass media and society* (pp. 55-67). London: Edward Arnold.

Fiske, J. (1989). *Understanding popular culture.* Boston: Unwin Hyman.

Foster, H. (1985). *Recodings: Art, spectacle, cultural politics.* Port Townsend, WA: Bay Press.

Friedberg, A. (1990). A denial of difference: Theories of cinematic identification. In E. A. Kaplan (Ed.), *Psychoanalysis and cinema.* London: Routledge.

Gaines, J. N. (1991). *Contested culture: The image, the voice, and the law.* Chapel Hill: University of North Carolina Press.

Gerbner, G., Gross, L., Morgan, M., & Signorielli, N. (1993). Growing up with television: The cultivation perspective. In J. Bryant & D. Zillmann (Eds.), *Media effects: Advances in theory and research.* Hillsdale, NJ: Lawrence Erlbaum.

Gever, M., Parmar, P., & Greyson, J. (1993). *Queer looks: Perspectives on lesbian and gay film and video.* New York: Routledge.

Gitlin, T. (1980). *The whole world is watching.* Berkeley: University of California Press.

Gitlin, T. (Ed.). (1986). *Watching television.* New York: Pantheon.

Golding, P., & Murdock, G. (1991). Culture, communication and political economy. In J. Curran & M. Gurrevitch (Eds.), *Mass media and society.* London: Edward Arnold.

Golding, P., Murdock, G., & Schlesinger, P. (Eds.). (1986). *Communicating politics: Mass communication and the political process.* Leicester: Leicester University Press.

Gray, A. (1987). Reading the audience. *Screen, 28*(3).

Gray, A. (1992). *Video playtime: The gendering of a leisure technology.* New York: Routledge.

Gross, L. (1988). Out of the mainstream: Sexual minorities and the mass media. In E. Seiter et al., *Remote control.* New York: Routledge.

Grossberg, L., Nelson, C., & Treichler, P. (Eds.). (1992). *Cultural studies.* New York: Routledge.

Hall, S. (1977). Culture, the media and the ideological effect. In J. Curran, M. Gurevitch, & J. Woollacot (Eds.), *Mass communication and society* (pp. 315-349). London: Edward Arnold.

Hall, S. (1980). Cultural studies: Two paradigms. *Media, Culture and Society, 2*(1).

Hall, S. (1981). Encoding/decoding in television discourse. In S. Hall et al. (Eds.), *Culture, media, language.* London: Hutchinson.

Hall, S., & Jefferson, T. (Eds.). (1976). *Resistance through rituals: Youth subcultures in postwar Britain.* London: University of Birmingham.

Herman, E., & Chomsky, N. (1988). *Manufacturing consent: The political economy of the mass media.* New York: Pantheon.

Jameson, F. (1981). *The political unconscious: Narrative as a socially symbolic act.* Ithaca, NY: Cornell University Press.

Jenkins, H. III. (1993). *Textual poachers: Television fans and participatory culture.* New York: Routledge.

Jhally, S., & Livant, B. (1986). Watching as working: The valorization of audience consciousness. *Journal of Communication, 36*(3).

Kaplan, E. A. (1983). *Regarding television: Critical approaches: An anthology* (Monograph Series, Vol. 2.). Los Angeles: American Film Institute, University Publications of America.

Kellner, D. (1989). *Critical theory, Marxism and modernity.* Cambridge, UK: Polity.

Kubey, R. et al. (Eds.). (1990). *Television and the quality of life.* Hillsdale, NJ: Lawrence Earlbaum.

Lee, M., & Solomon, N. (1990). *Unreliable sources: A guide to detecting bias in news media.* New York: Corol.

Lembo, R., & Tucker, K. H., Jr. (1990). Culture, television and opposition: Rethinking cultural studies. *Critical Studies in Mass Communication, 7*(2), 97-116.

Levine, L. W. (1988). *Highbrow/lowbrow: The emergence of cultural hierarchy in America.* Cambridge, MA: Harvard University Press.

Lewis, J. (1991). *The ideological octopus: An exploration of television and its audience* (Studies in Culture and Communication). New York: Routledge.

Lewis, L. A. (1992). *The adoring audience: Fan culture and popular media.* Winchester, MA: Unwin Hyman.

Lichter, S. R., Rothman, S., & Lichter, L. (1986). *The media elite.* Bethesda, MD: Adler & Adler.

Lipsitz, G. (1990). *Time passages: Collective memory and American popular culture.* Minneapolis: University of Minnesota Press.

Lull, J. (1990). *Inside family viewing: Ethnographic research on television audiences.* London: Routledge.

Lyotard, J.-F. (1986). *The postmodern condition: A report on knowledge* (G. Bennington, B. Massumi, & R. Durand, Trans.). Manchester, UK: Manchester University Press.

MacCabe, C. (Ed.). (1986). *High theory/low culture: Analyzing popular television and film.* New York: St. Martin's.

May, L. (1980). *Screening out the past: The birth of mass culture and the motion picture industry.* New York: Oxford University Press.

Mazzocco, D. W. (1994). *Networks of power: Corporate TV's threat to democracy.* Boston: South End Press.

Mellencamp, P. (1990). *Indiscretions: Avant-garde film, video television.* Bloomington: Indiana University Press.

Mellencamp, P. (Ed.). (1990). *The logics of television.* Bloomington: Indiana University Press.

Miller, M. C. (1988). *Boxed in: The culture of TV.* Evanston, IL: Northwestern University Press.

Montgomery, K. (1991). Gay activists and the networks. *Journal of Communication, 31*(3), 49-57.

Morgan, M. (1983). Symbolic victimization and real-world fear. *Human Communication Research, 9*(2), 146-157.

Morley, D. (1983). Cultural transformations: The politics of resistance. In H. David & P. Walton (Eds.), *Language, image, media* (pp. 104-117). New York: St. Martin's.

Morley, D. (1986). *Family television: Cultural power and domestic leisure.* London: Comedia.

Morley, D. (1992). *Television audiences and cultural studies.* London: Routledge.

Morley, D. (1993). Active audience theory: Pendulums and pitfalls. *Journal of Communication 43*(4), 13-19.

Murdock, G. (1989). Cultural studies: Missing links. *Critical Studies in Mass Communication, 6*(4).

Naremore, J., & Brantlinger, P. (Eds.). (1991). *Modernity and mass culture.* Bloomington: Indiana University Press.

O'Connor, A. (1989). The problem of American cultural studies. *Critical Studies in Mass Communication, 6*(4).

Parenti, M. (1992). *Make-believe media: The politics of entertainment.* New York: St. Martin's.

Postman, N. (1984). *Amusing ourselves to death.* New York: Viking.

Radway, J. (1986). Identifying ideological seams: Mass culture, analytical methods and political practice. *Communication, 9,* 93-123

Real, M. R. (1989). *Super media: A cultural studies approach.* Newbury Park: Sage.

Reed, B. (1994, March/April). The wealth of information: How media empires plan to amass it. *Dollars and Sense,* pp. 8-11, 35-36.

Rosaldo, R. (1980). *Culture and truth: The remaking of social analysis.* Boston: Beacon.

Ross, A. (1989). *No respect: Intellectuals and popular culture.* London: Routledge.

Ross, A., & Penley, C. (Eds.). (1991). *Technoculture.* Minneapolis: University of Minnesota Press.

Rutherford, J. (Ed.). (1990). *Identity: Community, culture, difference.* London: Lawrence and Wishart.

Ryan, C. (1991). *Prime time activism: Media strategies for grass roots organizing.* Boston: South End Press.

Sanders, C. R. (1990). *Marginal conventions: Popular culture, mass media and social deviance.* Bowling Green, OH: Bowling Green University Popular Press.

Schiller, H. (1989). *Culture Inc.: The corporate takeover of public expression.* New York: Oxford University Press.

Scott, J. (1990). *Domination and the arts of resistance.* New Haven, CT: Yale University Press.

Seiter, E., et al. (Eds.). (1989). *Remote control: Television audiences and cultural power.* New York: Routledge.

Shohat, E. (1991). Ethnicities in relation: Toward a multicultural reading of American cinema. In L. D. Friedman (Ed.), *Unspeakable images: Ethnicity and the American cinema* (pp. 215-250). Champaign: University of Illinois Press.

Sholle, D. (1990). Resistance: Pinning down a wandering concept in cultural studies discourse. *Journal of Urban and Cultural Studies, 1*(1), 87-105.

Spivak, G. (1987). *In other worlds: Essays in cultural politics.* New York: Methuen.

Stead, P. (1989). *Film and the working class.* New York: Routledge.

Suleiman, S. R. (1980). *The reader in the text: Essays on audience and interpretation.* Princeton, NJ: Princeton University Press.

Thomas, S., & Callahan, B. P. (1982). Allocating happiness: TV families and social class. *Journal of Communication, 32*(3), 184-189.

Toll, R. C. (1982). *The entertainment machine: American show business in the twentieth century.* New York: Oxford University Press.

Tomlinson, A. (1989). *Consumption, identity and style.* New York: Routledge.

Tompkins, J. P. (Ed.). (1980). *Reader-response criticism: From formalism to post-structuralism.* Baltimore, MD: Johns Hopkins University Press.

Tullock, J. (1990). *Television drama: Agency, audience and myth.* New York: Routledge.

Tunstall, J., & Palmer, M. (1991). *Media moguls.* New York: Routledge.

Turner, G. (1990). *British cultural studies.* London: Unwin Hyman.

Turow, J. (1992). The organizational underpinnings of contemporary media conglomerates. *Communications Research, 19*(6), 682-704.

VandeBerg, L. R., & Wenner, L. (1991). *Television criticism.* New York: Longman.

Weeks, J. (1981). *Sex, politics and society.* London: Longman.

Wenner, L. A. (Ed.). (1989). *Media, sports and society.* Newbury Park, CA: Sage.

West, C. (1991). *The ethical dimensions of Marxist thought.* New York: Monthly Review Press.

Williams, R. (1975). *Television: Technology and cultural form.* New York: Schocken.

Wolf, M. A., & Kielwasser, A. P. (1991). *Gay people, sex and the media.* New York: Harrington Park Press. (Originally published as *Journal of Homosexuality, 21[1/2]*)

Wood, W. C., & O'Hare, S. L. (1991). Paying for the video revolution: Consumer spending on the mass media. *Journal of Communication, 41*(1), 24-30.

B. Race, Gender, Class (Theory and General)

Abelove, H., Barale, M. A., & Halperin, D. M. (Eds.). (1993). *The lesbian and gay studies reader.* New York: Routledge.

Als, H. (1989, Summer). Negro faggotry. *Black Film Review,* pp. 18-19.

Ames, C. (1992). Restoring the Black man's lethal weapon: Race and sexuality in contemporary cop films. *Journal of Popular Film and Television, 20*(3), 52-60.

Anderson, T. (1990). *Black studies: Theory, method and cultural perspectives.* Pullman: Washington State University Press.

Ang, I. (1988, Winter). Feminist desire and female pleasure. *Camera Obscura,* pp. 179-190.

Baehr, H., & Dyer, G. (1987). *Boxed in: Women on and in television.* London: Routledge.

Bales, F. (1986). Television use and confidence in television by Blacks and Whites in four selected years. *Journal of Black Studies, 16,* 283-291.

Baker, H. A., & Redmond, P. (Eds.). (1989). *Afro-American literary study in the 1990s.* Chicago: University of Chicago Press.

Barlow, W. (1992). *Sounding out racism: The radio industry.* Washington, DC: Howard University Press.

Berry, G. L., & Asamen, J. K. (1993). *Children & television: Images in a changing sociocultural world.* Newbury Park, CA: Sage

Berry, G. L., & Mitchell-Kernan, C. (1982). *Television and socialization of the minority child.* New York: Academic Press.

Betterton, R. (1987). *Looking on: Images of femininity in the visual arts and media.* London: Pandora.

Blackman, I., & Perry, K. (1990, Spring). Skirting the issue: Lesbian fashion for the 1990s. *Feminist Review, 34,* 67-78.

Blount, M., & Cunningham, G. (in press). *Theorizing Black male subjectivity.* New York: Routledge.

Bobo, J. (1991). Black women in fiction and nonfiction: Images of power and powerlessness. *Wide Angle, 13*(3-4), 72-81.

Bobo, J. (1991). The subject is money: Reconsidering the Black film audience as a theoretical paradigm. *Black American Literature Forum, 25*(2), 421-432.

Bobo, J., & Seiter, E. (1991). Black feminism and media criticism: *The Women of Brewster Place. Screen, 32,* 286-302.

Bogle, D. (1980). *Brown sugar: Eighty years of America's Black female superstars.* New York: Harmony.

Bogle, D. (1988). *Blacks in films and television: An encyclopedia.* New York: Garland.

Bogle, D. (1992). *Toms, coons, mammies and bucks: An interpretive history of Blacks in American films.* New York: Continuum. (Original work published 1973)

Boime, A. (1990). *The art of exclusion: Representing Blacks in the nineteenth century.* Washington, DC: Smithsonian Institution Press.

Boskin, J. (1986). *Sambo: The rise and decline of an American jester.* New York: Oxford University Press.

Bourne, St. Clair. (1990). The African American image in American cinema. *The Black Scholar, 21*(2), pp. 12-19.

Bronski, M. (1984). *Culture clash: The making of gay sensibility.* Boston: South End Press.

Brown, M. E. (1990). *Television and women's culture: The politics of the popular.* Newbury Park, CA: Sage.

Brunsdon, C. (1991). Pedagogies of the feminine: Feminist teaching and women's genres, *Screen, 32*(4), 364-381.

Butler, J. (1990). *Gender trouble: Feminism and the subversion of identity.* New York: Routledge.

Butler, M., & Paisley, W. (1980). Women and the mass media: Sourcebook for research and action. New York: Human Sciences Press.

Byars, J. (Ed.). (1986, Autumn). Reading feminine discourse: Prime-time television in the US [Special issue]. *Communications.*

Byars, J. (1988). Gazes/voices/power: Expanding psychoanalysis for feminist film and television theory. In D. Pribam (Ed.), *Female spectators: Looking at film and television* (pp. 110-131). London: Verso.

Byars, J. (1993). All that Hollywood allows: Re-reading gender in 1950s melodrama. New York: Routledge.

Cantor, M., & Isber, C. (1975). *Report of the Task Force on Women in Public Broadcasting.* Washington, DC: Corporation for Public Broadcasting.

Carby, H. V. (1992). The multicultural wars. In G. Dent (Ed.), *Black popular culture: A project by Michele Wallace* (pp. 187-199). Seattle, WA: Bay Press.

Carby, H. (1987). *Reconstructing womanhood: The emergence of the Afro-American woman novelist.* New York: Oxford University Press.

Carson, D., Dittmar, L., & Welsch, J. R. (Eds.). (1994). *Multiple voices in feminist film.* Minneapolis: University of Minnesota Press.

Carter, E., & Watney, S. (1989). *Taking liberties: AIDS and cultural politics.* London: Serpent's Tail.

Cham, M. B., & Andrade-Watkins, C. (Eds.). (1988). *Blackframes: Critical perspectives on Black independent cinema.* Cambridge: MIT Press.

Chapman, C., & Rutherford, J. (1988). *Male order: Unwrapping masculinity.* London: Lawrence and Wishart.

Chrisman, R. (1990). What is the right thing? Notes on the deconstruction of Black ideology. *The Black Scholar, 21*(2), 53-57.

Churchill, W. (1992). *Fantasies of the master race.* Monroe, ME: Common Courage Press.

Cirksena, K. (1987). Politics and difference: Radical feminist epistemological premises for communication studies. *Journal of Communication Inquiry, 11*(1), 19-28.

Collins, P. H. (1990). *Black feminist thought: Knowledge consciousness and the politics of empowerment.* London: Harper Collins.

Craig, S. (1992). (Ed.). *Men, masculinity, and the media.* Newbury Park, CA: Sage.

Creedon, P. (1989). *Women in mass communication: Challenging gender values.* Newbury Park: Sage.

Cripps, T. (1978). *Black film as genre.* Bloomington: Indiana University Press.

Cross, W. E. (1991). *Shades of Black: Diversity in African-American identity.* Philadelphia: Temple University Press.

Cumberlatch, G., & Negine, R. (1992). *Images of disability on television.* London: Routledge.

Dates, J. L., & Barlow, W. (Eds.). (1990). *Split image: African Americans in the mass media.* Washington, DC: Howard University Press.

Davis, A. Y. (1985). *Violence against women and the ongoing challenge to racism.* Latham, NY: Kitchen Table/Women of Color Press.

Davis, A. Y. (1985). *Women, culture and politics.* New York: Random House.

Dearborn, M. (1989). *Pocahonatas's daughters: Gender and ethnicity in American culture.* New York: Random House.

de Lauretis, T. (1984). *Alice doesn't: Feminism, semiotics and the cinema.* London: Macmillan.

de Lauretis, T. (1987). *Technologies of gender: Essays on theory, film and fiction.* Bloomington: Indiana University Press.

Dervin, B. (1987, Fall). The potential contributions of feminist scholarship to the field of communication. *Journal of Communication.*

Diawara, M. (1988). Black spectatorship: Problems of identification and resistance. *Screen, 29*(4), 66-81.

Diawara, M. (Ed.). (in press). *Black American cinema: History and criticism.* New York: Routledge.

Doane, M. A. (1984). The women's film: Possession and address. M. A. Doane, P. Mellencamp, & L. Williams (Eds.), *Re-Vision: Essays in feminist film criticism.* Frederick, MD: University Publication of America in association with the American Film Institute.

Doane, M. A. (1988). Woman's stake: Filming the female body. In C. Penley (Ed.), *Feminism and film theory.* New York: Routledge.

Doane, M. A. (1991). *Femmes fatales: Feminism, film theory, Psychoanalysis.* New York: Routledge.

Doane, M. A. (1991). Film and the masquerade: Theorising the female spectator. *Screen, 23*(3-4).

Doane, M. A., Mellencamp, P., & Williams, L. (Eds.). (1984). *Re- Vision: Essays in feminist film criticism.* Frederick, MD: University Publication of America in association with the American Film Institute.

Donald, J., & Ratansi, A. (Eds.). (1992). *"Race," culture and difference.* London: Sage.

Doty, A. (1994). *Making things perfectly queer: Interpreting mass culture.* Minneapolis: University of Minnesota Press.

Downing, J. (1992). Latino media in greater New York. In S. Riggins (Ed.), *Minority languages and cultural survival.* Chicago: Aldine.

Dyer, R. (1988). White. *Screen, 29*(4), 44-64.

Early, G. (1990, Fall). Life with daughters: Watching the Miss America Pageant. *Kenyon Review, 12,* 132-145.

Ely, M. E. (1991). *The adventures of* Amos'n'Andy: *A social history of an American phenomenon.* New York: Maxwell Macmillan International.

Erens, P. (Ed.). (1990). *Issues in feminist film criticism.* Bloomington: Indiana University Press.

Fejes, F. (1989). Images of men in media research. *Critical Studies in Mass Communication, 6*(2), 215-221.

Fenster, M. (1993). Queer punk fanzines: Identity, community, and the articulation of homosexuality and hardcore. *Journal of Communication Inquiry, 17*(1), 73-94.

Ferguson, R., Gever, M., & Minh-ha, T. T. (Eds.). (1990). *Out there: Marginalization and contemporary cultures.* New York: New Museum of Contemporary Art.

Ferguson, M. (1983). *Forever feminine: Women's magazines and the cult of femininity.* London: Heinemann.

Flitterman-Lewis, S. (1987). Psychoanalysis, film and television. In R. C. Allen (Ed.), *Channels of discourse* (pp. 172-210). Chapel Hill: University of North Carolina Press.

Franklin, S., Lury, C., & Stacey, J. (Eds.). (1991). *Off-centre: Feminism and cultural studies.* London: Harper-Collins.

Franzwa, H. (1978). The image of women in television: An annotated bibliography. In G. Tuchman et al. (Eds.), *Hearth and home.* New York: Oxford University Press.

Friedman, L. D. (Ed.). (1991). *Unspeakable images: Ethnicity and the American cinema.* Champaign: University of Illinois Press.

Gaines, J. (1988, Winter). White privilege and looking relations: Race and gender in feminist film theory. *Screen, 29.*

Gaines, J. (1990). Women and representation: Can we enjoy alternative pleasure? In P. Erens (Ed.), *Issues in feminist film criticism.* Bloomington: Indiana University.

Gallagher, M. (1992). Women and men in the media [Special issue]. *Communication Research Trends, 12*(1).

Gamman, L., & Marshment, M. (Eds.). (1989). *The female gaze: Women as viewers of popular culture.* London: Women's Press.

Gates, H. L. (1987). *Figures in Black: Words, signs, and the racial self.* New York: Oxford University Press.

Gates, H. L., Jr. (1989, November 12). TV's Black world turns—But stays unreal. *New York Times.*

Gates, H. L. (1992). *Loose canons: Notes on the culture wars.* New York: Oxford University Press.

Gay, G., & Baber, W. L. (1987). *Expressively Black: The cultural basis of ethnic identity.* New York: Praeger.

Gays and Film [Special section]. (1977, November). *Jump Cut, 16,* 13-29.

Gever, M., & Magnan, N. (1986). The same difference: On lesbian representation, *Exposure, 24*(2), 27-35.

Gilman, S. L. (1985, Autumn). Black bodies, White bodies: Toward an iconography of female sexuality in late nineteenth-century art, medicine and literature. *Critical Inquiry, 12,* 204-242.

Gilman, S. L. (1985). *Difference and pathology: Stereotypes of sexuality.* Ithaca, NY: Cornell University Press.

Gledhill, C. (1988). Pleasurable negotiations. In D. Pribam (Ed.), *Female spectators: Looking at film and television* (pp. 64-89). London: Verso.

Gray, A. (1992). *Video playtime: The gendering of a leisure technology.* London: Routledge.

Gray, H. (1989). Television, Black Americans and the American dream. *Critical Studies in Mass Communication, 6,* 223-242.

Gray, H. (1991). Recodings: Possibilities and limitations in commercial television representations of African American culture. *Quarterly Review of Film and Video, 13,* 117-130.

Griffin, G. (Ed.). (1993). *Outwrite: Lesbianism and popular culture.* Boulder, CO: Pluto.

Gross, L. (1976, February 22). Television under pressure: Are a handful of activists serving or wrecking the medium? *TV Guide,* pp. 4-7.

Gross, L. (1984). The cultivation of intolerance: Television, Blacks and gays. In G. Melischeck et al. (Eds.), *Cultural indicators: An international symposium.* Vienna: Austrian Academy of Sciences.

Gross, L. (1993). *Contested closets: The politics and ethics of outing.* Minneapolis: University of Minnesota Press.

Guy-Sheftall, B. (1992). Black women's studies: The interface of women's studies and Black studies. *Phylon, 49*(1-2), 33-41.

Hall, S. (1980). Cultural studies: Two paradigms. In R. Collins et al. (Eds.), *Media, culture and society: A critical reader.* London: Sage.

Hall, S. (1980). Encoding and decoding. In S. Hall et al. (Eds.), *Culture, media, and language.* London: Hutchinson.

Hall, S. (1986). Gramsci's relevance for the study of race and ethnicity. *Journal of Communication Inquiry, 10*(2), 5-27.

Hall, S. (1991). Ethnicity: Identity and difference. *Radical America, 23*(4), 9-20.

Haskell, M. (1974). *From reverence to rape: The treatment of women in the movies.* Baltimore: Penguin.

Henry, C. P. (1990). *Culture and African American politics.* Bloomington: Indiana University Press.

Hine, D. C. (1992). The Black studies movement: Afrocentric-traditionalist-feminist paradigms for the next stage. *The Black Scholar, 22*(3), 11-18.

Hobson, D. (1980). Housewives and the mass media. In S. Hall et al. (Eds.), *Culture, media, and language.* London: Hutchinson.

Hobson, D. (1990). Women audiences and the workplace. In M. E. Brown (Ed.), *Television and women's culture.* Newbury Park, CA: Sage.

Hoch, P. (1979). *White hero, Black beast: Racism, sexism and the mask of masculinity.* London: Pluto Press.

hooks, b. (1981). *Ain't I a woman: Black women and feminism.* Boston: South End Press.

hooks, b. (1984). *Feminist theory: From margin to center.* Boston: South End Press.

hooks, b. (1990). *Yearning: Race, gender and cultural politics.* Boston: South End Press.

hooks, b. (1992). *Black looks: Essays on race and representation.* Boston: South End Press.

Hudson, B. (1984). Femininity and adolescence. In A. McRobbie & M. Nava (Eds.), *Gender and generation.* New York: Macmillan.

Iiyama, P., & Kitano, H.H.L. (1992). Asian Americans and the media. In G. L. Berry & C. Mitchell-Kernan (Eds.), *Television and socialization of the minority child* (pp. 151-185). New York: Academic Press.

Japp, P. M. (1991, Spring). Gender and work in the 1990s—Television's working women as displaced persons. *Women's Studies in Communication, 14,* 49-74.

Jeffords, S. (1989). *The remasculinization of America: Gender and the Vietnam War.* Bloomington: Indiana University Press.

Jeffords, S. (1994). *Hard bodies: Hollywood masculinity in the Reagan era.* New Brunswick, NJ: Rutgers University Press.

Jones, F. G. (1990, Fall). The Black audience and the BET channel. *Journal of Broadcasting and Electronic Media, 34,* 477-486.

Julien, I., & Mercer, K. (1988). True confessions: A discourse on images of Black male sexuality. In R. Chapman & J. Rutherford (Eds.), *Male order: Unwrapping masculinity.* London: Lawrence and Wishart.

Kaplan, E. A. (1978). *Women in film noir.* London: British Film Institute.

Kaplan, E. A. (1983). *Women and film: Both sides of the camera.* London: Methuen.

Kaplan, E. A. (1987). Feminist criticism and television. In R. C. Allen (Ed.), *Channels of discourse.* Chapel Hill: University of North Carolina Press.

King, C. (1992). The politics of representation: A democracy of the gaze. In F. Bonner et al. (Eds.), *Imagining women* (pp. 131-139). Cambridge, UK: Open University Press.

Kuhn, A. (1982). *Women's pictures, feminism and cinema.* Boston: Routledge & Kegan Paul.

Kuhn, A. (1984). Women's genres. *Screen, 25*(1), 18-28.

Kuhn, K. (1985). *The power of the image: Essays on representation and sexuality.* London: Routledge & Kegan Paul.

Kuhn, A. (1988). *Cinema, censorship and sexuality, 1909-1925.* London: Routledge.

Kuhn, A. with Radstone, S. (Ed.). (1991). *Women in film: An international guide.* New York: Fawcett Columbine.

LaCapra, D. (Ed.). (1991).*The bounds of race: Perspectives on hegemony and resistance.* Ithaca, NY: Cornell University Press.

Laermer, R. (1985, February 2). The televised gay: How we are pictured on the tube. *Advocate,* p. 2.

Laermer, R. (1987, January 16). Lesbian lives and AIDS crisis dominate gay imagery on the tube. *Advocate,* p. 62.

Ledwig, D. E. (1989). *To know ourselves: A report to the 101st Congress on public broadcasting and the needs of minorities and other groups.* Washington, DC: Corporation for Public Broadcasting.

Lee, E., & Browne, L. (1981), Television uses and gratifications among Black children, teenagers and adults. *Journal of Broadcasting, 25*(2), 203-207.

Leo, J. R. (1988). Television and homosexuality: Some problems of representation, discourse and melodrama. In R. L. Erenstein (Ed.), *Theatre and television.* Amsterdam: Institute for Theatre Research.

Leo, J. R. (1989). The familialism of "man" in American television melodrama. In R. R. Butters et al. (Eds.), *Displacing homophobia: Gay male perspectives in literature and culture* (pp. 31-51). Durham, NC: Duke University Press.

Leong, R. (Ed.). (1991). *The image: Independent Asian Pacific American media arts.* Los Angeles: UCLA Asian American Studies Center and Visual Communications, Southern California Asian American Studies Central, Inc.

Lesage, J. (1982). The hegemonic female fantasy. *Film Reader, 5,* 83-94.

Levine, L. (1978). *Black culture and Black consciousness: Afro- American folk thought from slavery to freedom.* New York: Oxford University Press.

Levine, R. (1981, May 30, June 6). How the gay lobby has changed television. *TV Guide,* pp. 2-6 and pp. 49-54.

Levine, R. (1984, October). Family affairs (gays on TV). *Esquire,* p. 225.

Long, E. (1986). Women, reading and cultural authority: Some implications of the audience perspective in cultural studies. *American Quarterly, 38,* 591-612.

Lott, T. L. (1991). A no-theory theory of contemporary Black cinema. *Black American Literature Forum, 25*(2), 221-236.

MacDonald, J. F. (1992). *Blacks and White TV: Afro-Americans in TV since 1948* (2nd ed.). Chicago: Nelson-Hall.

Maines, J. (1992, November). Black and White in color. *American Demographics, 14,* 9-10.

Mangin, M. (1989). College course file: The history of lesbians and gays on film. *Journal of Film and Video, 41*(3), 50-66.

Marable, M. (1985). *Black American politics: From the Washington marches to Jesse Jackson.* London: Verso.

Marable, M. (1992). *The crisis of color and democracy: Essays on race, class and power.* Monroe, ME: Common Courage Press.

Marchetti, G. (1991). Ethnicity, the cinema and cultural studies. In L. D. Friedman (Ed.), *Unspeakable images: Ethnicity and the American cinema* (pp. 277-307). Champaign: University of Illinois Press.

Massing, M. (1982, November-December). Black-out in television. *Columbia Journalism Review,* pp. 38-44.

Matabane, P. W. (1988, Autumn). Television and the Black audience: Cultivating moderate perspectives on racial integration. *Journal of Communication, 38,* 21-31.

Mayne, J. (1990). *The woman at the keyhole: Feminism and women's cinema.* Bloomington: Indiana University Press.

Mayne, J. (1993). *Cinema and spectatorship.* New York: Routledge.

Mayne, J. (1993). White spectatorship and genre-mixing. In J. Mayne, *Cinema and spectatorship.* New York: Routledge.

McCracken, E. (1993). *Decoding women's magazines: From Mademoiselle to Ms.* New York: St. Martin's.

McRobbie, A., & McCabe, T. (Eds.). (1981). *Feminism for girls: An adventure story.* London: Routledge.

McRobbie, A., & Nava, M. (Eds.). (1984). *Gender and generation.* New York: Macmillan.

Mercer, K. (1991). Skin head sex thing: Racial difference and the homoerotic imaginary. In Bad Object-Choices (Ed.), *How do I Look: Queer film and video* (pp. 169-210). Seattle, WA: Bay Press.

Mercer, K., Rose, J., Spivak, G. C., & McRobbie, A. (1988, Spring). Sexual identities: Questions of differences. *Undercut, 17,* 19-30.

Middleton, P. (1992). *The inward gaze: Masculinity and subjectivity in modern culture.* New York: Routledge.

Miller, R. M. (Ed.). (1978). *Ethnic images in American film and television.* Philadelphia: Balch Institute.

Miller, R. M. (Ed.). (1980). *The kaleidoscopic lense: How Hollywood views ethnic groups.* Englewood, NJ: Jerome S. Ozer.

Minh-ha, T. T. (1989). Outside in, inside out. In J. Pines (Ed.), *Questions of Third World cinema.* London: British Film Institute.

Minh-ha, T. T. (1992). *When the moon waxes red: Representation, gender and cultural politics.* New York: Routledge.

Miner, M. (1984). *Insatiable appetites: Twentieth-century American women's bestsellers.* Westport, CT: Greenwood.

Modleski, T. (1982). *Loving with a vengeance: Mass-produced fantasies for women.* New York: Methuen.

Modleski, T. (1986). Femininity as masquerade: A feminist approach to mass culture. In C. McCabe (Ed.), *High theory, low culture*. Manchester, UK: University of Manchester Press.

Modleski, T. (Ed.). (1986). *Studies in entertainment: Critical approaches to mass culture*. Bloomington: Indiana University Press.

Montgomery, K. (1979). *Gay activists and the networks: A case study of special interest pressure on television*. Doctoral dissertation, University of California at Los Angeles.

Montgomery, K. C. (1990). *Advocacy groups and the struggle over entertainment television*. New York: Oxford.

Morrison, T. (Ed.). (1992). *Race-ing justice, en-gendering power: Essays on Anita Hill, Clarence Thomas and the construction of social reality*. New York: Pantheon.

Mulvey, L. (1975). Visual pleasure and narrative cinema. *Screen, 16*(3), 6-18.

Mulvey, L. (1981). Afterthoughts on "Visual Pleasure and Narrative Cinema," .... *Framework*, nos. 15/16/17, pp. 12-15.

Mulvey, L. (1989). *Visual and other pleasures*. Bloomington: Indiana University Press.

Musser, C. (1991). Ethnicity, role-playing, and American film comedy: From Chinese laundry scene to whoopee (1894-1930). In L. D. Friedman (Ed.), *Unspeakable images: Ethnicity and the American cinema*. Champaign: University of Illinois Press.

Nain, G. T. (1991, Spring). Black women, sexism and racism: Black or antiracist feminism? *Feminist Review, 37*, 1-21.

Navarro, R. (1991). Shocking pink praxis: Race and gender on the ACT UP frontlines. In D. Fuss (Ed.), *Inside/out: Lesbian theories, gay theories*. New York: Routledge.

Navarro, R., & Saalfield, C. (1989). Not just Black and White: AIDS, media and people of color. *The Independent, 12*(6), 18-23.

Nesteby, J. R. (1982). *Black images in American films, 1896-1954: The interplay between civil rights and film culture*. Washington, DC: University Press of America.

Nichols, B. (1981). *Ideology and the image: Social representation in the cinema and other media*. Bloomington: Indiana University Press.

O'Connor, J. J. (1980). *The Hollywood Indian: Stereotypes of Native Americans in film*. Trenton: New Jersey State Museum.

O'Connor, J. J. (1991, May 19). Gay images: TV's mixed signals. *New York Times*.

Omi, M. (1986). *Racial formation in the United States: From the 1960s to the 1980s*. New York: Routledge.

Omi, M., & Winant, H. (1993). On the theoretical concept of race. In C. McCarthy & W. Crichlow (Eds.), *Race, identity and representation in education*. New York: Routledge.

Partington, A. (1991). Melodrama's gendered audience. In S. Franklin et al. (Eds.), *Off-centre: Feminism and cultural studies* (pp. 49-68). London: Harper Collins.

Penley, C. (Ed.). (1988). *Feminism and film theory*. New York: Routledge.

Peterson, R. E. (1987). Media consumption and girls who want to have fun. *Critical Studies in Mass Communication, 4*(1), 37-50.

Pieterse, J. N. (1992). *White on Black: Images of Africa and Blacks in Western popular culture*. New Haven, CT: Yale University Press.

Poindexter, P., & Stroman, C. (1981). Blacks and television: A review of the research literature. *Journal of Broadcasting, 25*(2), 103-122.

Preis, K. (1986). *Cheap amusements: Working women and leisure in turn-of-the-century New York*. Philadelphia: Temple University Press.

Press, A. L. (1991). Class and gender in the hegemonic process: Class differences in women's perceptions of realism and identification with television characters. *Media, Culture and Society, 11*(2), 229-252.

Press, A. L. (1991). *Women watching television: Gender, class and generation in the American television experience.* Philadelphia: University of Pennsylvania Press.

Pribam, D. (Ed.). (1988). *Female spectators: Looking at film and television.* London: Verso.

Rakow, L. F. (1986). Feminist approaches to popular culture: Giving patriarchy its due. *Communication, 9,* 19-41.

Rakow, L. F. (1987). Looking to the future: Five questions for gender research. *Women's Studies in Communication, 10,* 79-86.

Rakow, L. F. (Ed.). (1992). *Women making meaning: New Feminist directions in communication.* New York: Routledge.

Rapping, E. (1994). *Media icons: Forays into the culture and gender wars.* Boston: South End Press.

Raymond, D. (1990). *Sexual politics & popular culture.* Bowling Green, OH: Bowling Green University Popular Press.

Reid, M. A. (1991, May). African and Black diaspora film/video. *Jump Cut, 36,* 43-46.

Riggs, M. T. (1991). Black macho revisited: Reflections of a snap! queen. *Black American Literature Forum, 25*(2), 389-392.

Roach, J., & Felix, P. (1989). Black looks. In L. Gamman & M. Marshment (Eds.), *The female gaze* (pp. 130-142). London: Women's Press.

Roberts, J. W. (1989). *From trickster to badman: The Black folk hero in slavery and freedom.* Philadelphia: University of Pennsylvania Press.

Robinson, L. (1978). What's my line? Telefiction and women's work. In L. Roinson, *Sex, class & culture* (pp. 310-342). Bloomington: University of Indiana Press.

Rock, G. (1973, December). Same time, same station, same sexism, *Ms.,* pp. 24-28.

Rothenberg, P. S. (1992). *Race, class and gender in the United States.* New York: St. Martin's.

Rowland, C. (1986, April 1). A question of standards: Gay cable network vision or compromise. *Advocate,* pp. 49-50.

Roman, L., & Christian-Smith, L. K. (1988). *Becoming feminine: The politics of popular culture.* London: Falmer.

Rubin, B. (Ed.). (1980). *Small voices & great trumpets: Minorities & media.* New York: Praeger.

Russo, V. (Ed.). (1987). *The celluloid closet: Homosexuality in the movies* (2nd ed.). New York: Harper & Row.

Russo, V. (1984, January 24). Gay films: Gay reality vs. political correctness. *Advocate,* p. 36.

Rutherford, R. (Ed.). (1990). *Identity: Community, culture, difference.* London: Lawrence and Wishart.

Sabo, D., & Panepinto, J. (1990). Football ritual and the social reproduction of masculinity. In M. A. Messner & D. Sabo (Eds.), *Sport, men and the gender order.* Champaign, IL: Human Kinetics.

Schlesinger, P., et al. (1992). *Women viewing violence.* London: British Film Institute.

Schwichtenberg, C. (Ed.). (1993). *The Madonna connection: Representational politics, subcultural identities, and cultural theory.* Boulder, CO: Westview.

Shaw, H. B. (1990). *Perspectives on Black popular culture.* Bowling Green, OH: Bowling Green University Popular Press.

Shohat, E. (1991). Gender and culture of empire: Toward a feminist ethnography of the cinema. *Quarterly Review of Film and Video, 13*(1-3), 45-84.

Shoos, D. (1992, Spring). The female subject of popular culture. *Hypatia, 7,* 215-226.

Shrage, L. (1990). Feminist film aesthetics: A contextual approach. *Hypatia, 5,* 137-148.

Signorielli, N. (1989). Television and conceptions about sex roles: Maintaining conventionality and the status quo. *Sex Roles, 21*(5/6).

Silk, C. (1990). *Racism and anti-racism in American popular culture: Portrayals of African Americans in fiction and film.* New York: Manchester University Press.

Silverman, K. (1988). *The acoustic mirror: The female voice in psychoanalysis and cinema.* Bloomington: Indiana University Press .

Simmonds, F. N. (1992). *She's gotta have it: The representation of Black female sexuality on film.* In F. Bonner et al. (Eds.), *Imagining women* (pp. 210-220). Cambridge, UK: Open University Press.

Simms, S. A. (1981). Gay images on television. In J. W. Chesebro (Ed.), *Gayspeak: Gay male and lesbian communication* (pp. 153-162). New York: Pilgrim Press.

Sklar, R., & Musser, C. (Eds.). (1990). *Resisting images: Radical perspectives on film history.* Philadelphia: Temple University Press.

Smith, J. C. (Ed.). (1988). *Images of Blacks in American culture: A reference guide to information sources.* Westport, CT: Greenwood.

Smith, V. (1990). Black feminist theory and the representation of the other. In C. A. Wall (Ed.), *Changing our own words: Essays on criticism, theory and writing by Black women.* New Brunswick, NJ: Rutgers University Press.

Smitherman-Donaldson, G., & van Dijk, T. (1988). *Discourse and discrimination.* Detroit, MI: Wayne State University Press.

Snead, J. (1994). *White screens, Black images: Hollywood from the dark side* (C. MacCabe & C. West, Eds.). New York: Routledge.

Spigel, L., & Mann, D. (Eds.). (1993). *Private screenings: Television and the female consumer.* Minneapolis: University of Minnesota Press.

Spillers, H. J. (1992). *Comparative American identities: Race, sex, and nationality in the modern text.* New York: Routledge.

Stacey, S. (1990). Desperately seeking difference. In P. Erens (Ed.), *Issues in feminist film criticism* (pp. 365-379). Bloomington: Indiana University Press.

Stain, R., & Spence, L. (1983). Colonialism, racism and representation. *Screen, 24*(2), 2-20.

Stainchamps, E. (Ed.). (1974). *Rooms with no view: A woman's guide to the man's world of the media.* New York: Harper & Row.

Steeves, S. (1987). Feminist theories and media studies. *Critical Studies in Mass Communication, 4*(2).

Straayer, C. (1984, February). Lesbian/feminist audience. *Jump Cut, 29,* 40-44.

Straayer, C. (1990, April). The hypothetical lesbian heroine. *Jump Cut, 35,* 50-57.

Stuart, A. (1988). *The Color Purple:* In defence of happy endings. In D. Pribam (Ed.), *The Female Gaze* (pp. 60-75). London: Verso.

Tanenbaum, L. (1992, Winter). A look at feminist film in the '90s. *On the Issues,* pp. 12, 15, 17.

Tartaglia, J. (1979, Summer/Fall). The gay sensibility in American avant-garde film. *Millennium,* pp. 53-38.

Tasker, Y. (1991). Having it all: Feminism and the pleasures of the popular. In S. Franklin, C. Lury, & J. Stacey (Eds.), *Off centre: Feminism and cultural studies.* London: Harper Collins.

Tate, G. (1992). *Flyboy in the buttermilk: Essays on contemporary America.* New York: Simon & Schuster.

Taylor, C. (1989). The future of Black film: The debate continues. *Black Film Review, 5*(4), 6+

Taylor, C. (1992). The Malcolm ghost in the media machine. *The Black Scholar, 22*(4), 37-41.

Treichler, P. A., & Wartella, E. (1986). Interventions: Feminist theory and communication studies. *Communication, 9,* 1-18.

Tuchman, G., et al. (Eds.). (1978). *Hearth & home: Images of women in the mass media.* New York: Oxford University Press.

Tuchman, G. (1978). The symbolic annihilation of women in the mass media. In G. Tuchman et al. (Eds.), *Hearth & home: Images of women in the mass media* (pp. 4-38). New York: Oxford University Press.

Turner, P. A. (1991, Summer). From Homer to Hoke: A small step for African American mankind. *Journal of Negro Education, 60*(3), 342-353.

Turner, P. A. (1990, Spring). Tainted glory: Truth and fiction in contemporary Hollywood. *Trotter Institute Review,* pp. 5-9.

Turner, P. A. (1994). *Ceramic uncles and celluloid mammies: Black images and their influence on culture.* New York: Doubleday.

Turtell, S. (1979, February 8). Emerald city: New York's cable TV show for gays. *Advocate,* pp. 40-41.

U.S. Commission on Civil Rights. (1977, 1979). *Window dressing on the set: Minorities and women in television.* Washington, DC: Author.

Van Deburg, W. I. (1984). *Slavery and race in American popular culture.* Madison: University of Wisconsin Press.

Van Zoonan, L. (1994). *Feminist media studies.* London: Sage.

Vida, G. (1976). The lesbian image in the media. In G. Vida (Ed.), *Our right to love: A lesbian resource book* (pp. 240-245). Englewood Cliffs, NJ: Prentice Hall.

Wallace, W. (1990). Negative images: Towards a Black feminist cultural criticism. In M. Wallace (Ed.), *Invisibility blues: From pop to theory.* London: Verso.

Weibel, K. (1977). *Mirror, mirror: Images of women reflected in popular culture.* Garden City, NY: Doubleday.

West, C. (1988). Marxist theory and the specificity of Afro-American oppression. In C. Nelson & L. Grossberg (Eds.), *Marxism and the interpretation of culture.* Chicago: University of Chicago Press.

West, C. (1993). *Race matters.* Boston: Beacon.

West, J. (1972). Women, sex and class. In A. Kuhn & A. M. Wolpe (Eds.), *Feminism and materialism.* London: Routledge.

White, E. F. (1990). Africa on my mind: Gender, counter discourse and African-American nationalism. *Journal of Women's History, 2*(1).

Wiegman, R. (1991). Black bodies/American commodities: Gender, race and the bourgeois ideal in contemporary film. In L. D. Friedman (Ed.), *Unspeakable images: Ethnicity and the American cinema.* Champaign: University of Illinois Press.

Williams, L. (1984). When the woman looks. In M. A. Doane, P. Mellencamp, & L. Williams (Eds.), *Re-vision: Essays in feminist film criticism.* Frederick, MD: University Publication of America in association with the American Film Institute.

Willis, S. (1991). *A primer for daily life.* New York: Routledge.

Wilson, C. C., & Gutiérrez, F. (1985). *Minorities and media: Diversity and the end of mass communication.* Beverly Hills, CA: Sage.

Winokur, M. (1991). Black is White/White is Black: Passing as a strategy of racial compatibility in contemporary Hollywood comedy. In L. D. Friedman (Ed.), *Unspeakable images: Ethnicity and the American Cinema* (pp. 190-211). Champaign: University of Illinois Press.

Winston, M. R. (1982). Racial consciousness and the evolution of mass communication in the United States. *Daedalus, 111*(4), 171-182.

Woll, A. L., & Miller, R. M. (1987). (Eds.). *Ethnic and racial images in American film and television: Historical essays and bibliography.* New York: Garland.

Wong, E. F. (1978). *On visual media racism: Asians in American motion pictures.* New York: Arno.

Wood, R. (1978, January). Responsibilities of a gay film critic. *Film Comment,* pp. 12-17.

Wood, R. (1983, June). Is there camp after cruising. *Films and Filming,* pp. 26-29.

Yacowar, Y. (1989, March). *Die hard:* The White man's mythic invincibility, *Jump Cut, 34,* 2-4.

Zimmerman, B. (1981, March). *Daughters of darkness:* Lesbian vampires. *Jump Cut, 24/25,* 23-24.

PART II: ADVERTISING

Advertising directed to gays. (1982, May 25). *San Francisco Chronicle,* p. 15.

Advertising's black magic. (1986, February 10). *Newsweek,* p. 60.

Alperstein, N. M. (1989, Summer). The uses of television commercials in reporting everyday events and issues. *Journal of Popular Culture, 23,* 127-135.

Arlen, M. J. (1979). *Thirty seconds.* New York: Farrar, Strauss Giroux.

Arnheim, R. (1964). *Art and visual perception: A psychology of the creative eye.* Berkeley, CA: University of California Press.

Ascher, C. (1987). Selling to Ms. Consumer. In D. Lazere (Ed.), *American media and mass culture: Left perspectives* (pp. 43-52). Berkeley: University of California Press.

Banner, L. W. (1983). *American beauty.* Chicago: University of Chicago Press.

Barnouw, E. (1988). *The sponsor.* New York: Oxford University Press.

Barthel, C. (1988). *Putting on appearances: Gender and advertising.* Philadelphia: Temple University Press.

Barthes, R. (1983). *The fashion system* (M. Ward & R. Howard, Trans.). New York: Hill and Wang.

Bensen, S. P. (1979, Fall). Palaces of consumption and machines for selling: The American department store, 1880-1940. *Radical History Review,* pp. 199-221.

Berger, J. (1972). *Ways of seeing.* New York: Penguin.

Berger, J. (1974). *The look of things.* New York: Viking.

Best, S. (1986, September 26). The commodification of reality and the reality of commodification. *Chicago Literature Review,* pp. 14-15, 17.

Bhasin, K., & Malik, B. (1979, July/August). Don't sell our bodies to sell your products. *Manushi* [India], pp. 23-28.

Bretl, D. J., & Cantor, J. (1988). The portrayal of men and women in U.S. television commercials: A recent content analysis of trends over 15 years. *Sex Roles, 18*(9/10), 595-609.

Brown, B. M. (1993). Advertising influences on majority and minority youth: Images of inclusion and exclusion. *Journal of Communication Inquiry, 17,* 17-29.

Brown, B. W. (1992). Family intimacy in magazine advertising: 1920-1977. *Journal of Communication, 32*(3), 173-183.

Brown, M. E. (1987). The dialectic of the feminine: Melodrama and commodity in the Ferraro Pepsi commercial. *Communication, 9,* 335-354.

Browne, M. (1993, June). Dying to be thin. *Essence,* pp. 86-87, 124-127.

Brownlow, S., & Zebrowitz, L. A. (1990). Facial appearance, gender and credibility in television commercials. *Journal of Nonverbal Behavior, 14*(1), 51-60.

Burrell challenges assumptions about marketing to Blacks. (1986, February). *Madison Avenue,* pp. 44-45.

Chapkis, W. (1987). *Beauty secrets: Women and the politics of appearance.* Boston: South End Press.

Chapko, M. (1976, Autumn). Black ads are getting blacker. *Journal of Communication, 26*(4), 175-178.

Chineplou, M. (1991, December). No color in magazine ads. *Black Enterprise*, p. 11.

Circulation of magazines for gay males grows in size and publishers seek national advertisers. (1976, July 13). *The New York Times*, p. 55.

Compaine, B. M. (1980). The magazine industry: Developing the special audience. *Journal of Communication, 30*(2), 98-103.

Courtney, A. E., & Whipple, T. (1983). *Sex stereotyping in advertising*. Lexington, MA: D. C. Heath.

Coward, R. (1985). *Female desires: How they are sought, bought and packaged*. New York: Grove.

Crowley, J. H., & Pokrywczynski, J. (1991). Advertising practitioners look at a ban on tobacco advertising. *Journalism Quarterly, 68*, 329-337.

D'Amico, R. (1978, Spring). Desire and the commodity form. *Telos, 35* 88-123.

Dates, J. J. (1990). Advertising. In J. Dates & W. Barlow (Eds.), *Split image: African Americans in the mass media* (pp. 421-453). Washington, DC: Howard University Press.

Davis, K. (1991). Remaking the she-devil: A critical look at feminist approaches to beauty. *Hypatia, 6*(2), 21-43.

Davis, S. (1990, July). Men as success objects and women as sex objects: A study of personal advertisements. *Sex Roles, 23*, 43-50.

Despite less blatant sexism, ads still insult most women. (1985, August 1). *Wall Street Journal*, p. 19.

Douglas, D. (1988, September 7-13). Flex appeal, buns of steel and the body in question. *In These Times*, p. 19.

Downs, A. C., & Harrison, S. K. (1985). Embarrassing age spots or just plain ugly? Physical attractiveness stereotyping as an instrument of sexism on American television commercials. *Sex Roles, 13*(1/2), 9-19.

Earnshaw, S. (1984). Advertising and the media: The case of Women's magazines. *Media, Culture and Society, 6*, 411-421.

Ewen, S. (1976). *Captains of consciousness: Advertising and the social roots of the consumer culture*. New York: McGraw-Hill.

Ewen, S. (1988). *All consuming images*. New York: Basic Books.

Ewen, S. (1989). Advertising and the development of consumer society. In I. Angus & S. Jhally (Eds.), *Cultural politics in contemporary America* (pp. 82-95). New York: Routledge.

Ewen, S., & Ewen, E. (1982). *Channels of desire: Mass image and the shaping of American consciousness*. New York: McGraw-Hill.

Featherstone, M. (1983). The body in consumer culture. *Theory, Culture and Society, 1*(2), 18-33.

Ferguson, M. (1978). Imagery and ideology: The cover photographs of traditional women's magazines. In G. Tuchman et al. (Eds.), *Hearth and home* (pp. 97-115). New York: Oxford University Press.

Ferrante, C. L., et al. (1988). Images of women in television advertising. *Journal of Broadcasting and Electronic Media, 32*(2), 231-237.

Fisher, C. (1991). Ethnics gain market clout. *Advertising Age, 62*(3).

Flitterman, S. (1983). The real soap operas: Television commercials. In E. A. Kaplan (Ed.), *Regarding television* (pp. 84-96). Frederick, MD: University Publications of America.

Fox, R. W., & Lears, T. J. J. (Eds.). (1983). *The culture of consumption: Critical essays in American history, 1880-1980*. New York: Pantheon.

Fox, S. (1984). *The mirror makers: A history of American advertising and its creators*. New York: William Morrow.

Freedman, D. H. (1988, February 20). Why you watch some commercials—Whether you mean to or not. *TV Guide*, pp. 4-7.

Gagnard, A. (1989). Elements of timing and repetition in award-winning TV commercials. *Journalism Quarterly, 66,* 965-969.

Gays: A major force in the market place. (1979, September 3). *Business Week,* p. 118.

Gibson, D. P. (1969). *The $30 billion dollar Negro.* New York: Macmillan.

Gibson, D. P. (1978). *$70 billion in the black.* New York: Macmillan.

Gitlin, T. (1986). Car commercials and *Miami Vice.* In T. Gitlin (Ed.), *Watching television* (pp. 136-161). New York: Pantheon.

Gitter, G., O'Connell, S., & Mostofsky, D. (1972). Trends in appearance of models in *Ebony* ads over 17 years. *Journalism Quarterly, 49,* 547-550.

Gluckman, A., & Reed, B. (1993, November/December). The gay marketing moment: Leaving diversity in the dust. *Dollars and Sense,* pp. 16-19, 34-35.

Goffman, E. (1979). *Gender advertisements.* New York: Harper.

Goldman, R. (1987). Marketing fragrances: Advertising and the production of commodity signs. *Theory, Culture and Society, 4,* 691-725.

Goldman, R. (1992). *Reading ads socially.* New York: Routledge.

Goldsen, R. (1978, Winter). Why television advertising is deceptive and unfair. *Et Cetera,* pp. 354-375.

Gooch, B. (1985, July 23). The demise of the gay model. *Advocate,* p. 45.

Gottdiner, M. (1985). Hegemony and mass culture: A semiotic approach. *American Journal of Sociology, 90*(5), 979-1001.

Gregory, D., & Jacobs, P. (1993, September). The ugly side of the modeling business. *Essence,* pp. 89-90, 126-127.

Gutierrez, F. F. (1993). Advertising and the growth of minority markets and media. *Journal of Communication Inquiry, 17*(1), 6-16.

Haug, W. F. (1986). *Critique of commodity aesthetics: Appearance, sexuality and advertising in capitalist society.* Minnesota: University of Minnesota Press.

Hebdige, D. (1979). *Subculture: The meaning of style.* New York: Methuen.

Henkoff, R. (1979). Ads for advertisers: How advertisers see their audiences. In J. Wright (Ed.), *The commercial connection* (pp. 192-198). New York: Delta.

Herman, E. (1993). *Beyond hypocrisy: Decoding the news in an age of propaganda.* Boston: South End Press.

Himmelstein, H. (1989). Kodak's "America": Images from the American Eden. *Journal of Film and Video, 41*(2), 75-94.

Jacobs, S. (1994, March 7). Gay-oriented ads follow consumer out of the closet. *The Boston Globe.*

Jameson, F. (1983). Postmodernism and consumer society. In H. Foster (Ed.), *The anti-aesthetic essays on postmodern culture* (pp. 111-125). Port Townsend, WA: Bay Press.

Jennings, J., et al. (1980). Influence of television commercials on women's self-confidence and independent judgment. *Journal of Personality and Social Psychology, 38*(2), 203-210.

Jhally, S. (1990). *The codes of advertising: Fetishism and the political economy of meaning in the consumer society.* New York: Routledge.

Jhally, S. (1990, July). Image-based culture. *The World and I,* pp. 507-519.

Jones, S. A. (1978). *Subliminal advertising in American broadcast media.* New Haven, CT: Yale Law School, Yale Legislative Series.

Joseph, G. I., & Lewis, J. (1981). The media and Blacks—Selling it like it isn't. In G. I. Joseph & J. Lewis, *Common differences: Conflicts in Black and White feminist perspectives* (pp. 151-165). Garden City, NY: Anchor.

Joseph, G. I., & Lewis, J. (1981). Sexual subjects of media. In G. I. Joseph & J. Lewis, *Common differences: Conflicts in Black and White feminist perspectives* (pp. 166-177). Garden City, NY: Anchor.

Kane, K. (1993). The ideology of freshness in feminine hygiene commercials. *Journal of Communication Inquiry, 17*(1), 182-192.

Kellner, D. (1983). Critical theory, commodities and the consumer society. *Theory, Culture and Society, 1*(3), 66-83.

Kellner, D. (1990). Advertising and consumer culture. In J. Downing, A. Mohammadi, & A. Sreberny-Mohammadi (Eds.), *Questioning the media: A critical introduction* (pp. 242-254). Newbury Park, CA: Sage.

Kern-Foxworth, M. (1989, Winter). Ads pose dilemma for Black women. *Media&Values, 49*, 18.

Kervin, D. (1991). Gender ideology in television commercials. In L. R. Vande Berg & L. Wenner (Eds.), *Television criticism.* New York: Longman.

Kilbourne, J. (1989, Winter). Beauty . . . and the beast of advertising. *Media&Values,* pp., 8-49.

Kilbourne, J. (1991). The child as sex object: Images of children in the media. *Challenging Media Images of Women, 3*(3/4).

Kline, S., & Leiss, W. (1978). Advertising, needs, and commodity fetishism. *Canadian Journal of Political and Social Theory, 2*(1), 5-30.

Komisar, L. (1971). The image of woman in advertising. In V. Gornick & B. Moran, *Woman in sexist society* (pp. 207-217). New York: Basic Books.

Kuhn, A. (1985). *The power of the image.* Boston: Routledge and Kegan Paul.

Lakoff, R. T., & Scherr, R. L. (1984). *Face value: The politics of beauty.* Boston: Routledge and Kegan Paul.

Lears, T. J. J. (1984). Some versions of fantasy: Towards a cultural history of American advertising, 1880-1930. *Prospects, 9*, 349-405

Lebowitz, G. (1979, October). "Liberated woman" replaces sex as emphasis for fragrance ads. *Product Marketing,* p. 10.

Leiss, W., Kline, S., & Jhally, S. (1986). *Social communication in advertising: Persons, products and images of well-being.* New York: Methuen.

Leo, J. (1988, August). Take me, hurt me, smoke me. *Spy,* 106-109.

Leymore, V. L. (1975). *Hidden myth: Structure and symbolism in advertising.* New York: Basic Books.

Lovdal, L. T. (1989). Sex role messages in television commercials: An update. *Sex Roles, 21*(11/12), 715-724.

Marchand, R. (1985). *Advertising and the American dream: Making way for modernity, 1920-1940.* Berkeley: University of California Press.

Masse, M., & Rosenblum, K. (1988). Male and female created they them: The depiction of gender in the advertising of traditional women's and men's magazines. *Women's Studies International Forum, 11*(2), 127-144.

Matchan, L. (1984, October 15). A magazine's changing picture. *The Boston Globe.*

McCracken, E. (1993). *Decoding women's magazines: From* Mademoiselle *to* Ms. New York: St. Martin's.

McCune, J. C. (1990, December). Consumer activism means big business. *Management Review,* pp. 116-119.

Melton, G., & Fowler, G. (1987). Female roles in radio advertising. *Journalism Quarterly, 64*(1), 145-149.

Meyers, W. (1985). *The image-makers: Power and persuasion on Madison Avenue.* New York: Times Books.

Miller, C. (1992, July 6). Advertisers promote racial harmony; Nike criticized. *Marketing News,* p. 1.

Miller, M. C. (1994, March/April). Selling "power" to the powerless: How cigarette ads target youth. *Extra!,* pp. 22-23.

Millum, T. (1975). *Images of woman: Advertising in women's magazines.* Totawa, NJ: Rowan & Littlefield.

Morton, M. (1991, Fall). The tobacco pushers' marketing smokescreen. *Business and Society Review,* pp. 49-54.

Packard, V. (1957, August). The ad and the id. *Harper's Bazaar.*

Packard, V. (1957). *The hidden persuaders.* New York: David McKay.

Peck, J. (1993). Selling goods and selling God: Advertising, televangelism and the commodity form. *Journal of Communication Inquiry, 17*(1), 5-24.

Perimenis, L. (1991, Winter). The ritual of anorexia nervosa in cultural context. *Journal of American Culture, 14,* 49-59.

Pollay, R. W., et al. (1992, March). Separate, but not equal: Racial segmentation in cigarette advertising. *Journal of Advertising, 21,* 45-57.

Pope, D. (1983). *The making of modern advertising.* New York: Basic Books.

Price, J. (1978). *The best thing on TV: Commercials.* New York: Penguin.

Rapping, E. (1987). Commercials: Television's ultimate art form. In E. Rapping, *The looking glass world of nonfiction TV.* Boston: South End Press.

Riffe, D., et al. (1989, Spring). Females and minorities in TV ads in 1987 children's programs. *Journalism Quarterly, 66,* 129-136.

Robb, C. (1992, March 5). The myth of the model body. *The Boston Globe.*

Robertson, T. S., et al. (1989). Advertising and children: A cross-cultural study. *Communication Research, 16,* 459-485.

Root, J. (1984). *Pictures of women/sexuality.* Boston: Routledge & Kegan Paul.

Rosenblum, R. (1981, December). The hard sell: How TV ads talk tough in the new troubled times. *Mother Jones,* pp. 27-32.

Schudson, M. (1984). *Advertising: The uneasy persuasion: Its dubious impact on American society.* New York: Basic Books.

Schuetz, S., & Sprafkin, J. N. (1978). Spot messages appearing within Saturday morning television programs. In G. Tuchman et al. (Eds.), *Hearth & home: Images of women in the mass media* (pp. 69-77). New York: Oxford University Press.

Shields, V. R. (1990, Summer). Advertising visual images: Gendered ways of seeing and looking. *Journal of Communication Inquiry, 12,* 25-39.

Skelly, G., & Lundstrom, W. (1981). Male sex roles in magazine advertising, 1959-1979. *Journal of Communication, 31*(4), 52-57.

Slotkin, R. (1985). *The fatal environment: The myth of the frontier in the age of industrialization, 1800-1890.* New York: Atheneaum.

Spero, R. (1980). *The duping of the American voter: Dishonesty and deception in presidential television advertising.* New York: Lippincott & Crowell.

Spigel, L., & Mann, D. (1989). Women and consumer culture: A selective bibliography. *Quarterly Review of Film and Video, 111,* 85-105.

Stabiner, K. (1982, May 2). Tapping the homosexual market. *The New York Times Magazine,* pp. 34-35, 74-81.

Starr, M. E. (1984, Spring). The Marlboro Man: Cigarette smoking and masculinity in America. *Journal of Popular Culture, 17,* 45-57.

Stein, A. (1989). All dressed up, but no place to go? Style wars and the new lesbianism. *OUT/LOOK 1*(4), 34-42.

Steinem, G. (1990, July/August). Sex, lies and advertising. *Ms.,* pp. 18-28.

Steiner, L. (1988). Oppositional decoding as an act of resistance. *Critical Studies in Mass Communication, 5*(1), 1-15.

Strasser, S. (1990). *Satisfaction guaranteed.* New York: Pantheon.

Strate, L. (1992). Beer commercials: A manual on masculinity. In S. Craig (Ed.), *Men, masculinity and the media* (pp. 78-92). Newbury Park, CA: Sage.

Through the lenses of gender and ethnicity: Benetton's united colors ad campaign criticized in Toronto's *Globe Mail.* (1991, May 27). *MacLean's,* p. 21.

Timberg, B., & Himmelstein, H. (1989). Television commercials and the contradictions of everyday life: A follow-up to Himmelstein's production study of the Kodak "America" commercial. *Journal of Film and Video, 41*(3), 67-79.

Turim, M. (1983, September/October). Fashion shapes: Film, the fashion industry and the image of women. *Socialist Review, 71,* 79-96.

Vestergaard, T., & Schroder, K. (1985). *The language of advertising.* Oxford, UK: Basil Blackwell.

Waldman, D. (1984). From midnight shows to marriage vows: Women, exploitation and exhibition. *Wide Angle, 6*(2), 40-48.

Walsted, J. J., et al. (1980). Influence of television commercials on women's self-confidence and independent judgment. *Journal of Personality and Social Psychology, 38*(2), 203-210.

Wang, P. (1986, March). The rising cost of hype. New York.

Ward, A. (1992, August 10). What role do ads play in racial tension? *Advertising Age,* p. 1.

Warlaumont, H. G. (1993). Visual grammars of gender: The gaze and psychoanalytic theory in advertisements. *Journal of Communication Inquiry, 17*(1), 25-40.

Warner, F. (1992, March 16). Novello throws down the gauntlet: The surgeon general crusades to kill off Joe Cool. *AdWeek's Marketing Week,* pp. 4-5.

Weinstein, S. (1990, December 22). When gay means loss of revenue. *Los Angeles Times,* pp. F1, F5.

Wenner, L. (1991). One part alcohol, one part sport, one part dirt, stir gently: Beer commercials and television sports. In L. R. Vande Berg & L. Wenner (Eds.), *Television criticism.* New York: Longman.

Wernick, A. (1987). From voyeur to narcissist: Imaging men in contemporary advertising. In M. Kaufman (Ed.), *Beyond patriarchy: Essays by men on pleasure, power and change* (pp. 277-297). Toronto: Oxford University Press.

Williams, G. A. (1989). Enticing viewers: Sex and violence in *TV Guide* program advertisements. *Journalism Quarterly, 66,* 970-973.

Williams, R. (1980). Advertising: The magic system. In R. Williams, *Problems in materialism and culture* (pp. 170-195). London: Verso.

Williamson, J. (1978). *Decoding advertising: Ideology and meaning in advertising.* London: Marion Boyars.

Williamson, J. (1986). Woman is an island: Femininity and colonization. In T. Modleski (Ed.), *Studies in entertainment* (pp. 99-118). Bloomington: Indiana University Press.

Wilson, E. (1985). *Adorned in dreams: Fashions and modernity.* London: Virago.

Winship, J. (1980). Sexuality for sale. In Stuart Hall et al. (Eds.), *Culture, media and language.* London: Hutchinson.

Winship, J. (1983). Options—for the way you want to live now. Or a magazine for superwoman. *Theory, Culture and Society, 1*(3), 44-65.

Winship, J. (1987). *Inside women's magazines.* New York: Pandora.

Wolf, N. (1991). *The beauty myth: How Images of beauty are used against women* New York: Doubleday.

Wulfemeyer, K. T., & Mueller, B. (1992). Channel one and commercials in classrooms: Advertising content aimed at students. *Journalism Quarterly, 69,* 724-742.

Yanni, D. A. (1990, Summer). The social construction of women as mediated by advertising. *Journal of Communication Inquiry, 12.*

Young, B. M. (1991). *Television advertising and children.* New York: Oxford University Press.

Zinkhan, G. M., et al. (1990). The use of Blacks in magazine and television advertising: 1946-1986. *Journalism Quarterly, 67,* 547-553.

PART III: MODES OF SEXUAL REPRESENTATION 1—
ROMANCE NOVELS AND SLASHER FILMS

A. Slasher/Horror Film and Gender

Asselle, G., & Gandhy, B. (1983). Dressed to kill. *Screen, 23*(2), 4-18.

Barker, M. (Ed.). (1984). *The video nasties: Freedom and censorship in the media.* London: Pluto.

Barnes, A. S. (1977). *Dark dreams: A psychological history of modern horror films.* London: South Brunswick.

Bathrick, S. K. (1977, March). Ragtime: The horror of growing up female. *Jump Cut,* pp. 9-10.

Braudy, L. (1985). Genre and the resurrection of the past. In G. Slusser & E. S. Rabkin (Eds.), *Shadows of the magic lamp: Fantasy and science fiction in film.* Carbondale: Southern Illinois University Press.

Broeske, P. H. (1984, September 2). Killing is alive and well in Hollywood. *Los Angeles Times,* pp. 19-22.

Brophy, P. (1986). Horrality: The textuality of contemporary horror films. *Screen, 27*(1), 2-13.

Brown, R. S. (1980, Summer/Fall). Dress to kill: Myth and fantasy in the horror/suspense genre. *Film/Psychology Review, 4,* 169-182.

Carroll, N. (1981, Spring). Nightmare and the horror film: The symbolic biology of fantastic beings. *Film Quarterly, 34,* 16-25.

Clover, C. (1989). Her body, himself: Gender in the slasher film. In R. H. Bloch & F. Ferguson (Eds.), *Misogyny, misandry and misanthropy.* Berkeley: University of California Press.

Clover, C. (1993). *Women, men, and chainsaws.* Princeton, NJ: Princeton University Press.

Cohn, L. (1980, November 19). Horror, sci-fi pix earn 37% of rentals. *Variety,* pp. 5, 32.

Cowan, G., & O'Brien, M. (1990, August). Gender and survival vs. death in slasher films: A content analysis. *Sex Roles, 233,* 187-196.

Crane, J. (1988). Terror and everyday life. *Communication, 10,* 367-381.

Daniels, L. (1977). *Living in fear: A history of horror in the mass media.* New York: Scribner's.

Dickstein, M. (1980, September). The aesthetics of fright. *American Film, 5,* 32-37, 56-59.

Dika, V. (1987). The stalker film, 1978-81. In G. Waller (Ed.), *American horrors* (pp. 86-101). Champaign: University of Illinois Press.

Ebert, R. (1981). Why movie audiences aren't safe anymore. *American Film, 6*(5), 54-56.

Evans, W. (1973, Fall). Monster movies: A sexual theory. *Journal of Popular Film, 2,* 124-142.

Fischer, L., & Landy, M. (1987). Eyes of Laura Mars: A binocular critique. In G. Waller (Ed.), *American horrors* (pp. 62-78). Champaign: University of Illinois Press.

Franklin, P. (1991, September/October). Teen flicks since 50s: Girls still chicks and boys must get laid. *New Directions for Women, 20.*

Giles, D. (1984). Conditions of pleasure in horror film. In B. K. Grant (Ed.), *Planks of reason.* Metuchen, NJ: Scarecrow.

Gordon, N. G., & Gordon, A. (1982). Controversial issues in De Palma's *Dressed to Kill. Psychoanalytic Review, 69,* 435-442.

Grant, B. K. (1984). *Planks of reason: Essays on the horror film.* Metuchen, NJ: Scarecrow.

Greenspun, R. (1977). Carrie and Sally and Leatherface among the film buffs. *Film Comment, 13*(1), 14-17.

Kapsis, R. E. (1982). Dressed to kill. *American Film, 7*(5), 52-56.

Kawin, B. F. (1985). Children of the light. In G. Slusser & E. S. Rabkin (Eds.), *Shadows of the Magic Lamp: Fantasy and science fiction in film.* Carbondale: Southern Illinois University Press.

Kennedy, H. (1982). Things that go howl in the id. *Film Comment, 18*(2), 37-39.

Klinger, B. (1982). *Psycho:* The institutionalization of female sexuality. *Wide Angle, 5*(1), 49-55.

Koch, S. (1976, November). Fashions in pornography. *Harpers,* pp. 108-111.

Lowry, E. (1984). Genre and enunciation: The case of horror. *Journal of Film and Video, 36*(2), 13-20, 72.

Mackey, M. (1977, March 2). The meat hook mama, the nice girl, and Butch Cassidy in drag. *Jump Cut,* pp. 12-14.

Maslin, J. (1981, November 1). Tired blood claims the horror film as a fresh victim. *New York Times,* Sec. 2, pp. 15, 23.

Maslin, J. (1982, November 21). Bloodbaths debase movies and audiences. *New York Times,* Sec. 2, pp. 1, 13.

McCarthy, J. (1984). *Splatter movies: Breaking the last taboo of the screen.* New York: St. Martin's.

Meyers, R. (1983). *For one week only: The world of exploitation films.* Piscataway, NJ: New Century.

Modleski, T. (1986). The terror of pleasure: The contemporary horror film and postmodern theory. In T. Modleski (Ed.), *Studies in entertainment* (pp. 155-166). Bloomington: Indiana University Press.

Neale, S. (1981, Spring). *Halloween:* Suspense, aggression and the look. *Framework, 14,* 25-29.

Oliver, M. B. (1993). "Adolescents' enjoyment of graphic horror: Effects of viewers' attitudes and portrayals of victim. *Communication Research, 20*(1), 30-50.

Pannill, L. (1982). The woman artist as creature and creator. *Journal of Popular Culture, 16*(2), 26-29.

Polan, D. B. (1984). Eros and syphilization: The contemporary horror film. In B. K. Grant (Ed.), *Planks of reason: Essays on the horror film.* Metuchen, NJ: Scarecrow.

Rathgeb, D. L. (1991). Bogeyman from the id. *Journal of Popular Film and Television, 19*(1), 36-43.

Rickey, C. (1982, November). Hooked on horror: Why we like scary movies. *Mademoiselle,* pp. 168-170.

Rockett, W. H. (1982). The door ajar: Structure and convention in horror films that would terrify. *Journal of Popular Film and Television, 10*(3), 130-136.

Schatz, T. (1981). *Hollywood genres: Formulas, filmmaking, and the studio system.* New York: Random House.

Schatz, T. (1983). *Old Hollywood/new Hollywood: Ritual, art, and industry.* Ann Arbor: University of Michigan Research Press.

Stein, E. (1982, June 20). Have horror films gone too far? *New York Times,* Sec. 2, pp. 1, 21.

Tamborinin, R., & Stiff, J. (1987). Predictors of horror film attendance and appeal. *Communication Research, 14*(4), 415-436.

Telotte, J. P. (1980). Faith and idolatry in the horror film. *Literature/Film Quarterly, 8,* 143-155.

Telotte, J. P. (1982). Through a pumpkin's eye: The reflexive nature of horror. *Literary/Film Quarterly, 10,* 139-149.

Thomson, D. (1981). *Overexposures: The crisis in American filmmaking*. New York: William Morrow.

Twitchell, J. V. (1985). *Dreadful pleasures: An anatomy of modern horror*. New York: Oxford University Press.

Waller, G. A. (Ed.). (1987). *American horrors*. Champaign: University of Illinois Press.

Watkins, R. (1980, October 29). Demented revenge hits world films. *Variety*, pp. 3, 33.

Williams, L. (1984). When the woman looks. In M. A. Doane, P. Mellencamp, & L. Williams (Eds.), *Re-vision: Essays in feminist film criticism* (pp. 83-99). Frederick, MD: American Film Institute.

Williams, L. R. (1993). Erotic thrillers and rude women. *Sight and Sound, 3*(7), 12-14.

Williams, T. (1980, October). Horror in the family. *Focus on Film, 36,* 14-20.

Wood, R. (1978). Gods and monsters. *Film Comment, 14*(5).

Wood, R. (1978). Return of the repressed. *Film Comment, 14*(4), 25-32.

Wood, R. (1979). An introduction to the American horror film. In R. Wood & R. Lippe (Eds.), *The American nightmare*. Toronto: Festival of Festivals.

Wood, R. (1983). Beauty bests the beast. *American Film, 8*(10), 63-65.

Wood, R. (1986). *Hollywood from Vietnam to Reagan*. New York: Columbia University Press.

Wood, R. (1987). Returning the look: *Eyes of a Stranger*. In G. A. Waller (Ed.), *American Horrors* (pp. 79-85). Champaign: University of Illinois Press.

Zillmann, D. et al. (1993). Effects of an opposite-gender companion's affect of horror on distress, delight and attraction. *Journal of Personality and Social Psychology, 51*(3), 586-594.

Zimmerman, B. (1981, March). *Daughters of Darkness:* Lesbian vampires. *Jump Cut, 25-26,* 23-24.

B. Romance Novels

Barlow, L. (1992). The androgynous writer: Another point of view. In J. A. Krentz (Ed.), *Dangerous men and adventurous women* (pp. 45-52). Philadelphia: University of Pennsylvania Press.

Cohn, J. (1988). *Romance & the erotics of property: Mass market fiction for women*. Durham, NC: Duke University Press.

Elam, D. (1992). *Romancing the postmodern: Romance, history & the figure of woman*. New York: Routledge.

Ellis, K. (1987). Gimme shelter: Feminism, fantasy and women's popular fiction. In D. Lazere (Ed.), *American media and mass culture*. Berkeley: University of California Press.

Hazen, H. (1983). *Endless rapture: Rape, romance and the female image*. New York: Scribner's.

Howells, C. A. (1977, Winter). Love, mystery and misery: Feeling in gothic fiction. *New Literary History, 8,* 279-294.

Jensen, M. (1991). *Love's sweet return: The Harlequin story*. Bowling Green, OH: Bowling Green University Popular Press.

Krentz, J. A. (Ed.). (1991). *Dangerous men and adventurous women: Romance writers on the appeal of the romance*. Philadelphia: University of Pennsylvania Press.

Lewallen, A. (1989). Lace: Pornography for women? In L. Gamman & M. Marshment (Eds.), *The female gaze* (pp. 86-101). London: Women's Press.

Light, A. (1984, Summer). Returning to Manderly—Romance fiction, female sexuality and class. *Feminist Review, 16,* 7-25.

Linden, D. W., & Rees, M. (1992, July 6). I'm hungry but not for food. *Forbes.*

Lowery, M. M. (1983). *How to write romance novels that sell.* New York: Rawson Associates.

Mann, M. (1969). *The romantic novel: A survey of reading habits.* London: Mills and Boon.

Mann, P. H. (1974). *A new survey: The facts about romantic fiction.* London: Mills and Boon.

Mattelart, M. (1982). Women and the cultural industries. *Media, Culture and Society,* 4(2), 133-151.

Miner, M. (1984). *Insatiable appetites: Twentieth century American women's best sellers.* Westport, CT: Greenwood.

Modleski, T. (1982). *Loving with a vengeance: Mass-produced fantasies for women.* New York: Methuen.

Mussell, K. J. (1979). Beautiful and damned: The sexual woman in gothic fiction. *Journal of Popular Culture, 9(1),* 12-21.

Nelson, M. (1983, February). Sweet bondage: You and your romance habit. *Ms.*

Perebinossoff, P. (1985). What does a kiss mean? The love comic formula and the creation of the ideal teen-age girl. *Journal of Popular Culture, 18(4),* 825-835.

Pollack, R. (1992, March 16). What's in a pseudonym? Romance slaves of Harlequin. *Nation.*

Rabine, L. W. (1985). Romance in the age of electronics: Harlequin enterprises. *Feminist Studies, 11(1),* 39-60.

Rabine, L. W. (1985). *Reading the romantic heroine: Text, history, ideology.* Ann Arbor: University of Michigan Press.

Radway, J. (1983). Women read the romance: The interaction of text and context. *Feminist Studies, 9(1),* 53-78.

Radway, J. (1984, Summer). Interpretive communities and variable literacies: The function of romance reading. *Daedalus,* 113.

Radway, J. (1984). *Reading the romance: Women, patriarchy and popular literature.* Chapel Hill: University of North Carolina Press.

Russ, J. (1973). Somebody's trying to kill me and I think it's my husband: The modern gothic. *Journal of Popular Culture, 6(4),* 666-691.

Snitow, A. (1979, Summer). Mass market romance: Pornography for women is different. *Radical History Review,* pp. 141-161.

Thurston, C. (1987). *Romance revolution: Erotic novels for women & the quest for a new sexual identity.* Champaign: University of Illinois Press.

Waldman, D. (1984, Winter). At last I can tell it to someone: Feminine point of view and subjectivity in the gothic romance film of the 1940s. *Cinema Journal,* pp. 29-40.

PART IV: MODES OF SEXUAL REPRESENTATION 2—
PORNOGRAPHY

Allen, R. L. (1992). Time to heal the wounds of pornography. In R. Chrisman & R. Allen (Eds.), *Court of appeal: The Black community speaks out on the racial and sexual politics of* Thomas vs. Hill (pp. 29-32). New York: Ballantine.

American Civil Liberties Union. (1986). *Polluting the censorship debate: A summary and critique of the Final Report of the Attorney General's Commission on Pornography.* Washington, DC: Author.

Assiter, A., & Carol, A. (1993). *Bad girls and dirty pictures: The challenge to reclaim feminism.* London: Pluto.

Attorney General's Commission on Pornography. (1986). *Final report* (2 vols.). Washington, DC: U.S. Department of Justice.

Bell, L. (1987). *Good girls/bad girls: Feminists and sex trade workers face to face.* Toronto: Seal Press.

Berger, R. J., Searles, P., & Cottle, C. E. (1991). *Feminism and pornography.* New York: Praeger.

Betterton, R. (1987). *Looking on: Images of femininity in the visual arts and media.* London: Pandora.

Blakely, M. K. (1985, April). Is one woman's sexuality another woman's pornography? *Ms.,* pp. 37-47.

Bloom, C. (1988). Grinding with the bachelors: Pornography in a machine age. In G. Day & C. Bloom (Eds.), *Perspectives on pornography: Sexuality in film and literature.* New York: St. Martin's.

Brannigan, A., & Goldenberg, S. (1987). The study of aggressive pornography: The vicissitudes of relevance. *Critical Studies in Mass Communication, 4*(3), 262-283.

Brigman, W. (1983). Pornography as political expression. *Journal of Popular Culture, 17*(2), 129-134.

Brownmiller, S., et al. (1984, November). Forum: The place of pornography. *Harper's.*

Burstyn, V. (Ed.). (1985). *Women against censorship.* Toronto: Douglas & McIntyre.

Califa, P. (1980, April 17). The new puritans. *The Advocate.*

Carter, A. (1978). *The sadeian woman and the ideology of pornography.* New York: Pantheon.

Collins, B. G. (1990). Pornography and social policy—Three feminist approaches. *Affilia, 5*(4), 8-26.

Court, J. (1977). Pornography and sex crimes. *International Journal of Criminology and Penology, 5,* 129-157.

Coward, R. (1987). What is pornography? Two opposing feminist viewpoints. In R. Betterton (Ed.), *Looking on.* London: Pandora.

Delacoste, F., & Alexander, P. (Eds.). *Sex work: Writings by women in the sex industry.* London: Virago.

Diamond, S. (1985). Pornography: Image and reality. In V. Burstyn (Ed.), *Women against censorship* (pp. 40-57). Toronto: Douglas and McIntyre.

Dines, G. (1988). An analysis of pornography research. In A. W. Burgess (Ed.), *Rape and sexual assault II* (pp. 317-323). New York: Garland.

Dines, G. (1992). Pornography and the media: Cultural representations of violence against women. *Family Violence and Sexual Assault Bulletin, 8*(3), 17-20.

Dines, G., & Smith, G. W. H. (1988). Representations of women and men in *Playboy* sex cartoons. In C. Powell & G. Paton (Eds.), *Humour in society: Resistance and control.* New York: St. Martin's.

Donnerstein, E. E., Linz, D. G., & Penrod, S. (1987). *The question of pornography: Research findings and policy implications.* London: Collier Macmillan.

Douglas, A. (1980, August 30). Soft-porn culture. *The New Republic.*

DuBois, E., & Gordon, L. (1983, Spring). Seeking ecstasy on the battlefield: Danger and pleasure in nineteenth-century feminist thought. *Feminist Studies, 9,* 7-25.

Dworkin, A. (1977). *Pornography: Men possessing women.* New York: Peregree.

Dworkin, A. (1988). *Letters from a war zone.* New York: Penguin.

Dworkin, A., & MacKinnon, C. (1988). *Pornography and civil rights: A new day for women's equality.* Minneapolis: Organizing Against Pornography.

Dyer, R. (1982). Don't look now: The instability of the male pin-up. *Screen, 23*(3/4), 61-73.

Dyer, R. (1985, March). Male gay porn: Coming to terms. *Jump Cut, 30,* 27-29.

Dyer, R. (1990). Towards lesbian erotica, or pornography. In R. Dyer, *Now you see it: Studies on lesbian and gay film* (pp. 206-210). London: Routledge.

Echols, A. (1983, Spring). Cultural feminism: Feminist capitalism and the anti-porn movement. *Social Text, 7,* 34-53.

Ellis, J. (1980). On pornography. *Screen, 21*(1), 81-108.

Ellis, J. (1980). On pornography. *Screen, 21*(2), 65-66.

Ellis, K., et al. (Eds.). (1980). *Caught looking: Feminism, pornography and censorship.* New York: Caught Looking.

English, D., Hollibaugh, A., & Rubin, G. (1981). Talking sex: A conversation on sexuality and feminism. *Socialist Review, 11*(4), 43-62.

Eysenck, H. J., & Nias, D. K. (1980). *Sex, violence & the media.* New York: Granada.

Faust, B. (1980). *Women, sex and pornography.* New York: Macmillan.

Fisher, W. A., & Byrne, D. (1978). Sex differences in response to erotica? Love versus lust. *Journal of Personality and Social Psychology, 36*(2), 117-125.

Fritz, L. (1978-1979). Pornography as gynocidal propaganda. *New York University Review of Law and Social Change, 8*(2), 219-223.

Gaines, J. (1990). Women and representation: Can we enjoy alternative pleasure? In P. Erens (Ed.), *Issues in feminist film criticism* (pp. 75-92). Bloomington: Indiana University Press.

Gardner, T. (1980). Racism in pornography and the women's movement. In L. Lederer et al. (Eds.), *Take back the night: Women on pornography* (pp. 105-114). New York: William Morrow.

Garry, A. (1978). Pornography and respect for women. *Social Thought and Practice, 4,* 395-421.

Gibson, P. C., & Gibson, R. (Eds.). (1993). *Dirty looks: Women, pornography, power.* London: British Film Institute.

Greyson, J. (1985, March). Gay video: The present context. *Jump Cut, 30,* 36-38.

Griffin, S. (1982). *Pornography and silence: Culture's revenge against nature.* New York: Harper & Row.

Gubar, S., & Hoff, J. (1989). *For adult users only: The dilemma of violent pornography.* Bloomington: Indiana University Press.

Hartley, N. (1987). Confessions of a feminist porn star. In F. Delacoste & P. Alexander (Eds.), *Sex work: Writings by women in the sex industry.* Pittsburgh, PA: Cleis Press.

Henderson, L. (1991). Lesbian pornography: Cultural transgression and sexual demystification. *Women and Language, 14*(1), 3-12.

Hoff, J. (1989). Why is there no history of pornography? In S. Gubar & J. Hoff (Eds.), *For adult users only: The dilemma of violent pornography.* Bloomington: Indiana University Press.

Holbrook, D. (1973). *The case against pornography.* Chicago: Open Court.

Holbrook, D. (1973, March). The politics of pornography. *Socialist Commentary,* pp. 31-32.

Intons-Peterson, M. J., & Roskos-Ewoldsen, B. (1989). Mitigating the effects of violent pornography. In S. Gubar & J. Hoff (Eds.), *For adult users only: The dilemma of violent pornography.* Bloomington. Indiana University Press

Itzin, C. (Ed.). (1992). *Pornography: Women, violence and civil liberties.* Oxford: Oxford University Press.

Jaehne, K. (1983, Fall). Confessions of a feminist porn programmer. *Film Quarterly, 37,* 9-16.

Jameson, F., et al. (1983). *Formations of pleasure.* London: Routledge & Kegan Paul.

Jeffrey, S. (1985). *The spinster and her enemies: Feminism and sexuality, 1880-1930.* London: Pandora.

Jeffrey, S. (1987). *The sexuality debates.* London: Routledge.

Jensen, R. (1992). *Knowing pornography.* Unpublished doctoral dissertation, University of Minnesota.

Kappeler, K. (1986). *The pornography of representation.* Minneapolis: University of Minnesota Press.

Kelly, P. (1991, Winter). Pornography—A feminist-existentialist analysis. *Atlantis, 17,* 129-135.

Kerr, A. (1991). Pornography: What's to be done. *Canadian Women's Studies, 12*(1), 100-102.

Kimmel, M. (Ed.). (1990). *Men confront pornography.* New York: Crown.

Kipnis, L. (1990). (Male) desire and (female) disgust: Reading *Hustler.* In L. Grossberg, C. Nelson, & P. Treichler (Eds.), *Cultural studies.* New York: Routledge.

Kipnis, L. (1993). She-male fantasies and the aesthetics of pornography. In P. C. Gibson & R. Gibson (Eds.), *Dirty looks: Women, pornography, power.* London: British Film Institute.

Kittay, E. F. (1984). Pornography and the erotics of domination. In C. Gould (Ed.), *Beyond domination* (pp. 145-174). Totowa, NJ: Rowman & Allanheld.

Kleinhans, C., & Lesage, J. (1985, March). The politics of sexual representation. Introduction to special section on pornography and sexual images, *Jump Cut, 30,* 24-26.

Kuhn, A. (1982). The body in the machine. In A. Kuhn, *Women's pictures* (pp. 109-128). New York: Routledge.

Kuhn, A. (1989). *The power of the image: Essays on representation and sexuality.* Boston: Routledge & Kegan Paul.

Kutchinsky, B. (1990). Pornography and rape: Theory and practice? Evidence from crime data in four countries where pornography is easily available. *International Journal of Law and Society, 13*(4).

Lederer, L., et al. (Eds.). (1980). *Take back the night: Women on pornography.* New York: William Morrow.

Leidholdt, D., & Raymond, J. (1990). *The sexual liberals and the attack on feminism.* New York: Pergamon.

Leong, W.-T. (1991). The pornography problem: Disciplining women and young girls. *Media, Culture and Society, 13,* 91-117.

Lewin, L. (1984). *Naked is the best disguise: My life as a stripper.* New York: William Morrow.

Lesage, J. (1981, December). Women and pornography. *Jump Cut, 26,* 46-47.

Linden, R. R., et al. (Eds.). (1982). *Against sadomasochism: A radical feminist analysis.* E. Palo Alto, CA: Frog in the Well.

Linz, D. (1989). Exposure to sexually explicit materials and attitudes toward rape: A comparison of study results. *Journal of Sex Research, 26*(1), 50-84.

Linz, D., & Malamuth, N. (1993). *Pornography.* Newbury Park, CA: Sage.

Litewke, J. (1977). The socialized penis. In J. Snodgrass (Ed.), *For men against sexism* (pp. 16-35). Albion, CA: Times Change Press.

Longino, H. E. (1980). Pornography, oppression and freedom: A closer look. In L. Lederer et al. (Ed.), *Take back the night* (pp. 40-54). New York: William Morrow.

MacKinnon, C. A. (1987). *Feminism unmodified: Discourses on life and law.* Cambridge, MA: Harvard University Press.

MacKinnon, C. A. (1993). *Only words.* Cambridge, MA: Harvard University Press.

Malamuth, N. M., & Donnerstein, E. (Eds.). (1984). *Pornography and sexual aggression.* New York: Academic Press.

Malamuth, N., & Spinner, E. (1980). A longitudinal content analysis of sexual violence in the best-selling erotica magazines. *Journal of Sex Research, 16,* 226-237.

Mallowe, M. (1981, November). The business of porn. Philadelphia.

Marshall, W. L. (1988). The use of sexually explicit stimuli by rapists, child molesters and nonoffenders. *Journal of Sex Research, 25*(2), 267-288.

McClintock, A. (1992). Gonad the barbarian and the venus flytrap. In L. Segal & M. McIntosh (Eds.), *Sex exposed: Sexuality and the pornography debate*. London: Virago.

McCormack, T. (1985). Making sense of research on pornography. Appendix in V. Burstyn (Ed.), *Women against censorship* (pp. 183-205). Toronto: Douglas & McIntyre.

Mercer, K. (1987). Imaging the Black man's sex. In P. Holland, J. Spence, & S. Watney (Eds.), *Photography/politics: Two* (pp. 61-69). London: Comedia/Methuen.

Mercer, K. (1991). Skin head sex thing: Racial difference and the homoerotic imaginary. In Bad Object-Choices (Ed.), *How do I look: Queer film and video*. Seattle, WA: Bay Press.

Merck, M. (1992). *The sexual subject: Screen reader in sexuality*. New York: Routledge.

Moye, A. (1985). Pornography. In A. Metcalf & M. Humphries (Eds.), *The sexuality of men*. London: Macmillan.

Myers, K. (1982). Fashion'n'passion. *Screen, 23*(3-4).

Myers, K. (1987). Towards a feminist erotica. In R. Betterton (Ed.), *Looking on: Images of femininity in the visual arts and media* (pp. 189-202). London: Pandora.

Public hearings on the proposed Minneapolis civil rights anti-pornography ordinance. (1983). Minneapolis: Organizing Against Pornography.

Rich, B. R. (1981, March). *Maedchen in uniform:* From repressive tolerance to erotic liberation. *Jump Cut, 24/25,* 44-50.

Rose, T. (1994). *Black noise: Rap music and Black culture in contemporary America.* Hanover, NH: University Press of New England, Wesleyan University Press.

Ross, A. (1989). The popularity of pornography. In A. Ross (Ed.), *No respect: Intellectuals and popular culture* (pp. 171-208). New York: Routledge.

Russo, R. (1987). Conflicts and contradictions among feminists over issues of pornography and sexual freedom. *Women's Studies International Forum, 10*(2), 103-112.

Russell, D. E. H. (1988). Pornography and rape: A causal model. *Political Psychology, 9*(1), 41-73.

Russell, D. E. H. (Ed.). (1993). *Making violence sexy: Feminist views on pornography.* New York: Teachers College Press.

SAMOIS Collective. (Ed.). (1981). *Coming to power: Writings and graphics on lesbian S/M.* Palo Alto, CA: Up Press.

Santiago, R. (1990, November). Sex lies and videotape: How pornography affects Black couples. *Essence.*

Schwartz, T. (1981). The TV pornography boom. *New Times Magazine.*

Segal, L. (1993). Does pornography cause violence? The search for evidence. In P. C. Gibson & R. Gibson (Eds.), *Dirty looks: Women, pornography, power.* London: British Film Institute.

Segal, L. (1992). *Is the future female? Troubled thoughts on contemporary feminism.* London: Virago.

Segal, L., & McIntosh, M. (Eds.). (1992). *Sex exposed: Sexuality and the pornography debate.* London: Virago.

Slade, J. (1975). Recent trends in pornographic films. *Society, 12*(6), 77-84.

Small, F. (1989). Playboy: Violence in disguise? In M. S. Kimmel (Ed.), *Changing men.* Newbury Park, CA: Sage.

Snitow, A. B. (1970, Spring/Summer). Mass market romance: Pornography for women is different. *Radical History Review, 20,* 157.

Snitow, A., Stansell, C., & Thompson, S. (Eds.). *Powers of desire.* New York: Monthly Review Press.

Soble, A. (1986). *Pornography, Marxism, feminism, and the future of sexuality.* New Haven, CT: Yale University Press.

Steele, L. (1985). A capital idea: Gendering in the mass media. In V. Burstyn (Ed.), *Women against censorship* (pp. 58-78). Toronto: Douglas & McIntyre.

Steinem, G. (1980). Erotica and pornography: A clear and present difference. In L. Lederer et al. (Eds.), *Take back the night*. New York: William Morrow.

Steinem, G. (1980, May). Linda Lovelace's Ordeal. *Ms.*

Stoltenberg, J. (1990). Pornography and freedom. In J. Stoltenberg, *Refusing to be a man*. New York: Penguin.

Stewart, D. (1977). Pornography, obscenity and capitalism. *Antioch Review, 35*, 389-398.

Stock, W. (1983, August). *The effects of violent pornography on women*. Paper presented at the annual meeting of the American Psychological Association, Anaheim, CA.

Strossen, N. (1993, August). A feminist critique of "the" feminist critique of pornography. *Virginia Law Review.*

Swedberg, D. (1989). What do we see when we see woman/woman sex in pornographic movies. *National Women's Studies Association Journal, 1*(6), 2-16.

Thomas, S. (1986). Gender and social-class coding in popular photographic erotica. *Communication Quarterly, 34*(2), 103-112.

Tierney, J. (1994, January 9). Porn, the low-slung engine of progress. *New York Times.*

Tisdale, S. (1992, January/February). Talk dirty to me. *Harper's.*

Vance, C. S. (Ed.). (1984). *Pleasure and danger: Exploring female sexuality*. Boston: Routledge & Kegan Paul.

Vicinus, M. (1982). Sexuality and power. *Feminist Studies, 8*(1), 133-156.

Walker, A. (1980). Coming apart. In L. Lederer (Ed.), *Take back the night*. New York: William Morrow.

Walkowitz, J. (1980). The politics of prostitution. *Signs, 6*(1), 123-135.

Watney, S. (1987). *Policing desire: Pornography, AIDS and the media*. Minneapolis: University of Minnesota Press.

Waugh, T. (1985, March). Men's pornography: Gay versus straight. *Jump Cut, 30*, 30-35.

Weaver, J. (1992). The social science and psychological research evidence: Perceptual and behavioral consequences of exposure to pornography. In C. Itzin (Ed.), *Pornography: Women, violence and civil liberties*. Oxford, UK: Oxford University Press.

Webster, P. (1981). Pornography and pleasure. *Heresies, 3*(4), 48-51.

Weeks, J. (1981). *Sex, politics and society*. London: Longman.

Williams, L. (1989). *Hard core: Power, pleasure and the "frenzy of the visible."* Berkeley: University of California Press.

Williams, L. (1993). Second thoughts on hard core: American obscenity law and the scapegoating of deviance. In P. C. Gibson & R. Gibson (Eds.), *Dirty Looks*. London: British Film Institute.

Zillmann, D., & Bryant, J. (Eds.), *Pornography: Research advances and policy considera-tion*. Hillsdale, NJ: Lawrence Erlbaum.

Zita, J. (1988). Pornography and the male imaginary. *Enclitic, 17/18*, 28-44.

PART V: TV BY DAY

A. Soap Opera, TV Melodrama

Abernathy-Lear, G. (1992). *African-Americans' relationship with daytime serials*. Unpublished doctoral dissertation, University of Wisconsin—Madison.

Adams, M. (1980). *An American soap opera:* As the World Turns, *1956-1978.* Unpublished doctoral dissertation, University of Michigan.

Allen, R. C. (1983). The guiding light: Soap opera as economic product and cultural document. In J. E. O'Connor (Ed.), *American history/American television* (pp. 306-327). New York: Frederick Ungar.

Allen, R. C. (1983). On reading soap operas: A semiotic primer. In E. A. Kaplan (Ed.), *Regarding television* (pp. 97-108). Los Angeles: University Publications of America.

Allen, R. C. (1985). *Speaking of soap operas.* Chapel Hill: University of North Carolina Press.

Allen, R. C. (1989). Bursting bubbles: Soap opera, audiences, and the limits of genre. In E. Seiter et al. (Eds.), *Remote control: Television, audiences, and cultural power* (pp. 44-55). New York: Routledge, Chapman and Hall.

Ang, I. (1982). *Watching* Dallas: *Soap opera and the melodramatic imagination.* New York: Methuen.

Antoine, R. (1980, September). Blacks in daytime television. *Sepia,* pp. 76-79.

Archer, J. (1992). The fate of the subject in the narrative without end. In S. Frentz (Ed.), *Staying tuned: Contemporary soap opera criticism* (pp. 89-95). Bowling Green, OH: Bowling Green University Popular Press.

Asante, M., & Gonzalez, M. (1983, Fall). Sex and power on daytime television. *Journal of American Culture, 6,* 97-103.

Astrachan, A. (1975, March 23). Life can be beautiful/relevant: Social problems and soap operas. *The New York Times Magazine,* pp. 12-13, 54-64.

Barrios, L. (1988). Television, telenovellas, and family life in Venezuela. In J. Lull (Ed.), *World families watch television.* Newbury Park, CA: Sage.

Beurkel-Rothfuss, N. L., & Mayes, S. (1981). Soap opera viewing: The cultivation effect. *Journal of Communication, 31*(3), 108-115.

Birnbaum, J. (1989, March 27). A soap goes Black and White. *Time,* p. 85.

Blacks in the soaps. (1978, March). *Ebony,* pp. 32-36; (1982, November), pp. 123-128.

Bonner, F. (1992). Confession time: Women and game shows. In F. Bonner et al. (Ed.), *Imagining women* (pp. 237-236). Cambridge, UK: Open University Press.

Brothers, J. (1989, July 29). The shows that make you feel better. *TV Guide.*

Brown, M. E. (1990). Melodramatic identifications: Television fiction and women's fantasy. In M. E. Brown (Ed.), *Television and women's culture: The politics of the popular.* London: Sage.

Brown, M. E. (1994). *Soap opera and women's talk: The pleasure of resistance.* Thousand Oaks, CA: Sage.

Brown, W. J. (1992). Prodevelopment soap operas in the Third World. *Journal of Popular Film and Television, 19*(4).

Brunsdon, C. (1981). *Crossroads:* Notes on soap opera. *Screen, 22*(4), 32-37.

Bryant-Johnson, S. (1980). Blacks on TV soaps: Visible but neutralized. In R. M. Miller (Ed.), *The kaleidoscopic lens: How Hollywood views ethnic groups.* Englewood, NJ: Jerome S. Ozer.

Budge, B. (1989). Joan Collins and the wilder side of women: Exploring pleasure and representation. In L. Gamman & M. Marchmont (Eds.), *The female gaze* (pp. 102-111). London: Women's Press

Butler, J. (1986). Notes on the soap opera apparatus: Televisual style and *As the World Turns. Cinema Journal, 25*(3).

Campbell, B. M. (1978, November). Hooked on soaps. *Essence,* p. 100.

Cantor, M. G., & Pingree, S. (1983). *The soap opera.* Beverly Hills, CA: Sage.

Carter, A. (1992, August). All my sistuhs. *Essence,* p. 70.

Cassata, M., & Skill, T. (1983). *Life on daytime television: Tuning-in American serial drama.* Norwood, NJ: Ablex.

Cosby, C., & Fuller, M. (1976, December). Black image on television: Do "soapers" bring us the purest picture? *Soul*, p. 8.

Derry, C. (1983). Television soap opera: Incest, bigamy and fatal disease. *Journal of the University Film and Video Association, 35*(1), 4-16.

Edmondson, M., & Rounds, D. (1977). *From Mary Noble to Mary Hartman: The complete soap opera book.* New York: Stein & Day.

Fellman, A. C. (1978, Summer). Teaching with tears: Soap opera as a tool in teaching women's studies. *Signs, 3*, pp. 909-911.

Feuer, J. (1984). Melodrama, serial form and television today. *Screen, 25*(1), 4-16.

Feuer, J. (1989). Reading *Dynasty:* Television and reception theory. *South Atlantic Quarterly, 88*(2), 443-460.

Fine, M. G. (1981, Summer). Soap opera conversations: The talk that binds. *Journal of Communication, 31*, 97-107.

Flitterman, S. (1983). The real soap operas: TV commercials. In E. A. Kaplan (Ed.), *Regarding television* (pp. 84-96). Los Angeles: University Publications of America.

Flitterman-Lewis, S. (1987). Psychoanalysis, film, and television. In R. C. Allen (Ed.), *Channels of discourse: Television and contemporary criticism.* Chapel Hill: University of North Carolina Press.

Flitterman, S. (1988, Winter). All's well that doesn't end—Soap opera and the marriage motif. *Camera Obscura, 16*, 119-127.

Forkan, J. P. (1988, November 28). Can nets, sponsors still find happiness in daytime TV? *Television-Radio Age*, p. 45.

Fraser, C. G. (1991, March 5). Fans mourn cancellation of an interracial soap opera. *The New York Times*, pp. B3, C11.

Frentz, S. (1992). *Staying tuned: Contemporary soap opera criticism.* Bowling Green, OH: Bowling Green State University Popular Press.

Geraghty, C. (1991). *Women and soap operas: A study of prime time soaps.* London, UK: Blackwell.

Gray, A. (1987). Behind closed doors: Video recorders in the home. In H. Baehr & G. Dyer, *Boxed in: Women on and in television.* London: Routledge.

Gutcheon, B. R. (1974, August). There isn't anything wishy-washy about soaps. *Ms.*, p. 42.

Greenberg, B. S., Abelman, R., & Neuendorf, K. (1981, Summer). Sex on the soap operas: Afternoon delight. *Journal of Communication, 31*, 83-89.

Heating up: Network fight for leadership in daytime TV. (1974, June 3). *Broadcasting*, pp. 14-15.

Hennessee, J. A. (1978, May-June). The whole soap catalogue: Love and money in the afternoon. *Action*, pp. 16-22.

Herko, D. (1993, January). Get your fiction straight: How experts help the soaps with social issues. *Soap Opera Digest.*

Hill, G. H. (1990). *Coloring the soaps: Blacks on television and radio.* Los Angeles: Daystar.

Hobson, D. (1982). *Crossroads: The drama of a soap opera.* London: Methuen.

Hobson, D. (1989). Soap operas at work. In E. Seiter et al. (Eds.), *Remote control: Television, audiences and cultural power.* London: Routledge.

How ABC found happiness in daytime TV. (1981, August 24). *Business Week*, pp. 62, 64.

In search of those missing daytime viewers. (1977, November 7). *Broadcasting*, pp. 34-35.

Intintoli, M. J. (1984). *Taking soaps seriously.* New York: Praeger.

Jhirad, S. (1987, February). As the soaps turn. *Sojourner.*

Johnson, S. (1982). How soaps whitewash Blacks. *American Film, 7*(5), 36-37.

Kreutzner, G., & Seiter, E. (1991). Not all soaps are created equal: Towards a cross-cultural criticism of television serials. *Screen, 32*(2), 154-172.

Kuhn, A. (1984). Women's genres. *Screen, 25*(1).

Laguardia, R. (1974). *The wonderful world of soap operas.* New York: Ballantine.

Lee, M., & Cho, C. H. (1990). Women watching together: An ethnographic study of Korean soap opera fans in the U.S. *Cultural Studies, 4*(4), 30-44.

Leigh, A. (1988). Hotline: Hollywood. *Soap Opera Digest, 13*(9).

Lemish, D. (1985). Soap opera viewing in college: A naturalistic inquiry. *Journal of Broadcasting and Electronic Media, 29*(3), 97-116.

Liska, J. A. (1987, September 14). Lurid and torrid, daytime soaps keep nets rich. *Television-Radio Age,* p. 55.

Lopate, C. (1976). Day-time television: You'll never want to leave home. *Feminist Studies, 4*(6), 70-82.

Lowry, D. T., & Towles, D. E. (1989). Soap opera portrayals of sex, contraception and sexually transmitted diseases. *Journal of Communication, 39*(2).

MacDonald, J. F. (1979). Soap operas as a social force. In J. F. MacDonald, *Don't touch that dial.* Chicago: Nelson-Hall.

MacDonald, J. F. (1983). *Blacks and White TV.* Chicago: Nelson-Hall.

Mason, J. (1988, August). I wrote for the soaps. *Essence,* pp. 115-116.

Mateski, M. J. (1988). *Soap opera evolution: America's enduring romance with daytime drama.* Jefferson, NJ: McFarland.

Modleski, T. (1982). *Loving with a vengeance.* Hamden, CT: Archon.

Modleski, T. (1983). The rhythms of reception: Daytime television and women's work. In E. A. Kaplan (Ed.), *Regarding television* (pp. 67-75). Los Angeles: University Publications of America.

Mulvey, L. (1986). Melodrama in and out of the home. In C. McCabe (Ed.), *High theory/low culture: Analyzing popular television and film.* New York: St. Martin's.

Mumford, L. S. (1992, Winter). Plotting paternity: Looking for Dad on the daytime soaps. *Genders,* pp. 45-61.

NBC gets tangled in a storyline (interracial love). (1992, June 6). *Broadcasting,* p. 38.

Nelson, S. R. (1992). Pine Valley prostitute: The representation of *All My Children*'s Donna Tyler. In S. Frentz (Ed.), *Staying tuned* (pp. 103-109). Bowling Green, OH: Bowling Green State University Popular Press.

Newcomb, H. (1983). A humanist's view of daytime serial drama. In M. Cassata & T. Skill (Eds.), *Life on daytime TV.* Norwood, NJ: Ablex.

Nixon, A. E. (1972, Fall). In daytime TV, the golden age is now. *Television Quarterly, 10,* 49-54.

Nochimson, M. (1992). *No end to her: Soap opera and the female subject.* Berkeley: University of California Press.

Nuwer, H. (1980, November). Soaps lure male viewers. *Saturday Evening Post,* pp. 78-81.

O'Connor, J. J. (1980, January 20). Will soap opera find happiness in prime time. *The New York Times,* sec. 11, p. 33.

O'Connor, J. J. (1992, July 19). The young, the restless and the socially aware. *The New York Times,* sec. 2, p. 1.

Porter, D. (1982). Soap time: Thoughts on a commodity art form. In H. Newcomb (Ed.), *Television: The critical view* (pp. 122-131). New York: Oxford University Press.

Rabinovitz, L. (1992). Soap opera bridal fantasies. *Screen, 23,* 274-283.

Roane, A. (1980, September). Blacks in daytime television. *Sepia,* pp. 76-79.

Rogers, D. (1991, Winter). Daze of our lives: The soap opera as feminine text. *Journal of American Culture, 14,* pp. 29-41.

Rogers, D. (1992). Rockabye lady: Pregnancy as punishment in popular culture. *Journal of American Studies, 26*(1), 81.

Rose, B. (1979, Autumn). Thickening the plot. *Journal of Communication, 29,* 81-84.

Rosen, M. (1972). *Popcorn venus: Women, movies and the American dream.* New York: Coward, McCann and Geoghegan.

Rosen, R. (1986). Search for yesterday. In T. Gitlin (Ed.), *Watching television* (pp. 41-67). New York: Pantheon.

Rouse, M. G. (1979). Daytime radio programming for the homemaker, 1926-56. *Journal of Popular Culture, 12*(2), 315-327.

Rubin, A. M. (1986). Uses of daytime television, soap operas by college students. *Journal of Broadcasting and Electronic Media, 29,* 241-258.

Seiter, E. (1982, Winter). Promise and contradiction: The daytime television serials. *Film Reader, 5,* 150-153.

Seiter, E., et al. (1989). "Don't treat us like we're so stupid and naive": Toward an ethnography of soap opera viewers. In E. Seiter et al. (Eds.), *Remote control: Television audiences and cultural politics.* New York: Routledge.

Shapiro, S. (1983, December). My love-hate relationship with the soaps. *Sojourner.*

Soares, M. (1978). *The soap opera book.* New York: Harmony.

Tegler, P. (1982, Winter). The daytime serial: A bibliography of scholarly writings, 1981. *Journal of Popular Culture, 16.*

Torgerson, E. (1978, July 8). Heartache, illness, and crime do pay: High profits from carefully tailored soap operas bank roll costly nighttime programming. *TV Guide,* pp. 12-16.

Townley, R. (1975, May 3). She introduced a stranger to the world of soaps (Agnes Nixon, creator of several soap operas). *TV Guide,* pp. 12-16.

Turner, V. (1984, September). Blacks in the soaps: What's new and what's next? *Chocolate Singles,* pp. 10-13.

Waggett, G. (1989, May 27). A plea to the soaps: Let's stop turning rapists into heroes. *TV Guide.*

Waldrop, J., & Crispell, D. (1988). Daytime dramas, demographic dreams. *American Demographics, 10*(10).

Wander, P. (1979, Autumn). The angst of the upper class. *Journal of Communication, 29,* 85-88.

Waters, H. F. (1981, September 28). Television's hottest show. *Newsweek,* pp. 60-66.

Williams, C. T. (1992). *It's time for my story: Soap opera sources, structure, and response.* Westport, CT: Praeger.

Women making money: Scanning the soaps. (1975, July). *Ladies Home Journal,* p. 49.

B. Talk Shows

Berman, R. (1987). Talk shows. In R. Berman, *How television sees its audience.* Newbury Park, CA: Sage.

Carbaugh, D. (1988). *Talking American: Cultural discourse on Donahue.* Norwood, NJ: Ablex.

Carpignano, P., et al. (1990, Fall/Winter). Chatter in the age of electronic reproduction: Talk television and the public mind. *Social Text, 25-26,* 50, 52, 54.

Carter, B. (1992, June 22). Talk is cheap but profitable, on TV. *The New York Times,* p. C1, D1, col. 3.

Greenberg, H. R. (1989). Cinna the poet: *The Morton Downey, Jr. Show. Journal of Popular Film and Television, 17*(3), 123-125.

Harrison, B. G. (1989, June 11). The importance of being Oprah. *New York Times Magazine*, p. 28, col. 1.

Hirsch, A. (1991). *Talking heads: Political talkshows and their star pundits.* New York: St. Martin's.

Lehman, B. A. (1988, November 28). Oprah Winfrey sheds pounds but feeds a weight-loss myth. *The Boston Globe.*

Masciarotte, G.-J. (1991, Fall). C/mon, girl: Oprah Winfrey and the discourse of feminine talk. *Genders*, pp. 81-110.

McLaughlin, L. (1993, Winter). Chastity criminals in the age of electronic reproduction: Re-viewing talk television and the public sphere. *Journal of Communication Inquiry, 17*(1). 41-55.

Munson, W. (1993). *All talk: The talkshow in media culture.* Philadelphia: Temple University Press.

Prager, E. (1987, March 10). Oprah's opera. *Village Voice.*

Rapping, R. (1991, October). Daytime inquiries. *Progressive*, pp. 36-37.

Steenland, S. (1990). Those daytime talk shows. *Television Quarterly, 24*(4), 5-12.

Tuchman, G. (1974). Assembling a network talk-show. In G. Tuchman (Ed.), *The TV establishment: Programming for power and profit* (pp. 119-135). Englewood Cliffs, NJ: Prentice Hall.

Welles, S. (1992). My year with the talk shows and how I got hooked—Almost. *Television Quarterly, 26*(2), 47-59.

PART VI: TV BY NIGHT

Alcock, B., & Robson, J. (1990, Summer). *Cagney and Lacey* revisited. *Feminist Review*, pp. 42-53.

Atkin, A. (1992). An analysis of television series with minority-lead characters. *Critical Studies in Communication, 9.*

Atkin, D. J., et al. (1991). Ready for prime time: Network series devoted to working women in the 1980s. *Sex Roles, 25*(11/12), 677-685.

Backstage at the last *Cosby Show.* (1992, May). *Ebony*, 126-132.

Berry, V. T. (1992). From *Good Times* to *The Cosby Show:* Perceptions of changing televised images among Black fathers and sons. In S. Craig (Ed.), *Men, masculinity and the media.* Newbury Park, CA: Sage.

Block, A. (1985, November 26). *An Early Frost:* The story behind NBC's AIDS drama. *Advocate*, pp. 42-49.

Blum, L. (1982). Feminism and the mass media: A case study of *The Women's Room* as novel and television film. *Berkeley Journal of Sociology, 27*, 1-26.

Bobo, J., & Seiter, E. (1991). Black feminism and media criticism: *The Women of Brewster Place. Screen, 32*(3), 286-302.

Bodroghkozy, A. (1993). Is this what you mean by color TV? Race, gender, and contested meanings in NBC's *Julia.* In L. Spigel & D. Mann (Eds.), *Private screenings: Television and the female consumer* (pp. 143-167). Minneapolis: University of Minnesota Press.

Brown, H. G. (1986, August 2). How to outfox TV's new breed of macho men. *TV Guide.*

Budd, M., & Steinman, C. (1992, July). White racism and *The Cosby Show. Jump Cut*, pp. 5-14.

Butsch, R. (1990, July). *The Simpsons:* A breath of fresh air mixed with old pollutants. *In These Times.*

Butsch, R. (1992). Class and gender in four decades of television situation comedy: Plus ça change . . . *Critical Studies in Mass Communication, 9*, 387-399.

Byars, J. (1987). Reading feminine discourse: Prime-time television in the U.S. *Communication, 9*, 289-303.

Cantor, M. (1980). *Prime-time television*. Beverly Hills, CA: Sage.

D'Acci, J. (1987). The case of *Cagney and Lacey*. In H. Baehr & G. Dyer (Eds.), *Boxed in: Women in and on television*. London: Routledge.

Dates, J. L. (1987). Gimme a break: African-American women on prime-time television. In A. Wells (Ed.), *Mass media society* (pp. 450-459). Lexington, MA: D. C. Heath.

Deming, C. J., & Jenkins, M. M. (1991). Bar talk: Gender discourse in *Cheers*. In L. R. Vande Berg & L. Wenner, *Television criticism*. New York: Longman.

Deming, R. (1992). The return of the unrepressed: Male desire, gender and genre. *Quarterly Review of Film and Video, 14*(1-2), 125-147.

Dickerson, S. (1991). *Is Sapphire still alive? The image of Black women in television situation comedies in the 1990s*. Unpublished doctoral dissertation, Boston University.

Dow, B. J. (1992). Femininity and feminism in *Murphy Brown*. *Southern Communication Journal, 57*(2), 143-155.

Downing, J. (1988). *The Cosby Show* and American racial discourse. In G. Smitherman-Donaldson & T. A. van Dijk (Eds.), *Discourse and discrimination* (pp. 46-74). Detroit, MI: Wayne State University Press.

Dyson, M. (1989, September). Bill Cosby and the politics of race. *Zeta*.

Edmundson, M. (1986). Father still knows best. *Channels, 6*(3), 71-72.

Ehrenreich, B., & O'Reilly, J. (1984, November 24). No jiggles. No scheming. Just real women as friends. *TV Guide*.

Entman, R. (1990). Modern racism and the images of Blacks in local television news. *Critical Studies in Mass Communication, 7*(4).

Finch, M. (1986). Sex and address in *Dynasty*. *Screen, 27*(6), 24-42.

Finke, N. (1989, January 26). The blue-collar backgrounds behind a blue-collar hit. *Los Angeles Times*, sec. 6, p. 10.

Fiske, J. (1987). *Cagney and Lacey*: Reading character structurally and politically. *Communication, 9*, 399-426.

Fiske, J. (1987). *Television culture*. New York: Methuen.

Freeman, F. (1992). Social mobility in television comedies. *Critical Studies in Mass Communication, 9*, 400-406.

Gamman, L. (1991, Spring). Response: More *Cagney and Lacey*. *Feminist Review, 37*, 117-121.

Gates, H. L., Jr. (1989, November 12). TV's Black world turns—But stays unreal. *New York Times*.

Gitlin, T. (1982). Prime time ideology: The hegemonic process in television entertainment. In H. M. Newcomb (Ed.), *Television: The critical view* (3rd ed., pp. 426-454). New York: Oxford.

Gray, A. (1987). Reading the audience. *Screen, 28*(8).

Gray, H. (1986). Television and the new Black man: Black male images in prime-time situation comedy. *Media, Culture and Society, 8*, 223-242

Gray, H. (1991). Recodings: Possibilities and limitation in commercial television representations of African American culture. *Quarterly Review of Film and Video, 1-3*, 117-130.

Gregory, D. (1993, September). In your face: The new comediennes. *Essence*, pp. 85-86, 121.

Gross, L. (1984). The cultivation of intolerance: Television, Blacks and gays. In G. Melischeck et al. (Eds.), *Cultural indicators*. Vienna: Austrian Academy of Sciences.

Hanke, R. (1990). Hegemonic masculinity in *Thirtysomething*. *Critical Studies in Mass Communication, 7*(3), 231-248.

Hanson, C. A. (1990). The women of *China Beach*. *Journal of Popular Film and Television, 17*(4), 155-163.

Haralovich, M. B. (1989). Sitcoms and suburbs: Positioning the 1950s homemaker. *Quarterly Review of Film and Video, 11*, 61-83.

Hill, G., Raglin, L., & Johnson, C. F. (1990). *Black women in television: An illustrated history and bibliography*. New York: Garland.

Jenkins, H., III. (1991). It's not a fairy tale anymore. *Journal of Film and Video, 43*(1-2), 90-110.

Jhally, S., & Lewis, J. (1992). *Enlightened racism:* The Cosby Show, *audiences, and the myth of the American dream*. Boulder, CO: Westview.

Jones, G. (1992). *Honey, I'm home: Sitcoms, selling the American dream*. New York: Grove-Weidenfeld.

Kaler, A. K. (1990). *Golden Girls:* Feminine archetypal patterns of the complete woman. *Journal of Popular Culture, 24*(3), 49-60.

King, S. B. (1990). Sonny's virtues: The gender negotiations of *Miami Vice*. *Screen, 31*, 281-295.

Kolbert, E. (1993, August 23). Why late-night TV is a man's world. *New York Times*.

Lee, L. (1992). Subversive sitcoms: Roseanne as inspiration for feminist resistance. *Women's Studies, 21*, 87-101.

Lemon, J. (1978). Dominant or dominated? Women on prime-time television. In G. Tuchman (Ed.), *Hearth and Home* (pp. 51-68). New York: Oxford University Press.

Leo, J. R. (1991). Television and the narrative structures of discourse and difference. *Journal of Film and Video, 43*(4), 145-155.

Levinson, R., & Link, W. (1981). *Stay tuned: An inside look at the making of prime-time television*. New York: St. Martin's.

Levitt, S., Fisher, L., & Mills, B. K. (1993, November 29). Oprah's mission. *People Weekly*, pp. 107-112.

Lichter, R., Lichter L., & Rothman, S. (1986). The politics of the American dream—from Lucy to Lacey: TV's dream girls. *Public Opinion, 9*(3), 16-19.

Lindsey, K. (1983, October). Female friendships on TV. *Sojourner*.

Lipsitz, G. (1993). The meaning of memory: Family, class and ethnicity in early network television programs. In L. Spigel & D. Mann (Eds.), *Private screenings: Television and the female consumer* (pp. 71-108). Minneapolis: University of Minnesota Press.

Lull, J. (1990). *Inside family viewing: Ethnographic research on television's audiences*. New York: Routledge.

MacDonald, J. F. (1992). *Blacks and White TV* (2nd. ed.). Chicago: Nelson-Hall.

Mayerle, J. (1991). *Roseanne*—How did you get inside my house?—A case study of a hit blue-collar situation comedy. *Journal of Popular Culture, 24*(4), 71-88.

Mellencamp, P. (1986). Situation comedy, feminism, and Freud: Discourse of Gracie and Lucy. In T. Modleski (Ed.), *Studies in entertainment: Critical approaches to mass culture* (pp. 80-98). Bloomington: Indiana University Press.

Merritt, B. D. (1989). Bill Cosby: TV auteur? *Journal of Popular Culture, 24*(4), 89-102.

Miller, M. C. (1986). Prime time: Deride and conquer. In T. Gitlin (Ed.), *Watching television*. New York: Pantheon.

Miller, M. C. (1988). Cosby knows best. In M. C. Miller, *Boxed-in: The culture of TV* (pp. 69-78). Evanston, IL: Northwestern University Press.

Moore, M. (1980). Black face in prime time. In B. Rubin et al. (Eds.), *Small voices and great trumpets: Minorities and the media.* New York: Praeger.

More access for the Bundys. (1991, January 14). *Broadcasting,* p. 56.

O'Connor, J. J. (1991, May 19). Gay images: TV's mixed signals. *New York Times.*

O'Reilly, J. (1989, May 27). At last! Women worth watching. *TV Guide.*

Ozersky, J. (1992). TV's anti-families: Married . . . with malaise. *Tikkun, 6*(1), 11-14, 92-93.

Pouissant, A. (1988, October). The Huxtables: Fact or fantasy. *Ebony.*

Press, A. (1989). Class and gender in the hegemonic process: Class differences in women's perceptions of television realism and identification with television characters. *Media, Culture and Society, 11,* 229-251.

Press, A. L. (1990). Class, gender and the female viewer: Women's responses to *Dynasty.* In M. E. Brown (Ed.), *Television and women's culture* (pp. 158-182). Newbury Park, CA: Sage.

Press, A. L. (1991). *Women watching television: Gender, class and generation in the American television experience.* Philadelphia: University of Pennsylvania Press.

Rader, B. (1984). *In its own image: How television has transformed sports.* New York: Free Press.

Radner, H. (1990, Summer). Quality television and feminine narcissism: The shrew and the covergirl. *Genders, 8,* 110-128.

Rapping, E. (1985, April). A family affair. *The Progressive,* pp. 36-38.

Rapping, E. (1985, Fall). Made for TV movies: The domestication of social issues. *Cineaste,* pp. 30-33.

Rapping, E. (1991). TV lawyers with a conscience. *The Progressive,* p. 36-38.

Rapping, E. (1992). *The movie of the week: Private stories, public events.* Minneapolis: University of Minnesota Press.

Rapping, E. (1992, August). Tabloid TV and social reality. *The Progressive,* pp. 35-37.

Real, M. (1991). Bill Cosby and recoding ethnicity. In L. L. Vande Berg & L. Wenner (Eds.), *Television criticism.* New York: Longman.

Robinson, L. S. (1978). What's my line? Telefiction and women's work. In L. S. Robinson, *Sex, class and culture* (pp. 310-342). Bloomington: Indiana University Press.

Schlesinger, P., Dobash, R. E., Dobash, R. P., & Weaver, C. K. (1992). *Women viewing violence.* London: British Film Institute.

Schulze, L. J. (1986). Getting physical: Text/context/reading and the made-for-television movie. *Cinema Journal, 25*(2), 35-50.

Schuyler, S. (1988). Confessions of a sitcom junkie. In J. W. Cochran et al. (Eds.), *Changing our power: An introduction to women's studies.* Dubque, IA: Kendall Hunt.

Schwichtenberg, C. (1986). Sensual surfaces and stylistic excess: The pleasure and politics of *Miami Vice. Journal of Communication Inquiry, 10*(3), 45-65.

Schwichtenberg, C. (1987). Articulating the people's politics: Manhood and right-wing populism in *The A-Team. Communication, 9,* 379-398.

Seggar, J. F., Hafen, J. K., & Hannonen-Gladden, H. (1981). Television's portrayals of minorities and women in drama and comedy drama, 1971-80. *Journal of Broadcasting, 25*(3), 277-288.

Siegel, E. (1990, July 27). TV draws class lines from couch to kitchen. *The Boston Globe.*

Siegel, E. (1992, April 19). Sitcom alters face of TV. *The Boston Globe.*

Sklar, R. (1980). *Prime-time America: Life on and behind the television screen.* New York: Oxford University Press.

Spangler, L. C. (1989, Spring). A historical overview of female friendships on prime-time television. *Journal of Popular Culture, 22*(4), 13-23.

Spangler, L. C. (1992). Buddies and pals: A history of male friendships on prime-time television. In S. Craig (Ed.), *Men, masculinity and the media*. Newbury Park, CA: Sage.

Spigel, L. (1992). Installing the television set: Popular discourses on television and domestic space, 1948-1955. In L. Spigel & D. Mann (Eds.), *Private screenings: Television and the female consumer* (pp. 3-38). Minneapolis: University of Minnesota Press.

Spigel, L., & Mann, D. (Eds.) (1992). *Private screenings: Television and the female consumer.* Minneapolis: University of Minnesota.

Staples, R. (1977, May). Roots: Melodrama of the Black experience—forum: A symposium on *Roots. The Black Scholar, 88*, 36-42.

Steeves, H. L., & Smith, M. C. (1987). Class and gender in prime-time television entertainment: Observations from a socialist feminist perspective. *Journal of Communication Inquiry, 11*(1), 43-63.

Tankel, J. D., & Banks, B. J. (1986). The boys of prime time: An analysis of "new" male roles in television. In S. Thomas (Ed.), *Studies in communication* (Vol. 4, pp. 285-290). Norwood, NJ: Ablex.

Taylor, E. (1989). *Prime-time families: Television culture in post-war America.* Berkeley, CA: University of California Press.

Thomas, S., & Callahan, B. P. (1982). Allocating happiness: TV families and social class. *Journal of Communication, 32*(3), 184-189.

Torres, S. (1989). Melodrama, masculinity and the family: *Thirtysomething* as therapy. *Camera Obscura, 19*, 86-106.

Vidmar, N., & Rokeach, N. (1974). Archie Bunker's bigotry: A study in selective perception and exposure. *Journal of Communication, 24*, 36-47.

Washington, M. H. (1983, July 30). As their blackness disappears, so does their character (on Jeffersons). *TV Guide.*

Washington, M. H. (1986, March 22). Please, Mr. Cosby, build on your success. *TV Guide.*

Weiss, P. (1989, May/June). Bad rap for TV tabs. *Columbia Journalism Review*, pp. 38-42.

White, M. (1991). What's the difference: *Frank's Place* in television. *Wide Angle, 13*(3-4), 82-93.

Williams, J. P. (1992). "A bond stronger than friendship or love": Female psychological development and *Beauty and the Beast. National Women's Studies Association Journal, 4*(1), 59-72.

Wilson, B. J., Linz, D., Donnerstein, E., & Stipp, H. (1992). The impact of social issue television programming on attitudes toward rape. *Human Communication Research, 19*(2), 179-208.

Women on words and images. (1975). *Children and channelling: Sex stereotyping on prime-time TV.* Princeton, NJ: Carolignlan Press.

Woollacott, J. (1986). Fictions and ideologies: The case of situation comedy. In T. Bennett et al. (Eds.), *Popular culture and social relations* (pp. 196-218). Philadelphia: Milton Keynes.

PART VII: MUSIC VIDEOS AND RAP MUSIC:
CULTURAL CONFLICT AND CONTROL
IN THE AGE OF THE IMAGE

Abraham, K. (1991). *The politics of Black nationalism: From Harlem to Soweto.* Trenton, NJ: Africa World Press.

Abt, D. (1987). Music video: Impact of the visual dimension. In J. Lull (Ed.), *Popular music and communication* (pp. 96-111). Newbury Park, CA: Sage.

Allan, B. (1990). Musical cinema, music video, music television. *Film Quarterly, 43*(2).

Allen, H. (1989, April). Hip hop. *Essence,* pp. 78-80.

Aufderheide, P. (1986). The look of the sound. In T. Gitlin (Ed.), *Watching television.* New York: Pantheon.

Asante, M. K. (1988). *Afrocentricity.* Trenton, NJ: Africa World Press.

Baker, H. A., Jr. (1993). *Black studies, rap and the academy.* Chicago: University of Chicago Press.

Baudrillard, J. (1983). The ecstasy of communication. In H. Foster (Ed.), *The anti-aesthetic essays on postmodern culture* (pp. 126-134). Port Townsend, WA: Bay Press.

Baxter, R. L., et al. (1985). A content analysis of music videos. *Journal of Broadcasting and Electronic Media, 29*(5), 333-340.

Berg, C. M. (1987, Spring). Visualizing music: The archaeology of music video. *OneTwoThreeFour: A Rock'n'Roll Quarterly, 5,* 94-103.

Bernard, J. (1990). Rap and violence. *Reconstruction, 1*(2), 26-28.

Bernard, J. (1992, August 23). A newcomer abroad, rap speaks up. *New York Times.*

Blount, M., & Cunningham, G. (in press). *Theorizing Black male subjectivity.* New York: Routledge.

Bordo, S. (1990). Feminism, postmodernism and gender skepticism. In L. Nicholson (Ed.), *Feminism/postmodernism* (pp. 133-156). New York: Routledge.

Brown, J. D., & Campbell, K. C. (1986). Race and gender in music videos: The same beat but a different drummer. *Journal of Communication, 36*(1), 94-106.

Brown, J. D., & Schulze, L. (1990). The effects of race, gender fandom on audience interpretations of Madonna's music videos. *Journal of Communication, 40*(2).

Brown, M. E., & Fiske, J. (1987, Spring). Romancing the rock: Romance and representation in popular music videos. *OneTwoThreeFour: A Rock'n'Roll Quarterly,* pp. 61-73.

Burns, G. (1988). Dreams and mediation in music video. *Wide Angle, 10*(2), 41-61.

Campbell, L., & Miller, J. R. (1992). *As nasty as they wanna be: The uncensored story of Luther Campbell of the 2 Live Crew.* Fort Lee, NJ: Barricade.

Cantor, L. (1992). *Wheelin' on Beale: How WDIA-Memphis became the nation's first all-Black radio station and created the sound that changed America.* New York: Pharos.

Caplan, R. E. (1985). Violent program content in music video. *Journalism Quarterly, 62,* 144-147.

Chambers, G., & Morgan, J. (1992, September). Droppin' knowledge: A rap roundtable. *Essence,* 116-117, 120.

Costello, M., & Wallace, D. F. (Eds.). (1990). *Signifying rappers: Rap and race in the urban present.* New York: Ecco.

Craddock-Willis, A. (1989). Rap music and the Black musical tradition: A critical assessment. *Radical America, 23*(4), 29-38.

Curry, R. (1990). Madonna from Marilyn to Marlene—Pastiche or parody? *Journal of Film and Video, 42*(2), 15-30.

Davis, A. (1989). *Women, culture and politics.* New York: Random House.

Denisoff, R. S. (1988). *Inside MTV.* New Brunswick, NJ: Transaction.

Dennison, S. (1982). *Scandalize my name: Black imagery in American popular music* (Vol. 13). Critical Studies on Black Life and Culture. New York: Garland.

Denski, S., & Sholle, D. (1992). Metal men & glamour boys. In S. Craig (Ed.), *Men, masculinity and the media* (pp. 41-60). Newbury Park, CA: Sage.

Dority, B. (1990, September/October). The war on rock and rap music. *The Humanist,* pp. 25-26.

Dyson, M. E. (1989, June). The culture of hip hop. *Zeta Magazine,* pp. 45-50.

Dyson, M. E. (1989). Michael Jackson's postmodern spirituality. *Black Sacred Music,*
    3(2).

Dyson, M. E. (1993). Rap music and Black culture: An interview. In M. E. Dyson,
    Reflecting Black (pp. 16-22). Minneapolis: University of Minnesota Press.

Dyson, M. E. (1993). *Reflecting Black: African-American cultural criticism.* Minneapolis:
    University of Minnesota Press.

Ebron, P. (1991). Rapping between men: Performing gender. *Radical America, 23*(4),
    23-27.

Ehrenreich, B. (1986). Elizabeth Hess and Gloria Jacobs, Beatlemania: Girls just want
    to have fun. In B. Ehrenreich, *Remaking love: The feminization of sex* (pp. 10-38).
    Garden City, NY: Anchor/Doubleday.

Einhorn, J. (1991, January). The rap on rap. *Sojourner,* pp. 20-21.

Ellison, M. (1989). *Lyrical protest: Black music's struggle against discrimination.* New
    York: Praeger.

Fiske, J. (1986). MTV: Post-structural post-modern. *Journal of Communication Inquiry,*
    10(1).

Flores, J. (1993). Puerto Rican and proud, Boyee!: Rap, roots and America. *Centro de*
    Estudios Puertorriquenos, 5(1), 22-32.

Frith, S. (1987). The industrialization of popular music. In J. Lull (Ed.), *Popular music*
    and communication. Newbury Park, CA: Sage.

Frith, S. (1988). *Music for pleasure.* New York: Routledge & Kegan Paul.

Frith, S. (Ed.). (1991). *Facing the music.* New York: Pantheon.

Frith, S. (1993). Youth/music/television. In S. Frith, A. Goodwin, & L. Grossberg
    (Eds.), *Sound and Vision* (pp. 67-83). New York: Routledge.

Frith, S., Goodwin, A., & Grossberg, L. (1993). *Sound and vision: The music video reader.*
    New York: Routledge.

Gaines, J. (1991). *Contested culture: The image, the voice, and the law.* Chapel Hill:
    University of North Carolina Press.

Garofalo, R. (Ed.). (1992). *Rockin' the boat: Mass music and mass movements.* Boston:
    South End Press.

Gates, D. (1990, March 19). The rap attitude. *Newsweek,* pp. 56-63.

Gates, H. L., Jr. (1986). *Figures in Black: Words, signs and the "racial" self.* New York:
    Oxford University Press.

Gay, G., & Baber, W. L. (1987). *Expressively Black: The cultural basis of ethnic identity.*
    New York: Praeger.

George, N. (1988). *The death of rhythm and blues.* New York: Pantheon.

Gibbs, J. T. (1988). *Young, Black, and male in America: An endangered species.* Dover,
    MA: Auburn House.

Gilbert, M. (1993, July 25). The mighty cool world of MTV. *The Boston Globe.*

Gilroy, P. (1991). Sounds authentic: Black music, ethnicity, and the challenge of a
    changing game. *Black Music Research Journal, 11*(2), 111-137.

Goldstein, R. (1990, December 18). Free MTV! It's not the nipple: Madonna's new
    clip threatens the sexual order of music video. *Village Voice,* p. 2.

Goodwin, A. (1987). Music video in the (post) modern world. *Screen, 28*(3).

Goodwin, A. (1992). *Dancing in the distraction factory: Music television and popular*
    music. Minneapolis: University of Minnesota Press.

Goodwin, A. (1993). Fatal distractions: MTV meets postmodern theory. In S. Frith,
    A. Goodwin, & L. Grossberg (Eds.), *Sound and Vision* (pp. 45-66). New York:
    Routledge.

Gore, T. (1987). *Raising PG kids in an X-rated society.* Nashville, TN: Abingdon.

Gow, J. (1992). Making sense of music video: Research during the inaugural decade.
    Journal of American Culture, 15(3), 35-43.

Gow, J. (1992). Music video as communication: Popular formulas and emerging genres. *Journal of Popular Culture, 26*(2), 41-70.

Groce, S. B., & Cooper, M. (1990). Just me and the boys? Women in local-level rock and roll. *Gender and Society, 4*(2), 220-229.

Gross, R. L. (1990). Heavy metal music: A new subculture in American society. *Journal of Popular Culture, 24*(1), 119-130.

Grossberg, L. (1988). You still have to fight for your right to party: Music television as billboard of postmodern difference. *Popular Music, 7,* 315-332.

Hansen, C. H., & Hansen, R. D. (1990). The influence of sex and violence on the appeal of rock music videos. *Communication Research, 17*(2), 212-234.

Hansen, C. H., & Hansen, R. D. (1990). Rock music videos and antisocial behavior. *Basic and Applied Social Psychology, 11*(4), 357-369.

Harrison, D. D. (1988). *Black pearls: Blues queens of the 1920s.* New Brunswick, NJ: Rutgers University Press.

Hazzard-Gordon, K. (1990). *Jookin': The rise of social dance formations in African-American culture.* Philadelphia: Temple University Press.

Hebdige, D. (1983). *Subcultures: The meaning of style.* New York: Methuen.

Henderson, L. (1993). Justify our love: Madonna and the politics of queer sex. In C. Schwichtenberg (Ed.), *The Madonna connection* (pp. 107-128). Boulder, CO: Westview.

Henry, C. P. (1990). *Culture and African American politics.* Bloomington: Indiana University Press.

Hine, D. C. (1990). *Black women's history: Theory and practice.* Brooklyn, NY: Carlson.

Hip-hop madness. (1989, April). *Essence.*

Holden, S. (1990, December 3). That Madonna video: Realities and fantasies. *The New York Times,* pp. C18.

Holdstein, D. H. (1984, February). Music video messages and structure. *Jump Cut, 29,* 13-14.

hooks, b. (1990). *Yearning: Race, gender and cultural politics.* Boston: South End Press.

hooks, b. (1992, November). Speech: A love rap. *Essence,* pp. 81-82, 155-160.

Hudson, B. (1984). Femininity and adolescence. In A. McRobbie & M. Nava (Eds.), *Gender and generation* (pp. 31-51). London: Macmillan.

Indigo bans MTV and VH-1. (1992, March). *Sojourner,* pp. 7-8.

Is "As Nasty as They Wanna Be" obscene? *Reconstruction, 1*(2), 15-18.

Jameson, F. (1984, July-August). Postmodernism or the cultural logic of late capitalism. *New Left Review, 146,* 53-92.

Jones, A., & Deterline, K. (1994, March-April). Fear of a rap planet: Rappers face media double standard. *EXTRA!,* pp. 20-21.

Kalis, P., & Neuendorf, K. A. (1989). Aggressive cue prominence and gender participation in MTV. *Journalism Quarterly, 66*(1), 148-154, 229.

Kandel, M. (1990). Racist censorship and sexist rap. *Reconstruction, 1*(2), 21-25.

Kaplan, E. A. (1987). *Rocking around the clock: Music television, postmodernism and consumer culture.* London: Methuen.

Kaplan, E. A. (1988). Whose imaginary? The televisual apparatus, the female body and textual strategies in select rock videos on MTV. In D. Pribam (Ed.), *Female spectators.* London: Verso.

Kaplan, E. A. (1993). Madonna politics: Perversion, repression or subversion. In C. Schwichtenberg (Ed.), *The Madonna connection.* Boulder, CO: Westview.

Kellner, K. (1988). Postmodernism as social theory: Some challenges and problems. *Theory, Culture and Society, 5,* 239-270.

Kinder, M. (1984). Music video and the spectator: Television, ideology and dream. *Film Quarterly, 38*(1).

Kochman, T. (Ed.). (1972). *Rappin' and stylin' out: Communication in urban Black America*. Urbana: University of Illinois Press.

Kofsky, F. (1970). *Black nationalism and the revolution in music*. New York: Pathfinder.

Laing, D. (1985). Music video: Industrial product, cultural form. *Screen, 26*(2).

Laing, D. (1985). *Power and meaning in punk rock*. Milton Keynes, UK: Open University Press.

Ledbetter, J. (1992, Fall). Imitation of life. *Vibe*, pp. 112-114.

Lerner, E. (1990, Spring; 1990, Winter). Reply to Robin Roberts, "Sex as Weapon." *National Women's Studies Association Journal*, pp. 1-15 and pp. 329-339.

Levy, S. (1983, December). Ad nauseam: How MTV sells out rock and roll. *Rolling Stone*, p. 8.

Lewis, J. (1985, March). Purple rain: Music video comes of age. *Jump Cut, 30*, 1, 22, 43.

Lewis, L. A. (1987). Consumer girl culture: How music video appeals to girls. In M. E. Brown (Ed.), *Television and women's culture* (pp. 89-101). Newbury Park, CA: Sage.

Lewis, L. A. (1987). Female address in music video. *Journal of Communication Inquiry, 11*(1), 73-84.

Lewis, L. A. (1990, April). Being discovered: Female address on music television. *Jump Cut, 35*.

Lewis, L. A. (1990). *Gender politics and MTV: Voicing the difference*. Philadelphia: Temple University Press.

Light, A. (1991). About a salary or reality?—Rap's recurrent conflict. *South Atlantic Quarterly, 90*(4), 855-870.

Light, A. (1991, October 17). Queen Latifah's new gambit. *Rolling Stone*, pp. 19-20.

Lipsitz, G. (1987). World of confusion: Music video as modern myth. *OneTwoThree-Four: A Rock 'n' Roll Quarterly, 5*.

Lyotard, J-F. (1984). *The postmodern condition: A report on knowledge* (G. Bennington & B. Massumi, Trans.). Minneapolis: University of Minnesota Press.

Marable, M. (1985). *Black American politics: From the Washington marches to Jesse Jackson*. London: Verso.

Marable, M. (1991). *Race, reform and rebellion: The second reconstruction in Black America, 1945-1990*. Jackson: University Press of Mississippi.

Marlowe, A. (1992, March). Rap hermeneutics. *Artforum*.

Matthews, G. (1985). *Madonna*. New York: Wanderer Books/Simon & Schuster.

McClary, S. (1990, Spring). Living to tell—Madonna's resurrection of the fleshly. *Genders*, pp. 1-21.

McLaughlin, E. (1991). *Out of order? Policing Black people*. London: Routledge.

Mercer, K. (1993). Monster metaphors: Notes on Michael Jackson's *Thriller*. In S. Frith, A. Goodwin, & L. Grossberg (Eds.), *Sound and vision* (pp. 93-108). New York: Routledge.

Muro, M. (1992, January 22). Public enemy video sparks outrage. *The Boston Globe*.

MTV—Rock on. (1991, August 3). *The Economist*, p. 66.

Musto, M. (1991, March 20). Immaculate conception: Madonna and us. *Outweek*, pp. 35-41, 62.

National Coalition on Television Violence. (1984, January 14). *Rock music and MTV found increasingly violent* [Press release]. Champaign, IL: Author.

Pelka, F. (1991, Winter). Dreamworlds: How the media abuses women: Interview with Sut Jhally. *On the Issues, 21*.

Perkins, E. (Ed.). (in press). *Droppin' science: Critical essays on rap music and hip-hop culture*. Philadelphia: Temple University Press.

Peterson-Lewis, S., & Chennault, S. A. (1986, Winter). Black artists' music videos: Three success strategies. *Journal of Communication, 36*, 107-114.

Pfeil, F. (1988). Postmodernism as a "structure of feeling." In C. Nelson & L. Grossberg (Eds.), *Marxism and the interpretation of culture*. London: Macmillan.

Pittman, R. W. (1990, January 24). We're talking the wrong language to TV babies. *New York Times*, p. A15.

Pokskin, H. (1991, August 3). MTV at 10: The beat goes on. *TV Guide*, pp. 4-5, 7-8.

Powell, C. T. (1993). Music: An education with a beat from the street. *Journal of Negro Education, 60*(3).

Pratt, R. (1989). Popular music, free space and the quest for community. *Journal of Popular Music and Society, 13*(4), 59-76.

Rapping anti-gay violence. (1992, March 24). *Advocate*.

Rapping, E. (1991, June 5). Madonna makes the media play her game. *The Guardian*, p. 2.

Roberts, J. W. (1989). *From trickster to badman: The Black folk hero in slavery and freedom*. Philadelphia: University of Pennsylvania Press.

Roberts, R. (1990). Sex as a weapon: Feminist rock music videos. *National Women's Studies Association Journal, 2*(1), 1-15.

Roberts, R. (1991). Music videos, performance and resistance: Feminist rappers. *Journal of Popular Culture, 25*(2).

Roman, L. (1988). Intimacy, labor, and class: Ideologies of feminine sexuality in the punk slam dance. In L. Roman & L. K. Christian-Smith (Eds.), *Becoming feminine* (pp. 143-184). London: Falmer.

Rose, T. (1989). Orality and technology: Rap music and Afro-American cultural resistance. *Journal of Popular Music and Society, 13*(4), 35-44

Rose, T. (1990, May). Never trust a big butt and a smile. *Camera Obscura, 24*, 109-131.

Rose, T. (1991). Fear of a Black planet: Rap music and Black cultural politics in the 1990s. *Journal of Negro Education, 60*(3), 276-290.

Rose, T. (1994). *Black noise: Rap music and Black culture in contemporary America*. Hanover, NH: University of New England Press.

Rosenthal, D. (1992). *Hard bop: Jazz and Black music, 1955-1965*. New York: Oxford University Press.

Ross, A. (Ed.). (1988). *Universal abandon? The politics of postmodernism*. Minneapolis: University of Minnesota Press.

Rubey, D. (1991). Voguing at the carnival: Desire and pleasure on MTV. *South Atlantic Quarterly, 90*(4).

Saucier, K. (1986). Healers and heartbreakers: Images of women and men in country music. *Journal of Popular Culture, 20*(3), 147-166.

Sawchuch, K. A. (1980, Spring). Towards a feminist analysis of women in rock music: Patti Smith's Gloria. *Atlantis, 14*, 44-54.

Schwichtenberg, C. (Ed.). (1993). *The Madonna connection: Representational politics, subcultural identities, and cultural theory*. Boulder, CO: Westview.

Schwichtenberg, C. (1993). Madonna's postmodern feminism: Bringing the margins to the center. In C. Schwichtenberg (Ed.), *The Madonna connection* (pp. 129-148). Boulder, CO: Westview.

Scott, K. Y. (1991). *The habit of surviving: Black women's strategies for life*. New Brunswick, NJ: Rutgers University Press.

Scott, R. B. (1993). Images of race and religion in Madonna's video *Like a Prayer:* Prayer and praise. In C. Schwichtenberg (Ed.), *The Madonna connection*. Boulder, CO: Westview.

Seidman, S. A. (1992). An investigation of sex-role stereotyping in music videos. *Journal of Broadcasting and Electronic Media, 36*(2), 209-216.

Shaw, H. B. (1990). *Perspectives on Black popular culture*. Bowling Green, OH: Bowling Green University Popular Press.

Sherman, B. B., & Dominick, J. R. (1986). Violence and sex in music videos: TV and rock 'n' roll. *Journal of Communication, 36*(1), 79-93.

Shusterman, R. (1991). The fine art of rap. *New Literary History, 22,* 613-632.

Simels, S. (1985). *Gender chameleons: Androgyny in rock'n'roll.* New York: Timbre Books.

Sister Souljah's been getting a lot of bad rap. (1992, June). *Off Our Backs,* p. 7.

Smith, P. (1990, December 23). Taking the rap for women. *The Boston Globe.*

Stapleton, L. (1991, September/October). MTV: Flesh, flash and fantasy. *New Directions for Women, 20.*

Stockbridge, S. (1990). Rock video: Pleasure and resistance. In M. E. Brown (Ed.), *Television and women's culture: The politics of the popular* (pp. 102-113). Newbury Park, CA: Sage.

Sullivan, K. M. (1990). 2 Live Crew and the cultural contradictions of Miller. *Reconstruction, 1*(2), 19-20.

Sun, S-W., & Lull, J. (1986, Winter). The adolescent audience for music videos and why they watch. *Journal of Communication,* pp. 115-125.

Tate, G. (1988). The devil made 'em do it: Public enemy. In G. Tate, *Flyboy in the buttermilk* (pp. 123-129). New York: Simon & Schuster.

Tate, G. (1988). *Flyboy in the buttermilk: Essays on contemporary America.* New York: Simon & Schuster.

Teachout, T. (1990). Rap and racism. *Commentary, 89*(3), 60-62.

Tetzlaff, D. (1986). MTV and the politics of postmodern pop. *Journal of Communication Inquiry, 10*(1).

Toop, D. (1991). *Rap attack 2: African rap to global hip hop* (rev. ed.). New York: Serpent's Tail.

Vincent, R. C. (1989). Clio's consciousness raised? Portrayal of women in rock videos reexamined. *Journalism Quarterly, 66,* 155-160.

Vincent, R. C., Davis, D. K., & Boruszkowski, L. A. (1987). Sexism on MTV: The portrayal of women in rock video. *Journalism Quarterly, 64,* 750-755, 941.

Wallace, M. (1990). *Invisibility blues: From pop to theory.* London: Verso.

Wallace, M. (1990). Michael Jackson, Black modernisms and the ecstasy of communication. In M. Wallace, *Invisibility blues* (pp. 77-90). London: Verson.

Wallace, M. (1990, November). Women rap back. *Ms.,* pp. 60-61.

Walser, R. (1993). Forging masculinity: Heavy metal sound and images of gender. In S. Frith, A. Goodwin, & L. Grossberg (Eds.), *Sound and vision* (pp. 153-181). New York: Routledge.

Walser, R. (1993). *Running with the devil: Power, gender and madness in heavy metal music.* Hanover, NH: Wesleyan University Press.

Whitaker, C. (1990, June). Real story behind the rap revolution. *Ebony,* pp. 34, 36-37.

Williamson, J. (1985, October). The making of a material girl. *New Socialist,* pp. 46-47.

Wilson, J. L., & Markle, G. E. (1992). Justify my ideology: Madonna and traditional values. *Popular Music and Society, 16*(2), 75-84.

Wollen, P. (1986). Ways of thinking about music video (and postmodernism). *Critical Quarterly, 28*(1/2).

Zillmann, D., & Mundorf, N. (1987). Image effects in the appreciation of video rock. *Communication Research, 14*(3), 316-334.

Zook, K. B. (1992). Reconstructions of nationalist thought in Black music and culture. In R. Garofalo (Ed.), *Rockin' the boat.* Boston: South End Press.

Author Index

Abbey, A., 514
Adam, B., 67
Adams, W. J., 406
Allen, R. C., 320, 326, 328
Allen, W. R., 513
Altman, K., 319
Aptheker, H., 34
Arbogast, R., 110
Assael, S., 111
Assister, A., 244

Barlow, W., 438, 443
Barnouw, E., 407, 448
Barr, R., 470
Barrios, L., 364
Basil, M. D., 110
Bauman, K. E., 508
Behanna, W., 406
Bell, D., 489, 494
Bell, L., 282
Berger, D., 406
Berry, B., 293
Betterton, R., 263
Blum, A., 404
Blumler, J., 405, 406, 407, 410
Bobo, J., xix
Bogle, D., 38

Borchers, H., 342, 346
Bordo, B., 73
Bordo, S., 28
Bourdieu, P., 57
Brady, F., 256, 258
Braithwaite, R. L., 513
Brannigan, A., 300
Brod, H., 135
Bronski, M., 148
Brown, J. D., 483, 508
Brown, L., 406
Brown, M. E., 344, 345
Brunsdon, C., 343
Bryant, A., 405, 407
Bryant, J., 299, 300
Burns, G., 409
Burroughs, S., 106
Butsch, R., 3, 403, 408, 409
Byars, J., 165

Campbell, K. C., 483, 508
Campbell, R., 407
Cantor, M., 406, 409
Caploe, R., 384
Carby, H., 99, 524–525, 528
Carol, A., 244
Carpenter, J., 170

Cartland, B., 220
Castro, J., 110
Cawelti, J., 348
Check, J. V. P., 300
Chennault, S. A., 482
Childers, K. W., 508
Chodorow, N., 206
Chomsky, N., 86
Christian, B., 56, 57
Chuck D, 518
Clark, C., 384
Cobbey, R., 508
Cohen, D., 68
Comstock, G., 508
Connor, M. E., 513
Coward, R., 233
Craddock-Willis, A., 479
Cripps, T., 37, 38

Dagnoli, J., 109
D'Agostino, J., 536
Dakin, C., 292
Dates, J. L., 438, 443
Davies, J., 344
Davis, D. B., 538
Day, J., 218
De Certeau, M., 12
D'Emilio, J., 147
De Palma, B., 172
Diamant, A., 223
Diawara, M., 164
DiMaggio, P., 406
Dines-Levy, G., 300
Dinnerstein, D., 196–197, 351
Dominick, J. R., 37, 406
Donnerstein, E., 233, 299, 302
Dormon, J. H., 384
Douglas, C., 390
Downing, J., 399
Duff, C., 110
Dullea, G., 510
Dworkin, A., 247, 249, 250, 284, 299
Dworkin, S., 472
Dyer, R., 68, 100, 133, 232
Dyson, M. E., 399, 479, 482, 484, 485

Ebron, P., 485
Ehrenreich, B., 474
Ehrenstein, D., 147
Eisenstein, H., 280
Elliot, P., 410
Ellis, J., 448, 449
Ellsworth, E., 146
Emery, E., 37
Emery, M., 37

Entman, R. M., 399, 440, 443
Erens, P., 164, 165
Ewen, S., 85

Fanon, F., 33
Farber, S., 450
Farley, M., 289, 290
Faust, B., 208
Fausto-Sterling, A., 282
Feinberg, B., 110
Feuer, J., 344, 395, 432
Firestone, S., 239
Fisher, L., 508
Fiske, J., 12, 13, 57, 145, 328, 340, 357, 358,
        385, 387, 395, 430, 431, 432, 436, 441,
        443, 481, 509, 513
Flores, J., 479
Foucault, M., 283
Frederickson, G. M., 34
Freer, P., 67–68
Frye, M., 302

Gadsden, S., 106
Gaines, J., xix, 164
Gallagher, J. E., 110
Gamman, L., 164
Gans, H., 404
Gardner, F., 511
Gardner, T. A., 282, 289, 291, 296
Garofalo, R., 518
Gates, H. L., 399
Geraghty, C., 344
Gerbner, G., 62, 385, 546, 547, 550, 553
Gilman, S. L., 280, 281, 284
Giroux, H., 545
Giroy, P., 543
Gitlin, T., 406, 408, 409, 410, 427, 436, 450
Glasgow, D., 433
Gledhill, C., 164
Glennon, L. M., 403, 409
Goffman, E., 81, 328
Goldenberg, S., 300
Goldman, R., 130
Goodman, E., 510
Goodnance, A., 481
Goodwin, A., 482
Gould, S. J., 282
Goulding, P., 546
Graham, H., 225
Gramsci, A., 7
Gray, A., 356, 365
Gray, H., 398, 435, 436, 441
Greyson, J., 232
Gross, L., 63, 546, 547, 550, 553
Grossberg, L., 373, 516

Hachem, S., 67
Hall, S., 11, 13, 54, 57, 102, 103–104, 431, 435, 543
Hall, T. D., 282
Halpin, Z. T., 282, 284
Hamilton, R. F., 41
Hanke, R., 133, 134
Harding, S., 302
Haring, B., 533
Harms, J., 126
Hartley, J., 345, 395, 431
Hatchett, D., 390
Heim, C., 385
Herman, E., 71
Hill Collins, P., xix, 279, 390
Hirsch, E., 363
Hirsch, P., 406
Hodges, A., 66
Holden, S., 510
hooks, b., xix, 107, 537
Hooper, T., 170
Horsman, R., 34
Hutter, D., 66
Hymes, D., 57

Irigaray, L., 163
Itzin, C., 299

Jacobson, M., 110
Jameson, F., 430, 481
Janowitz, T., 509
Jensen, K., 362
Jensen, R., 303
Jhally, S., 134, 395, 399, 404
Jhirad, C., 319
Jones, R. R., 384
Jordon, W., 34
Joseph, G. I., 106

Kaplan, E. A., xix, 177, 480, 481, 482, 483, 511, 512, 514
Kappeler, S., 254
Keirsh, E., 503
Kellner, D., 7, 9, 10, 126
Kelly, L., 303
Kimmel, M. S., 303
Kipnis, L., 232, 254
Klein, A., 138
Kline, S., 83
Kluger, R., 35
Koch, G. G., 508
Kreutzner, G., 342, 346
Kristeva, J., 163
Kuhn, A., 149, 165, 233, 259, 271

Lacan, J., 163
Leidholdt, D., 291, 296
Leiss, W., 80
Levenkrom, S., 124
Levin, M., 110
Levine, L., 388
Levy, S., 482
Lewis, J., 395, 404
Lewis, L., 399, 480, 482, 509
Light, A., 479, 482, 485
Linden, D. W., 166
Lindlof, T., 366
Linz, D. G., 186, 187, 299, 302
Lipsitz, G., 536
London, L., 219
Longino, H. E., 229
Lopate, C., 320, 345
Lorde, A., 528
Lorenz, K., 238
Lovell, T., 107
Lowery, M., 162, 166, 215
Lull, J., 362, 363
Lynch, J., 408, 409

MacDonald, J. F., 384, 396, 399, 414
MacKinnon, C. A., 230, 247, 254, 261, 299, 301
Madonna, 509
Mailer, N., 541
Malamuth, N. M., 187, 233, 300
Mann, D., 413
Marchand, R., 148
Marchetti, G., 102
Marr, M., 293
Marriott, M., 534
Marshall, W. L., 303
Marshment, M., 164
Marx, K., 142
Mastro, J., 255
Mather, A., 198
Maxwell, B., 110
Mayerle, J., 400
Mayne, J., 164
McCaffrey, A., 217
McKenna, K., 513
McMahon, E. T., 110
McNall, S. G., 280, 283, 284
Mehler, M., 502, 503
Mellencamp, P., 340
Mercer, K., 482
Metz, C., 163
Meyers, K., 232
Miller, R., 258, 259, 260
Millett, K., 238
Minh-Ha, T., 527
Mitchell-Kernan, C., 388, 389

Modleski, T., 161, 233, 326, 343, 345, 346, 348
Montgomery, K., 64
Morgan, M., 546, 547, 550, 551, 553
Morley, D., 57, 363, 452
Morrison, T., 103
Mulvey, L., 163–164, 165, 348
Munson, W., 367
Murdock, G., 546
Myers, K., 233

Nochimson, M., 333
Nordin, K. D., 36

Omi, M., 439, 440
Owen, B., 405

Pallante, M., 224
Parisi, P., 193, 197
Parkin, F., 55
Pasquali, A., 66
Pekurny, R., 406, 407
Pelka, P., 482
Pelleck, C. J., 534
Penley, C., 164
Penrod, S., 299, 302
Perkins, T. E., 94, 100
Peterson, R. A., 406
Peterson-Lewis, S., 482
Pines, A. M., 302
Pollay, R. W., 109
Porter, D., 344
Press, A., 395

Radway, J., 12, 330
Ramsaye, T., 37
Rapping, E., 445, 450
Ravage, J., 406, 408, 409
Rees, M., 166
Reeves, J., 407, 408, 409
Reinharz, S., 302
Rhodes, J., 36
Rich, B. R., 232
Rieger, E., 502
Robinson, L., 320
Rogers, D. D., 326
Rogge, J., 362
Rokeach, M., 404, 439
Rosen, R., 320, 339
Ross, A., 254
Rule, S., 39
Russ, J., 195
Russell, D. E. H., 287, 294, 299, 301, 302

Russo, V., 64, 65
Ryan, B., 404
Ryan, M., 7

Said, E., 102
Salaam, K. Y., 385, 387
Saxton, A., 34, 35, 36
Schatzer, M., 366
Schemering, C., 384
Schoell, W., 178–179
Schooler, C., 110
Schudson, M., 94
Schulze, L., 148–149
Schwartz, T., 80
Seiter, E., xix, 321, 328, 342, 346
Shanahan, N., 550
Shayon, R. L., 417
Showalter, E., 351
Signorielli, N., 546, 547, 550, 551, 553
Silbert, M. H., 302
Silk, C., 37
Silk, J., 37
Silverstone, R., 363
Slaby, R. G., 186
Smitherman, G., 384, 389
Sommer, B., 499
Spelman, E. V., 283
Spicer, C., 405, 406, 407, 410
Spigel, L., 413
Stacey, J., 164
Staiger, J., 13
Steel, D., 225
Stein, A., 144
Stein, B., 409, 410
Steinem, G., 230
Stowe, H. B., 349
Sun, L., 550, 553
Sussman, C., 534
Swartley, A., 500

Tate, G., 479, 485
Taylor, P. A., 110
Teish, L., 289, 296
Tetzlaff, D., 481
Thompson, R., 409
Thorpe, K., 217
Toop, D., 479
Tuan, Y-F., 283–284
Tunstall, J., 406
Turow, J., 328, 406, 407, 409
Twitchell, J. B., 170

Van Deburg, W. L., 34, 35
Vidmar, N., 404, 439

Vincent, R. C., 483

Waggett, G., 333
Wakshlag, J., 406
Waldman, P., 109
Walker, A., 280, 281, 282, 285, 289
Walker, D., 406
Wallace, M., 56, 485
Walser, R., 482
Warth, E. M., 342, 346
Washington, M. H., 399
Washington, S., 294
Watney, S., 232
Waugh, T., 69, 232
Weaver, J. B., 233, 299
Weber, S. N., 388
Weiss, A., 66
West, C., 384
Weyr, T., 255, 257, 258, 261
Wiegman, R., 37

Wildavsky, B., 110
Wildman, S., 405
Wilkinson, D., 366
Williams, C. T., 320
Williams, L., 111, 233, 254
Williams, R., 67, 86, 431, 446
Williamson, J., 148
Wilson, J., 294
Winick, C., 406
Winspear, V., 220
Winston, M. R., 439
Wolf, N., 73
Wood, R., 170
Woodiwiss, K., 220

Yellin, J. F., 35

Zillmann, D., 233, 299, 300, 302
Zita, J., 233, 254

Subject Index

ABC network, 384, 405–407
Abolitionists, 35–36
Abuse: Black and Battered, 292–293
Acculturation process and MTV, 491
Accused, The, 453
Adolescence:
    beauty myth, 121–122
    empowerment sources, 12, 15
    narrowcast programming, 397
    Sassy, 119
    violent movies, 186–189
A.D.O.R. (rap music), 540
Adoration and pornography, 311
Adult bookstores, 243
Adventure theme in entertainment, 20–21
Advertising, 71–75. *See also* Print ads.
    appropriating black culture, 542
    beauty myth, 121–125
    blacks in charge of, 93–97, 105–107
    children, racial representations of, 99–105
    cigarette, racial segmentation in, 109–111
    commodity image-system, 79–86
    critical media literacy, 126–127
    early television, 47
    editorial content tied-in with, 112–113, 114, 116, 118, 119–120
    free association of meaning, 494
    history of, 78–79

Home Shopping Network/Club, 152–158
    institutional structuring through, 77–78
    lesbians targeted as consumers, 142–143
    masculinity/violence and, 133–136
    MTV, 489–492, 494–495
    public policy and, 130–131
    secular culture and capitalism united through, 488
    telefeatures, 447–448
    TV content influenced by, 407
Advertising: The Uneasy Persuasion (Schudson), 94
Advertising Age, 88, 113
Advocate, The, 143
Aesthetic inferiority and pornography, 311
Affiliates, 446, 447
African Americans. *See also* Black feminist thought in media studies; Race; Rap music.
    advertising by, 93–97, 105–107
    comedy series, 438–443
    female roles on TV, 424–429
    film industry depiction of, 36–38
    inferential racism, 20–22
    intertextual representations of black middle-class/urban poor on TV, 396, 430–437

magazines for, 110
mothers portrayed by Burrell agency, 106
pornography and female, 279–285
poverty, 107
resistance to symbolic annihilation, 383–390
soap operas, 332–337
Agrarian-based society, 78
AIDS, 65–66, 337–338
Airline industry, 117
Alcohol, 116
Alienation and pornography, 312
Aliens, 181
All in the Family, 406, 439, 459
All My Children, 338, 459
All Talk: The Talkshow in Media Culture (Munson), 367
Alternative media of African Americans, 35–36
Ambivalence about racist images, 22
American Airlines, 117
American Family Association (AFA), 509, 533
American Psychiatric Association, 64
Amos and Andy, 332, 425
Animals, black women compared to, 282–285, 294
Animal Sex Among Black Women (Washington), 293
Anonymity of images, 86
Anti-pornography politics, 244–251
Anti-Semitism, 471
Apparel industry, 112–113, 138, 144
Appropriating black culture, 542
Arousing the reader of romance novels, 221–222
Artificiality, creating, 122, 124
Ashes in the Wind (Woodiwiss), 220
Asian Americans, 289–290, 337
Association of National Advertisers, 127
As the World Turns, 334–335, 337, 339
Attorney General's Commission on Pornography (1986), 298, 303
Audience reception, 1, 3–4, 11–14
Cagney and Lacey, 461–463
Color Purple, 52–59
confession/explorations of a white/male/feminist porn watcher, 307–312
homosexuals, 66–69
Julia, 415–422
Korean fans of soap operas, 355–361
Madonna's music, 508–516
market research, TV, 447–448
pornography, 302–304
prostitute talks about pornography, former, 314–318

romance novels, 12, 202–212
slasher films, 178–179
violence on TV, 555
women as commodities, 88–92
women's genres, 162–163
Authors Guild, 226, 227
Autobiography of Miss Jane Pittman, The, 426
Automobiles, 113–114
Avedon, Barbara, 456

Bad Baron's Daughter (London), 219
Bad Girls and Dirty Pictures: The Challenge to Reclaim Feminism (Assiter & Carol), 244
Barr, Roseanne, 469–474
Bartmann, Sarah, 281
Beastie Boys, 540
Beauty Bound (Freedman), 124
Beauty myth, 121–125, 464, 472
Beavers, Louise, 425
Beavis and Butt-Head, 14
Beddoe, John, 25
Beer, 79, 116, 138
Bennett, Gordon, 35
Berlin Wall, collapse of, 81
Bernhard, Sandra, 30
Best Little Girl in the World, The (Levenkrom), 124
Big Daddy Kane, 522
Biological argument for male-supremacy, 237–238
Birds, The, 174
Birth of a Nation, 37
Black English, 388
Black Fashion Model (Wilson), 293
Black Feminist Thought (Hill Collins), 279
Black feminist thought in media studies, 2
Color Purple, 52–59
Madonna, 28–32
pornography, 279–285
white features glorified, 103
white feminist theory critiqued, xix
Black Ghetto Teens (Marr), 293
Black Head Nurse (Dakin), 292
Black Lyon, The, 209, 210
Blacks and White TV: Afro-Americans in Television Since 1948 (MacDonald), 414
Blending stylistic conventions, 62
Blues, the, 484–485
Bluest Eye, The (Morrison), 103
Bodybuilding, 138–139, 148
Body style, micro-politics of, 265–267
Bookers (talent coordinators), 367–368
Bookstores, adult, 243
Borman, Frank, 117
Born Out of Love (Mather), 198
Bortz, Paul, 369

Boss (rap music), 528–529
Boxed In: Women and Television (Gray), 365
Branch, Mark, 185
Brewer and Lord (insurance firm), 139
Brian's Song, 446
British cultural studies. *See* Cultural studies approach to media
Broadcasting & Cable, 554
Brother D (rap music), 520
Bryant, Anita, 64
Bugle Boycotts, 138
Burning Bed, The, 450, 452, 453
Burrell, Thomas J. (Burrell Advertising), 93–97, 105–107
Bush, George, 82
Butts, Rev. Calvin, 110

Cabin in the Sky, 57
Cable television, 396–397, 405, 489
Cabral, Francisco, 24
Cagney and Lacey, 454–465
Calvin Klein, 144
Camel cigarettes, 137–138
Camp humor, 68, 150
Canada, 225
Capital Cities, 9
Capitalism, 71, 493
Capital vs. working class, 44–45
Career women on soaps, 326
Caretakers, separating from, 206–207
Carillon Importers, 116
Carlin, Ann, 521
Carroll, Diahann, 416, 417–418, 425, 426
Carter, Nell, 426
Casting for roles on TV, 409
CBS network, 384, 405–407, 457–460
Center for Media and Values, 362
Centre for Research into Innovation, Culture and Technology, 363
Chambers, Marilyn, 115
Chamfort, Sebastien-Roch, 23
Changing Our Power: An Introduction to Women's Studies (Cochran), 476
Charlie's Angels, 457
Chicago Mercantile Exchange, 136
Children:
    image-system influencing, 83
    pornography using, 242, 315
    racial representations of, 99–105
    television watching, 549–550
    toy advertising, 115
    violent messages reaching, 188–189
China, 81
Chinese in 19th-century America, 25–26
Christianity justifying racism, 34
Christian Recorder, 36

Christopher, 143
Chuck D (rap music), 521, 522
Cigarettes, 109–111, 115–116, 127–130, 137–138
Cixous, Helene, 527
Clairol, 114
Clansmen, The (Dixon), 38
Class. *See also* Working class.
    black middle, 430–431, 435–437
    Cagney and Lacey, 460
    pornography and, 255
    Roseanne, 470–474
    sex, 239
    sitcom watching, 477–478
    soap operas, 338–339
    television's portrayal of working, 403–410
    underreporting issues of, xx, 13
    violence on TV, 134–135, 551
Close-ups on soap operas, 344
Clothing in romance novels, 191
Colonialism, 26
Color Purple, The, 4, 52–59
Colors, 431
Comedy series, 438–443, 469–478
Come-on look in pornography, 275–276
Commission on Obscenity and Pornography (1970), 298
Commodity image-system, 79–86, 134
Community-based public access channels, 397
Community formation, 12
Complementary articles, 112–113, 114, 116, 118, 119–120
Computers, 14, 137
Conde Nast package of women's magazines, 91, 93
Condom manufacturers, 137
Congress, U.S., 110, 556
Consciousness-raising groups, 379
Consumerism, policy decisions influencing, 45–50
Content analysis, 10
Contextual examination of pornography, 263–270
Cop shows, realistic, 426–427
Corday, Barbara, 456
Cornish, Samuel E., 36
Corporate control of film/television/music, 9, 71, 489–492, 494–495
Cosby, Bill, 431
Cosby Show, The, 107, 416, 430, 435–436, 449
Cosmetic products, 113, 117, 118–119
Cosmopolitan, 88–91
Counterhegemonic forces of resistance/struggle, 7
Cowboys vs. Indians metaphor, 137
Cox, Ida, 525

Creative personnel, work culture of, 408–410
Credit purchasing, government stimulating, 46
Crest toothpaste, 95
Crisis, 38
Crisis of Black America, The: The Vanishing Family, 430, 432–435
Critical media literacy, 15, 126–130
Cross-gender identification, 178–179
Crossover guests on talk shows, 368
Cullman, Joseph F., III, 110
Cultivation analysis, 551, 552–554
Cultural contradiction of capitalism, 493
Cultural Indicators project (CI), 551
Cultural politics, contemporary black, 531–538
Cultural studies approach to media, xviii–xxi, 5–8
    alternative media of African Americans, 35–36
    Color Purple, The, 52–59
    components of, 8–14
    Madonna, 28–32
    media history and ideas on race, 33–39
    multicultural nature of, 14–15
    oppressed peoples, similarities in treatment of, 23–26
    racist ideologies, 18–22
    sexual minorities, 63–69
    women's genres, 161–167
    working class, 40–50

Daily Variety, 459
Daly, Tyne, 454–464
Dann, Michael, 407
Darwinism, 36
Dash, Julie, 38–39
Day, Benjamin, 35
Days of Our Lives, 325, 350
DeBeers cartel, 77
Debt-encumbered home ownership, 46–47
Deferment and process on soap operas, 343–344
Dehumanizing the enemy, 26
Dell computers, 137
Dell's Candlelight Ecstasy line, 218
Dellums, Ron, 26
Democratizing the image-system, 86
Depression, Great, 43–44, 45
Dialectic of Sex (Firestone), 239
Dickinson, Angie, 456
Die Hard, 13
Documentaries, independent, 68–69
Dominant/preferred readings, 13, 55
Donahue, Phil, 369, 380–382
Do the Right Thing, 94

Double consciousness, 443
Douglass, Frederick, 36
Drama (TV), 424–429, 548–556
Dressed to Kill, 172
DuBois, W.E.B., 38
Dunning, William A., 37–38
Dworkin, Andrea, 247–248
Dworkin-MacKinnon Ordinance, 176, 231–232
Dyson, Marv, 385

Eastern Airlines, 117
Easy Riders, 243
Ebony, 113, 421
Economic expansion, 44–47, 80–81
Editorial content tied-in with advertising, 112–113, 114, 116, 118, 119–120
Educational reform movement, xviii–xix
Education and image-system, 85–86
Electoral politics, 82
Electronic Media, 555
Electronics industry, 114–115
Elias, Harry, 114–115
Elle, 146
Emotionalizing sex, 196–200
Empowerment sources, 12, 15
Encoding/decoding model, 54–55
English views of Ireland, 24–25
Esquire, 474
Essence, 113, 118
Estée Lauder, 118–119
Ethnic duality, 384
Ethnic targeting, 110
Ethnographic research, 321–322. *See also* Audience reception.
Europe, Eastern, 81
Executioner's Song, The, 450
Experience sold back to you, 80
Experimental research on pornography, 298–301

Faces of Death, 185, 186
Fairness Doctrine, 110
Fame, 426
Family:
    caretaker, separating from, 206–207
    early television's portrayal of, 47–50
    Roseanne, 469–474
    sitcoms' portrayal of, 476–478
    soap operas portrayal of, 326–327, 349–350
    telefeatures portraying, 449
    TV technology and power dynamics of, 362–366
Family Ties, 449

Famous Talent Agency, 535
Fandoms forming communities, 12
Fantasy identification, 12
Fatness, 472
Fawcett, Farrah, 450
Federal Bureau of Investigation (FBI), 133
Federal Communications Commission (FCC), 46, 110, 446
Female friendship and solidarity, 473
Female gaze in narrative film, 164, 451–453
Female Spectators: Looking at Film and Television (Pribam), 52
Feminine hygiene products, 115
Feminine Mystique (Friedan), xix
Femininity equated with passivity, 135–136
Feminist thought in media studies, xix. *See also* Black feminist thought in media studies; Pornography; Romance novels; Slasher films; Soap operas.
    Cagney and Lacey, 455, 456
    female gaze, 451–453
    gender identity, 163–164
    Roseanne, 469–474
    sitcoms, 477
    soap operas, 320–321, 325–326
    violence, 13–14
Feminization of women's roles on TV, 459–462
Fetishisation, 267–268
Film industry. *See also* Slasher films.
    audience reception, 13
    contemporary studies, xx–xxi, 7
    genre/semiotic analysis of, 10–11
    homosexuals, 64
    horror films, 169–170
    male/female gaze in narrative film, 164, 177, 451–453
    masculinity/violence in, 134, 139–140
    political economy of culture, 9
    racist ideology, 21–22, 36–38
    telefeatures, 445–453
    violence against women, 248
First Amendment to U.S. Constitution, 549
Fisher, Terry L., 427, 463–464
Flame and the Flower, The, 209
Flavor Flav (rap music), 522
Focus on the Family (FF), 533
Food products, 79, 112, 116, 191
Forbes, 242
Fortune, 46
Forty Acres enterprise, 521–522
Foster, Meg, 454–460
Fox network, 369
Fragmentary images of women, 267–268, 281
Frank's Place, 435

Frederick Douglass' Paper, 36
Free association of meaning in post-modernist culture, 494–496
Fresh Prince of Bel Air, The, 522
Freston, Tom, 489
Freud, Sigmund, 352
Friday the Thirteenth films, 173, 177
Friendship and solidarity, female, 473
From Reverence to Rape: The Treatment of Women in the Movies (Haskell), 456

Gallery, 242
Gay liberation movement, 64
Gay window advertising, 144–150
Gender. *See also* Men; Pornography; Romance novels; Slasher films; Soap operas.
    advertising, 81–82
    children and identification of, 100
    cross-gender identification, 178–179
    Madonna's music, 508–516
    television programming targeting, 319
General Electric (GE), 9
General Hospital, 327, 330, 332–333, 337
Generations, 333
Genre-based analysis of TV, 10–11, 395–400
Genres, women, 161–167
George, Nelson, 521
Get Christie Love, 426
Gilpatrick, Roswell, 117
Gimme a Break, 426
Girls on Film (Burchill), 29
Glamour, 124
Gless, Sharon, 454–464
Glitter Girl (Day), 218
Godfather, The, 452
Go-Gos, 501
Goldbergs, The, 47–48
Golden Girls, The, 459
Gold Told Me, 179
Good Housekeeping, 472
Government policies and consumerism, 45–46
Graham, Heather, 225
Grandmaster Flash and the Furious Five (rap music), 520
Grass-roots militancy, 44
Graves, Theresa, 426
Greek history and prostitution, 240, 241, 242, 250–251
Greeley, Horace, 35
Greenwald, Robert, 450
Griffith, D. W., 37–38
Guccione, Bob, 255, 259–260

Hair care, 114
Hallelujah, 57
Halloween, 170, 171, 173, 174–175
Hammer (rap music), 542
Happy violence, 550
Hard-core pornography, 260, 277–278
Harlequin novels. *See* Romance novels
Harper, Valerie, 426
Harper's Weekly, 25
Heartbeat, 459
Hearth and Home (Tuchman), xix
Hefner, Hugh, 255–258, 291
Hegemony and counterhegemony model, 7
Heroines/Heroes, 66, 139–140, 191–192, 216–219
Hill Street Blues, 426–427, 459
Hispanics, 337, 431, 552
Hollywood Caucus of Producers, Writers and Directors, 555
Hollywood Reporter, 459
Home ownership, debt-encumbered, 46–47
Home Shopping Network/Club, 152–158
Homosexuals, 15
    audience reception from, 66-69
    as sitcom watchers, 476–478
    Cagney and Lacey, 459, 462
    lesbians targeted as consumers, 142–150
    In Living Color, 442
    Madonna's relationship with, 29, 31–32
    Ms. advertising, 117
    pornography and, 245, 273
    soap operas' portrayal of, 337–338
    television's portrayal of, 63–66
Hooks, Benjamin, 110
Hoover, Herbert, 43
Horne, Lena, 57
Horror films, 169–170. *See also* Slasher films
Horse imagery, 219
House of Pain (music group), 540
Housewife theme dominant in advertising, 122
Housework theme on early television, 48
How to Write Romance Novels That Sell (Lowery), 162, 166, 215
Hudson, Rock, 65
Humor as mode of resistance, 387–390, 438–443
Hustler, 242, 260

I-camera in slasher films, 171, 178
Ice Cube (rap music), 522, 535, 542, 543
Identity formation, 5
Ideology, 1–2, 7
    defining, 18–20
    racist, 20–22
    textural analysis, 11

working class, perceptions of the, 404
I Love Lucy, 477
Image-system of the marketplace, 79–86, 134
Imaginative play, 83
Imagistic modes of representation, 2, 78, 84, 127–130
Imitation of Life, 333
Imperialism and entertainment, 20–21
Independent producers, 450
Indigenous soap operas, 360–361
Inequality, social, 26
Inferential racism, 20–22
In Living Color, 438–443, 522
Institutional policy analysis, 551, 554–555
Institutional structuring through advertising, 77–78
Insurance industry and rap music, 534–535
Integrity, independent, 61–62
Interdiscourse concept, 58
Internalizing dominant culture's values, 66–67
Interpellation concept, 58
Interracial sex, 292
Intolerance, 38
Invisibility of gay people, 64
Invisibility of whiteness, 100, 134
Ireland caricatured by English, 24–25

J. Crew, 146
Jackson, Michael, 431, 495
Jamieson, Judith, 111–112
Japanese, 24
Jewish people, 294–295, 471
Jim Crow segregation, 36
Joe Camel (ad mascot), 137–138
Jones, James Earl, 110
Jordan, Barbara, 110
Journal of Personality and Social Psychology (Linz), 185
Julia, 413–422, 425
JVC (electronics firm), 114–115

Kanter, Hal, 417
Kate and Allie, 459
Kearns, Michael, 67
Kefauver's Subcommittee on Juvenile Delinquency in 1954, 547
Kelly, Michael, 30
Kerner Commission Report on Civil Disorders, 414, 420
Killer role in slasher films, 172–173, 177, 179–181
Kipling, Rudyard, 26
Klein, Paul, 447–448

Koppel, Ted, 381–382
Korean fans of soap operas, 321–322, 355–361
Kosner, Ed, 117

L.A. Law, 427–428
Labeling violent films, 188
Ladies Home Journal, 470
Lady Audley's Secret, 351
Lang, Dale, 120
Language contrasted with ideology, 18–20
Lansing, Sherry, 457
Lauper, Cyndi, 501, 503, 504
Lear, Norman, 410, 425
Lee, Spike, 94, 521–522
Lennon, John, 24, 495
Lesbians. See Homosexuals
Le Shaun (entertainer), 526
Letters From a War Zone (Dworkin), 237
Liberal ideology, 18
Liberator, 35
Life and Times of Harvey Milk, 68
Life of Riley, The, 48
Lifestyle pornography magazines, 255–259, 260
Lionel, 115
Listen Up: The Lives of Quincy Jones, 522
Literacy in image-saturated society, 86
Literary-critical textural analysis, 10
Literary Digest, 26
Literary Market Place (LMP), 216
Literature of imperialism, 20–21
Local TV stations, 446, 447
Looking On: Images of Femininity in the Visual Arts and Media (Betterton), 263
Lord of La Pampa (Thorpe), 217
Los Angeles Times, 536
Loving With a Vengeance (Modleski), 348
Lucas, Reggie, 509
Lynching, 37

MacKinnon, Catherine, 247–248
MacNeil/Lehrer, 378
Made for Each Other, 209
Mademoiselle, 92
Madonna, 2
    audience reception, 508–516
    black feminist perspective on, 28–32
    blackness, feelings about, 540
    cultural studies approach to critiquing, 15
    political economy in analyzing, 10
    self fashioning, 491
Magazines:
    black, 110
    men's entertainment, 242, 246, 254–261
    women's, 88–92, 112–120
Mainstreaming feminist issues, 463–464
Making Violence Sexy (Russell), 287
Malcolm X, 523
Mama's Birthday, 49
Marketing and Media Decisions, 110
Market research, 447–448
Marlboro, 127–130
Marriage in romance novels/soap operas, 209, 342
Marshall, Gary, 407
Marshall Plan, 45
Marxism, xx, 11
Masturbation, 308
Maternal omnipotence on soaps, 326–327, 345
Mattel, 103
Maura (Granbeck), 220
Max Factor, 118
McDonald's, 95, 105, 107
MC Lyte (rap music), 526, 527–529
McNeil, Claudia, 425
McQueen, Butterfly, 425
Media Culture (Kellner), 14
Meese, Edwin, 187
Men. See also Gender; Patriarchal culture.
    biases of, xix
    biological argument for male-supremacy, 237–238
    fantasy identification, 12
    looking at other men, 310
    magazines for, 242, 246, 254–261
    male gaze in narrative film, 163–164, 177, 451–452
    masculinity, 127–128, 273, 345
    nurturing abilities, 207
    romantic feeling, 197–198
    Roseanne, 473–474
    soap operas, relationship patterns on, 327–328, 343, 344, 352
    TV technology in the home, 362–366
    violence of, normalizing, 133–140
Mermaid and the Minotaur (Dinnerstein), 196, 197
Message system analysis, 551–552
Micheaux, Oscar, 38
Michel Roux, 116
Middle-aged women on soap operas, 344
Middle-class:
    black, 430–431, 435–437
    cultural insularity of professional, 41–42
    televisions' portrayal of, 404, 469–474
Midwestern image and soap operas, 339
Military symbolism and masculine identification, 137–138
Miller, Merle, 67

Miller Brewing Company, 138
Mincer, Richard, 368
Minority-owned advertising agencies, 93–97, 105–107
Misogyny, Misandry, and Misanthropy (Bloch & Ferguson), 169
Mister Rogers, 104
Molinari, Gustave de, 24
Monie Love (rap music), 527
Moore, Mary Tyler, 426
Mork & Mindy, 407
Mortgage debt, 46–47
Motel Hell, 172
Mother Jones, 243
Mothers:
    on soap operas, 326–327, 345, 350
    Roseanne, 472–473
    viewers of soap operas as, 348–353
    working, 106
Motion Picture Association of America, 188
Movie of the Week, The (Rapping), 445
Moyers, Bill, 432–435
Moynihan report of the 1960s, 107
Ms., 88–90, 112–120
MTV, 84, 480–484, 488–496, 499–501, 504
Multiculturalism, 8, 14–15, 378, 379
Multistation owners, 405
Muscularity associated with masculinity, 138–139
Music commercials and race, 104
Music videos:
    critics of, 479
    female musicianship, 499–504
    image-system, 83
    MTV, 480–484, 488–496

Nabisco, 102–103
Narrowcast programming, 397
National Abortion Rights League, 456
National Association for the Advancement of Colored People (NAACP), 111
National Association of Educational Broadcasters, 547
National Black Caucus of State Legislators, 111
National Gay Task Force, The, 456
Nationalist thought in black music and culture, 518–523
National Organization for Women (NOW), 462
National Right to Life Committee, 456
National Urban League, 111
Native, popular culture's portrayal of the, 21–22, 102
NBC network, 9, 405–407, 414
Near-rape, 220–221

Necessary Illusions (Chomsky), 86
Negotiated reading, 55
Nestlé's Quik, 102
Network audience erosion, 369
Network domination and persistent images, 405–407
New Age Journal, 124
New Deal, 44, 45
Newsweek, 518–519
New Yorker, The, 113
New York Herald, 35
New York Post, 534
New York Sun, 35
New York Times, 50, 534
New York Times Magazine, 143
New York Tribune, 35
Nicholas, Denise, 425
Nigger, The, 37
Nightline, 378, 381–382
Nightmare on Elm Street, 172
1968 in America, 413
9 to 5, 458
No End to Her (Nochimson), 333
Nonhierarchical structure of talk shows, 380
Norwegian Cruise Line, 137
Nostalgic myth of America, 100–101
Not a Love Story, 246, 307
Novelists Inc., 226
N. W. Ayers (ad agency), 77

Objectification, 269–270, 280
Occasional Discourse on the Nigger Question (Carlyle), 34
Of Black America, 420
One Life to Live, 328, 333, 337, 338
Ono, Yoko, 495
Oppositional readings, 3, 13, 54–56, 58–59, 67–68
Oppressed peoples, similarities in treatment of, 23–26
Oprah Winfrey Show, 367
Oral culture, 358
Orion Television, 455
Oui, 242
Outing homosexuals, 147
Overt racism, 20

Palace of the Pomegranate (Winspear), 220
Pallante, Maria, 224
Parents, 104
Parent's Music Resource Center (PMRC), 533
Passivity, 135–136, 210, 249–250, 280, 328–329
Patriarchal culture, xix

anti-patriarchal advertising, 129
fragmentary images of women, 320
internalizing, 66
pornography, 237–243
religion, 251
soap operas, 325–330, 340–347
videos watched in the home, 357
visceral regression, 206–207
Penthouse, 242, 246, 255, 259–260, 289–290
Perfume, 118
Persian Gulf war, 9–10
Pfleger, Rev. Michael, 110
Phallic worship in romance novels, 190–191
Phil Donahue Show, 457
Philip Morris, 110–111, 115–116
Philippines, 26
Photographic pornography, 272–278
Pittman, Robert, 480, 489–490, 492
Planned Parenthood, 456, 510
Playboy, 242, 254–261, 291, 509
Police Woman, 456
Political correctness, 144–145, 378, 379
Political economy of culture, 1, 9–10, 14, 396
Politicized rap, 520
Politics and image-system, 82
Polysemic text, 3, 11
Pornography:
    anti-pornography politics, 244–251
    audience reception, 302–304
    black women, 279–285
    child, 242, 315
    circumscribed set of conventions, 271–278
    confession/explorations of a white male feminist, 307–312
    defining, 229–230
    experimental research, 298–301
    male-supremacist society, 237–243
    Playboy, 254–261
    political economy of culture, 10
    production/consumption issues *vs.* image analysis, 263–270
    prostitute talks about, former, 314–318
    racist, 287–297
    romance novels, 193–200
Pornography (Dworkin), 249, 250
Positive realism, 93–94
Positive stereotypes, 99
Postmodernism, 481–482, 488, 494–497
Postwar years, economic expansion in, 44–50
Poverty, 107, 430–435
Power of the Image: Essays on Representations and Sexuality (Kuhn), 271
Power/powerlessness dramatized by media, 5
    dramas on TV, 548–556

encoded words, 8
pornography, 277–278
soap operas, 349
TV technology in the home, 362–366
visibility in the media, 62
Powertots (talent coordinators), 368
Preteens and horror films, 186
Prime time television, 378, 379
Primitivism, 21–22, 102
Print ads:
    critical media literacy, 127–130
    lesbians targeted as consumers, 142–150
    masculinity/violence in, 136–140
    men's entertainment magazines, 255, 257, 258–260
    Ms., 112–120
    pornographic images compared to, 266–267
    women's magazines, 88–92
Private Screenings: Television and the Female Consumer (Spigel & Mann), 413, 454
Process emphasized on soap operas, 343–344
Producers, 368, 450
Program development (TV) around class issues, 405–410
Promiscuity, 195, 208, 211, 292
Prostitution, 239–241, 249, 314–318
Pseudonyms and romance novels, 223–224
Psycho, 170, 172, 174, 176
Psychoanalysis, 163–164, 268
Psychological distance, 93
Public agenda, defining the, 62
Public Broadcasting System (PBS), 69
Public Enemy (rap music), 521, 544
Public policy and advertising, 130–131
Publishers, contacting, 216
Punch, 24
Punishment Books, 291–292
Punk rock, 500

Qualitative analysis, 10

Race, 18–22. *See also* African Americans; Black feminist perspective.
    alternative media of African Americans, 35–36
    children, racial representations of, 99–105
    cigarette advertising, 109–111
    cultural politics, contemporary black, 531–538
    Julia, 413–422
    Korean fans of soap operas, 355–361
    Madonna's music, 508–516
    media history and ideas on, 33–39

Ms. and women models, 117–118
oppressed peoples, similarities in treat-
    ment of, 23–26
pornography, 287–297
Roseanne, 471
soap operas, 337
White-Black dichotomy, dominance of,
    xx–xxi
white hipsters (wanna-be's), 540–544
Radio, black-oriented, 385
Raiding of mainstream media culture, 323
Rake in soap operas, 330
Rambo, 10–11
Randolph, Lillian, 425
Randy of the Redwoods, 493
Rape:
    black women, 280
    film industry's portrayal of, 452
    historical representations, 137
    pornography, 293–294
    prostitution's relationship to, 239–241
    romance novels, 208, 220–221
    soap operas, 329–330
Rap music, 484–486
    black nationalist thought, 518–523
    cultural phenomena, 479–480
    cultural politics, contemporary black,
        531–538
    female rappers, 524–529
Ratings system, 447–448
Reagan, Nancy, 390
Reagan, Ronald, 9, 225, 390
Realism conveyed through media, 62–63,
    424, 426–429
Recipes tied-in with food ads, 116
Recurring crisis in sitcoms, 476–478
Redistribution of wealth, xviii, 44
Reed, Lou, 541
Regression, visceral, 206–207
Reinterpretation in romance novels, 210
Religion, 34, 237, 251
Remington Steele, 461
Remote-control devices, 362, 363, 364
Repetition compulsion theory, 352
Reproduction of Mothering (Chodorow), 206
Resistance to symbolic annihilation, 13–14,
    67–68, 383–390, 469–474
Resource distribution, xvii–xviii, 44
Reverse discrimination, 418
Revlon, 117
Right (politics), the, 64
Right-Wing Women (Dworkin), 249–250
Ring of Fear (McCaffrey), 217
Rivera, Geraldo, 369–374
*Rockin' the Beat: Mass Music and Mass Move-
    ments* (Garofalo), 518
Rock music industry. *See* Music videos

Rockwell, Norman, 100–101
Rocky films, 11
Rodgers, Nile, 509
Romance novels, 165–167
    audience reception, 12, 202–212
    distance between sexes glorified, 190–193
    guidelines for writing, 215–222
    pornography debated, 193–200
    writers of, 223–227
Romance Writers of America (R.W.A.), 226
Romanticized sex, 196–200
Romantic Times, 225
Roosevelt, Franklin D., 44
Roots, 426
Roseanne, 406–407, 469–474
Roseanne: My Life as a Woman (Barr), 470
Rosenbloom, Richard, 455
Rosenzweig, Barney, 456
Russwurm, John B., 35–36
Ryan's Hope, 337, 339, 350

Saab, 139
Sadomasochism (S&M), 246, 248, 277
Salt n' Pepa (rap music), 526, 527, 529
Sambo image, 35
Sand of Castle, The, 358–359
Sands, Diana, 425
Santa Barbara, 329–330, 337
Sassy, 119
Saturday Night Live, 541–542
Schiller, Lawrence, 450
Scientific American, 242
Scopophilia, 276
Sea Treasure, The, 209–210
Security at rap concerts, 531–532
SELF, 88–89
Self-defense against manipulation/control,
    86
Self fashioning, 491
Semen, 311
Semiotics, 10
Serious topics discussed on TV, 380–382,
    445–446, 449–450, 465
Servants on TV, 403
Sesame Street, 104
Seven-Up, 494
Sexual attitudes/representations, 124–125.
    See also Pornography; Romance nov-
    els; Slasher films.
    advertising, 122, 123
    image-system, 82, 84
    In Living Color, 442–443
    music videos, 499–500
    rap music, 524–529
    soap operas, 344–345
Sexual callousness model, 299

Sexual Politics (Millet), 238
Shanna, 209
Shayon, Robert L., 417
Shocklee, Hank, 521
Silent Witness, 452
Silhouette Books, 203
Sitcoms, 438–443, 469–478
Slasher films, 164–165
    examples of, 170–172
    final girl in, 175–181
    functional analysis of, 176–181
    killer role in, 172–173, 177, 179–181
    location, the terrible, 173–174, 179
    real-life violence and, 185–189
    victims in, 174–175
    weapons used in, 174
Slave-figure in films, 21
Slavery and pornography, 279–282
Slumber Party Massacre, 172–173
Sluts of the S.S, 294–295
Sneaker commercials and race, 104
Soap operas, 320–321
    African Americans resistance to symbolic
        annihilation, 383–390
    characterizations/plots, basic tenets of,
        325–330
    feminine values asserted in patriarchal
        culture, 340–347
    racial/social/sexual/minorities on, 332–
        339
    subject/spectator of, 348–353
    technological power dynamics in the
        home, 365–366
Social consciousness and ideology, 19
Social inequality, 26
Social issues on TV, 380–382, 445–446, 449–
    450, 465
Social movements of the 1960s, 378, 379, 413
Socialist ideology, 18–19
Soft-core pornography, 233, 255–259, 260,
    275
Soul Food (Berry), 293
Soul Slave, 291
Souls of Black Folk, The (DuBois), 443
Soviet Union, former, 116–117
Spectorsky, Auguste C., 258
Speed and fragmentation, 83–85
Spielberg, Steven, 55–56
Spin, 509
Split personality of MTVs model viewer, 493
Sport commercials and race, 104
Sports symbolism and masculine identifica-
    tion, 137–138
Status and *Playboy*, 256–257
Status quo and soap operas, 341–343
Steel, Danielle, 225
Steinem, Gloria, 457

Stereotypes, xviii
    appropriating, 439
    beauty myth, 121–125
    black advertisers and, 94
    black females on TV, 424–425, 428
    children, racial representations of, 99–105
    humiliating aspect of, 26
    negative, promulgating, 246–247
    political/social mood shifting, 36–37
    sexualization of black, 37
    time constraints and TV program devel-
        opment, 409
    working class, 41–42
Stern, Howard, 540
Stevenson, Bernard, 226
Stop the Violence movement, 521
Strikes, labor, 44–45
Style and surface, world of, 85
Subject/spectator of soap operas, 348–353
Substance, world of, 85–86
Suburban growth, 46–47
Subversion/appropriation of mainstream
    media, 68–69
Summers, Anne, 119–120
Symbolic annihilation, xviii, 4, 62, 383–390
Symbolic images in advertising, 127–130

Taft-Hartley Act of 1947, 45
Talk shows, 322, 367–382
Tandem productions, 425
Taste of Honey, A, 67–68
Technology, TV, 362–366
*Tele-Advising: Therapeutic Discourse in Amer-
    ica* (White), 152
Television. *See also* Advertising.
    black female characters, 424–429
    Cagney and Lacey, 454–465
    class portrayed on, 403–410
    comedy series, black, 438–443
    daytime, 319–323. *See also* Soap operas.
    economic expansion boosted by, 45–47
    family/class/ethnicity on early, 47–50
    fractionalized and competitive distribu-
        tion environment, 397
    genre-based analysis of, 10–11, 395–400
    homosexuals portrayed on, 63–66
    intertextual representations of black
        middle-class/urban poor, 396, 430–437
    Julia, 413–422, 425
    MTV, 84, 480–484, 488–496, 499–501, 504
    political economy of culture, 9
    role of, 61–63
    Roseanne, 469–474
    sitcoms, 406–407, 438–443, 469–474, 476–
        478
    speed and fragmentation, 84

talk shows, 322, 367–382
telefeatures, 445–453
TV technology and power dynamics in
    the home, 362–366
violence on, 247, 248, 547–556
working class portrayed on, 40, 403–410,
    469–474
Television Culture (Fiske), 340
Tenniel, Sir John, 24
Texas Chain Saw Massacre, 170–172, 173, 180,
    181
Textural analysis, 1, 10–11, 14
Thomas, Frank, 117
Three in the Attic, 54
Time constraints and TV production, 408–
    410
Time magazine, 416–417
Ti-rone (soap opera updates), 383–390
Tisch Financial Group, 9
Toms, Coons, Mulattoes, Mammies and Bucks
    (Bogle), 57
Torstar media conglomerate, 223
Touch a Star (Cartland), 220
Townsend, Robert, 522
Toy marketing, 83, 104–105, 115
TransAmerica (insurance), 533
Transnational corporations, 81
Transsexuals, 245
Trojan condoms, 137
Truman Doctrine, 45
Truth or Dare: In Bed With Madonna, 29,
    30–32
Turner, Tina, 30, 502–504
TV Guide, 459
Tyson, Cicely, 425

Uncle Tom's Cabin (Stowe), 37, 349
United Negro College Fund, 111
University of Birmingham Centre for Con-
    temporary Cultural Studies, 6, 54
Urry, Michelle, 257

Values and life styles research (VALS), 145
Vandervelde, Emiel, 23–24
Vanilla Ice (rap music), 542
VCRs, 365–366, 452
Venezuela, 66, 364
Venue availability for rap tours, 533–535
Victims in slasher films, 174–175
Video clubs, women operated, 357–360
Vietnam War, 26
Village Voice, 56, 144–145
Villainess/villain on soap operas, 345–347,
    351–353
Violence, 13–14. *See also* Rape; Slasher films.

advertising, 133–140
children and messages of, 188–189
pornographic, 245–247, 291–294, 298–304
rap music, 533–537
romance novels, 208, 211
TV marketing of, 247, 248, 547–556
Virginia Slims, 115–116, 127–130
Visceral regression, 206–207
Visibility and power, 62
Visual Pleasure and Narrative Cinema
    (Mulvey), 163
Vogue, 242
Voice-overs, male, 328
Volkswagen, 113
Voyeurism, 276
Vulnerability in romance novels, 217–218

Wachner, Linda, 118
Wade, Ernestine, 425
Walker, Alice, 52
Wall Street Journal, 124
Walters, Richard, 535
Warner Amex Cable Communications, 489,
    490
Watermelon Contest, 37
Waters, Ethel, 425
Wayans, Kennan Ivory, 438, 440, 522
Weapons in slasher films, 174
Wedding and Wooing of a Coon, 37
Weight, preoccupation with, 124
WHISPER (Women Hurt in Systems of
    Prostitution Engaged in Revolt), 317–
    318
White hipsters (wanna-be's), 540–544
White masculinity in advertising, violent,
    136–140
White Negro, The (Mailer), 541
Whiteness as ethnic category, 100–101, 133–
    134
*White on Black: Images of Blacks in Western
    Popular Culture* (Pieterse), 23
Wildmon, Rev. Donald E., 509
Women. *See also* Pornography; Romance
    novels; Slasher films; Soap operas.
animals, black women compared to, 282–
    285, 294
beauty myth in advertising, 121–125
black females on TV, 424–429
Cagney and Lacey, 454–464
career women on soaps, 326
cigarette advertising and, 109–110
family life on soaps, 326–327
female sexuality sold to, 265–267
fragmentary images of, 267–268, 274–275,
    281

housework portrayed on early television, 48

lesbians targeted as consumers, 142–150

magazines for, 88–92

mass cultural forms targeted for, xix, 161–167

Ms. advertising hardships, 112–120

music videos and female musicianship, 499–504

rap music performed by, 524–529

Roseanne, 469–474

subordination of, 135–136, 210, 249–250, 280, 328–329

TV technology in the home, 362–366

TV/video tastes influenced by men, 356–360

Women, Sex, and Pornography (Faust), 208

Women and the Mass Media (Butler & Paisley), xix

Women's Room, The, 447

Woodard, Alfre, 427

Word Is Out, 68

Working-class:
cinema heroes of, 134–135
cultural studies analysis of, 40–50
Roseanne, 470–474
soap operas, 338–339
television's portrayal of, 403–410, 469–474

Working Mother, 104

Working mothers, 106

World Families Watch Television (Lull), 362, 363

Worldview shaped by media, 5, 61–63

Writers Market, 191, 193, 216

Written text in advertising, 78–79

Yates, Sandra, 119–120

Yorkin, Bud, 425

The Young and the Restless, 335–336, 383–390

Young Black Teenagers (music group), 540

Zero-based programming, 490

Notes on Contributors

Gloria Abernathy-Lear is Assistant Professor at the University of Illinois—Chicago, where she teaches courses in mass media and popular culture. Her special research area is African Americans and television—especially the African American daytime serial audience.

Alison Bass is a staff writer for *The Boston Globe,* specializing in the coverage of mental health, human behavior and gender issues.

Jacqueline Bobo is Assistant Professor of Radio, Television and Motion Pictures at the University of North Carolina—Chapel Hill. She has written extensively on Black women and the media and is the author of *Credible Witness: Black Women, Film Theory, Spectatorship,* forthcoming from Columbia University Press, and editor of the forthcoming book, *Cultures of Resistance: Black Women Film and Video Artists.*

Aniko Bodroghkozy has completed her Ph.D. in communication arts at the University of Wisconsin—Madison and is currently working on a book examining youth rebellion of the 1960s and popular culture.

Jane D. Brown is Professor and Director of the Center for Research in Journalism and Mass Communication, School of Journalism, University of North Carolina—Chapel Hill. She studies how adolescents learn about themselves from the media.

Richard Butsch is Professor of Sociology, Rider University, Lawrenceville, New Jersey. He is the author of many articles on class, gender and race in television series and has recently edited *For Fun and Profit: The Transformation of Leisure into Consumption* (1990).

David Carter-Whitney received his MBA from the University of British Columbia, Vancouver.

Marsha Cassidy is Adjunct Professor, Communications at Elmhurst College in Illinois. She is interested in how narrative is used to persuade in advertising.

Chong Heup Cho is a doctoral student in the Department of Communication Arts at the University of Wisconsin—Madison. He is writing a study of the cultural politics and dependent economy of an authoritarian state, based on the violence of an Olympic boxing game in 1988.

Danae Clark is Assistant Professor of Media Studies in the Department of Communication at the University of Pittsburgh. She is the author of a forthcoming book on actors' labor in Hollywood.

Carol J. Clover is Professor of Scandinavian and Comparative Literature at the University of California, Berkeley. She is the author of *Men, Women, and Chainsaws: Gender in the Horror Film* (1992), as well as books on medieval and old Norse-Icelandic literature.

Patricia Hill Collins is Professor of African American Studies and Sociology at the University of Cincinnati. She is the author of *Black Feminist Thought: Knowledge, Consciousness, and the Politics of Empowerment* (1990) and coeditor of *Race, Class, and Gender: An Anthology* (1992). Her current work is on Black feminist thought as social theory and on the connections between racism, nationalism and reproduction.

Julie D'Acci is Assistant Professor in Communication Arts at the University of Wisconsin—Madison. She is the author of *Defining Women, Television and the Case of* Cagney and Lacey (1994).

Gail Dines is Assistant Professor of Sociology at Wheelock College, where she teaches courses in media and women's studies. She is author of several articles on media representations and she lectures on pornography at colleges and community groups throughout the United States.

Andrea Dworkin is the author of *Intercourse, Pornography: Men Possessing Women* and the novels *Mercy* and *Ice and Fire*. A collection of essays, *Letters From a War Zone,* was recently published in paperback by Lawrence Hill Books. She is coauthor of legislation recognizing pornography as a violation of the civil rights of women.

Barbara Ehrenreich is a writer and essayist for *Time Magazine*. She has published many articles and books on topics related to gender and class, including *Hearts of Men: American Dreams and the Flight from Commitment* (1984), *Fear of Falling: The Inner Life of the Middle Class* (1990), *The Worst Years of Our Lives: Irreverent Notes from a Decade of Greed* (1990) and most recently, the novel *Kipper's Game*.

John Fiske is Professor of Communication Arts at the University of Wisconsin—Madison. He writes widely on popular culture, and his latest books include *Power Plays, Power Works* (1993) and *Media Matters*.

George Gerbner is Professor and Dean Emeritus of the Annenberg School for Communication, at the University of Pennsylvania. He is director of U.S. and multinational media research projects. His most recent publications are *The Global Media Debate: Its Rise, Fall and Renewal* (1993), *Triumph of the Image: The Media's War in the Persian Gulf* (1992) and *Invisible Crises* (forthcoming).

Evelina Giobbe is founder of WHISPER and current director of Education and Public Policy. She has worked with community groups to end the harassment and sexual exploitation of neighborhood women and children, and she is the author of several articles on commercial sexual exploitation. She is currently collecting oral histories of women used in prostitution, pornography and on the strip circuit for a future book.

Robert Goldman is Associate Professor of Sociology at Lewis and Clark College, Portland, Oregon. He is the author of *Reading Ads Socially*, (1992), as well as *Mapping Hegemony* (1991).

Herman Gray teaches at the University of California—Santa Cruz (Stevenson College). He is the author of several articles on racial representations in U.S. television culture, as well as *Watching Race: Television and the Struggle for the Sign of Blackness* (forthcoming).

Larry Gross is Professor of Communications at the Annenberg School, University of Pennsylvania and editor of the Columbia University Press book series in lesbian and gay studies. His recent publications include *Contested Closets: The Politics and Ethics of Outing* (1993) and *On the Margins of Art Worlds* (1994).

Stuart Hall is Professor of Sociology at the Open University in Milton Keynes, England, and founder and editor of *New Left Review*. He is author of many articles, books and article collections. Most recently, he is the author or coauthor of *Culture, Media, Language* (1980), *The Hard Road to Renewal: Thatcherism and the Crisis of the Left* (1988) and *Formations of Modernity* (1992).

bell hooks is Distinguished Professor of English at City College in New York. A feminist theorist and cultural critic, writer and teacher, she speaks widely on issues of race, class and gender. Her most recent books include *Black Looks* (1992), *Teaching to Transgress* and *Outlaw Culture: Resisting Representation*.

Jean M. Humez is Associate Professor in the Women's Studies Program at the University of Massachusetts/Boston. Among other interdisciplinary humanities courses, she teaches an undergraduate course in Women and the Media, and an American Studies graduate course in Race and Gender in U.S. Cultural History. She has published books and articles on American women's spiritual and secular autobiographies, women in Shaker religion, and African-American women's life-storytelling texts, and is currently at work on a study of racial representation in the PBS-marketed series, *I'll Fly Away*.

Robert Jensen is an Assistant Professor in the Department of Journalism at the University of Texas at Austin. His research interests include feminist and lesbian/gay issues in media, law and ethics. He is coeditor of the forthcoming collection of essays, *Freeing the First Amendment: Critical Perspectives on Freedom of Expression*.

Sut Jhally is a Professor of Communications at the University of Massachusetts/Amherst. He has written broadly on media and popular culture and is creator of the educational videotape on music videos, *DreamWorlds*. He is author of *Codes of Advertising* and coauthor of *Social Communication in Advertising* and *Enlightened Racism:* The Cosby Show, *Audiences and the Myth of the American Dream*.

Richard Katula is Professor of Communications Studies, Northeastern University, Boston. He is the author of several books, including *Principles and Patterns of Public Speaking* (1987).

Jackson Katz is the creator and coordinator of the Mentors in Violence Prevention (MVP) Project at Northeastern University's Center for the Study of Sport in Society. He also is the founder and executive director of Real Men, an anti-sexist men's organization based in Boston. He lectures nationally on men's violence against women and images of violent masculinity in sports and media.

Douglas Kellner is Professor of Philosophy at the University of Texas at Austin and author of many books, including (with Michael Ryan) *Camera Politics: The Politics and Ideology of Contemporary Hollywood Film, Television and the Crisis of Democracy, The Persian Gulf TV War* and *Media Culture*.

Jean Kilbourne is creator of the award-winning films *Still Killing Us Softly* and *Calling the Shots*. She lectures internationally on alcohol and cigarette advertising, the image of women in advertising and other topics.

Annette Kuhn is a writer and lecturer in media and film studies and has also written scripts for television. She is author of *Women's Pictures* (1982),

The Power of the Image (1985), *Alien Zone: Cultural Theory and Contemporary Science Fiction* (1990), *Cinema, Censorship and Sexuality, 1909-1925* (1990) and *Women in Film* (1991).

James Ledbetter is a staff writer for the *Village Voice*. He has also published articles in *Mirabella*, the *Nation* and *Mother Jones*.

Janet Lee is Associate Professor of Women's Studies and Director of the Women's Studies Program at Oregon State University.

Jung S. Lee is a doctoral candidate at the School of Communications at the University of Wisconsin—Madison. She is interested in the social aspects of advertising.

Minu Lee is a former television broadcaster in Seoul, Korea. She earned an M.A. degree in communication arts at the University of Wisconsin—Madison in 1989 and is currently working on a book on soap operas and the politics of domestic leisure in Korea.

Lisa A. Lewis is the author of *Gender Politics and MTV: Voicing the Difference* and editor of *The Adoring Audience: Fan Culture and Popular Media* (1992).

Karen Lindsey is a feminist writer. She is coauthor of *Dr. Susan Love's Breast Book* and author of *Friends as Family* and the forthcoming *Divorced, Beheaded, Survived: A Feminist Reinterpretation of the Wives of Henry VIII*. She teaches at Emerson College and the University of Massachusetts—Boston. For two years she wrote a soap opera column for the *Middlesex News*.

George Lipsitz is Professor of Ethnic Studies at the University of California, San Diego, and the author of *Time Passages: Collective Memory and American Popular Culture* (1990) and *A Life in the Struggle: Ivory Perry and the Culture of Opposition* (1988).

Marilyn M. Lowery is author of romance novels such as *The Reluctant Duke* (as by Philippa Castle), as well as *How to Write Romance Novels That Sell*.

Scott MacDonald teaches film studies and American literature in the Division of Humanities at Utica College of Syracuse University. He is currently working on Volume 3 of *A Critical Cinema* (an ongoing series of interviews with independent filmmakers, published by the University of California Press). He considers his interview with Lizzie Borden in *Critical Cinema 2* the second part of "Confessions of a Feminist Porn Watcher."

Alice Mayall obtained a Ph.D. from Northern Illinois University and is currently employed as a clinical psychologist at Northeastern Center in Kendallville, Indiana.

Tania Modleski is Professor of English at the University of Southern California. She is the author of *Loving With a Vengeance, The Women Who Knew Too Much* and *Feminism Without Women* and the editor of *Studies in Entertainment*.

Wayne Munson is Assistant Professor of Communications and Media at Fitchburg State College in Massachusetts. He is author of *All Talk: The Talkshow in Media Culture* (1993).

Kathy Myers is the author of *Understains: The Sense and Seduction of Advertising* (1988).

Imani Perry graduated from Yale University with a double major in literature and American studies. She is currently a doctoral student at Harvard University in history of American civilization.

John Pettegrew currently teaches U.S. cultural history at Beloit College. His book, *The Mystique of American Manhood: Modern Conceptions of Masculinity and Gender, 1890-1920,* is forthcoming.

Jan Nederveen Pieterse is Senior Lecturer at the Institute of Social Studies, The Hague, and author of *Empire and Emancipation* (1989), as well as the more recent *White on Black: Images of Africa and Blacks in Western Popular Culture* (1992).

Richard Pollak is a journalist, novelist and teacher and at present is editor-at-large of *The Nation*. He is author of *Up Against Apartheid: The Role and Plight of the Press in South Africa* (1980) as well as of other books and articles. He is currently at work on a biography of Bruno Bettelheim.

Richard W. Pollay is Professor of Marketing at the University of British Columbia, Vancouver.

Janice A. Radway is Professor of Literature at Duke University and author of *Reading the Romance*.

Elayne Rapping is Professor of Communications at Adelphi University. Her books include *The Looking-Glass World of Non-Fiction TV* (1987), *The Movie of the Week: Private Stories, Public Culture* (1992) and the collection of essays, *Media tions: Forays into the Culture and Gender Wars* (1994). She is a regular columnist for *The Progressive* and *On the Issues: The Progressive Women's Journal*.

Jane Rhodes is Assistant Professor at the School of Journalism at Indiana University—Bloomington. Her research has focused on the historical representations of women and people of color in the mass media and on the Black press. Her book on the life of Mary Ann Shadd Cary, the first African

American woman newspaper publisher and editor, is forthcoming from Indiana University Press.

Deborah D. Rogers is Associate Professor of English at the University of Maine—Orono. She is the author of *Book Seller as Rogue: John Almon and the Politics of Eighteenth-Century Publishing* and editor of *The Critical Responses to Ann Radcliffe.*

Tricia Rose is Assistant Professor of Africana Studies and History at New York University. She is the author of *Black Noise: Rap Music and Black Culture in Contemporary America* and coeditor (with Andrew Ross) of *Microphone Fiends: Youth Music and Youth Culture.* Her essays and interviews have appeared in *Camera Obscura, Social Text, Journal of Popular Music and Society, Journal of Negro Education* and *The Village Voice.*

Gayle Rubin has written many essays on feminist theory, gay history and sexual politics. She is working on a book on the development of the gay male leather community in the United States after World War II.

Diana E. H. Russell is Emerita Professor of Sociology at Mills College, Oakland, California. She is the author/editor of 11 books, most of them about sexual violence, including *Sexual Exploitation* (1984), *Rape in Marriage* (1990), *Making Violence Sexy: Feminist Views on Pornography* (1993) and *Against Pornography: The Evidence of Harm* (1993).

Norma Miriam Schulman is Assistant Professor of Communication at George Mason University, Fairfax, Virginia. She has published articles on a wide variety of mass communication topics.

Laurie Schulze teaches courses in film history, feminist film criticism and television studies in the Department of Communication at the University of Denver. She has published articles on made-for-television movies, Madonna and female body builders, in *Cinema Journal* and several anthologies.

Sarah Schuyler lives in Seattle, where she received her doctorate in literature from the University of Washington.

Ellen Seiter is Professor of Telecommunication at Indiana University. She is coeditor of *Remote Control: Television, Audiences, and Cultural Power* (1989), and her latest book is *Sold Separately: Children and Parents in Consumer Culture* (1993).

Ann Barr Snitow is a Professor at Eugene Lang College, of the New School for Social Research in New York. She is coeditor of *Powers of Desire: The Politics of Sexuality* (1983). A founder of the Feminist Anti-Censorship Task Force, of the action group No More Nice Girls and of the Network East West Women (NEWW), her most recent writing and political work is about the changing situation of women in Eastern Europe.

Gloria Steinem was founding editor of *Ms.* in 1972 and is now its consulting editor. Author of many articles on women's issues and gender, she has also published *Outrageous Acts and Everyday Rebellions* (1986), *Revolution From Within: A Book of Self-Esteem* (1992) and *Living Beyond Words* (1994).

Mimi White is Associate Professor in the Radio, Television and Film department at Northwestern University. She is the author of *Tele-Advising: Therapeutic Discourse in American Television* (1992) and coauthor, with James Schwock and Susan Reilly, of *Media Knowledge: Readings in Popular Culture, Pedagogy and Critical Citizenship* (1992).

Kristal Brent Zook is completing her Ph.D. in the History of Consciousness Program at the University of California—Santa Cruz. She has published articles about film, television, literature and popular culture in such publications as *Emerge, The Village Voice* and the *L.A. Weekly* and is currently writing a book on the politics of Black television production.